ZAGAT
2013

New York City Restaurants

EDITORS
Curt Gathje and Carol Diuguid
COORDINATOR
Larry Cohn

Published and distributed by
Zagat Survey, LLC
76 Ninth Avenue
New York, NY 10011
T: 212.977.6000
E: newyork@zagat.com
plus.google.com/local

ACKNOWLEDGMENTS

We thank Anne Bauso, Carol Bialkowski, Jason Briker, Esther Brown, Simon Butler, Phil Carlucci, Katie Carroll, Leigh Crandall, Mikola de Roo, Kara Freewind, Danielle Harris, Lynn Hazlewood, Rebecca Marx, Bernard Onken, Rebecca Salois, Jamie Selzer, Alex Silberman, Hilary Sims, Stefanie Tuder, Alice Urmey, Miranda Van Gelder and Samantha Zalaznick, as well as the following members of our staff: Danielle Borovoy (editor), Brian Albert, Sean Beachell, Maryanne Bertollo, Reni Chin, Nicole Diaz, Kelly Dobkin, Jeff Freier, Alison Gainor, Matthew Hamm, Justin Hartung, Marc Henson, Anna Hyclak, Ryutaro Ishikane, Aynsely Karps, Natalie Lebert, Mike Liao, Vivian Ma, James Mulcahy, Polina Paley, Emily Rothschild, Amanda Spurlock, Chris Walsh, Jacqueline Wasilczyk, Sharon Yates, Anna Zappia and Kyle Zolner.

We also sincerely thank the thousands of people who participated in this survey – this guide is really "theirs."

ABOUT ZAGAT

In 1979, we asked friends to rate and review restaurants purely for fun. The term "user-generated content" had yet to be coined. That hobby grew into Zagat Survey; 34 years later, we have loyal surveyors around the globe and our content now includes nightlife, shopping, tourist attractions, golf and more. Along the way, we evolved from being a print publisher to a digital content provider. We also produce marketing tools for a wide range of corporate clients, and you can find us on Google+ and just about any other social media network.

Our reviews are based on public opinion surveys. The ratings reflect the average scores given by the survey participants who voted on each establishment. The text is based on quotes from, or paraphrasings of, the surveyors' comments. Phone numbers, addresses and other factual data were correct to the best of our knowledge when published in this guide.

Contents

OTHER USEFUL LISTS

Special Features:

RESTAURANT DIRECTORY

Ratings & Symbols

Zagat Top Spot	Name	Symbols		Cuisine	Zagat Ratings			
					FOOD	DECOR	SERVICE	COST
Area, Address & Contact	**Z Tim & Nina's** ◗			*Ozark*	▽ 23	9	13	$15

Chelsea | 76 Ninth Ave. (bet. 15th & 16th Sts.) | 212-977-6000 | www.zagat.com

Review, surveyor comments in quotes

Lowlifes love this "down-and-out" dump under the High Line, a "former food truck" turned restaurant after its customers stole the wheels; ignoring repeated "C-grade" health inspections, fans praise Nina's "haute hot plate" Ozarks cuisine, but concede that the "reclaimed cardboard" decor and Tim's "offhanded service" need work; it has just "a few seats", "charges bupkis" and "doesn't take rezzies", yet somehow there's "never a line."

Ratings

Food, Decor & **Service** are rated on a 30-point scale.

26	–	30	extraordinary to perfection
21	–	25	very good to excellent
16	–	20	good to very good
11	–	15	fair to good
0	–	10	poor to fair

▽   low response | less reliable

Cost

The price of dinner with a drink and tip; lunch is usually 25% to 30% less. For unrated **newcomers,** the price range is as follows:

| I | $25 and below | E | $41 to $65 |
| M | $26 to $40 | VE | $66 or above |

Symbols

Z	highest ratings, popularity and importance
◗	serves after 11 PM
⑤ Ⓜ	closed on Sunday or Monday
⊄	no credit cards accepted

Maps

Index maps show restaurants with the highest Food ratings and other notable places in those areas.

About This Survey

- 2,120 restaurants rated and reviewed
- 44,306 surveyors
- 119 notable openings, 60 closings
- Meals out per week per surveyor: 3.0
- Winners: **Le Bernardin** (Food, Most Popular), **Asiate** (Decor), **Per Se** (Service)
- No. 1 Newcomer for Food: **North End Grill**

SURVEY STATS: Compared to a year ago, 19% report eating out more often, 60% at the same frequency and 21% less; 34% feel they're spending more, 55% are spending the same and only 11% feel they're spending less . . . Restaurant mobile phone use is edging toward acceptability: 58% find it inappropriate, compared to 62% last year . . . The average tip holds steady at 19% . . . Service remains dining's top drawback (58%), though noise/crowd complaints are up three points to 27%; prices bring up the rear at 8% . . . On a 30-pt. scale, NYC rates 28 for culinary diversity, 26 for creativity, 18 for hospitality and 15 for table availability

TRENDS: Call it NYC's year of the happening Asian restaurant, with a bumper crop including the low-cost hipster magnets **Mission Chinese** and **Pok Pok Ny,** the more polished **Cafe China, Dong Chun Hong, Maharlika, Talde** and **Wong** and the flat-out swanky **Hakkasan, Jungsik** and **Kristalbelli.** North Brooklyn continued its ascendance with Williamsburg's white-hot **Reynard** and Bushwick's big-ticket tasting-menu mecca, **Blanca.** Citywide, a still-sluggish economy has many entrants following a familiar formula – comfort-oriented menus, palatable prices – but there have been a few splashier arrivals as well.

BIG-NAME OPENINGS: Alain Allegretti (**La Promenade des Anglais**), Floyd Cardoz (**North End Grill**), John DeLucie (**Bill's**), Alex Garcia (**A.G. Kitchen**), Daniel Humm (**NoMad**), Marcus Samuelsson (**Ginny's Supper Club**), Gabe Stulman (**Perla**), Michael White (**Nicoletta**), Galen Zamarra (**Mas La Grillade**)

HOT SCENES: Acme, Catch, Corner Social, Mission Chinese, Reynard, Rosemary's, Super Linda

HOT NABES: West Village (**Mas La Grillade, Rosemary's, Wong**); East Village (**Boukiés, Calliope, Nicoletta**); Smith Street (**Arthur on Smith, Battersby, Dassara**); NoHo (**Acme, Saxon & Parole**); Williamsburg (**Gwynnett St., Reynard**)

MAJOR CLOSINGS: Asia de Cuba, Ben Benson's, L'Atelier de Joël Robuchon, Matsuri

JOIN IN: To improve our guides, we solicit your comments – positive or negative; it's vital that we hear your opinions. Just contact us at **nina-tim@zagat.com.** We also invite you to share your opinions at plus.google.com/local.

New York, NY
October 10, 2012

Nina and Tim Zagat

KEY NEWCOMERS

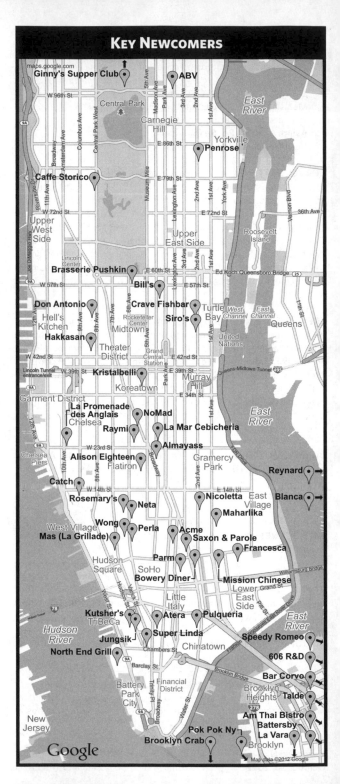

Ginny's Supper Club
ABV
Penrose
Caffe Storico
Brasserie Pushkin
Bill's
Don Antonio
Crave Fishbar
Siro's
Hakkasan
Kristalbelli
La Promenade des Anglais
NoMad
Raymi
La Mar Cebicheria
Almayass
Alison Eighteen
Reynard
Catch
Blanca
Rosemary's
Nicoletta
Neta
Maharlika
Wong
Perla
Acme
Mas (La Grillade)
Saxon & Parole
Francesca
Parm
Bowery Diner
Mission Chinese
Kutsher's
Atera
Pulqueria
Speedy Romeo
Jungsik
Super Linda
606 R&D
North End Grill
Bar Corvo
Talde
Am Thai Bistro
Battersby
Pok Pok Ny
La Vara
Brooklyn Crab

Google

Key Newcomers

Our editors' picks among this year's arrivals. See full list at p. 45.

BIG NAMES/BIG TICKETS

Atera
Blanca
Caffe Storico
La Promenade des Anglais
Mas (La Grillade)
Nicoletta
NoMad
North End Grill
Raymi
Reynard
Rosemary's

IMPORTS

Almayass
Brasserie Pushkin
Don Antonio
Hakkasan
Jungsik
La Mar Cebicheria
Mission Chinese
Pok Pok Ny
Siro's

NEIGHBORHOOD STARS

Battersby
Bowery Diner
La Vara
Saxon & Parole
606 R&D
Speedy Romeo
Super Linda

OLD NAMES, NEW LIFE

Acme
Alison Eighteen
Bill's
Kutsher's

ASIAN HEAT

Am Thai Bistro
Kristalbelli
Maharlika
Mission Chinese Food
Neta
Pok Pok Ny
Talde
Wong

CHIPS OFF THE OLD BLOCK

ABV
Bar Corvo
Francesca
Ginny's Supper Club
Parm
The Penrose
Perla
Pulqueria

FRESH CATCH

Catch
Crave Fishbar
Brooklyn Crab

PROJECTS ON TAP (See p. 46 for a complete list)

Beatrice Inn: Graydon Carter's revamp of the West Village hot spot

Carbone: The **Torrisi** team does white-tablecloth Italian in the Village

Juni: Shaun Hergatt partners with Jimmy Haber in Midtown's Hotel Chandler

Ladurée: Paris' macaron bastion opens a grand Gallic eatery in SoHo

Lady Mai: Loungey Chelsea sushi den from the **Bond Street** people

L'Apico: Another East Village Italian from the **Dell'anima/L'Artusi** team

Manzanilla: Flatiron Spaniard from Yann de Rochefort and Dani Garcia

The Marrow: West Village meatery from Harold Dieterle (**Perilla, Kin Shop**)

Sirio Ristorante: Sirio Maccioni (**Le Cirque**) brings his Vegas-born Tuscan concept to the Pierre's erstwhile **Le Caprice** quarters

TriBeCa Canvas: Masaharu Morimoto's long-awaited comfort-fooder

Yet-to-be-named French eatery from Andrew Carmellini (**The Dutch, Locanda Verde**) in NoHo's former **Chinatown Brasserie** digs

Branches on the way: Delmonico's (Garment District), **Ippudo** (West 50s), **Salumeria Rosi Parmacotto** (UES), **Tao** (Meatpacking)

Most Popular

This list is plotted on the map at the back of this book.

1. Le Bernardin | *French/Seafood*
2. Gramercy Tavern | *American*
3. Eleven Madison Park | *French*
4. Peter Luger (Bklyn) | *Steak*
5. Daniel | *French*
6. Gotham Bar & Grill | *American*
7. Babbo | *Italian*
8. Union Square Cafe* | *American*
9. 21 Club | *American*
10. Jean Georges | *French*
11. ABC Kitchen | *American*
12. 5 Napkin Burger | *Burgers*
13. Balthazar | *French*
14. Per Se | *American/French*
15. Bouley | *French*
16. Del Posto | *Italian*
17. Atlantic Grill | *Seafood*
18. Marea | *Italian/Seafood*
19. Rosa Mexicano | *Mexican*
20. Becco | *Italian*
21. Café Boulud | *French*
22. La Grenouille | *French*
23. Four Seasons | *American*
24. Palm | *Steak*
25. Blue Water Grill | *Seafood*
26. Nobu | *Japanese*
27. A Voce | *Italian*
28. Shake Shack | *Burgers*
29. Katz's Deli | *Deli*
30. Bar Boulud | *French*
31. Modern | *American/French*
32. Del Frisco's | *Steak*
33. Boulud Sud | *Mediterranean*
34. Jean Georges' Nougatine | *Fr.*
35. Carmine's | *Italian*
36. Aureole | *American*
37. Aquagrill | *Seafood*
38. 2nd Ave Deli | *Deli/Kosher*
39. Buddakan | *Asian*
40. Capital Grille | *Steak*
41. Maialino | *Italian*
42. Blue Hill | *American*
43. Bar Americain | *American*
44. Blue Smoke | *BBQ*
45. Il Mulino | *Italian*
46. Eataly | *Italian*
47. Aquavit | *Scandinavian*
48. Telepan | *American*
49. Felidia | *Italian*
50. Artisanal | *French*

Many of the above restaurants are among New York City's most expensive, but if popularity were calibrated to price, a number of other restaurants would surely join their ranks. To illustrate this, we have added two pages of Best Buys starting on page 22.

* Indicates a tie with restaurant above

Top Food

29 Le Bernardin | *French/Seafood*
Per Se | *American/French*

28 Bouley | *French*
Daniel | *French*
Eleven Madison Park | *French*
Jean Georges | *French*
La Grenouille | *French*
Mas (Farmhouse) | *American*
Sushi Yasuda | *Japanese*
Sushi Seki | *Japanese*
Grocery (Bklyn) | *American*
Gramercy Tavern | *American*
Marea | *Italian/Seafood*
Gotham Bar & Grill | *American*
Annisa | *American*

27 Peter Luger (Bklyn) | *Steak*
Lucali (Bklyn) | *Pizza*
Saul (Bklyn) | *American*
Picholine | *Fr./Med.*
Milos | *Greek/Seafood*
Il Mulino | *Italian*
Scalini Fedeli | *Italian*
Brooklyn Fare (Bklyn) | *French*
Torrisi Italian | *Italian*
L'Artusi | *Italian*
Blue Hill | *American*

Tanoreen (Bklyn) | *Med./Mid.*
Jean Georges' Nougatine | *Fr.*
Tratt. L'incontro (Qns) | *Italian*
Gari | *Japanese*
Pylos | *Greek*
Union Square Cafe | *American*
Masa/Bar Masa | *Japanese*
Nobu | *Japanese*
Perilla | *American*
Four Seasons | *American*
Tav. Kyclades (Qns) | *Gr./Sea.*
Al Di La (Bklyn) | *Italian*
Babbo | *Italian*
Pepolino | *Italian*
Café Boulud | *French*
Tocqueville | *American/French*
Telepan | *American*
Sripraphai (Qns) | *Thai*
Aquagrill | *Seafood*
Adour | *French*
Di Fara (Bklyn) | *Pizza*

26 Craft | *American*
Modern | *American/French*
Morimoto | *Japanese*
Corton | *French*
Momofuku Ko | *Amer.*

BY CUISINE

AMERICAN

29 Per Se
28 Mas (Farmhouse)
Grocery (Bklyn)
Gramercy Tavern
Gotham Bar & Grill
Annisa
27 Saul (Bklyn)
Blue Hill
Union Square Cafe
Perilla
Four Seasons
Tocqueville

ASIAN

25 Asiate
Buddakan
Talde (Bklyn)
24 Wong
Tao
Fatty Fish
1066 Eno
23 Wild Ginger

AUSTRIAN/GERMAN/ SWISS

26 Wallsé
25 Seäsonal
24 Zum Stammtisch (Qns)
23 Edi & the Wolf
22 Café Sabarsky
Zum Schneider
Blaue Gans
19 Heidelberg

BARBECUE

26 Fette Sau (Bklyn)
23 Dinosaur BBQ
Hill Country
Fatty 'Cue
Rub BBQ
Smoke Joint (Bklyn)
Blue Smoke
22 Rack & Soul

Excludes places with low votes, unless otherwise indicated

BURGERS

24 Burger Joint/Le Parker
   Burger Bistro (Bklyn)
   DuMont (Bklyn)
23 BareBurger
   Bonnie's Grill (Bklyn)
   Corner Bistro
22 Island Burgers
   B&B

CARIBBEAN

24 Sofrito
   Cuba
23 Negril
   Café Habana/Outpost
   Amor Cubano
   Cubana Café (Bklyn)
22 Victor's Cafe
   El Malecon

CHICKEN

26 Torishin▽
23 Pio Pio
22 El Malecon
   BonChon Chicken
21 Flor de Mayo
   Coco Roco
   Kyochon Chicken
20 Hill Country Chicken

CHINESE

26 RedFarm
24 Shanghai Café
   Chin Chin
   Xi'an Famous Foods
   Spicy & Tasty (Qns)
   Pacificana (Bklyn)
   Shun Lee Palace
   BaoHaus

DELIS

(see also Sandwiches)
25 Mile End (Bklyn)
   Katz's Deli
24 Barney Greengrass
23 Ben's Best (Qns)
   Carnegie Deli
   2nd Ave Deli
   Mill Basin (Bklyn)
22 Pastrami Queen

DESSERT

25 ChikaLicious
   Chocolate Room (Bklyn)
   L & B Spumoni (Bklyn)
24 Bouchon Bakery
   Veniero's

   Kyotofu
22 Momofuku Milk Bar
   Café Sabarsky

DIM SUM

26 RedFarm
24 Pacificana (Bklyn)
23 Lychee House
   Excellent Dumpling
   Oriental Garden
22 Nom Wah Tea
21 Golden Unicorn
   Ping's Seafood

ECLECTIC

27 Traif (Bklyn)
25 Graffiti
   Carol's Café (SI)
   WD-50
   Good Fork (Bklyn)
24 Stanton Social
23 Beauty & Essex
   Plaza Food Hall

FRENCH

29 Le Bernardin
28 Bouley
   Daniel
   Eleven Madison Park
   Jean Georges
   La Grenouille
27 Brooklyn Fare (Bklyn)
   Café Boulud

FRENCH BISTRO

25 Le Gigot
   Raoul's
   DB Bistro Moderne
   La Silhouette
24 JoJo
   Tournesol (Qns)
   Minetta Tavern
   Bar Boulud

GREEK

27 Milos Estiatorio
   Pylos
   Taverna Kyclades (Qns)
26 Eliá (Bklyn)
25 Avra
24 Thalassa
   Agnanti (Qns)
   Aegean Cove (Qns)

INDIAN

26 Tamarind
25 Amma
24 Junoon

Vatan
Banjara
Tulsi
23 Dhaba
Chola

ITALIAN

28 Marea
27 Il Mulino
Scalini Fedeli
Torrisi Italian
L'Artusi
Tratt. L'incontro (Qns)
Al Di La (Bklyn)
Babbo
Pepolino
Il Bambino (Qns)
26 Del Posto
Sistina

JAPANESE/SUSHI

29 Sasabune
28 Soto
Sushi Yasuda
Sushi Seki
Kajitsu
27 Kyo Ya
Gari
Masa/Bar Masa
Nobu
26 Sushi Zen
Morimoto
Blue Ribbon Sushi

KOREAN

26 Danji
25 HanGawi
23 Cho Dang Gol
Kang Suh
22 Do Hwa
Kum Gang San
BonChon Chicken
Gahm Mi Oak

KOSHER

26 Solo
25 Azuri Cafe
24 Caravan of Dreams
Prime Grill/KO
23 Ben's Best (Qns)
Peacefood Café
Colbeh
2nd Ave Deli

LOBSTER ROLLS

26 Pearl Oyster Bar
Red Hook Lobster (Bklyn)

25 Mary's Fish Camp
24 Luke's Lobster
Ed's Lobster Bar
23 Brooklyn Fish (Bklyn)
22 Mermaid
20 Ed's Chowder House

MEDITERRANEAN

27 Picholine
Tanoreen (Bklyn)
26 Alta
Solo
Il Buco
Little Owl
25 Convivium Osteria (Bklyn)
Boulud Sud

MEXICAN

24 Mercadito
Pampano
Toloache
El Paso Taqueria
Maya
Barrio Chino
Hell's Kitchen
23 Sueños

MIDDLE EASTERN

27 Tanoreen (Bklyn)
26 Taïm
Taci's Beyti (Bklyn)
25 Taboon
Ilili
Azuri Cafe
24 Balaboosta
23 Shalezeh

NOODLE SHOPS

26 Totto Ramen
Ippudo
25 Momofuku Noodle Bar
Soba Totto
Soba-ya
24 Xi'an Famous
23 Pho Bang
Great NY Noodle

PIZZA

27 Lucali (Bklyn)
Luzzo's/Ovest
Di Fara (Bklyn)
26 Denino's (SI)
Roberta's (Bklyn)
Basil Brick Oven Pizza (Qns)
25 Franny's (Bklyn)
Keste Pizza e Vino

RAW BARS

27 Aquagrill
26 Pearl Oyster Bar
25 Blue Ribbon
   Esca
24 Oceana
   Fishtail/David Burke
23 BLT Fish
   Oyster Bar

RUSSIAN

26 Brasserie Pushkin
21 Tatiana (Bklyn)▽
   Mari Vanna
   Russian Tea Room
   Russian Samovar
20 FireBird
18 Rasputin
 - Nasha Rasha

SANDWICHES

(see also Delis)
27 Il Bambino (Qns)
26 Leo's Lattacini/Corona (Qns)
25 Num Pang
   'Ino
   Porchetta
24 Parm
   Bouchon Bakery
   Meatball Shop

SEAFOOD

29 Le Bernardin
28 Marea
27 Milos Estiatorio
   Taverna Kyclades (Qns)
   Aquagrill
26 Pearl Oyster Bar
   Red Hook Lobster (Bklyn)
25 Mary's Fish

SMALL PLATES

28 Degustation
27 Traif (Bklyn)
26 Alta
   Zenkichi (Bklyn)
   Danji
   EN Japanese
25 Salumeria Rosi
   Sakagura

SOUTH AMERICAN

25 Caracas
   Buenos Aires
24 Arepas Café (Qns)
   La Mar Cebicheria
   Churrascaria

Empanada Mama
23 Circus
   Chimichurri Grill

SOUTHERN/SOUL

25 Pies-n-Thighs (Bklyn)
24 Peaches (Bklyn)
   Melba's
   Redhead
   Egg (Bklyn)
23 Char No. 4 (Bklyn)
   Seersucker* (Bklyn)
   Miss Mamie's/Maude's

SPANISH/TAPAS

28 Degustation
26 Tía Pol
25 Casa Mono
   Sevilla
24 Txikito
   Beso (SI)
   Tertulia
23 Boqueria

STEAKHOUSES

27 Peter Luger (Bklyn)
26 Sparks Steak
   Wolfgang's
   Keens
   Quality Meats
   Strip House
   Porter House NY
   Ruth's Chris
   Benjamin Steak
   Manzo
25 BLT Prime
   BLT Steak

THAI

27 Sripraphai (Qns)
26 Pure Thai Cookhouse
25 Kuma Inn
   Kin Shop
24 Erawan (Qns)
   Am Thai Bistro (Bklyn)
   Song (Bklyn)
   Kittichai

TURKISH

26 Taci's Beyti (Bklyn)
23 Sahara (Bklyn)
22 Hanci Turkish
   Akdeniz
   Beyoglu
   Turkish Kitchen
   Uskudar
   Bodrum

VEGETARIAN

28	Kajitsu
26	Taïm
	Dirt Candy
25	Pure Food & Wine
	HanGawi
	Candle 79
	Candle Cafe
24	Caravan of Dreams

VIETNAMESE

24	Omai
23	Pho Bang
	Nha Trang
22	Le Colonial
	Nicky's Viet.
	An Choi
	Bo-Ky
	Baoguette

BY SPECIAL FEATURE

BREAKFAST

27	Jean Georges' Nougatine
26	Clinton St. Baking Co.
	Maialino
25	Norma's
	Locanda Verde
	Marlow & Sons (Bklyn)
	Buvette
	Katz's Deli

BRUNCH DOWNTOWN

25	Prune
24	Minetta Tavern
	DBGB
	Balaboosta
	Fat Radish
23	Saxon & Parole
22	Five Points
21	Peels

BRUNCH MIDTOWN

26	Maialino
25	Ilili
23	Cookshop
22	Eatery
21	Resto
	Almond
	Lexington Brass▽
19	Friend of a Farmer

BRUNCH UPTOWN

25	Ouest
23	Red Rooster
22	Cafe D'Alsace
	Calle Ocho
21	Sarabeth's
20	Jones Wood Foundry
	Nice Matin
⌐	A.G. Kitchen

CELEBRITY SCENES

24	Minetta Tavern
	Spotted Pig
22	Da Silvano

	Lion
	Leopard at des Artistes
21	Crown
	Darby
⌐	Bill's

CHILD-FRIENDLY

25	Buttermilk Channel (Bklyn)
	L&B Spumoni (Bklyn)
23	Blue Smoke
	Max Brenner
21	Landmarc
20	Serendipity 3
19	Ninja
	Ruby Foo's

DINING AT THE BAR

28	Gramercy Tavern
	Gotham Bar & Grill
25	Hearth
	Colicchio & Sons
	Lincoln
23	Plaza Food Hall
	Oyster Bar
22	Freemans

DRINKS DOWNTOWN

28	Gramercy Tavern
	Gotham Bar & Grill
25	Bond Street
24	Stanton Social
	Minetta Tavern
	STK
	Balthazar
	Blue Water Grill

DRINKS MIDTOWN

27	Nobu
	Four Seasons
26	Modern
	Morimoto
	Keens
	Maialino
25	Le Cirque
	Del Frisco's

DRINKS UPTOWN

- __28__ Daniel
- Jean Georges
- __27__ Masa/Bar Masa
- __25__ Ouest
- __24__ Bar Boulud
- __23__ Mark
- Atlantic Grill
- Red Rooster

GROUP DINING

- __25__ Ilili
- Buddakan
- __24__ Stanton Social
- Tao
- Churrascaria
- Otto
- __23__ Rosa Mexicano
- __22__ Carmine's

HISTORIC PLACES

- __27__ Peter Luger (Bklyn)
- Four Seasons
- __26__ Keens
- __25__ Old Homestead
- Diner (Bklyn)
- Palm
- __23__ Oyster Bar
- __-__ Bill's

HOTEL DINING

- __28__ Jean Georges (Trump Int'l)
- Café Boulud (Surrey)
- Adour (St. Regis)
- __26__ Ai Fiori (Setai Fifth Ave.)
- Gilt (NY Palace)
- Benjamin Steak (Dylan)
- Maialino (Gramercy Park)
- __25__ Norma's (Le Parker Meridien)

HOT SERVERS

- __25__ Del Frisco's
- __24__ Spice Market
- __22__ Abe & Arthur's
- Indochine
- Cafe Gitane
- 44 & X/44½
- __21__ Miss Lily's
- __17__ Brother Jimmy's BBQ

HOT SPOTS

- __25__ Rosemary's▽
- __23__ Catch
- __22__ Acme
- Lavo
- __21__ Corner Social▽
- __-__ Bagatelle

- __-__ Mission Chinese
- __-__ Reynard (Bklyn)

HUSH-HUSH

- __26__ Bohemian▽
- __25__ Sakagura
- __24__ Burger Joint/Le Parker
- Hudson Clearwater
- __23__ Beecher's Cellar
- Kashkaval
- La Esquina
- __22__ Freemans

LATE DINING

- __25__ Blue Ribbon
- 'Ino
- __23__ Wollensky's Grill
- Covo
- __22__ Hop Kee
- Pastis
- Artichoke Basille's
- __21__ Cebu (Bklyn)

LOCAVORE

- __28__ Mas (Farmhouse)
- __27__ Blue Hill
- Telepan
- __26__ Craft
- ABC Kitchen
- Roberta's (Bklyn)
- __25__ Rosemary's▽
- Riverpark

MILESTONES

- 100th Oyster Bar
- 75th Brennan & Carr
- Heidelberg
- Wo Hop
- 25th Aureole
- Cafe Lalo
- Isabella's
- Trattoria Dell'Arte

NEWCOMERS (RATED)

- __25__ North End Grill
- Talde (Bklyn)
- La Promenade des Anglais
- __24__ Wong
- Don Antonio
- Parm
- Am Thai (Bklyn)
- La Mar Cebicheria

PRIVATE PARTIES

- __29__ Le Bernardin
- Per Se
- __28__ Daniel
- Eleven Madison Park

Jean Georges
La Grenouille
Gramercy Tavern
Marea

QUICK BITES

26 Leo's Latticini
Momofuku Ssäm Bar
25 Num Pang
Momofuku Noodle Bar
Azuri Cafe
Porchetta
24 Parm
Meatball Shop

SINGLES SCENES

25 Del Frisco's
Koi
Buddakan
24 Stanton Social
Hudson Clearwater
Tao
STK
23 Beauty & Essex

SOCIETY WATCH

25 David Burke Townhouse
24 Elio's
Arabelle
22 Leopard at des Artistes
Sant Ambroeus
21 Ze Café
Crown
18 Swifty's

24/7

24 Sanford's (Qns)
Empanada Mama

23 Coppelia
Kang Suh
21 Cafeteria
20 Veselka (First Ave.)
Bubby's (TriBeCa)
18 Bowery Diner

VISITORS ON EXPENSE ACCOUNT

29 Le Bernardin
Per Se
28 Bouley
Daniel
Eleven Madison Park
Jean Georges
La Grenouille
Sushi Yasuda

WINE BARS

26 Danny Brown (Qns)
Il Buco Alimentari
25 SD26
24 Peasant
Bar Boulud
23 Bar Jamon
21 Felice
Terroir

WINNING WINE LISTS

29 Le Bernardin
Per Se
28 Bouley
Daniel
Eleven Madison Park
Jean Georges
Mas (Farmhouse)
Gramercy Tavern

BY LOCATION

CHELSEA

26 Morimoto
Del Posto
Scarpetta
Tía Pol
25 Da Umberto
Ilili
La Bergamote
Colicchio & Sons

CHINATOWN

24 Xi'an Famous Foods
23 Great NY Noodle
Nice Green Bo
Nha Trang
Peking Duck

Wo Hop
Excellent Dumpling
Oriental Garden

EAST 40s

28 Sushi Yasuda
26 Sparks Steak
Benjamin Steak
25 Aburiya Kinnosuke
Sakagura
Num Pang
Avra
Grifone

EAST 50s

28 La Grenouille
27 Four Seasons

Adour
26 Gilt
Wolfgang's
Felidia
Solo
25 Caviar Russe

EAST 60s
28 Daniel
Sushi Seki
26 Tiella
25 Scalinatella
David Burke Townhouse
Rouge Tomate
Park Avenue
24 JoJo

EAST 70s
29 Sasabune
27 Gari
Café Boulud
26 Caravaggio
25 Candle 79
Candle Cafe
24 Numero 28
V-Note

EAST 80s
26 Sistina
Sandro's
25 Giovanni
Poke
Erminia
24 Toloache
Spigolo
Elio's

EAST 90s & 100s
24 El Paso Taqueria
Pinocchio
Nick's
Sfoglia
23 Pio Pio
Paola's
Rizzo's Pizza
Square Meal

FINANCIAL DISTRICT
25 North End Grill
Capital Grille
24 Toloache
Adrienne's Pizza
Luke's Lobster
MarkJoseph Steak
Harry's Cafe/Steak
Delmonico's

FLATIRON/UNION SQ.
28 Eleven Madison Park
Gramercy Tavern
27 Union Square Cafe
Tocqueville
26 Craft
Tamarind
15 East
ABC Kitchen

GARMENT DISTRICT
26 Ai Fiori
Keens
24 Mercato
Uncle Jack's
23 Cho Dang Gol
Frankie & Johnnie's
Colbeh
Szechuan Gourmet

GRAMERCY
26 Maialino
25 BLT Prime
Casa Mono
Pure Food & Wine
Novitá
24 Posto
Defonte's
Yama

GREENWICH VILLAGE
28 Gotham Bar & Grill
27 Il Mulino
Blue Hill
Babbo
26 Alta
Strip House
Tomoe Sushi
25 Num Pang

HARLEM
24 Melba's
23 Dinosaur BBQ
Lido*
Covo
Miss Mamie's/Maude's
5 & Diamond
Red Rooster
22 Amy Ruth's

LITTLE ITALY
25 Pellegrino's
24 Shanghai Café
Ferrara
Vincent's
23 Angelo's, Mulberry St.
Nyonya

Pho Bang
La Esquina

LOWER EAST SIDE

26 Clinton St. Baking Co.
25 Ápizz
Kuma Inn
WD-50
Katz's Deli
24 Stanton Social
Meatball Shop
Barrio Chino

MEATPACKING

25 Valbella
Old Homestead
24 STK
Spice Market
23 Catch
Sea
Macelleria
22 Abe & Arthur's

MURRAY HILL

26 Marcony
Wolfgang's
25 HanGawi
SD26
Primehouse NY
Ben & Jack's
Riverpark
24 Villa Berulia

NOHO

26 Bianca
Il Buco
25 Bond Street
Mile End
23 Aroma Kitchen & Winebar
Forcella
Hecho en Dumbo
Saxon & Parole

NOLITA

27 Torrisi Italian
25 Lombardi's
24 Peasant
Parm
Balaboosta
Ed's Lobster Bar
23 Café Habana
Public

SOHO

27 Aquagrill
26 Blue Ribbon Sushi
25 Blue Ribbon

Raoul's
24 L'Ecole
Numero 28
Osteria Morini
David Burke Kitchen

TRIBECA

28 Bouley
27 Scalini Fedeli
Nobu
Pepolino
26 Corton
Tamarind
Wolfgang's
25 Brushstroke

WEST 40s

27 Gari
26 Sushi Zen
Aureole
Wolfgang's
25 Del Frisco's
Esca
DB Bistro Moderne
Koi

WEST 50s

29 Le Bernardin
28 Marea
27 Milos Estiatorio
Nobu
26 Modern
Totto Ramen
Quality Meats
Danji

WEST 60s

29 Per Se
28 Jean Georges
27 Picholine
Jean Georges' Nougatine
Masa/Bar Masa
Telepan
26 Porter House NY
25 Asiate

WEST 70s

27 Gari
25 Salumeria Rosi
Dovetail
24 Ocean Grill
'Cesca
23 Saravanaa Bhavan
FishTag
Hummus Place

WEST 80s

27 Recipe
  Candle Cafe
  Ouest
24 Momoya
  Barney Greengrass
  Celeste
  Luke's Lobster
  Prime Ko

WEST 90s & UP

25 Pisticci
24 Gennaro
  Thai Market
  Max SoHa/Caffe

23 Pio Pio
  Community Food
  Vareli
  Hummus Place

WEST VILLAGE

28 Soto
  Mas (Farmhouse)
  Annisa
27 L'Artusi
  Perilla
26 Pearl Oyster Bar
  Taïm
  RedFarm

BROOKLYN

BAY RIDGE

27 Tanoreen
26 Eliá
  Tuscany Grill
25 Areo
24 Chadwick's
  Burger Bistro
23 Fushimi
  Embers

BKLYN HTS/DUMBO

26 River Café
  Colonie
25 Henry's End
  Noodle Pudding
  Queen
24 Grimaldi's
  Jack the Horse
22 Rice

CARROLL GARDENS/ BOERUM & COBBLE HILLS

28 Grocery
27 Lucali
  Saul
25 Chocolate Room
  Ki Sushi
  Buttermilk Channel
  Mile End
  Fragole

FORT GREENE/ PROSPECT HEIGHTS

25 Franny's
  James
24 Abistro

  606 R&D
  Madiba
23 Caffe e Vino
  Habana Outpost
  No. 7

PARK SLOPE

27 Al Di La
26 Rose Water
25 Blue Ribbon Brooklyn
  Chocolate Room
  Convivium Osteria
  Bogota Latin
  Applewood
  Talde

WILLIAMSBURG

27 Peter Luger
  Traif
26 Fette Sau
  Dressler
  Zenkichi
25 Caracas
  Diner
  Marlow & Sons

OTHER AREAS

27 Brooklyn Fare (Downtown)
  Di Fara (Midwood)
26 Taci's Beyti (Midwood)
  Five Leaves (Greenpoint)
  Red Hook Lobster (Red Hook)
  Locanda Vini/Olii (Clinton Hill)
  Roberta's (Bushwick)
25 Totonno Pizza (Coney Island)

OTHER BOROUGHS

BRONX

26 Roberto
25 Patricia's
24 Jake's
Zero Otto Nove
Dominick's
Sammy's Shrimp Box
Enzo's
Artie's

QUEENS: ASTORIA/LIC

27 Tratt. L'incontro
Taverna Kyclades
Il Bambino
26 Basil Brick Oven Pizza
25 Piccola Venezia
Christos
24 Tournesol
Arepas Café

QUEENS: OTHER AREAS

27 Sripraphai (Woodside)
26 Salt & Fat (Sunnyside)
Leo's Latticini (Corona)
Danny Brown (Forest Hills)
Don Peppe (Ozone Park)
25 Park Side (Corona)
24 Zum Stammtisch (Glendale)
Erawan (Bayside)

STATEN ISLAND

26 Denino's
Trattoria Romana
Bocelli
25 Carol's Cafe
24 Beso
Da Noi
Angelina's
Joe & Pat's

Top Decor

PATIOS/GARDENS

Aurora
Barbetta
Battery Gardens
B Bar & Grill
Boathouse
Brasserie Ruhlmann
Bryant Park
Cávo (Qns)
Château Cherbuliez
Gran Electrica (Bklyn)
I Trulli
New Leaf
Pure Food & Wine
Raoul's
Salinas
ViceVersa

PRIVATE ROOMS

Breslin
City Hall
Del Posto
Eleven Madison Park
Felidia
Ilili
Keens
Le Grenouille
Lincoln
Megu
Patroon
Public
River Café (Bklyn)
SD26
21 Club
Valbella

ROMANCE

Erminia
Flor de Sol
Gascogne
House
Il Buco
Kings' Carriage
La Lanterna di Vittorio
Lambs Club
Mas (Farmhouse)
One if by Land
Peasant
Place
River Café (Bklyn)
Valentino's on the Green (Qns)
Wallsé
Zenkichi (Bklyn)

VIEWS

Asiate
A Voce
Battery Gardens
Boathouse
Brooklyn Crab (Bklyn)
Gigino
Lincoln
Michael Jordan's

Modern
Per Se
River Café (Bklyn)
Robert
Sea Grill
View
Water Club
Water's Edge (Qns)

Top Service

29 Per Se
Le Bernardin

28 Eleven Madison Park
Daniel
La Grenouille
Jean Georges

27 Bouley
Four Seasons
Gramercy Tavern
Mas (Farmhouse)
Annisa
Grocery (Bklyn)
Adour
Carlyle
Scalini Fedeli

26 Del Posto
Gotham Bar & Grill
Tocqueville
Marea
Union Square Cafe

Picholine
Corton
Blue Hill
River Café (Bklyn)
Asiate
Brushstroke
Il Tinello
Jean Georges' Nougatine
Café Boulud
Tratt. L'incontro (Qns)
North End Grill
Ai Fiori

25 Le Cirque
Craft
Veritas
Le Gigot
Modern
Aureole
One if by Land
Danny Brown (Qns)

Best Buys

Everyone loves a bargain, and NYC offers plenty of them. Bear in mind: (1) lunch typically costs 25 to 30% less than dinner, (2) outer-borough dining is far less costly than in Manhattan, (3) most Indian restaurants offer incredibly inexpensive prix fixe lunch buffets and (4) biannual Restaurant Weeks (in January and July) are big bargains.

ALL YOU CAN EAT

- 24 La Baraka (Qns)
- Churrascaria
- 23 Chola
- Dhaba
- Tony's Di Napoli
- Becco
- 22 Indus Valley
- Yuka
- Darbar
- 19 East Buffet (Qns)

BYO

- 27 Lucali (Bklyn)
- Di Fara (Bklyn)
- 26 Taci's Beyti (Bklyn)
- 25 Kuma Inn
- Tea & Sympathy
- Poke
- 23 Tartine
- Phoenix Garden
- Nook
- Lychee House

CHEAP DATES

- 26 Sauce▽
- Bianca
- 25 Keste Pizza e Vino
- Soba-ya
- 24 Don Antonio
- 23 26 Seats
- Uva
- 22 Social Eatz
- 21 Corner Social▽
- La Lanterna di Vittorio

EARLY-BIRD

- 25 Ouest
- 24 JoJo
- Chadwick's (Bklyn)
- La Mar Cebicheria
- Kittichai
- 23 Italianissimo
- Sueños
- Kefi
- China Grill
- 19 Orsay

FAMILY-STYLE

- 26 Piccolo Angolo
- Don Peppe (Qns)
- 25 Pisticci
- 24 Dominick's (Bronx)
- 23 Tony's Di Napoli
- Rao's
- 22 La Mela
- Carmine's
- Osso Buco
- 21 Sambuca

PRE-THEATER

- 28 Sugiyama▽
- 27 Jean Georges' Nougatine
- 25 DB Bistro Moderne
- Maze
- 24 Circo
- 23 Molyvos
- Atlantic Grill
- 22 Indochine
- 21 Thalia
- 20 Maria Pia

PRIX FIXE LUNCH

- 28 Bouley ($49)
- Jean Georges ($38)
- Gotham Bar & Grill ($25)
- 27 Milos, Estiatorio ($24)
- Four Seasons ($35)
- Tocqueville ($29)
- 26 Aureole ($36)
- 25 Del Frisco's ($34)
- 24 21 Club ($37)
- 23 Philippe ($20)

PRIX FIXE DINNER

- 28 Sushi Yasuda ($23)
- 25 Poke ($35)
- 24 Periyali ($35)
- 23 Apiary ($37)
- Etcetera Etcetera ($35)
- La Mangeoire ($35)
- 22 Abboccato ($35)
- 21 Docks Oyster Bar ($34)
- Le Relais/Venise L'Entrecôte ($25)
- 20 Nice Matin ($35)

BEST BUYS: FULL MENU

Azuri Cafe | *Israeli/Kosher*
Big Wong | *Chinese*
Bo-Ky | *Noodle Shop*
Brennan & Carr (Bkln) | *Sandwiches*
Café Habana | *Cuban/Mexican*
Calexico | *Mexican*
Chai Home Kitchen | *Thai*
Chef Yu | *Chinese*
Chickpea | *Mideastern*
Cubana Café (Bkln) | *Cuban*
Dos Toros | *Mexican*
Egg (Bkln) | *Southern*
Eisenberg's | *Sandwiches*
El Malecon | *Dominican*
Friedman's Lunch | *American*
Hill Country Chicken | *Southern*
Hummus Place | *Israeli/Kosh/Veg.*
Il Bambino (Qns) | *Italian*
Joe & Pat's (S.I.) | *Italian/Pizza*
Joya (Bkln) | *Thai*
Lime Jungle | *Mexican*
Little Poland | *Diner/Polish*
Maoz | *Mideastern/Veg.*
Menkui Tei | *Japanese/Noodles*
Mexicue | *BBQ/Mexican*

Mission Chinese| *Chinese*
Noodle Bar | *Asian/Noodle Shop*
Num Pang | *Cambodian/Sandwiches*
Oaxaca | *Mexican*
Omonia Café (Qns) | *Coffee/Greek*
Parm | *Italian/Sandwiches*
Peacefood Café | *Kosh/Vegan/Veg.*
Peaches (Bkln) | *Southern*
Penelope | *American*
Peter's Since 1969 | *American*
Pho Bang | *Noodles/Vietnamese*
Pies-n-Thighs (Bkln) | *Soul Food*
Piper's Kilt | *Burgers/Pub Food*
Pok Pok Ny (Bkln) | *Thai*
Pure Thai | *Thai*
Rice | *Eclectic*
Sanford's (Qns) | *American*
Song (Bkln) | *Thai*
Taïm | *Israeli/Veg.*
Tasty Hand-Pulled | *Noodle Shop*
Tiffin Wallah | *Indian/Veg.*
Tom's (Bkln) | *Diner*
Totto Ramen | *Japanese/Noodles*
Xi'an | *Chinese*
Zaytoons (Bkln) | *Mideastern*

BEST BUYS: SPECIALTY SHOPS

Arepas Café (Qns) | *Arepas*
Artichoke Basille's | *Pizza*
Baoguette | *Sandwiches*
BaoHaus | *Sandwiches*
BareBurger | *Burgers*
Bark (Bkln) | *Hot Dogs*
Best Pizza (Bkln) | *Pizza*
Black Iron | *Burgers*
Blue 9 | *Burgers*
Brgr | *Burgers*
Burger Joint | *Burgers*
Caracas | *Arepas*
Carl's | *Cheesesteaks*
ChikaLicious | *Dessert*
Chocolate Room (Bkln) | *Dessert*
Creperie | *Crêpes*
Crif Dogs | *Hot Dogs*
Defonte's | *Sandwiches*
Dumpling Man | *Dumplings*
Empanada Mama | *Empanadas*
Five Guys | *Burgers*
Goodburger | *Burgers*
Gray's Papaya | *Hot Dogs*
Hampton Chutney | *Dosas*
Hanco's (Bkln) | *Sandwiches*

Island | *Burgers*
Joe's Pizza | *Pizza*
Kati Roll Co. | *Kati Wraps*
Leo's Latticini (Qns) | *Sandwiches*
Lucky's | *Burgers*
Momofuku Milk Bar | *Dessert*
Nicky's Viet. | *Sandwiches*
99 Miles to Philly | *Cheesesteaks*
Papaya King | *Hot Dogs*
Peanut Butter | *Sandwiches*
Pizza 33 | *Pizza*
Porchetta | *Sandwiches*
Potbelly | *Sandwiches*
Rizzo's | *Pizza*
Rocket Pig | *Sandwiches*
Roll-n-Roaster (Bkln) | *Sandwiches*
Shake Shack | *Burgers*
Shorty's | *Cheesesteaks*
67 Burger (Bkln) | *Burgers*
S'MAC | *Mac 'n' Cheese*
SNice | *Sandwiches*
Steak 'n Shake | *Burgers*
Sweet Melissa (Bkln) | *Dessert*
Two Boots | *Pizza*
'Wichcraft | *Sandwiches*

Latest openings, menus, photos and more on plus.google.com/local

OTHER USEFUL LISTS*

LOCATION MAPS

---

* These lists include low vote places that do not qualify for top lists.

Special Features

Listings cover the best in each category and include names, locations and Food ratings. Multi-location restaurants' features may vary by branch.

BAR/SINGLES SCENES

NEW Rosemary's | **W Vill**	25
Blue Ribbon | **multi.**	25
Del Frisco's | **W 40s**	25
Koi | **W 40s**	25
Buddakan | **Chelsea**	25
Stanton Social | **LES**	24
Hudson Clearwater | **W Vill**	24
Tao | **E 50s**	24
STK | **Meatpacking**	24
DBGB | **E Vill**	24
Blue Water | **Union Sq**	24
Breslin | **Chelsea**	24
Boca Chica | **E Vill**	24
Spice Market | **Meatpacking**	24
Otto | **G Vill**	24
Dutch | **SoHo**	24
Joya | **Cobble Hill**	23
NEW Catch | **Meatpacking**	23
Hillstone | **multi.**	23
Butter | **E Vill**	23
Bobo | **W Vill**	23
Lure Fishbar | **SoHo**	23
Beauty & Essex | **LES**	23
NEW Saxon & Parole | **NoHo**	23
La Esquina | **L Italy**	23
SushiSamba | **multi.**	23
Atlantic Grill | **E 70s**	23
Cabana | **multi.**	23
Betel | **W Vill**	22
Abe/Arthur | **Meatpacking**	22
Social Eatz | **E 50s**	22
Freemans | **LES**	22
Pastis | **Meatpacking**	22
Standard Grill | **Meatpacking**	22
Lion | **G Vill**	22
NEW Perla | **G Vill**	22
Lavo | **E 50s**	22
'Inoteca | **LES**	22
NEW Corner Social | **Harlem**	21
NEW Sons of Essex | **LES**	21
Hurricane Club | **Flatiron**	21
Miss Lily's | **G Vill**	21
Pulino's | **NoLita**	21
Peels | **E Vill**	21
Smith | **E Vill**	21
Citrus B&G | **W 70s**	21
NEW Pulqueria | **Chinatown**	20

Macao Trading | **TriBeCa**	20
Dos Caminos | **multi.**	20
Schiller's | **LES**	20
Cafe Noir | **SoHo**	20
Delicatessen | **NoLita**	20
Baraonda | **E 70s**	20
Bill's Bar | **Meatpacking**	20
Bryant Park | **W 40s**	19
NEW Bowery Diner | **LES**	18
Brother Jimmy's | **multi.**	17
Coffee Shop | **Union Sq**	17
NEW Pounds & Ounces | **Chelsea**	16
NEW A.G. Kitchen | **W 70s**	–
NEW Bagatelle | **Meatpacking**	–
NEW Crave Fishbar | **E 50s**	–
NEW Ken & Cook | **NoLita**	–
NEW Noir | **E 50s**	–
NEW Penrose | **E 80s**	–
NEW Toy | **Meatpacking**	–

BREAKFAST

Jean Georges Noug. | **W 60s**	27
Five Leaves | **Greenpt**	26
Clinton St. Baking | **LES**	26
Maialino | **Gramercy**	26
Norma's | **W 50s**	25
Locanda Verde | **TriBeCa**	25
Marlow/Sons | **W'burg**	25
Buvette | **W Vill**	25
Katz's Deli | **LES**	25
Barney Greengrass | **W 80s**	24
Joseph Leonard | **W Vill**	24
Egg | **W'burg**	24
Balthazar | **SoHo**	24
Breslin | **Chelsea**	24
Lambs Club | **W 40s**	24
Cafe Mogador | **E Vill**	23
Coppelia | **Chelsea**	23
Tartine | **W Vill**	23
Morandi | **W Vill**	23
Casa Lever | **E 50s**	23
Penelope | **Murray Hill**	23
Carnegie Deli | **W 50s**	23
City Bakery | **Flatiron**	22
Café Sabarsky | **E 80s**	22
Jeffrey's Grocery | **W Vill**	22
Pastis | **Meatpacking**	22
Michael's | **W 50s**	22

Standard Grill | **Meatpacking**	22
Wall/Water | **Financial**	22
Brasserie | **E 50s**	22
Tom's | **Prospect Hts**	22
Good Enough/Eat | **W 80s**	22
Asellina | **Murray Hill**	22
Sant Ambroeus | **multi.**	22
Cafe Luxembourg | **W 70s**	22
Landmarc | **W 60s**	21
Teresa's | **Bklyn Hts**	21
Taste | **E 80s**	21
Pulino's | **NoLita**	21
Peels | **E Vill**	21
Sarabeth's | **multi.**	21
Untitled | **E 70s**	21
Veselka | **E Vill**	20
Naples 45 | **E 40s**	20
E.A.T. | **E 80s**	20
Rue 57 | **W 50s**	20
Nice Matin | **W 70s**	20
NoHo Star | **NoHo**	20
Bubby's | **TriBeCa**	20
Le Pain Q. | **multi.**	20
Kitchenette | **multi.**	20

BRUNCH

Union Sq. Cafe | **Union Sq**	27
Perilla | **W Vill**	27
Telepan | **W 60s**	27
Aquagrill | **SoHo**	27
Five Leaves | **Greenpt**	26
Rose Water | **Park Slope**	26
River Café | **Dumbo**	26
Colonie | **Bklyn Hts**	26
Dressler | **W'burg**	26
Wallsé | **W Vill**	26
Clinton St. Baking | **LES**	26
Maialino | **Gramercy**	26
Dell'anima | **W Vill**	26
Norma's | **W 50s**	25
Prune | **E Vill**	25
Locanda Verde | **TriBeCa**	25
Le Gigot | **W Vill**	25
David Burke Townhse. | **E 60s**	25
Buttermilk | **Carroll Gdns**	25
Ilili | **Chelsea**	25
Blue Ribbon Bakery | **W Vill**	25
Mile End | **Boerum Hill**	25
Applewood | **Park Slope**	25
JoeDoe | **E Vill**	25
Colicchio/Sons | **Chelsea**	25
Diner | **W'burg**	25
Betto | **W'burg**	25

Ouest | **W 80s**	25
Riverpark | **Murray Hill**	25
La Silhouette | **W 50s**	25
Stone Park | **Park Slope**	24
Stanton Social | **LES**	24
Mercadito | **multi.**	24
JoJo | **E 60s**	24
Minetta | **G Vill**	24
Petrossian | **W 50s**	24
Spasso | **W Vill**	24
Spotted Pig | **W Vill**	24
Joseph Leonard | **W Vill**	24
Sanford's | **Astoria**	24
Tertulia | **W Vill**	24
Ocean Grill | **W 70s**	24
Jack Horse | **Bklyn Hts**	24
Balthazar | **SoHo**	24
Carlyle | **E 70s**	24
Celeste | **W 80s**	24
Beaumarchais | **Meatpacking**	24
DBGB | **E Vill**	24
Blue Water | **Union Sq**	24
Bocca Lupo | **Cobble Hill**	24
Northern Spy | **E Vill**	24
Balaboosta | **NoLita**	24
Mesa Grill | **Flatiron**	24
Dutch | **SoHo**	24
Fat Radish | **LES**	24
Capsouto Frères | **TriBeCa**	23
Seersucker | **Carroll Gdns**	23
Cafe Mogador | **E Vill**	23
FishTag | **W 70s**	23
Tribeca Grill | **TriBeCa**	23
Mark | **E 70s**	23
Cookshop | **Chelsea**	23
Extra Virgin | **W Vill**	23
Tartine | **W Vill**	23
Artisanal | **Murray Hill**	23
Water Club | **Murray Hill**	23
NEW Saxon & Parole | **NoHo**	23
Back Forty | **E Vill**	23
Miss Mamie/Maude | **Harlem**	23
Community Food | **W 100s**	23
Public | **NoLita**	23
Brasserie 8½ | **W 50s**	23
Square Meal | **E 90s**	23
Edi & the Wolf | **E Vill**	23
Home | **W Vill**	23
Penelope | **Murray Hill**	23
Atlantic Grill | **multi.**	23
Ofrenda | **W Vill**	23
No. 7 | **Ft Greene**	23

Scottadito | **Park Slope**	23
Maggie Brown | **Clinton Hill**	23
Red Rooster | **Harlem**	23
Empellón | **W Vill**	23
Vanderbilt | **Prospect Hts**	22
Black Whale | **City Is**	22
Amy Ruth's | **Harlem**	22
La Follia | **Gramercy**	22
Pastis | **Meatpacking**	22
44 & X/44½ | **W 40s**	22
Alfama | **E 50s**	22
Lion | **G Vill**	22
Waverly Inn | **W Vill**	22
Tom's | **Prospect Hts**	22
Cafe Cluny | **W Vill**	22
Café d'Alsace | **E 80s**	22
Lavo | **E 50s**	22
Miriam | **Park Slope**	22
Turkish Kitchen | **Murray Hill**	22
Good Enough/Eat | **W 80s**	22
Bridge Cafe | **Financial**	22
Tipsy Parson | **Chelsea**	22
Leopard/des Artistes | **W 60s**	22
Jane | **G Vill**	22
Lorenzo's | **Bloomfield**	22
Rocking Horse | **Chelsea**	22
Eatery | **W 50s**	22
Olea | **Ft Greene**	22
5 Points | **NoHo**	22
Calle Ocho | **W 80s**	22
Cafe Luxembourg | **W 70s**	22
Astor Room | **Astoria**	22
Palm Court | **W 50s**	21
Mon Petit Cafe | **E 60s**	21
Resto | **Murray Hill**	21
Hundred Acres | **SoHo**	21
Taste | **E 80s**	21
Miss Lily's | **G Vill**	21
Locale | **Astoria**	21
Peels | **E Vill**	21
Isabella's | **W 70s**	21
Cafeteria | **Chelsea**	21
Good | **W Vill**	21
Fatty Crab | **W Vill**	21
Cebu | **Bay Ridge**	21
Sarabeth's | **multi.**	21
Untitled | **E 70s**	21
Les Halles | **multi.**	21
Great Jones Cafe | **NoHo**	21
Cafe Luluc | **Cobble Hill**	21
Almond | **Flatiron**	21
NEW Lexington Brass | **E 40s**	21
Thistle Hill | **Park Slope**	21
Cafe Ronda | **W 70s**	20
Sylvia's | **Harlem**	20
Ed's Chowder | **W 60s**	20
Jones Wood Foundry | **E 70s**	20
Delta Grill | **W 40s**	20
Schiller's | **LES**	20
Caffe Cielo | **W 50s**	20
Nice Matin | **W 70s**	20
Puttanesca | **W 50s**	20
Cafe Loup | **W Vill**	20
A.O.C. | **W Vill**	20
Bubby's | **multi.**	20
Delicatessen | **NoLita**	20
Odeon | **TriBeCa**	20
Kitchenette | **multi.**	20
Cornelia St. Cafe | **W Vill**	20
Lyon | **W Vill**	19
Friend/Farmer | **Gramercy**	19
Arté Café | **W 70s**	19
View | **W 40s**	18
NEW Parish Hall | **W'burg**	-

BYO

Lucali | **Carroll Gdns**	27
Di Fara | **Midwood**	27
Taci's Beyti | **Midwood**	26
NEW Butcher Bar | **Astoria**	25
Kuma Inn | **LES**	25
Tea & Sympathy | **W Vill**	25
Poke | **E 80s**	25
Lomzynianka | **Greenpt**	24
Tartine | **W Vill**	23
La Sirène | **Hudson Square**	23
Phoenix Gdn. | **Murray Hill**	23
Nook | **W 50s**	23
Mezzaluna/Pizza | **G Vill**	22
Gazala's | **W 40s**	21
Oaxaca | **multi.**	21
Afghan Kebab | **multi.**	21
Zaytoons | **multi.**	21
Wondee Siam | **W 50s**	21
Little Poland | **E Vill**	21
Gen. Greene | **Ft Greene**	20
Baluchi's | **Murray Hill**	20
NEW Brooklyn Seoul | **W'burg**	-

CELEBRITY CHEFS

Gastón Acurio	
NEW La Mar | **Flatiron**	24
Alain Allegretti	
NEW La Promenade/	25
Anglais | **Chelsea**	

Michael Anthony
  Gramercy Tavern | **Flatiron** 28

Julieta Ballesteros
  Crema | **Chelsea** 23

Dan Barber
  Blue Hill | **G Vill** 27

Lidia Bastianich
  Felidia | **E 50s** 26
  Manzo | **Flatiron** 26
  Eataly | **Flatiron** 24

Mario Batali
  Babbo | **G Vill** 27
  Del Posto | **Chelsea** 26
  Manzo | **Flatiron** 26
  Casa Mono | **Gramercy** 25
  Lupa | **G Vill** 25
  Esca | **W 40s** 25
  Eataly | **Flatiron** 24
  Otto | **G Vill** 24

Jonathan Benno
  Lincoln | **W 60s** 25

April Bloomfield
  Spotted Pig | **W Vill** 24
  John Dory | **Chelsea** 24
  Breslin | **Chelsea** 24

Saul Bolton
  Saul | **Boerum Hill** 27
  Vanderbilt | **Prospect Hts** 22

David Bouley
  Bouley | **TriBeCa** 28
  Brushstroke | **TriBeCa** 25

Daniel Boulud
  Daniel | **E 60s** 28
  Café Boulud | **E 70s** 27
  Boulud Sud | **W 60s** 25
  DB Bistro Moderne | **W 40s** 25
  Bar Boulud | **W 60s** 24
  DBGB | **E Vill** 21

Antoine Bouterin
  Le Perigord | **E 50s** 25

Danny Bowien
  NEW Mission Chinese Food | ⎯
    LES

Jimmy Bradley
  Harrison | **TriBeCa** 23

Terrance Brennan
  Picholine | **W 60s** 27
  Artisanal | **Murray Hill** 23

Scott Bryan
  Apiary | **E Vill** 23

David Burke
  David Burke Townhse. | **E 60s** 25
  Fishtail/David Burke | **E 60s** 24

David Burke Kitchen | 24
    SoHo
David Burke/Bloom. | 20
    E 50s

Joey Campanaro
  Little Owl | **W Vill** 26

Marco Canora
  Hearth | **E Vill** 25
  Terroir | **multi.** 21

Floyd Cardoz
  North End Grill | **Financial** 25

Andrew Carmellini
  Locanda Verde | **TriBeCa** 25
  Dutch | **SoHo** 24

Michael Cetrulo
  Scalini Fedeli | **TriBeCa** 27

David Chang
  Momofuku Ko | **E Vill** 26
  Momofuku Ssäm | **E Vill** 26
  Momofuku Noodle | **E Vill** 25
  Má Pêche | **W 50s** 24
  Momofuku Milk Bar | **multi.** 22

Rebecca Charles
  Pearl Oyster | **W Vill** 26

Amanda Cohen
  Dirt Candy | **E Vill** 26

Tom Colicchio
  Craft | **Flatiron** 26
  Colicchio/Sons | **Chelsea** 25
  Riverpark | **Murray Hill** 25
  Craftbar | **Flatiron** 24
  'Wichcraft | **multi.** 20

Scott Conant
  Scarpetta | **Chelsea** 26

Christian Delouvrier
  La Mangeoire | **E 50s** 23

John DeLucie
  Lion | **G Vill** 22
  Crown | **E 80s** 21
  NEW Bill's | **E 50s** ⎯

Alain Ducasse
  Adour | **E 50s** 27
  Benoit | **W 50s** 22

Wylie Dufresne
  WD-50 | **LES** 25

Todd English
  Olives | **Union Sq** 23
  Plaza Food Hall | **W 50s** 23
  Ça Va | **W 40s** 22
  NEW Château Cherbuliez | ⎯
    Flatiron

Sandro Fioriti
  Sandro's | **E 80s** 26

Bobby Flay
Mesa Grill | **Flatiron** — 24
Bar Americain | **W 50s** — 24

Marc Forgione
Marc Forgione | **TriBeCa** — 25

Shea Gallante
Ciano | **Flatiron** — 25

Alex Garcia
NEW A.G. Kitchen | **W 70s** — –

Alex Guarnaschelli
Butter | **E Vill** — 23
Darby | **W Vill** — 21

Kurt Gutenbrunner
Wallsé | **W Vill** — 26
Café Sabarsky | **E 80s** — 22
Blaue Gans | **TriBeCa** — 22

Gabrielle Hamilton
Prune | **E Vill** — 25

Kerry Heffernan
South Gate | **W 50s** — 22

Peter Hoffman
Back Forty | **multi.** — 23

Daniel Humm
Eleven Madison | **Flatiron** — 28
NEW NoMad | **Chelsea** — 26

Michael Huynh
Baoguette | **multi.** — 22

Hung Hyunh
NEW Catch | **Meatpacking** — 23

Sara Jenkins
Porchetta | **E Vill** — 25
Porsena | **E Vill** — 22

Gavin Kaysen
Café Boulud | **E 70s** — 27

Thomas Keller
Per Se | **W 60s** — 29
Bouchon Bakery | **multi.** — 24

Gabriel Kreuther
Modern | **W 50s** — 26

Mark Ladner
Del Posto | **Chelsea** — 26

Paul Liebrandt
Corton | **TriBeCa** — 26

Anita Lo
Annisa | **W Vill** — 28

Maria Loi
NEW Loi | **W 70s** — 22

Michael Lomonaco
Porter House | **W 60s** — 26

Waldy Malouf
Beacon | **W 50s** — 23
NEW High Heat | **G Vill** — –

Nobu Matsuhisa
Nobu | **multi.** — 27

Jehangir Mehta
Graffiti | **E Vill** — 25
Mehtaphor | **TriBeCa** — 24

Carlo Mirarchi
Roberta's | **Bushwick** — 26
NEW Blanca | **Bushwick** — –

Marco Moreira
Tocqueville | **Union Sq** — 27
15 East | **Union Sq** — 26

Masaharu Morimoto
Morimoto | **Chelsea** — 26

Charlie Palmer
Aureole | **W 40s** — 26

David Pasternack
Esca | **W 40s** — 25

Zak Pelaccio
Fatty 'Cue | **W Vill** — 23
Fatty Crab | **W Vill** — 21

Alfred Portale
Gotham B&G | **G Vill** — 28

Michael Psilakis
FishTag | **W 70s** — 23
Kefi | **W 80s** — 23

Cesar Ramirez
Brooklyn Fare | — 27
Downtown Bklyn

Mary Redding
Mary's Fish | **W Vill** — 25
Brooklyn Fish | **Park Slope** — 23

Mads Refslund
NEW Acme | **NoHo** — 23

Andy Ricker
NEW Pok Pok Ny | **Red Hook** — 22

Eric Ripert
Le Bernardin | **W 50s** — 29

Missy Robbins
A Voce | **multi.** — 24

Marcus Samuelsson
Red Rooster | **Harlem** — 23
NEW Ginny's Supper Club | — –
Harlem

Richard Sandoval
Pampano | **E 40s** — 24
Maya | **E 60s** — 24
Zengo | **E 40s** — 23
NEW Raymi | **Flatiron** — –

Angelo Sosa
NEW Añejo | **W 40s** — 23
Social Eatz | **E 50s** — 22

Alex Stupak
Empellón | **E Vill** — 23

Gari Sugio
  Gari/Sushi | **multi.** 27

Nao Sugiyama
  Sugiyama | **W 50s** 28

Masayoshi Takayama
  Masa/Bar Masa | **W 60s** 27

Dale Talde
  NEW Talde | **Park Slope** 25

Bill Telepan
  Telepan | **W 60s** 27

Sue Torres
  Sueños | **Chelsea** 23

Christina Tosi
  Momofuku Milk Bar | **multi.** 22

Tom Valenti
  Ouest | **W 80s** 25

Jean-Georges Vongerichten
  Jean Georges | **W 60s** 28
  ABC Kitchen | **Flatiron** 26
  Perry St. | **W Vill** 26
  JoJo | **E 60s** 24
  Spice Market | **Meatpacking** 24
  Mark | **E 70s** 23
  Mercer Kitchen | **SoHo** 22

Jonathan Waxman
  Barbuto | **W Vill** 24

Michael White
  Marea | **W 50s** 28
  Ai Fiori | **Garment** 26
  Osteria Morini | **SoHo** 24
  NEW Nicoletta | **E Vill** ─

Jody Williams
  Buvette | **W Vill** 25

Geoffrey Zakarian
  Lambs Club | **W 40s** 24
  National | **E 50s** 21

Galen Zamarra
  Mas | **W Vill** 28
  NEW Mas (La Grillade) | **W Vill** 24

CHILD-FRIENDLY

(* children's menu available)

Blue Ribbon* | **multi.** 25
Buttermilk* | **Carroll Gdns** 25
L&B Spumoni* | **Bensonhurst** 25
Noodle Pudding | **Bklyn Hts** 25
Zum Stammtisch* | **Glendale** 24
Zero Otto | **Fordham** 24
Farm/Adderley* | **Ditmas Pk** 24
DBGB* | **E Vill** 24
Bocca Lupo* | **Cobble Hill** 24
Gargiulo's | **Coney Is** 24
Otto | **G Vill** 24

London Lennie* | **Rego Pk** 24
Nick's | **multi.** 24
Joe & Pat's | **Castleton Corners** 24
Beecher's Cellar | **Flatiron** 23
Tony's Di Napoli | **W 40s** 23
Brooklyn Fish* | **Park Slope** 23
Riverview* | **LIC** 23
Café Habana/Outpost | **Ft Greene** 23
Miss Mamie/Maude* | **Harlem** 23
Amorina* | **Prospect Hts** 23
Beacon* | **W 50s** 23
Bamonte's | **W'burg** 23
La Villa Pizzeria | **multi.** 23
Blue Smoke* | **Murray Hill** 23
Pinche Taqueria | **NoHo** 22
Amy Ruth's | **Harlem** 22
Rack & Soul* | **W 100s** 22
Brennan | **Sheepshead** 22
Max Brenner* | **G Vill** 22
Shake Shack | **multi.** 22
BLT Burger* | **G Vill** 22
Carmine's* | **W 40s** 22
Good Enough/Eat* | **W 80s** 22
Arirang Hibachi* | **multi.** 22
Osso Buco | **E 90s** 22
Max* | **multi.** 22
Pig Heaven | **E 80s** 21
Landmarc* | **multi.** 21
Peanut Butter Co. | **G Vill** 21
Pulino's* | **NoLita** 21
Virgil's BBQ* | **W 40s** 21
Sarabeth's | **multi.** 21
Sambuca* | **W 70s** 21
ChipShop* | **multi.** 21
Whole Foods | **multi.** 21
Sylvia's* | **Harlem** 20
Serendipity 3 | **E 60s** 20
Rock Ctr.* | **W 50s** 20
Junior's* | **multi.** 20
Bubby's* | **multi.** 20
Two Boots* | **multi.** 20
Ninja* | **TriBeCa** 19
Jackson Hole* | **multi.** 19
Ruby Foo's* | **W 40s** 19
Friend/Farmer* | **Gramercy** 19
Boathouse* | **E 70s** 19
View* | **W 40s** 18
Cowgirl* | **W Vill** 17

COLLEGE-CENTRIC

Columbia
  Pisticci | **W 100s** 25
  Thai Market | **W 100s** 24

Max SoHa/Caffe | **W 100s**	24
Miss Mamie/Maude | **Harlem**	23
Community Food | **W 100s**	23
Rack & Soul | **W 100s**	22
Sezz Medi' | **W 100s**	22
Maoz | **W 100s**	22
Symposium | **W 100s**	20
Havana Central | **multi.**	20
Kitchenette | **multi.**	20

NYU

Ippudo | **E Vill**	26
Num Pang | **G Vill**	25
Caracas | **E Vill**	25
S'MAC | **E Vill**	24
BaoHaus | **E Vill**	24
Otto | **G Vill**	24
Crif Dogs | **E Vill**	23
La Esquina | **L Italy**	23
Café Habana/Outpost | **NoLita**	23
Angelica Kit. | **E Vill**	22
Artichoke Basille | **E Vill**	22
John's/12th St. | **E Vill**	22
Dos Toros | **E Vill**	22
99 Mi. to Philly | **E Vill**	22
Café Henri | **W Vill**	22
Gyu-Kaku | **E Vill**	22
Vanessa's Dumpling | **E Vill**	22
Smith | **E Vill**	21
Spice | **G Vill**	21
Veselka | **E Vill**	20
Republic | **Union Sq**	20

COMMUTER OASES

Grand Central

🚇 Sushi Yasuda | **E 40s**	28
Sparks | **E 40s**	26
Benjamin Steak | **E 40s**	26
Sakagura | **E 40s**	25
Num Pang | **E 40s**	25
Pietro's | **E 40s**	25
Morton's | **E 40s**	25
Nanni | **E 40s**	25
Soba Totto | **E 40s**	25
🚇 Capital Grille | **E 40s**	25
Hatsuhana | **E 40s**	24
Fabio Piccolo | **E 40s**	24
Tulsi | **E 40s**	24
Bobby Van's | **E 40s**	23
Naya | **E 40s**	23
La Fonda/Sol | **E 40s**	23
Pepe | **E 40s**	23
Oyster Bar | **E 40s**	23

Zengo | **E 40s**	23
Patroon | **E 40s**	23
Cipriani Dolci | **E 40s**	22
Sinigual | **E 40s**	22
Ammos | **E 40s**	22
Pera | **E 40s**	21
Cafe Centro | **E 40s**	21
Docks Oyster | **E 40s**	21
Michael Jordan | **E 40s**	21
🆕 Lexington Brass | **E 40s**	21
Naples 45 | **E 40s**	20
Junior's | **E 40s**	20
Two Boots | **E 40s**	20
Menchanko-tei | **E 40s**	20

Penn Station

Keens | **Garment**	26
Uncle Jack's | **Garment**	24
Lazzara's | **Garment**	23
Biricchino | **Chelsea**	21
Uncle Nick's | **Chelsea**	21
Chef Yu | **Garment**	21
Stage Door Deli | **Garment**	21
Mooncake Foods | **Chelsea**	21
Chickpea | **Garment**	19
Brother Jimmy's | **Garment**	17

Port Authority

Esca | **W 40s**	25
Mercato | **Garment**	24
Shula's | **W 40s**	24
Chimichurri Grill | **W 40s**	23
Peter's 1969 | **W 40s**	23
Lil'/Shorty's | **W 40s**	23
John's Pizzeria | **W 40s**	23
Etcetera Etcetera | **W 40s**	23
Qi | **W 40s**	22
🚇 Shake Shack | **W 40s**	22
Casa Nonna | **Garment**	22
Ça Va | **W 40s**	22
🚇 5 Napkin Burger | **W 40s**	22
Marseille | **W 40s**	21
Chez Josephine | **W 40s**	21
Don Giovanni | **W 40s**	21
Dafni Greek | **W 40s**	20
Schnipper´s | **W 40s**	20
West Bank | **W 40s**	20
🆕 Clyde Frazier's | **Garment**	18

CRITIC-PROOF

(Gets lots of business despite so-so food)

La Bonne Soupe | **W 50s**	19
Jackson Hole | **multi.**	19

Fairway Cafe | **multi.**	19
Ruby Foo's | **W 40s**	19
Goodburger | **multi.**	19
Big Nick's | **W 70s**	19
Sardi's | **W 40s**	19
Bistro Le Steak | **E 70s**	19
Bryant Park | **W 40s**	19
Joe Allen | **W 40s**	19
Arté Café | **W 70s**	19
Boathouse | **E 70s**	19
Fraunces Tavern | **Financial**	18
Brother Jimmy's | **multi.**	17
Cowgirl | **multi.**	17
Coffee Shop | **Union Sq**	17

DANCING/ ENTERTAINMENT

(Call for days and
times of performances)

River Café | **Dumbo**	26
Tommaso | **Dyker Hts**	24
Sofrito | **E 50s**	24
Blue Water | **Union Sq**	24
Blue Fin | **W 40s**	23
NEW Son Cubano | **Chelsea**	23
Blue Smoke | **Murray Hill**	23
Flor/Sol | **TriBeCa**	22
Knickerbocker | **G Vill**	21
Cávo | **Astoria**	21
Chez Josephine | **W 40s**	21
La Lanterna | **G Vill**	21
Sylvia's | **Harlem**	20
Delta Grill | **W 40s**	20
Cornelia St. Cafe | **W Vill**	20
Walker's | **TriBeCa**	19
Cafe Steinhof | **Park Slope**	19

DESSERT SPECIALISTS

ChikaLicious | **E Vill**	25
Chocolate Room | **multi.**	25
La Bergamote | **multi.**	25
L&B Spumoni | **Bensonhurst**	25
Bouchon Bakery | **multi.**	24
Veniero's | **E Vill**	24
Ferrara | **L Italy**	24
Kyotofu | **W 40s**	24
Ristorante/Settepani | **W'burg**	24
Momofuku Milk Bar | **multi.**	22
City Bakery | **Flatiron**	22
Café Sabarsky | **E 80s**	22
Max Brenner | **G Vill**	22
Sant Ambroeus | **multi.**	22
Sweet Melissa | **Park Slope**	21

Lady Mendl's | **Gramercy**	21
Serendipity 3 | **E 60s**	20
Junior's | **multi.**	20
Cafe Lalo | **W 80s**	20

FIREPLACES

Per Se | **W 60s**	29
Bouley | **TriBeCa**	28
Alta | **G Vill**	26
Sud Vino & Cucina | **Bed-Stuy**	26
NEW NoMad | **Chelsea**	26
Keens | **Garment**	26
Quality Meats | **W 50s**	26
Benjamin Steak | **E 40s**	26
Piccola Venezia | **Astoria**	25
Locanda Verde | **TriBeCa**	25
Ciano | **Flatiron**	25
WD-50 | **LES**	25
Applewood | **Park Slope**	25
Vinegar Hill Hse. | **Vinegar Hill**	25
Christos | **Astoria**	25
Moim | **Park Slope**	24
One if by Land | **W Vill**	24
Club A Steak | **E 50s**	24
Alberto | **Forest Hills**	24
STK | **Meatpacking**	24
Aegean Cove | **Astoria**	24
Triomphe | **W 40s**	24
Antica Venezia | **W Vill**	24
21 Club | **W 50s**	24
Lambs Club | **W 40s**	24
Dutch | **SoHo**	24
Tosca Café | **Throgs Neck**	23
Blossom | **W Vill**	23
Ovelia | **Astoria**	23
Frankie/Johnnie | **Garment**	23
Molly's | **Gramercy**	23
Nurnberger | **New Brighton**	23
Manducatis | **LIC**	23
Water Club | **Murray Hill**	23
A Casa Fox | **LES**	23
Place | **W Vill**	23
Telly's Taverna | **Astoria**	23
Vareli | **W 100s**	23
Public | **NoLita**	23
Pearl Room | **Bay Ridge**	23
Manetta's | **LIC**	23
Scottadito | **Park Slope**	23
F & J Pine | **Morris Park**	23
Black Duck | **Murray Hill**	23
I Trulli | **Murray Hill**	22

Sea Shore | **City Is**	22
Lattanzi | **W 40s**	22
Salinas | **Chelsea**	22
Waverly Inn | **W Vill**	22
Trattoria Cinque | **TriBeCa**	22
E&E Grill House | **W 40s**	22
South Gate | **W 50s**	22
Ça Va | **W 40s**	22
Lorenzo's | **Bloomfield**	22
Asellina | **Murray Hill**	22
Marco Polo | **Carroll Gdns**	22
House | **Gramercy**	21
Lady Mendl's | **Gramercy**	21
Cebu | **Bay Ridge**	21
Ali Baba | **E 40s**	21
McCormick/Schmick | **W 50s**	21
Greenhouse | **Bay Ridge**	21
44 | **W 40s**	21
Donovan's | **Woodside**	21
Sidetracks | **Sunnyside**	21
La Lanterna | **G Vill**	21
Glass House | **W 40s**	20
Delta Grill | **W 40s**	20
FireBird | **W 40s**	20
5 9th | **Meatpacking**	20
St. Andrews | **W 40s**	20
Vivolo/Cucina | **E 70s**	20
Lobster Box | **City Is**	20
Cornelia St. Cafe | **W Vill**	20
Battery Gdns. | **Financial**	19
Bourbon St. Café | **Bayside**	19
Friend/Farmer | **Gramercy**	19
Boathouse | **E 70s**	19
Park | **Chelsea**	18
NEW Joanne | **W 60s**	18

GLUTEN-FREE OPTIONS

(Call to discuss specific needs)

Keste Pizza | **W Vill**	25
Caracas | **multi.**	25
NEW Don Antonio | **W 50s**	24
V-Note | **E 70s**	24
S'MAC | **E Vill**	24
Risotteria | **W Vill**	23
Hill Country | **Flatiron**	23
Hummus Pl. | **multi.**	23
Rubirosa | **NoLita**	22
Friedman's Lunch | **Chelsea**	22
Bistango | **Murray Hill**	22
Sambuca | **W 70s**	21
Nice Matin | **W 70s**	20
Nizza | **W 40s**	20

GREEN/LOCAL/ ORGANIC

Per Se | **W 60s**	29
Eleven Madison | **Flatiron**	28
Mas | **W Vill**	28
Grocery | **Carroll Gdns**	28
Gramercy Tavern | **Flatiron**	28
Degustation | **E Vill**	28
Gotham B&G | **G Vill**	28
Saul | **Boerum Hill**	27
L'Artusi | **W Vill**	27
Blue Hill | **G Vill**	27
Union Sq. Cafe | **Union Sq**	27
Babbo | **G Vill**	27
Telepan | **W 60s**	27
Craft | **Flatiron**	26
Momofuku Ko | **E Vill**	26
Pearl Oyster | **W Vill**	26
Tortilleria Nixtamal | **Corona**	26
Vesta | **Astoria**	26
Rose Water | **Park Slope**	26
Fette Sau | **W'burg**	26
Paulie Gee's | **Greenpt**	26
NEW NoMad | **Chelsea**	26
Colonie | **Bklyn Hts**	26
Aureole | **W 40s**	26
ABC Kitchen | **Flatiron**	26
Il Buco | **NoHo**	26
Roberta's | **Bushwick**	26
Dirt Candy | **E Vill**	26
Clinton St. Baking | **LES**	26
Juventino | **Park Slope**	26
Dell'anima | **W Vill**	26
Momofuku Ssäm | **E Vill**	26
Prune | **E Vill**	25
NEW Rosemary's | **W Vill**	25
Locanda Verde | **TriBeCa**	25
Dovetail | **W 70s**	25
Pure Food/Wine | **Gramercy**	25
Marc Forgione | **TriBeCa**	25
Recipe | **W 80s**	25
Aldea | **Flatiron**	25
Franny's | **Prospect Hts**	25
James | **Prospect Hts**	25
Lupa | **G Vill**	25
Esca | **W 40s**	25
Buttermilk | **Carroll Gdns**	25
Candle 79 | **E 70s**	25
Rouge Tomate | **E 60s**	25
Hearth | **E Vill**	25
Rucola | **Boerum Hill**	25
Good Fork | **Red Hook**	25

Applewood | **Park Slope**	25
Momofuku Noodle | **E Vill**	25
Diner | **W'burg**	25
Marlow/Sons | **W'burg**	25
Candle Cafe | **E 70s**	25
Riverpark | **Murray Hill**	25
Lincoln | **W 60s**	25
Stone Park | **Park Slope**	24
NEW Wong | **W Vill**	24
Barbuto | **W Vill**	24
Caravan/Dreams | **E Vill**	24
Peaches | **Bed-Stuy**	24
Farm/Adderley | **Ditmas Pk**	24
Bar Boulud | **W 60s**	24
Egg | **W'burg**	24
NEW La Mar | **Flatiron**	24
Arabelle | **E 60s**	24
Frankies | **multi.**	24
Gobo | **multi.**	24
Northern Spy | **E Vill**	24
Prime Meat | **Carroll Gdns**	24
Eataly | **Flatiron**	24
Market Table | **W Vill**	24
Fat Radish | **LES**	24
Sfoglia | **E 90s**	24
Aroma Kitchen | **NoHo**	23
Seersucker | **Carroll Gdns**	23
Blossom | **Chelsea**	23
Forcella | **NoHo**	23
Aurora | **multi.**	23
Harrison | **TriBeCa**	23
Cookshop | **Chelsea**	23
BareBurger | **multi.**	23
Café Habana/Outpost | **Ft Greene**	23
Back Forty | **E Vill**	23
Community Food | **W 100s**	23
Home | **W Vill**	23
Print | **W 40s**	23
Angelica Kit. | **E Vill**	22
Momofuku Milk Bar | **multi.**	22
City Bakery | **Flatiron**	22
NEW Veatery | **E 80s**	22
Fornino | **W'burg**	22
NEW Arthur on Smith | **Boerum Hill**	22
Barbetta | **W 40s**	22
Bark Hot Dogs | **Park Slope**	22
Lunetta | **Boerum Hill**	22
Zito's | **Park Slope**	22
Bell Book/Candle | **W Vill**	22
5 Points | **NoHo**	22
Palo Santo | **Park Slope**	22

New Leaf | **Wash. Hts**	21
Hundred Acres | **SoHo**	21
NEW Amali | **E 60s**	21
Isabella's | **W 70s**	21
Flatbush Farm | **Park Slope**	21
Whole Foods | **multi.**	21
Gen. Greene | **Ft Greene**	20
Zen Palate | **W 40s**	20
Le Pain Q. | **Flatiron**	20
Josie's | **multi.**	20

GROUP DINING

Peter Luger | **W'burg**	27
Tanoreen | **Bay Ridge**	27
Nobu | **multi.**	27
Morimoto | **Chelsea**	26
Alta | **G Vill**	26
Don Peppe | **Ozone Pk**	26
Fette Sau | **W'burg**	26
Sparks | **E 40s**	26
Tamarind | **multi.**	26
Wolfgang's | **multi.**	26
Quality Meats | **W 50s**	26
Momofuku Ssäm | **E Vill**	26
BLT Prime | **Gramercy**	25
BLT Steak | **E 50s**	25
Del Frisco's | **multi.**	25
Kuma Inn | **LES**	25
Ilili | **Chelsea**	25
L&B Spumoni | **Bensonhurst**	25
Colicchio/Sons | **Chelsea**	25
Palm | **multi.**	25
Buddakan | **Chelsea**	25
Capital Grille | **multi.**	25
Stanton Social | **LES**	24
Smith/Wollensky | **E 40s**	24
Dominick's | **Fordham**	24
Tao | **E 50s**	24
Pacificana | **Sunset Pk**	24
Balthazar | **SoHo**	24
Churrascaria | **multi.**	24
DBGB | **E Vill**	24
Blue Water | **Union Sq**	24
Breslin | **Chelsea**	24
Craftbar | **Flatiron**	24
Má Pêche | **W 50s**	24
Crispo | **W Vill**	24
Spice Market | **Meatpacking**	24
Bar Americain | **W 50s**	24
Otto | **G Vill**	24
Tony's Di Napoli | **W 40s**	23
Dinosaur BBQ | **Harlem**	23
Tribeca Grill | **TriBeCa**	23

Becco | **W 40s**	23
Blue Fin | **W 40s**	23
Beauty & Essex | **LES**	23
Artisanal | **Murray Hill**	23
Oyster Bar | **E 40s**	23
Kefi | **W 80s**	23
Public | **NoLita**	23
Brasserie 8½ | **W 50s**	23
Atlantic Grill | **multi.**	23
Rosa Mexicano | **multi.**	23
Zengo | **E 40s**	23
China Grill | **W 50s**	23
Red Rooster | **Harlem**	23
Peking Duck | **multi.**	23
Beacon | **W 50s**	23
F & J Pine | **Morris Park**	23
Cabana | **multi.**	23
Blue Smoke | **multi.**	23
Victor's Cafe | **W 50s**	22
Pastis | **Meatpacking**	22
Standard Grill | **Meatpacking**	22
Blaue Gans | **TriBeCa**	22
Flor/Sol | **TriBeCa**	22
Carmine's | **multi.**	22
Kum Gang San | **multi.**	22
Arirang Hibachi | **multi.**	22
Casa Nonna | **Garment**	22
Osso Buco | **E 90s**	22
Fig & Olive | **multi.**	22
Calle Ocho | **W 80s**	22
Gyu-Kaku | **multi.**	22
Golden Unicorn | **Chinatown**	21
Landmarc | **multi.**	21
Redeye Grill | **W 50s**	21
Jing Fong | **Chinatown**	21
Saigon Grill | **W 90s**	21
Hurricane Club | **Flatiron**	21
East Manor | **Flushing**	21
Sambuca | **W 70s**	21
Citrus B&G | **W 70s**	21
Congee | **LES**	21
Bond 45 | **W 40s**	20
Sammy's | **LES**	20
Hill Country Chicken | **Flatiron**	20
Dos Caminos | **multi.**	20
Wildwood BBQ | **Flatiron**	20
Havana Central | **multi.**	20
Republic | **Union Sq**	20
Cilantro | **multi.**	20
Ninja | **TriBeCa**	19
Ruby Foo's | **W 40s**	19
Boathouse | **E 70s**	19

HIPSTER

St. Anselm | **W'burg**	27
Traif | **W'burg**	27
Momo Sushi Shack | **Bushwick**	26
Five Leaves | **Greenpt**	26
Fette Sau | **W'burg**	26
Rye | **W'burg**	26
Ippudo | **E Vill**	26
Roberta's | **Bushwick**	26
James | **Prospect Hts**	25
Motorino | **E Vill**	25
Do or Dine | **Bed-Stuy**	25
La Superior | **W'burg**	25
Mile End | **multi.**	25
Good Fork | **Red Hook**	25
Diner | **W'burg**	25
Marlow/Sons | **W'burg**	25
Pies-n-Thighs | **W'burg**	25
Vinegar Hill Hse. | **Vinegar Hill**	25
NEW Littleneck | **Gowanus**	24
Meatball Shop | **multi.**	24
Egg | **W'burg**	24
Prime Meat | **Carroll Gdns**	24
Breslin | **Chelsea**	24
NEW 606 R&D | **Prospect Hts**	24
DuMont | **W'burg**	24
NEW Allswell | **W'burg**	24
Hecho en Dumbo | **NoHo**	23
Café Habana/Outpost | **NoLita**	23
Fatty 'Cue | **W Vill**	23
No. 7 | **multi.**	23
Fedora | **W Vill**	23
Walter Foods | **multi.**	22
Smile | **SoHo**	22
Freemans | **LES**	22
Vanderbilt | **Prospect Hts**	22
Isa | **W'burg**	22
NEW Pok Pok Ny | **Red Hook**	22
Peels | **E Vill**	21
Chez Oskar | **Ft Greene**	21
Gen. Greene | **Ft Greene**	20
NEW ABV | **E 90s**	20
NEW Blue Collar | **W'burg**	–
NEW Governor | **Dumbo**	–
NEW Gran Electrica | **Dumbo**	–
NEW Grey Lady | **LES**	–
NEW Mission Chinese Food | **LES**	–
NEW Reynard | **W'burg**	–

HISTORIC PLACES

(Year opened; * building)

1787 | One if by Land* | **W Vill**	24
1794 | Bridge Cafe* | **Financial**	22

1868	Old Homestead	**Meatpacking**	25
1868	Landmark Tavern*	**W 40s**	19
1884	P.J. Clarke's	**E 50s**	18
1885	Keens	**Garment**	26
1887	Peter Luger	**W'burg**	27
1888	Katz's Deli	**LES**	25
1892	Ferrara	**L Italy**	24
1894	Veniero's	**E Vill**	24
1896	Rao's	**Harlem**	23
1900	Bamonte's	**W'burg**	23
1902	Angelo's/Mulberry	**L Italy**	23
1904	Vincent's	**L Italy**	24
1906	Barbetta	**W 40s**	22
1907	Gargiulo's	**Coney Is**	24
1908	Barney Greengrass	**W 80s**	24
1908	John's/12th St.	**E Vill**	22
1910	Wolfgang's*	**Murray Hill**	26
1910	Totonno Pizza*	**Coney Is**	25
1911	Commerce*	**W Vill**	24
1913	Oyster Bar	**E 40s**	23
1919	Mario's	**Fordham**	23
1920	Leo's Latticini/Corona	**Corona**	26
1920	Waverly Inn	**W Vill**	22
1921	Sardi's	**W 40s**	19
1922	Defonte's	**Red Hook**	24
1926	Palm	**E 40s**	25
1926	Frankie/Johnnie	**W 40s**	23
1927	Diner*	**W'burg**	25
1927	El Faro	**W Vill**	23
1927	Gallagher's	**W 50s**	22
1927	Ann & Tony's	**Fordham**	22
1929	Eleven Madison*	**Flatiron**	28
1929	21 Club	**W 50s**	24
1929	John's Pizzeria	**W Vill**	23
1929	Russian Tea	**W 50s**	21
1930	Carlyle	**E 70s**	24
1930	El Quijote	**Chelsea**	22
1933	Patsy's	**Harlem**	21
1936	Tom's	**Prospect Hts**	22
1936	Monkey Bar*	**E 50s**	21
1937	Denino	**Port Richmond**	26
1937	Minetta	**G Vill**	24
1937	Carnegie Deli	**W 50s**	23
1937	Stage Deli	**W 50s**	20
1938	Wo Hop	**Chinatown**	23
1938	Brennan	**Sheepshead**	22
1938	Heidelberg	**E 80s**	19
1939	L&B Spumoni	**Bensonhurst**	25
1941	Sevilla	**W Vill**	25
1943	Forlini's	**Chinatown**	20
1944	Patsy's	**W 50s**	23

1945	Ben's Best	**Rego Pk**	23
1946	Lobster Box	**City Is**	20
1950	Junior's	**Downtown Bklyn**	20
1953	Liebman's Deli	**Riverdale**	22
1954	Veselka	**E Vill**	20
1954	Serendipity 3	**E 60s**	20
1957	Arturo's	**G Vill**	23
1957	La Taza de Oro	**Chelsea**	22
1958	Queen	**Bklyn Hts**	25
1959	Four Seasons	**E 50s**	27
1959	London Lennie	**Rego Pk**	24
1959	El Parador Cafe	**Murray Hill**	23
1959	Rizzo's Pizza	**Astoria**	23
1959	Brasserie	**E 50s**	22
1960	Joe & Pat's	**Castleton Corners**	24
1960	Molly's	**Gramercy**	23
1960	Bull & Bear	**E 40s**	23
1960	Chez Napoléon	**W 50s**	23
1961	Corner Bistro	**W Vill**	23
1962	La Grenouille	**E 50s**	28
1962	Sylvia's	**Harlem**	20
1962	Big Nick's	**W 70s**	19

HOTEL DINING

Ace Hotel	
John Dory	**Chelsea**	24
Breslin	**Chelsea**	24
No. 7	**Chelsea**	23
Americano Hotel	
NEW Americano	**Chelsea**	22
Amsterdam Court Hotel	
Natsumi	**W 50s**	23
Andaz Wall St. Hotel	
Wall/Water	**Financial**	22
Benjamin Hotel	
National	**E 50s**	21
Blakely Hotel	
Abboccato	**W 50s**	22
Bowery Hotel	
Gemma	**E Vill**	21
Bryant Park Hotel	
Koi	**W 40s**	25
Carlton Hotel	
Millesime	**Murray Hill**	20
Carlyle Hotel	
Carlyle	**E 70s**	24
Chambers Hotel	
Má Pêche	**W 50s**	24
Momofuku Milk Bar	**W 50s**	22
Chatwal Hotel	
Lambs Club	**W 40s**	24

City Club Hotel
  DB Bistro Moderne | **W 40s** 25

Dream Downtown Hotel
  Marble Lane | **Chelsea** 23

Dream Hotel
  Serafina | **W 50s** 20

Duane Street Hotel
  Mehtaphor | **TriBeCa** 24

Dylan Hotel
  Benjamin Steak | **E 40s** 26

Elysée Hotel
  Monkey Bar | **E 50s** 21

Empire Hotel
  Ed's Chowder | **W 60s** 20

Eventi Hotel
  NEW Humphrey | **Chelsea** ‒

Excelsior Hotel
  Calle Ocho | **W 80s** 22

Fashion 26 Hotel
  Rare B&G | **Chelsea** 22

Gansevoort Hotel
  NEW Toy | **Meatpacking** ‒

Gansevoort Park Avenue Hotel
  Asellina | **Murray Hill** 22

Gem Hotel
  NEW Foragers City Table | 20
  Chelsea

Gramercy Park Hotel
  Maialino | **Gramercy** 26

Greenwich Hotel
  Locanda Verde | **TriBeCa** 25

Hyatt 48 Lex Hotel
  NEW Lexington Brass | 21
  E 40s

Ink48 Hotel
  Print | **W 40s** 23

Inn at Irving Pl.
  Lady Mendl's | **Gramercy** 21

InterContinental NY Times Sq.
  Shake Shack | **W 40s** 22
  Ça Va | **W 40s** 22

Iroquois Hotel
  Triomphe | **W 40s** 24

James Hotel
  David Burke Kitchen | **SoHo** 24

Jane Hotel
  Cafe Gitane | **W Vill** 22

Jumeirah Essex Hse.
  South Gate | **W 50s** 22

Le Parker Meridien
  Norma's | **W 50s** 25
  Burger Joint | **W 50s** 24

London NYC Hotel
  Maze | **W 50s** 25
  Gordon Ramsay | **W 50s** 24

Lowell Hotel
  Post House | **E 60s** 24

Mandarin Oriental Hotel
  Asiate | **W 60s** 25

Maritime Hotel
  La Bottega | **Chelsea** 22

Mark Hotel
  Mark | **E 70s** 23

Marriott Marquis Hotel
  View | **W 40s** 18

Mela Hotel
  Saju Bistro | **W 40s** 21

Mercer Hotel
  Mercer Kitchen | **SoHo** 22

Mondrian SoHo Hotel
  NEW Isola | **SoHo** ‒

NoMad Hotel
  NEW NoMad | **Chelsea** 26

NY Palace Hotel
  Gilt | **E 50s** 26

On the Ave Hotel
  Serafina | **W 70s** 20

Out NYC Hotel
  NEW Ktchn | **W 40s** ‒

Park South Hotel
  Black Duck | **Murray Hill** 23

Pearl Hotel
  E&E Grill House | **W 40s** 22

Plaza Athénée Hotel
  Arabelle | **E 60s** 24

Plaza Hotel
  Plaza Food Hall | **W 50s** 23
  Palm Court | **W 50s** 21

Ritz-Carlton Battery Park
  2 West | **Financial** 23

Royalton Hotel
  44 | **W 40s** 21

Setai Fifth Avenue Hotel
  Ai Fiori | **Garment** 26

Setai Wall Street Hotel
  NEW The Exchange | **Financial** ‒

Shelburne Murray Hill Hotel
  Rare B&G | **Murray Hill** 22

Sherry-Netherland Hotel
  Harry Cipriani | **E 50s** 22

6 Columbus Hotel
  Blue Ribbon Sushi B&G | **W 50s** 25

60 Thompson
  Kittichai | **SoHo** 24

Standard Hotel	
Standard Grill | **Meatpacking**	22
St. Regis Hotel	
Adour | **E 50s**	27
Surrey Hotel	
Café Boulud | **E 70s**	27
Thompson LES Hotel	
NEW Blue Ribbon/Izakaya | **LES**	–
Time Hotel	
Serafina | **W 40s**	20
Trump Int'l Hotel	
Jean Georges | **W 60s**	28
Jean Georges Noug. | **W 60s**	27
Waldorf-Astoria	
Bull & Bear | **E 40s**	23
Wales Hotel	
Paola's | **E 90s**	23
Washington Sq. Hotel	
North Sq. | **G Vill**	23
Westin Times Sq. Hotel	
Shula's | **W 40s**	24
W Hotel Downtown	
BLT B&G | **Financial**	22
W Hotel Times Sq.	
Blue Fin | **W 40s**	23
W Hotel Union Sq.	
Olives | **Union Sq**	23
Wythe Hotel	
NEW Reynard | **W'burg**	–

HOT SPOTS

NEW NoMad | **Chelsea**	26
NEW Rosemary's | **W Vill**	25
Stanton Social | **LES**	24
Minetta | **G Vill**	24
Hudson Clearwater | **W Vill**	24
Tao | **E 50s**	24
DBGB | **E Vill**	24
Eataly | **Flatiron**	24
Dutch | **SoHo**	24
NEW Catch | **Meatpacking**	23
Beauty & Essex | **LES**	23
NEW Saxon & Parole | **NoHo**	23
NEW Acme | **NoHo**	23
Red Rooster | **Harlem**	23
Empellón | **W Vill**	23
Rubirosa | **NoLita**	22
Abe/Arthur | **Meatpacking**	22
Standard Grill | **Meatpacking**	22
Lion | **G Vill**	22
NEW Perla | **G Vill**	22
Lavo | **E 50s**	22

NEW Pok Pok Ny | **Red Hook**	22
NEW Corner Social | **Harlem**	21
Crown | **E 80s**	21
NEW Sons of Essex | **LES**	21
Hurricane Club | **Flatiron**	21
Miss Lily's | **G Vill**	21
Peels | **E Vill**	21
NEW Pulqueria | **Chinatown**	20
NEW Super Linda | **TriBeCa**	19
NEW Bowery Diner | **LES**	18
NEW A.G. Kitchen | **W 70s**	–
NEW Bagatelle | **Meatpacking**	–
NEW Bill's | **E 50s**	–
NEW Ken & Cook | **NoLita**	–
NEW Mission Chinese Food | **LES**	–
NEW Nicoletta | **E Vill**	–
NEW Penrose | **E 80s**	–
NEW Reynard | **W'burg**	–

JACKET REQUIRED

Le Bernardin | **W 50s**	29
Per Se | **W 60s**	29
Bouley | **TriBeCa**	28
Daniel | **E 60s**	28
Jean Georges | **W 60s**	28
La Grenouille | **E 50s**	28
Four Seasons | **E 50s**	27
River Café | **Dumbo**	26
Le Cirque | **E 50s**	25
Carlyle | **E 70s**	24
21 Club | **W 50s**	24

LATE DINING

(Weekday closing hour)

Sushi Seki | 2:30 AM | **E 60s**	28
Traif | 2 AM | **W'burg**	27
Momofuku Ko | 1 AM | **E Vill**	26
Blue Ribbon Sushi | varies | **SoHo**	26
NEW Sauce | 2 AM | **LES**	26
Five Leaves | 12 AM | **Greenpt**	26
NEW NoMad | 12:30 AM | **Chelsea**	26
Bohemian | 1 AM | **NoHo**	26
Colonie | varies | **Bklyn Hts**	26
Kanoyama | 12 AM | **E Vill**	26
Roberta's | 12 AM | **Bushwick**	26
NEW Atera | 1 AM | **TriBeCa**	26
Omen | 1 AM | **SoHo**	26
Supper | varies | **E Vill**	26
Danji | varies | **W 50s**	26
Dell'anima | 2 AM | **W Vill**	26
San Matteo | varies | **multi.**	26
Momofuku Ssäm | 2 AM | **E Vill**	26

NEW Brasserie Pushkin | 12:30 AM | **W 50s**	26
NEW Rosemary's | 12 AM | **W Vill**	25
Aburiya Kinnosuke | 12 AM | **E 40s**	25
Casa Mono | 12 AM | **Gramercy**	25
Blue Ribbon Sushi B&G | 2 AM | **W 50s**	25
Blue Ribbon | varies | **multi.**	25
ChikaLicious | 12 AM | **E Vill**	25
Del Frisco's | 12 AM | **W 40s**	25
Avra | 12 AM | **E 40s**	25
Lupa | 12 AM | **G Vill**	25
'Ino | 2 AM | **W Vill**	25
Motorino | varies | **E Vill**	25
NEW Boukiés | varies | **E Vill**	25
Do or Dine | 2 AM | **Bed-Stuy**	25
La Superior | varies | **W'burg**	25
Raoul's | 1 AM | **SoHo**	25
Yakitori Totto | varies | **W 50s**	25
Blue Ribbon Bakery | varies | **W Vill**	25
Rucola | 12 AM | **Boerum Hill**	25
Diner | 12 AM | **W'burg**	25
Marlow/Sons | 12 AM | **W'burg**	25
Bahari Estiatorio | 12 AM | **Astoria**	25
Betto | 1 AM | **W'burg**	25
Pies-n-Thighs | 12 AM | **W'burg**	25
Buenos Aires | varies | **E Vill**	25
Takahachi | varies | **E Vill**	25
Buddakan | 12 AM | **Chelsea**	25
Buvette | 2 AM | **W Vill**	25
NEW Talde | 12 AM | **Park Slope**	25
Sevilla | varies | **W Vill**	25
Christos | 12 AM | **Astoria**	25
Stanton Social | 3 AM | **LES**	24
Mercadito | varies | **W Vill**	24
Numero 28 | 12 AM | **E Vill**	24
Minetta | 2 AM | **G Vill**	24
Sorella | 2 AM | **LES**	24
NEW Parm | varies | **NoLita**	24
South Brooklyn Pizza | varies | **multi.**	24
Best Pizza | 12 AM | **W'burg**	24
Spasso | varies | **W Vill**	24
Hudson Clearwater | 12 AM | **W Vill**	24
Spotted Pig | 2 AM | **W Vill**	24
Sofrito | varies | **E 50s**	24
Perbacco | 1 AM | **E Vill**	24
Meatball Shop | varies | **multi.**	24
Joseph Leonard | 2 AM | **W Vill**	24
Veniero's | varies | **E Vill**	24
Adrienne's | 12 AM | **Financial**	24
Mont Blanc | varies | **W 40s**	24
Elio's | varies | **E 80s**	24
Barrio Chino | 1 AM | **LES**	24
Farm/Adderley | 1 AM | **Ditmas Pk**	24
Sanford's | 24 hrs. | **Astoria**	24
Tertulia | 12 AM | **W Vill**	24
Tao | 1 AM | **E 50s**	24
New WonJo | 24 hrs. | **Garment**	24
STK | varies | **Meatpacking**	24
John Dory | 12 AM | **Chelsea**	24
Balthazar | 1 AM | **SoHo**	24
Ferrara | varies | **L Italy**	24
Mercato | 1 AM | **Garment**	24
Churrascaria | 12 AM | **multi.**	24
Sammy's Shrimp Box | varies | **City Is**	24
Frankies | varies | **W Vill**	24
Beaumarchais | varies | **Meatpacking**	24
DBGB | varies | **E Vill**	24
Emporio | 2 AM | **NoLita**	24
Bar Pitti | 12 AM | **G Vill**	24
Vincent's | 1:30 AM | **L Italy**	24
Bocca Lupo | varies | **Cobble Hill**	24
Prime Meat | 2 AM | **Carroll Gdns**	24
Breslin | 12 AM | **Chelsea**	24
Empanada Mama | 1 AM | **W 50s**	24
Kyotofu | varies | **W 40s**	24
Banjara | 12 AM | **E Vill**	24
El Quinto Pino | varies | **Chelsea**	24
Harry's Cafe & Steak | 12 AM | **Financial**	24
Spice Market | varies | **Meatpacking**	24
Max SoHa/Caffe | 12 AM | **W 100s**	24
Queens Kickshaw | 1 AM | **Astoria**	24
NEW 1066 Eno | varies | **E 50s**	24
Lil' Frankie | 2 AM | **E Vill**	24
Otto | 12:30 AM | **G Vill**	24
Dutch | 2 AM | **SoHo**	24
Sik Gaek | 4 AM | **multi.**	24
DuMont | 2 AM | **W'burg**	24
Redhead | 1 AM | **E Vill**	24
Fat Radish | 12 AM | **LES**	24
NEW Allswell | varies | **W'burg**	24
Marble Lane | varies | **Chelsea**	23
Boqueria | 12 AM | **SoHo**	23
Tosca Café | 1 AM | **Throgs Neck**	23

Roll-n-Roaster | 1 AM | **Sheepshead** 23]

Wollensky's | 2 AM | **E 40s** 23]

Bar Jamon | 2 AM | **Gramercy** 23]

Natsumi | 11:30 PM | **W 50s** 23]

Joe's Pizza | 5 AM | **W Vill** 23]

Negril | 12 AM | **G Vill** 23]

Tony's Di Napoli | 12 AM | **multi.** 23]

Campagnola | 12 AM | **E 70s** 23]

Char No. 4 | 1 AM | **Cobble Hill** 23]

Cafe Mogador | varies | **multi.** 23]

Lucien | 1 AM | **E Vill** 23]

Cipriani D'twn | 12 AM | **SoHo** 23]

La Masseria | 12 AM | **W 40s** 23]

Crab Shanty | varies | **City Is** 23]

Great NY Noodle | 4 AM | **Chinatown** 23]

Las Ramblas | 1 AM | **W Vill** 23]

Becco | 12 AM | **W 40s** 23]

Crif Dogs | varies | **multi.** 23]

Lil'/Shorty's | varies | **multi.** 23]

Sidecar | 4 AM | **Park Slope** 23]

Stamatis | varies | **Astoria** 23]

Philippe | 12 AM | **E 60s** 23]

Frank | 1 AM | **E Vill** 23]

Arturo's | 1 AM | **G Vill** 23]

Mark | 1 AM | **E 70s** 23]

CamaJe | 12 AM | **G Vill** 23]

Molly's | 12 AM | **Gramercy** 23]

Elias Corner | 12 AM | **Astoria** 23]

Macondo | varies | **LES** 23]

Coppelia | 24 hrs | **Chelsea** 23]

Mesa Coyoacan | varies | **W'burg** 23]

Blue Fin | varies | **W 40s** 23]

Beauty & Essex | 1 AM | **LES** 23]

Covo | 12 AM | **Harlem** 23]

Morandi | 12 AM | **W Vill** 23]

Hecho en Dumbo | varies | **NoHo** 23]

Sojourn | 1 AM | **E 70s** 23]

Kellari Tav./Parea | 12 AM | **W 40s** 23]

Riverview | 12 AM | **LIC** 23]

Sahara | 2 AM | **Gravesend** 23]

La Esquina | 2 AM | **multi.** 23]

Café Habana/Outpost | 12 AM | **multi.** 23]

Telly's Taverna | 12 AM | **Astoria** 23]

Primola | 12 AM | **E 60s** 23]

NEW Añejo | varies | **W 40s** 23]

Gastroarte | varies | **W 60s** 23]

Sea | 12:30 AM | **W'burg** 23]

Bistro Les Amis | varies | **SoHo** 23]

Vareli | varies | **W 100s** 23]

Fuleen | 2:30 AM | **Chinatown** 23]

Kang Suh | 24 hrs. | **Garment** 23]

Le Comptoir | varies | **W'burg** 23]

Shun Lee West | 12 AM | **W 60s** 23]

Edi & the Wolf | 12 AM | **E Vill** 23]

Fatty 'Cue | varies | **W Vill** 23]

Tacombi/Fonda Nolita | varies | **NoLita** 23]

Chai Home Kitchen | varies | **W'burg** 23]

SushiSamba | varies | **multi.** 23]

Carnegie Deli | 3:30 AM | **W 50s** 23]

2nd Ave Deli | varies | **multi.** 23]

No. 7 | 12 AM | **Ft Greene** 23]

Bull & Bear | 12 AM | **E 40s** 23]

Hummus Pl. | varies | **multi.** 23]

Tratt. Dell'Arte | 1:30 AM | **W 50s** 23]

Uva | 2 AM | **E 70s** 23]

Corner Bistro | varies | **multi.** 23]

Macelleria | 12 AM | **Meatpacking** 23]

Kati Roll | varies | **G Vill** 23]

Moustache | 12 AM | **multi.** 23]

Fedora | varies | **W Vill** 23]

Creperle | 4 AM | **multi.** 23]

NEW Viv | varies | **W 40s** 23]

Haveli | 12 AM | **E Vill** 22]

Momofuku Milk Bar | 12 AM | **E Vill** 22]

Roc | varies | **TriBeCa** 22]

Walter Foods | varies | **multi.** 22]

Rai Rai Ken | 2:30 AM | **E Vill** 22]

Sea Shore | varies | **City Is** 22]

Victor's Cafe | 12 AM | **W 50s** 22]

Yuca Bar | varies | **E Vill** 22]

508 | 12 AM | **Hudson Square** 22]

Nicola's | 12 AM | **E 80s** 22]

Smile | 12 AM | **NoHo** 22]

Corsino | 2 AM | **W Vill** 22]

Jeffrey's Grocery | 12 AM | **W Vill** 22]

Hop Kee | varies | **Chinatown** 22]

Vanderbilt | varies | **Prospect Hts** 22]

Island Burgers | 12 AM | **W 50s** 22]

Ponty Bistro | 12 AM | **Gramercy** 22]

La Palapa | 12 AM | **E Vill** 22]

Brennan | 1 AM | **Sheepshead** 22]

Pastis | varies | **Meatpacking** 22]

12th St. B&G | 4 AM | **Park Slope** 22]

Standard Grill | 4 AM | **Meatpacking** | 22

Miss Korea BBQ | 24 hrs. | **Garment** | 22

Centro Vinoteca | 2 AM | **W Vill** | 22

Lattanzi | 12 AM | **W 40s** | 22

Harry's Italian | varies | **Financial** | 22

Zabb Elee | varies | **Jackson Hts** | 22

Zum Schneider | varies | **E Vill** | 22

Max Brenner | varies | **G Vill** | 22

Artichoke Basille | varies | **multi.** | 22

Gallagher's | 12 AM | **W 50s** | 22

Riposo | varies | **multi.** | 22

El Malecon | varies | **multi.** | 22

Salinas | 12 AM | **Chelsea** | 22

Stonehome | 12 AM | **Ft Greene** | 22

Lion | varies | **G Vill** | 22

Rice 'n' Beans | 12 AM | **W 50s** | 22

Waverly Inn | varies | **W Vill** | 22

Beagle | varies | **E Vill** | 22

Carl's Steaks | varies | **Murray Hill** | 22

Mexicue | 2 AM | **LES** | 22

NEW Perla | varies | **G Vill** | 22

NEW Whitehall | varies | **W Vill** | 22

Cafe Cluny | 12 AM | **W Vill** | 22

Piper's Kilt | 12:30 AM | **multi.** | 22

Lavo | 1 AM | **E 50s** | 22

Henry Public | 1 AM | **Cobble Hill** | 22

Shake Shack | 12 AM | **W 40s** | 22

La Mela | 2 AM | **L Italy** | 22

Carmine's | 12 AM | **W 40s** | 22

Kum Gang San | 24 hrs. | **multi.** | 22

'Inoteca | 3 AM | **multi.** | 22

Maoz | varies | **multi.** | 22

BonChon Chicken | varies | **multi.** | 22

Calexico | 4 AM | **Greenpt** | 22

Barbetta | 12 AM | **W 40s** | 22

Gahm Mi Oak | 24 hrs. | **Garment** | 22

Cascabel Taqueria | 12 AM | **multi.** | 22

Mercer Kitchen | varies | **SoHo** | 22

Sammy's Fishbox | 2 AM | **City Is** | 22

Eatery | varies | **W 50s** | 22

El Quijote | varies | **Chelsea** | 22

Birreria | 2 AM | **Flatiron** | 22

Umberto's | 4 AM | **L Italy** | 22

99 Mi. to Philly | 1 AM | **E Vill** | 22

Asellina | varies | **Murray Hill** | 22

Café Henri | 12 AM | **multi.** | 22

Cafe Gitane | varies | **multi.** | 22

Lucky's Famous Burgers | varies | **multi.** | 22

5 Napkin Burger | 12 AM | **multi.** | 22

Bice | 12 AM | **E 50s** | 22

Due | varies | **E 70s** | 21

Flor/Mayo | 12 AM | **multi.** | 21

Landmarc | 2 AM | **multi.** | 21

Guantanamera | varies | **W 50s** | 21

NEW Corner Social | 2 AM | **Harlem** | 21

Robert | 12 AM | **W 50s** | 21

Saju Bistro | varies | **W 40s** | 21

Coppola's | 12 AM | **Murray Hill** | 21

Tenzan | varies | **E 50s** | 21

Knickerbocker | 1 AM | **G Vill** | 21

Shun Lee Cafe | varies | **W 60s** | 21

NEW Steak 'n Shake | 12 AM | **W 50s** | 21

Bocca/Bacco | varies | **multi.** | 21

Haru | 12 AM | **multi.** | 21

NEW Sons of Essex | varies | **LES** | 21

Tiny's | varies | **TriBeCa** | 21

J.G. Melon | 2:30 AM | **E 70s** | 21

Oaxaca | varies | **Park Slope** | 21

Saigon Grill | 12 AM | **W 90s** | 21

Da Tommaso | 12 AM | **W 50s** | 21

Gottino | 2 AM | **W Vill** | 21

Gemma | varies | **E Vill** | 21

NEW Dong Chun Hong | 24 hrs | **Garment** | 21

Maruzzella | varies | **E 70s** | 21

Tratt. Pesce | 12 AM | **W Vill** | 21

Pulino's | 2 AM | **NoLita** | 21

Ayza Wine | varies | **W Vill** | 21

Tatiana | 1 AM | **Brighton Bch** | 21

Felice | 12 AM | **E 80s** | 21

Virgil's BBQ | 12 AM | **W 40s** | 21

Black Iron | varies | **E Vill** | 21

Stage Door Deli | 2 AM | **Garment** | 21

NEW Jacob's Pickles | varies | **W 80s** | 21

Le Grainne Cafe | 12 AM | **Chelsea** | 21

MexiBBQ | varies | **Astoria** | 21

Cafeteria | 24 hrs. | **Chelsea** | 21

National | 1 AM | **E 50s** | 21

Fatty Crab | varies | **W Vill** | 21

Mari Vanna | 1 AM | **Flatiron** | 21

Cebu | 3 AM | **Bay Ridge** | 21

Sarge's Deli | 24 hrs. | **Murray Hill** | 21

Chez Oskar | 12 AM | **Ft Greene** | 21

Mamajuana | varies | **multi.** 21

Smith | varies | **multi.** 21

Kyochon | varies | **multi.** 21

Les Halles | 12 AM | **Murray Hill** 21

Hummus Kitchen | 12 AM | **W 50s** 21

Great Jones Cafe | varies | **NoHo** 21

Vesuvio | 12 AM | **Bay Ridge** 21

NEW Ngam | 12 AM | **E Vill** 21

Five Guys | varies | **multi.** 21

Cafe Luluc | 12 AM | **Cobble Hill** 21

ChipShop | 12 AM | **Bklyn Hts** 21

Flatbush Farm | 1 AM | **Park Slope** 21

Thalia | 12 AM | **W 50s** 21

Cávo | 2 AM | **Astoria** 21

Chez Josephine | 1 AM | **W 40s** 21

Tolani | 2 AM | **W 70s** 21

Donovan's | varies | **Woodside** 21

Cafe Español | varies | **multi.** 21

Russian Samovar | 2 AM | **W 50s** 21

Terroir | varies | **multi.** 21

Monkey Bar | 12 AM | **E 50s** 21

NEW Lexington Brass | 1 AM | **E 40s** 21

Pizza 33 | varies | **multi.** 21

Thistle Hill | 2 AM | **Park Slope** 21

Don Giovanni | varies | **multi.** 21

El Centro | varies | **W 50s** 21

Congee | varies | **LES** 21

La Lanterna | 3 AM | **G Vill** 21

NEW Jack's Wife Freda | 12 AM | **SoHo** 20

Stage Deli | 2 AM | **W 50s** 20

Papaya King | varies | **E 80s** 20

Glass House | 12 AM | **W 40s** 20

Cafe Fiorello | 1 AM | **W 60s** 20

Bread | varies | **NoLita** 20

NEW Pulqueria | 2 AM | **Chinatown** 20

Veselka | varies | **E Vill** 20

Bombay Palace | 12 AM | **W 50s** 20

Jones Wood Foundry | varies | **E 70s** 20

Gray's Papaya | 24 hrs. | **multi.** 20

Macao Trading | 4 AM | **TriBeCa** 20

Delta Grill | 12 AM | **W 40s** 20

Forlini's | 12 AM | **Chinatown** 20

St. Andrews | 4 AM | **W 40s** 20

Serendipity 3 | varies | **E 60s** 20

NEW ABV | varies | **E 90s** 20

Rue 57 | 12 AM | **W 50s** 20

Omonia | 4 AM | **Astoria** 20

Schiller's | 1 AM | **LES** 20

NEW Claw | 12 AM | **W 50s** 20

Nice Matin | 12 AM | **W 70s** 20

Junior's | varies | **multi.** 20

Cafe Loup | varies | **W Vill** 20

Nizza | 2 AM | **W 40s** 20

Lobster Box | varies | **City Is** 20

NoHo Star | 12 AM | **NoHo** 20

A.O.C. | varies | **W Vill** 20

Bubby's | 24 hrs. | **TriBeCa** 20

Brasserie Cognac | 12 AM | **W 50s** 20

Cercle Rouge | varies | **TriBeCa** 20

Cafe Noir | 2 AM | **SoHo** 20

Cafe Lalo | 2 AM | **W 80s** 20

Delicatessen | 1 AM | **NoLita** 20

Two Boots | varies | **multi.** 20

Odeon | 1 AM | **TriBeCa** 20

Cilantro | 12 AM | **multi.** 20

Baraonda | 1 AM | **E 70s** 20

Barbès | 12 AM | **Murray Hill** 20

Bill's Bar | 12 AM | **Meatpacking** 20

Pranna | varies | **Murray Hill** 20

Serafina | varies | **multi.** 20

Per Lei | 12 AM | **E 70s** 20

West Bank | 12 AM | **W 40s** 20

Jackson Hole | varies | **multi.** 19

B Bar & Grill | 1 AM | **NoHo** 19

Blue 9 Burger | varies | **E Vill** 19

Chickpea | 12 PM | **Garment** 19

Walker's | 1 AM | **TriBeCa** 19

Big Nick's | varies | **W 70s** 19

Bamboo 52 | 2 AM | **W 50s** 19

Bar Italia | varies | **E 60s** 19

Landmark Tavern | varies | **W 40s** 19

NEW Bowery Diner | 24 hrs. | **LES** 18

NEW Clyde Frazier's | 12 AM | **Garment** 18

P.J. Clarke's | varies | **multi.** 18

Park | 1 AM | **Chelsea** 18

Fraunces Tavern | 1 AM | **Financial** 18

Neary's | 1 AM | **E 50s** 18

Brother Jimmy's | varies | **multi.** 17

Coffee Shop | varies | **Union Sq** 17

NEW Pounds & Ounces | varies | **Chelsea** 16

NEW A.G. Kitchen | varies | **W 70s** –

NEW Arabesque | varies | **Murray Hill** –

NEW Bagatelle | varies | **Meatpacking** –

NEW Blue Collar | varies | **W'burg**	⌐
NEW Blue Ribbon/Izakaya | 2 AM | **LES**	⌐
NEW Brooklyn Seoul | 12 AM | **W'burg**	⌐
NEW Calliope | 12 AM | **E Vill**	⌐
NEW Casa Enrique | 12 AM | **LIC**	⌐
NEW Château Cherbuliez | 2 AM | **Flatiron**	⌐
NEW Dans Le Noir | 12 AM | **Garment**	⌐
NEW Extra Fancy | 4 AM | **W'burg**	⌐
NEW Francesca | 12 AM | **LES**	⌐
NEW Ginny's Supper Club | varies | **Harlem**	⌐
NEW Goodwin | 12 AM | **W Vill**	⌐
NEW Governor | 12 AM | **Dumbo**	⌐
NEW Gran Electrica | 12 AM | **Dumbo**	⌐
NEW Grey Lady | varies | **LES**	⌐
NEW High Heat | varies | **G Vill**	⌐
NEW Isola | varies | **SoHo**	⌐
NEW Ken & Cook | 1:30 AM | **NoLita**	⌐
NEW Nasha Rasha | varies | **Flatiron**	⌐
NEW Nicoletta | 3 AM | **E Vill**	⌐
NEW Noir | 4 AM | **E 50s**	⌐
NEW Penrose | 4 AM | **E 80s**	⌐
NEW Purple Fig | 12 AM | **W 70s**	⌐
NEW Reynard | 12 AM | **W'burg**	⌐
NEW Toy | 2 AM | **Meatpacking**	⌐

MEET FOR A DRINK

(Most top hotels, bars and the following standouts)

Daniel | **E 60s**	28
Jean Georges | **W 60s**	28
Gramercy Tavern | **Flatiron**	28
Gotham B&G | **G Vill**	28
Masa/Bar Masa | **W 60s**	27
Nobu | **W 50s**	27
Four Seasons | **E 50s**	27
Modern | **W 50s**	26
Morimoto | **Chelsea**	26
Five Leaves | **Greenpt**	26
NEW NoMad | **Chelsea**	26
Keens | **Garment**	26
Dressler | **W'burg**	26
Maialino | **Gramercy**	26
Le Cirque | **E 50s**	25
Bond St. | **NoHo**	25
Del Frisco's | **W 40s**	25

SD26 | **Murray Hill**	25
North End Grill | **Financial**	25
Rucola | **Boerum Hill**	25
Colicchio/Sons | **Chelsea**	25
Koi | **W 40s**	25
Maze | **W 50s**	25
Pies-n-Thighs | **W'burg**	25
Buddakan | **Chelsea**	25
Ouest | **W 80s**	25
Stone Park | **Park Slope**	24
Stanton Social | **LES**	24
Minetta | **G Vill**	24
Bar Boulud | **W 60s**	24
Tao | **E 50s**	24
STK | **Meatpacking**	24
Balthazar | **SoHo**	24
Maloney/Porcelli | **E 50s**	24
Blue Water | **Union Sq**	24
21 Club | **W 50s**	24
Harry's Cafe & Steak | **Financial**	24
Spice Market | **Meatpacking**	24
Boqueria | **Flatiron**	23
Wollensky's | **E 40s**	23
Natsumi | **W 50s**	23
Hillstone | **multi.**	23
Aurora | **W'burg**	23
Mark | **E 70s**	23
Blue Fin | **W 40s**	23
La Fonda/Sol | **E 40s**	23
Kellari Tav./Parea | **W 40s**	23
Artisanal | **Murray Hill**	23
NEW Saxon & Parole | **NoHo**	23
Back Forty | **SoHo**	23
Casa Lever | **E 50s**	23
Atlantic Grill | **multi.**	23
Bull & Bear | **E 40s**	23
Zengo | **E 40s**	23
Red Rooster | **Harlem**	23
Patroon | **E 40s**	23
Betel | **W Vill**	22
Freemans | **LES**	22
Rayuela | **LES**	22
Pastis | **Meatpacking**	22
Barbounia | **Flatiron**	22
Standard Grill | **Meatpacking**	22
Centro Vinoteca | **W Vill**	22
City Hall | **TriBeCa**	22
'Inoteca | **LES**	22
South Gate | **W 50s**	22
Le Colonial | **E 50s**	22
Brick Cafe | **Astoria**	22
Cafe Luxembourg | **W 70s**	22

Amaranth	**E 60s**	22
Landmarc	**W 60s**	21
NEW Corner Social	**Harlem**	21
Pera	**E 40s**	21
Crown	**E 80s**	21
NEW Sons of Essex	**LES**	21
J.G. Melon	**E 70s**	21
House	**Gramercy**	21
Hudson River	**Harlem**	21
Mari Vanna	**Flatiron**	21
Michael Jordan	**E 40s**	21
Flatbush Farm	**Park Slope**	21
Monkey Bar	**E 50s**	21
Glass House	**W 40s**	20
Mad Dog	**Financial**	20
Henry's	**W 100s**	20
NEW Pulqueria	**Chinatown**	20
Macao Trading	**TriBeCa**	20
Dos Caminos	**multi.**	20
Markt	**Flatiron**	20
Odeon	**TriBeCa**	20
B Bar & Grill	**NoHo**	19
Orsay	**E 70s**	19
Bryant Park	**W 40s**	19
Cafe Steinhof	**Park Slope**	19
NEW Clyde Frazier's	**Garment**	18
P.J. Clarke's	**multi.**	18
Park	**Chelsea**	18
NEW A.G. Kitchen	**W 70s**	–
NEW Bellwether	**W'burg**	–
NEW Bill's	**E 50s**	–
NEW Ginny's Supper Club	**Harlem**	–
NEW Goodwin	**W Vill**	–
NEW Grey Lady	**LES**	–
NEW Noir	**E 50s**	–
NEW Penrose	**E 80s**	–
NEW Reynard	**W Burg**	–
NEW Toy	**Meatpacking**	–

NEWCOMERS

Gwynnett St.	**W'burg**	28
Bar Corvo	**Prospect Hts**	28
Pete Zaaz	**Prospect Hts**	27
Battersby	**Carroll Gdns**	27
Sauce	**LES**	26
NoMad	**Chelsea**	26
Jungsik	**TriBeCa**	26
Maharlika	**E Vill**	26
Atera	**TriBeCa**	26
Brasserie Pushkin	**W 50s**	25
Rosemary's	**W Vill**	25
Butcher Bar	**Astoria**	25

Boukiés	**E Vill**	25
North End Grill	**Financial**	25
Talde	**Park Slope**	25
Almayass	**Flatiron**	25
La Promenade/Anglais	**Chelsea**	25
Wong	**W Vill**	24
Don Antonio	**W 50s**	24
Parm	**NoLita**	24
Yefsi Estiatorio	**E 70s**	24
Littleneck	**Gowanus**	24
Speedy Romeo	**Clinton Hill**	24
Am Thai Bistro	**multi.**	24
La Mar	**Flatiron**	24
Mas (La Grillade)	**W Vill**	24
606 R&D	**Prospect Hts**	24
1066 Eno	**E 50s**	24
Sushi Shop	**E 50s**	24
Allswell	**W'burg**	24
Catch	**Meatpacking**	23
Son Cubano	**Chelsea**	23
Saxon & Parole	**NoHo**	23
Acme	**NoHo**	23
Añejo	**W 40s**	23
Hakkasan	**W 40s**	23
Alison Eighteen	**Flatiron**	23
Viv	**W 40s**	23
Loi	**W 70s**	22
1 Bite Med.	**E 50s**	22
Americano	**Chelsea**	22
Veatery	**E 80s**	22
Perla	**G Vill**	22
Whitehall	**W Vill**	22
Arthur on Smith	**Boerum Hill**	22
Pok Pok Ny	**Red Hook**	22
Desi Shack	**Murray Hill**	22
Corner Social	**Harlem**	21
Steak 'n Shake	**W 50s**	21
Sons of Essex	**LES**	21
Amali	**E 60s**	21
Dong Chun Hong	**Garment**	21
Biang	**Flushing**	21
Jacob's Pickles	**W 80s**	21
Kutsher's	**TriBeCa**	21
Ngam	**E Vill**	21
Lexington Brass	**E 40s**	21
Jack's Wife Freda	**SoHo**	20
Caffe Storico	**W 70s**	20
Pulqueria	**Chinatown**	20
ABV	**E 90s**	20
Claw	**W 50s**	20
Foragers City Table	**Chelsea**	20
Bigoli	**W Vill**	19

Super Linda | **TriBeCa**	19
Bowery Diner | **LES**	18
Clyde Frazier's | **Garment**	18
Yunnan Kitchen | **LES**	18
Joanne | **W 60s**	18
Pounds & Ounces | **Chelsea**	16
A.G. Kitchen | **W 70s**	⌐
Arabesque | **Murray Hill**	⌐
Bagatelle | **Meatpacking**	⌐
Bellwether | **W'burg**	⌐
Bill's | **E 50s**	⌐
Blanca | **Bushwick**	⌐
Blue Collar | **W'burg**	⌐
Blue Ribbon/Izakaya | **LES**	⌐
Brooklyn Crab | **Red Hook**	⌐
Brooklyn Seoul | **W'burg**	⌐
Bugs | **E Vill**	⌐
Calliope | **E Vill**	⌐
Casa Enrique | **LIC**	⌐
Château Cherbuliez | **Flatiron**	⌐
Cómodo | **SoHo**	⌐
Crave Fishbar | **E 50s**	⌐
Dans Le Noir | **Garment**	⌐
Dassara | **Carroll Gdns**	⌐
The Exchange | **Financial**	⌐
Extra Fancy | **W'burg**	⌐
Francesca | **LES**	⌐
Ginny's Supper Club | **Harlem**	⌐
Goodwin | **W Vill**	⌐
Governor | **Dumbo**	⌐
Gran Electrica | **Dumbo**	⌐
Grey Lady | **LES**	⌐
High Heat | **G Vill**	⌐
Humphrey | **Chelsea**	⌐
Isola | **SoHo**	⌐
Jezebel | **SoHo**	⌐
Ken & Cook | **NoLita**	⌐
Kristalbelli | **Garment**	⌐
Ktchn | **W 40s**	⌐
La Vara | **Cobble Hill**	⌐
Mission Chinese Food | **LES**	⌐
Nasha Rasha | **Flatiron**	⌐
Neta | **G Vill**	⌐
Nicoletta | **E Vill**	⌐
Noir | **E 50s**	⌐
Parish Hall | **W'burg**	⌐
Penrose | **E 80s**	⌐
Purple Fig | **W 70s**	⌐
Raymi | **Flatiron**	⌐
Reynard | **W'burg**	⌐
Rocket Pig | **Chelsea**	⌐
Siro's | **E 40s**	⌐

Toy | **Meatpacking**	⌐
Vic & Anthony's | **Flatiron**	⌐

NEWCOMERS ON TAP

(keep posted at zagat.com)

Aamanns | *Danish* | **TriBeCa**
Ainsworth Park | *Steak* | **Gramercy**
American Table Cafe | *American* | **W 60s**
Angolo | *Italian* | **SoHo**
Antica Pesa | *Italian* | **W'burg**
Arlington Club | *Steak* | **E 70s**
Auden | *American* | **W 50s**
Bao | *Vietnamese* | **W Vill**
Barraca | *Spanish/Tapas* | **W Vill**
Beatrice Inn | *Steak* | **W Vill**
The Boil | *Seafood* | **LES**
Brooklyn Central | *Pizza* | **Park Slope**
Brooklyn Fare Manhattan | *Med.* | **Garment**
The Butterfly | *American* | **TriBeCa**
Cafe Tallulah | *Sm. Plates* | **W 70s**
Carbone | *Italian* | **G Vill**
Casa Pomona | *Tapas* | **W 80s**
Center Bar | *Sm. Plates* | **W 60s**
China Latina | *Latin* | **Chelsea**
Clarkson Social Club | *American* | **W Vill**
Corvo Bianco | *Italian* | **W 80s**
Courgette | *Mediterranean* | **W 50s**
Desnuda | *S. American* | **W'burg**
Distilled NY | *American* | **TriBeCa**
83½ | *American* | **E 80s**
El Toro Blanco | *Mexican* | **W Vill**
Finale | *SE Asian* | **LES**
Fletcher's | *BBQ* | **Gowanus**
The Fourth | *American* | **E Vill**
Gannouri | *Korean BBQ* | **Garment**
Ganso | *Japanese* | **Downtown Bklyn**
Giovanni Rana | *Italian* | **Chelsea**
GRK | *Greek* | **Financial**
Guy's American Kitchen | *American* | **W 40s**
Hanjan | *Korean* | **Flatiron**
Harvist | *Southern* | **Harlem**
Houston Hall | *American* | **W Vill**
Hudson Common | *Gastropub* | **W 50s**
Jeepney | *Filipino* | **E Vill**
Juliana's | *Pizza* | **Dumbo**
Kittery | *Seafood* | **Carroll Gdns.**
Krescendo | *Pizza* | **Boerum Hill**

Lady Mai | *Japanese* | **Chelsea**

L&W Oyster Co. | *Seafood* | **Murray Hill**

L'Apicio | *Italian* | **E Vill**

The Lobster Club | *Sandwiches* | **G Vill**

LT Burger | *Burgers* | **W 40s**

Maison Harlem | *French* | **Harlem**

Manzanilla | *Spanish* | **Murray Hill**

The Marrow | *Italian/German* | **W Vill**

Melibea | *Spanish* | **W Vill**

Mighty Quinn's | *BBQ* | **W Vill**

MP Tavena | *Greek* | **Astoria**

Mundo NY | *Mediterranean* | **LES**

M. Wells Dinette | *Diner* | **LIC**

Near and Far | *American* | **LES**

Near East Oven | *Mideastern* | **Bklyn Hts**

Nightingale 9 | *Vietnamese* | **Carroll Gdns.**

Niu Noodle House | *Chinese* | **W Vill**

Paulaner | *German* | **TriBeCa**

Pig & Khao | *Asian* | **E Vill**

The Pines | *American* | **Park Slope**

Porcellino | *Italian* | **E Vill**

Prospect | *American* | **Fort Greene**

Ramen Yebisu | *Noodle Shop* | **W'burg**

Red Gravy | *Italian* | **Bklyn Hts**

Ristorante Morini | *Italian* | **E 80s**

Rosamunde | *Hot Dogs* | **W'burg**

Roy | *French* | **Carroll Gdns.**

Rustic | *American* | **LES**

Schapiro's | *American* | **LES**

Sen | *Japanese* | **Flatiron**

Sirio | *Italian* | **E 60s**

Suzume | *Japanese* | **W'burg**

Taras Bulba | *Russian* | **SoHo**

Tetsu | *Japanese* | **TriBeCa**

The Third Man | *Austrian* | **E Vill**

Tiny Fork | *Seafood* | **LES**

Todd's Mill | *American* | **LES**

Tommy Bahama | *Caribbean* | **E 40s**

Toro | *Tapas* | **Chelsea**

Tribeca Canvas | *American* | **TriBeCa**

The Wallace | *American* | **Clinton Hill**

Willow Rd | *American* | **Chelsea**

Zona Rosa | *Mexican* | **W'burg**

NOTEWORTHY CLOSINGS

Accademia di Vino
Aja
Angelo & Maxie's
APL
Asia de Cuba
Bar Basque
Bar Breton
Bar Henry
Belcourt
Ben Benson's
Bino
BLT Market
Centolire
Chestnut
Chinatown Brasserie
CrossBar
Elevation Burger
Ellabess
FoodParc
Heartbreak
Holy Basil
Hotel Griffou
Hung Ry
Imperial No. Nine
Itzocan
Kenmare
La Petite Auberge
L'Atelier de Joel Robuchon
Le Caprice
Little Giant
Mama Mexico
Mama's Food Shop
Mary Queen of Scots
Masten Lake
Matsuri
Mercat
Mia Dona
Milk Street Cafe
Mizu Sushi
Nam
Niko
9
900
Nuela
Old Town Hot Pot
Persephone
Quattro Gastronomia Italiana
Quercy
Rocco
Romera
Sala Thai

Shang
SHO Shaun Hergatt
Tanuki Tavern
10 Downing
Terrace in the Sky
Tse Yang
Vandaag
Walle
York Grill

OUTDOOR DINING

Grocery | **Carroll Gdns**	28
Sripraphai | **Woodside**	27
Aquagrill | **SoHo**	27
Pure Food/Wine | **Gramercy**	25
Conviv. Osteria | **Park Slope**	25
Avra | **E 40s**	25
Esca | **W 40s**	25
Bogota | **Park Slope**	25
Raoul's | **SoHo**	25
Primehouse | **Murray Hill**	25
L&B Spumoni | **Bensonhurst**	25
San Pietro | **E 50s**	25
Pampano | **E 40s**	24
Sea Grill | **W 40s**	24
Farm/Adderley | **Ditmas Pk**	24
Il Gattopardo | **W 50s**	24
Ocean Grill | **W 70s**	24
Bar Pitti | **G Vill**	24
Blue Water | **Union Sq**	24
Wollensky's | **E 40s**	23
Aurora | **W'burg**	23
Bobo | **W Vill**	23
Fonda | **Park Slope**	23
I Coppi | **E Vill**	23
Tartine | **W Vill**	23
Gnocco | **E Vill**	23
Portofino | **City Is**	23
Riverview | **LIC**	23
Water Club | **Murray Hill**	23
Sahara | **Gravesend**	23
Back Forty | **E Vill**	23
Square Meal | **E 90s**	23
Home | **W Vill**	23
ViceVersa | **W 50s**	23
Trestle on 10th | **Chelsea**	23
Cabana | **Seaport**	23
La Mangeoire | **E 50s**	23
I Trulli | **Murray Hill**	22
Gascogne | **Chelsea**	22
Da Silvano | **G Vill**	22
Pastis | **Meatpacking**	22
44 & X/44½ | **W 40s**	22

Lattanzi | **W 40s**	22
Zum Schneider | **E Vill**	22
Salinas | **Chelsea**	22
Tom's | **Prospect Hts**	22
Shake Shack | **Flatiron**	22
Water's Edge | **LIC**	22
La Bottega | **Chelsea**	22
Barbetta | **W 40s**	22
Da Nico | **L Italy**	22
Bacchus | **Boerum Hill**	22
New Leaf | **Wash. Hts**	21
Gigino | **multi.**	21
Surya | **W Vill**	21
Gottino | **W Vill**	21
Gemma | **E Vill**	21
Cafe Centro | **E 40s**	21
Isabella's | **W 70s**	21
Marina Cafe | **Great Kills**	21
Alma | **Carroll Gdns**	21
Cafe Luluc | **Cobble Hill**	21
Cacio e Pepe | **E Vill**	21
Flatbush Farm | **Park Slope**	21
Cávo | **Astoria**	21
Bottino | **Chelsea**	21
La Lanterna | **G Vill**	21
Cafe Fiorello | **W 60s**	20
5 9th | **Meatpacking**	20
Rock Ctr. | **W 50s**	20
A.O.C. | **W Vill**	20
Markt | **Flatiron**	20
B Bar & Grill | **NoHo**	19
Battery Gdns. | **Financial**	19
Brass. Ruhlmann | **W 50s**	19
Bryant Park | **W 40s**	19
Boathouse | **E 70s**	19
Park | **Chelsea**	18
Coffee Shop | **Union Sq**	17
NEW Château Cherbuliez | **Flatiron**	-

PEOPLE-WATCHING

Marea | **W 50s**	28
Four Seasons | **E 50s**	27
Café Boulud | **E 70s**	27
NEW NoMad | **Chelsea**	26
Sparks | **E 40s**	26
Gilt | **E 50s**	26
NEW Rosemary's | **W Vill**	25
Le Cirque | **E 50s**	25
David Burke Townhse. | **E 60s**	25
Katz's Deli | **LES**	25
Minetta | **G Vill**	24
Spotted Pig | **W Vill**	24

Elio's | **E 80s**	24
Sette Mezzo | **E 70s**	24
Balthazar | **SoHo**	24
Via Quadronno | **multi.**	24
21 Club | **W 50s**	24
Breslin | **Chelsea**	24
Orso | **W 40s**	24
Spice Market | **Meatpacking**	24
Cipriani D'twn | **SoHo**	23
Philippe | **E 60s**	23
🆕 Acme | **NoHo**	23
Casa Lever | **E 50s**	23
Carnegie Deli | **W 50s**	23
Rao's | **Harlem**	23
Red Rooster | **Harlem**	23
Harry Cipriani | **E 50s**	22
Nicola's | **E 80s**	22
Freemans | **LES**	22
Da Silvano | **G Vill**	22
Pastis | **Meatpacking**	22
Michael's | **W 50s**	22
Le Bilboquet | **E 60s**	22
Standard Grill | **Meatpacking**	22
Lion | **G Vill**	22
Lavo | **E 50s**	22
Leopard/des Artistes | **W 60s**	22
Sant Ambroeus | **multi.**	22
Indochine | **E Vill**	22
Cafe Gitane | **NoLita**	22
Bice | **E 50s**	22
Amaranth | **E 60s**	22
Ze Café | **E 50s**	21
Crown | **E 80s**	21
Isabella's | **W 70s**	21
Fred's at Barneys | **E 60s**	21
Cafe Fiorello | **W 60s**	20
Orsay | **E 70s**	19
Joe Allen | **W 40s**	19
Swifty's | **E 70s**	18
Nello | **E 60s**	18
🆕 Bagatelle | **Meatpacking**	-

POWER SCENES

Le Bernardin | **W 50s**	29
Daniel | **E 60s**	28
Jean Georges | **W 60s**	28
La Grenouille | **E 50s**	28
Marea | **W 50s**	28
Gotham B&G | **G Vill**	28
Peter Luger | **W'burg**	27
Nobu | **multi.**	27
Four Seasons | **E 50s**	27
Adour | **E 50s**	27

Del Posto | **Chelsea**	26
Ai Fiori | **Garment**	26
Sparks | **E 40s**	26
Gilt | **E 50s**	26
Keens | **Garment**	26
Solo | **E 50s**	26
Norma's | **W 50s**	25
BLT Prime | **Gramercy**	25
Le Cirque | **E 50s**	25
BLT Steak | **E 50s**	25
Del Frisco's | **W 40s**	25
North End Grill | **Financial**	25
Morton's | **E 40s**	25
San Pietro | **E 50s**	25
Smith/Wollensky | **E 40s**	24
Elio's | **E 80s**	24
Il Gattopardo | **W 50s**	24
Carlyle | **E 70s**	24
Megu | **multi.**	24
21 Club | **W 50s**	24
Harry's Cafe & Steak | **Financial**	24
Bar Americain | **W 50s**	24
Bobby Van's | **E 40s**	23
Cipriani Wall Street | **Financial**	23
Casa Lever | **E 50s**	23
Fresco | **E 50s**	23
Bull & Bear | **E 40s**	23
Rao's | **Harlem**	23
China Grill | **W 50s**	23
Patroon | **E 40s**	23
Michael's | **W 50s**	22
Gallagher's | **W 50s**	22
Lion | **G Vill**	22
City Hall | **TriBeCa**	22
Sant Ambroeus | **multi.**	22
Bice | **E 50s**	22
Russian Tea | **W 50s**	21
44 | **W 40s**	21

PRIVATE ROOMS/ PARTIES

Le Bernardin | **W 50s**	29
Per Se | **W 60s**	29
Daniel | **E 60s**	28
Eleven Madison | **Flatiron**	28
Jean Georges | **W 60s**	28
La Grenouille | **E 50s**	28
Gramercy Tavern | **Flatiron**	28
Marea | **W 50s**	28
Picholine | **W 60s**	27
Milos | **W 50s**	27
Blue Hill | **G Vill**	27
Nobu | **multi.**	27

Four Seasons | **E 50s**	27
Tocqueville | **Union Sq**	27
Craft | **Flatiron**	26
Modern | **W 50s**	26
Del Posto | **Chelsea**	26
Sparks | **E 40s**	26
River Café | **Dumbo**	26
NEW Jungsik | **TriBeCa**	26
Keens | **Garment**	26
Felidia | **E 50s**	26
Solo | **E 50s**	26
Il Buco | **NoHo**	26
EN Japanese | **W Vill**	26
Maialino | **Gramercy**	26
BLT Prime | **Gramercy**	25
Le Cirque | **E 50s**	25
BLT Steak | **E 50s**	25
Del Frisco's | **W 40s**	25
Valbella | **Meatpacking**	25
Raoul's | **SoHo**	25
SD26 | **Murray Hill**	25
Ilili | **Chelsea**	25
Ponte's | **TriBeCa**	25
Buddakan | **Chelsea**	25
Le Perigord | **E 50s**	25
Ben & Jack's | **E 40s**	25
Capital Grille | **E 40s**	25
Lincoln | **W 60s**	25
Oceana | **W 40s**	24
Thalassa | **TriBeCa**	24
A Voce | **W 60s**	24
Tao | **E 50s**	24
Arabelle | **E 60s**	24
Maloney/Porcelli | **E 50s**	24
Megu | **TriBeCa**	24
Periyali | **Flatiron**	24
Blue Water | **Union Sq**	24
21 Club | **W 50s**	24
Breslin | **Chelsea**	24
Shun Lee Palace | **E 50s**	24
Harry's Cafe & Steak | **Financial**	24
Spice Market | **Meatpacking**	24
Delmonico's | **Financial**	24
BLT Fish | **Flatiron**	23
Palma | **W Vill**	23
Gabriel's | **W 60s**	23
Tribeca Grill | **TriBeCa**	23
Mr. K's | **E 50s**	23
Water Club | **Murray Hill**	23
Remi | **W 50s**	23
Public | **NoLita**	23
Casa Lever | **E 50s**	23
Fresco | **E 50s**	23

Il Cortile | **L Italy**	23
Beacon | **W 50s**	23
Patroon | **E 40s**	23
Blue Smoke | **Murray Hill**	23
Mr. Chow | **E 50s**	22
Michael's | **W 50s**	22
Le Zie | **Chelsea**	22
City Hall | **TriBeCa**	22
'Inoteca | **LES**	22
Cellini | **E 50s**	22
Parlor Steak | **E 90s**	22
Barbetta | **W 40s**	22
Redeye Grill | **W 50s**	21
Hurricane Club | **Flatiron**	21
Sambuca | **W 70s**	21
FireBird | **W 40s**	20
Rock Ctr. | **W 50s**	20
Battery Gdns. | **Financial**	19
Landmark Tavern | **W 40s**	19
Park | **Chelsea**	18

QUICK BITE

Leo's Latticini/Corona | **Corona**	26
San Matteo | **E Vill**	26
Momofuku Ssäm | **E Vill**	26
Num Pang | **G Vill**	25
Momofuku Noodle | **E Vill**	25
Azuri Cafe | **W 50s**	25
Porchetta | **E Vill**	25
NEW Parm | **NoLita**	24
Meatball Shop | **LES**	24
Defonte's | **multi.**	24
Press 195 | **Bayside**	24
Empanada Mama | **W 50s**	24
Eataly | **Flatiron**	24
Joe's Pizza | **W Vill**	23
Crif Dogs | **multi.**	23
Naruto Ramen | **E 80s**	23
La Esquina | **L Italy**	23
Fresco | **multi.**	23
No. 7 | **Chelsea**	23
Hummus Pl. | **multi.**	23
Kati Roll | **multi.**	23
Momofuku Milk Bar | **multi.**	22
Pastrami Queen | **E 70s**	22
City Bakery | **Flatiron**	22
Island Burgers | **multi.**	22
A Salt & Battery | **W Vill**	22
Brennan | **Sheepshead**	22
Carl's Steaks | **Murray Hill**	22
Shake Shack | **multi.**	22
Daisy May's | **W 40s**	22
Bark Hot Dogs | **Park Slope**	22

Zito's	**Park Slope**	22	Kyotofu	**W 40s**	24
Dos Toros	**multi.**	22	Sfoglia	**E 90s**	24
Nicky's	**Boerum Hill**	22	Aroma Kitchen	**NoHo**	23
Hampton Chutney	**SoHo**	22	Circus	**E 60s**	23
99 Mi. to Philly	**E Vill**	22	Montebello	**E 50s**	23
Baoguette	**multi.**	22	North Sq.	**G Vill**	23
NEW Desi Shack	**Murray Hill**	22	Toledo	**Murray Hill**	23
Noodle Bar	**W Vill**	22	Solera	**E 50s**	23
Oaxaca	**multi.**	21	Mr. K's	**E 50s**	23
Kyochon	**multi.**	21	Remi	**W 50s**	23
Hummus Kitchen	**multi.**	21	Brasserie 8½	**W 50s**	23
Dumpling Man	**E Vill**	21	**NEW** Alison Eighteen	**Flatiron**	23
Whole Foods	**multi.**	21	Square Meal	**E 90s**	23
Little Poland	**E Vill**	21	Dawat	**E 50s**	23
Papaya King	**E 80s**	20	La Gioconda	**E 50s**	23
'Wichcraft	**multi.**	20	12 Chairs	**SoHo**	23
Gray's Papaya	**multi.**	20	Beacon	**W 50s**	23
Schnipper´s	**W 40s**	20	Trattoria Cinque	**TriBeCa**	22
David Burke/Bloom.	**E 50s**	20	Canaletto	**E 60s**	22
Two Boots	**multi.**	20	Cellini	**E 50s**	22
Blue 9 Burger	**E Vill**	19	Kings' Carriage	**E 80s**	22
NEW High Heat	**G Vill**	–	Palm Court	**W 50s**	21
		Ze Café	**E 50s**	21
QUIET CONVERSATION		Fiorini	**E 50s**	21
		Teodora	**E 50s**	21
Le Bernardin	**W 50s**	29	Paul & Jimmy's	**Gramercy**	21
Per Se	**W 60s**	29	Henry's	**W 100s**	20
Jean Georges	**W 60s**	28	Madison Bistro	**Murray Hill**	20
La Grenouille	**E 50s**	28	Bombay Palace	**W 50s**	20
Mas	**W Vill**	28	Caffe Cielo	**W 50s**	20
Marea	**W 50s**	28		
Annisa	**W Vill**	28	**RAW BARS**	
Picholine	**W 60s**	27	Jack's Lux.	**E Vill**	28
Brooklyn Fare	**Downtown Bklyn**	27	Aquagrill	**SoHo**	27
Masa/Bar Masa	**W 60s**	27	Pearl Oyster	**W Vill**	26
Tocqueville	**Union Sq**	27	Momofuku Ssäm	**E Vill**	26
Adour	**E 50s**	27	Caviar Russe	**E 50s**	25
NEW Jungsik	**TriBeCa**	26	Blue Ribbon	**multi.**	25
Aureole	**W 40s**	26	Esca	**W 40s**	25
Zenkichi	**W'burg**	26	Primehouse	**Murray Hill**	25
Perry St.	**W Vill**	26	Marlow/Sons	**W'burg**	25
EN Japanese	**W Vill**	26	Stanton Social	**LES**	24
Da Umberto	**Chelsea**	25	Oceana	**W 40s**	24
Asiate	**W 60s**	25	**NEW** Littleneck	**Gowanus**	24
Giovanni	**E 80s**	25	Fishtail/David Burke	**E 60s**	24
Il Tinello	**W 50s**	25	Ocean Grill	**W 70s**	24
Pietro's	**E 40s**	25	John Dory	**Chelsea**	24
Rosanjin	**TriBeCa**	25	Balthazar	**SoHo**	24
Petrossian	**W 50s**	24	Uncle Jack's	**W 50s**	24
Villa Berulia	**Murray Hill**	24	Blue Water	**Union Sq**	24
Il Gattopardo	**W 50s**	24	21 Club	**W 50s**	24
Arabelle	**E 60s**	24	Má Pêche	**W 50s**	24
Basso56	**W 50s**	24	Ed's Lobster	**multi.**	24
Periyali	**Flatiron**	24		

SPECIAL FEATURES

Bar Americain | **W 50s**	24
Dutch | **SoHo**	24
London Lennie | **Rego Pk**	24
Tosca Café | **Throgs Neck**	23
BLT Fish | **Flatiron**	23
NEW Catch | **Meatpacking**	23
Flex Mussels | **multi.**	23
Fulton | **E 70s**	23
Sushi Damo | **W 50s**	23
Mark | **E 70s**	23
Lure Fishbar | **SoHo**	23
Blue Fin | **W 40s**	23
Riverview | **LIC**	23
Plaza Food Hall | **W 50s**	23
Oyster Bar | **E 40s**	23
Fish | **W Vill**	23
Pearl Room | **Bay Ridge**	23
SushiSamba | **multi.**	23
Atlantic Grill | **multi.**	23
Fedora | **W Vill**	23
Walter Foods | **multi.**	22
Jeffrey's Grocery | **W Vill**	22
Jordan's Lobster | **Sheepshead**	22
Standard Grill | **Meatpacking**	22
Wall/Water | **Financial**	22
Mermaid | **multi.**	22
City Hall | **TriBeCa**	22
Flor/Sol | **TriBeCa**	22
Ammos | **E 40s**	22
Parlor Steak | **E 90s**	22
Fig & Olive | **Meatpacking**	22
Mercer Kitchen | **SoHo**	22
Umberto's | **Fordham**	22
Olea | **Ft Greene**	22
Darby | **W Vill**	21
City Lobster | **W 40s**	21
Marina Cafe | **Great Kills**	21
Docks Oyster | **E 40s**	21
McCormick/Schmick | **W 50s**	21
Ed's Chowder | **W 60s**	20
Millesime | **Murray Hill**	20
Macao Trading | **TriBeCa**	20
Lobster Box | **City Is**	20
Brasserie Cognac | **W 50s**	20
Pier 9 | **W 50s**	20
City Crab | **Flatiron**	20
Markt | **Flatiron**	20
East Buffet | **Flushing**	19
NEW Bowery Diner | **LES**	18
P.J. Clarke's | **multi.**	18
NEW Toy | **Meatpacking**	-

ROMANTIC PLACES

Bouley | **TriBeCa**	28
Daniel | **E 60s**	28
Eleven Madison | **Flatiron**	28
La Grenouille | **E 50s**	28
Mas | **W Vill**	28
Jack's Lux. | **E Vill**	28
Saul | **Boerum Hill**	27
Scalini Fedeli | **TriBeCa**	27
Blue Hill | **G Vill**	27
Four Seasons | **E 50s**	27
Tocqueville | **Union Sq**	27
Del Posto | **Chelsea**	26
Sistina | **E 80s**	26
Alta | **G Vill**	26
River Café | **Dumbo**	26
Rye | **W'burg**	26
Aureole | **W 40s**	26
Dressler | **W'burg**	26
Il Buco | **NoHo**	26
Wallsé | **W Vill**	26
Zenkichi | **W'burg**	26
Perry St. | **W Vill**	26
Piccola Venezia | **Astoria**	25
Caviar Russe | **E 50s**	25
Le Gigot | **W Vill**	25
Asiate | **W 60s**	25
Conviv. Osteria | **Park Slope**	25
David Burke Townhse. | **E 60s**	25
James | **Prospect Hts**	25
Raoul's | **SoHo**	25
Blue Ribbon Bakery | **W Vill**	25
Erminia | **E 80s**	25
JoJo | **E 60s**	24
Peasant | **NoLita**	24
Petrossian | **W 50s**	24
One if by Land | **W Vill**	24
Pinocchio | **E 90s**	24
Dylan Prime | **TriBeCa**	24
Balthazar | **SoHo**	24
Periyali | **Flatiron**	24
Antica Venezia | **W Vill**	24
Kyotofu | **W 40s**	24
Spiga | **W 80s**	24
Lambs Club | **W 40s**	24
Spice Market | **Meatpacking**	24
Capsouto Frères | **TriBeCa**	23
Aurora | **multi.**	23
Ovelia | **Astoria**	23
Mr. K's | **E 50s**	23
I Coppi | **E Vill**	23
CamaJe | **G Vill**	23

Paola's | **E 90s**	23
Riverview | **LIC**	23
Water Club | **Murray Hill**	23
Place | **W Vill**	23
26 Seats | **E Vill**	23
August | **W Vill**	23
Uva | **E 70s**	23
La Mangeoire | **E 50s**	23
I Trulli | **Murray Hill**	22
Roc | **TriBeCa**	22
Tre Dici/Steak | **Chelsea**	22
Sacred Chow | **G Vill**	22
Gascogne | **Chelsea**	22
L'Absinthe | **E 60s**	22
Valentino's/Green | **Bayside**	22
Flor/Sol | **TriBeCa**	22
Water's Edge | **LIC**	22
Kings' Carriage | **E 80s**	22
Barbetta | **W 40s**	22
Duane Park | **TriBeCa**	22
Olea | **Ft Greene**	22
Firenze | **E 80s**	21
Gigino | **Financial**	21
Nino's | **E 70s**	21
House | **Gramercy**	21
Teodora | **E 50s**	21
Lady Mendl's | **Gramercy**	21
Locale | **Astoria**	21
Pasha | **W 70s**	21
Mari Vanna | **Flatiron**	21
Alma | **Carroll Gdns**	21
Chez Josephine | **W 40s**	21
Bottino | **Chelsea**	21
La Lanterna | **G Vill**	21
FireBird | **W 40s**	20
Philip Marie | **W Vill**	20
Maria Pia | **W 50s**	20
Battery Gdns. | **Financial**	19
Boathouse | **E 70s**	19
View | **W 40s**	18

SENIOR APPEAL

Saul | **Boerum Hill**	27
Del Posto | **Chelsea**	26
Piccolo Angolo | **W Vill**	26
Aureole | **W 40s**	26
Felidia | **E 50s**	26
Giovanni | **E 80s**	25
Il Tinello | **W 50s**	25
Grifone | **E 40s**	25
Pietro's | **E 40s**	25
Ponte's | **TriBeCa**	25
DeGrezia | **E 50s**	25

Le Perigord | **E 50s**	25
Ponticello | **Astoria**	25
San Pietro | **E 50s**	25
Barney Greengrass | **W 80s**	24
Fabio Piccolo | **E 40s**	24
Rossini's | **Murray Hill**	24
Triomphe | **W 40s**	24
Artie's | **City Is**	24
Lusardi's | **E 70s**	24
Delmonico's | **Financial**	24
Gabriel's | **W 60s**	23
Embers | **Bay Ridge**	23
Mr. K's | **E 50s**	23
Mark | **E 70s**	23
Nippon | **E 50s**	23
Remi | **W 50s**	23
Primola | **E 60s**	23
Shun Lee West | **W 60s**	23
Dawat | **E 50s**	23
Beacon | **W 50s**	23
La Mirabelle | **W 80s**	23
Bamonte's | **W'burg**	23
Chez Napoléon | **W 50s**	23
La Mangeoire | **E 50s**	23
Nicola's | **E 80s**	22
Quattro Gatti | **E 80s**	22
Lattanzi | **W 40s**	22
Gallagher's | **W 50s**	22
Leopard/des Artistes | **W 60s**	22
Kings' Carriage | **E 80s**	22
Barbetta | **W 40s**	22
Shanghai Pavilion | **E 70s**	22
Due | **E 70s**	21
Palm Court | **W 50s**	21
Fiorini | **E 50s**	21
Quatorze Bis | **E 70s**	21
Russian Tea | **W 50s**	21
Scaletta | **W 70s**	21
Ithaka | **E 80s**	20
La Bonne Soupe | **W 50s**	19
Sardi's | **W 40s**	19

SLEEPERS

(Good food, but little known)

Saraghina | **Bed-Stuy**	27
SushiAnn | **E 50s**	26
Momo Sushi Shack | **Bushwick**	26
Tortilleria Nixtamal | **Corona**	26
Nove | **Eltingville**	26
Sud Vino & Cucina | **Bed-Stuy**	26
Bohemian | **NoHo**	26
Roman's | **Ft Greene**	26
Torishin | **E 60s**	26
Juventino | **Park Slope**	26

San Matteo | **multi.**	26
Tevere | **E 80s**	26
Rouge et Blanc | **SoHo**	25
Watawa | **Astoria**	25
Do or Dine | **Bed-Stuy**	25
La Superior | **W'burg**	25
Ricardo | **Harlem**	25
Suteishi | **Seaport**	25
Ponte's | **TriBeCa**	25
Uvarara | **MiddlE Vill**	25
Betto | **W'burg**	25
Ponticello | **Astoria**	25
Rosanjin | **TriBeCa**	25
Tra Di Noi | **Fordham**	24
Malagueta | **Astoria**	24
Siam Sq. | **Riverdale**	24
Sorella | **LES**	24
Taro Sushi | **Prospect Hts**	24
Thai Pavilion | **Astoria**	24
Pho Viet Huong | **Chinatown**	24
Loukoumi Taverna | **Astoria**	24
Rin Thai Cuisine | **Chelsea**	24
Mable's Smokehouse & Banquet Hall | **W'burg**	24
New Hawaii Sea | **Westchester Hts**	24
Cannibal | **Murray Hill**	24
Lomzynianka | **Greenpt**	24
Ristorante/Settepani | **multi.**	24
Minca | **E Vill**	24
Piadina | **G Vill**	24
Marble Lane | **Chelsea**	23
Yuba | **E Vill**	23
Mundo | **Astoria**	23
New Malaysia | **Chinatown**	23
Toledo | **Murray Hill**	23
Shiro of Japan | **Glendale**	23
Macondo | **LES**	23
Nurnberger | **New Brighton**	23
La Piazzetta | **W'burg**	23
Mesa Coyoacan | **W'burg**	23
Zebú Grill | **E 90s**	23
Mémé | **W Vill**	23
Fuleen | **Chinatown**	23
Le Comptoir | **W'burg**	23
Scalino | **Park Slope**	23
Tacombi/Fonda Nolita | **NoLita**	23
Scottadito | **Park Slope**	23
Zuzu Ramen | **Park Slope**	23
Maggie Brown | **Clinton Hill**	23

STARGAZING

Marea | **W 50s**	28
Bond St. | **NoHo**	25
Minetta | **G Vill**	24

Spotted Pig | **W Vill**	24
Elio's | **E 80s**	24
Balthazar | **SoHo**	24
Bar Pitti | **G Vill**	24
Philippe | **E 60s**	23
Rao's | **Harlem**	23
Abe/Arthur | **Meatpacking**	22
Da Silvano | **G Vill**	22
Lion | **G Vill**	22
Waverly Inn | **W Vill**	22
Leopard/des Artistes | **W 60s**	22
Cafe Luxembourg | **W 70s**	22
Crown | **E 80s**	21
Darby | **W Vill**	21
Joe Allen | **W 40s**	19
NEW Bill's | **E 50s**	-

THEME RESTAURANTS

Ninja | **TriBeCa**	19
Ruby Foo's | **W 40s**	19
NEW Clyde Frazier's | **Garment**	18
Cowgirl | **W Vill**	17
NEW Nasha Rasha | **Flatiron**	-

TOUGH TICKETS

Il Mulino | **G Vill**	27
Brooklyn Fare | **Downtown Bklyn**	27
Torrisi | **NoLita**	27
Momofuku Ko | **E Vill**	26
NEW NoMad | **Chelsea**	26
ABC Kitchen | **Flatiron**	26
Minetta | **G Vill**	24
NEW Acme | **NoHo**	23
Rao's | **Harlem**	23
Lion | **G Vill**	22
Crown | **E 80s**	21
NEW Bill's | **E 50s**	-
NEW Blanca | **Bushwick**	-

TRANSPORTING EXPERIENCES

Per Se | **W 60s**	29
La Grenouille | **E 50s**	28
Masa/Bar Masa | **W 60s**	27
Keens | **Garment**	26
Il Buco | **NoHo**	26
Asiate | **W 60s**	25
Ilili | **Chelsea**	25
Buddakan | **Chelsea**	25
One if by Land | **W Vill**	24
Tao | **E 50s**	24
Vatan | **Murray Hill**	24
Balthazar | **SoHo**	24
Megu | **TriBeCa**	24
Lambs Club | **W 40s**	24

Spice Market | **Meatpacking** 24
Beauty & Essex | **LES** 23
Rao's | **Harlem** 23
Qi | **Union Sq** 22
Cafe China | **Murray Hill** 22
Waverly Inn | **W Vill** 22
Water's Edge | **LIC** 22
Le Colonial | **E 50s** 22
Monkey Bar | **E 50s** 21
FireBird | **W 40s** 20
Ninja | **TriBeCa** 19
Boathouse | **E 70s** 19
NEW Dans Le Noir | **Garment** –

VIEWS

Per Se | **W 60s** 29
Modern | **W 50s** 26
River Café | **Dumbo** 26
Porter House | **W 60s** 26
Asiate | **W 60s** 25
Suteishi | **Seaport** 25
Ponte's | **TriBeCa** 25
Riverpark | **Murray Hill** 25
Lincoln | **W 60s** 25
Bouchon Bakery | **W 60s** 24
Sea Grill | **W 40s** 24
A Voce | **W 60s** 24
Antica Venezia | **W Vill** 24
Angelina's | **Tottenville** 24
2 West | **Financial** 23
City Is. Lobster | **City Is** 23
Portofino | **City Is** 23
Riverview | **LIC** 23
Water Club | **Murray Hill** 23
Cabana | **Seaport** 23
Roc | **TriBeCa** 22
Sea Shore | **City Is** 22
Cipriani Dolci | **E 40s** 22
Jordan's Lobster | **Sheepshead** 22
Rare B&G | **multi.** 22
Water's Edge | **LIC** 22
Landmarc | **W 60s** 21
Robert | **W 50s** 21
Gigino | **Financial** 21
Hudson River | **Harlem** 21
Marina Cafe | **Great Kills** 21
Michael Jordan | **E 40s** 21
Alma | **Carroll Gdns** 21
Rock Ctr. | **W 50s** 20
Lobster Box | **City Is** 20
Bubby's | **Dumbo** 20
Fairway Cafe | **Red Hook** 19
Battery Gdns. | **Financial** 19

Bryant Park | **W 40s** 19
Boathouse | **E 70s** 19
P.J. Clarke's | **Financial** 18
View | **W 40s** 18
NEW Brooklyn Crab | **Red Hook** –

VISITORS ON EXPENSE ACCOUNT

Le Bernardin | **W 50s** 29
Per Se | **W 60s** 29
Bouley | **TriBeCa** 28
Daniel | **E 60s** 28
Eleven Madison | **Flatiron** 28
Jean Georges | **W 60s** 28
La Grenouille | **E 50s** 28
Kuruma Zushi | **E 40s** 28
Sushi Yasuda | **E 40s** 28
Gramercy Tavern | **Flatiron** 28
Marea | **W 50s** 28
Peter Luger | **W'burg** 27
Picholine | **W 60s** 27
Milos | **W 50s** 27
Il Mulino | **G Vill** 27
Gari/Sushi | **W 40s** 27
Union Sq. Cafe | **Union Sq** 27
Masa/Bar Masa | **W 60s** 27
Nobu | **multi.** 27
Four Seasons | **E 50s** 27
Babbo | **G Vill** 27
Café Boulud | **E 70s** 27
Adour | **E 50s** 27
Craft | **Flatiron** 26
Modern | **W 50s** 26
Corton | **TriBeCa** 26
Del Posto | **Chelsea** 26
Ai Fiori | **Garment** 26
Scarpetta | **Chelsea** 26
River Café | **Dumbo** 26
Aureole | **W 40s** 26
Keens | **Garment** 26
Le Cirque | **E 50s** 25
Veritas | **Flatiron** 25
Del Frisco's | **W 40s** 25
Colicchio/Sons | **Chelsea** 25
Palm | **multi.** 25
NEW La Mar | **Flatiron** 24
Lambs Club | **W 40s** 24
Spice Market | **Meatpacking** 24
Gordon Ramsay | **W 50s** 24
Montebello | **E 50s** 23

WINNING WINE LISTS

Le Bernardin | **W 50s** 29
Per Se | **W 60s** 29

Bouley | **TriBeCa**	28
Daniel | **E 60s**	28
Eleven Madison | **Flatiron**	28
Jean Georges | **W 60s**	28
Mas | **W Vill**	28
Gramercy Tavern | **Flatiron**	28
Marea | **W 50s**	28
Gotham B&G | **G Vill**	28
Annisa | **W Vill**	28
Picholine | **W 60s**	27
Milos | **W 50s**	27
Scalini Fedeli | **TriBeCa**	27
Blue Hill | **G Vill**	27
Union Sq. Cafe | **Union Sq**	27
Babbo | **G Vill**	27
Café Boulud | **E 70s**	27
Adour | **E 50s**	27
Craft | **Flatiron**	26
Modern | **W 50s**	26
Del Posto | **Chelsea**	26
Alta | **G Vill**	26
Scarpetta | **Chelsea**	26
NEW NoMad | **Chelsea**	26
Sparks | **E 40s**	26
River Café | **Dumbo**	26
Aureole | **W 40s**	26
Gilt | **E 50s**	26
Felidia | **E 50s**	26
Il Buco | **NoHo**	26
Wallsé | **W Vill**	26
Porter House | **W 60s**	26
Tía Pol | **Chelsea**	26
Maialino | **Gramercy**	26
Dell'anima | **W Vill**	26
BLT Prime | **Gramercy**	25
Salumeria Rosi | **W 70s**	25
Le Cirque | **E 50s**	25
Casa Mono | **Gramercy**	25
Asiate | **W 60s**	25
Veritas | **Flatiron**	25
BLT Steak | **E 50s**	25
Del Frisco's | **W 40s**	25
Aldea | **Flatiron**	25
Franny's | **Prospect Hts**	25
David Burke Townhse. | **E 60s**	25
Lupa | **G Vill**	25
'Ino | **W Vill**	25
Esca | **W 40s**	25
Motorino | **E Vill**	25
Buttermilk | **Carroll Gdns**	25
Valbella | **Meatpacking**	25
Rouge Tomate | **E 60s**	25

Raoul's | **SoHo**	25
SD26 | **Murray Hill**	25
Hearth | **E Vill**	25
Primehouse | **Murray Hill**	25
DB Bistro Moderne | **W 40s**	25
San Pietro | **E 50s**	25
Ouest | **W 80s**	25
Capital Grille | **E 40s**	25
Vinegar Hill Hse. | **Vinegar Hill**	25
Oceana | **W 40s**	24
Smith/Wollensky | **E 40s**	24
Tommaso | **Dyker Hts**	24
Txikito | **Chelsea**	24
Osteria Morini | **SoHo**	24
Thalassa | **TriBeCa**	24
Junoon | **Flatiron**	24
A Voce | **Flatiron**	24
Bar Boulud | **W 60s**	24
Post House | **E 60s**	24
Balthazar | **SoHo**	24
Megu | **TriBeCa**	24
Frankies | **multi.**	24
21 Club | **W 50s**	24
Eataly | **Flatiron**	24
Harry's Cafe & Steak | **Financial**	24
'Cesca | **W 70s**	24
Otto | **G Vill**	24
BLT Fish | **Flatiron**	23
Bobby Van's | **multi.**	23
Solera | **E 50s**	23
Tribeca Grill | **TriBeCa**	23
Delco | **W 40s**	23
Blue Fin | **W 40s**	23
Artisanal | **Murray Hill**	23
La Pizza Fresca | **Flatiron**	23
Rothmann's | **E 50s**	23
Uva | **E 70s**	23
Trestle on 10th | **Chelsea**	23
I Trulli | **Murray Hill**	22
Michael's | **W 50s**	22
Café d'Alsace | **E 80s**	22
Benoit | **W 50s**	22
City Hall | **TriBeCa**	22
'Inoteca | **LES**	22
Water's Edge | **LIC**	22
Barbetta | **W 40s**	22
Bottega/Vino | **E 50s**	22
Bacchus | **Boerum Hill**	22
Landmarc | **multi.**	21
Terroir | **multi.**	21
Nice Matin | **W 70s**	20

Cuisines

Includes names, locations and Food ratings.

AFGHAN

Afghan Kebab | **multi.**	21

AFRICAN

Abistro | **Ft Greene**	24
Ponty Bistro | **Gramercy**	22

AMERICAN

Per Se | **W 60s**	29
Mas | **W Vill**	28
Grocery | **Carroll Gdns**	28
Gramercy Tavern | **Flatiron**	28
NEW Gwynnett St. | **W'burg**	28
Gotham B&G | **G Vill**	28
Annisa | **W Vill**	28
Saul | **Boerum Hill**	27
St. Anselm | **W'burg**	27
Blue Hill | **G Vill**	27
Union Sq. Cafe | **Union Sq**	27
Perilla | **W Vill**	27
Four Seasons | **E 50s**	27
NEW Battersby | **Carroll Gdns**	27
Tocqueville | **Union Sq**	27
Telepan | **W 60s**	27
Salt & Fat | **Sunnyside**	26
Craft | **Flatiron**	26
Modern | **W 50s**	26
Momofuku Ko | **E Vill**	26
Five Leaves | **Greenpt**	26
Rose Water | **Park Slope**	26
NEW NoMad | **Chelsea**	26
River Café | **Dumbo**	26
Rye | **W'burg**	26
Colonie | **Bklyn Hts**	26
Aureole | **W 40s**	26
Gilt | **E 50s**	26
Wolfgang's | **W 40s**	26
Dressler | **W'burg**	26
Quality Meats | **W 50s**	26
ABC Kitchen | **Flatiron**	26
Strip House | **G Vill**	26
NEW Atera | **TriBeCa**	26
Perry St. | **W Vill**	26
Clinton St. Baking | **LES**	26
Little Owl | **W Vill**	26
Momofuku Ssäm | **E Vill**	26
Norma's | **W 50s**	25
Henry's End | **Bklyn Hts**	25
Prune | **E Vill**	25

Caviar Russe | **E 50s**	25
Dovetail | **W 70s**	25
Mike's Bistro | **W 70s**	25
Blue Ribbon | **multi.**	25
Marc Forgione | **TriBeCa**	25
Recipe | **W 80s**	25
Asiate | **W 60s**	25
Veritas | **Flatiron**	25
Del Frisco's | **W 50s**	25
David Burke Townhse. | **E 60s**	25
James | **Prospect Hts**	25
Recette | **W Vill**	25
Buttermilk | **Carroll Gdns**	25
Rouge Tomate | **E 60s**	25
Park Avenue | **E 60s**	25
Hearth | **E Vill**	25
North End Grill | **Financial**	25
Blue Ribbon Bakery | **W Vill**	25
WD-50 | **LES**	25
Applewood | **Park Slope**	25
Momofuku Noodle | **E Vill**	25
JoeDoe | **E Vill**	25
Colicchio/Sons | **Chelsea**	25
Diner | **W'burg**	25
Marlow/Sons | **W'burg**	25
Ouest | **W 80s**	25
Riverpark | **Murray Hill**	25
Vinegar Hill Hse. | **Vinegar Hill**	25
Stone Park | **Park Slope**	24
Oceana | **W 40s**	24
Bouchon Bakery | **multi.**	24
Hudson Clearwater | **W Vill**	24
Melba's | **Harlem**	24
Fishtail/David Burke | **E 60s**	24
Joseph Leonard | **W Vill**	24
Chadwick's | **Bay Ridge**	24
One if by Land | **W Vill**	24
S'MAC | **E Vill**	24
Farm/Adderley | **Ditmas Pk**	24
Sanford's | **Astoria**	24
David Burke Kitchen | **SoHo**	24
Arabelle | **E 60s**	24
Dylan Prime | **TriBeCa**	24
Jack Horse | **Bklyn Hts**	24
Maloney/Porcelli | **E 50s**	24
Northern Spy | **E Vill**	24
21 Club | **W 50s**	24
Prime Meat | **Carroll Gdns**	24
Commerce | **W Vill**	24

CUISINES

Craftbar	**Flatiron**	24	Abe/Arthur	**Meatpacking**	22
Má Pêche	**W 50s**	24	Smile	**NoHo**	22
Lambs Club	**W 40s**	24	Social Eatz	**E 50s**	22
Market Table	**W Vill**	24	Freemans	**LES**	22
NEW Mas (La Grillade)	**W Vill**	24	Jeffrey's Grocery	**W Vill**	22
Queens Kickshaw	**Astoria**	24	Vanderbilt	**Prospect Hts**	22
NEW 606 R&D	**Prospect Hts**	24	Black Whale	**City Is**	22
Bar Americain	**W 50s**	24	BandB	**SoHo**	22
Dutch	**SoHo**	24	12th St. B&G	**Park Slope**	22
DuMont	**W'burg**	24	BLT B&G	**Financial**	22
NEW Allswell	**W'burg**	24	T-Bar Steak	**E 70s**	22
Apiary	**E Vill**	23	44 & X/44½	**W 40s**	22
Westville	**multi.**	23	Standard Grill	**Meatpacking**	22
Beecher's Cellar	**Flatiron**	23	Friedman's Lunch	**Chelsea**	22
Red Cat	**Chelsea**	23	Wall/Water	**Financial**	22
Peter's 1969	**multi.**	23	101	**Bay Ridge**	22
Hillstone	**multi.**	23	Max Brenner	**G Vill**	22
2 West	**Financial**	23	Stonehome	**Ft Greene**	22
Butter	**E Vill**	23	Lion	**G Vill**	22
North Sq.	**G Vill**	23	Waverly Inn	**W Vill**	22
Harrison	**TriBeCa**	23	Beagle	**E Vill**	22
Tribeca Grill	**TriBeCa**	23	Cafe Cluny	**W Vill**	22
Sidecar	**Park Slope**	23	Henry Public	**Cobble Hill**	22
Mark	**E 70s**	23	Good Enough/Eat	**W 80s**	22
CamaJe	**G Vill**	23	South Gate	**W 50s**	22
Cookshop	**Chelsea**	23	Water's Edge	**LIC**	22
Beauty & Essex	**LES**	23	Bridge Cafe	**Financial**	22
Riverview	**LIC**	23	Kings' Carriage	**E 80s**	22
Water Club	**Murray Hill**	23	NEW Arthur on Smith	**Boerum Hill**	22
NEW Saxon & Parole	**NoHo**	23	Duane Park	**TriBeCa**	22
Place	**W Vill**	23	Jane	**G Vill**	22
NEW Acme	**NoHo**	23	Mercer Kitchen	**SoHo**	22
Back Forty	**multi.**	23	Bell Book/Candle	**W Vill**	22
Community Food	**W 100s**	23	Eatery	**W 50s**	22
Le Comptoir	**W'burg**	23	5 Points	**NoHo**	22
NEW Alison Eighteen	**Flatiron**	23	Astor Room	**Astoria**	22
Square Meal	**E 90s**	23	New Leaf	**Wash. Hts**	21
Home	**W Vill**	23	NEW Corner Social	**Harlem**	21
Penelope	**Murray Hill**	23	Palm Court	**W 50s**	21
5 & Diamond	**Harlem**	23	Robert	**W 50s**	21
No. 7	**Ft Greene**	23	Redeye Grill	**W 50s**	21
Maggie Brown	**Clinton Hill**	23	Knickerbocker	**G Vill**	21
Red Rooster	**Harlem**	23	Crown	**E 80s**	21
Print	**W 40s**	23	Hundred Acres	**SoHo**	21
Corner Bistro	**multi.**	23	Darby	**W Vill**	21
12 Chairs	**SoHo**	23	NEW Sons of Essex	**LES**	21
Trestle on 10th	**Chelsea**	23	Tiny's	**TriBeCa**	21
Beacon	**W 50s**	23	Cibo	**E 40s**	21
Patroon	**E 40s**	23	House	**Gramercy**	21
Fedora	**W Vill**	23	Hudson River	**Harlem**	21
Black Duck	**Murray Hill**	23	Taste	**E 80s**	21
Walter Foods	**multi.**	22	Benchmark	**Park Slope**	21

Peels | **E Vill**	21
NEW Jacob's Pickles | **W 80s**	21
Isabella's | **W 70s**	21
Cafeteria | **Chelsea**	21
National | **E 50s**	21
Garden Café | **Inwood**	21
Good | **W Vill**	21
Sarabeth's | **multi.**	21
Untitled | **E 70s**	21
Smith | **multi.**	21
Fred's at Barneys | **E 60s**	21
NEW Kutsher's | **TriBeCa**	21
Flatbush Farm | **Park Slope**	21
Thalia | **W 50s**	21
Greenhouse | **Bay Ridge**	21
44 | **W 40s**	21
Alice's Tea | **multi.**	21
Monkey Bar | **E 50s**	21
NEW Lexington Brass | **E 40s**	21
Sidetracks | **Sunnyside**	21
Thistle Hill | **Park Slope**	21
NEW Jack's Wife Freda | **SoHo**	20
Glass House | **W 40s**	20
Gen. Greene | **Ft Greene**	20
Henry's | **W 100s**	20
5 9th | **Meatpacking**	20
E.A.T. | **E 80s**	20
NEW ABV | **E 90s**	20
Table d'Hôte | **E 90s**	20
Philip Marie | **W Vill**	20
NEW Foragers City Table | **Chelsea**	20
Rock Ctr. | **W 50s**	20
NoHo Star | **NoHo**	20
Schnipper´s | **multi.**	20
Bubby's | **multi.**	20
David Burke/Bloom. | **E 50s**	20
Delicatessen | **NoLita**	20
Odeon | **TriBeCa**	20
East End Kitchen | **E 80s**	20
Whym | **W 50s**	20
Bistro Ten 18 | **W 100s**	20
Cornelia St. Cafe | **W Vill**	20
West Bank | **W 40s**	20
Jackson Hole | **multi.**	19
B Bar & Grill | **NoHo**	19
Fairway Cafe | **multi.**	19
Battery Gdns. | **Financial**	19
Walker's | **TriBeCa**	19
Morgan | **Murray Hill**	19
Friend/Farmer | **Gramercy**	19
Bryant Park | **W 40s**	19
Joe Allen | **W 40s**	19

Boathouse | **E 70s**	19
NEW Bowery Diner | **LES**	18
NEW Clyde Frazier's | **Garment**	18
NEW Joanne | **W 60s**	18
View | **W 40s**	18
Fraunces Tavern | **Financial**	18
Swifty's | **E 70s**	18
Coffee Shop | **Union Sq**	17
NEW Pounds & Ounces | **Chelsea**	16
NEW A.G. Kitchen | **W 70s**	-
NEW Bellwether | **W'burg**	-
NEW Blanca | **Bushwick**	-
NEW The Exchange | **Financial**	-
NEW Ginny's Supper Club | **Harlem**	-
NEW Goodwin | **W Vill**	-
NEW Governor | **Dumbo**	-
NEW Humphrey | **Chelsea**	-
NEW Jezebel | **SoHo**	-
NEW Ken & Cook | **NoLita**	-
NEW Ktchn | **W 40s**	-
NEW Noir | **E 50s**	-
NEW Parish Hall | **W'burg**	-
NEW Penrose | **E 80s**	-
NEW Reynard | **W'burg**	-

ARGENTINEAN

Buenos Aires | **E Vill**	25
Mundo | **Astoria**	23
Chimichurri Grill | **W 40s**	23
Sosa Borella | **W 50s**	21

ARMENIAN

NEW Almayass | **Flatiron**	25

ASIAN

Asiate | **W 60s**	25
Buddakan | **Chelsea**	25
NEW Talde | **Park Slope**	25
Shi | **LIC**	25
NEW Wong | **W Vill**	24
Tao | **E 50s**	24
Fatty Fish | **E 60s**	24
Spice Market | **Meatpacking**	24
NEW 1066 Eno | **E 50s**	24
Wild Ginger | **multi.**	23
Fatty 'Cue | **W Vill**	23
Cafe Asean | **W Vill**	23
Zengo | **E 40s**	23
China Grill | **W 50s**	23
Qi | **Union Sq**	22
Betel | **W Vill**	22
Social Eatz | **E 50s**	22
Purple Yam | **Ditmas Pk**	22

CUISINES

East Pacific | **multi.**	22
Alpha Fusion | **Garment**	22
Mooncake Foods | **multi.**	21
Citrus B&G | **W 70s**	21
Amber | **multi.**	20
Pranna | **Murray Hill**	20
Ruby Foo's | **W 40s**	19
East Buffet | **Flushing**	19
NEW Toy | **Meatpacking**	-

AUSTRIAN

Wallsé | **W Vill**	26
Seäsonal | **W 50s**	25
Mont Blanc | **W 40s**	24
Edi & the Wolf | **E Vill**	23
Café Sabarsky | **E 80s**	22
Blaue Gans | **TriBeCa**	22
Cafe Steinhof | **Park Slope**	19

BAKERIES

Clinton St. Baking | **LES**	26
La Bergamote | **multi.**	25
Bouchon Bakery | **multi.**	24
Veniero's | **E Vill**	24
Ferrara | **L Italy**	24
Eataly | **Flatiron**	24
Ristorante/Settepani | **W'burg**	24
Momofuku Milk Bar | **multi.**	22
City Bakery | **Flatiron**	22
Sweet Melissa | **Park Slope**	21
Andre's Café | **E 80s**	21
Le Pain Q. | **multi.**	20

BARBECUE

Fette Sau | **W'burg**	26
NEW Butcher Bar | **Astoria**	25
Mable's Smokehouse & Banquet Hall | **W'burg**	24
Dinosaur BBQ | **Harlem**	23
Hill Country | **Flatiron**	23
Fatty 'Cue | **W Vill**	23
Rub BBQ | **Chelsea**	23
Smoke Joint | **Ft Greene**	23
Blue Smoke | **multi.**	23
Rack & Soul | **W 100s**	22
Mexicue | **multi.**	22
Daisy May's | **W 40s**	22
Virgil's BBQ | **W 40s**	21
MexiBBQ | **Astoria**	21
Wildwood BBQ | **Flatiron**	20
Brother Jimmy's | **multi.**	17

BELGIAN

Cannibal | **Murray Hill**	24
Resto | **Murray Hill**	21

B. Café | **multi.**	21
Markt | **Flatiron**	20
Le Pain Q. | **multi.**	20
Petite Abeille | **multi.**	20
BXL | **multi.**	19

BRAZILIAN

Ipanema | **W 40s**	26
Malagueta | **Astoria**	24
Churrascaria | **multi.**	24
Circus | **E 60s**	23
Zebú Grill | **E 90s**	23
SushiSamba | **multi.**	23
Rice 'n' Beans | **W 50s**	22
Via Brasil | **W 40s**	22
Coffee Shop | **Union Sq**	17

BRITISH

Tea & Sympathy | **W Vill**	25
Breslin | **Chelsea**	24
Fat Radish | **LES**	24
A Salt & Battery | **W Vill**	22
NEW Whitehall | **W Vill**	22
ChipShop | **multi.**	21
Jones Wood Foundry | **E 70s**	20

BURGERS

DB Bistro Moderne | **W 40s**	25
Minetta | **G Vill**	24
Burger Joint | **W 50s**	24
Spotted Pig | **W Vill**	24
Burger Bistro | **multi.**	24
DuMont | **W'burg**	24
Molly's | **Gramercy**	23
BareBurger | **multi.**	23
Bonnie's Grill | **Park Slope**	23
Back Forty | **E Vill**	23
Corner Bistro | **multi.**	23
Social Eatz | **E 50s**	22
Island Burgers | **multi.**	22
BandB | **SoHo**	22
Zaitzeff | **multi.**	22
Piper's Kilt | **multi.**	22
Shake Shack | **multi.**	22
BLT Burger | **G Vill**	22
67 Burger | **multi.**	22
Rare B&G | **multi.**	22
Lucky's Famous Burgers | **multi.**	22
5 Napkin Burger | **multi.**	22
NEW Steak 'n Shake | **W 50s**	21
J.G. Melon | **E 70s**	21
Black Iron | **E Vill**	21
Counter | **W 40s**	21

Five Guys	**multi.**	21
Donovan's	**multi.**	21
Schnipper´s	**multi.**	20
Bill's Bar	**multi.**	20
Jackson Hole	**multi.**	19
Blue 9 Burger	**multl.**	19
Goodburger	**multi.**	19
Brgr	**multi.**	19
Big Nick's	**W 70s**	19
Go Burger	**multi.**	19
P.J. Clarke's	**multi.**	18
NEW Blue Collar	**W'burg**	-
NEW High Heat	**G Vill**	-

CAJUN

Bayou	**Rosebank**	23
Sugar Freak	**Astoria**	22
Great Jones Cafe	**NoHo**	21
Delta Grill	**W 40s**	20
Two Boots	**Park Slope**	20
Bourbon St. Café	**Bayside**	19

CALIFORNIAN

Michael's	**W 50s**	22

CAMBODIAN

Num Pang	**multi.**	25

CARIBBEAN

Don Pedro's	**E 90s**	21

CAVIAR

Caviar Russe	**E 50s**	25
Petrossian	**W 50s**	24
Russian Tea	**W 50s**	21

CHEESE SPECIALISTS

Picholine	**W 60s**	27
Artisanal	**Murray Hill**	23
Beecher's Cellar	**Flatiron**	23

CHEESESTEAKS

Lil'/Shorty's	**multi.**	23
Carl's Steaks	**Murray Hill**	22
99 Mi. to Philly	**E Vill**	22

CHICKEN

Torishin	**E 60s**	26
Yakitori Totto	**W 50s**	25
Pies-n-Thighs	**W'burg**	25
Peter's 1969	**W'burg**	23
Pio Pio	**multi.**	23
El Malecon	**multi.**	22
BonChon Chicken	**multi.**	22
Flor/Mayo	**multi.**	21

Coco Roco	**multi.**	21
Kyochon	**multi.**	21
Hill Country Chicken	**Flatiron**	20

CHINESE

(* dim sum specialist)

RedFarm*	**W Vill**	26
Shanghai Café	**L Italy**	24
Chin Chin	**E 40s**	24
Xi'an	**multi.**	24
Spicy & Tasty	**Flushing**	24
Pacificana*	**Sunset Pk**	24
New Hawaii Sea	**Westchester Hts**	24
Shun Lee Palace	**E 50s**	24
BaoHaus	**E Vill**	24
Wa Jeal	**E 80s**	23
Great NY Noodle	**Chinatown**	23
Philippe	**E 60s**	23
Mr. K's	**E 50s**	23
Tang Pavilion	**W 50s**	23
Nice Green Bo	**Chinatown**	23
Szechuan Gourmet	**multi.**	23
Wu Liang Ye	**W 40s**	23
NEW Hakkasan	**W 40s**	23
Phoenix Gdn.	**Murray Hill**	23
Fuleen	**Chinatown**	23
Shun Lee West	**W 60s**	23
Peking Duck	**multi.**	23
Lychee Hse.*	**E 50s**	23
Wo Hop	**Chinatown**	23
Excellent Dumpling*	**Chinatown**	23
Oriental Gdn.*	**Chinatown**	23
Mr. Chow	**multi.**	22
Legend	**Chelsea**	22
Amazing 66	**Chinatown**	22
Joe's Shanghai	**multi.**	22
Tasty Hand-Pulled	**Chinatown**	22
Hop Kee	**Chinatown**	22
Chef Ho's	**E 80s**	22
Cafe China	**Murray Hill**	22
X.O.*	**L Italy**	22
Nom Wah Tea*	**Chinatown**	22
Shanghai Pavilion	**E 70s**	22
Bo-Ky	**multi.**	22
Big Wong	**Chinatown**	22
Vanessa's Dumpling	**multi.**	22
Golden Unicorn*	**Chinatown**	21
Flor/Mayo	**multi.**	21
Pig Heaven	**E 80s**	21
Ping's Sea.*	**multi.**	21
Shun Lee Cafe*	**W 60s**	21
Jing Fong*	**Chinatown**	21
Dim Sum Go Go*	**Chinatown**	21

CUISINES

NEW Dong Chun Hong | Garment	21
Red Egg* | L Italy	21
Chef Yu | Garment	21
NEW Biang | Flushing	21
Sammy's | G Vill	21
Joe's | Chinatown	21
Grand Sichuan | multi.	21
King Yum | Fresh Meadows	21
East Manor* | Flushing	21
Dumpling Man | E Vill	21
Congee | LES	21
Macao Trading | TriBeCa	20
Our Place* | E 70s	20
NoHo Star | NoHo	20
China Chalet | multi.	20
Au Mandarin | Financial	20
NEW Yunnan Kitchen | LES	18
NEW Mission Chinese Food | LES	-

COFFEEHOUSES

Saraghina | Bed-Stuy	27
Via Quadronno | multi.	24
Queens Kickshaw | Astoria	24
Café Sabarsky | E 80s	22
Smile | NoHo	22
Tarallucci | multi.	21
Untitled | E 70s	21
Andre's Café | E 80s	21
Yura on Madison | E 90s	20
Omonia | Astoria	20
Cafe Lalo | W 80s	20
Le Pain Q. | multi.	20

CONTINENTAL

Jack's Lux. | E Vill	28
Petrossian | W 50s	24
Astor Room | Astoria	22
Cebu | Bay Ridge	21
Russian Tea | W 50s	21
Russian Samovar | W 50s	21
Sardi's | W 40s	19
NEW Siro's | E 40s	-

CREOLE

Sugar Freak | Astoria	22
Delta Grill | W 40s	20

CRÊPES

Creperie | G Vill	23

CUBAN

Cuba | G Vill	24
NEW Son Cubano | Chelsea	23
Café Habana/Outpost | multi.	23
Amor Cubano | Harlem	23
Cubana Café | multi.	23
Victor's Cafe | W 50s	22
Havana Alma | W Vill	22
Guantanamera | W 50s	21
Havana Central | multi.	20

CZECH

Hospoda | E 70s	23

DELIS

(See also Sandwiches)

Mile End | Boerum Hill	25
Katz's Deli | LES	25
Barney Greengrass | W 80s	24
Ben's Best | Rego Pk	23
Carnegie Deli | W 50s	23
2nd Ave Deli | multi.	23
Mill Basin | Mill Basin	23
Pastrami Queen | E 70s	22
Liebman's Deli | Riverdale	22
Stage Door Deli | multi.	21
Sarge's Deli | Murray Hill	21
Stage Deli | W 50s	20
Ben's Kosher | multi.	20

DESSERT

ChikaLicious | E Vill	25
Chocolate Room | multi.	25
L&B Spumoni | Bensonhurst	25
Bouchon Bakery | multi.	24
Veniero's | E Vill	24
Kyotofu | W 40s	24
Momofuku Milk Bar | multi.	22
Café Sabarsky | E 80s	22
Max Brenner | G Vill	22
Sant Ambroeus | multi.	22
Sweet Melissa | Park Slope	21
Lady Mendl's | Gramercy	21
Serendipity 3 | E 60s	20
Omonia | Astoria	20
Junior's | multi.	20
Cafe Lalo | W 80s	20

DINER

Diner | W'burg	25
Coppelia | Chelsea	23
Bonnie's Grill | Park Slope	23
La Taza de Oro | Chelsea	22
Tom's | Prospect Hts	22
Teresa's | Bklyn Hts	21
Little Poland | E Vill	21
Junior's | multi.	20

| Schnipper´s | **multi.** | 20 |
| **NEW** Bowery Diner | **LES** | 18 |

DOMINICAN

| El Malecon | **multi.** | 22 |
| Mamajuana | **multi.** | 21 |

EASTERN EUROPEAN

| Sammy's | **LES** | 20 |

ECLECTIC

Smorgasburg	**W'burg**	28
Traif	**W'burg**	27
Juventino	**Park Slope**	26
Graffiti	**E Vill**	25
Carol's	**Dongan Hills**	25
Do or Dine	**Bed-Stuy**	25
WD-50	**LES**	25
Good Fork	**Red Hook**	25
Stanton Social	**LES**	24
Mehtaphor	**TriBeCa**	24
Harry's Cafe & Steak	**Financial**	24
Beauty & Essex	**LES**	23
Sojourn	**E 70s**	23
Plaza Food Hall	**W 50s**	23
Public	**NoLita**	23
Nook	**W 50s**	23
Rice	**Dumbo**	22
Abigael's	**Garment**	21
107 West	**W 100s**	21
Tolani	**W 70s**	21
Whole Foods	**multi.**	21
Schiller's	**LES**	20
Josie's	**multi.**	20
East Buffet	**Flushing**	19
Rasputin	**Sheepshead**	18
NEW Dans Le Noir	**Garment**	-

ETHIOPIAN

Zoma	**Harlem**	24
Meskerem	**multi.**	23
Queen of Sheba	**W 40s**	23
Awash	**multi.**	23

EUROPEAN

Danny Brown	**Forest Hills**	26
NEW NoMad	**Chelsea**	26
Spotted Pig	**W Vill**	24
August	**W Vill**	23

FILIPINO

| **NEW** Maharlika | **E Vill** | 26 |
| Kuma Inn | **LES** | 25 |

FISH 'N' CHIPS

| A Salt & Battery | **W Vill** | 22 |
| ChipShop | **multi.** | 21 |

FONDUE

Chocolate Room	**multi.**	25
Mont Blanc	**W 40s**	24
Kashkaval	**W 50s**	23
Artisanal	**Murray Hill**	23

FRENCH

Le Bernardin	**W 50s**	29
Per Se	**W 60s**	29
Bouley	**TriBeCa**	28
Daniel	**E 60s**	28
Eleven Madison	**Flatiron**	28
Jean Georges	**W 60s**	28
La Grenouille	**E 50s**	28
Jack's Lux.	**E Vill**	28
Degustation	**E Vill**	28
Picholine	**W 60s**	27
Brooklyn Fare	**Downtown Bklyn**	27
Jean Georges Noug.	**W 60s**	27
Café Boulud	**E 70s**	27
Tocqueville	**Union Sq**	27
Adour	**E 50s**	27
Modern	**W 50s**	26
Corton	**TriBeCa**	26
Le Cirque	**E 50s**	25
Rouge et Blanc	**SoHo**	25
La Bergamote	**multi.**	25
Maze	**W 50s**	25
Le Perigord	**E 50s**	25
Buvette	**W Vill**	25
NEW La Promenade/Anglais	**Chelsea**	25
L'Ecole	**SoHo**	24
Petrossian	**W 50s**	24
Bouchon Bakery	**multi.**	24
Arabelle	**E 60s**	24
La Baraka	**Little Neck**	24
Carlyle	**E 70s**	24
Triomphe	**W 40s**	24
Gordon Ramsay	**W 50s**	24
Bobo	**W Vill**	23
Le Comptoir	**W'burg**	23
NEW Alison Eighteen	**Flatiron**	23
Fedora	**W Vill**	23
Creperie	**LES**	23
La Mangeoire	**E 50s**	23
Ponty Bistro	**Gramercy**	22
NEW Americano	**Chelsea**	22
La Boîte en Bois	**W 60s**	22

CUISINES

Le Rivage | **W 40s**	22
Le Colonial | **E 50s**	22
Mercer Kitchen | **SoHo**	22
Chez Lucienne | **Harlem**	22
Brick Cafe | **Astoria**	22
Indochine | **E Vill**	22
Café Henri | **multi.**	22
Cafe Gitane | **multi.**	22
Pascalou | **E 90s**	21
Ze Café | **E 50s**	21
Le Marais | **W 40s**	21
Breeze | **W 40s**	21
La Mediterranée | **E 50s**	21
Ayza Wine | **multi.**	21
Le Grainne Cafe | **Chelsea**	21
Le Relais/Venise | **E 50s**	21
Café du Soleil | **W 100s**	20
Nizza | **W 40s**	20
Cafe Noir | **SoHo**	20
Barbès | **Murray Hill**	20
Lyon | **W Vill**	19
NEW Bagatelle | **Meatpacking**	-
NEW Calliope | **E Vill**	-
NEW Château Cherbuliez | **Flatiron**	-

FRENCH (BISTRO)

Le Gigot | **W Vill**	25
Raoul's | **SoHo**	25
DB Bistro Moderne | **W 40s**	25
La Silhouette | **W 50s**	25
JoJo | **E 60s**	24
Tournesol | **LIC**	24
Minetta | **G Vill**	24
Bar Boulud | **W 60s**	24
DBGB | **E Vill**	24
Le Parisien | **Murray Hill**	24
Capsouto Frères | **TriBeCa**	23
Lucien | **E Vill**	23
CamaJe | **G Vill**	23
Tartine | **W Vill**	23
26 Seats | **E Vill**	23
La Sirène | **Hudson Square**	23
Bistro Les Amis | **SoHo**	23
La Mirabelle | **W 80s**	23
Chez Napoléon | **W 50s**	23
Gascogne | **Chelsea**	22
Pastis | **Meatpacking**	22
Le Bilboquet | **E 60s**	22
Bistro Vendôme | **E 50s**	22
Cafe Cluny | **W Vill**	22
Benoit | **W 50s**	22
La Lunchonette | **Chelsea**	22

Bacchus | **Boerum Hill**	22
Cafe Luxembourg | **W 70s**	22
Landmarc | **multi.**	21
Saju Bistro | **W 40s**	21
Mon Petit Cafe | **E 60s**	21
Bistro Citron | **W 80s**	21
Quatorze Bis | **E 70s**	21
Chez Oskar | **Ft Greene**	21
Les Halles | **multi.**	21
Cafe Luluc | **Cobble Hill**	21
Chez Josephine | **W 40s**	21
Almond | **Flatiron**	21
Le Veau d'Or | **E 60s**	21
Steak Frites | **Union Sq**	20
Madison Bistro | **Murray Hill**	20
Bistro Cassis | **W 70s**	20
Deux Amis | **E 50s**	20
Table d'Hôte | **E 90s**	20
Bistro Chat Noir | **E 60s**	20
Nice Matin | **W 70s**	20
Cafe Loup | **W Vill**	20
Chez Jacqueline | **G Vill**	20
A.O.C. | **multi.**	20
Cercle Rouge | **TriBeCa**	20
Odeon | **TriBeCa**	20
Cornelia St. Cafe | **W Vill**	20
Bistro 61 | **E 60s**	20
La Bonne Soupe | **W 50s**	19
Cafe Joul | **E 50s**	19
Bistro Le Steak | **E 70s**	19
NEW Purple Fig | **W 70s**	-

FRENCH (BRASSERIE)

Balthazar | **SoHo**	24
Beaumarchais | **Meatpacking**	24
Artisanal | **Murray Hill**	23
Brasserie 8½ | **W 50s**	23
L'Absinthe | **E 60s**	22
Brasserie | **E 50s**	22
Café d'Alsace | **E 80s**	22
Ça Va | **W 40s**	22
Marseille | **W 40s**	21
Rue 57 | **W 50s**	20
Brasserie Cognac | **W 50s**	20
Orsay | **E 70s**	19
Brass. Ruhlmann | **W 50s**	19

GASTROPUB

Spotted Pig | Euro. | **W Vill**	24
Cannibal | Belgian | **Murray Hill**	24
Beagle | Amer. | **E Vill**	22
Resto | Belgian | **Murray Hill**	21

Thistle Hill | American | **Park Slope** 21
NEW Penrose | Amer. | **E 80s** ⌐

GERMAN

Zum Stammtisch	**Glendale**	24
Schnitzel Haus	**Bay Ridge**	24
Prime Meat	**Carroll Gdns**	24
Nurnberger	**New Brighton**	23
Zum Schneider	**E Vill**	22
Blaue Gans	**TriBeCa**	22
Heidelberg	**E 80s**	19
Rolf's	**Gramercy**	17

GREEK

Milos	**W 50s**	27
Pylos	**E Vill**	27
Taverna Kyclades	**Astoria**	27
Eliá	**Bay Ridge**	26
Avra	**E 40s**	25
NEW Boukiés	**E Vill**	25
Bahari Estiatorio	**Astoria**	25
NEW Yefsi Estiatorio	**E 70s**	24
Thalassa	**TriBeCa**	24
Agnanti	**Astoria**	24
Aegean Cove	**Astoria**	24
Loukoumi Taverna	**Astoria**	24
Periyali	**Flatiron**	24
Molyvos	**W 50s**	23
FishTag	**W 70s**	23
Ovelia	**Astoria**	23
Stamatis	**Astoria**	23
Elias Corner	**Astoria**	23
Kellari Tav./Parea	**W 40s**	23
Telly's Taverna	**Astoria**	23
Snack	**multi.**	23
Kefi	**W 80s**	23
Parea Bistro	**Flatiron**	23
NEW Loi	**W 70s**	22
Ammos	**E 40s**	22
Ethos	**multi.**	22
Agora Taverna	**Forest Hills**	22
Uncle Nick's	**multi.**	21
Greek Kitchen	**W 50s**	21
Cávo	**Astoria**	21
Symposium	**W 100s**	20
Dafni Greek	**W 40s**	20
Omonia	**Astoria**	20
Okeanos	**Park Slope**	20
Ithaka	**E 80s**	20

HEALTH FOOD

(See also Vegetarian)

Community Food	**W 100s**	23
Qi	**multi.**	22

Spring/Natural	**multi.**	21
Mooncake Foods	**multi.**	21
Josie's	**multi.**	20

HOT DOGS

Crif Dogs	**multi.**	23
Shake Shack	**multi.**	22
Bark Hot Dogs	**multi.**	22
Papaya King	**E 80s**	20
Gray's Papaya	**multi.**	20
Go Burger	**multi.**	19

HUNGARIAN

Andre's Café | **E 80s** 21

ICE CREAM PARLOR

Serendipity 3 | **E 60s** 20

INDIAN

Tamarind	**multi.**	26
Seva Indian Cuisine	**Astoria**	25
Amma	**E 50s**	25
Yuva	**E 50s**	24
Junoon	**Flatiron**	24
Vatan	**Murray Hill**	24
Tiffin Wallah	**Murray Hill**	24
Banjara	**E Vill**	24
Tulsi	**E 40s**	24
Dhaba	**Murray Hill**	23
Chola	**E 50s**	23
Saravanaa Bhavan	**multi.**	23
Pongal	**Murray Hill**	23
Dawat	**E 50s**	23
Kati Roll	**multi.**	23
Haveli	**E Vill**	22
Indus Valley	**W 100s**	22
Nirvana	**Murray Hill**	22
Brick Ln. Curry	**multi.**	22
Darbar	**multi.**	22
Hampton Chutney	**multi.**	22
NEW Desi Shack	**Murray Hill**	22
Mughlai	**W 70s**	21
Surya	**W Vill**	21
Utsav	**W 40s**	21
Sapphire	**W 60s**	21
Bukhara Grill	**E 40s**	21
Jackson Diner	**multi.**	21
Bombay Talkie	**Chelsea**	21
Bombay Palace	**W 50s**	20
Baluchi's	**multi.**	20

ISRAELI

Taïm	**multi.**	26
Azuri Cafe	**W 50s**	25

CUISINES

Hummus Pl. | **multi.**	23
Miriam | **Park Slope**	22

ITALIAN

(N=Northern; S=Southern)

NEW Bar Corvo | **Prospect Hts**	28
Marea | **W 50s**	28
Il Mulino | S | **G Vill**	27
Scalini Fedeli | N | **TriBeCa**	27
Luzzo's/Ovest | S | **E Vill**	27
Torrisi | **NoLita**	27
L'Artusi | **W Vill**	27
Tratt. L'incontro | **Astoria**	27
Al Di La | N | **Park Slope**	27
Babbo | **G Vill**	27
Saraghina | **Bed-Stuy**	27
Pepolino | N | **TriBeCa**	27
Il Bambino | **Astoria**	27
Del Posto | **Chelsea**	26
Leo's Latticini/Corona | **multi.**	26
Ai Fiori | **Garment**	26
Sistina | N | **E 80s**	26
Marcony | **Murray Hill**	26
NEW Sauce | S | **LES**	26
Vesta | **Astoria**	26
Nove | **Eltingville**	26
Roberto | **Fordham**	26
Don Peppe | **Ozone Pk**	26
Sud Vino & Cucina | **Bed-Stuy**	26
Scarpetta | **Chelsea**	26
Sandro's | S | **E 80s**	26
Bianca | N | **NoHo**	26
Piccolo Angolo | **W Vill**	26
Tratt. Romana | **Dongan Hills**	26
Felidia | **E 50s**	26
Locanda Vini | N | **Clinton Hill**	26
Roman's | **Ft Greene**	26
Pó | **W Vill**	26
Il Buco | **NoHo**	26
Gradisca | **W Vill**	26
Roberta's | **Bushwick**	26
Tiella | S | **E 60s**	26
Supper | N | **E Vill**	26
Bocelli | **Grasmere**	26
Maialino | S | **Gramercy**	26
Caravaggio | **E 70s**	26
Dell'anima | **W Vill**	26
Tuscany Grill | N | **Bay Ridge**	26
San Matteo | S | **multi.**	26
Tevere | S | **E 80s**	26
Manzo | **Flatiron**	26
Piccola Venezia | **Astoria**	25
NEW Rosemary's | **W Vill**	25

Spina | **E Vill**	25
Locanda Verde | **TriBeCa**	25
Salumeria Rosi | N | **W 70s**	25
Da Umberto | N | **Chelsea**	25
Scalinatella | **E 60s**	25
Trattoria Toscana | N | **W Vill**	25
Ápizz | **LES**	25
Il Giglio | N | **TriBeCa**	25
Franny's | **Prospect Hts**	25
Patricia's | **Morris Park**	25
Lupa | S | **G Vill**	25
'Ino | **W Vill**	25
Esca | S | **W 40s**	25
Pisticci | S | **W 100s**	25
Ciano | **Flatiron**	25
Giovanni | N | **E 80s**	25
Il Tinello | N | **W 50s**	25
I Sodi | **W Vill**	25
Valbella | N | **multi.**	25
Grifone | N | **E 40s**	25
SD26 | **Murray Hill**	25
Hearth | N | **E Vill**	25
Il Bagatto | **E Vill**	25
Rucola | N | **Boerum Hill**	25
Pietro's | **E 40s**	25
L&B Spumoni | **Bensonhurst**	25
Ponte's | **TriBeCa**	25
Novitá | N | **Gramercy**	25
Uvarara | **MiddlE Vill**	25
Noodle Pudding | **Bklyn Hts**	25
Betto | **W'burg**	25
Padre Figlio | **E 40s**	25
Nanni | N | **E 40s**	25
Pellegrino's | **L Italy**	25
DeGrezia | **E 50s**	25
Queen | **Bklyn Hts**	25
Ponticello | N | **Astoria**	25
San Pietro | S | **E 50s**	25
Areo | **Bay Ridge**	25
Park Side | **Corona**	25
NEW La Promenade/Anglais | **Chelsea**	25
Lincoln | **W 60s**	25
Porchetta | **E Vill**	25
Erminia | S | **E 80s**	25
Fragole | **Carroll Gdns**	25
Malatesta | N | **W Vill**	25
Tra Di Noi | **Fordham**	24
Barbuto | **W Vill**	24
NEW Don Antonio | **W 50s**	24
Peasant | **NoLita**	24
Zero Otto | S | **multi.**	24
Tommaso | **Dyker Hts**	24

Acappella | N | **TriBeCa**	24
Sorella | **LES**	24
Villa Berulia | N | **Murray Hill**	24
Osteria Morini | N | **SoHo**	24
NEW Parm | S | **NoLita**	24
Alloro | **E 70s**	24
Spasso | **W Vill**	24
Via Emilia | N | **Flatiron**	24
Spigolo | **E 80s**	24
Perbacco | **E Vill**	24
Veniero's | **E Vill**	24
NEW Speedy Romeo | **Clinton Hill**	24
Pinocchio | **E 90s**	24
Dominick's | **Fordham**	24
Elio's | **E 80s**	24
Defonte's | **multi.**	24
Vezzo | **Murray Hill**	24
Gennaro | **W 90s**	24
Sette Mezzo | **E 70s**	24
A Voce | **multi.**	24
Villa Mosconi | **G Vill**	24
Il Gattopardo | S | **W 50s**	24
Alberto | N | **Forest Hills**	24
Mercato | **Garment**	24
Fabio Piccolo | **E 40s**	24
Frankies | **multi.**	24
Celeste | S | **W 80s**	24
Basso56 | S | **W 50s**	24
Miranda | **W'burg**	24
Rossini's | N | **Murray Hill**	24
Via Quadronno | N | **multi.**	24
Emporio | **NoLita**	24
Bar Pitti | **G Vill**	24
Vincent's | **L Italy**	24
Enzo's | **multi.**	24
Antica Venezia | **W Vill**	24
Bocca Lupo | **Cobble Hill**	24
Gargiulo's | S | **Coney Is**	24
Da Noi | N | **multi.**	24
Lusardi's | N | **E 70s**	24
Lavagna | **E Vill**	24
Angelina's | **Tottenville**	24
Eataly | **Flatiron**	24
Spiga | **W 80s**	24
Crispo | N | **W Vill**	24
'Cesca | S | **W 70s**	24
Orso | N | **W 40s**	24
Nocello | N | **W 50s**	24
Max SoHa/Caffe | **W 100s**	24
Ristorante/Settepani | S | **multi.**	24
Circo | N | **W 50s**	24
Lil' Frankie | **E Vill**	24

Otto | **G Vill**	24
Joe & Pat's | **Castleton Corners**	24
Sfoglia | N | **E 90s**	24
Piadina | **G Vill**	24
Aroma Kitchen | **NoHo**	23
Caffe e Vino | **Ft Greene**	23
Tosca Café | **Throgs Neck**	23
Il Postino | **E 40s**	23
Italianissimo | **E 80s**	23
Angelo's/Mulberry | S | **L Italy**	23
Da Andrea | N | **G Vill**	23
Tony's Di Napoli | S | **multi.**	23
Campagnola | **E 70s**	23
Lido | N | **Harlem**	23
Montebello | N | **E 50s**	23
Basta Pasta | **Flatiron**	23
Cipriani D'twn | **SoHo**	23
Palma | S | **W Vill**	23
La Masseria | S | **W 40s**	23
Forcella | S | **W'burg**	23
Aurora | **multi.**	23
Il Cantinori | N | **G Vill**	23
Gabriel's | N | **W 60s**	23
Becco | **W 40s**	23
Cipriani Wall Street | **Financial**	23
Mario's | S | **Fordham**	23
Frank | **E Vill**	23
Arturo's | **G Vill**	23
Barbone | **E Vill**	23
I Coppi | N | **E Vill**	23
Luna Piena | **E 50s**	23
Ecco | **TriBeCa**	23
Patsy's | S | **W 50s**	23
57 Napoli Pizza e Vino | **E 50s**	23
La Piazzetta | **W'burg**	23
Cotta | **W 80s**	23
Gnocco | N | **E Vill**	23
Risotteria | **W Vill**	23
Covo | **Harlem**	23
Manducatis | S | **LIC**	23
Portofino | N | **City Is**	23
Morandi | **W Vill**	23
Paola's | **E 90s**	23
Antonucci | **E 80s**	23
Beccofino | **Riverdale**	23
La Pizza Fresca | **Flatiron**	23
Pepe | **multi.**	23
Remi | **W 50s**	23
Primola | **E 60s**	23
Armani Rist. | N | **E 50s**	23
La Vigna | **Forest Hills**	23
Casa Lever | **E 50s**	23

CUISINES

Scalino | **Park Slope** 23

Da Ciro | **Murray Hill** 23

Fresco | N | **multi.** 23

Il Fornaio | **L Italy** 23

Manetta's | **LIC** 23

Rao's | S | **Harlem** 23

Scottadito | N | **Park Slope** 23

Il Cortile | **L Italy** 23

ViceVersa | **W 50s** 23

Amorina | **Prospect Hts** 23

Etcetera Etcetera | **W 40s** 23

Tratt. Dell'Arte | N | **W 50s** 23

Uva | **E 70s** 23

La Gioconda | **E 50s** 23

Macelleria | N | **Meatpacking** 23

Bamonte's | **W'burg** 23

La Villa Pizzeria | **multi.** 23

F & J Pine | **Morris Park** 23

I Trulli | **Murray Hill** 22

Roc | **TriBeCa** 22

Cipriani Dolci | **E 40s** 22

Rubirosa | **NoLita** 22

Tre Dici/Steak | **Chelsea** 22

Testaccio | S | **LIC** 22

508 | **Hudson Square** 22

Harry Cipriani | N | **E 50s** 22

Nicola's | **E 80s** 22

Corsino | **W Vill** 22

Mezzaluna/Pizza | **E 70s** 22

La Follia | **Gramercy** 22

Girasole | **E 80s** 22

Da Silvano | N | **G Vill** 22

Cola | S | **Chelsea** 22

Quattro Gatti | **E 80s** 22

Valentino's/Green | **Bayside** 22

Bocca | S | **Flatiron** 22

Bella Via | **LIC** 22

Le Zie | N | **Chelsea** 22

Centro Vinoteca | **W Vill** 22

Lattanzi | S | **W 40s** 22

Harry's Italian | **multi.** 22

101 | **Bay Ridge** 22

Bistango | **Murray Hill** 22

Riposo | N | **multi.** 22

Abboccato | **W 50s** 22

John's/12th St. | **E Vill** 22

NEW Perla | **G Vill** 22

Lavo | **E 50s** 22

La Mela | S | **L Italy** 22

Pasquale's | **Fordham** 22

Carmine's | S | **multi.** 22

Trattoria Cinque | **TriBeCa** 22

Ann & Tony's | **Fordham** 22

'Inoteca | **multi.** 22

Barosa | **Rego Pk** 22

Bella Blu | N | **E 70s** 22

Fornino | **multi.** 22

Parma | N | **E 70s** 22

Casa Nonna | **Garment** 22

La Bottega | **Chelsea** 22

Fiorentino's | S | **Gravesend** 22

Osso Buco | **E 90s** 22

Canaletto | N | **E 60s** 22

Leopard/des Artistes | S | **W 60s** 22

Cellini | N | **E 50s** 22

NEW Arthur on Smith | **Boerum Hill** 22

Pomodoro Rosso | **W 70s** 22

Barbetta | N | **W 40s** 22

Angelo's Pizza | **multi.** 22

Lunetta | **Boerum Hill** 22

Zito's | **Park Slope** 22

Bottega/Vino | **E 50s** 22

Da Nico | **L Italy** 22

Lorenzo's | **Bloomfield** 22

Max | S | **multi.** 22

Trattoria Trecolori | **W 40s** 22

Tre Otto | **E 90s** 22

Birreria | **Flatiron** 22

Umberto's | **multi.** 22

Asellina | **Murray Hill** 22

Brick Cafe | N | **Astoria** 22

Sant Ambroeus | N | **multi.** 22

Osteria Laguna | **E 40s** 22

Porsena | **E Vill** 22

Monte's | **Gowanus** 22

Anthony's | **Park Slope** 22

Marco Polo | **Carroll Gdns** 22

Bice | N | **E 50s** 22

Due | N | **E 70s** 21

Cara Mia | **W 40s** 21

PizzArte | S | **W 50s** 21

Biricchino | N | **Chelsea** 21

Bistro Milano | N | **W 50s** 21

Noi Due | **W 60s** 21

Ze Café | **E 50s** 21

Grand Tier | **W 60s** 21

Coppola's | **multi.** 21

Firenze | N | **E 80s** 21

Gigino | **multi.** 21

Nino's | N | **multi.** 21

Mezzogiorno | N | **SoHo** 21

Bocca/Bacco | **multi.** 21

Fiorini | S | **E 50s** 21

Giorgio's | **Flatiron**	21
Tarallucci | **multi.**	21
Bricco | **W 50s**	21
Cibo | N | **E 40s**	21
Teodora | N | **E 50s**	21
Da Tommaso | N | **W 50s**	21
Gottino | **W Vill**	21
Gemma | **E Vill**	21
Alfredo/Rome | S | **W 40s**	21
SottoVoce | **Park Slope**	21
Maruzzella | N | **E 70s**	21
Marinella | **W Vill**	21
Tratt. Pesce | **multi.**	21
Acqua | S | **W 90s**	21
Felice | **multi.**	21
Locale | **Astoria**	21
S.P.Q.R. | S | **L Italy**	21
Paul & Jimmy's | **Gramercy**	21
Pescatore | **E 50s**	21
Fred's at Barneys | N | **E 60s**	21
Osteria al Doge | N | **W 40s**	21
Sambuca | S | **W 70s**	21
Vesuvio | **Bay Ridge**	21
Meson Sevilla | **W 40s**	21
Cacio e Pepe | S | **E Vill**	21
Scaletta | N | **W 70s**	21
Amarone | **W 40s**	21
Grace's Tratt. | **E 70s**	21
Bottino | N | **Chelsea**	21
Brio | **multi.**	21
Terroir | **multi.**	21
Sosa Borella | **W 50s**	21
Al Forno Pizza | **E 70s**	21
Fratelli | **Pelham Gardens**	21
La Lanterna | **G Vill**	21
NEW Caffe Storico | **W 70s**	20
Cafe Fiorello | **W 60s**	20
Bread | **TriBeCa**	20
Il Vagabondo | **E 60s**	20
Naples 45 | S | **E 40s**	20
Arno | N | **Garment**	20
Forlini's | N | **Chinatown**	20
Destino | S | **E 50s**	20
Bond 45 | **W 40s**	20
Il Riccio | S | **E 70s**	20
Vivolo/Cucina | **E 70s**	20
Caffe Grazie | **E 80s**	20
Regional | **W 90s**	20
Pappardella | **W 70s**	20
Caffe Cielo | **W 50s**	20
Madison's | **Riverdale**	20
Puttanesca | **W 50s**	20

Nizza | **W 40s**	20
Divino | N | **E 80s**	20
Baraonda | **E 70s**	20
Serafina | **multi.**	20
Maria Pia | **W 50s**	20
Per Lei | **E 70s**	20
NEW Bigoli | **W Vill**	19
Bettola | **W 70s**	19
Arté Café | **W 70s**	19
Bar Italia | **E 60s**	19
Petaluma | **E 70s**	18
NEW Joanne | **W 60s**	18
Nello | N | **E 60s**	18
NEW Calliope | **E Vill**	-
NEW Isola | **SoHo**	-
NEW Nicoletta | **E Vill**	-

JAMAICAN

Negril | **G Vill**	23
Miss Llly's | **G Vill**	21

JAPANESE

(* sushi specialist)

Sasabune* | **E 70s**	29
Ushiwakamaru* | **G Vill**	28
Soto* | **W Vill**	28
Sugiyama | **W 50s**	28
Kuruma Zushi* | **E 40s**	28
Sushi Yasuda* | **E 40s**	28
Sushi Seki* | **E 60s**	28
Kajitsu | **E Vill**	28
Kyo Ya | **E Vill**	27
Gari/Sushi* | **multi.**	27
Takashi | **W Vill**	27
Masa/Bar Masa* | **W 60s**	27
Nobu* | **multi.**	27
Sushi Zen* | **W 40s**	26
Morimoto | **Chelsea**	26
SushiAnn* | **E 50s**	26
Momo Sushi Shack* | **Bushwick**	26
Blue Ribbon Sushi* | **SoHo**	26
Totto Ramen | **W 50s**	26
Bohemian | **NoHo**	26
15 East* | **Union Sq**	26
Sushi Sen-nin* | **Murray Hill**	26
Torishin | **E 60s**	26
Kanoyama* | **E Vill**	26
Ippudo | **E Vill**	26
Zenkichi | **W'burg**	26
Omen | **SoHo**	26
EN Japanese | **W Vill**	26
Jewel Bako* | **E Vill**	26
Tomoe Sushi* | **G Vill**	26

CUISINES

Donguri | **E 80s**	25
Brushstroke | **TriBeCa**	25
Aburiya Kinnosuke | **E 40s**	25
Blue Ribbon Sushi B&G* | **W 50s**	25
Blue Ribbon* | **Park Slope**	25
Sakagura | **E 40s**	25
Robataya | **E Vill**	25
Bond St.* | **NoHo**	25
Ki Sushi* | **Boerum Hill**	25
Watawa* | **Astoria**	25
Hibino* | **Cobble Hill**	25
Yakitori Totto | **W 50s**	25
Suteishi* | **Seaport**	25
Koi* | **W 40s**	25
Aki* | **W Vill**	25
Takahachi* | **multi.**	25
Soba Totto | **E 40s**	25
Rosanjin | **TriBeCa**	25
Poke* | **E 80s**	25
Sushiden* | **multi.**	25
Soba-ya | **E Vill**	25
Hasaki* | **E Vill**	24
Hatsuhana* | **E 40s**	24
Momoya* | **multi.**	24
Taro Sushi | **Prospect Hts**	24
one or eight* | **W'burg**	24
Megu | **multi.**	24
Kyotofu | **W 40s**	24
Prime Grill/KO | **W 80s**	24
Yama* | **multi.**	24
NEW Sushi Shop* | **E 50s**	24
Minca | **E Vill**	24
Fushimi | **multi.**	23
Yuba* | **E Vill**	23
Natsumi* | **W 50s**	23
Shiro of Japan* | **Glendale**	23
Sushi Damo* | **W 50s**	23
Soba Nippon | **W 50s**	23
Nippon* | **E 50s**	23
Japonica* | **G Vill**	23
Naruto Ramen | **E 80s**	23
SushiSamba* | **multi.**	23
Zuzu Ramen | **Park Slope**	23
Shabu-Shabu 70* | **E 70s**	23
Rai Rai Ken | **E Vill**	22
Shabu-Tatsu | **E Vill**	22
Katsu-Hama | **multi.**	22
Sushiya* | **W 50s**	22
Yuka* | **E 80s**	22
Arirang Hibachi | **multi.**	22
Inakaya | **W 40s**	22
Ko Sushi* | **multi.**	22

Ise* | **multi.**	22
Gyu-Kaku | **multi.**	22
Hide-Chan | **E 50s**	21
Tenzan* | **multi.**	21
Blue Ginger* | **Chelsea**	21
Haru* | **multi.**	21
Aji Sushi* | **Murray Hill**	21
Menkui Tei | **multi.**	21
Kouzan* | **W 90s**	20
Ramen Setagaya | **E Vill**	20
Menchanko-tei | **E 40s**	20
Ninja | **TriBeCa**	19
Bamboo 52* | **W 50s**	19
NEW Blue Ribbon/Izakaya | **LES**	-
NEW Bugs* | **E Vill**	-
NEW Dassara | **Carroll Gdns**	-
NEW Neta* | **G Vill**	-

JEWISH

Mile End | **Boerum Hill**	25
Katz's Deli | **LES**	25
Barney Greengrass | **W 80s**	24
Ben's Best | **Rego Pk**	23
Carnegie Deli | **W 50s**	23
2nd Ave Deli | **multi.**	23
Mill Basin | **Mill Basin**	23
Pastrami Queen | **E 70s**	22
Lattanzi | **W 40s**	22
Sarge's Deli | **Murray Hill**	21
NEW Kutsher's | **TriBeCa**	21
Stage Deli | **W 50s**	20
Sammy's | **LES**	20
Ben's Kosher | **multi.**	20

KOREAN

(* barbecue specialist)

NEW Jungsik | **TriBeCa**	26
Danji | **W 50s**	26
HanGawi | **Murray Hill**	25
Moim | **Park Slope**	24
New WonJo* | **Garment**	24
Sik Gaek | **multi.**	24
Cho Dang Gol | **Garment**	23
Kang Suh* | **Garment**	23
Do Hwa* | **W Vill**	22
Miss Korea BBQ* | **Garment**	22
Kum Gang San* | **multi.**	22
BonChon Chicken | **multi.**	22
Gahm Mi Oak | **Garment**	22
Bann | **W 50s**	22
NEW Dong Chun Hong | **Garment**	21
Kyochon | **multi.**	21
Mandoo Bar | **Garment**	20

NEW Brooklyn Seoul | W'burg	⌐
NEW Kristalbelli* | Garment	⌐

KOSHER/ KOSHER-STYLE

Solo | E 50s	26
Tevere | E 80s	26
Mike's Bistro | W 70s	25
Azuri Cafe | W 50s	25
Caravan/Dreams | E Vill	24
Tiffin Wallah | Murray Hill	24
Prime Grill/KO | multi.	24
Ben's Best | Rego Pk	23
Peacefood Café | W 80s	23
Pongal | Murray Hill	23
Colbeh | Garment	23
2nd Ave Deli | multi.	23
Hummus Pl. | multi.	23
Mill Basin | Mill Basin	23
Pastrami Queen | E 70s	22
Sacred Chow | G Vill	22
Liebman's Deli | Riverdale	22
Noi Due | W 60s	21
Le Marais | W 40s	21
Abigael's | Garment	21
Hummus Kitchen | multi.	21
Ben's Kosher | multi.	20
NEW Jezebel | SoHo	⌐

LEBANESE

Ilili | Chelsea	25
NEW Almayass | Flatiron	25
Naya | multi.	23
Al Bustan | E 50s	21

MALAYSIAN

Nyonya | multi.	23
New Malaysia | Chinatown	22
Laut | Union Sq	22
Sentosa | Flushing	22
Fatty Crab | W Vill	21
Penang | W 70s	21

MEDITERRANEAN

Picholine | W 60s	27
Tanoreen | Bay Ridge	27
Alta | G Vill	26
Solo | E 50s	26
Il Buco | NoHo	26
Little Owl | W Vill	26
Conviv. Osteria | Park Slope	25
Boulud Sud | W 60s	25
Aldea | Flatiron	25

Taboon | multi.	25
NEW Boukiés | E Vill	25
Balaboosta | NoLita	24
Bistro de la Gare | W Vill	24
Red Cat | Chelsea	23
Olives | Union Sq	23
Extra Virgin | W Vill	23
Mémé | W Vill	23
Kashkaval | W 50s	23
Place | W Vill	23
Vareli | W 100s	23
508 | Hudson Square	22
Smile | multi.	22
NEW 1 Bite Med. | E 50s	22
Dee's | Forest Hills	22
Barbounia | Flatiron	22
Miriam | Park Slope	22
Sezz Medi' | W 100s	22
Fig & Olive | multi.	22
Bodrum | W 80s	22
Isa | W'burg	22
Olea | Ft Greene	22
5 Points | NoHo	22
Antique Garage | SoHo	22
Amaranth | E 60s	22
Pera | multi.	21
Marseille | W 40s	21
NEW Amali | E 60s	21
Cafe Centro | E 40s	21
Ayza Wine | multi.	21
Isabella's | W 70s	21
Hummus Kitchen | multi.	21
Cafe Ronda | W 70s	20
Café du Soleil | W 100s	20
Epices/Traiteur | W 70s	20
Nice Matin | W 70s	20
Nick & Toni | W 60s	20
Dervish | W 40s	19
Park | Chelsea	18
NEW Arabesque | Murray Hill	⌐

MEXICAN

Tortilleria Nixtamal | Corona	26
La Superior | W'burg	25
Mercadito | multi.	24
Pampano | E 40s	24
Toloache | multi.	24
El Paso Taqueria | multi.	24
Maya | E 60s	24
Barrio Chino | LES	24
Hell's Kitchen | W 40s	24
Sueños | Chelsea	23

CUISINES

Crema | **Chelsea**	23
Mexicana Mama | **multi.**	23
Pachanga Patterson | **Astoria**	23
Fonda | **multi.**	23
Mesa Coyoacan | **W'burg**	23
El Parador Cafe | **Murray Hill**	23
Hecho en Dumbo | **NoHo**	23
La Esquina | **multi.**	23
Café Habana/Outpost | **multi.**	23
NEW Añejo | **W 40s**	23
Mexico Lindo | **Gramercy**	23
Tacombi/Fonda Nolita | **NoLita**	23
Ofrenda | **W Vill**	23
Rosa Mexicano | **multi.**	23
Mexican Radio | **NoLita**	23
Noche Mex. | **W 100s**	23
Empellón | **multi.**	23
Pinche Taqueria | **multi.**	22
La Palapa | **E Vill**	22
Móle | **multi.**	22
Mexicue | **multi.**	22
Sinigual | **E 40s**	22
Café Frida | **multi.**	22
Calexico | **multi.**	22
Dos Toros | **multi.**	22
Cascabel Taqueria | **multi.**	22
Rocking Horse | **Chelsea**	22
Pequena | **multi.**	22
Maz Mezcal | **E 80s**	21
Oaxaca | **multi.**	21
MexiBBQ | **Astoria**	21
Alma | **Carroll Gdns**	21
El Centro | **W 50s**	21
Mad Dog | **Financial**	20
NEW Pulqueria | **Chinatown**	20
Dos Caminos | **multi.**	20
Centrico | **TriBeCa**	20
Lime Jungle | **W 50s**	20
NEW Casa Enrique | **LIC**	-
NEW Gran Electrica | **Dumbo**	-

MIDDLE EASTERN

Tanoreen | **Bay Ridge**	27
Mimi's Hummus | **Ditmas Pk**	26
Taboon | **multi.**	25
Balaboosta | **NoLita**	24
12 Chairs | **SoHo**	23
Moustache | **multi.**	23
Maoz | **multi.**	22
Gazala's | **multi.**	21
Zaytoons | **multi.**	21
Chickpea | **multi.**	19
NEW Arabesque | **Murray Hill**	-

MOROCCAN

Cafe Mogador | **multi.**	23
Mémé | **W Vill**	23
Cafe Gitane | **multi.**	22
Cafe Noir | **SoHo**	20
Barbès | **Murray Hill**	20

NEW ENGLAND

Pearl Oyster | **W Vill**	26
NEW Littleneck | **Gowanus**	24
Luke's Lobster | **multi.**	24
Ed's Lobster | **multi.**	24
Mermaid | **multi.**	22
NEW Claw | **W 50s**	20
NEW Extra Fancy | **W'burg**	-

NOODLE SHOPS

Totto Ramen | **W 50s**	26
Ippudo | **E Vill**	26
Donguri | **E 80s**	25
Momofuku Noodle | **E Vill**	25
Soba Totto | **E 40s**	25
Soba-ya | **E Vill**	25
Xi'an | **multi.**	24
Pho Viet Huong | **Chinatown**	24
Minca | **E Vill**	24
Pho Bang | **multi.**	23
Great NY Noodle | **Chinatown**	23
Soba Nippon | **W 50s**	23
Naruto Ramen | **E 80s**	23
Zuzu Ramen | **Park Slope**	23
Rai Rai Ken | **E Vill**	22
Tasty Hand-Pulled | **Chinatown**	22
Bo-Ky | **multi.**	22
Noodle Bar | **multi.**	22
Hide-Chan | **E 50s**	21
Menkui Tei | **multi.**	21
NEW Biang | **Flushing**	21
Sammy's | **G Vill**	21
Bao Noodles | **Gramercy**	20
Ramen Setagaya | **E Vill**	20
Republic | **Union Sq**	20
Menchanko-tei | **E 40s**	20
NEW Brooklyn Seoul | **W'burg**	-

NUEVO LATINO

Luz | **Ft Greene**	23
Coppelia | **Chelsea**	23
Cabana | **multi.**	23
Calle Ocho | **W 80s**	22
Mamajuana | **multi.**	21
Citrus B&G | **W 70s**	21
NEW A.G. Kitchen | **W 70s**	-

PAKISTANI

NEW Desi Shack | **Murray Hill** 22

PAN-LATIN

Bogota | **Park Slope** 25
Yerba Buena | **multi.** 24
Miranda | **W'burg** 24
Boca Chica | **E Vill** 24
Macondo | **LES** 23
A Casa Fox | **LES** 23
Zengo | **E 40s** 23
Yuca Bar | **E Vill** 22
Rayuela | **LES** 22
Palo Santo | **Park Slope** 22
Hudson River | **Harlem** 21
NEW Cómodo | **SoHo** ⌐

PERSIAN

Shalezeh | **E 80s** 23
Colbeh | **Garment** 23
Ravagh | **multi.** 23
Persepolis | **E 70s** 22

PERUVIAN

Nobu | **multi.** 27
NEW La Mar | **Flatiron** 24
Pio Pio | **multi.** 23
Flor/Mayo | **multi.** 21
Coco Roco | **multi.** 21
NEW Raymi | **Flatiron** ⌐

PIZZA

Lucali | **Carroll Gdns** 27
Luzzo's/Ovest | **E Vill** 27
NEW Pete Zaaz | **Prospect Hts** 27
Saraghina | **Bed-Stuy** 27
Di Fara | **Midwood** 27
Denino | **Port Richmond** 26
Vesta | **Astoria** 26
Paulie Gee's | **Greenpt** 26
Roberta's | **Bushwick** 26
Basil Brick Oven Pizza | **Astoria** 26
San Matteo | **E 90s** 26
Ápizz | **LES** 25
Franny's | **Prospect Hts** 25
Keste Pizza | **W Vill** 25
Totonno Pizza | **Coney Is** 25
Motorino | **E Vill** 25
Lombardi's | **NoLita** 25
Posto | **Gramercy** 24
Numero 28 | **multi.** 24
NEW Don Antonio | **W 50s** 24
Zero Otto | **multi.** 24
South Brooklyn Pizza | **multi.** 24

Best Pizza | **W'burg** 24
Co. | **Chelsea** 24
Adrienne's | **Financial** 24
NEW Speedy Romeo | **Clinton Hill** 24
Vezzo | **Murray Hill** 24
Grimaldi's | **multi.** 24
Eataly | **Flatiron** 24
Lil' Frankie | **E Vill** 24
Otto | **G Vill** 24
Nick's | **multi.** 24
Joe & Pat's | **Castleton Corners** 24
Joe's Pizza | **W Vill** 23
Forcella | **multi.** 23
Spunto | **W Vill** 23
Arturo's | **G Vill** 23
57 Napoli Pizza e Vino | **E 50s** 23
Covo | **Harlem** 23
La Pizza Fresca | **Flatiron** 23
Rizzo's Pizza | **multi.** 23
John's Pizzeria | **multi.** 23
Da Ciro | **Murray Hill** 23
Lazzara's | **Garment** 23
Amorina | **Prospect Hts** 23
La Villa Pizzeria | **multi.** 23
Rubirosa | **NoLita** 22
Mezzaluna/Pizza | **multi.** 22
Dee's | **Forest Hills** 22
Bella Via | **LIC** 22
Harry's Italian | **multi.** 22
Artichoke Basille | **multi.** 22
Sezz Medi' | **W 100s** 22
Bella Blu | **E 70s** 22
Fornino | **multi.** 22
La Bottega | **Chelsea** 22
Angelo's Pizza | **multi.** 22
Anthony's | **Park Slope** 22
PizzArte | **W 50s** 21
Gigino | **multi.** 21
Nino's | **E 40s** 21
Bricco | **W 50s** 21
Pulino's | **NoLita** 21
Acqua | **W 90s** 21
Patsy's | **multi.** 21
Brio | **multi.** 21
Donatella | **Chelsea** 21
Pizza 33 | **multi.** 21
Don Giovanni | **multi.** 21
Al Forno Pizza | **E 70s** 21
Naples 45 | **E 40s** 20
Two Boots | **multi.** 20
Pintaile's Pizza | **E 80s** 20
Bettola | **W 70s** 19

CUISINES

NEW High Heat | **G Vill**	–
NEW Nicoletta | **E Vill**	–

POLISH

Lomzynianka | **Greenpt**	24
Teresa's | **Bklyn Hts**	21
Little Poland | **E Vill**	21

POLYNESIAN

Hurricane Club | **Flatiron**	21
King Yum | **Fresh Meadows**	21

PORTUGUESE

Ipanema | **W 40s**	26
Alfama | **E 50s**	22
Macao Trading | **TriBeCa**	20

PUB FOOD

Molly's | **Gramercy**	23
BandB | **SoHo**	22
Piper's Kilt | **Kingsbridge**	22
Henry Public | **Cobble Hill**	22
J.G. Melon | **E 70s**	21
Donovan's | **multi.**	21
Walker's | **TriBeCa**	19
Landmark Tavern | **W 40s**	19
P.J. Clarke's | **multi.**	18
Fraunces Tavern | **Financial**	18
Neary's | **E 50s**	18

PUERTO RICAN

Sofrito | **E 50s**	24
Sazon | **TriBeCa**	24
La Taza de Oro | **Chelsea**	22

QUÉBÉCOIS

Le Pescadeux | **SoHo**	22

RUSSIAN

NEW Brasserie Pushkin | **W 50s**	26
Tatiana | **Brighton Bch**	21
Mari Vanna | **Flatiron**	21
Russian Tea | **W 50s**	21
Russian Samovar | **W 50s**	21
FireBird | **W 40s**	20
NEW Nasha Rasha | **Flatiron**	–

SANDWICHES

(See also Delis)

Il Bambino | **Astoria**	27
Leo's Latticini/Corona | **multi.**	26
San Matteo | **E Vill**	26
Num Pang | **multi.**	25
'Ino | **W Vill**	25
Taboon | **G Vill**	25
Mile End | **NoHo**	25

Porchetta | **E Vill**	25
NEW Parm | **NoLita**	24
Bouchon Bakery | **multi.**	24
Meatball Shop | **multi.**	24
Defonte's | **multi.**	24
Press 195 | **Bayside**	24
Via Quadronno | **multi.**	24
Queens Kickshaw | **Astoria**	24
DuMont | **W'burg**	24
Roll-n-Roaster | **Sheepshead**	23
Beecher's Cellar | **Flatiron**	23
No. 7 | **multi.**	23
Smile | **SoHo**	22
Social Eatz | **E 50s**	22
Brennan | **Sheepshead**	22
Zaitzeff | **multi.**	22
Zito's | **Park Slope**	22
Nicky's | **multi.**	22
An Choi | **LES**	22
Baoguette | **multi.**	22
Sweet Melissa | **Park Slope**	21
Peanut Butter Co. | **G Vill**	21
sNice | **multi.**	21
Untitled | **E 70s**	21
Yura on Madison | **E 90s**	20
'Wichcraft | **multi.**	20
Bread | **NoLita**	20
Hanco's | **multi.**	20
E.A.T. | **E 80s**	20
Potbelly | **multi.**	20
Eisenberg's Sandwich | **Flatiron**	18
NEW Parish Hall | **W'burg**	–
NEW Rocket Pig | **Chelsea**	–

SCANDINAVIAN

Aquavit | **E 50s**	25
Smorgas Chef | **multi.**	20

SEAFOOD

Le Bernardin | **W 50s**	29
Jack's Lux. | **E Vill**	28
Marea | **W 50s**	28
Milos | **W 50s**	27
Taverna Kyclades | **Astoria**	27
Aquagrill | **SoHo**	27
Pearl Oyster | **W Vill**	26
Red Hook Lobster | **Red Hook**	26
Bocelli | **Grasmere**	26
Mary's Fish | **W Vill**	25
Avra | **E 40s**	25
Esca | **W 40s**	25
North End Grill | **Financial**	25
Oceana | **W 40s**	24

Pampano | **E 40s**	24
NEW Littleneck | **Gowanus**	24
Sea Grill | **W 40s**	24
Fishtail/David Burke | **E 60s**	24
Thalassa | **TriBeCa**	24
Francisco's | **Chelsea**	24
Ocean Grill | **W 70s**	24
John Dory | **Chelsea**	24
Sammy's Shrimp Box | **City Is**	24
Luke's Lobster | **multi.**	24
Periyali | **Flatiron**	24
Blue Water | **Union Sq**	24
Artie's | **City Is**	24
Ed's Lobster | **multi.**	24
Sik Gaek | **multi.**	24
London Lennie | **Rego Pk**	24
BLT Fish | **Flatiron**	23
NEW Catch | **Meatpacking**	23
FishTag | **W 70s**	23
Flex Mussels | **multi.**	23
Crab Shanty | **City Is**	23
Brooklyn Fish | **Park Slope**	23
Fulton | **E 70s**	23
City Is. Lobster | **City Is**	23
Elias Corner | **Astoria**	23
Lure Fishbar | **SoHo**	23
Blue Fin | **W 40s**	23
Portofino | **City Is**	23
Kellari Tav./Parea | **W 40s**	23
Telly's Taverna | **Astoria**	23
Oyster Bar | **E 40s**	23
Fish | **W Vill**	23
Fuleen | **Chinatown**	23
Pearl Room | **Bay Ridge**	23
Atlantic Grill | **multi.**	23
Black Duck | **Murray Hill**	23
Oriental Gdn. | **Chinatown**	23
Sea Shore | **City Is**	22
Jordan's Lobster | **Sheepshead**	22
Mermaid | **multi.**	22
City Hall | **TriBeCa**	22
Water's Edge | **LIC**	22
Ammos | **E 40s**	22
Parlor Steak | **E 90s**	22
Sammy's Fishbox | **City Is**	22
Le Pescadeux | **SoHo**	22
Umberto's | **multi.**	22
Ping's Sea. | **multi.**	21
Redeye Grill | **W 50s**	21
Tratt. Pesce | **multi.**	21
City Lobster | **W 40s**	21
Marina Cafe | **Great Kills**	21

Docks Oyster | **E 40s**	21
Pescatore | **E 50s**	21
McCormick/Schmick | **W 50s**	21
Ed's Chowder | **W 60s**	20
Millesime | **Murray Hill**	20
St. Andrews | **W 40s**	20
NEW Claw | **W 50s**	20
Lobster Box | **City Is**	20
Pier 9 | **W 50s**	20
Ithaka | **E 80s**	20
City Crab | **Flatiron**	20
Sagaponack | **Flatiron**	19
Cowgirl | **Seaport**	17
NEW Bellwether | **W'burg**	-
NEW Brooklyn Crab | **Red Hook**	-
NEW Crave Fishbar | **E 50s**	-
NEW Extra Fancy | **W'burg**	-
NEW Grey Lady | **LES**	-
NEW Vic & Anthony's | **Flatiron**	-

SMALL PLATES

(See also Spanish tapas specialist)

Degustation | French/Spanish | **E Vill**	28
Traif | Eclectic | **W'burg**	27
Alta | Med. | **G Vill**	26
Zenkichi | Japanese | **W'burg**	26
Danji | Korean | **W 50s**	26
EN Japanese | Japanese | **W Vill**	26
Salumeria Rosi | Italian | **W 70s**	25
Sakagura | Japanese | **E 40s**	25
Robataya | Japanese | **E Vill**	25
Recette | Amer. | **W Vill**	25
NEW Boukiés | Greek | **E Vill**	25
Ilili | Lebanese | **Chelsea**	25
Marlow/Sons | Amer. | **W'burg**	25
Maze | French | **W 50s**	25
Buvette | French | **W Vill**	25
NEW Almayass | Armenian/Lebanese | **Flatiron**	25
Stanton Social | Eclectic | **LES**	24
Mercadito | Mex. | **multi.**	24
NEW Wong | Asian | **W Vill**	24
Pampano | Mexican | **E 40s**	24
Sorella | Italian | **LES**	24
NEW Yefsi Estiatorio | Greek | **E 70s**	24
Mehtaphor | Eclectic | **TriBeCa**	24
Bocca Lupo | Italian | **Cobble Hill**	24
Prime Meat | Amer. | **Carroll Gdns**	24
Macondo | Pan-Latin | **LES**	23
Beauty & Essex | Amer. | **LES**	23

Sojourn | Eclectic | **E 70s**	23
NEW Añejo | Mexican | **W 40s**	23
Uva | Italian | **E 70s**	23
Corsino | Italian | **W Vill**	22
NEW 1 Bite Med. | Med. | **E 50s**	22
Vanderbilt | Amer. | **Prospect Hts**	22
Rayuela | Pan-Latin | **LES**	22
Centro Vinoteca | Italian | **W Vill**	22
NEW Whitehall | British | **W Vill**	22
Beyoglu | Turkish | **E 80s**	22
'Inoteca | Italian | **multi.**	22
Lunetta | Italian | **Boerum Hill**	22
Fig & Olive | Med. | **multi.**	22
Olea | Med. | **Ft Greene**	22
Gottino | Italian | **W Vill**	21
44 | Amer. | **W 40s**	21
Terroir | Italian | **multi.**	21
Gen. Greene | Amer. | **Ft Greene**	20
NEW Caffe Storico | Italian | **W 70s**	20
Macao Trading | Chinese/Portug. | **TriBeCa**	20
NEW Foragers City Table | Amer./Asian | **Chelsea**	20
NEW Bellwether | Amer. | **W'burg**	-
NEW Bugs | Japanese | **E Vill**	-
NEW Ginny's Supper Club | Amer. | **Harlem**	-
NEW Goodwin | Amer. | **W Vill**	-
NEW Neta | Japanese | **G Vill**	-
NEW Purple Fig | French | **W 70s**	-

SOUL FOOD

Pies-n-Thighs | **W'burg**	25
Miss Mamie/Maude | **Harlem**	23
Amy Ruth's | **Harlem**	22
Rack & Soul | **W 100s**	22
Sylvia's | **Harlem**	20

SOUP

La Bonne Soupe | **W 50s**	19

SOUTH AFRICAN

Madiba | **Ft Greene**	24
Braai | **W 50s**	20

SOUTH AMERICAN

Empanada Mama | **W 50s**	24
Cafe Ronda | **W 70s**	20
NEW Super Linda | **TriBeCa**	19

SOUTHERN

Peaches | **Bed-Stuy**	24
Melba's | **Harlem**	24
Egg | **W'burg**	24
Redhead | **E Vill**	24
Char No. 4 | **Cobble Hill**	23
Seersucker | **Carroll Gdns**	23
Miss Mamie/Maude | **Harlem**	23
Red Rooster | **Harlem**	23
Amy Ruth's | **Harlem**	22
Rack & Soul | **W 100s**	22
Tipsy Parson | **Chelsea**	22
Sylvia's | **Harlem**	20
Hill Country Chicken | **Flatiron**	20
B. Smith's | **W 40s**	20
Kitchenette | **multi.**	20
Bourbon St. Café | **Bayside**	19

SOUTHWESTERN

Mesa Grill | **Flatiron**	24
Mojave | **Astoria**	23
Agave | **W Vill**	20
Cilantro | **multi.**	20
Cowgirl | **multi.**	17

SPANISH

(* tapas specialist)

Degustation | **E Vill**	28
Tía Pol* | **Chelsea**	26
Casa Mono* | **Gramercy**	25
Sevilla | **W Vill**	25
Txikito* | **Chelsea**	24
Beso* | **St. George**	24
Tertulia* | **W Vill**	24
Francisco's | **Chelsea**	24
El Quinto Pino* | **Chelsea**	24
Boqueria* | **multi.**	23
Bar Jamon* | **Gramercy**	23
El Faro* | **W Vill**	23
El Pote | **Murray Hill**	23
El Porrón* | **E 60s**	23
Toledo | **Murray Hill**	23
Las Ramblas* | **W Vill**	23
Solera* | **E 50s**	23
1492 Food* | **LES**	23
La Fonda/Sol | **E 40s**	23
NEW Son Cubano | **Chelsea**	23
Gastroarte* | **W 60s**	23
Alcala | **E 40s**	23
Socarrat* | **multi.**	23
Real Madrid | **Mariners Harbor**	22
Salinas* | **Chelsea**	22
Flor/Sol* | **TriBeCa**	22

El Quijote	**Chelsea**	22	Bobby Van's	**multi.**	23
Meson Sevilla	**W 40s**	21	Embers	**Bay Ridge**	23
Cafe Español	**multi.**	21	Frankie/Johnnie	**multi.**	23
NEW Francesca*	**LES**	-	NYY Steak	**Yankee Stadium**	23
NEW La Vara*	**Cobble Hill**	-	Rothmann's	**E 50s**	23

STEAKHOUSES

Peter Luger	**W'burg**	27	Bull & Bear	**E 40s**	23
Sparks	**E 40s**	26	Macelleria	**Meatpacking**	23
Wolfgang's	**multi.**	26	Tre Dici/Steak	**Chelsea**	22
Keens	**Garment**	26	T-Bar Steak	**E 70s**	22
Quality Meats	**W 50s**	26	Gallagher's	**W 50s**	22
Strip House	**G Vill**	26	City Hall	**TriBeCa**	22
Porter House	**W 60s**	26	E&E Grill House	**W 40s**	22
Ruth's Chris	**W 50s**	26	Arirang Hibachi	**multi.**	22
Benjamin Steak	**E 40s**	26	Parlor Steak	**E 90s**	22
Manzo	**Flatiron**	26	Via Brasil	**W 40s**	22
BLT Prime	**Gramercy**	25	Le Marais	**W 40s**	21
BLT Steak	**E 50s**	25	Nino's	**W 50s**	21
Del Frisco's	**multi.**	25	Benchmark	**Park Slope**	21
Ricardo	**Harlem**	25	Michael Jordan	**E 40s**	21
Old Homestead	**Meatpacking**	25	Les Halles	**multi.**	21
Primehouse	**Murray Hill**	25	McCormick/Schmick	**W 50s**	21
Empire Steakhouse	**E 50s**	25	Le Relais/Venise	**E 50s**	21
Pietro's	**E 40s**	25	Steak Frites	**Union Sq**	20
Morton's	**E 40s**	25	St. Andrews	**W 40s**	20
Padre Figlio	**E 40s**	25	Fairway Cafe	**W 70s**	19
Buenos Aires	**E Vill**	25	Bistro Le Steak	**E 70s**	19
Palm	**multi.**	25	**NEW** Vic & Anthony's	**Flatiron**	-
Ben & Jack's	**multi.**	25		
Capital Grille	**multi.**	25		

SWISS

Mont Blanc	**W 40s**	24

Christos	**Astoria**	25
Jake's	**Riverdale**	24

TEAHOUSES

Tea & Sympathy	**W Vill**	25
Radiance Tea House	**W 50s**	22
Sweet Melissa	**Park Slope**	21
Lady Mendl's	**Gramercy**	21
Alice's Tea	**multi.**	21

Smith/Wollensky	**E 40s**	24
Club A Steak	**E 50s**	24
Post House	**E 60s**	24
Dylan Prime	**TriBeCa**	24
STK	**multi.**	24
Churrascaria	**multi.**	24
Maloney/Porcelli	**E 50s**	24

THAI

Sripraphai	**Woodside**	27
Ayada	**Woodside**	26
Pure Thai Cookhouse	**W 50s**	26
Kuma Inn	**LES**	25
Kin Shop	**W Vill**	25
Siam Sq.	**Riverdale**	24
Erawan	**Bayside**	24
Thai Pavilion	**Astoria**	24
NEW Am Thai Bistro	**multi.**	24
Song	**Park Slope**	24
Kittichai	**SoHo**	24
Rin Thai Cuisine	**Chelsea**	24
Thai Market	**W 100s**	24
Joya	**Cobble Hill**	23
Sea	**multi.**	23

Uncle Jack's	**multi.**	24
Prime Meat	**Carroll Gdns**	24
Artie's	**City Is**	24
Prime Grill/KO	**multi.**	24
MarkJoseph	**Financial**	24
Harry's Cafe & Steak	**Financial**	24
Delmonico's	**Financial**	24
Shula's	**W 40s**	24
A.J. Maxwell's	**W 40s**	23
Marble Lane	**Chelsea**	23
Circus	**E 60s**	23
Wollensky's	**E 40s**	23
Chimichurri Grill	**W 40s**	23

CUISINES

Land | **multi.** 23
Topaz Thai | **W 50s** 23
Chai Home Kitchen | **multi.** 23
NEW Viv | **W 40s** 23
Jaiya | **multi.** 22
Qi | **W 40s** 22
Laut | **Union Sq** 22
Sookk | **W 100s** 22
Zabb Elee | **multi.** 22
Pam Real Thai | **W 40s** 22
Room Service | **multi.** 22
Ember Room | **W 40s** 22
NEW Pok Pok Ny | **Red Hook** 22
Breeze | **W 40s** 21
Pongsri Thai | **multi.** 21
Wondee Siam | **multi.** 21
NEW Ngam | **E Vill** 21
Spice | **multi.** 21
Bann Thai | **Forest Hills** 20
Lemongrass | **multi.** 20

TUNISIAN

Epices/Traiteur | **W 70s** 20

TURKISH

Taci's Beyti | **Midwood** 26
Turkish Grill | **Sunnyside** 24
Mundo | **Astoria** 23
Sahara | **Gravesend** 23
Hanci | **W 50s** 22
Akdeniz | **W 40s** 22
Beyoglu | **E 80s** 22
Turkish Kitchen | **Murray Hill** 22
Uskudar | **E 70s** 22
Bodrum | **W 80s** 22
Pera | **multi.** 22
Turkish Cuisine | **W 40s** 21
Seven's Turkish Grill | **W 70s** 21
Pasha | **W 70s** 21
Ali Baba | **multi.** 21
Turkuaz | **W 100s** 21
Sip Sak | **E 40s** 21
A La Turka | **E 70s** 20

UKRAINIAN

Veselka | **E Vill** 20

VEGETARIAN
(* vegan)

Kajitsu | **E Vill** 28
Taïm | **multi.** 26
Dirt Candy | **E Vill** 26
Pure Food/Wine* | **Gramercy** 25
HanGawi | **Murray Hill** 25
Candle 79* | **E 70s** 25
Candle Cafe* | **multi.** 25
Caravan/Dreams* | **E Vill** 24
Vatan | **Murray Hill** 24
Tiffin Wallah | **Murray Hill** 24
Gobo* | **multi.** 24
Peacefood Café* | **W 80s** 23
Saravanaa Bhavan | **multi.** 23
Blossom* | **multi.** 23
Pongal | **Murray Hill** 23
Wild Ginger* | **multi.** 23
Hummus Pl. | **multi.** 23
Angelica Kit.* | **E Vill** 22
Sacred Chow* | **G Vill** 22
Maoz | **multi.** 22
Quantum Leap | **G Vill** 22
sNice | **multi.** 21
Zen Palate | **multi.** 20

VENEZUELAN

Caracas | **multi.** 25
Arepas Café | **Astoria** 24

VIETNAMESE

Rouge et Blanc | **SoHo** 25
Pho Viet Huong | **Chinatown** 24
Omai | **Chelsea** 24
Pho Bang | **multi.** 23
Nha Trang | **Chinatown** 23
NEW Veatery | **E 80s** 22
Le Colonial | **E 50s** 22
Nicky's | **multi.** 22
An Choi | **LES** 22
Bo-Ky | **multi.** 22
Baoguette | **multi.** 22
Indochine | **E Vill** 22
Saigon Grill | **W 90s** 21
Bao Noodles | **Gramercy** 20
Hanco's | **multi.** 20

Locations

Includes names, street locations and Food ratings. Abbreviations key:
(a=Avenue, s=Street, e.g. 1a/116s=First Ave. at 116th St.;
3a/82-83s=Third Ave. between 82nd & 83rd Sts.)

Manhattan

CHELSEA

(26th to 30th Sts., west of 5th; 14th
to 26th Sts., west of 6th)

Morimoto	10a/15-16s	26
Del Posto	10a/15-16s	26
Scarpetta	14s/8-9a	26
NEW NoMad	Bway/28s	26
Tía Pol	10a/22-23s	26
Da Umberto	17s/6-7a	25
Ilili	5a/27-28s	25
La Bergamote	9a/20s	25
Colicchio/Sons	10a/15-16s	25
Buddakan	9a/15-16s	25
NEW La Promenade/Anglais	23s/9-10a	25
Momoya	7a/21s	24
Txikito	9a/24-25s	24
Co.	9a/24s	24
Omai	9a/19-20s	24
Francisco's	23s/6-7a	24
John Dory	Bway/29s	24
Rin Thai Cuisine	23s/7-8a	24
Breslin	29s/Bway-5a	24
El Quinto Pino	24s/9-10a	24
Marble Lane	16s/8-9a	23
Westville	18s/7-8a	23
Sueños	17s/8-9a	23
Red Cat	10a/23-24s	23
Crema	17s/6-7a	23
Blossom	multi.	23
Cookshop	10a/20s	23
Coppelia	14s/7-8a	23
NEW Son Cubano	27s/10-11a	23
BareBurger	8a/17-18s	23
Pepe	10a/24-25s	23
No. 7	Bway/28-29s	23
Rub BBQ	23s/7-8a	23
Socarrat	19s/7-8a	23
Trestle on 10th	10a/24s	23
Legend	7a/15-16s	22
Tre Dici/Steak	26s/6-7a	22
Gascogne	8a/17-18s	22
Eolo	7a/21-22s	22
La Taza de Oro	8a/14-15s	22
Le Zie	7a/20-21s	22

Friedman's Lunch	9a/15-16s	22
NEW Americano	27s/10-11a	22
Artichoke Basille	10a/17s	22
Salinas	9a/18-19s	22
Mexicue	7a/29-30s	22
Rare B&G	26s/6-7a	22
La Lunchonette	10a/18s	22
La Bottega	9a/17s	22
Room Service	8a/18-19s	22
Tipsy Parson	9a/19-20s	22
Rocking Horse	8a/19-20s	22
El Quijote	23s/7-8a	22
Lucky's Famous Burgers	23s/7-8a	22
Biricchino	29s/8a	21
Blue Ginger	8a/15-16s	21
Uncle Nick's	8a/29s	21
Pongsri Thai	23s/6-7a	21
Le Grainne Cafe	9a/21s	21
Cafeteria	7a/17s	21
Mooncake Foods	30s/8a	21
Grand Sichuan	multi.	21
Sarabeth's	9a/15-16s	21
Patsy's	23s/8-9a	21
Bombay Talkie	9a/21 22s	21
Bottino	10a/24-25s	21
Spice	multi.	21
Donatella	8a/19-20s	21
Pizza 33	23s/7-8a	21
Don Giovanni	10a/22-23s	21
'Wichcraft	multi.	20
Potbelly	14s/5-6a	20
NEW Foragers City Table	22s/8a	20
Brgr	7a/26-27s	19
Park	10a/17-18s	18
NEW Pounds & Ounces	8a/18s	16
NEW Humphrey	6a/29s	-
NEW Rocket Pig	24s/10a	-

CHINATOWN

(Canal to Pearl Sts., east of B'way)

Xi'an	multi.	24
Pho Viet Huong	Mulberry/Bayard-Canal	24
New Malaysia	Bowery/Bayard	23
Great NY Noodle	Bowery/Bayard	23

Nice Green Bo | *Bayard/Elizabeth-Mott*	23
Nha Trang | *multi.*	23
Fuleen | *Division/Bowery*	23
Peking Duck | *Mott/Mosco-Pell*	23
Wo Hop | *Mott/Chatham-Mosco*	23
Excellent Dumpling | *Lafayette/Canal-Walker*	23
Oriental Gdn. | *Elizabeth/Bayard-Canal*	23
Amazing 66 | *Mott/Bayard-Canal*	22
Joe's Shanghai | *Pell/Bowery-Mott*	22
Tasty Hand-Pulled | *Doyers/Bowery*	22
Hop Kee | *Mott/Chatham-Mosco*	22
Nom Wah Tea | *Doyers/Bowery-Pell*	22
Bo-Ky | *Bayard/Mott-Mulberry*	22
Big Wong | *Mott/Bayard-Canal*	22
Golden Unicorn | *E Bway/Catherine*	21
Ping's Sea. | *Mott/Chatham-Mosco*	21
Jing Fong | *Elizabeth/Bayard-Canal*	21
Dim Sum Go Go | *E Bway/Chatham*	21
Pongsri Thai | *Bayard/Baxter*	21
Joe's | *Pell/Doyers*	21
NEW Pulqueria | *Dyers/Bowery-Pell*	20
Forlini's | *Baxter/Walker*	20

EAST 40s

Kuruma Zushi | *47s/5a-Mad*	28
Sushi Yasuda | *43s/2-3a*	28
Sparks | *46s/2-3a*	26
Benjamin Steak | *41s/Mad-Park*	26
Aburiya Kinnosuke | *45s/2-3a*	25
Sakagura | *43s/2-3a*	25
Num Pang | *41s/Lex-3a*	25
Avra | *48s/Lex-3a*	25
Grifone | *46s/2-3a*	25
Pietro's | *43s/2-3a*	25
Morton's | *5a/45s*	25
Padre Figlio | *44s/1-2a*	25
Nanni | *46s/Lex-3a*	25
Soba Totto | *43s/2-3a*	25
Palm | *2a/44-45s*	25
Ben & Jack's | *44s/2-3a*	25
Sushiden | *49s/5a-Mad*	25
Capital Grille | *42s/Lex-3a*	25

Hatsuhana | *multi.*	24
Pampano | *multi.*	24
Smith/Wollensky | *3a/49s*	24
Chin Chin | *49s/2-3a*	24
Fabio Piccolo | *44s/2-3a*	24
Megu | *1a/47s*	24
Prime Grill/KO | *49s/Mad-Park*	24
Yama | *49s/1-2a*	24
Tulsi | *46s/2-3a*	24
Il Postino | *49s/1-2a*	23
Wollensky's | *49s/3a*	23
Bobby Van's | *Park/46s*	23
Naya | *3a/43s*	23
La Fonda/Sol | *Park/44s*	23
Pepe | *42s/Vanderbilt*	23
Oyster Bar | *42s/Vanderbilt*	23
Alcala | *46s/1-2a*	23
Bull & Bear | *Lex/49s*	23
Zengo | *3a/40s*	23
Patroon | *46s/Lex-3a*	23
Cipriani Dolci | *42s/Vanderbilt*	22
Katsu-Hama | *47s/5a-Mad*	22
Sinigual | *3a/41s*	22
Ammos | *Vanderbilt/44-45s*	22
Darbar | *46s/Lex-3a*	22
Osteria Laguna | *42s/2-3a*	22
Ise | *49s/Lex-3a*	22
Gyu-Kaku | *3a/49-50s*	22
Nino's | *2a/47-48s*	21
Pera | *Mad/41-42s*	21
Cibo | *2a/41s*	21
Cafe Centro | *Park/45s*	21
Bukhara Grill | *49s/2-3a*	21
Docks Oyster | *3a/40s*	21
Ali Baba | *2a/46s*	21
Mamajuana | *48s/Lex-3a*	21
Michael Jordan | *43s/Vanderbilt*	21
Five Guys | *3a/43-44s*	21
NEW Lexington Brass | *Lex/48s*	21
Sip Sak | *2a/49-50s*	21
'Wichcraft | *multi.*	20
Naples 45 | *Park/45s*	20
Potbelly | *Rock Plaza*	20
Junior's | *42s/Vanderbilt*	20
Two Boots | *42s/Vanderbilt*	20
Menchanko-tei | *45s/Lex-3a*	20
Chickpea | *45s/Mad-Vanderbilt*	19
Goodburger | *2a/42s*	19
NEW Siro's | *2a/47s*	-

EAST 50s

La Grenouille | *52s/5a-Mad*	28
Four Seasons | *52s/Lex-Park*	27

Adour	*55s/5a-Mad*	27
SushiAnn	*51s/Mad-Park*	26
Gilt	*Mad/50-51s*	26
Wolfgang's	*54s/3a*	26
Felidia	*58s/2-3a*	26
Solo	*Mad/55-56s*	26
Caviar Russe	*Mad/54-55s*	25
Le Cirque	*58s/Lex-3a*	25
BLT Steak	*57s/Lex-Park*	25
Aquavit	*55s/Mad-Park*	25
Amma	*51s/2-3a*	25
Valbella	*53s/5a-Mad*	25
Empire Steakhouse	*52s/5-6a*	25
DeGrezia	*50s/2-3a*	25
Le Perigord	*52s/FDR-1a*	25
San Pietro	*54s/5a-Mad*	25
Yuva	*58s/2-3a*	24
Sofrito	*57s/1a-Sutton*	24
Club A Steak	*58s/2-3a*	24
Tao	*58s/Mad-Park*	24
Maloney/Porcelli	*50s/Mad-Park*	24
Via Quadronno	*5a/59s*	24
Shun Lee Palace	*55s/Lex-3a*	24
NEW 1066 Eno	*1a/58-59s*	24
NEW Sushi Shop	*Mad/54-55s*	24
Chola	*58s/2-3a*	23
Montebello	*56s/Lex-Park*	23
Peter's 1969	*Lex/55-56s*	23
Bobby Van's	*54s/Lex-Park*	23
Hillstone	*3a/54s*	23
Solera	*53s/2-3a*	23
Mr. K's	*Lex/51s*	23
Luna Piena	*53s/2-3a*	23
Naya	*2a/55-56s*	23
57 Napoli Pizza e Vino	*57/Lex-Park*	23
Nippon	*52s/Lex-3a*	23
Rothmann's	*54s/5a-Mad*	23
Armani Rist.	*5a/56s*	23
Casa Lever	*53s/Mad-Park*	23
Dawat	*58s/2-3a*	23
Fresco	*52s/Mad-Park*	23
Rosa Mexicano	*1a/58s*	23
Peking Duck	*53s/2-3a*	23
Socarrat	*2a/50-51a*	23
Lychee Hse.	*55s/Lex-3a*	23
La Gioconda	*53s/2-3a*	23
Kati Roll	*53s/2-3a*	23
La Mangeoire	*2a/53-54s*	23
Mr. Chow	*57s/1-2a*	22
Harry Cipriani	*5a/59-60s*	22
Social Eatz	*53s/2-3a*	22

NEW 1 Bite Med.	*1a/58-59s*	22
Bistro Vendôme	*58s/1a-Sutton*	22
Brick Ln. Curry	*53s/2-3a*	22
Alfama	*52s/2-3a*	22
Brasserie	*53s/Lex-Park*	22
Lavo	*58s/Mad-Park*	22
BonChon Chicken	*2a/51s*	22
Cellini	*54s/Mad-Park*	22
Angelo's Pizza	*2a/55s*	22
Darbar	*55s/Lex-3a*	22
Bottega/Vino	*59s/5a-Mad*	22
Fig & Olive	*52s/5a-Mad*	22
Le Colonial	*57s/Lex-3a*	22
Ethos	*1a/51s*	22
Bice	*54s/5a-Mad*	22
Hide-Chan	*52s/2-3a*	21
Ze Café	*52s/FDR-1a*	21
Tenzan	*2a/52-53s*	21
La Mediterranée	*2a/50-51s*	21
Fiorini	*56s/2-3a*	21
Teodora	*57s/Lex-3a*	21
Al Bustan	*53s/1-2a*	21
National	*Lex/50s*	21
Grand Sichuan	*2a/55-56s*	21
Pescatore	*2a/50-1s*	21
Smith	*2a/50-51s*	21
Le Relais/Venise	*Lex/52s*	21
Whole Foods	*57s/2-3a*	21
Monkey Bar	*54s/Mad-Park*	21
Destino	*1a/50s*	20
Deux Amis	*51s/1-2a*	20
Dos Caminos	*3a/50-51s*	20
David Burke/Bloom.	*59s/Lex-3a*	20
Serafina	*58s/Mad-Park*	20
BXL	*51s/2-3a*	19
Chickpea	*Lex/54s*	19
Goodburger	*Lex/54s*	19
Cafe Joul	*1a/58-59s*	19
P.J. Clarke's	*3a/55s*	18
Neary's	*57s/1a*	18
NEW Bill's	*54s/Mad-Park*	-
NEW Crave Fishbar	*2a/50-51s*	-
NEW Noir	*50s/Lex-3a*	-

EAST 60s

Daniel	*65s/Mad-Park*	28
Sushi Seki	*1a/62-63s*	28
Torishin	*1a/64-65s*	26
Tiella	*1a/60-61s*	26
Scalinatella	*61s/3a*	25

LOCATIONS

David Burke Townhse. | *61s/Lex-Park* — 25

Rouge Tomate | *60s/5a-Mad* — 25

Park Avenue | *63s/Lex-Park* — 25

JoJo | *64s/Lex-3a* — 24

Fishtail/David Burke | *62s/Lex-Park* — 24

Maya | *1a/64-65s* — 24

Arabelle | *64s/Mad-Park* — 24

Post House | *63s/Mad-Park* — 24

Fatty Fish | *64s/1a-York* — 24

Circus | *61s/Lex-Park* — 23

El Porrón | *1a/61-62s* — 23

Tony's Di Napoli | *3a/63-64s* — 23

Philippe | *60s/Mad-Park* — 23

Ravagh | *1a/66-67s* — 23

Primola | *2a/64-65s* — 23

John's Pizzeria | *64s/1a-York* — 23

Cabana | *3a/60-61s* — 23

L'Absinthe | *67s/2-3a* — 22

Le Bilboquet | *63s/Mad-Park* — 22

Canaletto | *60s/2-3a* — 22

Fig & Olive | *Lex/62-63s* — 22

Amaranth | *62s/5a-Mad* — 22

Mon Petit Cafe | *Lex/62s* — 21

NEW Amali | *60s/Park* — 21

Felice | *1a/64s* — 21

Patsy's | *multi.* — 21

Fred's at Barneys | *Mad/60s* — 21

Brio | *61s/Lex* — 21

Alice's Tea | *64s/Lex* — 21

Le Veau d'Or | *60s/Lex-Park* — 21

Il Vagabondo | *62s/1-2a* — 20

Serendipity 3 | *60s/2-3a* — 20

Bistro Chat Noir | *66s/5a-Mad* — 20

Le Pain Q. | *Lex/63-64s* — 20

Serafina | *61s/Mad-Park* — 20

Bistro 61 | *1a/61s* — 20

Jackson Hole | *64s/2-3a* — 19

Brgr | *3a/60-61s* — 19

Bar Italia | *Mad/66s* — 19

Nello | *Mad/62-63s* — 18

EAST 70s

Sasabune | *73s/1a-York* — 29

Gari/Sushi | *78s/1a-York* — 27

Café Boulud | *76s/5a-Mad* — 27

Caravaggio | *74s/5a-Mad* — 26

Candle 79 | *79s/Lex-3a* — 25

Candle Cafe | *3a/74-75s* — 25

Numero 28 | *1a/74-75s* — 24

V-Note | *1a/79-80s* — 24

Alloro | *77s/1-2a* — 24

NEW Yefsi Estiatorio | *York/78-79s* — 24

Sette Mezzo | *Lex/70-71s* — 24

Carlyle | *76s/Mad* — 24

Via Quadronno | *73s/5a-Mad* — 24

Lusardi's | *2a/77-78s* — 24

Campagnola | *1a/73-74s* — 23

Fulton | *75s/2-3a* — 23

Mark | *77s/5a-Mad* — 23

Szechuan Gourmet | *2a/72-73s* — 23

BareBurger | *1a/73s* — 23

Sojourn | *79s/2-3a* — 23

Hospoda | *73s/1-2a* — 23

Atlantic Grill | *3a/76-77s* — 23

2nd Ave Deli | *1a/75s* — 23

Uva | *2a/77-78s* — 23

Shabu-Shabu 70 | *70s/1-2a* — 23

Pastrami Queen | *Lex/78-79s* — 22

Mezzaluna/Pizza | *3a/74-75s* — 22

T-Bar Steak | *3a/73-74s* — 22

Bella Blu | *Lex/70-71s* — 22

Uskudar | *2a/73-74s* — 22

Parma | *3a/79-80s* — 22

Shanghai Pavilion | *3a/78-79s* — 22

Dos Toros | *Lex/77-78s* — 22

Persepolis | *2a/73-74s* — 22

Ko Sushi | *2a/70s* — 22

Sant Ambroeus | *Mad/77-78s* — 22

Due | *3a/79-80s* — 21

Nino's | *1a/72-73s* — 21

Bocca/Bacco | *2a/78s* — 21

Haru | *3a/76s* — 21

J.G. Melon | *3a/74s* — 21

Afghan Kebab | *2a/70-71s* — 21

B. Café | *75s/2-3a* — 21

Maruzzella | *1a/77-78s* — 21

Quatorze Bis | *79s/1-2a* — 21

Untitled | *Mad/75s* — 21

Grace's Tratt. | *71s/2-3a* — 21

Spice | *multi.* — 21

Al Forno Pizza | *2a/77-78s* — 21

Jones Wood Foundry | *76s/1a-York* — 20

Our Place | *79s/2-3a* — 20

Il Riccio | *79s/Lex-3a* — 20

Vivolo/Cucina | *74s/Lex-Park* — 20

Le Pain Q. | *77s/2-3a* — 20

Cilantro | *1a/71s* — 20

Baraonda | *2a/75s* — 20

Serafina | *Mad/79s* — 20

Per Lei | *2a/71s* — 20

A La Turka | *2a/74s* — 20

Blue 9 Burger | *2a/73-74s* — 19

Orsay | *Lex/75s*	19
Bistro Le Steak | *3a/75s*	19
Go Burger | *2a/75-76s*	19
Boathouse | *Central Pk/72s*	19
Petaluma | *1a/73s*	18
Swifty's | *Lex/72-73s*	18
Brother Jimmy's | *2a/77-78s*	17

EAST 80s

Sistina | *2a/80-81s*	26
Sandro's | *81s/1-2a*	26
Tevere | *84s/Lex-3a*	26
Donguri | *83s/1-2a*	25
Giovanni | *83s/5a-Mad*	25
Poke | *85s/1-2a*	25
Erminia | *83s/2-3a*	25
Toloache | *82s/Lex-3a*	24
Spigolo | *2a/81s*	24
Elio's | *2a/84-85s*	24
Luke's Lobster | *81s/2-3a*	24
Gobo | *3a/81s*	24
Italianissimo | *84s/1-2a*	24
Wa Jeal | *2a/82-83s*	23
Flex Mussels | *82s/Lex-3a*	23
Shalezeh | *3a/80-81s*	23
Antonucci | *81s/Lex-3a*	23
Naruto Ramen | *3a/89-90s*	23
Land | *2a/81-82s*	23
Jaiya | *2a/80-81s*	23
Café Sabarsky | *5a/86s*	22
Nicola's | *84s/Lex-3a*	22
Girasole | *82s/Lex-3a*	22
Chef Ho's | *2a/89-90s*	22
Quattro Gatti | *81s/2-3a*	22
Móle | *2a/89-90s*	22
NEW Veatery | *2a/88-89s*	22
Café d'Alsace | *2a/88s*	22
Beyoglu | *3a/81s*	22
Shake Shack | *86s/Lex-3a*	22
Yuka | *2a/80-81s*	22
Kings' Carriage | *82s/2-3a*	22
Cascabel Taqueria | *2a/80s*	22
Ko Sushi | *York/85s*	22
Pig Heaven | *2a/80-81s*	21
Tenzan | *2a/89s*	21
Firenze | *2a/82-83s*	21
Maz Mezcal | *86s/1-2a*	21
Crown | *81s/5a-Mad*	21
Taste | *3a/80s*	21
Tratt. Pesce | *3a/87-88s*	21
Felice | *1a/83s*	21
Hummus Kitchen | *2a/83-84s*	21
Alice's Tea | *81s/2-3a*	21

Andre's Café | *2a/84-85s*	21
Papaya King | *86s/3a*	20
E.A.T. | *Mad/80-81s*	20
Caffe Grazie | *84s/5a-Mad*	20
Baluchi's | *2a/89-90s*	20
Amber | *3a/80s*	20
Ithaka | *86s/1-2a*	20
Two Boots | *2a/84s*	20
Pintaile's Pizza | *York/83-84s*	20
Le Pain Q. | *Mad/84-85s*	20
Cilantro | *2a/88-89s*	20
East End Kitchen | *81s/E End-York*	20
Divino | *2a/80-81s*	20
Jackson Hole | *2a/83-84s*	19
Heidelberg | *2a/85-86s*	19
Fairway Cafe | *86s/2a*	19
NEW Penrose | *2a/82-83s*	–

EAST 90s & 100s

(90th to 110th Sts.)

San Matteo | *2a/90s*	26
El Paso Taqueria | *multi.*	24
Pinocchio | *1a/90-91s*	24
Nick's | *2a/94s*	24
Sfoglia | *Lex/92s*	24
Pio Pio | *1a/90-91s*	23
Zebú Grill | *92s/1-2a*	23
Paola's | *Mad/92s*	23
Rizzo's Pizza | *Lex/93s*	23
Square Meal | *92s/5a-Mad*	23
Moustache | *Lex/102s*	23
Brick Ln. Curry | *3a/93-94s*	22
Maoz | *Harlem Meer*	22
Osso Buco | *3a/93s*	22
Parlor Steak | *3a/90s*	22
Tre Otto | *Mad/97-98s*	22
Pascalou | *Mad/92-93s*	21
Don Pedro's | *2a/96s*	21
Sarabeth's | *Mad/92*	21
Yura on Madison | *Mad/92s*	20
NEW ABV | *Lex/97s*	20
Table d'Hôte | *92s/Mad-Park*	20
Jackson Hole | *Mad/91s*	19
Chickpea | *Mad/98s*	19

EAST VILLAGE

(14th to Houston Sts., east of B'way, excluding NoHo)

Jack's Lux. | *2a/5-6s*	28
Degustation | *5s/2-3a*	28
Kajitsu | *9s/Ave A-1a*	28
Luzzo's/Ovest | *1a/12-13s*	27
Kyo Ya | *7s/1a*	27
Pylos | *7s/Ave A-1a*	27

Restaurant	Rating
Momofuku Ko	*1a/10-11s*	26
NEW Maharlika	*1a/6-7s*	26
Kanoyama	*2a/11-12s*	26
Ippudo	*4a/9-10s*	26
Supper	*2s/Aves A-B*	26
Dirt Candy	*9s/Ave A-1a*	26
Jewel Bako	*5s/2-3a*	26
San Matteo	*St Marks/Ave A*	26
Momofuku Ssäm	*2a/13s*	26
Prune	*1s/1-2a*	25
Spina	*Ave B/11s*	25
Robataya	*9s/2-3a*	25
ChikaLicious	*10s/1-2a*	25
Graffiti	*10s/1-2a*	25
Caracas	*multi.*	25
Motorino	*12s/1-2a*	25
NEW Boukiés	*2s/2a*	25
Hearth	*12s/1a*	25
Il Bagatto	*2s/Aves A-B*	25
Momofuku Noodle	*1a/10-11s*	25
JoeDoe	*1s/1-2a*	25
Buenos Aires	*6s/Aves A-B*	25
Takahachi	*Ave A/5-6s*	25
Porchetta	*7s/Ave A-1a*	25
Soba-ya	*9s/2-3a*	25
Hasaki	*9s/2-3a*	24
Mercadito	*Ave B/11-12s*	24
Numero 28	*2a/11-12s*	24
Caravan/Dreams	*6s/1a*	24
South Brooklyn Pizza	*1a/7-8s*	24
Yerba Buena	*Ave A/Houston-2s*	24
Perbacco	*4s/Aves A-B*	24
Xi'an	*St Marks/1a*	24
Veniero's	*11s/1-2A*	24
S'MAC	*multi.*	24
DBGB	*Bowery/1s-Houston*	24
Luke's Lobster	*7s/Ave A-1a*	24
Northern Spy	*12s/Aves A-B*	24
Lavagna	*5s/Aves A-B*	24
Banjara	*1a/6s*	24
Boca Chica	*1a/1s*	24
BaoHaus	*14s/2-3a*	24
Lil' Frankie	*1a/1-2s*	24
Redhead	*13s/1-2a*	24
Minca	*5s/Aves A-B*	24
Apiary	*3a/10-11s*	23
Westville	*Ave A/11s*	23
Yuba	*9s/3-4a*	23
Cafe Mogador	*St Marks/Ave A-1a*	23
Lucien	*1a/1s*	23
Butter	*Lafayette/Astor-4s*	23
Crif Dogs	*St Marks/Ave A-1a*	23
Frank	*2a/5-6s*	23
Barbone	*Ave B/11-12s*	23
Fonda	*Ave B/3s*	23
I Coppi	*9s/Ave A-1a*	23
Gnocco	*10s/Aves A-B*	23
BareBurger	*2a/5s*	23
26 Seats	*Ave B/10-11s*	23
Back Forty	*Ave B/11-12s*	23
Edi & the Wolf	*Ave C/6-7s*	23
Hummus Pl.	*St Marks/Ave A-1a*	23
Awash	*6s/1-2a*	23
Moustache	*10s/Ave A-1a*	23
Empellón	*1a/6-7s*	23
Angelica Kit.	*12s/2a*	22
Haveli	*2a/5-6s*	22
Momofuku Milk Bar	*13s/2-3a*	22
Rai Rai Ken	*10s/1-2a*	22
Shabu-Tatsu	*10s/1-2a*	22
Yuca Bar	*Ave A/7s*	22
La Palapa	*St Marks/1-2a*	22
Brick Ln. Curry	*6s/1-2a*	22
Zabb Elee	*2a/4-5s*	22
Zum Schneider	*Ave C/7s*	22
Artichoke Basille	*14s/1-2a*	22
Beagle	*Ave A/10-11s*	22
John's/12th St.	*12s/2a*	22
Mermaid	*2a/5-6s*	22
Dos Toros	*4a/13s*	22
Max	*Ave B/3-4s*	22
99 Mi. to Philly	*3a/12-13s*	22
Porsena	*7s/2-3a*	22
Indochine	*Lafayette/Astor-4s*	22
Gyu-Kaku	*Cooper/Astor-4s*	22
Vanessa's Dumpling	*14s/2-3a*	22
5 Napkin Burger	*14s/3-4a*	22
Tarallucci	*1a/10-11s*	21
Oaxaca	*Extra/Bowery-2a*	21
Gemma	*Bowery/2-3s*	21
Menkui Tei	*Cooper/7s-St Marks*	21
Black Iron	*5s/Aves A-B*	21
Peels	*Bowery/2s*	21
Grand Sichuan	*St Marks/2-3a*	21
Smith	*3a/10-11s*	21
NEW Ngam	*3a/12-13s*	21
Cacio e Pepe	*2a/11-12s*	21
Dumpling Man	*St Marks/Ave A-1a*	21
Spice	*multi.*	21
Terroir	*12s/Ave A-1a*	21
Little Poland	*2a/12-13s*	21
Veselka	*multi.*	20
Ramen Setagaya	*St Marks/2-3a*	20
Two Boots	*Ave A/3s*	20

Blue 9 Burger | *3A/12-3s* 19

Chickpea | *14s/2-3a* 19

NEW Bugs | *12s/Aves A-B* -

NEW Calliope | *4s/2a* -

NEW Nicoletta | *2a/10s* -

FINANCIAL DISTRICT

(South of Murray St.)

North End Grill | 25
N End/Murray-Vesey

Capital Grille | 25
Bway/Nassau-Pine

Toloache | 24
Maiden/Gold-William

Adrienne's | 24
Pearl/Coenties-Hanover

Luke's Lobster | *William/Stone* 24

MarkJoseph | 24
Water/Dover-Peck

Harry's Cafe & Steak | 24
Hanover/Pearl Stone

Delmonico's | *Beaver/William* 24

Bobby Van's | *Broad/Exchange* 23

2 West | *West/Battery* 23

Cipriani Wall Street | 23
Wall/Hanover-William

Fresco | *Pearl/Hanover* 23

Blue Smoke | *Vesey/N End-West* 23

BLT B&G | *Wash/Albany-Carlisle* 22

Wall/Water | *Wall/Water* 22

Harry's Italian | *multi.* 22

Zaitzeff | *Nassau/John* 22

Shake Shack | 22
Murray/N End-West

BonChon Chicken | *John/Cliff* 22

Bridge Cafe | *Water/Dover* 22

Nicky's | *Nassau/Ann-Fulton* 22

Ise | *Pine/Pearl-William* 22

Baoguette | *Nassau/Fulton-John* 22

Gigino | *Battery/West* 21

Haru | *Wall/Beaver-Pearl* 21

Stage Door Deli | 21
Vesery/Bway-Church

Les Halles | *John/Bway-Nassau* 21

Mad Dog | 20
Pearl/Coenties-Hanover

Smorgas Chef | *Stone/William* 20

Potbelly | *multi.* 20

China Chalet | 20
Bway/Exchange-Morris

Au Mandarin | *Vesey/West* 20

Chickpea | *William/John* 19

Battery Gdns. | *Battery Pk* 19

Goodburger | *Maiden/Pearl* 19

P.J. Clarke's | *World Fin/Vesey* 18

Fraunces Tavern | *Pearl/Broad* 18

NEW The Exchange | -
Broad/Beaver-Exchange

FLATIRON

(14th to 26th Sts., 6th Ave. to
Park Ave. S., excluding Union Sq.)

Eleven Madison | *Mad/24s* 28

Gramercy Tavern | 28
20s/Bway-Park

Craft | *19s/Bway-Park* 26

Tamarind | *22s/Bway-Park* 26

ABC Kitchen | *18s/Bway-Park* 26

Manzo | *5a/23-24s* 26

Veritas | *20s/Bway-Park* 25

Aldea | *17s/5-6a* 25

Ciano | *22s/Bway-Park* 25

NEW Almayass | 25
21s/Bway-Park

Zero Otto | *21s/5-6a* 24

Via Emilia | *21s/Bway-Park* 24

Junoon | *24s/5-6a* 24

Grimaldi's | *6a/20-21s* 24

A Voce | *Mad/26s* 24

NEW La Mar | *Mad/25s* 24

Periyali | *20s/5-6a* 24

Craftbar | *Bway/19 20s* 24

Eataly | *5a/23-24s* 24

Mesa Grill | *5a/15-16s* 24

Boqueria | *19s/5-6a* 23

Beecher's Cellar | *Bway/20s* 23

BLT Fish | *17s/5-6a* 23

Basta Pasta | *17s/5-6a* 23

La Pizza Fresca | *20s/Bway-Park* 23

NEW Alison Eighteen | 23
18s/5-6a

Hill Country | *26s/Bway-6a* 23

SushiSamba | *Park/19-20s* 23

Rosa Mexicano | *18s/Bway-5a* 23

Parea Bistro | *20s/Bway-Park* 23

City Bakery | *18s/5-6a* 22

Bocca | *19s/Bway-Park* 22

Barbounia | *Park/20s* 22

Shake Shack | *23s/Mad* 22

Birreria | *5a/23-24s* 22

Haru | *Park/18s* 21

Giorgio's | *21s/Bway-Park* 21

Tarallucci | *18s/Bway-5a* 21

Hurricane Club | *Park/26s* 21

Mari Vanna | *20s/Bway-Park* 21

Brio | *Bway/21s* 21

Almond | *22s/Bway-Park* 21

'Wichcraft | *20s/Bway-5a* 20

Hill Country Chicken | Bway/25s — 20

Wildwood BBQ | Park/18-19s — 20

Schnipper´s | 23s/Mad-Park — 20

City Crab | Park/19s — 20

Markt | 6a/21s — 20

Le Pain Q. | 19s/Bway-Park — 20

Petite Abeille | 17s/5-6a — 20

Chickpea | 6a/21-22s — 19

Goodburger | Bway/17-18s — 19

Sagaponack | 22s/5-6a — 19

Eisenberg's Sandwich | 5a/22-23s — 18

NEW Château Cherbuliez | 20s/5-6a — ‒

NEW Nasha Rasha | 19s/5-6a — ‒

NEW Raymi | 24s/5-6a — ‒

NEW Vic & Anthony's | Park/19s — ‒

GARMENT DISTRICT

(30th to 40th Sts., west of 5th)

Ai Fiori | 5a/36-7s — 26

Keens | 36s/5-6a — 26

New WonJo | 32s/Bway-5a — 24

Mercato | 39s/8-9a — 24

Uncle Jack's | 9a/34-35s — 24

Cho Dang Gol | 35s/5-6a — 23

Frankie/Johnnie | 37s/5-6a — 23

Colbeh | 39s/5-6a — 23

Szechuan Gourmet | 39s/5-6a — 23

Kang Suh | Bway/32s — 23

Lazzara's | 38s/7-8a — 23

Kati Roll | 39s/5-6a — 23

Miss Korea BBQ | 32s/Bway-5a — 22

Alpha Fusion | 34s/8-9a — 22

Kum Gang San | 32s/Bway-5a — 22

BonChon Chicken | 38s/7-8a — 22

Casa Nonna | 38s/8-9a — 22

Gahm Mi Oak | 32s/Bway-5a — 22

NEW Dong Chun Hong | 5a/31-32s — 21

Ayza Wine | 31s/Bway-5a — 21

Chef Yu | 8a/36-37s — 21

Stage Door Deli | Penn Plaza/33s — 21

Abigael's | Bway/38-39s — 21

Sarabeth's | 5a/38-39s — 21

Arno | 38s/Bway-7a — 20

Mandoo Bar | 32s/Bway-5a — 20

Ben's Kosher | 38s/7-8a — 20

Potbelly | multi. — 20

Chickpea | 8a/34s — 19

Go Burger | 38s/8-9a — 19

NEW Clyde Frazier's | 10a/37s — 18

Brother Jimmy's | 8a/31s — 17

NEW Dans Le Noir | 38s/7-8a — ‒

NEW Kristalbelli | 36s/5-6a — ‒

GRAMERCY PARK

(14th to 23rd Sts., east of Park Ave. S.)

Maialino | Lex/21s — 26

BLT Prime | 22s/Lex-Park — 25

Casa Mono | Irving/17s — 25

Pure Food/Wine | Irving/17-18s — 25

Novitá | 22s/Lex-Park — 25

Posto | 2a/18s — 24

Defonte's | 3a/21s — 24

Yama | 17s/Irving — 24

Bar Jamon | 17s/Irving — 23

Molly's | 3a/22-23s — 23

Mexico Lindo | 2a/26s — 23

La Follia | 3a/19s — 22

Ponty Bistro | 3a/18-19s — 22

Ko Sushi | 3a/18-19s — 22

House | 17s/Irving-Park — 21

Lady Mendl's | Irving/17-18s — 21

Paul & Jimmy's | 18s/Irving-Park — 21

Bao Noodles | 2a/22-23s — 20

Zen Palate | 18s/Irving-Park — 20

Petite Abeille | 20s/1a — 20

Friend/Farmer | Irving/18-19s — 19

Brother Jimmy's | 16s/Irving-Union Sq — 17

Rolf's | 3a/22s — 17

GREENWICH VILLAGE

(Houston to 14th Sts., west of B'way, east of 6th Ave.)

Ushiwakamaru | Houston/MacDougal-Sullivan — 28

Gotham B&G | 12s/5a-Uni — 28

Il Mulino | 3s/Sullivan-Thompson — 27

Blue Hill | Wash pl/MacDougal-6a — 27

Babbo | Waverly/MacDougal-6a — 27

Alta | 10s/5-6a — 26

Strip House | 12s/5a-Uni — 26

Tomoe Sushi | Thompson/Blkr-Houston — 26

Num Pang | 12s/5a-Uni — 25

Lupa | Thompson/Blkr-Houston — 25

Taboon | 13s/5a-Uni — 25

Minetta | MacDougal/Blkr-3s — 24

Cuba | Thompson/Blkr-3s — 24

Villa Mosconi	*MacDougal/Blkr-Houston*	24	Le Pain Q.	*multi.*	20
Bar Pitti	*6a/Blkr-Houston*	24	**NEW** High Heat	*Blkr/Thompson*	-
Otto	*8s/5a-Uni*	24	**NEW** Neta	*8s/6a*	-
Piadina	*10s/5-6a*	24		
Da Andrea	*13s/5-6a*	23	**HARLEM/**	
Meskerem	*MacDougal/Blkr-3s*	23	**EAST HARLEM**	
Negril	*3s/La Guardia-Thompson*	23	(110th to 155th Sts., excluding	
Mexicana Mama	*12s/Bway-Uni*	23	Columbia U. area)	
North Sq.	*Waverly/MacDougal*	23	Ricardo	*2A/110-1s*	25
Il Cantinori	*10s/Bway-Uni*	23	Zoma	*Douglass/113s*	24
Arturo's	*Houston/Thompson*	23	Melba's	*114s/Douglass*	24
CamaJe	*MacDougal/Blkr-Houston*	23	El Paso Taqueria	*116s/2-3a*	24
Japonica	*Uni/12s*	23	Ristorante/Settepani	*Lenox/120s*	24
BareBurger	*Laguardia/Blkr-3s*	23	Dinosaur BBQ	*125s/12a*	23
Kati Roll	*MacDougal/Blkr-3s*	23	Lido	*Douglass/117s*	23
Creperie	*MacDougal/Blkr-3s*	23	Covo	*135s/12a*	23
Sacred Chow	*Sullivan/Blkr-3s*	22	Miss Mamie/Maude	*multi.*	23
Mezzaluna/Pizza	*Houston/MacDougal*	22	5 & Diamond	*Douglass/112s*	23
Da Silvano	*6a/Blkr*	22	Rao's	*114s/Pleasant*	23
Max Brenner	*Bway/13-14s*	22	Amor Cubano	*3a/111s*	23
Artichoke Basille	*MacDougal/Blkr-3s*	22	Red Rooster	*Lenox/125-126s*	23
Lion	*9s/5-6a*	22	Amy Ruth's	*116s/Lenox-7a*	22
NEW Perla	*Minetta/MacDougal-6a*	22	Chez Lucienne	*Lenox/125-126s*	22
Mermaid	*MacDougal/Blkr-Houston*	22	**NEW** Corner Social	*Lenox/126s*	21
BLT Burger	*6a/11-12s*	22	Hudson River	*133s/12a*	21
Maoz	*8s/Mercer*	22	Patsy's	*1a/117-118s*	21
Jane	*Houston/La Guardia-Thompson*	22	Sylvia's	*Lenox/126-127s*	20
Quantum Leap	*Thompson/Blkr-3s*	22	**NEW** Ginny's Supper Club	*Lenox/125-126s*	-
Knickerbocker	*Uni/9s*	21	**HUDSON SQUARE**	
Peanut Butter Co.	*Sullivan/Blkr-3s*	21	(Canal to Houston Sts.,	
Miss Lily's	*Houston/Sullivan*	21	west of 6th Ave.)	
Jackson Diner	*Uni/10-11s*	21	La Sirène	*Broome/Varick*	23
Sammy's	*6A/11s*	21	508	*Greenwich s/Canal-Spring*	22
Patsy's	*Uni/10-11s*	21	**LITTLE ITALY**	
Five Guys	*La Guardia/Blkr-Houston*	21	(Canal to Kenmare Sts.,	
Cafe Español	*Blkr/MacDougal-Sullivan*	21	Bowery to Lafayette St.)	
Spice	*13s/Bway-Uni*	21	Pellegrino's	*Mulberry/Grand-Hester*	25
La Lanterna	*MacDougal/3-4s*	21	Shanghai Café	*Mott/Canal-Hester*	24
'Wichcraft	*8s/Mercer*	20	Ferrara	*Grand/Mott-Mulberry*	24
Gray's Papaya	*6a/8s*	20	Vincent's	*Mott/Hester*	24
Chez Jacqueline	*MacDougal/Blkr-Houston*	20	Angelo's/Mulberry	*Mulberry/Grand-Hester*	23
Amber	*6a/9-10s*	20	Nyonya	*Grand/Mott-Mulberry*	23
			Pho Bang	*Mott/Broome-Grand*	23
			La Esquina	*Kenmare/Cleveland-Lafayette*	23
			Wild Ginger	*Broome/Mott*	23

Il Fornaio | *Mulberry/Grand-Hester* 23

Il Cortile | *Mulberry/Canal-Hester* 23

X.O. | *Hester/Bowery-Elizabeth* 22

La Mela | *Mulberry/Broome-Grand* 22

Da Nico | *Mulberry/Broome-Grand* 22

Umberto's | *Mulberry/Grand-Hester* 22

Bo-Ky | *Grand/Elizabeth* 22

Red Egg | *Centre/Howard* 21

S.P.Q.R. | *Mulberry/Grand-Hester* 21

LOWER EAST SIDE

(Houston to Canal Sts., east of Bowery)

🆕 Sauce | *Riv/Allen* 26

Clinton St. Baking | *Clinton/Houston Stanton* 26

Ápizz | *Eldridge/Riv-Stanton* 25

Kuma Inn | *Ludlow/Delancey-Riv* 25

WD-50 | *Clinton/Riv-Stanton* 25

Katz's Deli | *Houston/Ludlow* 25

Stanton Social | *Stanton/Ludlow-Orchard* 24

Sorella | *Allen/Broome-Delancey* 24

Meatball Shop | *Stanton/Allen-Orchard* 24

Barrio Chino | *Broome/Ludlow-Orchard* 24

Ed's Lobster | *Clinton/Houston-Stanton* 24

Fat Radish | *Orchard/Canal-Hester* 21

Macondo | *Houston/Allen-Eldridge* 23

1492 Food | *Clinton/Riv-Stanton* 23

Beauty & Essex | *Essex/Riv-Stanton* 23

A Casa Fox | *Orchard/Stanton* 23

Creperie | *Ludlow/Riv-Stanton* 23

Freemans | *Riv/Bowery-Chrystie* 22

Rayuela | *Allen/Riv-Stanton* 22

Móle | *Allen/Houston* 22

Mexicue | *Forsyth/Broome-Grand* 22

'Inoteca | *Riv/Ludlow* 22

An Choi | *Orchard/Broome* 22

Lucky's Famous Burgers | *Houston/Eldridge/Forsyth* 22

Vanessa's Dumpling | *Eldridge/Broome-Grand* 22

Noodle Bar | *Orchard/Stanton* 22

🆕 Sons of Essex | *Essex/Riv-Stanton* 21

Whole Foods | *Houston/Bowery-Chrystie* 21

Congee | *multi.* 21

Sammy's | *Chrystie/Delancey* 20

Schiller's | *Riv/Norfolk* 20

🆕 Bowery Diner | *Bowery/Prince* 18

🆕 Yunnan Kitchen | *Clinton/Riv* 18

🆕 Blue Ribbon/Izakaya | *Orchard/Houston-Stanton* -

🆕 Francesca | *Clinton/Houston-Stanton* -

🆕 Grey Lady | *Delancey/Allen* -

🆕 Mission Chinese Food | *Orchard/Riv-Stanton* -

MEATPACKING

(Gansevoort to 15th Sts., west of 9th Ave.)

Valbella | *13s/9a-Wash* 25

Old Homestead | *9a/14-15s* 25

STK | *Little W 12s/9a-Wash* 24

Beaumarchais | *13/9a-Wash* 24

Spice Market | *13s/9a* 24

🆕 Catch | *13s/9a-Wash* 23

Sea | *Wash/Little W 12s* 23

Macelleria | *Gansevoort/Greenwich s-Wash* 23

Abe/Arthur | *14s/9a-Wash* 22

Pastis | *9a/Little W 12s* 22

Standard Grill | *Wash/Little W 12-13s* 22

Fig & Olive | *13s/9a-Wash* 22

5 9th | *9a/Gansevoort-Little W 12s* 20

Dos Caminos | *Hudson/14s* 20

Bill's Bar | *9a/13s* 20

Serafina | *9a/Little W 12s* 20

🆕 Bagatelle | *Little W 12s/9a* -

🆕 Toy | *9a/13s* -

MURRAY HILL

(26th to 40th Sts., east of 5th; 23rd to 26th Sts., east of Park Ave. S.)

Marcony | *Lex/31-32s* 26

Wolfgang's | *Park/33s* 26

Sushi Sen-nin | *33s/Mad-Park* 26

HanGawi | *32s/5a-Mad* 25

SD26 | *26s/5a-Mad* 25

Primehouse | *Park/27s* 25

Ben & Jack's | *5a/28-29s* 25

Riverpark | *29s/FDR-1a* 25

Villa Berulia | *34s/Lex-Park* 24

Vezzo	*Lex/31s*	24
Vatan	*3a/29s*	24
Tiffin Wallah	*28s/Lex-Park*	24
Rossini's	*38s/Lex-Park*	24
Cannibal	*29s/Lex-Park*	24
Le Parisien	*33s/Lex-3a*	24
El Pote	*2a/38-39s*	23
Dhaba	*Lex/27-28s*	23
Saravanaa Bhavan	*Lex/26s*	23
Hillstone	*Park/27s*	23
Toledo	*36s/5a-Mad*	23
Pongal	*Lex/27-28s*	23
Lil'/Shorty's	*multi.*	23
Pio Pio	*34s/2-3a*	23
El Parador Cafe	*34s/1-2a*	23
BareBurger	*3a/34-35s*	23
Ravagh	*30s/5a-Mad*	23
Artisanal	*32s/Mad-Park*	23
Water Club	*E River/23s*	23
Phoenix Gdn.	*40s/2-3a*	23
Penelope	*Lex/30s*	23
Da Ciro	*Lex/33-34s*	23
2nd Ave Deli	*33s/Lex-3a*	23
Black Duck	*28s/Lex-Park*	23
Blue Smoke	*27s/Lex-Park*	23
I Trulli	*27s/Lex-Park*	22
Jaiya	*3a/28s*	22
Cafe China	*37s/5a-Mad*	22
Nirvana	*Lex/39-40s*	22
East Pacific	*34s/Lex-Park*	22
Bistango	*3u/29s*	22
Carl's Steaks	*3a/34s*	22
Zaitzeff	*2a/38-39s*	22
Turkish Kitchen	*3a/27-28s*	22
'Inoteca	*3a/24s*	22
Rare B&G	*Lex/37s*	22
BonChon Chicken	*5a/32-33s*	22
Ethos	*3a/33-34s*	22
Asellina	*Park/29s*	22
Baoguette	*Lex/25-26s*	22
NEW Desi Shack	*Lex/39s*	22
Coppola's	*3a/27-28s*	21
Resto	*29s/Lex-Park*	21
Aji Sushi	*3a/34-35s*	21
Sarge's Deli	*3a/36-37s*	21
Grand Sichuan	*Lex/33-34s*	21
Ali Baba	*34s/2-3a*	21
Kyochon	*5a/32-33s*	21
Les Halles	*Park/28-29s*	21
Hummus Kitchen	*3a/30-31s*	21
Patsy's	*3a/34-35s*	21
Terroir	*3a/30-31s*	21

Pizza 33	*3a/33s*	21
Smorgas Chef	*Park/37-38s*	20
Millesime	*Mad/29s*	20
Madison Bistro	*Mad/37-38s*	20
Zen Palate	*3a/34-35s*	20
Baluchi's	*3a/24-25s*	20
Dos Caminos	*Park/26-27s*	20
Lemongrass	*34s/Lex-3a*	20
Potbelly	*Park/24-25s*	20
Amber	*3a/27-28s*	20
Barbès	*36s/5a-Mad*	20
Pranna	*Mad/28-29s*	20
Josie's	*3a/37s*	20
Jackson Hole	*3a/35s*	19
Morgan	*Mad/36-37s*	19
Brother Jimmy's	*Lex/31s*	17
NEW Arabesque	*36s/5a-Mad*	—

NOHO

(Houston to 4th Sts.,
Bowery to B'way)

Bianca	*Blkr/Bowery-Elizabeth*	26
Bohemian	*Gr Jones/ Bowery-Lafayette*	26
Il Buco	*multi.*	26
Bond St.	*Bond/Bway-Lafayette*	25
Mile End	*Bond/Bowery-Lafayette*	25
Aroma Kitchen	*4s/Bowery-Lafayette*	23
Forcella	*Bowery/Bond-Gr Jones*	23
Hecho en Dumbo	*Bowery/4s-Gr Jones*	23
NEW Saxon & Parole	*Bowery/Blkr*	23
NEW Acme	*Gr. Jones/Lafayette*	23
Pinche Taqueria	*Lafayette/Blkr*	22
Smile	*Bond/Bowery-Lafayette*	22
5 Points	*Gr Jones/ Bowery-Lafayette*	22
Great Jones Cafe	*Gr Jones/ Bowery-Lafayette*	21
NoHo Star	*Lafayette/Blkr*	20
Two Boots	*Blkr/Bway*	20
B Bar & Grill	*4s/Bowery-Lafayette*	19

NOLITA

(Houston to Kenmare Sts.,
Bowery to Lafayette St.)

Torrisi	*Mulberry/Prince-Spring*	27
Taïm	*Spring/Mulberry*	26
Lombardi's	*Spring/Mott-Mulberry*	25

Peasant | *Elizabeth/Prince-Spring* — 24

NEW Parm | *Mulberry/Prince-Spring* — 24

Emporio | *Mott/Prince-Spring* — 24

Balaboosta | *Mulberry/Prince-Spring* — 24

Ed's Lobster | *Lafayette/Kenmare-Spring* — 24

Café Habana/Outpost | *Prince/Elizabeth* — 23

Public | *Elizabeth/Prince-Spring* — 23

Tacombi/Fonda Nolita | *Elizabeth/Houston-Prince* — 23

Socarrat | *Mulberry/Houston-Prince* — 23

Mexican Radio | *Cleveland/Kenmare-Spring* — 23

Pinche Taqueria | *Mott/Prince-Spring* — 22

Rubirosa | *Mulberry/Prince-Spring* — 22

Cafe Gitane | *Mott/Prince* — 22

Spring/Natural | *Spring/Lafayette* — 21

Pulino's | *Bowery/Houston* — 21

Bread | *Spring/Elizabeth-Mott* — 20

Delicatessen | *Prince/Lafayette* — 20

NEW Ken & Cook | *Kenmare/Bowery-Elizabeth* — -

SOHO

(Canal to Houston Sts., west of Lafayette St.)

Aquagrill | *Spring/6a* — 27

Blue Ribbon Sushi | *Sullivan/Prince-Spring* — 26

Omen | *Thompson/Prince-Spring* — 26

Blue Ribbon | *Sullivan/Prince-Spring* — 25

Rouge et Blanc | *MacDougal/Houston-Prince* — 25

Raoul's | *Prince/Sullivan-Thompson* — 25

L'Ecole | *Bway/Grand* — 24

Numero 28 | *Spring/Sullivan-Thompson* — 24

Osteria Morini | *Lafayette/Kenmare-Spring* — 24

David Burke Kitchen | *Grand/6a* — 24

Balthazar | *Spring/Bway-Crosby* — 24

Kittichai | *Thompson/Broome-Spring* — 24

Dutch | *Sullivan/Prince* — 24

Boqueria | *Spring/Thompson-W Bway* — 23

Cipriani D'twn | *W Bway/Broome-Spring* — 23

Aurora | *Broome/Thompson-Bway* — 23

Lure Fishbar | *Mercer/Prince* — 23

Pepe | *Sullivan/Houston-Prince* — 23

Snack | *Thompson/Prince-Spring* — 23

Back Forty | *Prince/Crosby* — 23

Bistro Les Amis | *Spring/Thompson* — 23

12 Chairs | *MacDougal/Houston-Prince* — 23

Smile | *Howard/Crosby-Lafayette* — 22

BandB | *Houston/Greene-Mercer* — 22

Mercer Kitchen | *Prince/Mercer* — 22

Hampton Chutney | *Prince/Crosby-Lafayette* — 22

Le Pescadeux | *Thompson/Prince-Spring* — 22

Antique Garage | *Mercer/Broome-Grand* — 22

Pera | *Thompson/Broome-Spring* — 21

Mezzogiorno | *Spring/Sullivan* — 21

Hundred Acres | *MacDougal/Prince* — 21

sNice | *Sullivan/Houston-Prince* — 21

Mooncake Foods | *Watts/6a-Thompson* — 21

NEW Jack's Wife Freda | *Lafayette/Kenmare-Spring* — 20

Dos Caminos | *W Bway/Houston-Prince* — 20

Cafe Noir | *Grand/Thompson* — 20

Le Pain Q. | *Grand/Greene-Mercer* — 20

NEW Cómodo | *MacDougal/Houston-King* — -

NEW Isola | *Crosby/Grand-Howard* — -

NEW Jezebel | *W Bway/Canal-Grand* — -

SOUTH STREET SEAPORT

Suteishi | *Peck/Front* — 25

Cabana | *South/Fulton* — 23

Cowgirl | *Front/Dover* — 17

TRIBECA

(Canal to Murray Sts., west of B'way)

Bouley | *Duane/ Greenwich s-Hudson* — 28

Scalini Fedeli | *Duane/Greenwich s-Hudson* — 27

Nobu | *multi.* — 27

Pepolino | *W Bway/Canal-Lispenard* | 27

Corton | *W Bway/Walker-White* | 26

Tamarind | *Hudson/Franklin-Harrison* | 26

NEW Jungsik | *Harrison/Hudson* | 26

Wolfgang's | *Greenwich s/Beach-Hubert* | 26

NEW Atera | *Worth/Bway-Church* | 26

Brushstroke | *Hudson/Duane* | 25

Locanda Verde | *Greenwich s/N Moore* | 25

Marc Forgione | *Reade/Greenwich s-Hudson* | 25

Il Giglio | *Warren/Greenwich s-W Bway* | 25

Ponte's | *Desbrosses/Wash-West* | 25

Takahachi | *Duane/Church-W Bway* | 25

Palm | *West/Chambers-Warren* | 25

Rosanjin | *Duane/Church-W Bway* | 25

Acappella | *Hudson/Chambers* | 24

Mehtaphor | *Duane/Church* | 24

Thalassa | *Franklin/Greenwich s-Hudson* | 24

Dylan Prime | *Laight/Greenwich s* | 24

Sazon | *Reade/Church-W Bway* | 24

Churrascaria | *W Bway/Franklin-White* | 24

Megu | *Thomas/Church-W Bway* | 24

Capsouto Frères | *Wash/Watts* | 23

Harrison | *Greenwich s/Harrison* | 23

Tribeca Grill | *Greenwich s/Franklin* | 23

Ecco | *Chambers/Church-W Bway* | 23

Mr. Chow | *Hudson/N Moore* | 22

Roc | *Duane/Greenwich s* | 22

Blaue Gans | *Duane/Church-W Bway* | 22

City Hall | *Duane/Church-W Bway* | 22

Flor/Sol | *Greenwich s/Franklin-Harrison* | 22

Trattoria Cinque | *Greenwich s/Franklin-Harrison* | 22

Duane Park | *Duane/Hudson-W Bway* | 22

Max | *Duane/Greenwich s-Hudson* | 22

Landmarc | *W Bway/Leonard-Worth* | 21

Gigino | *Greenwich s/Duane-Reade* | 21

Tiny's | *W Bway/Duane-Thomas* | 21

Sarabeth's | *Greenwich s/Harrison-Jay* | 21

NEW Kutsher's | *Franklin/Greenwich s-Hudson* | 21

Whole Foods | *Greenwich s/Murray-Warren* | 21

Terroir | *Harrison/Greenwich s-Hudson* | 21

'Wichcraft | *Greenwich s/Beach* | 20

Bread | *Church/Walker* | 20

Macao Trading | *Church/Lispenard-Walker* | 20

Baluchi's | *Greenwich s/Murray-Warren* | 20

Potbelly | *W Bway/Chambers-Reade* | 20

Centrico | *W Bway/Franklin* | 20

Bubby's | *Hudson/N Moore* | 20

Cercle Rouge | *W Bway/N Moore* | 20

Odeon | *W Bway/Duane-Thomas* | 20

Kitchenette | *Chambers/Greenwich a-W Bway* | 20

Petite Abeille | *W Bway/Duane-Thomas* | 20

Ninja | *Hudson/Duane-Reade* | 19

Walker's | *N Moore/Varick* | 19

NEW Super Linda | *Broadway/Reade* | 19

UNION SQUARE

(14th to 17th Sts., 5th Ave. to Union Sq. E.)

Union Sq. Cafe | *16s/5a-Union Sq* | 27

Tocqueville | *15s/5a-Union Sq* | 27

15 East | *15s/5a-Union Sq* | 26

Blue Water | *Union Sq/16s* | 24

Olives | *Park/17s* | 23

Qi | *14s/5-6a* | 22

Laut | *17s/Bway-5a* | 22

Maoz | *Union Sq/16-17s* | 22

Whole Foods | *Union Sq/Bway-Uni* | 21

Steak Frites | *16s/5a-Union Sq. W.* | 20

Potbelly | *17s/Bway-5a* | 20

Republic | *Union Sq/16-17s* | 20

Coffee Shop | *Union Sq/16s* | 17

WASHINGTON HTS./ INWOOD

(North of W. 155th St.)

El Malecon | *Bway/175-176s* | 22

Piper's Kilt | *Bway/207s* | 22

New Leaf | *Corbin/190s* | 21

Garden Café | *Bway/Isham-207s* | 21

Mamajuana | *Dyckman/Payson-Seaman* | 21

LOCATIONS

Gari/Sushi | 46s/8-9a — 27

Sushi Zen | 44s/Bway-6a — 26

Aureole | 42s/Bway-6a — 26

Wolfgang's | 41s/7-8a — 26

Ipanema | 46s/5-6a — 26

Del Frisco's | 6a/48-49s — 25

Esca | 43s/9a — 25

DB Bistro Moderne | 44s/5-6a — 25

Koi | 40s/5-6a — 25

Sushiden | 49s/6-7a — 25

Oceana | 49s/6-7a — 24

Bouchon Bakery | 48s/5-6a — 24

Sea Grill | 49s/5-6a — 24

Mont Blanc | 48s/8-9a — 24

STK | 6a/42-43s — 24

Churrascaria | 49s/8-9a — 24

Hell's Kitchen | 9a/46-47s — 24

Triomphe | 44s/5-6a — 24

Kyotofu | 9a/48-49s — 24

Lambs Club | 44s/6-7a — 24

Orso | 46s/8-9a — 24

Shula's | 43s/Bway-8a — 24

A.J. Maxwell's | 48s/5-6a — 23

Chimichurri Grill | 9a/43-44s — 23

Meskerem | 47s/9-10a — 23

Tony's Di Napoli | 43s/Bway-6a — 23

Peter's 1969 | 9a/42-43s — 23

Bobby Van's | 45s/6-7a — 23

La Masseria | 48s/Bway-8a — 23

Blossom | 9a/43-44s — 23

Becco | 46s/8-9a — 23

Lil'/Shorty's | 9a/41-42s — 23

Pio Pio | 10a/43-44s — 23

Frankie/Johnnie | 45s/Bway-8a — 23

Blue Fin | Bway/47s — 23

Wu Liang Ye | 48s/5-6a — 23

Kellari Tav./Parea | 44s/5-6a — 23

NEW Añejo | 10a/47s — 23

NEW Hakkasan | 43s/8-9a — 23

John's Pizzeria | 44s/Bway-8a — 23

Queen of Sheba | 10a/45-46s — 23

Etcetera Etcetera | 44s/8-9a — 23

Print | 11a/47-48s — 23

NEW Viv | 9a/49s — 23

Qi | 8a/43s — 22

44 & X/44½ | multi. — 22

Lattanzi | 46s/8-9a — 22

Harry's Italian | 6a/49-50s — 22

Riposo | 9a/46-47s — 22

Akdeniz | 46s/5-6a — 22

Pam Real Thai | multi. — 22

Shake Shack | 8a/44s — 22

Carmine's | 44s/Bway-8a — 22

E&E Grill House | 49s/Bway-8a — 22

Maoz | multi. — 22

Le Rivage | 46s/8-9a — 22

Room Service | 9a/47-48s — 22

Ça Va | 44s/8-9a — 22

Daisy May's | 11a/46s — 22

Inakaya | 40s/7-8a — 22

Barbetta | 46s/8-9a — 22

Ember Room | 9a/45-46s — 22

Trattoria Trecolori | 47s/Bway-8a — 22

Via Brasil | 46s/5-6a — 22

Gyu-Kaku | 44s/8-9a — 22

5 Napkin Burger | 9a/44-45s — 22

Cara Mia | 9a/45-46s — 21

Le Marais | 46s/6-7a — 21

Saju Bistro | 44s/Bway-6a — 21

Breeze | 9a/45-46s — 21

Turkish Cuisine | 9a/44-45s — 21

Haru | 43s/Bway-8a — 21

Utsav | 46s/6-7a — 21

Marseille | 9a/44-45s — 21

Gazala's | 9a/48-49s — 21

Alfredo/Rome | 49s/5-6a — 21

City Lobster | 49s/6a — 21

Pongsri Thai | 48s/Bway-8a — 21

Virgil's BBQ | 44s/Bway-6a — 21

Counter | Bway/41s — 21

Grand Sichuan | 46s/8-9a — 21

Wondee Siam | 10a/45-46s — 21

Osteria al Doge | 44s/Bway-6a — 21

Five Guys | multi. — 21

Meson Sevilla | 46s/8-9a — 21

44 | 44s/5-6A — 21

Amarone | 9a/47-48s — 21

Chez Josephine | 42s/9-10a — 21

Don Giovanni | 44s/8-9a — 21

'Wichcraft | multi. — 20

Glass House | 47s/Bway-8a — 20

Zen Palate | 9a/46s — 20

Delta Grill | 9a/48s — 20

FireBird | 46s/8-9a — 20

St. Andrews | 44s/Bway-6A — 20

Bond 45 | 45s/6-7a — 20

B. Smith's | 46s/8-9a — 20

Dafni Greek | 42s/8-9a — 20

Junior's | 45s/Bway-8a — 20

Nizza | 9a/44-45s — 20

Havana Central | 46s/6-7a — 20

Schnipper's | 8a/41s — 20

Two Boots	*9a/44-45s*	20
Serafina	*49s/Bway-8a*	20
West Bank	*42s/9-10a*	20
BXL	*43s/Bway-6a*	19
Ruby Foo's	*Bway/49s*	19
Dervish	*47s/6-7u*	19
Sardi's	*44s/Bway-8a*	19
Bryant Park	*40s/5-6a*	19
Joe Allen	*46s/8-9a*	19
Landmark Tavern	*11a/46s*	19
View	*Bway/45-46s*	18
NEW Ktchn	*42s/10-1a*	–

WEST 50s

Le Bernardin	*51s/6-7a*	29
Sugiyama	*55s/Bway-8a*	28
Marea	*CPS/Bway-7a*	28
Milos	*55s/6-7a*	27
Gari/Sushi	*59s/5a*	27
Nobu	*57s/5-6a*	27
Modern	*53s/5-6a*	26
Totto Ramen	*52s/8-9a*	26
Quality Meats	*58s/5-6a*	26
Danji	*52s/8-9a*	26
Ruth's Chris	*51s/6-7u*	26
Pure Thai Cookhouse	*9a/51-52s*	26
NEW Brasserie Pushkin	*57s/5-6a*	26
Norma's	*56s/6-7a*	25
Blue Ribbon Sushi B&G	*58s/8-9a*	25
Del Frisco's	*51s/5-6a*	25
Seäsonal	*58s/6-7a*	25
Taboon	*10a/52s*	25
Il Tinello	*56s/5-6a*	25
Yakitori Totto	*55s/Bway-8a*	25
La Bergamote	*52s/10-11a*	25
Azuri Cafe	*51s/9-10a*	25
Maze	*54s/6-7a*	25
Palm	*50s/Bway-8a*	25
Capital Grille	*51s/6-7a*	25
La Silhouette	*53s/8-9a*	25
NEW Don Antonio	*50s/8-9a*	24
Burger Joint	*56s/6-7a*	24
Toloache	*50s/Bway-8a*	24
Petrossian	*58s/7a*	24
Il Gattopardo	*54s/5-6a*	24
Uncle Jack's	*56s/5-6a*	24
Basso56	*56s/Bway-8a*	24
Luke's Lobster	*59s/5a*	24
21 Club	*52s/5-6a*	24
Empanada Mama	*9a/51-52s*	24

Má Pêche	*56s/5-6a*	24
Nocello	*55s/Bway-8a*	24
Gordon Ramsay	*54s/6-7a*	24
Bar Americain	*52s/6-7a*	24
Circo	*55s/6-7a*	24
Natsumi	*50s/Bway-8a*	23
Molyvos	*7a/55-56s*	23
Bobby Van's	*50s/6-7a*	23
Sushi Damo	*58s/8-9a*	23
Tang Pavilion	*55s/5-6a*	23
Patsy's	*56s/Bway-8a*	23
Soba Nippon	*52s/5-6a*	23
Szechuan Gourmet	*56s/Bway-8a*	23
Kashkaval	*9a/56s*	23
Plaza Food Hall	*59s/5a*	23
Remi	*53s/6-7a*	23
Brasserie 8½	*57s/5-6a*	23
Topaz Thai	*56s/6-7a*	23
Chai Home Kitchen	*8a/55s*	23
Carnegie Deli	*7a/55s*	23
No. 7	*59s/5a*	23
China Grill	*53s/5-6a*	23
Nook	*9a/50-51s*	23
ViceVersa	*51s/8-9a*	23
Tratt. Dell'Arte	*7a/56-57s*	23
Beacon	*56s/5-6a*	23
Chez Napoléon	*50s/8-9a*	23
Momofuku Milk Bar	*56s/5-6a*	22
Victor's Cafe	*52s/Bway-8a*	22
Joe's Shanghai	*56s/5-6a*	22
Island Burgers	*9a/51-52s*	22
Michael's	*55s/5-6a*	22
Gallagher's	*52s/Bway-8a*	22
Rice 'n' Beans	*9a/50-51s*	22
Abboccato	*55s/6-7a*	22
Hanci	*10a/56-57s*	22
Katsu-Hama	*55s/5-6a*	22
Sushiya	*56s/5-6a*	22
Benoit	*55s/5-6a*	22
South Gate	*CPS/6-7a*	22
Angelo's Pizza	*multi.*	22
Radiance Tea House	*55s/6-7a*	22
Eatery	*9a/53s*	22
Bann	*50s/8-9a*	22
Ise	*56s/5-6a*	22
Lucky's Famous Burgers	*52s/8-9a*	22
PizzArte	*55s/5-6a*	21
Bistro Milano	*55s/5-6a*	21
Guantanamera	*8a/55-56s*	21
Palm Court	*5a/59s*	21
Robert	*Bway/8a*	21

Redeye Grill | *7a/56s*	21
Nino's | *58s/6-7a*	21
NEW Steak 'n Shake | *Bway/53-54s*	21
Bocca/Bacco | *9a/54-55s*	21
Bricco | *56s/8-9a*	21
Afghan Kebab | *9a/51-52s*	21
Da Tommaso | *8a/53-54s*	21
Uncle Nick's | *9a/50-51s*	21
Menkui Tei | *56s/5-6a*	21
Mooncake Foods | *54s/8-9a*	21
Sarabeth's | *CPS/5-6a*	21
Hummus Kitchen | *9a/51-52s*	21
Wondee Siam | *multi.*	21
McCormick/Schmick | *52s/6-7a*	21
Five Guys | *55s/5-6a*	21
Greek Kitchen | *10a/58s*	21
Russian Tea | *57s/6-7a*	21
Thalia | *8a/50s*	21
Russian Samovar | *52s/Bway-8a*	21
Sosa Borella | *8a/50s*	21
El Centro | *9a/54s*	21
Stage Deli | *7a/53-54s*	20
Bombay Palace | *52s/5-6a*	20
Braai | *51s/8-9a*	20
Rue 57 | *57s/6a*	20
Potbelly | *56s/5-6a*	20
Caffe Cielo | *8a/52-53s*	20
NEW Claw | *9a/50-51s*	20
Rock Ctr. | *50s/5-6a*	20
Puttanesca | *9a/56s*	20
Brasserie Cognac | *Bway/55s*	20
Pier 9 | *9a/53-54s*	20
Le Pain Q. | *7a/58s*	20
Bill's Bar | *51s/5-6a*	20
Whym | *9a/57-58s*	20
Lime Jungle | *multi.*	20
Serafina | *55s/Bway*	20
Maria Pia | *51s/8-9a*	20
La Bonne Soupe | *55s/5-6a*	19
Blue 9 Burger | *9a/52-53s*	19
Goodburger | *8a/57-58s*	19
Brass. Ruhlmann | *50s/5-6a*	19
Bamboo 52 | *52s/8-9a*	19

WEST 60s

Per Se | *60s/Bway*	29
Jean Georges | *CPW/60-61s*	28
Picholine | *64s/Bway-CPW*	27
Jean Georges Noug. | *CPW/60-61s*	27

Masa/Bar Masa | *60s/Bway*	27
Telepan | *69s/Colum-CPW*	27
Porter House | *60s/Bway*	26
Asiate | *60s/Bway*	25
Boulud Sud | *64s/Bway-CPW*	25
Lincoln | *65s/Amst-Bway*	25
Bouchon Bakery | *60s/Bway*	24
A Voce | *60s/Bway*	24
Bar Boulud | *Bway/63-64s*	24
Blossom | *Amst/67-68s*	23
Gabriel's | *60s/Bway-Colum*	23
Gastroarte | *69s/Bway-Colum*	23
Shun Lee West | *65s/Colum-CPW*	23
Atlantic Grill | *64s/Bway-CPW*	23
Rosa Mexicano | *Colum/62s*	23
La Boîte en Bois | *68s/Colum-CPW*	22
Leopard/des Artistes | *67s/Colum-CPW*	22
Landmarc | *60s/Bway*	21
Noi Due | *69s/Bway-Colum*	21
Grand Tier | *Lincoln Ctr/63-65s*	21
Shun Lee Cafe | *65s/Colum-CPW*	21
Sapphire | *Bway/60-61s*	21
Whole Foods | *60s/Bway*	21
'Wichcraft | *62s/Bway-Colum*	20
Cafe Fiorello | *Bway/63-64s*	20
Ed's Chowder | *63s/Bway-Colum*	20
Nick & Toni | *67s/Bway-Colum*	20
Le Pain Q. | *65s/Bway-CPW*	20
P.J. Clarke's | *63s/Colum*	18
NEW Joanne | *68s/Colum-CPW*	18

WEST 70s

Gari/Sushi | *Colum/77-78s*	27
Salumeria Rosi | *Amst/73-74s*	25
Dovetail | *77s/Colum*	25
Mike's Bistro | *72s/Bway-W End*	25
Ocean Grill | *Colum/78-79s*	24
'Cesca | *75s/Amst*	24
Saravanaa Bhavan | *Amst/79-80s*	23
FishTag | *79s/Amst-Bway*	23
Hummus Pl. | *Amst/74-75s*	23
NEW Loi | *70s/Amst-W End*	22
Riposo | *72s/Colum-CPW*	22
Shake Shack | *Colum/77s*	22
Café Frida | *Colum/77-78s*	22
Maoz | *Amst/70-71s*	22
Pomodoro Rosso | *Colum/70-71s*	22

Cafe Luxembourg | 70s/Amst-W End 22
Coppola's | 79s/Amst-Bway 21
Tenzan | Colum/73s 21
Mughlai | Colum/75s 21
Gazala's | Colum/78s 21
Seven's Turkish Grill | 72s/Amst-Colum 21
Isabella's | Colum/77s 21
Pasha | 71s/Colum-CPW 21
Grand Sichuan | Amst/74-75s 21
Penang | 72s/Amst-Colum 21
Patsy's | 74s/Colum-CPW 21
Sambuca | 72s/Colum-CPW 21
Scaletta | 77s/Colum-CPW 21
Tolani | Amst/79-80s 21
Citrus B&G | Amst/75s 21
Alice's Tea | 73s/Amst-Colum 21
Cafe Ronda | Colum/71-72s 20
NEW Caffe Storico | CPW/77s 20
Gray's Papaya | Bway/72s 20
Bistro Cassis | Colum/70-71s 20
Pappardella | Colum/75s 20
Epices/Traiteur | 70s/Colum 20
Nice Matin | 79s/Amst 20
Amber | Colum/70s 20
Le Pain Q. | 72s/Colum-CPW 20
Serafina | Bway/77s 20
Josie's | Amst/74s 20
Fairway Cafe | Bway/74s 19
Big Nick's | multi. 19
Bettola | Amst/79-80s 19
Arté Café | 73s/Amst-Colum 19
NEW A.G. Kitchen | Colum/72-73s -
NEW Purple Fig | 72s/Bway-W End -

WEST 80s

Recipe | Amst/81-82s 25
Candle Cafe | Bway/98-90s 25
Ouest | Bway/84s 25
Momoya | Amst/80-81s 24
Barney Greengrass | Amst/86-87s 24
Celeste | Amst/84-85s 24
Luke's Lobster | Amst/80-81s 24
Prime Grill/KO | 85s/Amst-Bway 24
Spiga | 84s/Amst-Bway 24
Peacefood Café | Amst/82a 23
Blossom | Colum/82-83s 23
Cotta | Colum/84-85s 23
Kefi | Colum/84-85s 23
Land | Amst/81-82s 23

La Mirabelle | 86s/Amst-Colum 23
Momofuku Milk Bar | Colum/87s 22
Island Burgers | Amst/80s 22
Mermaid | Amst/87-88s 22
Good Enough/Eat | Amst/83s-84s 22
Hampton Chutney | Amst/82-83s 22
Bodrum | Amst/88-89s 22
Calle Ocho | 81s/Colum-CPW 22
5 Napkin Burger | Bway/84s 22
Flor/Mayo | Amst/83-84s 21
Haru | Amst/80-81s 21
Tarallucci | Colum/83s 21
B. Café | Amst/87-88s 21
Spring/Natural | Colum/83s 21
Bistro Citron | Colum/82-83s 21
NEW Jacob's Pickles | Amst/84-85s 21
Sarabeth's | Amst/80-81s 21
Mamajuana | Amst/87-88s 21
Hummus Kitchen | Amst/80s 21
Spice | Amst/81s 21
Cafe Lalo | 83s/Amst-Bway 20
Cilantro | Colum/83-84s 20
Jackson Hole | Colum/85s 19
Brother Jimmy's | Amst/80-81s 17

WEST 90s

Gennaro | Amst/92-93s 24
Pio Pio | Amst/94s 23
Hummus Pl. | Bway/98-99s 23
El Malecon | Amst/97-98s 22
Carmine's | Bway/90-91s 22
Café Frida | Amst/97-98s 22
Saigon Grill | Amst/90s 21
Tratt. Pesce | Colum/90-91s 21
Acqua | Amst/95s 21
Whole Foods | Colum/97-100 21
Kouzan | Amst/93s 20
Regional | Bway/98-9s 20
Two Boots | Bway/95-96s 20

WEST 100s

(See also Harlem/East Harlem)
Pisticci | La Salle/Bway 25
Thai Market | Amst/107-108s 24
Max SoHa/Caffe | multi. 24
Community Food | Bway/112-113s 23
Vareli | Bway/111-112s 23
Noche Mex. | Amst/101-102s 23
Awash | Amst/106-107s 23

LOCATIONS

Indus Valley	*Bway/100s*	22
Rack & Soul	*109s/Bway*	22
Sookk	*Bway/102-103s*	22
Sezz Medi'	*Amst/122s*	22
Maoz	*Bway/110-111s*	22
Cascabel Taqueria	*Bway/108s*	22
Flor/Mayo	*Bway/100-101s*	21
Wondee Siam	*Amst/107-108s*	21
107 West	*Bway/107-108s*	21
Turkuaz	*Bway/100s*	21
Symposium	*113s/Amst-Bway*	20
Henry's	*Bway/105s*	20
Zen Palate	*105s/Bway*	20
Café du Soleil	*Bway/104s*	20
Havana Central	*Bway/113-114s*	20
Kitchenette	*Amst/122-123s*	20
Bistro Ten 18	*Amst/110s*	20

WEST VILLAGE

(Houston to 14th Sts., west of 6th Ave., excluding Meatpacking)

Soto	*6a/4s-Wash*	28
Mas	*Downing/Bedford-Varick*	28
Annisa	*Barrow/7a-4s*	28
L'Artusi	*10s/Blkr-Hudson*	27
Takashi	*Hudson/Barrow-Morton*	27
Perilla	*Jones/Blkr-4s*	27
Pearl Oyster	*Cornelia/Blkr-4s*	26
Taïm	*Waverly/Perry-11s*	26
RedFarm	*Hudson/Charles-10s*	26
Piccolo Angolo	*Hudson/Jane*	26
Pó	*Cornelia/Blkr-4s*	26
Wallsé	*11s/Wash*	26
Gradisca	*13s/6-7a*	26
Perry St.	*Perry/West*	26
EN Japanese	*Hudson/Leroy*	26
Dell'anima	*8a/Jane*	26
Little Owl	*Bedford/Grove*	26
NEW Rosemary's	*Greenwich a/10s*	25
Le Gigot	*Cornelia/Blkr-4s*	25
Trattoria Toscana	*Carmine/Bedford-7a*	25
Mary's Fish	*Charles/4s*	25
Keste Pizza	*Blkr/Morton*	25
'Ino	*Bedford/Downing-6a*	25
Recette	*12s/Greenwich s*	25
I Sodi	*Christopher/Blkr-Hudson*	25
Blue Ribbon Bakery	*Downing/Bedford*	25
Aki	*4s/Barrow-Jones*	25
Tea & Sympathy	*Greenwich a/12-13s*	25

Buvette	*Grove/Bedford-Blkr*	25
Kin Shop	*6a/11-12s*	25
Sevilla	*Charles/4s*	25
Malatesta	*Wash/Christopher*	25
Mercadito	*7a/Blkr-Grove*	24
NEW Wong	*Cornelia/Blkr-4s*	24
Numero 28	*Carmine/Bedford-Blkr*	24
Barbuto	*Wash/Jane-12s*	24
Yerba Buena	*Perry/Greenwich a*	24
Spasso	*Hudson/Perry*	24
Hudson Clearwater	*Hudson/Morton*	24
Spotted Pig	*11s/Greenwich s*	24
Meatball Shop	*Greenwich a/Perry*	24
Joseph Leonard	*Waverly/Grove*	24
One if by Land	*Barrow/7a-4s*	24
Tertulia	*6a/Wash*	24
Frankies	*Hudson/11s*	24
Antica Venezia	*West/10s*	24
Gobo	*6a/8s-Waverly*	24
Commerce	*Commerce/Barrow*	24
Market Table	*Carmine/Bedford*	24
Crispo	*14s/7-8a*	24
Yama	*Carmine/Bedford-Blkr*	24
NEW Mas (La Grillade)	*7a/Bedford-Leroy*	24
Bistro de la Gare	*Hudson/Jane*	24
Westville	*10s/Blkr-4s*	23
El Faro	*Greenwich s/Horatio-Jane*	23
Joe's Pizza	*Carmine/Blkr-6a*	23
Mexicana Mama	*Hudson/Charles-10s*	23
Palma	*Cornelia/Blkr-4s*	23
Blossom	*Carmine/Bedford-Blkr*	23
Flex Mussels	*13s/6-7s*	23
Las Ramblas	*4s/Cornelia-Jones*	23
Spunto	*Carmine/7a*	23
Bobo	*10s/7a*	23
Extra Virgin	*4s/Perry*	23
Tartine	*11s/4s*	23
Risotteria	*Blkr/Morton*	23
Mémé	*Hudson/Bank*	23
Morandi	*Waverly/Charles*	23
Place	*4s/Bank-12s*	23
Pepe	*Hudson/Perry-11s*	23
Snack	*Bedford/Morton*	23
Fish	*Blkr/Jones*	23
John's Pizzeria	*Blkr/6-7a*	23
Home	*Cornelia/Blkr-4s*	23
Fatty 'Cue	*Carmine/Bedford-Blkr*	23
SushiSamba	*7a/Barrow*	23

Cafe Asean	10s/Greenwich-6a	23
Ofrenda	7a/Christopher-10s	23
Hummus Pl.	7a/Barrow-Blkr	23
August	Blkr/Charles-10s	23
Corner Bistro	4s/Jane	23
Moustache	Bedford/Grove	23
Fedora	4s/Charles-10s	23
Empellón	4s/10s	23
Do Hwa	Carmine/Bedford	22
Betel	Grove/Blkr-7a	22
Corsino	Hudson/Horatio	22
Jeffrey's Grocery	Waverly/Christopher	22
A Salt & Battery	Greenwich a/12-3s	22
Centro Vinoteca	7a/Barrow	22
Móle	Jane/Hudson	22
Waverly Inn	Bank/Waverly	22
NEW Whitehall	Greenwich a/10s	22
Cafe Cluny	12s/4s	22
Havana Alma	Christopher/Bedford-Blkr	22
Dos Toros	Carmine/Blkr-6a	22
Bell Book/Candle	10s/Greenwich a-Waverly	22
Sant Ambroeus	4s/Perry	22
Baoguette	Christopher/Bedford	22
Café Henri	Bedford/Downing	22
Cafe Gitane	Jane/Wash-West	22
Noodle Bar	Carmine/Bedford-Blkr	22
Surya	Blkr/Grove-7a	21
Darby	14s/7-8a	21
Oaxaca	Greenwich a/Charles-Perry	21
Gottino	Greenwich a/Charles-Perry	21
Marinella	Carmine/Bedford	21
Tratt. Pesce	Blkr/6-7a	21
Ayza Wine	7a/Carmine	21
sNice	8a/Horatio-Jane	21
Good	Greenwich a/Bank-12s	21
Fatty Crab	Hudson/Gansevoort-Horatio	21
Grand Sichuan	7a/Carmine-Leroy	21
Five Guys	Blkr/Barrow	21
Cafe Español	Carmine/Bedford-7a	21
Smorgas Chef	12s/4s	20
Agave	7a/Charles-10s	20
Philip Marie	Hudson/11s	20
Cafe Loup	13s/6-7a	20
A.O.C.	Blkr/Grove	20
Two Boots	11s/7a	20
Cornelia St. Cafe	Cornelia/Blkr-4s	20
Petite Abeille	Hudson/Barrow	20
Lyon	Greenwich a/13s	19
NEW Bigoli	13s/6-7a	19
Cowgirl	Hudson/10s	17
NEW Goodwin	Hudson/Leroy-Morton	-

Bronx

CITY ISLAND

Sammy's Shrimp Box	City Is/Horton	24
Artie's	City Is/Ditmars	24
Crab Shanty	City Is/Tier	23
City Is. Lobster	Bridge/City Is	23
Portofino	City Is/Cross	23
Sea Shore	City Is/Cross	22
Black Whale	City Is/Hawkins	22
Sammy's Fishbox	City Is/Rochelle	22
Lobster Box	City Is/Belden-Rochelle	20

FORDHAM

Roberto	Crescent/Hughes	26
Tra Di Noi	187s/Belmont-Hughes	24
Zero Otto	Arthur/186s	24
Dominick's	Arthur/Crescent-187s	24
Enzo's	Arthur/Crescent-186s	24
Mario's	Arthur/184-186s	23
Pasquale's	Arthur/Crescent	22
Ann & Tony's	Arthur/187-188s	22
Umberto's	Arthur/186s	22

KINGSBRIDGE

| El Malecon | Bway/231-233s | 22 |
| Piper's Kilt | 231s/Albany Crescent | 22 |

MORRIS PARK

Patricia's	Morris Pk/Haight-Lurting	25
Enzo's	Williamsbridge/Neill	24
F & J Pine	Bronxdale/Matthews-Muliner	23

MOTT HAVEN

| Pio Pio | Cypress/138-139s | 23 |

PELHAM GARDENS

| Fratelli | Eastchester/Mace | 21 |

RIVERDALE

| Jake's | Bway/242s | 24 |
| Siam Sq. | Kappock/Henry | 24 |

LOCATIONS

Beccofino | *Mosholu/Fieldston-Spencer* 23

Liebman's Deli | *235s/Johnson* 22

Madison's | *Riverdale/259s* 20

THROGS NECK

Tosca Café | *Tremont/Miles-Sampson* 23

WESTCHESTER HEIGHTS

New Hawaii Sea | *Williamsbridge/Raymond-Silver* 24

YANKEE STADIUM

NYY Steak | *161s/River* 23

Brooklyn

BAY RIDGE

Tanoreen | *3a/76s* 27

Eliá | *3a/86-87s* 26

Tuscany Grill | *3a/86-87s* 26

Areo | *3a/84-85s* 25

Chadwick's | *3a/89s* 24

Schnitzel Haus | *5a/74s* 24

Burger Bistro | *3a/72s* 24

Fushimi | *4a/93-94s* 23

Embers | *3a/95-96s* 23

Pearl Room | *3a/82s* 23

101 | *4a/101s* 22

Arirang Hibachi | *4a/88-89s* 22

Cebu | *3a/88s* 21

Vesuvio | *3a/73s* 21

Five Guys | *5a/85-86s* 21

Greenhouse | *3a/77-78s* 21

BEDFORD-STUYVESANT

Saraghina | *Halsey/Lewis* 27

Sud Vino & Cucina | *Bedford/Lex* 26

Do or Dine | *Bedford/Lex-Quincy* 25

Peaches | *multi.* 24

BENSONHURST

L&B Spumoni | *86s/10-11s* 25

Nyonya | *86s/23-24a* 23

Tenzan | *18a/71s* 21

BOERUM HILL

Saul | *Smith/Bergen-Dean* 27

Ki Sushi | *Smith/Dean-Pacific* 25

Mile End | *Hoyt/Atlantic-Pacific* 25

Rucola | *Dean/Bond* 25

NEW Arthur on Smith | *Smith/Degraw-Sackett* 22

Lunetta | *Smith/Dean-Pacific* 22

Bacchus | *Atlantic/Bond-Nevins* 22

Nicky's | *Atlantic/Hoyt-Smith* 22

Hanco's | *Bergen/Hoyt-Smith* 20

BOROUGH PARK

Nyonya | *8a/53-54s* 23

BRIGHTON BEACH

Tatiana | *Brighton 6s/Brightwater* 21

BROOKLYN HEIGHTS

Colonie | *Atlantic/Clinton-Henry* 26

Henry's End | *Henry/Cranberry-Middagh* 25

Noodle Pudding | *Henry/Cranberry-Middagh* 25

Queen | *Court/Livingston-Schermerhorn* 25

Jack Horse | *Hicks/Cranberry* 24

Teresa's | *Montague/Hicks* 21

Five Guys | *Montague/Clinton-Henry* 21

ChipShop | *Atlantic/Clinton-Henry* 21

Hanco's | *Montague/Clinton-Henry* 20

Baluchi's | *Henry/Cranberry-Middagh* 20

BUSHWICK

Momo Sushi Shack | *Bogart/Moore* 26

Roberta's | *Moore/Bogart* 26

NEW Blanca | *Moore/Bogart* -

CARROLL GARDENS

Grocery | *Smith/Sackett-Union* 28

Lucali | *Henry/Carroll-1pl* 27

NEW Battersby | *Smith/Degraw-Sackett* 27

Buttermilk | *Court/Huntington* 25

Fragole | *Court/Carroll-1pl* 25

South Brooklyn Pizza | *Court/4pl-Lucquer* 24

Frankies | *Court/4pl-Luquer* 24

Prime Meat | *Court/Luquer* 24

Seersucker | *Smith/Carroll-President* 23

Cubana Café | *Smith/Degraw-Sackett* 23

Momofuku Milk Bar | *Smith/2pl* 22

Calexico | *Union/Columbia-Hicks* 22

Marco Polo | *Court/Union* 22

Zaytoons | *Smith/Sackett* 21

Alma | *Columbia/Degraw* `21`
NEW Dassara | `-`
   Smith/Degraw-Sackett

CLINTON HILL

Locanda Vini | `26`
   Gates/Cambridge-Grand
NEW Speedy Romeo | `24`
   Classon/Greene
Maggie Brown | `23`
   Myrtle/Wash-Waverly

COBBLE HILL

Chocolate Room | `25`
   Court/Butler-Douglass
Hibino | *Henry/Pacific* `25`
Bocca Lupo | *Henry/Warren* `24`
Joya | *Court/Warren-Wyckoff* `23`
Char No. 4 | `23`
   Smith/Baltic-Warren
Wild Ginger | `23`
   Smith/Dean-Pacific
Awash | *Court/Baltic-Kane* `23`
Henry Public | `22`
   Henry/Atlantic-Pacific
Coco Roco | *Smith/Bergen-Dean* `21`
Oaxaca | `21`
   Smith/Degraw-Douglass
Cafe Luluc | *Smith/Baltic* `21`
Lemongrass | `20`
   Court/Dean-Pacific
NEW La Vara | `-`
   Clinton/Verandah-Warren

CONEY ISLAND

Totonno Pizza | *Neptune/15-16s* `25`
Grimaldi's | *Surf/Stillwell* `24`
Gargiulo's | *15s/Mermaid-Surf* `24`

DITMAS PARK

Mimi's Hummus | `26`
   Cortelyou/Westmin
NEW Am Thai Bistro | `24`
   Church/10-11s
Farm/Adderley | `24`
   Cortelyou/Stratford-Westmin
Purple Yam | `22`
   Cortelyou/Argyle-Rugby

DOWNTOWN BROOKLYN

Brooklyn Fare | `27`
   Schermerhorn/Hoyt
Shake Shack | *Fulton/Adams* `22`
Five Guys | `21`
   Metrotech/Bridge-Lawrence
Junior's | *Flatbush/DeKalb* `20`

DUMBO

River Café | *Water/* `26`
   Furman-Old Fulton
Grimaldi's | *Front/Old Fulton* `24`
Rice | *Wash/Front-York* `22`
Bark Hot Dogs | *Pier 6/Main* `22`
Bubby's | *Main/Plymouth-Water* `20`
NEW Governor | `-`
   Main/Plymouth-Water
NEW Gran Electrica | *Front/* `-`
   Old Fulton

DYKER HEIGHTS

Tommaso | *86s/Bay 8s-15a* `24`

FORT GREENE

Roman's | `26`
   DeKalb/Clermont-Vanderbilt
Abistro | *DeKalb/Vanderbilt* `24`
Madiba | *DeKalb/Carlton* `24`
Caffe e Vino | `23`
   Dekalb/Ashland-St Felix
Luz | `23`
   Vanderbilt/Myrtle-Willoughby
Café Habana/Outpost | `23`
   Fulton/Portland
No. 7 | `23`
   Greene/Cumberland-Fulton
Smoke Joint | *Elliott/Lafayatte* `23`
Walter Foods | `22`
   Dekalb/Cumberland
Stonehome | `22`
   Lafayette/Portaland
67 Burger | *Lafayette/Fulton* `22`
Olea | *Lafayette/Adelphi* `22`
Pequena | *Portland/Lafayette* `22`
Chez Oskar | *DeKalb/Adelphi* `21`
Zaytoons | *Myrtle/Hall-Wash* `21`
Gen. Greene | *DeKalb/Clermont* `20`

GOWANUS

NEW Littleneck | `24`
   3a/Carroll-President
Monte's | *Carroll/Nevins-3a* `22`

GRAVESEND

Sahara | *Coney Is/Aves T-U* `23`
Fiorentino's | *Ave U/* `22`
   McDonald-West

GREENPOINT

Five Leaves | `26`
   Bedford/Lorimer-Manhattan
Paulie Gee's | `26`
   Greenpoint/Franklin-West
Lomzynianka | `24`
   Manhattan/Nassau-Norman

LOCATIONS

No. 7 | *Manhattan/Java-Kent* | 23

Calexico | *Manhattan/Bedford* | 22

KENSINGTON

NEW Am Thai Bistro |
McDonald/Albermale-Caton | 24

MIDWOOD

Di Fara | *Ave J/15s* | 27

Taci's Beyti | *Coney Is/Ave P-Kings* | 26

MILL BASIN

Mill Basin | *Ave T/59s* | 23

La Villa Pizzeria | *Ave U/66-67s* | 23

PARK SLOPE

Al Di La | *5a/Carroll* | 27

Rose Water | *Union/6a* | 26

Juventino | *5a/5-6s* | 26

Blue Ribbon | *5a/1s-Garfield* | 25

Chocolate Room |
5a/Propsect-St Marks | 25

Conviv. Osteria | *5a/
Bergen-St Marks* | 25

Bogota | *5a/Lincoln-St Johns* | 25

Applewood | *11s/7-8a* | 25

NEW Talde | *7a/11s* | 25

Stone Park | *5a/3s* | 24

South Brooklyn Pizza | *multi.* | 24

Moim | *Garfield/7-8a* | 24

Song | *5a/1-2s* | 24

Burger Bistro | *5a/Berkeley-Lincoln* | 24

Brooklyn Fish |
5a/Degraw-Douglass | 23

Sidecar | *5a/15-16s* | 23

Fonda | *7a/14-15s* | 23

BareBurger | *7a/1s* | 23

Bonnie's Grill | *5A/1s-Garfield* | 23

Scalino | *7a/10s* | 23

Scottadito | *Union/6-7a* | 23

Zuzu Ramen | *4a/Degraw* | 23

La Villa Pizzeria | *5a/1s-Garfield* | 23

Cubana Café | *6a/St Marks* | 23

12th St. B&G | *8a/12s* | 22

Miriam | *5a/Prospect* | 22

67 Burger | *Flatbush/Bergen-6a* | 22

Fornino | *5a/Carroll-Garfield* | 22

Bark Hot Dogs |
Bergen/5a-Flatbush | 22

Zito's | *multi.* | 22

Palo Santo | *Union/4-5a* | 22

Anthony's | *7a/14-15s* | 22

Coco Roco | *5a/6-7s* | 21

Oaxaca | *4a/Carroll/President* | 21

Sweet Melissa | *7a/1-2s* | 21

SottoVoce | *7a/4s* | 21

Benchmark | *2s/4-5a* | 21

sNice | *5a/2-3s* | 21

Five Guys | *7a/6-7s* | 21

ChipShop | *5a/6-7s* | 21

Flatbush Farm |
St Marks/Flatbush | 21

Spice | *7a/Berkeley-Lincoln* | 21

Thistle Hill | *7a/15s* | 21

Hanco's | *7a/10s* | 20

Baluchi's | *5a/2-3s* | 20

Okeanos | *7a/8s* | 20

A.O.C. | *5a/Garfield* | 20

Two Boots | *2s/7-8a* | 20

Cafe Steinhof | *7a/14s* | 19

PROSPECT HEIGHTS

NEW Bar Corvo |
Wash/Lincoln-St John | 28

NEW Pete Zaaz |
Classon/Sterling-St John | 27

Franny's | *Flatbush/
Prospect-St Marks* | 25

James | *Carlton/St Marks* | 25

Taro Sushi | *Flatbush/St Marks* | 24

NEW 606 R&D |
Vanderbilt/Prospect-St Marks | 24

Amorina | *Vanderbilt/Prospect* | 23

Vanderbilt | *Vanderbilt/Bergen* | 22

Tom's | *Wash/Sterling* | 22

Pequena | *Vanderbilt/Bergen* | 22

Zaytoons | *Vanderbilt/St Marks* | 21

RED HOOK

Red Hook Lobster | *Van Brunt/
Verona-Visitation* | 26

Good Fork | *Van Brunt/
Coffey-Van Dyke* | 25

Defonte's | *Columbia/Luquer* | 24

NEW Pok Pok Ny |
Columbia/Degraw-Kane | 22

Fairway Cafe | *Van Brunt/Reed* | 19

NEW Brooklyn Crab |
Reed/Conover-Van Brunt | -

SHEEPSHEAD BAY

Roll-n-Roaster |
Emmons/Nostrand-29s | 23

Jordan's Lobster |
Harkness/Plumb 2-3s | 22

Brennan | *Nostrand/Ave U* | 22

Rasputin | *Coney Island/Ave X* | 18

SUNSET PARK

Pacificana | *55s/8a* | 24

VINEGAR HILL

Vinegar Hill Hse. | *Hudson/Front-Water* — 25

WILLIAMSBURG

NEW Gwynnett St. | *Graham/Ainslie-Devoe* — 28

Smorgasburg | *E River/6-7s* — 28

Peter Luger | *Bway/Driggs* — 27

St. Anselm | *Metro/Havemeyer* — 27

Traif | *S 4s/Havemeyer-Roebling* — 27

Fette Sau | *Metro/Havemeyer-Roebling* — 26

Rye | *S 1s/Havemeyer-Roebling* — 26

Dressler | *Bway/Bedford-Driggs* — 26

Zenkichi | *N 6s/Wythe* — 26

Caracas | *Grand/Havemeyer-Roebling* — 25

La Superior | *Berry/S 2-3s* — 25

Diner | *Bway/Berry* — 25

Marlow/Sons | *Bway/Berry-Whythe* — 25

Betto | *8s/Bedford/Berry* — 25

Pies-n-Thighs | *4s/Driggs* — 25

Best Pizza | *Havemeyer/7-8s* — 24

Meatball Shop | *Bedford/7-8s* — 24

one or eight | *2s/Kent-Wythe* — 24

Egg | *5s/Bedford-Berry* — 24

Miranda | *Berry/N 9s* — 24

Mable's Smokehouse & Banquet Hall | *11s/Berry-Wythe* — 24

Ristorante/Settepani | *Lorimer/Conselyea-Skillman* — 24

DuMont | *multi.* — 24

NEW Allswell | *Bedford/10s* — 24

Fushimi | *Driggs/10-11s* — 23

Peter's 1969 | *Bedford/7-8s* — 23

Cafe Mogador | *Wythe/7-8s* — 23

Forcella | *Lorimer/Grand-Powers* — 23

Aurora | *Grand/Wythe* — 23

Crif Dogs | *Driggs/7s* — 23

La Piazzetta | *Graham/Frost-Richardson* — 23

Mesa Coyoacan | *Graham/Conselyea-Skillman* — 23

La Esquina | *Wythe/Metro-3s* — 23

Sea | *N 6s/Berry* — 23

Le Comptoir | *Grand/Driggs-Roebling* — 23

Wild Ginger | *Bedford/5-6s* — 23

Chai Home Kitchen | *6s/Berry* — 23

Bamonte's | *Withers/Lorimer-Union* — 23

Momofuku Milk Bar | *Matro/Havemeyer-Marcy* — 22

Walter Foods | *Grand/Roebling* — 22

Móle | *Kent/4s* — 22

Fornino | *Bedford/6-7s* — 22

Isa | *Wythe/S 2s* — 22

Vanessa's Dumpling | *Bedford/1-2s* — 22

NEW Bellwether | *Union/Richardson* — –

NEW Blue Collar | *Havemeyer/2-3s* — –

NEW Brooklyn Seoul | *Metro/Graham-Humboldt* — –

NEW Extra Fancy | *Metro/Roebling* — –

NEW Parish Hall | *3a/Berry-Wythe* — –

NEW Reynard | *Wythe/12s* — –

Queens

ASTORIA

Tratt. L'incontro | *31s/Ditmars* — 27

Taverna Kyclades | *Ditmars/33-35s* — 27

Il Bambino | *31a/34-35s* — 27

Vesta | *30a/21s* — 26

Basil Brick Oven Pizza | *Astoria/27-29s* — 26

Piccola Venezia | *28a/42s* — 25

NEW Butcher Bar | *30a/37-38s* — 25

Watawa | *Ditmars/33-35s* — 25

Seva Indian Cuisine | *34s/30a* — 25

Bahari Estiatorio | *Bway/31-32s* — 25

Ponticello | *Bway/46-47s* — 25

Christos | *23a/41s* — 25

Malagueta | *36a/28s* — 24

Thai Pavilion | *multi.* — 24

Arepas Café | *36a/34s* — 24

Sanford's | *Bway/30-31s* — 24

Agnanti | *Ditmars/19s* — 24

Aegean Cove | *Steinway/20a* — 24

Loukoumi Taverna | *Ditmars/45-46s* — 24

Queens Kickshaw | *Bway/41-Steinway* — 24

Mundo | *Bway/32s* — 23

Ovelia | *30a/34s* — 23

Pachanga Patterson | *31a/33-34s* — 23

Stamatis | *23a/29-31s* — 23

Elias Corner | *31s/24a* — 23

BareBurger | *multi.* — 23

Telly's Taverna | *23a/28-29s* — 23

Rizzo's Pizza | *Steinway/30-31a* — 23

Mojave | *31s/Ditmars-23a* — 23

LOCATIONS

Sugar Freak | *30a/36-37s* 22

Brick Cafe | *33s/31a* 22

5 Napkin Burger | *36s/35a* 22

Astor Room | *36s/35-36a* 22

Locale | *34a/33s* 21

MexiBBQ | *30a/37-38s* 21

Cávo | *31a/42-43s* 21

Omonia | *Bway/33s* 20

BAYSIDE

Erawan | *Bell/42-43a* 24

Press 195 | *Bell/40-41a* 24

Uncle Jack's | *Bell/40a* 24

BareBurger | *Bell/42-43s* 23

Valentino's/Green | *Cross
Is/Clear-Utopia* 22

BonChon Chicken |
Bell/45dr-45r 22

Donovan's | *41a/Bell* 21

Ben's Kosher | *26a/Bell* 20

Jackson Hole | *Bell/35a* 19

Bourbon St. Café | *Bell/40-41a* 19

CORONA

Leo's Latticini/Corona |
104s/46a 26

Tortilleria Nixtamal |
47a/104-108s 26

Park Side | *Corona/51a-108s* 25

DOUGLASTON

Grimaldi's |
61a/Douglaston-244s 24

Fairway Cafe | *61a//LI Expy.* 19

ELMHURST

Pho Bang | *Bway/Elmhurst* 23

Ping's Sea. | *Queens/Goldsmith* 21

FLUSHING

Leo's Latticini/Corona |
126s/Roosevelt 26

Xi'an | *Main/41r* 24

Spicy & Tasty |
Prince/Roosevelt-39a 24

Sik Gaek | *Crocheron/162s* 24

Pho Bang | *Kissena/Main* 23

Szechuan Gourmet |
37a/Main-Prince 23

Blue Smoke | *126s/Roosevelt* 23

Joe's Shanghai |
37a/Main-Union 22

Sentosa | *Prince/Roosevelt-39a* 22

Shake Shack | *126s/Roosevelt* 22

Kum Gang San |
Northern/Bowne-Union 22

NEW Biang | *Main/41a-41r* 21

East Manor |
Kissena/Kalmia-Lanburnum 21

Kyochon | *Northern/156-157s* 21

East Buffet |
Main/Franklin-Maple 19

FOREST HILLS

Danny Brown | *Metro/71dr* 26

Alberto | *Metro/69-70a* 24

Nick's | *Ascan/Austin-Burns* 24

BareBurger | *Austin/71r-72a* 23

La Vigna | *Metro/70a* 23

Cabana | *70r/Austin-Queens* 23

Dee's | *Metro/74a* 22

Agora Taverna | *Austin/71a* 22

Bann Thai |
Austin/69r-Yellowstone 20

Baluchi's | *Queens/76a-76r* 20

FRESH MEADOWS

King Yum | *Union/181s* 21

GLENDALE

Zum Stammtisch |
Myrtle/69pl-70s 24

Shiro of Japan | *Cooper/80s* 23

HOWARD BEACH

La Villa Pizzeria | *153a/82s* 23

JACKSON HEIGHTS

Pio Pio | *Northern/84-85s* 23

Zabb Elee | *Roosevelt/72s* 22

Afghan Kebab | *37a/74-75s* 21

Jackson Diner |
74s/Roosevelt-37a 21

Jackson Hole | *Astoria/70s* 19

JAMAICA

Bobby Van's | *JFK/Amer. Air* 23

Papaya King | *LaGuardia Rd* 20

LITTLE NECK

La Baraka | *Northern/Little Neck* 24

LONG ISLAND CITY

Shi | *Ctr./Vernon* 25

Tournesol | *Vernon/50-51a* 24

Manducatis | *multi.* 23

Riverview | *49a/Ctr.* 23

Manetta's | *Jackson/49a* 23

Corner Bistro | *Vernon/47r* 23

Testaccio | *Vernon/47r* 22

Bella Via | *Vernon/48a* 22

Water's Edge | *E River/44dr* 22

Café Henri | *50a/Jackson-Vernon* `22`

NEW Casa Enrique | *49a/5s-Vernon* `-`

MIDDLE VILLAGE

Uvarara | *Metro/79-80s* `25`

OZONE PARK

Don Peppe | *Lefferts/135-149a* `26`

REGO PARK

London Lennie | *Woodhaven/Fleet-Penelope* `24`

Ben's Best | *Queens/63r-64a* `23`

Pio Pio | *Woodhaven/62r* `23`

Barosa | *Woodhaven/62r* `22`

Grand Sichuan | *Queens/66r-67a* `21`

SUNNYSIDE

Salt & Fat | *Queens/41-42s* `26`

Turkish Grill | *Queens/42s* `24`

Sidetracks | *Queens/45s* `21`

WOODSIDE

Sripraphai | *39a/64-65s* `27`

Ayada | *Woodside/77-78s* `26`

Sik Gaek | *Roosevelt/50s* `24`

Mamajuana | *56s/Bway-Northern* `21`

Donovan's | *Roosevelt/58s* `21`

Staten Island

BLOOMFIELD

Lorenzo's | *South/Lois* `22`

CASTLETON CORNERS

Joe & Pat's | *Victory/Manor* `24`

DONGAN HILLS

Tratt. Romana | *Hylan/Benton* `26`

Carol's | *Richmond/ Four Crnrs-Seaview* `25`

ELTINGVILLE

Nove | *Richmond/Amboy* `26`

China Chalet | *Amboy/Armstrong-Rich* `20`

GRANT CITY

Fushimi | *Richmond/Lincoln* `23`

GRASMERE

Bocelli | *Hylan/Old Town-Parkinson* `26`

GREAT KILLS

Arirang Hibachi | *Nelson/Locust* `22`

Marina Cafe | *Mansion/Hillside* `21`

MARINERS HARBOR

Real Madrid | *Forest/Union* `22`

NEW BRIGHTON

Nurnberger | *Castleton/Davis-Pelton* `23`

NEW SPRINGVILLE

East Pacific | *Richmond a/Richmond Hill* `22`

PORT RICHMOND

Denino | *Port Richmond/Hooker-Walker* `26`

ROSEBANK

Bayou | *Bay/Chestnut-St Mary* `23`

SHORE ACRES

Da Noi | *Fingerboard/Tompkins* `24`

ST. GEORGE

Beso | *Schuyley/Richmond* `24`

TOTTENVILLE

Angelina's | *Ellis/Arthur Kill* `24`

TRAVIS

Da Noi | *Victory/Service* `24`

LOCATIONS

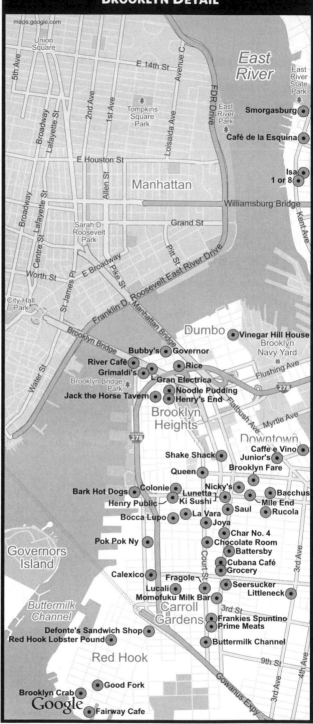

BROOKLYN DETAIL

maps.google.com

Union Square

5th Ave

2nd Ave

Lafayette St

Broadway

1st Ave

E 14th St

Avenue C

FDR Drive

East River

East River State Park

Smorgasburg

Tompkins Square Park

Café de la Esquina

E Houston St

Allen St

Manhattan

Isa
1 or 8

Kent Ave

Williamsburg Bridge

Broadway

Lafayette St

Centre St

Sarah D. Roosevelt Park

Grand St

Worth St

St James Pl

E Broadway

Pike St

Pitt St

Franklin D Roosevelt East River Drive

City Hall Park

Water St

Brooklyn Bridge

Franklin D. Roosevelt East River Drive

Manhattan Bridge

Dumbo

Vinegar Hill House

Brooklyn Navy Yard

Flushing Ave

278

Brooklyn Bridge Park

Bubby's   Governor

River Café   Rice

Grimaldi's   Gran Electrica

Jack the Horse Tavern   Noodle Pudding
Henry's End

Brooklyn Heights

Flatbush Ave

Myrtle Ave

278

Downtown

Caffe e Vino

Shake Shack   Junior's

Queen   Brooklyn Fare

Bark Hot Dogs   Colonie   Nicky's   Bacchus

Henry Public   Lunetta   Mile End
Ki Sushi   Saul   Rucola

Bocca Lupo   La Vara
Joya

Pok Pok Ny   Char No. 4
Chocolate Room
Battersby

Court St

Cubana Café
Grocery

Calexico   Fragole
Seersucker
Littleneck

Lucali   Momofuku Milk Bar

Governors Island

Carroll Gardens

3rd St

3rd Ave

Buttermilk Channel

Frankies Spuntino
Prime Meats

Defonte's Sandwich Shop
Red Hook Lobster Pound

Buttermilk Channel

9th St

Red Hook

Gowanus Expy

3rd Ave

4th Ave

Good Fork

Brooklyn Crab

Google   Fairway Cafe

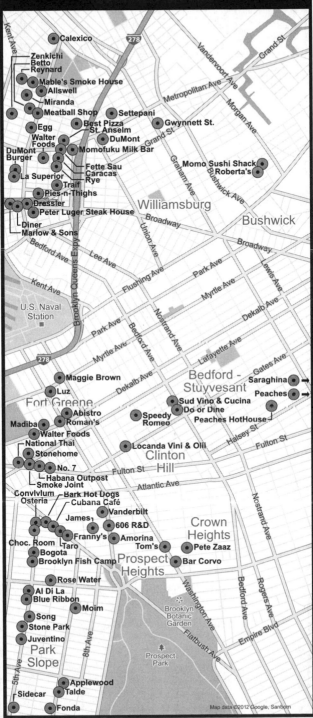

BROOKLYN DETAIL

Calexico

Zenkichi
Betto
Reynard
Mable's Smoke House
Allswell
Miranda
Meatball Shop
Settepani
Gwynnett St.
Egg
Best Pizza
St. Anselm
Walter
Foods
DuMont
Momofuku Milk Bar
DuMont
Burger
Momo Sushi Shack
Fette Sau
Roberta's
Caracas
La Superior
Rye
Traif
Pies-n-Thighs
Dressler
Peter Luger Steak House

Williamsburg

Bushwick

Diner
Marlow & Sons

U.S. Naval
Station

Maggie Brown
Luz
Bedford -
Stuyvesant
Saraghina
Peaches
Fort Greene
Sud Vino & Cucina
Abistro
Do or Dine
Madiba
Roman's
Speedy
Peaches HotHouse
Walter Foods
Romeo
National Thai
Stonehome
Locanda Vini & Olii
No. 7
Clinton
Hill
Habana Outpost
Smoke Joint
Fulton St
Atlantic Ave
Convivium
Bark Hot Dogs
Osteria
Cubana Café
James
Vanderbilt
Crown
Heights
Franny's
606 R&D
Choc. Room
Amorina
Taro
Tom's
Pete Zaaz
Bogota
Brooklyn Fish Camp
Prospect
Bar Corvo
Rose Water
Heights
Al Di La
Blue Ribbon
Brooklyn
Botanic
Moim
Garden
Song
Stone Park
Juventino
Park
Slope
Prospect
Park
Applewood
Talde
Sidecar
Fonda

Map data ©2012 Google, Sanborn

MAPS

MANHATTAN NEIGHBORHOODS

maps.google.com

Morningside Heights
Harlem
East Harlem
West 100s
East 100s
West 90s
East 90s
West 80s
Central Park
East 80s
Carl Schurz Park
West 70s
East 70s
Hudson River
West 60s
East 60s
West 50s
East 50s
East River
West 40s
East 40s
Bryant Park
Garment District
Murray Hill
Madison Square
Chelsea
Flatiron
Gramercy Park
Union Sq
Meatpacking
Greenwich Village
East Village
Tompkins Square Park
East River Park
West Village
Washington Square Park
NoHo
Hudson River Park
Hudson Square
SoHo
NoLita
Lower East Side
Little Italy
TriBeCa
Chinatown
Rutgers Park
North Park
City Hall
Hudson River
East River
Financial District
South Street Seaport
Battery Park

Google

Map data ©2012 Google

RESTAURANT
DIRECTORY

Abboccato *Italian*

22 | 20 | 21 | $56

W 50s | Blakely Hotel | 136 W. 55th St. (bet. 6th & 7th Aves.) |
212-265-4000 | www.abboccato.com

Besides "convenient" coordinates – near both "City Center and Carnegie
Hall" – this Midtown Italian "sleeper" follows through with "dependably
good" eats, "prompt" service and "intimate" environs; the $35 dinner
prix fixe is a "bargain" vis-à-vis the otherwise "higher-end" tabs.

☑ ABC Kitchen *American*

26 | 24 | 23 | $58

Flatiron | ABC Carpet & Home | 35 E. 18th St. (bet. B'way & Park Ave. S.) |
212-475-5829 | www.abckitchennyc.com

"Farm fresh" is the mantra at Jean-Georges Vongerichten's "killer"
Flatiron American in ABC Carpet putting forth "thoughtfully composed" "organic", "sustainable" dishes in white-on-white, "Nordic-
chic" digs; "hip, friendly" service adds to the "charming" vibe, though
the "tough-to-get reservations" are even tougher now that "Obama
has been here."

Abe & Arthur's *American*

22 | 23 | 21 | $66

Meatpacking | 409 W. 14th St. (bet. 9th Ave. & Washington St.) |
646-289-3930 | www.abeandarthursrestaurant.com

"Atmo is key" at this "total Meatpacking scene" where the "solid"
American surf 'n' turf takes a backseat to the "insanely loud", "Vegas"-
like goings-on; the staff is "gorgeous", the prices as "beefy" as the
steaks and the crowd's a mix of "Bravo *Housewives*", "*Jersey Shore* cast
members" and "B&T wannabes."

Abigael's *Eclectic/Kosher*

21 | 17 | 20 | $47

Garment District | 1407 Broadway (bet. 38th & 39th Sts.) |
212-575-1407 | www.abigaels.com

A menu spanning "short ribs to sushi" gives kosher cuisine an "upscale" gloss at this double-decker Garment District Eclectic overseen
by "creative" chef Jeff Nathan, "bland" atmospherics and spotty service" detract, but it remains a "staple" for observant folks.

Abistro *African*

24 | 20 | 21 | $33

Fort Greene | 250 DeKalb Ave. (Vanderbilt Ave.) | Brooklyn | 347-384-2972

"Heart and soul" abound at this "satisfying" Fort Greene cafe where
French-accented West African food – including a "worth-the-trip"
Senegalese fried chicken – is rendered with a "home-cooked" touch;
recently transplanted to bigger, "nicer" digs, it retains its "friendly"
mien, moderate tabs and "tasty" weekend brunch.

Aburiya Kinnosuke ● *Japanese*

25 | 20 | 22 | $55

E 40s | 213 E. 45th St. (bet. 2nd & 3rd Aves.) | 212-867-5454 |
www.aburiyakinnosuke.com

"Outstanding" robata-grilled dishes and "ethereal" homemade tofu
bring an "authentic" taste of "Tokyo" to Midtown at this "top-quality",
sushi-free izakaya; value-seekers tout the "bargain" lunch specials
since those "little dishes can add up" at suppertime.

NEW ABV ● *American*

▽ 20 | 20 | 21 | $31

E 90s | 1504 Lexington Ave. (97th St.) | 212-722-8959 | www.abvny.com

This "offbeat" new wine bar from the Earl's Beer & Cheese team plants
"hipster" seeds in north Carnegie Hill via "quirky" American eats ("foie

gras fluffernutter", anyone?); a "boutique" vino list, communal tables and industrial looks lead locals to welcome it to the neighborhood.

Acappella ☒ *Italian*   24 | 22 | 24 | $68

TriBeCa | 1 Hudson St. (Chambers St.) | 212-240-0163 | www.acappella-restaurant.com

Dining is "an event" at this "old-world" TriBeCa Northern Italian renowned for "excellent" food, "over-the-top" service and *Godfather* opulent" decor; "try not to faint when you get the check" or you'll miss out on the complimentary grappa.

A Casa Fox ☒ *Pan-Latin*   23 | 21 | 21 | $34

LES | 173 Orchard St. (Stanton St.) | 212-253-1900 | www.acasafox.com

What this "little" LES Pan-Latin joint lacks in legroom is made up for in "homey", "candlelit" ambiance and a "fab assortment" of tapas and clay pots; given the "friendly" hospitality, modest tabs and "cozy fireplace", it's sure to "warm your soul."

NEW Acme *American*   23 | 19 | 19 | $55

NoHo | 9 Great Jones St. (Lafayette St.) | 212-203-2121 | www.acmenyc.com

Longtime NoHo staple Acme Bar & Grill has undergone a name shortening and a total "revamp", starting with a "culinary resuscitation" by Danish star chef Mads Refslund, whose "sophisticated", "earthy" American menu is a "forager's dream"; approachable pricing, a "beautiful" deco-ish setting and a "fashionable" crowd make it arguably the 'it' arrival of the year.

Acqua *Italian/Pizza*   21 | 18 | 20 | $39

W 90s | 718 Amsterdam Ave. (95th St.) | 212-222-2752 | www.acquanyc.com

This "casual" UWS Italian "staple" keeps it simple and "satisfying" with a "dependable" outlay of "really good" brick-oven pizzas and "hearty" trattoria standards; "reasonable" prices, "friendly" service and convenience to Symphony Space make the "uninspired" decor easy to overlook.

☒ Adour ☒☒ *French*   27 | 27 | 27 | $115

E 50s | St. Regis Hotel | 2 E. 55th St. (bet. 5th & Madison Aves.) | 212-710-2277 | www.adour-stregis.com

Alain Ducasse earns an effusive "*merci*" from fans of his "adourable" Midtown French where "impeccable" cuisine and "redoubtable" wines are presented by "suave" servers in "opulent", David Rockwell–designed digs; since the tabs are geared toward "onepercenters", most people "save it for a special occasion" and say it should be better known.

Adrienne's Pizzabar ◐ *Pizza*   24 | 17 | 18 | $25

Financial District | 87 Pearl St. (bet. Coenties Slip & Hanover Sq.) | 212-248-3838 | www.adriennespizzabar.com

Brace yourself for "lunchtime madness" when "Wall Street suits" and "casual passersby" descend on this FiDi pizzeria for its "outstanding" thin-crust pies; "adequate" service and "nonexistent decor" are part of the package, making it best enjoyed at an alfresco seat on "picturesque Stone Street."

Aegean Cove *Greek*   24 | 20 | 23 | $39

Astoria | 20-01 Steinway St. (20th Ave.) | Queens | 718-274-9800
Although parked "in the middle of nowhere", this "hidden" Astoria
Greek rewards intrepid types with "top-notch" takes on "classic"
Hellenica and "eager-to-please" hospitality; pluses include moderate
prices, a "rooftop garden" and "easy parking" anytime.

Afghan Kebab House *Afghan*   21 | 15 | 19 | $26

E 70s | 1345 Second Ave. (bet. 70th & 71st Sts.) | 212-517-2776
W 50s | 764 Ninth Ave. (bet. 51st & 52nd Sts.) | 212-307-1612
Jackson Heights | 74-16 37th Ave. (bet. 74th & 75th Sts.) | Queens |
718-565-0471 | www.afghankebabhouse4.com
"Mouthwatering" kebabs get skewered at this "authentic" Afghan
trio hailed for "flavorful", "substantial" grub for "bargain-basement"
dough; "no-frills" service and "dark", "shabby" settings reminiscent of
a tour of duty are the downsides.

Agave *Southwestern*   20 | 19 | 19 | $36

W Village | 140 Seventh Ave. S. (bet. Charles & W. 10th Sts.) |
212-989-2100 | www.agaveny.com
Sure, the chow is "decent" enough, but this Village Southwesterner's
"young" fan base reports that it's the "killer margaritas" that "keep the
place buzzing"; though service skews "slow", time is on your side during the "all-you-can-drink" weekend brunch.

NEW **A.G. Kitchen** *Nuevo Latino*   - | - | - | M

W 70s | 269 Columbus Ave. (bet. 72nd & 73rd Sts.) | 212-873-9400 |
www.agkitchen.com
Chef Alex Garcia (Calle Ocho, Copacabana) lends his initials and
culinary derring-do to this casual new Upper Westsider fielding Nuevo
Latino comfort fare along with some north-of-the-border dishes; separate bar, lounge and dining areas draw spirited young folk who dig the
vibe and friendly price points.

Agnanti *Greek*   24 | 15 | 20 | $35

Astoria | 19-06 Ditmars Blvd. (19th St.) | Queens | 718-545-4554 |
www.agnantimeze.com
A "notch above the typical Astorian", this "tried-and-true" Hellenic
taverna rolls out "delicious", "reasonably priced" meals that conjure
up the "Greek isles"; since the decor is "forgettable", regulars request
seats on the "wonderful" patio facing Astoria Park and the East River.

Agora Taverna *Greek*   22 | 19 | 19 | $35

Forest Hills | 70-09 Austin St. (71st Ave.) | Queens | 718-793-7300 |
www.agorataverna.com
Forest Hills' limited dining scene gets a boost via this "welcome"
Greek yearling purveying "tasty" taverna standards, though "fresh fish
is the star of the show"; "helpful" service, "cheery" vibes and a "reasonable" price point are further incentives.

Z Ai Fiori *Italian*   26 | 25 | 26 | $89

Garment District | Setai Fifth Avenue Hotel | 400 Fifth Ave., 2nd fl.
(bet. 36th & 37th Sts.) | 212-613-8660 | www.aifiorinyc.com
This "heavenly" Garment District Italian in the Setai Fifth Avenue Hotel
showcases Michael White's "pitch-perfect", "Riviera-inspired" cooking,

especially its "ethereal pasta"; "polished" service, "top-notch" wines and a "soothing", "stylish" setting make for high prices, while ensuring a steady flow of "expense-account" and "special-occasion" traffic.

Aji Sushi *Japanese*

FOOD	DECOR	SERVICE	COST
21	17	20	$30

Murray Hill | 519 Third Ave. (bet. 34th & 35th Sts.) | 212-686-2055 | www.ajisushinyc.com

Maybe it's "just a standard sushi spot", but Murray Hill locals swear by this "reliable" Japanese for its "good variety" and "value" tabs; "swift delivery" seems the preferred way to go, given the "bland" atmosphere and just "adequate" service.

A.J. Maxwell's Steakhouse *Steak*

FOOD	DECOR	SERVICE	COST
23	21	23	$61

W 40s | 57 W. 48th St. (bet. 5th & 6th Aves.) | 212-262-6200 | www.ajmaxwells.com

"Big guys" attack "hefty" cuts of beef at this Rock Center chop shop where the "pricey" steaks and sides arrive in a storied setting that was once the "Forum of the Twelve Caesars"; cynics find the going pretty "typical", though the location makes it handy "pre-theater."

Akdeniz *Turkish*

FOOD	DECOR	SERVICE	COST
22	14	19	$31

W 40s | 19 W. 46th St. (bet. 5th & 6th Aves.) | 212-575-2307 | www.akdenizturkishusa.com

It's all about "value" at this Midtown Turk offering a "can't-be-beat" $25 dinner prix fixe that's a showstopper for theatergoers; the "tiny" room can be "claustrophobic" and the decor's "shabby", but the grub's "tasty" and the service "accommodating."

Aki *Japanese*

FOOD	DECOR	SERVICE	COST
25	16	23	$41

W Village | 181 W. Fourth St. (bet. Barrow & Jones Sts.) | 212-989-5440

"Not your regular sushi place", this "atypical" Villager plies a "creative" East-meets–West Indies "fusion" concept that "sounds crazy but actually works"; smooth service and "affordable" tabs make the "smaller-than-a-studio-apartment" dimensions more bearable.

A La Turka *Turkish*

FOOD	DECOR	SERVICE	COST
20	15	18	$37

E 70s | 1417 Second Ave. (74th St.) | 212-744-2424 | www.alaturkarestaurant.com

"Surprisingly good" Turkish food is yours at this "change-of-pace" Upper Eastsider where the prices are "affordable" and the noise level "manageable"; those who find "nothing exceptional" going on cite "drab" decor and "spotty" service.

Alberto *Italian*

FOOD	DECOR	SERVICE	COST
24	20	23	$42

Forest Hills | 98-31 Metropolitan Ave. (bet. 69th & 70th Aves.) | Queens | 718-268-7860 | www.albertorestaurant.com

Now in its 40th year, this "tried-and-true" Forest Hills Northern Italian has earned "institution" status thanks to an "excellent", "extensive" menu, "personable" service and a "warm" milieu; though a tad "pricey" for Queens, it compensates by "taking a special interest" in its clientele.

Al Bustan *Lebanese*

FOOD	DECOR	SERVICE	COST
21	20	20	$48

E 50s | 319 E. 53rd St. (bet. 1st & 2nd Aves.) | 212-759-5933 | www.albustanny.com

"Hidden" on an East Midtown side street, this upscale double-decker delivers "succulent" Lebanese classics in a "modern", chandeliered room; although the "big space" can feel "empty" at dinner, at least it's "comfortable" and you can "hear yourself speak."

Alcala *Spanish*

23 | 20 | 22 | $48

E 40s | 342 E. 46th St. (bet. 1st & 2nd Aves.) | 212-370-1866 | www.alcalarestaurant.com

"Basque country" comes to a residential block near the U.N. via this "*muy bueno*" Spaniard that's touted for its "excellent" tapas, "flavorful" large plates and "liquid-courage" sangria; "caring" service and an "attractive" setting embellish the "low-key" vibe, while a "romantic" back garden seals the deal.

Aldea *Mediterranean*

25 | 22 | 24 | $68

Flatiron | 31 W. 17th St. (bet. 5th & 6th Aves.) | 212-675-7223 | www.aldearestaurant.com

George Mendes' "astutely prepared" modern Med cooking focuses on Iberian Coast cuisine at this Flatiron "foodie destination"; the best seats are at the bar facing the "open kitchen", but wherever you land, count on a "sleek" setting, savvy service and serious tabs.

▨ Al Di La *Italian*

27 | 19 | 22 | $48

Park Slope | 248 Fifth Ave. (Carroll St.) | Brooklyn | 718-783-4565 | www.aldilatrattoria.com

Still "damn popular" after 15 years in business, this "delightful" Park Slope trattoria is touted for its "superlative" Venetian fare and "ridiculously reasonable" rates; since the "annoying" no-rez rule leads to "insane waits", regulars either opt for its "annex" wine bar, "go for lunch" or just "bring a Kindle" and get in line.

Alfama *Portuguese*

22 | 19 | 22 | $48

E 50s | 214 E. 52nd St. (bet. 2nd & 3rd Aves.) | 212-759-5552 | www.alfamanyc.com

With its midpriced "modern" spins on "classic" Portuguese food, this "friendly" East Midtowner is a "tasty" reminder that "there's more to Europe than France and Italy"; maybe the digs are a bit "stark", but most appreciate experiencing "Lisbon in the heart of NYC."

Al Forno Pizzeria *Pizza*

21 | 14 | 18 | $24

E 70s | 1484 Second Ave. (bet. 77th & 78th Sts.) | 212-249-5103 | www.alfornopizzeria77.com

"Neighborhood" Yorkville pizzeria churning out "quality" brick-oven pies on the "quick" for low dough; "typical" Italian pastas and salads are also on hand, but given "lots of kids" and little atmosphere, "home delivery" may be the way to go.

Alfredo of Rome *Italian*

21 | 20 | 21 | $50

W 40s | 4 W. 49th St. (bet. 5th & 6th Aves.) | 212-397-0100 | www.alfredos.com

"Tourists" are as much a fixture as the "delightful Al Hirshfeld drawings on the wall" at this Rock Center Italian where the "serviceable" chow is "basic" but "tasty"; seasonal proximity to the "Christmas tree" offsets prices that may seem "expensive for what you get."

Ali Baba *Turkish*

21 | 16 | 18 | $35

E 40s | 862 Second Ave. (46th St.) | 212-888-8622 | www.alibabasterrace.com

FOOD	DECOR	SERVICE	COST

(continued)

Ali Baba

Murray Hill | 212 E. 34th St. (bet. 2nd & 3rd Aves.) | 212-683-9206 |
www.alibabaturkishcuisine.com

Ottoman expats say these "convivial" Midtown Turks "taste like home",
then up the ante with "generous portions" at real-"value" tabs; propo-
nents praise Second Avenue's "lovely roofdeck", though the "neon sign",
"seedy" looks and "so-so service" are another story.

Alice's Tea Cup *Teahouse*

21 | 22 | 20 | $26

E 60s | 156 E. 64th St. (Lexington Ave.) | 212-486-9200
E 80s | 220 E. 81st St. (bet. 2nd & 3rd Aves.) | 212-734-4832
W 70s | 102 W. 73rd St. (bet. Amsterdam & Columbus Aves.) | 212-799-3006
www.alicesteacup.com

"Mother-daughter bonding" takes a "whimsical" turn at these "sweet
little" American tearooms where the "scrumptious" scones and "ther-
apeutic" teas highlight an otherwise "uneven" menu; "kitschy" furnishings (one part "Miss Havisham", one part "Timothy Leary") add
appeal, but "no reservations", "long waits" and "slow" service are
strictly "down the rabbit hole."

NEW Alison Eighteen *American*

23 | 22 | 21 | $70

Flatiron | 15 W. 18th St. (bet. 5th & 6th Aves.) | 212-366-1818 |
www.alisoneighteen.com

Fans of the defunct Alison on Dominick Street (1989–2002) "welcome
back" this Flatiron "reincarnation" that rolls out "excellent" French-
accented Americana prepared by the original chef; "steep" tabs and a
"serene", "conversation-friendly" mien play to a "grown-up" crowd
who see "lots of potential" here.

Alloro *Italian*

24 | 18 | 24 | $57

E 70s | 307 E. 77th St. (bet. 1st & 2nd Aves.) | 212-535-2866 |
www.alloronyc.com

"Original" is the consensus on this "small" UES Italian "sleeper" where
"imaginative", "ambitious" dishes from a "skilled" chef are conveyed
by an "eager-to-please" crew; loyalists are so grateful it's "not just another red-sauce joint" that they overlook the "bland" setting.

NEW Allswell ● *American*

∇ 24 | 19 | 21 | $42

Williamsburg | 124 Bedford Ave. (N. 10th St.) | Brooklyn |
347-799-2743 | www.allswellnyc.tumblr.com

"Just like the name says", this new Williamsburg pub fields a
"tasty" American menu that showcases "local ingredients" and
"changes daily"; a "small", old-timey setting equipped with a communal table makes its "hipster" following feel at home, despite a few
gripes about the pricing.

Alma *Mexican*

21 | 22 | 19 | $36

Carroll Gardens | 187 Columbia St., 2nd fl. (Degraw St.) | Brooklyn |
718-643-5400 | www.almarestaurant.com

"Mind-altering" Manhattan skyline views from a "year-round" rooftop
are the bait at this "youthful" Carroll Gardens Mexican where the
chow is as "solid" as the margaritas are "strong"; an "off-the-beaten-
path" address "not close to public transportation" makes "walking
shoes" the footwear of choice.

	FOOD	DECOR	SERVICE	COST

NEW Almayass ● *Armenian/Lebanese*   ∇ 25 | 24 | 23 | $33

Flatiron | 24 E. 21st St. (bet. B'way & Park Ave. S.) | 212-473-3100 |
www.almayassnyc.com

A Lebanese-Armenian chain founded in Beirut makes its U.S. debut at this easily affordable new Flatiron venture, showcasing "tasty" cuisine focusing on shareable meze, with plenty of vegetarian options; the banquetlike setting includes a "beautiful" dining room along with sizable bar and lounge areas.

Almond *French*   21 | 20 | 20 | $45

Flatiron | 12 E. 22nd St. (bet. B'way & Park Ave. S.) | 212-228-7557 |
www.almondnyc.com

"Comforting" French fare meets "rustic charm" at this "buzzing" Flatiron bistro, a Bridgehampton spin-off where the tabs are "reasonable" and the crowd "young"; it's an "easy choice" for "big groups", so expect "noisy" decibels and a "happening", *Sex and the City*-esque brunch.

Alpha Fusion *Asian*   22 | 18 | 20 | $30

Garment District | 365 W. 34th St. (bet. 8th & 9th Aves.) |
212-279-8887 | www.alpha34.com

Fielding "quick", "tasty" renditions of sushi, pad Thai and more for a "great price", this "unassuming" Garment District Asian is a "safe bet" provided you don't mind the ultra-"simple" setting; proximity to "MSG" is a further incentive.

Alta *Mediterranean*   26 | 23 | 21 | $52

G Village | 64 W. 10th St. (bet. 5th & 6th Aves.) | 212-505-7777 |
www.altarestaurant.com

"Sharing" is the thing at this "rustic" bi-level Villager known for its "succulent" Med small plates, "incredible Brussels sprouts" and "solve-all-your-problems" sangria; though a "substantial bill" is to be expected, what-the-hell types order the "whole shebang" for $480.

NEW Amali *Mediterranean*   ∇ 21 | 20 | 21 | $58

E 60s | 115 E. 60th St. (Park Ave.) | 212-339-8363 | www.amalinyc.com

This "upscale" Bloomie's-area newcomer from the Periyali team gives Mediterranean cooking a locavore-friendly, "farm-fresh" gloss; early adapters like the "sophisticated" mood and sleek furnishings, the "noise level" and "pricey" tariffs not so much.

Amaranth *Mediterranean*   22 | 19 | 19 | $63

E 60s | 21 E. 62nd St. (bet. 5th & Madison Aves.) | 212-980-6700 |
www.amaranthrestaurant.com

Aka "air-kissing central", this "buzzy" Madison Avenue–area Med is the kind of place where the "better-than-average" food is incidental to the "social scene"; service is "diffident" if you've got a "European title", "inattentive" if you don't, but the "expensive" pricing extends to all.

Amarone ● *Italian*   21 | 16 | 21 | $43

W 40s | 686 Ninth Ave. (bet. 47th & 48th Sts.) | 212-245-6060 |
www.amaroneristorantenyc.com

"Unassuming" is the word on this "reliable" Hell's Kitchen trattoria that supplies "reasonably priced" Italian standards in a setting that's "pleasant" though "hardly exciting"; "convenience to the theater" is its trump card, and "timely" staffers "get you in and out" on time.

	FOOD	DECOR	SERVICE	COST

Amazing 66 *Chinese*
22 | 14 | 17 | $24

Chinatown | 66 Mott St. (bet. Bayard & Canal Sts.) | 212-334-0099
"Cheap and filling" says it all about this "solid" C-town Cantonese plying an encyclopedic menu of "familiar" items in "old"-looking digs; the
"pushy" service comes with language-barrier issues, but no one no-
tices when its "kick-ass lunch specials" are being served.

Amber ● *Asian*
20 | 19 | 19 | $36

E 80s | 1406 Third Ave. (80th St.) | 212-249-5020 |
www.amberuppereast.com
G Village | 432 Sixth Ave. (bet. 9th & 10th Sts.) | 212-477-5880 |
www.ambernyc.com
Murray Hill | 381 Third Ave. (bet. 27th & 28th Sts.) | 212-686-6388 |
www.ambergramercy.com
W 70s | 221 Columbus Ave. (70th St.) | 212-799-8100 |
www.amberwestside.com
This "up-tempo" Pan-Asian mini-chain provides "right-on-the-money"
sushi and "consistent" entrees in "dark", "trying-to-be-trendy" settings (with "Buddha watching over you"); "noisy" decibels and "party"
atmospherics are part of the experience.

NEW The Americano *French*
▽ 22 | 23 | 22 | $45

Chelsea | Americano Hotel | 518 W. 27th St. (bet. 10th & 11th Aves.) |
212-525-0000 | www.hotel-americano.com
Located in Chelsea's High Line–adjacent Americano Hotel, this newcomer offers midpriced Latin-inflected French fare amid "cooler than-
cool" digs decorated with black leather banquettes, minimalist
marble-topped tables and polished concrete floors, adjoined by a
roomy patio; a "trendy" crowd keeps the feel "fun."

Amma *Indian*
25 | 18 | 22 | $45

E 50s | 246 E. 51st St. (bet. 2nd & 3rd Aves.) | 212-644-8330 |
www.ammanyc.com
"Breaking away from the clichés", this Midtown "contender" provides
a "tantalizing array" of "refined" Northern Indian fare served by a
"kind, calm" crew in a setting that falls somewhere between "intimate"
and "cramped"; tabs skew a bit "high", but the $12 prix fixe lunch is
an "excellent value."

Ammos *Greek/Seafood*
22 | 21 | 21 | $52

E 40s | 52 Vanderbilt Ave. (bet. 44th & 45th Sts.) | 212-922-9999 |
www.ammosnewyork.com
The "only thing missing is the plate-breaking" at this "authentic"
Grand Central–area Greek that offers a "hustle-bustle" lunch for "expense account"–wielding "suits" as well as a more "quiet" dinner hour;
while tabs are on the "high" end, expect serious "sticker shock" if you
order whole fish, priced by the pound.

Amor Cubano *Cuban*
23 | 18 | 21 | $31

Harlem | 2018 Third Ave. (111th St.) | 212-996-1220 |
www.amorcubanorestaurant.com
Giving "Miami" a run for its money, this "hopping" East Harlem Cuban
doles out "tasty, traditional" chow right out of "pre-Castro Havana",
lubricated with "amazing" mojitos; "live music" via a "loud band" adds
"authenticity" and distracts from the just "ok" ambiance.

Amorina *Italian/Pizza* 23 | 16 | 19 | $27

Prospect Heights | 624 Vanderbilt Ave. (Prospect Pl.) | Brooklyn | 718-230-3030 | www.amorinapizza.com

When in the mood for "delicious" Roman-style pizzas and pastas, all at "low, low prices", fans turn to this Prospect Heights Italian; the "small", red-checkered-tablecloth setting exudes "homey" vibes and is patrolled by a "hard-working" staff.

ⓃⒺⓌ Am Thai Bistro *Thai* 24 | 17 | 23 | $27

Ditmas Park | 1003 Church Ave. (bet. E. 10th & 11th Sts.) | Brooklyn | 718-287-8888 | www.amthaibistro.com

ⓃⒺⓌ Am-Thai Chili Basil Kitchen ⌁ *Thai*

Kensington | 359 McDonald Ave. (bet. Albemarle Rd. & Caton Ave.) | Brooklyn | 718-871-9115 | www.amthaikitchen.com

"Hole-in-the-wall culinary experiences" are alive and well at these new Brooklyn Thai twins vending "excellent versions of familiar dishes" along with some "elevated specials"; the "small" Ditmas Park outlet has limited seating, while cash-only Kensington is strictly a take-out affair.

Amy Ruth's *Soul Food* 22 | 15 | 20 | $26

Harlem | 113 W. 116th St. (bet. Lenox & 7th Aves.) | 212-280-8779 | www.amyruthsharlem.com

Those jonesing for a taste of "classic Harlem" head to this 15-year-old, low-budget soul food "stalwart" for "hearty" cooking highlighted by "amazing" chicken and waffles; regulars "ignore the decor" and "lackadaisical" service, and get there early "before the tourist buses arrive."

An Choi *Vietnamese* 22 | 17 | 20 | $29

LES | 85 Orchard St. (Broome St.) | 212-226-3700 | www.anchoinyc.com

There's an "authentic" feel pervading this "funky" LES Vietnamese touted for its "original", "delicious" takes on pho and banh mi; low prices and Saigon "back alley" decor add extra legitimacy.

Andre's Café *Bakery/Hungarian* 21 | 13 | 18 | $26

E 80s | 1631 Second Ave. (bet. 84th & 85th Sts.) | 212-327-1105 | www.andrescafeny.com

The "main event is pastry and coffee" at this "little" bakery/cafe, though its "basic" Hungarian menu is "hearty" and "authentic" enough; it's "one of the last bastions" of the genre in Yorkville with "easy-to-digest" tabs and "hole-in-the-wall" decor that makes "take-out a viable option."

ⓃⒺⓌ Añejo ⬤Ⓜ *Mexican* ▽ 23 | 22 | 22 | $43

W 40s | 668 10th Ave. (47th St.) | 212-920-4770 | www.anejonyc.com

Chef Angelo Sosa's "cool" new Hell's Kitchen haute Mexican is an "excellent concept" that matches "crazy-good" small plates with "inventive" tequila and mezcal cocktails; "enthusiastic" staffers and "fair prices" outshine the "too-small" setting.

Angelica Kitchen ⌁ *Vegan/Vegetarian* 22 | 17 | 20 | $25

E Village | 300 E. 12th St. (2nd Ave.) | 212-228-2909 | www.angelicakitchen.com

A longtime East Village "standard bearer" for vegan grazing, this "go-with-the-flow" BYO is a "wholesome" destination for "your-body-as-a-temple" dining at a "reasonable" (cash-only) cost; though the decor is "spartan" and the service "loose", there's "always a line for a table."

Angelina's Ⓜ *Italian* `24` `23` `21` `$58`

Tottenville | 399 Ellis St. (off Arthur Kill Rd.) | Staten Island | 718-227-2900 | www.angelinasristorante.com

"Fine dining" comes to Tottenville at this "highly recommended" Italian offering "fabulous" food and "professional" service in a "stunning" tri-level mansion; sure, it's "expensive" for SI and the crowd can be a bit "Jersey Shore", but most call it a bona fide "special-occasion" hub.

Angelo's of Mulberry Street Ⓜ *Italian* `23` `17` `20` `$45`

Little Italy | 146 Mulberry St. (bet. Grand & Hester Sts.) | 212-966-1277 | www.angelomulberry.com

It doesn't get more "old-school" than this circa-1902 Little Italy "favorite" that's still popular thanks to "good, old-fashioned" Italian cooking and "top-notch" service; perhaps the "stereotypical" decor could use "a little touching up", but otherwise fans "feel the love" – "maybe the tourists know something" after all.

Angelo's Pizzeria *Pizza* `22` `15` `18` `$25`

E 50s | 1043 Second Ave. (55th St.) | 212-521-3600 | www.angelospizzany.com

W 50s | 117 W. 57th St. (bet. 6th & 7th Aves.) | 212-333-4333 | www.angelospizzany.com

W 50s | 1697 Broadway (bet. 53rd & 54th Sts.) | 212-245-8811 | www.angelosnyc.com

These "family-friendly" Midtown pizzerias turn out "worthy" brick-oven pies with "generous" toppings for "economical" dough; since "ambiance is not their strong point" and service skews "hit-or-miss", regulars feel a "glass of wine always helps."

Ann & Tony's Ⓜ *Italian* `22` `17` `21` `$36`

Fordham | 2407 Arthur Ave. (bet. 187th & 188th Sts.) | Bronx | 718-933-1469 | www.annandtonysonline.com

Talk about "classic", this circa-1927 Arthur Avenue Italian remains a steady "favorite" for "healthy portions" of "old-fashioned" food served by a "treat-you-like-family" crew; "great prices" help blot out "decor from the '70s.

🅉 Annisa *American* `28` `24` `27` `$86`

W Village | 13 Barrow St. (bet. 7th Ave. S. & W. 4th St.) | 212-741-6699 | www.annisarestaurant.com

"Adult dining experiences" don't get much more "top-drawer" than Anita Lo's West Village "temple of food" where "adventurous", Asian-accented New Americana is backed up by "polished" service; the "tiny", "minimalist" room is "serene" enough to "hear your dinner companion and no one else's."

Anthony's *Italian/Pizza* `22` `17` `21` `$28`

Park Slope | 426 Seventh Ave. (bet. 14th & 15th Sts.) | Brooklyn | 718-369-8315 | www.anthonysbrooklyn.com

"Disguised as a pizza joint", this "comfortable" Park Slope Italian goes beyond pies with "classic" red-sauce dishes that are "tasty" and "priced right"; too bad about the "meh" decor, but compensations include a "can't-do-enough-to-please-you" staff.

| | FOOD | DECOR | SERVICE | COST |

Antica Venezia *Italian*   24 | 22 | 24 | $53

W Village | 396 West St. (W. 10th St.) | 212-229-0606 | www.avnyc.com
"Venice" comes to the West Side Highway via this "romantic" Village
Italian overlooking the Hudson and known for "*molto bene*", "old-world"
dishes, often finished off tableside; "complimentary" appetizers and
cordials make the "pricey" tabs easier to digest.

Antique Garage *Mediterranean*   22 | 25 | 20 | $46

SoHo | 41 Mercer St. (bet. Broome & Grand Sts.) | 212-219-1019 |
www.antiquegaragesoho.com
It's all about the "delightful" decor at this former SoHo auto-body shop
that's been turned into a Med eatery where the "cool" antique furnishings are for sale; maybe the service "needs work" and the chow's just
"slightly above average", but the "funky" ambiance is fine as is.

Antonucci *Italian*   23 | 18 | 21 | $57

E 80s | 170 E. 81st St. (bet. Lexington & 3rd Aves.) | 212-570-5100 |
www.antonuccicafe.com
In a "neighborhood filled with Italian restaurants", this "nice and easy"
UES trattoria holds its own with "authentic" cooking highlighted by especially "excellent pastas"; "tight seating" and "pricey-for-everyday"
tabs detract, but "warm" vibes and "unhurried" service are pluses.

A.O.C. ❶ *French*   20 | 18 | 19 | $39

W Village | 314 Bleecker St. (Grove St.) | 212-675-9463 | www.aocnyc.com

A.O.C. Bistro *French*

Park Slope | 259 Fifth Ave. (Garfield Pl.) | Brooklyn | 718-788-1515 |
www.aocbistro.com
"Genuinely French", these "straightforward" West Village–Park Slope
bistros roll out "better-than-expected" Gallic menus for A-ok tabs;
service may skew "indifferent" and the decor "could use an update",
but all is forgiven in Bleecker Street's "lovely" back garden "escape."

Apiary *American*   23 | 20 | 21 | $53

E Village | 60 Third Ave. (bet. 10th & 11th Sts.) | 212-254-0888 |
www.apiarynyc.com
Buzzy folks "make a beeline" to Scott Bryan's "bustling" East Village
New American, a "gem in a kebab neighborhood" boasting "exceptional" cooking, "polished service" and "modern", "stylish" looks; but
since this "hive has a loud hum", conversationalists "go early."

Ápizz *Italian*   25 | 22 | 23 | $48

LES | 217 Eldridge St. (bet. Rivington & Stanton Sts.) | 212-253-9199 |
www.apizz.com
One of the "coziest" joints in town, this "sexy" LES Italian purveys "excellent" pizza and other "melt-in-your-mouth" items straight from a
"wood-burning oven"; despite "quality" service, "accessible" rates and
"unexpectedly beautiful" digs, it remains something of a "hidden
gem" – maybe because of the "sketchy" address.

Applewood ⓜ *American*   25 | 21 | 23 | $47

Park Slope | 501 11th St. (bet. 7th & 8th Aves.) | Brooklyn |
718-788-1810 | www.applewoodny.com
"Inventively prepared farm-fresh ingredients" lure "locals and foodies"
alike to this "charming" New American that's "like going to the country

without leaving Park Slope"; sure, it's "a tad pricey", but "detailed service", "cozy" atmospherics and a "fabulous brunch" compensate.

☑ Aquagrill *Seafood*   27 | 20 | 24 | $61
SoHo | 210 Spring St. (6th Ave.) | 212-274-0505 | www.aquagrill.com
Finatics get "aquathrills" at this "memorable" SoHo seafooder that enjoys a "well-deserved reputation" thanks to a "shucking good" raw bar and "straight-out-of-the-water" catch ferried by an "energetic" crew; "expensive" tabs and "acoustic challenges" aside, it's "always packed."

☑ Aquavit ⊠ *Scandinavian*   25 | 24 | 25 | $111
E 50s | 65 E. 55th St. (bet. Madison & Park Aves.) | 212-307-7311 |
www.aquavit.org
"Sublime" Scandinavian fare and the namesake spirit highlight this "distinctive" Midtowner that's enhanced by "first-class" service and a "sparse", Nordic-"chic" setting; though the prix fixe–only tabs are as "stunning" as the cooking, the front cafe is "less expensive."

Arabelle *American/French*   24 | 26 | 25 | $70
E 60s | Plaza Athénée Hotel | 37 E. 64th St. (bet. Madison & Park Aves.) |
212-606-4647 | www.arabellerestaurant.com
"Civility" is alive and well at this "sumptuous" Franco-American "secluded" in the Plaza Athénée Hotel and patronized by "ladies of a certain age"; while the "refined" menu exhibits "no culinary pyrotechnics", the "elegant" environs and "sky-high" tabs make more of an impression.

NEW Arabesque ● *Mediterranean/Mideastern*   - | - | - | M
Murray Hill | 4 E. 36th St. (bet. 5th & Madison Aves.) | 212-532-2210 |
www.arabesquenewyork.com
Sibling to nearby Barbès, this exotic Murray Hill newcomer blends Mediterranean and Mideastern cuisines with "excellent" results, ditto decor that mixes Moorish and Moroccan elements; a small-plates emphasis and "pretty reasonable" tabs tell the rest of the story.

Areo Ⓜ *Italian*   25 | 20 | 22 | $53
Bay Ridge | 8424 Third Ave. (bet. 84th & 85th Sts.) | Brooklyn | 718-238-0079
"Delicious" Italian food accompanied by a "huge dollop of noise" is yours at this 25-year-old Bay Ridge Italian "scene out of *The Godfather*"; the "dated" decor and "friendly" service is incidental to the "colorful local crowd", flashing "more skin than at Jones Beach."

Arepas Café *Venezuelan*   24 | 15 | 20 | $17
Astoria | 33-07 36th Ave. (34th St.) | Queens | 718-937-3835 |
www.arepascafe.com
"Flavors straight out of Caracas" are stuffed into "fluffy", easily affordable arepas at this "something-different" Astoria Venezuelan; a "diner atmosphere" and sometime "slow service" make it worth considering for "takeout."

Arirang Hibachi Steakhouse *Japanese*   22 | 20 | 22 | $39
Bay Ridge | 8814 Fourth Ave. (bet. 88th & 89th Sts.) | Brooklyn |
718-238-9880
Great Kills | 23 Nelson Ave. (Locust Pl.) | Staten Island | 718-966-9600
www.partyonthegrill.com
"Interactive" is the philosophy of these cross-borough "Benihana wannabes", where the Japanese steaks and sides arrive "projectile-style"

| | | FOOD | DECOR | SERVICE | COST |

from "amusing" hibachi chefs "swinging their implements around"; "kids can't get enough of it", but adults sigh "hokey" even though the pricing's pretty "reasonable for dinner and a show."

Armani Ristorante *Italian*
23 | 25 | 23 | $70

E 50s | Armani/5th Ave. | 717 Fifth Ave., 3rd fl. (56th St.) | 212-207-1902 | www.armanilifestyle.com

"Serious shoppers" in Giorgio Armani's Fifth Avenue flagship unwind at this "hidden" third-floor Italian whose "slick" looks are a match for its "eye-candy" crew; the food's pretty "delectable", the pricing less so, but it's "better for lunch" as it's usually underpopulated at the dinner hour.

Arno 🖾 *Italian*
20 | 17 | 21 | $50

Garment District | 141 W. 38th St. (bet. B'way & 7th Ave.) | 212-944-7420 | www.arnoristorante.com

A "go-to place" in the Garment District "culinary desert", this "old-fashioned" Northern Italian is targeted to the "garmento" business-lunch trade; the "down-to-earth" cooking is "fine" though "not exotic", but the decor seems a bit "tired" given the tabs.

Aroma Kitchen & Winebar ● *Italian*
23 | 19 | 21 | $43

NoHo | 36 E. Fourth St. (bet. Bowery & Lafayette St.) | 212-375-0100 | www.aromanyc.com

Recently "expanded" – "what a difference a back room makes!" – this "neighborhood" NoHo Italian remains as "rustic" and "cozy" as ever, purveying "delicious" dishes paired with a "fine" wine list; "hospitable" service and "amazing" private rooms downstairs add appeal.

Arté Café *Italian*
19 | 18 | 18 | $36

W 70s | 106 W. 73rd St. (bet. Amsterdam & Columbus Aves.) | 212-501-7014 | www.artecafenyc.com

It's all about "bang for the buck" at this UWS Italian, renowned for its $13 "blue-liah special" early-bird and "amazing" bottomless-booze brunch; since the chow is not so special, the service "slow" and the decor "nothing to brag about", "don't expect inspiration", just "excellent value."

NEW Arthur on Smith *American*
∇ 22 | 20 | 21 | $57

Boerum Hill | 276 Smith St. (bet. Degraw & Sackett Sts.) | Brooklyn | 718-360-2340 | www.arthuronsmith.com

Farm-to-fork dining is the thing at this new Smith Street American offering an Italian-accented seasonal menu paired with craft beers and a local wine list; the eco-chic setting features the exposed brick, reclaimed wood and dish-towel napkins typical of the genre.

Artichoke Basille's Pizza ● *Pizza*
22 | 10 | 15 | $14

Chelsea | 114 10th Ave. (17th St.) | 212-792-9200
E Village | 328 E. 14th St. (bet. 1st & 2nd Aves.) | 212-228-2004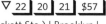
G Village | 111 MacDougal St. (bet. Bleecker & W. 3rd Sts.) | 646-278-6100
www.artichokepizza.com

"Unique", "creamy" pizzas slathered with artichoke dip are the signature of this mini-chain that answers "after-midnight cravings" with late-late hours; sure, there's "zero decor", service is "smug" and the "calorie-bomb" slices may "lose appeal when sober", but "long lines" at all hours testify to its "popularity."

	FOOD	DECOR	SERVICE	COST

Artie's *Seafood/Steak*
City Island | 394 City Island Ave. (Ditmars St.) | Bronx |
718-885-9885 | www.artiesofcityisland.com

24 | 19 | 23 | $38

"Actual City Island residents" eat at this "been-there-forever" surf 'n'
turfer offering a "retro" Italian-accented menu; true, it's "not on the
water" and the decor is "generic seafooder", yet "unhurried" service
and fair pricing keep locals "happy as clams."

❷ Artisanal *French*
Murray Hill | 2 Park Ave. (enter on 32nd St., bet. Madison & Park Aves.) |
212-725-8585 | www.artisanalbistro.com

23 | 21 | 20 | $55

"Cheese is a way of life" at Terrance Brennan's "time-tested" Murray
Hill "lactic heaven", renowned for its "astonishingly diverse" fromage
selection backed up by a roster of "tasty" French brasserie standards;
the "ultimate" fondues and "authentic Parisian" decor distract from
occasional "clattery" sound levels and "absentminded" service.

Arturo's Pizzeria ● *Pizza*
G Village | 106 W. Houston St. (Thompson St.) | 212-677-3820

23 | 16 | 19 | $26

"Old Greenwich Village" endures at this 1957-vintage pizzeria where
a "slice of the past" comes via "delicious, no-nonsense" pies straight
out of a coal oven; a live "jazz combo" and an "unpretentious" mood
compensate for decor that's somewhere between "faded" and "dingy."

A Salt & Battery *British*
W Village | 112 Greenwich Ave. (bet. 12th & 13th Sts.) |
212-691-2713 | www.asaltandbattery.com

22 | 13 | 19 | $20

Fish 'n' chips fanciers say this cutely named Village "hole-in-the-wall"
does a "jolly good" rendition of the British staple for an "affordable"
sum; "anti-health food" treats like "deep-fried candy bars" fill out the
"greasy" bill, but since there's "no decor" and seating's just a "few
stools", most get the goods to go.

Asellina ● *Italian*
Murray Hill | Gansevoort Park Avenue Hotel | 420 Park Ave. S. (29th St.) |
212-317-2908 | www.togrp.com

22 | 24 | 19 | $56

Designed with "the Kardashians" in mind, this "big" Murray Hill Italian is
"more about atmosphere than food", leading some to declare the "bar
scene's the thing" here; fans praise the "stylish" setting, but the "inex-
perienced service" and "expense-account pricing" are another matter.

❷ Asiate *American/Asian*
W 60s | Mandarin Oriental Hotel | 80 Columbus Circle, 35th fl.
(60th St. at B'way) | 212-805-8881 | www.mandarinoriental.com

25 | 28 | 26 | $117

"Splendid" vistas of Central Park and the UWS make for literally "over-
the-top" dining at this "luxurious" Asian–New American in the Mandarin
Oriental, voted NYC's No. 1 for Decor; while the "art-on-a-plate" menu
is delivered by a "class-act" crew, "sky-high", prix fixe–only tabs provide some "double takes", ergo the $34 lunch is the way to go.

Astor Room Ⓜ *American/Continental*
Astoria | Kaufman Astoria Studios | 34-12 36th St. (bet. 35th & 36th Aves.) |
Queens | 718-255-1947 | www.astorroom.com

22 | 23 | 22 | $42

It "feels like the 1920s" at this American-Continental, once the
Paramount Pictures commissary during the silent film era and now a

supper club in Kaufman Astoria Studios; "retro" eats (e.g. oysters Rockefeller, beef Wellington), "speakeasy" looks and "vintage cocktails" embellish the "old-school" vibe.

	FOOD	DECOR	SERVICE	COST

NEW Atera 🖼️ Ⓜ️ American ▽ 26 | 22 | 21 | $195

TriBeCa | 77 Worth St. (bet. B'way & Church St.) | 212-226-1444 | www.ateranyc.com

Portland toque Matthew Lightner helms this 18-seat TriBeCa "foodie destination" offering an avant-garde multicourse American tasting menu served at a counter opposite an open kitchen; the approach is "modernist" with an emphasis on foraging (typical ingredients include moss, nettles and birch sap), the "delectable" menu ever evolving and the cost $150 for the prix fixe–only spectacle.

⏣ Atlantic Grill Seafood 23 | 20 | 21 | $55

E 70s | 1341 Third Ave. (bet. 76th & 77th Sts.) | 212-988-9200
W 60s | 49 W. 64th St. (bet. B'way & CPW) | 212-787-4663
www.atlanticgrill.com

Steve Hanson's "everyman" poisson palaces are "big", "brassy" affairs offering "rock-solid" catch presented in cacophonous digs where "shouting" is often the norm; a "busy brunch", "crisp service" and "pretty-penny" tabs complete the overall "terrific" picture, and there's burgers and such for non-fish fanciers.

August European 23 | 21 | 20 | $48

W Village | 359 Bleecker St. (bet. Charles & W. 10th Sts.) | 212-929-8727 | www.augustny.com

"Really romantic", this beyond-"small" West Village European seduces diners with "candlelight", "charming" service and "quality", wood-fired-oven cooking that's "adventuresome without being bizarre"; insiders tout the "delightful" all-seasons back garden for "intimate dining."

Au Mandarin Chinese 20 | 16 | 19 | $34

Financial District | World Financial Ctr. | 200-250 Vesey St. (West St.) | 212-385-0313 | www.aumandarin.com

"Convenient" for "captive-audience" suits in the World Financial Center, this "legitimate" Chinese offers "consistently good" food in a marble "mall"-like setting; some feel it's "overpriced", but it's a no-brainer for a "take-out dinner at your desk" or when you can't make it to C-town.

⏣ Aureole American 26 | 24 | 25 | $88

W 40s | Bank of America Tower | 135 W. 42nd St. (bet. B'way & 6th Ave.) | 212-319-1660 | www.charliepalmer.com

"Elegant" dining comes to the "unlikely neighborhood" between Times Square and Bryant Park at Charlie Palmer's flagship New American, a "high-up-the-food-chain" place where the cooking's "inventive" and the service "smart"; the "sedate", "ultracorporate" main dining room offers only "top-dollar" prix fixes, but the menu's "more reasonable" (and à la carte) in the "energetic" front bar room.

Aurora Italian 23 | 21 | 22 | $46

SoHo | 510 Broome St. (bet. Thompson St. & W. B'way) | 212-334-9020
Williamsburg | 70 Grand St. (Wythe Ave.) | Brooklyn | 718-388-5100 ⬀
www.auroraristorante.com

At this "quaint" Italian duo, the "delectable" rustic cooking is a match for the "Tuscan countryside" settings (the cash-only Williamsburg original also boasts a "lovely garden"); "hip" crowds, midrange prices and "helpful" service ensure "enjoyable" repasts.

A Voce *Italian* | 24 | 24 | 23 | $66 |

Flatiron | 41 Madison Ave. (26th St.) | 212-545-8555 🖥
W 60s | Time Warner Ctr. | 10 Columbus Circle, 3rd fl. (60th St. at B'way) | 212-823-2523
www.avocerestaurant.com

These "sophisticated" yet "accessible" Italians "shine" thanks to chef Missy Robbins' "delectable" cuisine backed up by "cosseting" service; both the Flatiron original and Columbus Circle spin-off are "corporate" but "comfortable", but there's "more buzz" – and a "park view" – at the larger TWC satellite.

Avra ◐ *Greek/Seafood* | 25 | 22 | 21 | $62 |

E 40s | 141 E. 48th St. (bet. Lexington & 3rd Aves.) | 212-759-8550 | www.avrany.com

The "freshest" catch "grilled to perfection" is "served with panache" at this "Mykonos"-like Hellenic seafooder that's "popular with Midtown business" people who don't mind "by-the-pound" pricing geared to "Greek ship owners"; regulars sidestep the "noise" and "tight tables" by "eating outside."

Awash *Ethiopian* | 23 | 15 | 19 | $26 |

E Village | 338 E. Sixth St. (bet. 1st & 2nd Aves.) | 212-982-9589
W 100s | 947 Amsterdam Ave. (bet. 106th & 107th Sts.) | 212-961-1416
NEW **Cobble Hill** | 242 Court St. (bet. Baltic & Kane Sts.) | Brooklyn | 718-243-2151
www.awashny.com

"Different experience" seekers tout this "unsung", utensil-free Ethiopian trio where "delectable" stews are scooped up with injera flatbread; "dingy" settings and "decidedly relaxed" service come with the territory, but at least you'll walk out awash with cash.

Ayada *Thai* | ▽ 26 | 15 | 20 | $23 |

Woodside | 77-08 Woodside Ave. (bet. 77th & 78th Sts.) | Queens | 718-424-0844

"Setting a standard of excellence" in Woodside, this "tiny", "unassuming" Thai purveys "complex", "real-deal" Siamese dishes from an encyclopedic menu rife with "tongue-numbing goodness"; even better, it's "so affordable you can try everything" and come back for more.

Ayza Wine & | 21 | 20 | 20 | $35 |
Chocolate Bar *French/Mediterranean*

Garment District | 11 W. 31st St. (bet. B'way & 5th Ave.) | 212-714-2992
NEW **W Village** | 1 Seventh Ave. S. (Carmine St.) | 212-365-2992 ◐
www.ayzanyc.com

Made for a "night out with the girls", these "novel" French-Med wine bars put out the "perfect trifecta" of "wine, cheese and chocolate" in "chic" albeit "tiny", "crowded" settings; "decadent" cocktails and "nice energy" keep things "always hopping."

Azuri Cafe *Israeli/Kosher* | 25 | 10 | 14 | $17 |

W 50s | 465 W. 51st St. (bet. 9th & 10th Aves.) | 212-262-2920
Falafel "from heaven" and other "cheap", "delicious" Israeli eats offset the "dumpy" decor at this Hell's Kitchen "hole-in-the-wall"; just "don't

expect a warm welcome" – the "short-tempered" owner is the neighborhood's "favorite curmudgeon."

☑ Babbo ●Ⓜ *Italian*

FOOD	DECOR	SERVICE	COST
27	23	24	$81

G Village | 110 Waverly Pl. (bet. MacDougal St. & 6th Ave.) |
212-777-0303 | www.babbonyc.com

The "hype is true" about this 15-year-old Batali-Bastianich "powerhouse" where the "assertive", "adventurous" Italian menu "takes pasta to the next level" and is plied in a "convivial" Village carriage house to the tune of a "loud" rock soundtrack; ignore the "high-end" tabs, "tight" dimensions and "calluses-on-your-redial-finger" reservations: this "exceptional experience" approaches "culinary perfection."

Bacchus *French*

22	19	20	$40

Boerum Hill | 409 Atlantic Ave. (bet. Bond & Nevins Sts.) | Brooklyn |
718-852-1572 | www.bacchusbistro.com

Francophiles tout the "wonderful" French comfort cooking at this "charming little" Boerum Hill bistro near BAM; "reasonable" rates, "no pretension" and a "beautiful" back garden lend "lazy-day" appeal, even if a few Francophobes feel it has "no particular distinction."

Back Forty *American*

23	19	21	$38

E Village | 190 Ave. B (bet. 11th & 12th Sts.) | 212-388-1990

NEW Back Forty West *American*

SoHo | 70 Prince St. (Crosby St.) | 212-219-8570
www.backfortynyc.com

"Locavore" pioneer Peter Hoffman fields a "fab" "farm-to-table" New American menu (highlighted by a "spot-on" burger) at this "hipster"-friendly East Villager also known for its moderate rates and "idyllic" back garden; the new SoHo spin-off set in Savoy's former space is open all day.

NEW Bagatelle ●Ⓩ *French*

-	-	-	E

Meatpacking | 1 Little W. 12th St. (9th Ave.) | 212-488-2110 |
www.bistrotbagatelle.com

Back on the Meatpacking scene at a new address, this notorious Euro party palace purveys pricey, perfectly respectable French chow but is much better known for its no-holds-barred displays of joie de vivre; an epic weekend champagne brunch mixes techno music and table dancing with stilettos and jeroboams of bubbly.

Bahari Estiatorio ● *Greek*

▽ 25	19	22	$34

Astoria | 31-14 Broadway (bet. 31st & 32nd Sts.) | Queens |
718-204-8968 | www.bahariestiatorio.com

"Great bang for the buck" is the secret weapon of this "always busy" Astoria taverna that follows through with "delicious" Hellenica in "large portions"; fans overlook the "kitschy" decor given the "polite" service and overall "pleasant mood."

Balaboosta *Mediterranean/Mideastern*

24	18	21	$49

NoLita | 214 Mulberry St. (bet. Prince & Spring Sts.) | 212-966-7366 |
www.balaboostanyc.com

"Artful", "original" Med-Mideastern dishes fill out the menu of this "different" NoLita crowd-pleaser via the Taim team that "lives up to its name": 'perfect housewife'; granted, the dining room's "small" and the vibe "trendy", but there's "no attitude" and pricing is not bad.

	FOOD	DECOR	SERVICE	COST

⊉ Balthazar ● *French* | 24 | 24 | 21 | $57 |

SoHo | 80 Spring St. (bet. B'way & Crosby St.) | 212-965-1414 |
www.balthazarny.com

"What's the point of flying to Paris?" when there's Keith McNally's "always entertaining" SoHo brasserie, where "cut-above" French cooking, "Parisian-cafe-movie-set" decor and an "NY hip" vibe draw a "great mix of humanity" – think "tourists", "Eurotrash", "Victoria Beckham"; "fever-pitch" noise levels and "polite if harried" service show it "hasn't lost its bounce", and insiders tout its "soulful breakfasts" and "manna-from-heaven" bread basket.

Baluchi's *Indian* | 20 | 16 | 18 | $30 |

E 80s | 1724 Second Ave. (bet. 89th & 90th Sts.) | 212-996-2600
Murray Hill | 329 Third Ave. (bet. 24th & 25th Sts.) | 212-679-3434
TriBeCa | 275 Greenwich St. (bet. Murray & Warren Sts.) | 212-571-5343
NEW Brooklyn Heights | 46 Henry St. (bet. Cranberry & Middagh Sts.) |
Brooklyn | 718-858-6700
Park Slope | 310 Fifth Ave. (bet. 2nd & 3rd Sts.) | Brooklyn | 718-832-5555
Forest Hills | 113-30 Queens Blvd. (bet. 76th Ave. & 76th Rd.) |
Queens | 718-520-8600
www.baluchis.com

This "Americanized" Indian chain is popular for its "serviceable" food and "economical" tabs (lunch is a particular "bargain"); but critics citing "conventional" cooking, "mundane" settings and "dull-witted" service say "don't expect nirvana."

Bamboo 52 ● *Japanese* | 19 | 18 | 18 | $32 |

W 50s | 344 W. 52nd St. (bet. 8th & 9th Aves.) | 212-315-2777 |
www.bamboo52nyc.com

Whether "restaurant or disco", this Hell's Kitchen Japanese is a decided "break from the Midtown norm", with "respectable" sushi fighting for attention with the "garish", "clublike" setting and "way-too-loud music"; "moderate" tabs keep it packed with "gay-friendly" types.

Bamonte's *Italian* | 23 | 18 | 23 | $44 |

Williamsburg | 32 Withers St. (bet. Lorimer St. & Union Ave.) |
Brooklyn | 718-384-8831

"Auld Brooklyn" lives on at this circa-1900 Williamsburg Italian, an "old-world" source of "red-sauce" fare and "lots of it" (the "only things locally sourced are the waiters"); ok, it may be "short on decor", but the tabs are "reasonable" and the ambiance "right out of *The Godfather*."

B&B *Pub Food* | 22 | 19 | 19 | $35 |
(fka Burger & Barrel)

SoHo | 25 W. Houston St. (bet. Greene & Mercer Sts.) |
212-334-7320 | www.burgerandbarrel.com

"Trendy" burgers, "barrel beers" and "wine on tap" collide in a "high-energy" setting at this "happy" SoHo pub from the Lure Fishbar folks; sure, it's "loud", with "lighting so low you can barely see your food", but its "cool", cost-conscious crowd considers it fine as is.

Banjara ● *Indian* | 24 | 16 | 21 | $34 |

E Village | 97 First Ave. (6th St.) | 212-477-5956 | www.banjaranyc.com

"Different" from its round-the-corner Curry Hill competitors, this "upscale" subcontinental "doesn't bow to American tastes", purveying "authentic" Northern Indian fare that "stands out from the rest"; "worn" decor and "so-so service" are trumped by "low prices."

Bann *Korean*
22 | 21 | 20 | $45

W 50s | Worldwide Plaza | 350 W. 50th St. (bet. 8th & 9th Aves.) | 212-582-4446 | www.bannrestaurant.com

"Classy" Korean barbecue is no oxymoron at this Theater District "change of pace" where smokeless tabletop grills impress do-it-yourselfers and the "modern" setting thrills aesthetes; maybe the tabs skew "upscale", but the food's "exciting", the service "caring" and the overall experience "satisfying."

Bann Thai *Thai*
20 | 19 | 20 | $29

Forest Hills | 69-12 Austin St. (bet. 69th Rd. & Yellowstone Blvd.) | Queens | 718-544-9999 | www.bannthairestaurant.com

Admittedly "off the beaten path", this "reliable" Forest Hills Siamese is worth seeking out for "zesty" vittles that are "as fresh as the decor is colorful" – and "reasonably priced" to boot; purists find the cooking a bit "Americanized", but ultimately "not bad for the neighborhood."

Baoguette *Vietnamese*
22 | 9 | 15 | $14

NEW Financial District | 75 Nassau St. (bet. Fulton & John Sts.) | 212-510-8787 🖾
Murray Hill | 61 Lexington Ave. (bet. 25th & 26th Sts.) | 212-532-1133 🖾
W Village | 120 Christopher St. (Bedford St.) | 212-929-0877 ❶ www.baoguette.com

"Nontraditional" banh mi sandwiches assembled from "ultrafresh bread" and "fiery fillings" are the hook at Michael 'Bao' Huynh's "no-frills" Vietnamese mini-chain; "cheap" tabs make the "rude" service and "hole-in-the-wall" looks easier to swallow.

BaoHaus *Chinese*
24 | 11 | 16 | $13

E Village | 238 E. 14th St. (bet. 2nd & 3rd Aves.) | 646-669-8889 | www.baohausnyc.com

Ignore the "blaring hip-hop music" and "fast-food vibe" – the "savory" Taiwanese bao are "seriously delicious" ("even when sober") at this East Village steamed-bun specialist from enfant terrible Eddie Huang; despite "teenage" service and "no decor to speak of", "cheap" checks keep its "college" crowd content.

Bao Noodles *Noodle Shop/Vietnamese*
20 | 14 | 16 | $25

Gramercy | 391 Second Ave. (bet. 22nd & 23rd Sts.) | 212-725-7770 | www.baonoodles.com

"Vietnam's answer to Jewish penicillin", the "comforting" pho ladled out at this "bargain" Gramercy noodle house "will cure whatever ails you"; the rest of the menu is equally "delicious", leaving "no atmosphere" and "slow" service as the only downsides.

☒ Bar Americain *American*
24 | 23 | 23 | $63

W 50s | 152 W. 52nd St. (bet. 6th & 7th Aves.) | 212-265-9700 | www.baramericain.com

There's plenty of "buzz" in the air at Bobby Flay's "very NY" Midtown brasserie where "after-work" and "pre-theater" crowds convene for "upscale" New Americana, unfazed by the "splurge-worthy" tabs; a

	FOOD	DECOR	SERVICE	COST

"snazzy", "soaring" setting, "superb service" and a "smoking bar scene" burnish the "sophisticated" mood.

Baraonda ◐ *Italian*   20 | 19 | 18 | $50
E 70s | 1439 Second Ave. (75th St.) | 212-288-8555 | www.baraondany.com

"Euro types" gravitate to this longtime UES Italian where the "good but not sensational" chow plays second fiddle to late-night "rowdy" reveling involving "loud music" and "dancing on tables"; critics say it's "past its prime", unless "plastic surgery and pasta" is your thing.

Barbès ◐ *French/Moroccan*   20 | 17 | 21 | $42
Murray Hill | 21 E. 36th St. (bet. 5th & Madison Aves.) | 212-684-0215 | www.barbesrestaurantnyc.com

An "exotic escape from *la vie ordinaire*", this Murray Hill "sure thing" purveys "toothsome" French-Moroccan vittles in a setting akin to an "Algerian bistro in Marseilles"; it may be "cramped" and "noisy", but "pleasant" service and "value" pricing help to distract.

Barbetta ◐ⓜ *Italian*   22 | 23 | 23 | $65
W 40s | 321 W. 46th St. (bet. 8th & 9th Aves.) | 212-246-9171 | www.barbettarestaurant.com

For "upscale Theater District dining", there's always this "gracious", 1906-vintage Northern Italian offering an "old-world" blend of "tasty" food, "elegant" decor, "refined" service and a "transporting", "escape-from-Manhattan" garden; sure, it's "pricey", but worth it.

Barbone *Italian*   23 | 17 | 22 | $47
E Village | 186 Ave. B (bet. 11th & 12th Sts.) | 212-254-6047 | www.barbonenyc.com

"Hidden away in the East Village", this "no-tourists" Italian sleeper earns raves for "well-prepared" classic dishes ferried by "friendly" folks overseen by a "charismatic" chef-owner; "good overall value" and a "great backyard patio" ice the cake.

ⓩ Bar Boulud *French*   24 | 21 | 22 | $62
W 60s | 1900 Broadway (bet. 63rd & 64th Sts.) | 212-595-0303 | www.danielnyc.com

"Mouthwatering charcuterie" is a highlight of this "outstanding" French bistro–cum–wine bar that allows a taste of "Daniel Boulud's artistry" in a more "casual", "not terribly expensive" milieu; the "long, narrow" room strikes some as "sterile", but the "sidewalk" seats facing Lincoln Center feel like a "Parisian cafe."

Barbounia *Mediterranean*   22 | 23 | 20 | $49
Flatiron | 250 Park Ave. S. (20th St.) | 212-995-0242 | www.barbounia.com

"Stylish" and "upbeat", this "cacophonous" Flatiron Med lures "see-and-be-seen" "Gen-X" types with a "tasty", "something-for-everyone" menu (and one "crazy brunch"); still, it's the "beautiful", "airy" setting – replete with vaulted ceilings – that's the star of the show.

Barbuto *Italian*   24 | 19 | 21 | $54
W Village | 775 Washington St. (bet. Jane & W. 12th Sts.) | 212-924-9700 | www.barbutonyc.com

Parked in a "chic converted garage", this "unpretentious" West Village Italian showcases Jonathan Waxman's "simple but classy" cooking highlighted by a "life-changing" roasted chicken; the atmosphere's "upbeat" – ok, "noisy" – but it's somewhat quieter in summer when they roll up the doors and it becomes "semi-alfresco."

NEW Bar Corvo *Italian* ▽ | 28 | 22 | 24 | $37 |

Prospect Heights | 791 Washington Ave. (bet. Lincoln & St. Johns Pls.) | Brooklyn | 718-230-0940 | www.barcorvo.com

The owners of Park Slope's beloved Al Di La have done it again in Prospect Heights with this wonderful new "neighborhood game changer" serving "straightforward", very "affordable" Italiana; its "cramped", narrow space is done up in a warm, rustic style, equipped with an open kitchen and long communal table.

BareBurger *Burgers* | 23 | 18 | 20 | $22 |

NEW **Chelsea** | 153 Eighth Ave. (bet. 17th & 18th Sts.) | 212-414-2273
NEW **E 70s** | 1370 First Ave. (73rd St.) | 212-510-8559
NEW **E Village** | 85 Second Ave. (5th St.) | 212-510-8610
G Village | 535 La Guardia Pl. (bet. Bleecker & W. 3rd Sts.) | 212-477-8125
Murray Hill | 514 Third Ave. (bet. 34th & 35th Sts.) | 212-679-2273
Park Slope | 170 Seventh Ave. (bet. 1st St. & Garfield Pl.) | Brooklyn | 718-768-2273
NEW **Astoria** | 23-01 31st St. (23rd Ave.) | Queens | 718-204-7167
Astoria | 33-21 31st Ave. (34th St.) | Queens | 718-777-7011
NEW **Bayside** | 42-38 Bell Blvd. (bet. 42nd & 43rd Aves.) | Queens | 718-279-2273
NEW **Forest Hills** | 71-49 Austin St. (bet. 71st Rd. & 72nd Ave.) | Queens | 718-275-2273
www.bareburger.com

Rapidly expanding, this "special" burger chain focuses on "natural, organic" beef (plus elk, bison, ostrich and wild boar) with "delicious" results; maybe it's "a bit expensive" for the genre, but in return "you get quality" and the satisfaction of eating "healthy."

Bar Italia ● *Italian* | 19 | 18 | 18 | $50 |

E 60s | 768 Madison Ave. (66th St.) | 212-249-5300 | www.baritalianyc.com

"Wanna-be-seen" Euros flock to this "fashion-forward" Madison Avenue Italian where the "better-than-expected" cooking takes a backseat to the "sleek" white setting and "*Real Housewives*" people-watching; expect serious tabs and "lots of attitude."

Bar Jamon ● *Spanish* | 23 | 20 | 20 | $43 |

Gramercy | 125 E. 17th St. (Irving Pl.) | 212-253-2773

Mario Batali's "convivial" Gramercy tapas bar–cum–"holding pen" for his 'round-the-corner Casa Mono puts out "top-of-the-line" Spanish small plates paired with an "extensive" wine list; it's a "tight squeeze" and the tabs are "not cheap", but fans like its "sexy-time" mood.

Bark Hot Dogs *Hot Dogs* | 22 | 17 | 19 | $16 |

Dumbo | Brooklyn Bridge Park | Pier 6 (Main St.) | Brooklyn | No phone Ⓜ
Park Slope | 474 Bergen St. (bet. 5th & Flatbush Aves.) | Brooklyn | 718-789-1939
www.barkhotdogs.com

The "dogs are hot and the crowd cool" at this Park Slope wiener wonderland where the haute dawgs have "great snap" and are made from "locally sourced", "pedigreed ingredients"; the seasonal terrace in

Brooklyn Bridge Park's Pier Six features "picnic tables" and drop-dead Manhattan vistas.

Barney Greengrass Deli — 24 | 9 | 16 | $30

W 80s | 541 Amsterdam Ave. (bet. 86th & 87th Sts.) | 212-724-4707 | www.barneygreengrass.com

Still "as good as when grandpa ate here", this UWS institution has been slinging "old-style Jewish deli food" and "gold-standard" smoked fish since 1908; "fading" decor, "no credit cards" and "borderline rude service" are all "part of the charm", as the "lines out the door" attest.

Barosa *Italian* — 22 | 19 | 21 | $42

Rego Park | 62-29 Woodhaven Blvd. (62nd Rd.) | Queens | 718-424-1455 | www.barosas.com

"Tasty" red-sauce fare "like mom used to make" comes at a "good price" at this "neighborhood favorite" Rego Park Italian; its "upscale" ambitions are apparent in the "polite" service, while "fantastic specials" seal the deal.

Bar Pitti ● *Italian* — 24 | 16 | 18 | $44

G Village | 268 Sixth Ave. (bet. Bleecker & Houston Sts.) | 212-982-3300

Home to "many a celeb sighting", this "jet-set" Village Italian is best known for its "excellent people-watching", even if the "easygoing" menu is pretty "delicious"; no reservations, no plastic, "no discernible decor" and "far-from-friendly" service don't faze its "paparazzi"-ready patrons.

Barrio Chino ● *Mexican* — 24 | 18 | 19 | $31

LES | 253 Broome St. (bet. Ludlow & Orchard Sts.) | 212-228-6710 | www.barriochinonyc.com

The Spanish name translates as 'Chinese neighborhood', so it's no surprise that this "rustic", "microscopic" LES cantina offers "unusual" Mexican-Sino fusion fare; it's still "something of a scene" after 10 years, maybe because of its "highly affordable" price point and "lay-you-out-flat" tequila list.

Basil Brick Oven Pizza *Pizza* — 26 | 19 | 21 | $23

Astoria | 28-17 Astoria Blvd. (bet 27th & 29th Sts.) | Queens | 718-204-1205 | www.basilbrickoven.com

"Great pizza" emerges from the "wood-burning oven" of this "tiny" Astoria yearling that also vends "delicious" pasta and panini; a "good location", "reliably fast delivery" and affordable tabs make fans wonder why it's so "little known."

Basso56 *Italian* — 24 | 19 | 23 | $51

W 50s | 234 W. 56th St. (bet. B'way & 8th Ave.) | 212-265-2610 | www.basso56.com

An "excellent Carnegie Hall resource", this Midtown Italian features a "nicely put-together menu" with "modern flair" ferried by an "accommodating" team; some sniff at the "narrow", "nothing-fancy" setting, but admit the prices are "reasonable for the quality."

Basta Pasta *Italian* — 23 | 17 | 21 | $43

Flatiron | 37 W. 17th St. (bet. 5th & 6th Aves.) | 212-366-0888 | www.bastapastanyc.com

"Japanese-style Italian food" begs the question "where else but NY?", but this "unusual" Flatiron "change of pace" comes through with "interesting" vittles led by a signature "pasta tossed in a Parmesan wheel"; if the decor's getting "dated", the "hospitable" service and "reasonable" costs are fine as is.

NEW Battersby ⓜ *American*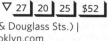

Carroll Gardens | 255 Smith St. (bet. Degraw & Douglass Sts.) | Brooklyn | 718-852-8321 | www.battersbybrooklyn.com

"Creative" yet "approachable", this new Smith Street breakaway "phenomenon" fields a "highly refined", "ever-changing" American menu highlighted by a "standout" kale salad; sure, it's "tiny" and "no reservations" lead to "long waits", but given pricing that's a bargain by Manhattan standards, fans "see a bright future" ahead.

Battery Gardens *American/Continental* `19` `25` `20` `$50`

Financial District | SW corner of Battery Park (State St.) | 212-809-5508 | www.batterygardens.com

The "harbor is at your feet" at this "shoreline" Battery Park American-Continental where the "peerless" views of the harbor and Lady Liberty are matched with "better-than-expected" food; for the most "priceless" experience, go for "outdoor cocktails at sunset."

Bayou *Cajun* `23` `23` `23` `$41`

Rosebank | 1072 Bay St. (bet. Chestnut & St. Mary's Aves.) | Staten Island | 718-273-4383 | www.bayounyc.com

"Ragin' Cajun" cooking comes to Staten Island's Rosebank via this Bay Street "favorite" where the "tasty" cooking is as "true" to N'Awlins as the "Big Easy" decor; "affordable" tabs and "designated-driver-recommended" drinks ratchet up the "festive" vibrations.

B Bar & Grill ⓞ *American*

NoHo | 40 E. Fourth St. (bet. Bowery & Lafayette St.) | 212-475-2220 | www.bbarandgrill.com

One of the first settlers on the now-happening Bowery, this circa-'94 bar/lounge/eatery purveys "above-ordinary" American chow at below-average prices in a "big" indoor-outdoor setting; the "leisurely" party mood is a match for the "slow-motion service", but regulars say it's "all about the patio" here.

B. Café *Belgian* `21` `16` `19` `$39`

E 70s | 240 E. 75th St. (bet. 2nd & 3rd Aves.) | 212-249-3300
W 80s | 566 Amsterdam Ave. (bet. 87th & 88th Sts.) | 212-873-0003
www.bcafe.com

"Belgian pub grub" is yours at these "satisfying" crosstown "reliables" offering "consistently fine" mussels and frites washed down with "high-test" brews; ok, the "railroad" settings are a bit "drab" and "squashed", but the staff "tries its best" and you do get "lots for your money."

Beacon *American* `23` `21` `22` `$59`

W 50s | 25 W. 56th St. (bet. 5th & 6th Aves.) | 212-332-0500 | www.beaconnyc.com

"Everything shines" at Waldy Malouf's "spacious" Midtown New American where the "superb" wood-fired cuisine tastes even better in a "warm", "Frank Lloyd Wright"–esque setting "quiet enough for conversation"; though it's "best on an expense account", "value" prix fixe deals are available.

	FOOD	DECOR	SERVICE	COST

Beagle ● *American* ▽ 22 | 20 | 22 | $47

E Village | 162 Ave. A (bet. 10th & 11th Sts.) | 212-228-6900 |
www.thebeaglenyc.com

This cocktail-centric East Village American gastropub supplies a "well-prepared" menu heavy on small plates, but it's the "interesting old-school" tipples that garner the most response; sure, it's "tiny" and rather "pricey for what it is", yet fans insist this one deserves "more hype."

Beaumarchais ● *French* ▽ 24 | 22 | 20 | $60

Meatpacking | 409 W. 13th St. (bet. 9th Ave. & Washington St.) |
212-675-2400 | www.brasseriebeaumarchais.com

"French food" meets "French kissing" at this Meatpacking District "Eurotrash" magnet better known for its "blaring music", "party vibe" and "hot brunch" than the "surprisingly good" grub; all the "grinding", "champagne spraying" and "dancing on tables" distracts from the sticker shock.

✓ Beauty & Essex ● *American* 23 | 27 | 21 | $59

LES | 146 Essex St. (bet. Rivington & Stanton Sts.) | 212-614-0146 |
www.beautyandessex.com

A "scene-and-a-half" hidden behind a "functioning pawn shop", this LES phenom seduces "beautiful" folks with "sexy" Americana served in an "over-the-top", AvroKO-designed duplex; it may come at a "high price", but "free bubbly in the ladies' room" compensates.

✓ Becco ● *Italian* 23 | 19 | 22 | $46

W 40s | 355 W. 46th St. (bet. 8th & 9th Aves.) | 212-397-7597 |
www.becco-nyc.com

It's all about "price performance" at this Bastianich Restaurant Row Italian, a 20-year-old vet famed for its $23 all-you-can-eat "pasta-coma" dinner paired with a $25 wine list; "flexible" staffers and "congenial" digs fuel the "bustling" scene of value-seekers and "theatergoers."

Beccofino *Italian* 23 | 18 | 20 | $33

Riverdale | 5704 Mosholu Ave. (bet. Fieldston Rd. & Spencer Ave.) |
Bronx | 718-432-2604

Pretty "happening" for Riverdale, this "traditional" Italian offers "Manhattan-quality" red-sauce cooking at Bronx prices; its "neighborly atmosphere" draws huzzahs, but "no reservations" and "small" dimensions mean you must "come early or be prepared to wait."

Beecher's Cellar *American* 23 | 19 | 20 | $28

Flatiron | 900 Broadway (20th St.) | 212-466-3340 |
www.beechershandmadecheese.com

Upstairs, this Flatiron cheese factory vends "artisanal" varieties "made right in front of your eyes", while downstairs a "secret" lounge/eatery features a "limited" but "tasty" American menu highlighted by a "magical mac 'n' cheese"; "personable" service and a "candlelit" setting with "cozy armchairs" make for "low-key dining."

Bella Blu *Italian* 22 | 19 | 20 | $57

E 70s | 967 Lexington Ave. (bet. 70th & 71st Sts.) | 212-988-4624 |
www.bellabluny.com

"Well-to-do" Upper Eastsiders "get happy" at this "popular" Italian serving a "high-quality" menu led by "fantastic" pizzas; granted, it's

| | FOOD | DECOR | SERVICE | COST |

"pricey", the seating's "cheek-by-jowl" and service depends on "how familiar you look", but "superior people-watching" saves the day.

Bella Via *Italian*   `22` `19` `20` `$32`

LIC | 47-46 Vernon Blvd. (48th Ave.) | Queens | 718-361-7510 | www.bellaviarestaurant.com

"Funky LIC" is home to this "reliable" Italian known for its well-done pastas and coal-fired pizzas at prices that "won't break the bank"; set in a big-windowed storefront, it features "simple" decor that contributes to its "pleasant", "friendly" mien.

Bell Book & Candle *American* `22` `20` `20` `$48`

W Village | 141 W. 10th St., downstairs (bet. Greenwich Ave. & Waverly Pl.) | 212-414-2355 | www.bbandcnyc.com

Best known for an aeroponic "roof garden" that supplies most of its produce, this "cozy-chic" West Villager dispenses "seasonal" Americana that's quite "delicious"; the "dark" basement setting has "great date" potential, provided the "high noise level" doesn't get to you.

NEW Bellwether *American* `-` `-` `-` `M`

Williamsburg | 594 Union Ave. (Richardson St.) | Brooklyn | 347-529-4921 | www.bellwetherbrooklyn.com

Seafood-centric small plates are the hook at this sprawling new Williamsburg arrival that morphs into a lounge late-night when the tables are removed and a disco ball is lowered; moderate tabs, Danish modern design and a serious cocktail program are further inducements.

Ben & Jack's Steak House *Steak* `25` `20` `23` `$69`

E 40s | 219 E. 44th St. (bet. 2nd & 3rd Aves.) | 212-682-5678
Murray Hill | 255 Fifth Ave. (bet. 28th & 29th Sts.) | 212-532-7600
www.benandjackssteakhouse.com

Among the "best of the Luger's imitators", these East Side carnivoriums feature "cooked-to-perfection" steaks and "man-size" sides; "boys'-club" looks and "friendly" staffers offset the typically "expensive" tabs.

Benchmark *American/Steak* `21` `21` `21` `$47`

Park Slope | 339 Second St. (bet. 4th & 5th Aves.) | Brooklyn | 718-965-7040 | www.benchmarkrestaurant.com

Nestled in an "intimate" carriage house, this "somewhat overlooked" Park Slope steakhouse offers "terrific" chops as well as "quite good" American accompaniments; fans admire its "calm" mood and midrange tabs, while a "lovely patio" allows it to "double in size" in good weather.

Benjamin Steak House *Steak* `26` `22` `24` `$75`

E 40s | Dylan Hotel | 52 E. 41st St. (bet. Madison & Park Aves.) | 212-297-9177 | www.benjaminsteakhouse.com

Luger alums are behind this "not well-known" hotel steakhouse where the "top-end" chops are priced for "corporate credit cards"; further assets include "engaging" service, a "high-ceilinged", fireplace-equipped setting and convenience to Grand Central, just one block away.

Benoit *French* `22` `21` `21` `$63`

W 50s | 60 W. 55th St. (bet. 5th & 6th Aves.) | 646-943-7373 | www.benoitny.com

After some "ups and downs", Alain Ducasse's Midtown French bistro has "hit its stride", fielding "classic", "true-to-its-roots" dishes (in-

| | FOOD | DECOR | SERVICE | COST |

cluding a "roast chicken of the gods") in a "well-lit" room that feels "like Paris"; though on the "pricey" side, most agree it's "worth a try."

Ben's Best   *Deli/Kosher* | 23 | 11 | 18 | $24 |

Rego Park | 96-40 Queens Blvd. (bet. 63rd Rd. & 64th Ave.) | Queens | 718-897-1700 | www.bensbest.com

For an "authentic artery-clogging experience", look no further than this circa-1945 Jewish deli known for "old-time" kosher fare "and lots of it"; the "oy!"-inducing decor is "just what you'd expect", but "Queens prices" and "ok service" compensate.

Ben's Kosher Deli   *Deli/Kosher* | 20 | 13 | 17 | $27 |

Garment District | 209 W. 38th St. (bet. 7th & 8th Aves.) | 212-398-2367
Bayside | Bay Terrace | 211-37 26th Ave. (Bell Blvd.) | Queens | 718-229-2367
www.bensdeli.net

"Sandwiches built for two" and other fresser's delights turn up at this "decent" kosher deli duo in Bayside and the Garment District; "luncheonette" looks and "uneven" service lead critics to pronounce the overall going "routine", but the tourists don't seem to care.

Beso   *Spanish* | 24 | 23 | 23 | $44 |

St. George | 11 Schuyler St. (Richmond Terr.) | Staten Island | 718-816-8162 | www.besonyc.com

A "short walk from the ferry", this St. George Spaniard rolls out "outstanding tapas" and "wonderful sangria" in a "relaxed" setting that "feels very far away from Staten Island"; admirers "wish it was bigger", though the price tags are fine as is.

Best Pizza ◑ *Pizza* | 24 | 15 | 19 | $15 |

Williamsburg | 33 Havemeyer St. (bet. N. 7th & 8th Sts.) | Brooklyn | 718-599-2210 | www.best.piz.za.com

The Roberta's team is behind this "funky" Williamsburg pizzeria where the "perfectly executed" pies are fired in a century-old brick oven and available by the slice; "paper plates", "hand-hewn" decor and "hip-hop on the stereo" exemplify the "new Brooklyn aesthetic."

Betel   *SE Asian* | 22 | 22 | 21 | $51 |

W Village | 51 Grove St. (bet. Bleecker St. & 7th Ave. S.) | 212-352-0460 | www.betelnyc.com

"Unique spins" on SE Asian street food are slung at this "cool" West Villager; its "stiletto"-clad fan base likes the "dark, dimly lit" setting and "jumping scene", the "tight tables" and "pricey" tabs not so much.

Betto ◑ Ⓜ *Italian*   ▽ | 25 | 23 | 22 | $41 |

Williamsburg | 138 N. Eighth St. (bet. Bedford Ave. & Berry St.) | Brooklyn | 718-384-1904 | www.bettonyc.com

Bringing his "delicious" Italian small-plates concept to Williamsburg, Jason Denton ('Ino, 'Inoteca) adds some Brooklyn touches to the mix like "bespoke cocktails", a "long communal table" and a roll-up front door; the end result is both "easygoing" and "affordable."

Bettola ◑ *Italian* | 19 | 16 | 19 | $37 |

W 70s | 412 Amsterdam Ave. (bet. 79th & 80th Sts.) | 212-787-1660 | www.bettolanyc.com

"Comfortable" is the word on this "popular" UWS trattoria, offering "simple but tasty" Italiana highlighted by thin-crust pizzas; given the "reasonable" tabs, its "neighborhood" following ignores the "inconsistent" service and so-so decor.

Beyoglu *Turkish*
| 22 | 17 | 18 | $37 |

E 80s | 1431 Third Ave. (81st St.) | 212-650-0850

"Craveable" meze is the calling card of this "perennially popular" UES Turk; those who want to "hear their tablemates" opt for the upstairs dining room, but wherever you sit, the tabs are "affordable", the mood "upbeat" and the service "variable."

Bianca ⊄ *Italian*
| 26 | 19 | 22 | $32 |

NoHo | 5 Bleecker St. (bet. Bowery & Elizabeth St.) | 212-260-4666 | www.biancanyc.com

"Low prices", "low lighting" and "outstanding" Emilia-Romagna fare draw the "hipster" trade to this "constantly jammed", cash-only NoHo Italian; "tiny" digs and a no-rezzie policy make for inevitable "long lines", but the "next-door wine bar" is a pleasant enough holding pen.

NEW Biang ⊄ *Chinese/Noodle Shop*
| ∇ 21 | 22 | 19 | $28 |

Flushing | 41-10 Main St. (bet. 41st Ave. & 41st Rd.) | Queens | 718-888-7713 | www.biang-nyc.com

There's plenty of biang for the buck at this new, cash-only Flushing spot from the owner of Xi'an Famous Foods, slinging spicy, Western Chinese–style bowls of hand-ripped noodles along with skewered meats for ultracheap sums; it gets bonus points for waiter service and a semi-upscale setting.

Bice ◑ *Italian*
| 22 | 20 | 20 | $64 |

E 50s | 7 E. 54th St. (bet. 5th & Madison Aves.) | 212-688-1999 | www.bicenewyork.com

For "entertaining" people-watching, there's always this "elite" Midtown Italian where the "lively" crowd ranges from blasé "Euros" to wide-eyed "tourists" and "power"-lunchers; you don't last this long without having reliably good food, but it helps to "look like a big spender" and have a couple of Bellinis to "ease the pain of the bill."

Big Nick's
Burger Joint *Burgers*
| 19 | 9 | 16 | $18 |

W 70s | 2175 Broadway (77th St.) | 212-362-9238 ◑
W 70s | 70 W. 71st St. (bet. Columbus Ave. & CPW) | 212-799-4444
www.bignicksny.com

"Hangover burgers" highlight the "everything-but-the-kitchen-sink" menu of these separately owned UWS "grease museums" where "cheap", "sinful" diner eats, "bus-terminal" decor and "cranky" service are part of the "old-school" experience.

NEW Bigoli Ⓜ *Italian*
| ∇ 19 | 19 | 21 | $58 |

W Village | 140 W. 13th St. (bet. 6th & 7th Aves.) | 212-647-1001 | www.bigolirestaurant.com

Although "still finding its way" following a chef change, this midpriced West Village Italian offers "fine if not very interesting" pizzas, pastas and tapas from a massive wood-burning oven; "noisy" acoustics are offset by "well-meaning" service and a "comfortable" setting replete with palm trees and a skylight.

	FOOD	DECOR	SERVICE	COST

Big Wong ≠ *Chinese*   **22** | **6** | **12** | **$15**

Chinatown | 67 Mott St. (bet. Bayard & Canal Sts.) | 212-964-0540 |
www.bigwongking.com

"Genuine, moan-provoking" Cantonese fare ("amazing congee", "outstanding roast meats") explains the "mob scene" at this cash-only
C-towner; given the "insanely inexpensive" checks, it's easy to overlook
the "nonexistent" decor, "rushed" service and unfortunate name.

NEW Bill's 🅂🅼 *American*   **-** | **-** | **-** | **E**

E 50s | 57 E. 54th St. (bet. Madison & Park Aves.) | 212-518-2727
The legendary, circa-1924 speakeasy Bill's Gay Nineties is back, now
transformed into a chic Midtown triplex promising an American grill
menu heavy on steaks and oysters; chef-to-the-stars John DeLucie
(Crown, The Lion) is behind the burners, so expect his Page Six–ready
following, especially in the impregnable third-floor inner sanctum.

Bill's Bar & Burger *Burgers*   **20** | **16** | **18** | **$25**

Meatpacking | 22 Ninth Ave. (13th St.) | 212-414-3003 ◑
W 50s | 16 W. 51st St. (bet. 5th & 6th Aves.) | 212-705-8510
www.billsbarandburger.com

"Good ol' fashioned burgers" and "craft beer on tap" are the highlights
at Steve Hanson's "hopping" hamburger hamlets, where "authentic"
disco fries and "creative" alcoholic shakes add zest; both outlets share
"efficient service" and "fair pricing", but look out for "tourist hordes"
at Rock Center.

Biricchino 🅂 *Italian*   **21** | **16** | **22** | **$39**

Chelsea | 260 W. 29th St. (8th Ave.) | 212-695-6690 | www.biricchino.com
Set in a "neighborhood with few choices", this MSG-convenient Chelsea
vet rolls out "real-deal" Northern Italiana, particularly its "incredible"
housemade sausages; true, the decor may leave "much to be desired",
but service is "attentive" and the pricing as "low-key" as the mood.

Birreria ◑ *Italian*   **22** | **21** | **19** | **$42**

Flatiron | Eataly | 200 Fifth Ave., 15th fl. (bet. 23rd & 24th Sts.) |
212-937-8910 | www.eataly.com

Perched on Eataly's rooftop, this all-seasons, retractable-roofed beer
garden dispenses a "wonderful" selection of cask ales backed up by a
"simple" Italian menu heavy on cheese and salumi; it would "feel like
a secret" Flatiron hideaway except that "every tourist in the universe"
knows about it, so "to actually gain access, go early."

Bistango *Italian*   **22** | **18** | **24** | **$40**

Murray Hill | 415 Third Ave. (29th St.) | 212-725-8484 |
www.bistangonyc.com

While the Italian offerings at this "old-school" Murray Hill perennial
are certainly "tasty", it's the "wonderful gluten-free" options – "even
beer" – that earn the most praise; "reasonable" pricing and "accommodating" service led by an "engaging host" seal the deal.

Bistro Cassis *French*   **20** | **18** | **18** | **$47**

W 70s | 225 Columbus Ave. (bet. 70th & 71st Sts.) | 212-579-3966 |
www.bistrocassis.com

For a serving of "old Paris on the UWS", this French bistro can be
counted on for "traditional", "satisfying" dishes that are fairly priced;

the "no-reservations" policy is a turn-off, but the "intimate" interior and "expeditious" service make it "good pre–Lincoln Center", an "easy walk" away.

	FOOD	DECOR	SERVICE	COST

Bistro Chat Noir *French*

20 | 20 | 21 | $55

E 60s | 22 E. 66th St. (bet. 5th & Madison Aves.) | 212-794-2428 | www.bistrochatnoir.com

A "low-key fave" in a "chic" address off Madison Avenue, this Gallic Eastsider caters to "fashionable" folk with "Parisian intimacy" and "quite good" French bistro fare dispensed in a "snug" setting; tabs are "expensive", but a "fantastic" owner and "convivial staff" keep customers satisfied.

Bistro Citron *French*

21 | 18 | 21 | $47

W 80s | 473 Columbus Ave. (bet. 82nd & 83rd Sts.) | 212-400-9401 | www.bistrocitronnyc.com

Upper Westsiders fancying a "taste of Paree" head to this "re-laxed", "old-style" bistro purveying "reliably good" French country cooking in a "happy" milieu; it "won't drain your bank account" and is a "great place to take your mom or girlfriend du jour", hence it's a "neighborhood favorite."

Bistro de la Gare Ⓜ *Mediterranean*

24 | 19 | 23 | $53

W Village | 626 Hudson St. (Jane St.) | 212-242-4420 | www.bistrodelagarenyc.com

"Grown-up dining" comes to the "oh-so-trendy" West Village via this "quaint little" Med boîte offering an "informal", "down-to-earth" menu of "lovingly prepared" items; "intimate" environs, "personal ser-vice" and not-bad tabs embellish its "enjoyable" vibe, while a "best-kept secret" back garden seals the deal.

Bistro Les Amis ❷ *French*

23 | 20 | 23 | $47

SoHo | 180 Spring St. (Thompson St.) | 212-226-8645 | www.bistrolesamis.com

Bringing a soupçon of the "Left Bank" to SoHo, this 15-year-old French bistro lures fans with its "comforting" cooking vs. cost ratio; ok, there's "no scene" going on, but sidewalk seats provide prime people-watching and the "*charmant*" staff lives up to the promise of its name.

Bistro Le Steak *French*

19 | 16 | 19 | $48

E 70s | 1309 Third Ave. (75th St.) | 212-517-3800 | www.bistrolesteak.com

A "neighborhood anchor" for the "10021 set", this "not trendy" UES bistro dispenses "simple", "understated" French food "without sky-high prices" or attitude; although certainly "nothing fancy" (and per-haps "in need of renovation"), this perennial "has been here for years" and is a favorite of Mayor Bloomberg.

Bistro Milano *Italian*

21 | 20 | 21 | $47

W 50s | 1350 Sixth Ave. (enter on 55th St., bet. 5th & 6th Aves.) | 212-757-2600 | www.bistromilanonyc.com

"Fresh pasta", "excellent pizza" and a "spacious" outdoor terrace combine to make this "midpriced" Northern Italian from the Bice folks a "reliable" drop-in; given its modern looks and "convenience to City Center" and "Fifth Avenue shopping", it's a natural for theatergoers and "tourists" alike.

	FOOD	DECOR	SERVICE	COST

Bistro 61 *French*   20 | 16 | 20 | $44

E 60s | 1113 First Ave. (61st St.) | 212-223-6220 | www.bistro61.com
UES locals tout this "everyday" French bistro near the Queensborough
Bridge for its "flavorful", Moroccan-accented cooking "served with a
smile" by an "earnest" crew; "decent" pricing and a "relaxing", brick-
walled setting add to the overall "charming" effect.

Bistro Ten 18 *American*   20 | 18 | 20 | $39

W 100s | 1018 Amsterdam Ave. (110th St.) | 212-662-7600 |
www.bistroten18.com
It's "slim pickings" for decent dining in Morningside Heights, and this
"shabby-chic" American is "one of the better options" given its "solid"
menu and "relaxed" service; while tabs are "budget-friendly", the view
of St. John the Divine from its sidewalk seats is "priceless."

Bistro Vendôme *French*   22 | 20 | 21 | $56

E 50s | 405 E. 58th St. (bet. 1st Ave. & Sutton Pl.) | 212-935-9100 |
www.bistrovendomenyc.com
"Sutton seniors" gather at this "upscale bistro" for French specialties
dispatched by "Gallic-accented staffers" who are as "charming" as the
tri-level townhouse setting; though the noise level and tabs can be "a
bit much", dining on the "particularly pretty" terrace is "delightful."

Black Duck *American/Seafood*   23 | 20 | 22 | $49

Murray Hill | Park South Hotel | 122 E. 28th St. (bet. Lexington Ave. &
Park Ave. S.) | 212-448-0888 | www.blackduckny.com
"Dark" and "cozy", this "sleeper" hotel tavern on a "nothing" Murray
Hill block provides "upmarket" New Americana with a seafood slant for
a "fair price"; service is "spot-on", while a "mood-setting fireplace",
"wonderful weekend jazz" and "clubby but not stuffy" vibe add allure.

Black Iron Burger Shop ◑⇤ *Burgers*   21 | 15 | 18 | $19

E Village | 540 E. Fifth St. (bet. Aves. A & B) | 212-677-6067 |
www.blackironburger.com
"Pretty damn good" "no-frills" burgers paired with draft pints "go
down easy" at this cash-only East Village "hole-in-the-wall"; though
the "earthy" setting's on the "small" side, the staff is "fun", the tabs
"reasonable" and the late-night hours a bonus.

Black Whale *American*   22 | 20 | 22 | $30

City Island | 279 City Island Ave. (Hawkins St.) | Bronx | 718-885-3657
The "offbeat" nautical decor conjures up "Cape Cod in the Bronx" at
this "cute" City Island vet where the "inexpensive" New American
menu includes some notably "decadent desserts"; fans find the Sunday
brunch and back patio equally "memorable."

NEW Blanca ⊠Ⓜ *American*   - | - | - | VE

Bushwick | 261 Moore St. (Bogart St.) | Brooklyn | 646-703-2715 |
www.blancanyc.com
Bushwick's beloved Roberta's goes upscale with the addition of this
fine-dining destination set in a spare, 12-seat loft space where an
open kitchen sends out a lavish tasting menu – offered at a single 6 PM
seating – to the lucky few able to snag reservations; chef Carlo Mirarchi's
meticulously wrought New American courses arrive artfully presented
on high-end china, appropriate to the $180 price tag.

Blaue Gans   *Austrian/German*

FOOD	DECOR	SERVICE	COST
22	19	20	$48

TriBeCa | 139 Duane St. (bet. Church St. & W. B'way) |
212-571-8880 | www.kg-ny.com

"First-rate" Wiener schnitzel heads the list of "hearty" Austro-German dishes at Kurt Gutenbrunner's "down-to-earth" "neighborhood" TriBeCan, abetted by "wonderful" Teutonic brews; the poster-lined room is "simple" but "cool", while "fair prices" and "pleasant" staffers add to the "gemütlich" mood.

Blossom   *Vegan/Vegetarian*

FOOD	DECOR	SERVICE	COST
23	19	21	$34

Chelsea | 187 Ninth Ave. (bet. 21st & 22nd Sts.) | 212-627-1144
W 80s | 466 Columbus Ave. (bet. 82nd & 83rd Sts.) | 212-875-2600
NEW **W Village** | 41 Carmine St. (bet. Bedford & Bleecker Sts.) |
646-438-9939

Blossom du Jour   *Vegan/Vegetarian*

Chelsea | 174 Ninth Ave. (bet. 20th & 21st Sts.) | 212-229-2595
NEW **W 40s** | 617 Ninth Ave. (bet. 43rd & 44th Sts.) | 646-998-3535
NEW **W 60s** | 165 Amsterdam Ave. (bet. 67th & 68th Sts.) | 212-799-9010
www.blossomdujour.com

"Plant-based food" gets a "delicious" spin at these "guilt-free" vegans known for dishes so "inventive" they could "convert meat eaters"; "friendly" staffers and "peaceful" digs come along with the affordable tabs, while the du Jour take-out venues vend "healthy meals on the run."

BLT Bar & Grill   *American*

FOOD	DECOR	SERVICE	COST
22	20	20	$50

Financial District | W Hotel Downtown | 123 Washington St. (bet. Albany & Carlisle Sts.) | 646-826-8666 | www.bltrestaurants.com

A "classier" option in the "barren Financial District", this American tavern in the W Downtown serves "upscale" standards to "expense-account" wielders and "9/11 Memorial" visitors; the ceilings in this duplex are as "high" as the bills, but the after-work scene is "lively."

BLT Burger   *Burgers*

FOOD	DECOR	SERVICE	COST
22	16	19	$29

G Village | 470 Sixth Ave. (bet. 11th & 12th Sts.) | 212-243-8226 |
www.bltburger.com

"High-end burgers" are flipped in a "low-key" setting at this "diner"-esque Villager where "decadence" comes in the form of "big, juicy" patties, "top-notch" sides and "thick shakes" (some of them "boozy"); service lies somewhere between "prompt" and "rushed", while critics call it "overpriced" for what it is.

BLT Fish   ⊠ *Seafood*

FOOD	DECOR	SERVICE	COST
23	21	22	$62

Flatiron | 21 W. 17th St. (bet. 5th & 6th Aves.) | 212-691-8888 |
www.bltfish.com

"Straight-out-of-the-water" seafood is the bait at this Flatiron fish-monger famed for its "expertly prepared" catch, "exceptional" service and "stylish" setting beneath a "giant skylight"; brace for "a whopper of a tab" in the "more genteel" upstairs room, or set your anchor in the more "funky" ground-floor Fish Shack where it's "cheaper" and "louder."

BLT Prime   *Steak*

FOOD	DECOR	SERVICE	COST
25	23	23	$75

Gramercy | 111 E. 22nd St. (bet. Lexington Ave. & Park Ave. S.) |
212-995-8500 | www.bltprime.com

"They know their way around a cow" at this "chic" Gramercy steak-house touted for "perfectly cooked" chops and "light-as-a-feather" popovers; "stellar" wines, "solicitous" service and "sleek" decor add to the overall "special experience" and help explain tabs that may "leave your credit card smoking."

BLT Steak *Steak*
25 | 23 | 23 | $79

E 50s | 106 E. 57th St. (bet. Lexington & Park Aves.) | 212-752-7470 | www.bltsteak.com

Frequented by "suits", "big spenders and pretty ladies", this Midtown chop shop sizzles with "outstanding" steaks accompanied by "first-rate" sides and popovers "on steroids"; "super service" and a "swanky" setting amplify the "power-scene" vibes, but "bring lots of money" – the pricing's "sky high."

NEW Blue Collar ● *Burgers*
- | - | - | I

Williamsburg | 160 Havemeyer St. (bet. S. 2nd & 3rd Sts.) | Brooklyn | 347-725-3837

West Coast–style, flat top–griddled burgers come at a neighborhood-appropriate price – four bucks for the most basic version – at this funky new Williamsburg patty palace; not much decor and hipster service are part of the unpretentious package.

Blue Fin ● *Seafood*
23 | 22 | 21 | $56

W 40s | W Hotel Times Sq. | 1567 Broadway (47th St.) | 212-918-1400 | www.bluefinnyc.com

A safe "harbor" in "hectic" Times Square, Steve Hanson's "hoppin'" Broadway seafooder offers "fin-tastic" food to showgoers and "visiting relatives", dispensed by a "courteous" if "somewhat frenzied" crew; in case the "big, brassy" setting becomes "raucous", note that it's "calmer" in the mezzanine seats, but up or down, you'll have to take a deep dive into your wallet.

Blue Ginger *Asian*
21 | 17 | 20 | $32

Chelsea | 106 Eighth Ave. (bet. 15th & 16th Sts.) | 212-352-0911

Handy for a "quick bite before a show" at the nearby Joyce Theater, this "fun" Chelsea Pan-Asian slices sushi that's "pleasing to the eye" and also offers "mouthwatering" cooked items, all "well priced"; "friendly" staffers take your mind off the "typical" decor.

Z Blue Hill *American*
27 | 24 | 26 | $87

G Village | 75 Washington Pl. (bet. MacDougal St. & 6th Ave.) | 212-539-1776 | www.bluehillfarm.com

A locavore "pioneer", Dan Barber's "sublime" Village American is famed for its "vibrant flavors" and "amazing ingredients" bursting with "straight-from-the-farm" freshness; the "calming" setting, "above-and-beyond" service and "peace-and-quiet" acoustics help mute the "expensive" tabs, though reservations are more "difficult" since "Barack and Michelle" showed up.

Blue 9 Burger *Burgers*
19 | 10 | 15 | $14

E 70s | 1415 Second Ave. (bet. 73rd & 74th Sts.) | 212-988-8171 ●
E Village | 92 Third Ave. (bet. 12th & 13th Sts.) | 212-979-0053 | www.orderbluenine.com ●
W 50s | 789 Ninth Ave. (bet. 52nd & 53rd Sts.) | 212-333-3042

Though the mood's "fast food", the burgers are "quite delectable" at this "tasty" trio and come at you "fast and cheap"; the East Village original is an "after-hours" magnet for the "student-hipster" set, though snobs reserve it for "delivery" given the "indifferent service" and "unexciting" digs.

Blue Ribbon ● *American*   25 | 20 | 23 | $54

SoHo | 97 Sullivan St. (bet. Prince & Spring Sts.) | 212-274-0404
Blue Ribbon Brooklyn ● *American*
Park Slope | 280 Fifth Ave. (bet. 1st St. & Garfield Pl.) | Brooklyn | 718-840-0404
www.blueribbonrestaurants.com

The Bromberg brothers "deserve a blue ribbon" for these "nifty" SoHo–Park Slope New Americans rolling out a "sublime", "a-to-z" menu that runs the gamut "from foie gras to matzo ball soup"; "personable service", "unpretentious" settings and "night-owl" hours balance out "loud" acoustics, "pricey" tabs and "long waits" due to the "no-rezzie challenge."

Blue Ribbon Bakery ● *American*   25 | 19 | 21 | $42

W Village | 35 Downing St. (Bedford St.) | 212-337-0404 | www.blueribbonrestaurants.com

The "wonderful smell" of bread perfumes the air at the Bromberg brothers' "crusty" West Village American, a bistro-bakery combo supplying the "epitome of comfort food", "enthusiastic" service and a particularly "standout" brunch; both its "shoebox"-size ground floor and bigger "wine-cellar"-esque basement are equally "long on charm."

Blue Ribbon Sushi ● *Japanese*   26 | 20 | 23 | $59

SoHo | 119 Sullivan St. (bet. Prince & Spring Sts.) | 212-343-0404 | www.blueribbonrestaurants.com

Long a "standard bearer of cool" in SoHo, this Bromberg brothers Japanese slices "top-flight", "work-of-art" sushi along with a "wonderful array" of cooked items; "proactive service" and "cozy", "denlike" digs offset "pretty-penny" price tags and that "frustrating" no-rez thing.

Blue Ribbon Sushi Bar & Grill ● *Japanese*   25 | 21 | 23 | $61

W 50s | 6 Columbus Hotel | 308 W. 58th St. (bet. 8th & 9th Aves.) | 212-397-0404 | www.blueribbonrestaurants.com

Somewhat "swankier" than its "bohemian kin", this "inviting" Japanese "tucked away" in a Columbus Circle hotel is touted for its "fresh-off-the-boat" sushi and "impeccable" grilled fare; it shares the "mellow" vibes, late-night hours and "steep tabs" of its Downtown siblings.

NEW Blue Ribbon   – | – | – | E
Sushi Izakaya ● *Japanese*

LES | Thompson LES Hotel | 187 Orchard St. (bet. Houston & Stanton Sts.) | 212-466-0404 | www.blueribbonrestaurants.com

The Blue Ribbon brand burgeons on at this latest entry in the Thompson LES Hotel, where the extensive Japanese menu includes a signature fried chicken along with eight varieties of fried rice; the wide-open, two-room setting is dimly lit and is outfitted with a mix of communal tables and more private booths.

Ⓩ Blue Smoke *BBQ*   23 | 19 | 21 | $42

NEW Financial District | 255 Vesey St. (bet. North End Ave. & West St.) | 212-889-2005
Murray Hill | 116 E. 27th St. (bet. Lexington Ave. & Park Ave. S.) | 212-447-7733

(continued)

Blue Smoke

Flushing | Citi Field | 126th St. & Roosevelt Ave. (behind the scoreboard) | Queens | No phone
www.bluesmoke.com

Danny Meyer's "enjoyable" rib joints sling "finger-lickin'", "four-napkin" BBQ washed down with an "extensive" range of beers and bourbons, all for "down-home" dough; while the "waits can be a pain" and there's debate about authenticity ("respectful" vs. "commercialized"), the hallmark "hospitality" keeps the mood "effervescent"; P.S. the Murray Hill original is set atop a "smoking" live jazz cellar.

☒ Blue Water Grill *Seafood* | 24 | 23 | 22 | $58 |

Union Sq | 31 Union Sq. W. (16th St.) | 212-675-9500 |
www.bluewatergrillnyc.com

Set in a former bank building with "soaring ceilings, grand columns" and "plenty of marble", Steve Hanson's "roomy" Union Square seafooder follows through with "top-flight" catch, "welcoming" service and prices on the "premium" side of the scale; "high decibels" come with the "energetic" territory, but bonuses include smooth jazz downstairs and "unbeatable people-watching."

☒ Boathouse *American* | 19 | 26 | 19 | $54 |

E 70s | Central Park | Central Park Lake, enter on E. 72nd St. (Park Dr. N.) | 212-517-2233 | www.thecentralparkboathouse.com

A "tranquil" "retreat from the urban jungle", this "sun-soaked", lake-adjacent American with a Central Park setting right out of an "Impressionist painting" is a natural for "soirees" and "celebrations"; maybe the eats are "forgettable", the service "uneven" and the crowd "touristy", but no one cares: the scenery's "wow factor" makes it "special."

Bobby Van's Steakhouse *Steak* | 23 | 20 | 22 | $66 |

E 40s | 230 Park Ave. (46th St.) | 212-867-5490 🛪
E 50s | 131 E. 54th St. (bet. Lexington & Park Aves.) | 212-207-8050
Financial District | 25 Broad St. (Exchange Pl.) | 212-344-8463 🛪
John F. Kennedy Airport | Terminal 8, Across from Gate 14 | JFK Access Rd. | Queens | 718-553-2100

Bobby Van's Grill *Steak*

W 40s | 120 W. 45th St. (bet. 6th & 7th Aves.) | 212-575-5623
W 50s | 135 W. 50th St. (bet. 6th & 7th Aves.) | 212-957-5050
www.bobbyvans.com

"Manly-man" steaks toted by "experienced waiters" are trademarks at this "testosterone-city" mini-chain; "clubby" looks make it just the ticket for "business lunches" (especially in the Financial District branch's "cool old bank vault"), but when the check arrives, it helps to be a "hedge-fund manager."

Bobo *French* | 23 | 24 | 21 | $53 |

W Village | 181 W. 10th St. (7th Ave. S.) | 212-488-2626 | www.bobonyc.com

The "ambiance is the selling point" at this "low-lit" West Village townhouse, now serving a "well-prepared" French menu to a "Euro"-heavy following either in an "ornate dining room", outdoor terrace or "more youthful" downstairs bar; it may be a tad "expensive", but service is "friendly" and the vibrations "charming."

	FOOD	DECOR	SERVICE	COST

Boca Chica *Pan-Latin* 24 | 18 | 20 | $32

E Village | 13 First Ave. (1st St.) | 212-473-0108 | www.bocachicanyc.com
"Large portions" of "flavorful" Pan-Latin chow chased with "home-made sangria" keep this East Village "hole-in-the-wall" hopping with "fun" young folks; no one minds the "loud music" and "close-together" tables given the "affordable" tabs and good company.

Bocca 🌢 *Italian* 22 | 19 | 21 | $46

Flatiron | 39 E. 19th St. (bet. B'way & Park Ave. S.) | 212-387-1200 | www.boccanyc.com
It "feels like Rome" at this "enjoyable" Cacio e Pepe sibling in the Flatiron known for its "expert" Italian cooking, "appealing" modern look and "reasonable" rates; regulars say "pasta is the thing to eat" here, notably its "cool" signature dish tossed tableside in a wheel of pecorino.

Bocca 🌢 *Italian* 21 | 21 | 19 | $44

E 70s | 1496 Second Ave. (78th St.) | 212-249-1010 | www.boccadibaccoeast.com
Bocca di Bacco 🌢 *Italian*
W 50s | 828 Ninth Ave. (bet. 54th & 55th Sts.) | 212-265-8828 | www.boccadibacconyc.com
"Old-world Italy" comes to Hell's Kitchen and the UES via this Italian duo vending "jazzed-up" standards bolstered by "sure-hit" wines by the glass and a "rustic", brick-walled setting; "uneven" quality and "up-and-down" service strike off-notes, but given the "decent prices" and "positive energy", most "go home happy."

Bocca Lupo 🌢 *Italian* 24 | 21 | 22 | $36

Cobble Hill | 391 Henry St. (Warren St.) | Brooklyn | 718-243-2522
A "wine-lovers' mecca", this "neighborhood" Cobble Hill enoteca pairs "delectable" Italian small plates with an "extensive" list of "reasonably priced" vinos; early evening, it's full of "kiddies getting their first foodie training", but later the mood gets "groovier" when the hipsters toddle in.

Bocelli *Italian/Seafood* 26 | 23 | 23 | $50

Grasmere | 1250 Hylan Blvd. (bet. Old Town Rd. & Parkinson Ave.) | Staten Island | 718-420-6150 | www.bocellirest.com
"Can't-miss" dining comes to Grasmere via this longtime "fine Italian" specializing in "city-quality" seafood served by a "top-notch" team; its "central-casting" following doesn't mind the "high prices" given extras like "valet parking", live entertainment and swanky, "palazzo"-ish digs.

Bodrum *Mediterranean/Turkish* 22 | 16 | 20 | $37

W 80s | 584 Amsterdam Ave. (bet. 88th & 89th Sts.) | 212-799-2806 | www.bodrumnyc.com
"Small and cozy", this UWS "neighborhood" Med is the "real deal" for "inexpensive" dining on "stellar" Turkish meze and "tasty thin-crust pizza"; though service is "speedy", it's often "crowded and cramped", so insiders flee to the "outside tables."

Bogota Latin Bistro *Pan-Latin* 25 | 21 | 23 | $29

Park Slope | 141 Fifth Ave. (bet. Lincoln & St. Johns Pls.) | Brooklyn | 718-230-3805 | www.bogotabistro.com
There's "big energy" aplenty at this Park Slope Pan-Latin, a "crazy-popular" spot for an "expertly seasoned", Colombia-centric menu

washed down with "killer" cocktails; "quick service" and "ridiculously affordable" tabs enhance the "festive" (verging on "raucous") vibe.

Bohemian ● ⑤ *Japanese* ∇ 26 | 26 | 26 | $70

NoHo | 57 Great Jones St. (bet. Bowery & Lafayette St.) | No phone
"Knowing someone" is the only way to access this "secret", "bucket-list" Japanese lurking behind a NoHo butcher shop – the "phone number is unlisted", so a referral (and a reservation) are musts; once inside the "tiny", "living room–style" setting, the "lucky few" find "delectable" cuisine, "meticulously" crafted cocktails and "charming hosts"; granted, the experience is "not cheap", but then again, the dining is "sublime."

Bo-Ky ⊅ *Noodle Shop* 22 | 8 | 13 | $15

Chinatown | 80 Bayard St. (bet. Mott & Mulberry Sts.) | 212-406-2292
Little Italy | 216 Grand St. (Elizabeth St.) | 212-219-9228
www.bokynyc.com
One of the few "good things about jury duty" is the chance to lunch at these Chinatown–Little Italy noodle shops churning out "authentic" Chinese and Vietnamese soups for ultra-"cheap" tabs; "dreary" decor, "busy" atmospherics and "poor" (albeit "quick") service come with the territory.

Bombay Palace ● *Indian* 20 | 19 | 19 | $42

W 50s | 30 W. 52nd St. (bet. 5th & 6th Aves.) | 212-541-7777 |
www.bombay-palace.com
On the Midtown scene since 1979, this "spacious" spot supplies subcontinental "standards" served by "slow" staffers; maybe the once-"sumptuous" surroundings are getting "a little tired", but no one's weary of its "good-value" $16 lunch buffet.

Bombay Talkie *Indian* 21 | 18 | 18 | $39

Chelsea | 189 Ninth Ave. (bet. 21st & 22nd Sts.) | 212-242-1900 |
www.bombaytalkie.com
"Change-of-pace" seekers tout this "not-typical" Chelsea Indian for its "original" takes on "less commonly seen" street food items; a "fun vibe" and semi-"stylish" digs decorated with "Bollywood" murals compensate for the slightly "upscale" pricing.

BonChon Chicken *Chicken* 22 | 13 | 15 | $21

E 50s | 957 Second Ave. (bet. 50th & 51st Sts.) | 212-308-8810
Financial District | 104 John St. (Cliff St.) | 646-682-7747 ●
Garment District | 207 W. 38th St. (bet. 7th & 8th Aves.) | 212-221-3339
Murray Hill | 325 Fifth Ave. (bet. 32nd & 33rd Sts.) | 212-686-8282 ●
Bayside | 45-37 Bell Blvd. (bet. 45th Dr. & 45th Rd.) | Queens |
718-225-1010 ●
www.bonchon.com
"Habit-forming" is the verdict on the "out-of-sight" Korean fried chicken with "crispy, parchmentlike skin" vended at this international chain; since the birds are cooked to order, expect "forever" waits, not to mention "slipshod" service, "no decor" and just-"decent" prices.

Bond 45 ● *Italian* 20 | 19 | 20 | $52

W 40s | 154 W. 45th St. (bet. 6th & 7th Aves.) | 212-869-4545 |
www.bond45.com
Shelly Fireman's "cavernous" Times Square trattoria in the old Bond clothing store provides a "straight-up", "something-for-everybody"

Italian menu dispensed in a "well-decorated barn" of a setting; "service with alacrity" suits theatergoers, though penny-pinchers may be pained by the tariffs.

Bond Street *Japanese*   25 | 23 | 22 | $66

NoHo | 6 Bond St. (bet. B'way & Lafayette St.) | 212-777-2500 | www.bondstrestaurant.com

"Everyone's fabulous" at this "too-hip-for-words" NoHo Japanese where a "snappy" staff serves "designer sushi" to "models", "i-bankers" and "celebs"; it's a "hot scene" – with prices to match – played out in a "chic" upstairs room or the kissy, "dimly lit" downstairs lounge.

Bonnie's Grill   *Burgers*   23 | 14 | 20 | $22

Park Slope | 278 Fifth Ave. (bet. 1st St. & Garfield Pl.) | Brooklyn | 718-369-9527 | www.bonniesgrill.com

Park Slopers refuel at this "short-order joint" slinging "damn good burgers" in "classic diner" digs; it's "fun sitting at the counter" and the grub's "well priced", but since the dimensions are "slim", "good luck getting a seat on the weekend."

Boqueria   *Spanish*   23 | 20 | 20 | $46

Flatiron | 53 W. 19th St. (bet. 5th & 6th Aves.) | 212-255-4160
SoHo | 171 Spring St. (bet. Thompson St. & W. B'way) | 212-343-4255
www.boquerianyc.com

"Graze your way" through "top-class tapas" at these "happening" Spaniards bringing a "transported-to-Barcelona" feel to the Flatiron and SoHo; a "competent" crew navigates the "no-room-to-spare" settings and "well-priced" wines offset tabs that "add up pretty quickly", but the no-rez rule results in "discouraging" waits.

Bottega del Vino   *Italian*   22 | 21 | 21 | $63

E 50s | 7 E. 59th St. (bet. 5th & Madison Aves.) | 212-223-2724 | www.bottegadelvinonyc.com

"Situated near everything" – or at least Bergdorf's, the Plaza and the Apple Store – this "relaxed" Midtown "replica of the Venice original" dispenses "tasty" Italiana bolstered by an "immense" wine selection; buoyant staffers maintain the "happy mood" . . . until the "priced-for-the-neighborhood" bill arrives.

Bottino   *Italian*   21 | 21 | 20 | $46

Chelsea | 246 10th Ave. (bet. 24th & 25th Sts.) | 212-206-6766 | www.bottinonyc.com

Convenient to West Chelsea's "gallery district" and the High Line, this "all-around pleasant" Tuscan "pioneer" delivers "solid" meals at "fair prices"; the "unhurried" pace suits its "arty" constituents, though the "charming", "spacious" garden is bound to please everyone.

Bouchon Bakery   *American/French*   24 | 17 | 20 | $25

W 40s | 1 Rockefeller Plaza (48th St., bet. 5th & 6th Aves.) | 212-782-3890
W 60s | Time Warner Ctr. | 10 Columbus Circle, 3rd fl. (60th St. at B'way) | 212-823-9366
www.bouchonbakery.com

Bringing the "Thomas Keller touch" to the masses, these cafe/patisserie combos purvey "transcendent pastries" and "fancy sandwiches" in "mall"-like settings; the mainly takeout Rock Center branch features

"*Today Show*" convenience, while its sit down–friendly Columbus Circle sibling boasts "scenic" Central Park vistas.

NEW Boukiés ● *Greek* ▽ 25 | 23 | 24 | $37

E Village | 29 E. Second St. (2nd Ave.) | 212-777-2502 | www.boukiesrestaurant.com

From the owners of the East Village favorite Pylos comes this nearby arrival specializing in "delicious", moderately priced Greek meze; the roomy setting feels more "grown-up" than the norm in these parts, with blond-wood tables and a Hellenic blue-and-white color scheme.

Z Bouley ✂ *French* 28 | 27 | 27 | $111

TriBeCa | 163 Duane St. (bet. Greenwich & Hudson Sts.) | 212-964-2525 | www.davidbouley.com

Starting with the "lovely scent of apples in the foyer", David Bouley's TriBeCa "trailblazer" is the epitome of "refined", "grown-up" dining, from the "superlative" New French fare to the "extraordinary" service and "sumptuous", jackets-required setting; granted, it can be "expensive", but in return you get a "priceless", near-"perfection" experience; P.S. the midday $55 prix fixe is "one of the best fancy lunch deals" in town.

Z Boulud Sud *Mediterranean* 25 | 23 | 24 | $74

W 60s | 20 W. 64th St. (bet. B'way & CPW) | 212-595-1313 | www.danielnyc.com

"Refined" dining comes to Lincoln Center-land via this "first-class" yearling from Daniel Boulud, plying "creative interpretations" of Med fare in an "elegant" venue adjacent to Bar Boulud; its "grown-up" fan base digs the "exquisite" cooking and "adroit" service, and the "big-bucks" tabs suggest there's "no sign of recession here."

Bourbon Street Café *Cajun/Southern* 19 | 18 | 20 | $31

Bayside | 40-12 Bell Blvd. (bet. 40th & 41st Aves.) | Queens | 718-224-2200 | www.bourbonstreetny.com

Bayside's take on a "N'Awlins dive", this "fun" pub dishes up "ample portions" of "solid" Cajun grub along with "decent" Southern-accented plates, all at "best-buy" rates; "blaring TVs" compete with the "big noisy bar scene" and overall "Mardi Gras" vibe.

NEW Bowery Diner ● *Diner* 18 | 17 | 17 | $29

LES | 241 Bowery (Prince St.) | 212-388-0052 | www.bowerydiner.com

Parked next to the New Museum, this LES newcomer conjures up "nostalgia" with "diner standards" dispensed 24/7 in retro digs equipped with an old-fashioned soda fountain counter; critics contend the chow is "just ok" and rather "overpriced", but supporters say it's still working out the kinks.

Braai *S African* 20 | 20 | 21 | $38

W 50s | 329 W. 51st St. (bet. 8th & 9th Aves.) | 212-315-3315 | www.braainyc.com

Diners with a "taste for adventure" mingle with "homesick expats" at this "different" Hell's Kitchen outpost specializing in South African barbecue; the "flavorful", "unique" eats (think ostrich and venison) arrive in a "hut"-like, "thatched-roof" setting that adds to the "novelty."

	FOOD	DECOR	SERVICE	COST

Brasserie *French*
22 | 22 | 22 | $53

E 50s | Seagram Bldg. | 100 E. 53rd St. (bet. Lexington & Park Aves.) | 212-751-4840 | www.patinagroup.com

Descending its "sleek catwalk" entrance makes fans feel "cosmopolitan" at this "ultracool" brasserie in the Seagram Building, a "longtime favorite" for "top-notch", all-day French dining; "high" prices and a "cacophonous" racket are counterbalanced by "pro" service and "streamlined", "spaceship" decor.

Brasserie Cognac ❶ *French*
20 | 19 | 18 | $46

W 50s | 1740 Broadway (55th St.) | 212-757-3600 | www.cognacrestaurant.com

"Homesick Parisians" feel at home at this "proper" Midtown brasserie offering "simple, tasty" standards at prices that "suit most budgets"; Carnegie Hall and City Center convenience make it a "good option" for theatergoers, though the "attractive", mirrored space also works for a "romantic" tête-à-tête.

Brasserie 8½ *French*
23 | 24 | 23 | $60

W 50s | 9 W. 57th St. (bet. 5th & 6th Aves.) | 212-829-0812 | www.patinagroup.com

"Glamorous" is the word on this Midtown brasserie accessed by a "Gloria Swanson"–style "grand stairway", where the equally "spiffy" French fare is served in a room lined with artwork by "Matisse and Leger"; it's "sedate" enough for "conversation without shouting", though very "active at the bar" after work.

NEW Brasserie Pushkin ❶ *Russian*
∇ 26 | 27 | 25 | $76

W 50s | 41 W. 57th St. (bet. 5th & 6th Aves.) | 212-465-2400 | www.brasseriepushkin.com

Crystal chandeliers, "ornate" ceilings and a "strikingly beautiful" crowd set the tone at this new Midtown triplex spun off from Moscow's "famed Cafe Pushkin"; the "delicious" French-accented Russian cuisine comes courtesy of a "welcoming" team, but take note that "you need to be an oligarch to afford it."

Brasserie Ruhlmann *French*
19 | 21 | 20 | $56

W 50s | 45 Rockefeller Plaza (enter on 50th St., bet. 5th & 6th Aves.) | 212-974-2020 | www.brasserieruhlmann.com

"Hobnob with the NBC crowd" and others "happily expensing their meals" at Laurent Tourondel's "heart-of-Rock-Center" brasserie, where the "old-world" art deco look is as "delightful" as the French cooking; service is "gracious", and "prime people-watching" from its patio ices the cake.

Bread Tribeca *Italian*
20 | 17 | 18 | $32

TriBeCa | 301 Church St. (Walker St.) | 212-334-0200 | www.breadtribeca.com

Bread ❶ *Sandwiches*

NoLita | 20 Spring St. (bet. Elizabeth & Mott Sts.) | 212-334-1015 | www.orderbreadsoho.com

There's "much more than bread" available at this "low-key" duo dishing up "affordable" Italiana highlighted by "satisfying" panini and "wonderful tomato soup"; service and "elbow room" may be in short supply, but its "cool hipster" fan base doesn't seem to mind.

	FOOD	DECOR	SERVICE	COST

Breeze *French/Thai*
21 | 15 | 18 | $28

W 40s | 661 Ninth Ave. (bet. 45th & 46th Sts.) | 212-262-7777 |
www.breezenyc.com

"Bright-orange decor" draws attention to this "unique" Hell's Kitchen
venue that plies "serious" Thai-French fusion vittles along with "fruity
drinks" in "long, narrow" digs; "rapid" service and "too-good-to-be-
true" pricing make it a "great first act" pre-theater.

Brennan & Carr ●⊅ *Sandwiches*
22 | 12 | 19 | $18

Sheepshead Bay | 3432 Nostrand Ave. (Ave. U) | Brooklyn | 718-646-9559
Now in its 75th year, this cash-only Sheepshead Bay "tradition" still
"rocks" thanks to "outrageous" double-dipped roast beef sandwiches
"drowned in au jus"; it's something of a "dive" with "table-mat menus",
but enthusiasts of "old-fashioned goodness" keep returning "with the
new generation in tow."

The Breslin ● *British*
24 | 22 | 19 | $49

Chelsea | Ace Hotel | 16 W. 29th St. (bet. B'way & 5th Ave.) |
212-679-1939 | www.thebreslin.com

"Sceney but satisfying", this "dark, woody" Ace Hotel destination
from Ken Friedman and April Bloomfield offers "heavenly" "meat in all
of its forms" on its "decadent" British menu, but the "beautiful" "hipster" crowd steals the "show"; "noise", "too-cool-for-school" service
and no rez–induced "waits" come with the territory.

Brgr *Burgers*
19 | 14 | 15 | $17

Chelsea | 287 Seventh Ave. (bet. 26th & 27th Sts.) | 212-488-7500
E 60s | 1026 Third Ave. (bet. 60th & 61st Sts.) | 212-588-0080
www.brgr.com

"Brgr lvrs" plug this "highbrow fast-food" duo for its "solid" "grass-fed
beef" version "made to order" with "neat toppings" and augmented
with "excellent" shakes; but critics find "only average" patties that
"can be pricey" for their "abbreviated" size.

Bricco *Italian*
21 | 19 | 22 | $45

W 50s | 304 W. 56th St. (bet. 8th & 9th Aves.) | 212-245-7160 |
www.bricconyc.com

This Hell's Kitchen Italian hideaway is a "steady" source of "well-
prepared" pasta and wood-oven pizza delivered by the "nicest staff";
"reasonable rates" and "warm" atmospherics (check out the lipsticked
kisses on the ceiling) buttress its "reliable" rep.

Brick Cafe *French/Italian*
22 | 20 | 21 | $34

Astoria | 30-95 33rd St. (31st Ave.) | Queens | 718-267-2735 |
www.brickcafe.com

Astorians assemble at this "neighborhood standby" for "tasty" French-
Italian eats served in rustic digs so atmospheric that it's "hard to believe
you're in Queens"; "reasonable" rates, weekly "live jazz" and "can't-
be-beat" alfresco tables are further reasons why it's "always packed."

Brick Lane Curry House *Indian*
22 | 16 | 19 | $29

E 50s | 235 E. 53rd St. (bet. 2nd & 3rd Aves.) | 212-339-8353 |
www.bricklanetoo.com
NEW **E 90s** | 1664 Third Ave. (bet. 93rd & 94th Sts.) | 646-998-4440 |
www.bricklanecurryhouse.com

(continued)

(continued)

Brick Lane Curry House

E Village | 306-308 E. Sixth St. (bet. 1st & 2nd Aves.) | 212-979-2900 | www.bricklanecurryhouse.com

There's "no need to go to London – let alone India" – thanks to this curry-savvy East Side mini-chain purveying "real-deal" dishes with heat levels ranging from "mild to crazy hot" (the "fiery phaal" requires "extra napkins to wipe away the sweat and tears"); like the decor, the tabs are distinctly "low budget."

Bridge Cafe *American*

| 22 | 20 | 22 | $45 |

Financial District | 279 Water St. (Dover St.) | 212-227-3344 | www.bridgecafenyc.com

"Longevity" in a site "hidden below the Brooklyn Bridge" is the claim to fame of this circa-1794 tavern, fielding "feel-good" American chow along with a heaping side of "bygone" NY "nostalgia"; "cordial" staffers and moderate tabs please regulars who say the "way-back", "slightly ramshackle" mood is the real draw here.

Brio *Italian*

| 21 | 17 | 19 | $44 |

E 60s | 137 E. 61st St. (Lexington Ave.) | 212-980-2300 | www.brionyc.com
Flatiron | 920 Broadway (21st St.) | 212-673-2121 | www.flatiron.brionyc.com

These "bustling" Italians in the Flatiron and near Bloomie's are "handy" options for "basic" refueling on "relatively inexpensive" pastas and pizzas; "efficient" service compensates for "dark", "lacking" settings, but then again the dining is "grown-up" and "civilized."

NEW Brooklyn Crab *Seafood*

| - | - | - | M |

Red Hook | 24 Reed St. (bet. Conover & Van Brunt Sts.) | Brooklyn | 718-643-2722 | www.brooklyncrab.com

From the owners of Alma, this new triple-decker Red Hook seafooder fields a moderately priced menu of fish-shack classics and raw bar snacks; additional attractions include mini-golf and free peak-hour shuttle service from the Carroll Street F/G subway stop.

⛫ Brooklyn Fare Kitchen *French*

| 27 | 19 | 25 | $293 |

Downtown Bklyn | 200 Schermerhorn St. (Hoyt St.) | Brooklyn | 718-243-0050 | www.brooklynfare.com

A "must on any foodie's bucket list", this Downtown Brooklyn "gastronomic temple" showcases chef Cesar Ramirez's Japanese-inspired French cooking via 20-plus "out-of-this-world" small plates served in the "spartan" prep kitchen of a gourmet grocery; no question, the $225 prix fixe-only menu is "very expensive", yet it's still the "toughest reservation in the city" with only 18 counterside stools (arranging to "have dinner with the president would be easier"); P.S. it "now has wine" so you needn't BYO.

Brooklyn Fish Camp ⛫ *Seafood*

| 23 | 17 | 20 | $42 |

Park Slope | 162 Fifth Ave. (bet. Degraw & Douglass Sts.) | Brooklyn | 718-783-3264 | www.brooklynfishcamp.com

"Peerless freshness" makes for happy campers at this "laid-back" Park Slope sequel to Mary's Fish Camp that "hits the mark" with "robust" whole fish and "spot-on" lobster rolls; the tabs may be "pricey" considering its "clam-shack", "wine-in-a-juice-glass" approach, but that backyard garden sure is "fantastic."

	FOOD	DECOR	SERVICE	COST

NEW Brooklyn Seoul ⏪ Korean/Noodle Shop — — — | I |

Williamsburg | 749 Metropolitan Ave. (bet. Graham Ave. & Humboldt St.) |
Brooklyn | 718-576-3050 | www.brooklynseoul.com

Williamsburg's ramen shortage is answered at this new Korean noodle
shop offering chicken, pork and veggie varieties, along with pork-belly
buns and build-your-own bibimbop; cheap tabs make up for the lack
of space and seats.

Brother Jimmy's BBQ *BBQ* 17 | 14 | 16 | $28

E 70s | 1485 Second Ave. (bet. 77th & 78th Sts.) | 212-288-0999 ◑
Garment District | 416 Eighth Ave. (31st St.) | 212-967-7603
Gramercy | 116 E. 16th St. (bet. Irving Pl. & Union Sq. E.) | 212-673-6465
Murray Hill | 181 Lexington Ave. (31st St.) | 212-779-7427 ◑
W 80s | 428 Amsterdam Ave. (bet. 80th & 81st Sts.) | 212-501-7515 ◑
www.brotherjimmys.com

"Totally fratty" throngs pile into this "trashy" BBQ chainlet for "filling"
snoutfuls of "edible" grub served in "redneck Riviera" settings; the
"weak service", "franchise feel" and "stale beer smell" can detract, but
at least the pricing's "decent" for a hoot and a howl.

☑ Brushstroke ☒ *Japanese* 25 | 26 | 26 | $123

TriBeCa | 30 Hudson St. (Duane St.) | 212-791-3771 |
www.davidbouley.com

From David Bouley and the "serious chefs" from Osaka's Tsuji Culinary
Institute comes this "haute" TriBeCa Japanese, where "brilliant",
"detail"-oriented kaiseki spreads are "smoothly" served in a "soothing, wood-enveloped" space arranged around an open kitchen; some
say the "long", "elaborate" prix fixe–only meals are "better than sex",
but the "small" sushi bar area offers limited à la carte foreplay.

Bryant Park Grill/Cafe *American* 19 | 23 | 19 | $48

W 40s | behind NY Public Library | 25 W. 40th St. (bet. 5th & 6th Aves.) |
212-840-6500 | www.arkrestaurants.com

"Primo" Bryant Park scenery is the main "selling point" of this American
pair, where "location, location, location" trumps the "pricey" tabs and
rather "average" food and service; the Grill's the more "handsome" of
the pair with both indoor and outdoor seats, while the alfresco-only
Cafe is more of a "tourist magnet."

B. Smith's Restaurant Row *Southern* 20 | 20 | 20 | $48

W 40s | 320 W. 46th St. (bet. 8th & 9th Aves.) | 212-315-1100 |
www.bsmith.com

For a "change of pace" on Restaurant Row, check out this "slick"
Southern comfort-food practitioner from TV personality Barbara
Smith; maybe it's "not what it used to be" and "pricier than it should
be", but a "great location" for showgoers and a solid overall performance keep it humming.

Bubby's *American* 20 | 17 | 17 | $33

TriBeCa | 120 Hudson St. (N. Moore St.) | 212-219-0666 ◑
Dumbo | 1 Main St. (bet. Plymouth & Water Sts.) | Brooklyn |
718-222-0666 ⏪
www.bubbys.com

"Wholesome" breakfast fare served in "glorified diner" digs sums up the
scene at these "unfussy" bastions of American "home cooking", best

known for its "weekend brunch crunch", replete with "crazy lines", "slow service" and "ill-behaved" kids; the TriBeCa branch is open 24/7, while the cash-only Dumbo outlet boasts "gorgeous" Manhattan views.

☑ Buddakan ● *Asian* | 25 | 27 | 22 | $66 |

Chelsea | 75 Ninth Ave. (bet. 15th & 16th Sts.) | 212-989-6699 | www.buddakannyc.com

"Beautiful folks" are lured by the "lavish" setting and *Sex and the City* style" of Stephen Starr's Chelsea "crowd-pleaser", but this "mega"-scene follows through with "absolutely delicious" Asian fare dispatched by an "accommodating", "model"-like crew; sure, the pricing's "high" and the volume "loud", but if you're in the mood for "pomp and circumstance", look no further.

Buenos Aires ● *Argentinean/Steak* | 25 | 16 | 22 | $44 |

E Village | 513 E. Sixth St. (bet. Aves. A & B) | 212-228-2775 | www.buenosairesnyc.com

Beef eaters convene at this East Village Argentine steakhouse for "mouthwatering", chimichurri-slathered chops that you can "cut with a fork" and wash down with a "great selection of Malbecs"; forget the "don't-judge-a-book-by-its-cover" decor: "super" service and "gentle" tabs make this often-crowded spot a "keeper."

NEW Bugs ☒Ⓜ *Japanese* | - | - | - | M |

E Village | 504 E. 12th St. (bet. Aves. A & B) | 646-918-7981

A Jewel Bako vet is behind this new East Villager vending sushi and Japanese small plates in a minuscule, 15-seat room; the owner hopes locals will be drawn to it like bugs to a bright light, hence the nutty moniker.

Bukhara Grill *Indian* | 21 | 16 | 18 | $40 |

E 40s | 217 E. 49th St. (bet. 2nd & 3rd Aves.) | 212-888-2839 | www.bukharany.com

They "spice it up" at this "authentic" North Indian near the U.N., where the cooking's "tasty" and the service "courteous"; if it seems a bit "pricey" given the "dowdy" digs, at least the $17 lunch buffet is a "terrific bargain."

Bull & Bear ● *Steak* | 23 | 23 | 23 | $80 |

E 40s | Waldorf-Astoria | 301 Park Ave. (enter on Lexington Ave. & 49th St.) | 212-872-1275 | www.bullandbearsteakhouse.com

"Time travel" to *"Mad Men"* days at this circa-1960 Waldorf-Astoria steakhouse where "professional" servers ply *"Wall Street Journal"* subscribers with "superb" cuts ("strong" cocktails gratify those on a "liquid diet"); it's a NYC "tradition", assuming one can "bear what they charge" for those bulls.

Burger Bistro *Burgers* | 24 | 18 | 21 | $21 |

Bay Ridge | 7217 Third Ave. (72nd St.) | Brooklyn | 718-833-5833
NEW Park Slope | 177 Fifth Ave. (bet. Berkeley & Lincoln Pls.) | Brooklyn | 718-398-9800
www.theburgerbistro.com

"So many options to choose from" is the hallmark of this "build-your-own-burger" duo in Bay Ridge and Park Slope, offering "perfectly cooked" patties accessorized with "every topping imaginable"; "friendly" service and "Brooklyn prices" keep the trade brisk.

	FOOD	DECOR	SERVICE	COST

Burger Joint at
Le Parker Meridien ◑⇴ *Burgers* | 24 | 13 | 15 | $17

W 50s | Le Parker Meridien | 119 W. 56th St. (bet. 6th & 7th Aves.) |
212-708-7414 | www.parkermeridien.com

Probably NYC's "worst-kept secret", this burger "speakeasy" hidden
behind a "giant curtain" in the Parker Meridien lobby flips "damn fine"
patties in "tacky" digs quite at odds with its "luxurious" hotel setting;
"lacking" service, "really long" lines and a "cash-only policy" come
with the territory – and "good luck getting a table."

NEW Butcher Bar *BBQ* | ▽ 25 | 24 | 22 | $26

Astoria | 37-08 30th Ave. (bet. 37th & 38th Sts.) | Queens |
718-606-8140 | www.butcherbar.com

"Organic" is the mantra of this tiny new barbecue joint/butcher
shop combo in Astoria, offering "excellent" St. Louis–style smoked
ribs responsibly sourced from "grass-fed beef" and served alongside
sides that are "better than they should be"; the wood and subway
tile–lined digs have "limited seating", but a back patio allows more room
to spread out.

Butter ⊠ *American* | 23 | 24 | 22 | $61

E Village | 415 Lafayette St. (bet. Astor Pl. & 4th St.) | 212-253-2828 |
www.butterrestaurant.com

A "beautiful" setting, "creative" cookery and "slinky" staffers lend
"sophistication" to this New American duplex near the Public Theater
overseen by chef Alex Guarnaschelli; the "dramatic", birch-forest decor on the ground floor gives way to a "dark", "sceney" cellar that's a
magnet for *"Gossip Girl"* fans, but wherever you wind up, expect to lay
out serious bread.

Buttermilk Channel *American* | 25 | 21 | 22 | $41

Carroll Gardens | 524 Court St. (Huntington St.) | Brooklyn |
718-852-8490 | www.buttermilkchannelnyc.com

This "refreshing" Carroll Gardens American "hits the spot" with
"addictive" brunches featuring "unique spins" on comfort-food classics, delivered by an "aim-to-please" team; "limited" space and a "no-
reservations" rule can make for "exhausting" waits, but once you're in,
it's "always a good experience."

Buvette ◑ *French* | 25 | 23 | 22 | $46

W Village | 42 Grove St. (bet. Bedford & Bleecker Sts.) |
212-255-3590 | www.ilovebuvette.com

"Ooh-la-la!", this West Village "godsend" "oozes charm" thanks to
chef-owner Jody Williams' "glorious" French tapas served in "cute",
"pint-sized" quarters by an "easygoing" crew; the "upbeat" mood
keeps "chairs bumping" at peak hours, but given the ultra-"tight"
space it's probably not for pro basketball players.

BXL Café ◑ *Belgian* | 19 | 14 | 18 | $32

W 40s | 125 W. 43rd St. (bet. B'way & 6th Ave.) | 212-768-0200
BXL East ◑ *Belgian*
E 50s | 210 E. 51st St. (bet. 2nd & 3rd Aves.) | 212-888-7782
www.bxlcafe.com

"Moules frites done right" chased with "awesome beers" explain
the "crush" at these "friendly" Belgian pubs in Midtown; the decor's

"nothing fancy" and it can be "way too noisy" at prime times, but the "price is right", particularly the "endless mussel" special on Sunday and Monday nights.

Cabana _Nuevo Latino_ | 23 | 19 | 19 | $36 |

E 60s | 1022 Third Ave. (bet. 60th & 61st Sts.) | 212-980-5678
Seaport | Pier 17 | 89 South St. (Fulton St.) | 212-406-1155
Forest Hills | 107-10 70th Rd. (bet. Austin St. & Queens Blvd.) |
Queens | 718-263-3600
www.cabanarestaurant.com

It "always feels like a party" at these "casual", "colorful" Nuevo Latinos where "nicely spiced" chow and "rocket-fuel" mojitos make for a "happening" vibe; the "noise factor" and "erratic" service may be sore points, but tabs are "reasonable" and the Seaport outlet sports "gorgeous" water views.

Cacio e Pepe _Italian_ | 21 | 15 | 18 | $42 |

E Village | 182 Second Ave. (bet. 11th & 12th Sts.) | 212-505-5931 |
www.cacioepepe.com

The "titular" signature pasta served in a "massive round" of pecorino is the star of the "traditional Roman" menu at this "sweet" East Village Italian; "pleasant" service and "fair prices" keep things "bustling", so regulars take "respite" in the "pretty" back garden.

Cafe Asean ⌷ _SE Asian_ | 23 | 15 | 20 | $29 |

W Village | 117 W. 10th St. (bet. Greenwich & 6th Aves.) |
212-633-0348 | www.cafeasean.com

"Modest" looks belie the "well-crafted" SE Asian lineup purveyed at this "tiny" West Villager where the "inexpensive", cash-only menu "takes you further East with every bite"; "easy vibes", "accommodating" service and a "serene" garden round out this "offbeat find."

⊿ Café Boulud _French_ | 27 | 24 | 26 | $80 |

E 70s | Surrey Hotel | 20 E. 76th St. (bet. 5th & Madison Aves.) |
212-772-2600 | www.danielnyc.com

Daniel Boulud's "magic touch" is in evidence at this UES "class act", a showcase for chef Gavin Kaysen's "sophisticated", "pristine" French cooking, "impeccably served" in a "cosmopolitan" milieu; the "premium" pricing doesn't faze its "upper-crusty", "old-money" crowd, but lesser mortals say the "wonderful prix fixe lunch" is "a steal" at $37; P.S. there's also a "lovely" lounge next door, Bar Pleiades, that shakes smart cocktails.

Cafe Centro ⊠ _Mediterranean_ | 21 | 20 | 21 | $49 |

E 40s | MetLife Bldg. | 200 Park Ave. (45th St.) | 212-818-1222 |
www.patinagroup.com

There's always a "big hubbub" at lunchtime at this "steady" Grand Central–area magnet for "networking" suits who dig the "satisfying" Med cooking, "prompt" service and "modern", patio-equipped setting; it's "quieter" at dinner, despite a weeknight $35 prix fixe "deal."

Cafe China _Chinese_ | ▽ 22 | 18 | 17 | $33 |

Murray Hill | 13 E. 37th St. (bet. 5th & Madison Aves.) |
212-213-2810 | www.cafechinanyc.com

"Big flavors" come for "modest" sums at this new Murray Hill Chinese where the "authentic", "high-quality" Sichuan dishes make for "numb tongues"; in contrast to the fiery cuisine, the "nostalgic" decor channels 1930s Shanghai, though the so-so service is very much present-day New York.

	FOOD	DECOR	SERVICE	COST

Cafe Cluny ❶ *American/French*

| 22 | 21 | 20 | $46 |

W Village | 284 W. 12th St. (4th St.) | 212-255-6900 | www.cafecluny.com
A "wonderful vibe" has evolved at this "cute" West Village bistro, a once-"trendy" joint that's now a bona fide "neighborhood favorite" thanks to "terrific" Franco-American cooking served in a "charming", "sun-filled" space; since the weekend brunch can be a "free-for-all", regulars say "arrive early."

Café d'Alsace *French*

| 22 | 19 | 19 | $46 |

E 80s | 1695 Second Ave. (88th St.) | 212-722-5133 | www.cafedalsace.com
Particularly "great on a cold winter day", this "Euro-authentic" Yorkville brasserie rolls out "hearty" Alsatian eats backed by an "endless" beer list curated by a suds sommelier; given the "on-top-of-each-other" tables and "intense" prime-time "clamor", the sidewalk seats are "a plus."

Café du Soleil *French/Mediterranean*

| 20 | 18 | 18 | $38 |

W 100s | 2723 Broadway (104th St.) | 212-316-5000 | www.cafedusoleilny.com
"Simple but tasty" French-Med staples priced for "value" make this "upbeat" Columbia-area entry a "popular neighborhood" fallback, though service skews "spotty"; when the "bistro-ish" interior gets too "cramped and loud", insiders flee to the "wonderful" sidewalk terrace.

Cafe Español ❶ *Spanish*

| 21 | 16 | 21 | $38 |

G Village | 172 Bleecker St. (bet. MacDougal & Sullivan Sts.) | 212-505-0657 | www.cafeespanol.com
W Village | 78 Carmine St. (bet. Bedford St. & 7th Ave. S.) | 212-675-3312 | www.cafeespanolny.com
When you "don't want to spend much" on "traditional" Spanish fare, these separately owned, "been-there-forever" Villagers provide "satisfying" basics doled out in "generous", "paella-for-days" portions; "tight quarters" and "hokey decor" detract, but the sangria "always calls you back."

Cafe Fiorello ❶ *Italian*

| 20 | 18 | 20 | $51 |

W 60s | 1900 Broadway (bet. 63rd & 64th Sts.) | 212-595-5330 | www.cafefiorello.com
Lincoln Center ticket-holders like this "long-standing" Italian "workhorse" for "dependable" classics including "scrumptious" pizza and a "surefire" antipasti bar; insiders "go after curtain time" and request "outside tables" to sidestep the "cheek-by-jowl seating", "rushed service" and overall "hullabaloo."

Café Frida *Mexican*

| 22 | 19 | 20 | $37 |

W 70s | 368 Columbus Ave. (bet. 77th & 78th Sts.) | 212-712-2929
W 90s | 768 Amsterdam Ave. (bet. 97th & 98th Sts.) | 212-749-2929
www.cafefrida.com
"Young" folks consider these "uncomplicated" UWS Mexicans "well worth the money" for "flavorful", "hearty" dining lubricated with "killer margaritas" (the "*mañana*" service is another story); the Amsterdam Avenue site adds a rear garden "oasis" to the incentives.

| | FOOD | DECOR | SERVICE | COST |

Cafe Gitane ⬤ *French/Moroccan* | 22 | 20 | 18 | $30 |

NoLita | 242 Mott St. (Prince St.) | 212-334-9552 ⊟
W Village | Jane Hotel | 113 Jane St. (bet. Washington & West Sts.) | 212-255-4113
www.cafegitanenyc.com

The food's a match for the "trendy vibe" at these "fashionable" French-Moroccan lairs where "affordable" bites like "fabulous" couscous are dispensed by a "gorgeous" staff; the NoLita original is on the "tight" side, but the more spread-out Jane Hotel spin-off is just as "energetic."

Café Habana ⬤ *Cuban/Mexican* | 23 | 18 | 17 | $21 |

NoLita | 17 Prince St. (Elizabeth St.) | 212-625-2001 | www.cafehabana.com

Habana Outpost ⬤⊟ *Cuban/Mexican*

Fort Greene | 755-757 Fulton St. (S. Portland Ave.) | Brooklyn | 718-858-9500 | www.habanaoutpost.com

Don't miss the "killer grilled corn" at these "lovable" Mexican-Cuban "hipster paradises"; "happening" hordes endure "long waits" for a table at the "funky" NoLita original and its "environmentally friendly" Fort Greene sibling, while "economic" tabs and "amazing" libations keep this duo *"muy caliente."*

Café Henri ⬤ *French*

W Village | 27 Bedford St. (Downing St.) | 212-243-2846
LIC | 10-10 50th Ave. (bet. Jackson Ave. & Vernon Blvd.) | Queens | 718-383-9315

"Wonderful" crêpes "any time of day" and other "well-executed" French faves evoke the "5th *arrondissement*" at these "low-key" boîtes in the West Village and LIC; though both are "small" and "often overlooked", prices are "reasonable" and "you'll never be hurried."

Cafe Joul *French* | 19 | 14 | 18 | $45 |

E 50s | 1070 First Ave. (bet. 58th & 59th Sts.) | 212-759-3131 | www.cafejoul.com

Very much a "local" enclave, this "relaxed" Sutton Place bistro does the job with "consistent" French cooking and "no-rush" service; but holdouts observe the "close quarters" are looking "worn" and conclude "nothing to write home about."

Cafe Lalo ⬤ *Coffeehouse/Dessert* | 20 | 22 | 17 | $23 |

W 80s | 201 W. 83rd St. (bet. Amsterdam Ave. & B'way) | 212-496-6031 | www.cafelalo.com

Famously "featured in *You've Got Mail*", this 25-year-old UWS "sweetery" is ever a "tempting" rendezvous for "decadent desserts"; despite "wall-to-wall" tourists and "can't-be-bothered" service, it still makes fans "fall in love with NYC all over again."

Cafe Loup ⬤ *French* | 20 | 18 | 21 | $45 |

W Village | 105 W. 13th St. (bet. 6th Ave. & 7th Ave. S.) | 212-255-4746 | www.cafeloupnyc.com

Long a Village "neighborhood standby", this "timeless" bistro is a "grown-up" nexus for "fairly priced" French fare "like *grand-mère* used to make" dispatched by a "personable" crew; the room may need "updating", but loyalists attest it's "worth repeating", especially for "Sunday jazz brunch."

	FOOD	DECOR	SERVICE	COST

Cafe Luluc ●⇥ *French* | 21 | 15 | 19 | $30

Cobble Hill | 214 Smith St. (Baltic St.) | Brooklyn | 718-625-3815
An "easy way to feel Parisian", this "cash-only" Cobble Hill French bistro offers "satisfying" food served "sans attitude" at "Brooklyn prices"; just "be ready to wait" on weekends – it's a renowned "brunch destination", flipping some of the "world's best pancakes."

Cafe Luxembourg *French* | 22 | 20 | 21 | $54

W 70s | 200 W. 70th St. (bet. Amsterdam & West End Aves.) | 212-873-7411 | www.cafeluxembourg.com
"Still a real show", this long-standing "bastion of UWS hip" is catnip for a crowd of "good-lookers" and "A-listers" who show up for its "terrific" French bistro cooking, "legitimate Paris" mien and cool "insider vibe"; "intelligentsia" celeb sightings compensate for the "loud", "shoulder-to-shoulder" conditions at prime times.

Cafe Mogador ● *Moroccan* | 23 | 17 | 19 | $30

E Village | 101 St. Marks Pl. (bet. Ave. A & 1st Ave.) | 212-677-2226
NEW **Williamsburg** | 133 Wythe Ave. (bet. N. 7th & 8th Sts.) | Brooklyn | 718-486-9222 **Ⓜ**
www.cafemogador.com
Popular with the "tattooed, leathered" set, this "go-to" East Village Moroccan and its new Williamsburg sibling "have it down to a science", providing "memorable" tagines for "super-affordable" dough; to avoid "long waits" for the "delicious" brunch, go for "early dinner."

Cafe Noir ● *French/Moroccan* | 20 | 19 | 19 | $36

SoHo | 32 Grand St. (Thompson St.) | 212-431-7910 | www.cafenoirny.com
A "fun Eurotrash" crowd frequents this "sultry" SoHo French-Moroccan where "tasty tapas" and sangria are served in "small" but atmospheric digs; it's a "good value" that grows more "flirty" after dark.

Cafe Ronda *Mediterranean/S American* | 20 | 17 | 18 | $35

W 70s | 249-251 Columbus Ave. (bet. 71st & 72nd Sts.) | 212-579-9929 | www.caferonda.com
"Very UWS", this Med–South American "port in a storm" is a "local" magnet for "delicious" tapas and "refreshing" sangria that "won't break the bank"; since the quarters are "cramped" and it's "always busy" ("especially for brunch"), claustrophobes "sit outside" and watch the Columbus Avenue parade go by.

Café Sabarsky/Café Fledermaus *Austrian* | 22 | 25 | 21 | $44

E 80s | Neue Galerie | 1048 Fifth Ave. (86th St.) | 212-288-0665 | www.kg-ny.com
Kurt Gutenbrunner's "civilized" Neue Galerie cafes transport you to "fin de siècle Vienna", with "exquisite pastries" and "vonderful" Austrian savories dispensed in "glorious", "old-worldy" settings; Sabarsky is the "prettier" of the pair while Fledermaus is "easier to get into", but both are "pretty expensive."

Cafe Steinhof *Austrian* | 19 | 17 | 19 | $28

Park Slope | 422 Seventh Ave. (14th St.) | Brooklyn | 718-369-7776 | www.cafesteinhof.com
Park Slopers "raise a stein" to this Austrian "change of pace" purveying "stick-to-your-ribs" grub for comfortably "low" dough (Monday's

	FOOD	DECOR	SERVICE	COST

$7 goulash night may be the "best deal in the 'hood"); "fantastic" brews and a "spirited" "bar culture" shore up the "informal" mood.

Cafeteria ● *American*   21 | 19 | 18 | $33

Chelsea | 119 Seventh Ave. (17th St.) | 212-414-1717 | www.cafeteriagroup.com

With a 24/7 open-door policy, this longtime Chelsea "after-the-clubs" spot serves "dressed-up" American comfort classics with "unwarranted attitude" to a crowd that "clearly expects to be watched"; though it's lost the "allure of years past", it's reassuring to know that's it's there when you feel like "meatloaf and a Cosmopolitan at 3 AM."

Caffe Cielo ● *Italian* 20 | 16 | 20 | $47

W 50s | 881 Eighth Ave. (bet. 52nd & 53rd Sts.) | 212-246-9555 | www.caffecielonyc.com

With its "well-rounded menu" and "caring service", this "longtime" Hell's Kitchen Italian is a "dependable neighborhood" go-to as well as a "not-so-busy" pre-theater option; the "tired" room could "use some sprucing up", but the "reasonable" costs are fine as is.

Caffe e Vino *Italian* 23 | 17 | 21 | $40

Fort Greene | 112 DeKalb Ave. (bet. Ashland Pl. & St. Felix St.) | Brooklyn | 718-855-6222 | www.caffeevino.com

"Delightful", "rustic" Italian food is the thing at this "tiny but terrific" Fort Greene trattoria near BAM; the "unpretentious" setting (complete with "requisite brick wall") can be "cramped", but the "attentive" servers will "get you out well-fed" before curtain time.

Caffe Grazie *Italian* 20 | 18 | 21 | $49

E 80s | 26 E. 84th St. (bet. 5th & Madison Aves.) | 212-717-4407 | www.caffegrazie.com

With its "dignified" townhouse setting and "quite creditable" Italian cooking, this 20-year-old Upper East Side duplex off Museum Mile is a "restful" respite "before, after or instead of the Met"; maybe it's "a bit pricey", but the $16 set-price lunch is a "bargain considering the neighborhood."

NEW Caffe Storico Ⓜ *Italian* ∇ 20 | 21 | 20 | $46

W 70s | NY Historical Society | 170 CPW (77th St.) | 212-485-9211 | www.caffestorico.com

From restaurateur Stephen Starr comes this UWS newcomer that "hits all the right marks" with an "innovative", Venetian-influenced Italian menu featuring "delicious" *cicchetti* (small plates); set in the New-York Historical Society, the "airy", white-on-white room is lined with "antique dishes from the museum's collection."

Calexico *Mexican* 22 | 13 | 17 | $20

Carroll Gardens | 122 Union St. (bet. Columbia & Hicks Sts.) | Brooklyn | 718-488-8226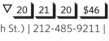
Greenpoint | 645 Manhattan Ave. (Bedford Ave.) | Brooklyn | 347-763-2129 ●
www.calexicocart.com

Mexican mavens "all abuzz" over these "rough-and-ready" street-cart spin-offs call out its "outstanding", "Cali-inspired" tacos, tortas and burritos; "fabulous prices" and "fast service" offset the typical Brooklyn "hole-in-the-wall" settings.

Calle Ocho *Nuevo Latino*

22	21	20	$43

W 80s | Excelsior Hotel | 45 W. 81st St. (bet. Columbus Ave. & CPW) | 212-873-5025 | www.calleochonyc.com

The vibe may be a tad "more relaxed" since this longtime UWS Nuevo Latino moved to the Excelsior Hotel, but the "explosive flavors" of its "adventuresome" menu and "beyond-delicious" mojitos remain in place – and its bottomless-sangria Sunday brunch still draws droves of "hair-of-the-dog-that-bit-you" types.

NEW Calliope *French/Italian*

-	-	-	M

E Village | 84 E. Fourth St. (2nd Ave.) | 212-260-8484 | www.calliopenyc.com

Set in the former Belcourt digs, this new East Village French bistro offers a short-and sweet menu of rustic dishes made from carefully sourced ingredients; the spacious setting is done up in no-frills farmhouse style (dishcloth napkins, mismatched chairs) and framed by floor-to-ceiling windows that lend an airy feel.

CamaJe ❶ *American/French*

▽ 23	17	22	$36

G Village | 85 MacDougal St. (bet. Bleecker & Houston Sts.) | 212-673-8184 | www.camaje.com

This "little" Village bistro showcases chef Abigail Hitchcock's "beautifully presented" Franco-American fare ferried by "attentive" staffers in "arty", "laid-back" quarters; added attractions include "intimate cooking classes" and blindfolded "dining in the dark", an "experience unlike any other."

Campagnola ❶ *Italian*

23	19	21	$69

E 70s | 1382 First Ave. (bet. 73rd & 74th Sts.) | 212-861-1102

All eyes are on the "floor show" at this "old-school" UES veteran where the stellar people-watching is on par with the "excellent", "garlicky" Italian cooking and "all-business" service; for best results, "go with somebody they know" – it's much "better if you're a regular" – and better yet if you bring "someone else's expense account."

Canaletto *Italian*

22	17	23	$59

E 60s | 208 E. 60th St. (bet. 2nd & 3rd Aves.) | 212-317-9192

This "genuine" Northern Italian near Bloomie's purveys "dependable", "traditional" dishes to an "older crowd"; a "well-seasoned staff" and "comfortable" environs that are "not unduly loud" mute "pricey" tariffs.

Candle Cafe *Vegan/Vegetarian*

25	17	21	$32

E 70s | 1307 Third Ave. (bet. 74th & 75th Sts.) | 212-472-0970

Candle Cafe West *Vegan/Vegetarian*

NEW **W 80s** | 2427 Broadway (bet. 89th & 90th Sts.) | 212-769-8900 www.candlecafe.com

Candle 79's "cheaper", "more utilitarian" cousins, these Uptown joints feature "intriguing" vegan eats "prepared with love" in "cramped", "unpretentious" digs; though they're "often crowded" with "Gwyneth Paltrow wannabes", the "right-on" cooking is "worth the wait."

Candle 79 *Vegan/Vegetarian*

25	22	23	$47

E 70s | 154 E. 79th St. (bet. Lexington & 3rd Aves.) | 212-537-7179 | www.candle79.com

"Tasting is believing" at this UES vegan "fine-dining" "phenom" that "sets the standard" with "quality-sourced", "distinctive" dishes delivered by "enthusiastic" servers in "intimate", "classic" digs; a "pleasant departure from meaty fare", it's "so worth" the "premium price."

The Cannibal ● *Belgian*   ▽ 24 | 20 | 23 | $41

Murray Hill | 113 E. 29th St. (bet. Lexington & Park Aves.) | 212-686-5480 | www.thecannibalnyc.com

A spin-off of Murray Hill's Resto, this next-door butcher shop–cum-Belgian gastropub plies a "meat-heavy" menu of "superlative" small plates backed up by an "amazing" selection of brews; maybe the snug, communal table–equipped setting is "not comfortable", but few "headhunters" mind given the "swoon"-inducing chow.

❼ Capital Grille   *Steak*   25 | 23 | 24 | $71

E 40s | Chrysler Ctr. | 155 E. 42nd St. (bet. Lexington & 3rd Aves.) | 212-953-2000

Financial District | 120 Broadway (Nassau & Pine Sts.) | 212-374-1811
W 50s | Time-Life Building | 120 W. 51st St. (bet. 6th & 7th Aves.) | 212-246-0154
www.thecapitalgrille.com

"Business-oriented" yet "swanky" enough for a date, this "clubby" steakhouse trio plies "perfectly cooked" chops in "roomy" settings (the "glassy, brassy" Chrysler Center outpost is the most "beautiful" of the bunch); sure, it's part of a national chain, but "you'd never know it" given the overall "quality"; P.S. the "food tastes better with an expense account."

Capsouto Frères   *French*   23 | 22 | 24 | $61

TriBeCa | 451 Washington St. (Watts St.) | 212-966-4900 | www.capsoutofreres.com

"Escape from NY to France" via this TriBeCa "pioneer" that's "old-school in a good way" thanks to "toothsome" French bistro fare, *très* "polished" service and a "high-ceilinged", "not-too-noisy" setting; ok, it's on the "pricey" side and you'll need a "GPS" to find it, but payoffs include "no parking problems" and "wonderful" signature soufflés.

Caracas Arepa Bar   *Venezuelan*   25 | 16 | 19 | $20

E Village | 93½ E. Seventh St. (bet. Ave. A & 1st Ave.) | 212-529-2314

Caracas Brooklyn   *Venezuelan*

Williamsburg | 291 Grand St. (bet. Havemeyer & Roebling Sts.) | Brooklyn | 718-218-6050

Caracas to Go   *Venezuelan*

E Village | 91 E. Seventh St. (1st Ave.) | 212-228-5062
www.caracasarepabar.com

"Transcendent corn pockets" stuffed with "fresh fillings" spark "arepa mania" at these Venezuelan "cheap-eats" joints; fans brave the "squeeze" and "inevitable line" at the East Village "walk-in closet" or cross the river to Williamsburg to "get a seat" either indoors or outdoors.

Cara Mia   *Italian*   21 | 16 | 21 | $38

W 40s | 654 Ninth Ave. (bet. 45th & 46th Sts.) | 212-262-6767 | www.caramiany.com

"Not fancy but plenty comfortable", this Hell's Kitchen "red-sauce" Italian is a Theater District "standby" for "homemade pasta" and "spot-on" service; granted, it's "space-challenged" and "crazy busy" pre-curtain, but at least you can mangia "without paying an arm and a leg."

	FOOD	DECOR	SERVICE	COST

Caravaggio *Italian*
26 | 24 | 26 | $84

E 70s | 23 E. 74th St. (bet. 5th & Madison Aves.) | 212-288-1004 | www.caravaggioristorante.com

More than "just dining out", this "refined" UES Italian is a "special-occasion" nexus owing to its "sophisticated" cooking, "flawless" service and "exquisite" modern setting; "money is no object" for most of its "mature" fan base, though frugal folks find the $28 prix fixe lunch quite "enticing."

Caravan of Dreams *Kosher/Vegan/Vegetarian*
24 | 18 | 21 | $28

E Village | 405 E. Sixth St. (1st Ave.) | 212-254-1613 | www.caravanofdreams.net

A dream come true for "healthy food" fanatics, this East Village vet offers "transformative" kosher vegan fare in "mellow", "bohemian" quarters; fair prices and occasional "live music" enhance its "aura of peace and satisfaction", making followers "feel good inside and out."

Carl's Steaks ❶ *Cheesesteaks*
22 | 8 | 14 | $15

Murray Hill | 507 Third Ave. (34th St.) | 212-696-5336 | www.carlssteaks.com

"Hangover food" is the specialty of this "small" Murray Hill joint slinging "gooey", "indulgent" cheesesteaks that may be the "best outside of Philly"; party animals seeking "late-night eats" don't mind the "Camden" decor and service that "leaves much to be desired."

❷ Carlyle Restaurant *French*
24 | 27 | 27 | $90

E 70s | Carlyle Hotel | 35 E. 76th St. (Madison Ave.) | 212-570-7192 | www.thecarlyle.com

"Synonymous with class", this "old-world" room in the Carlyle Hotel holds "fond memories" for a "blue-blood" fan base in thrall to its "refined" New French fare, "royal-treatment" service and "Dorothy Draper"-esque digs; plan to wear your "finest baubles" (jackets required for dinner) and be prepared for "super-premium prices."

❷ Carmine's *Italian*
22 | 18 | 20 | $43

W 40s | 200 W. 44th St. (bet. B'way & 8th Ave.) | 212-221-3800 ❶
W 90s | 2450 Broadway (bet. 90th & 91st Sts.) | 212-362-2200
www.carminesnyc.com

"Big appetites" are sated at this family-style Italian duo where the "solid" red-sauce fare arrives in "feed-an-army"-size portions for "affordable" dough (just brace yourself for a "garlic hangover"); naturally, "tourists abound" at the "crazy busy" Theater District outlet, though the more "neighborhoody" Upper West Side original can be equally "hectic."

Carnegie Deli ❶⋔ *Deli*
23 | 12 | 15 | $30

W 50s | 854 Seventh Ave. (55th St.) | 212-757-2245 | www.carnegiedeli.com

"Obesity beckons" at this circa-1937 Midtown deli known for "lip-smacking", "larger-than-life" sandwiches representing "every-thing you love about NY between two slices of bread"; sure, the staff is "impatient", the digs "tattered" and the cash-only tabs "reflect the portion sizes", but there's a reason for the perpetual "long waits" at prime times; natives "sit next to tourists for entertainment value" (and vice-versa).

Carol's Cafe ☒Ⓜ Eclectic
25 | 21 | 22 | $47

Dongan Hills | 1571 Richmond Rd. (bet. 4 Corners Rd. & Seaview Ave.) | Staten Island | 718-979-5600 | www.carolscafe.com

"Thoughtful", "Manhattan-quality" cooking via chef Carol Frazzetta is yours at this "pretty" Staten Island Eclectic in Dongan Hills; maybe the tabs run "a little high" for these parts, but "perfect-ending" desserts and weekly "cooking lessons" sweeten the pot.

NEW Casa Enrique ❶ Mexican
- | - | - | M

LIC | 5-48 49th Ave. (bet. 5th St. & Vernon Blvd.) | Queens | 347-448-6040
The Cafe Henri crew heads south of the border at this new LIC Mexican, serving a menu inspired by the cuisine of the Chiapas region; the sleek, white-on-white setting is pretty chic for Queens, yet tabs are moderate and the mood laid-back.

Casa Lever ☒ Italian
23 | 24 | 23 | $77

E 50s | Lever House | 390 Park Ave. (enter on 53rd St., bet. Madison & Park Aves.) | 212-888-2700 | www.casalever.com
Luring Park Avenue "power" players, this Midtown Milanese from the Sant Ambroeus team offers "delicious" chow together with "attentive" service; set in the "historic" Lever House, the "modernist" room lined with "wall-to-wall Warhols" is so "fashionable" that many say "you pay for the style" here.

Casa Mono ❶ Spanish
25 | 19 | 20 | $62

Gramercy | 52 Irving Pl. (17th St.) | 212-253-2773 | www.casamononyc.com
"Robust" tapas meet a "beautifully curated" wine list at Mario Batali's 10-year-old Gramercy Spaniard, where "inspired" cooking and a beyond-"intimate" layout make for "tough reservations"; for the "best experience", snag "counter seats overlooking the open kitchen" and try to ignore the "steep" prices.

Casa Nonna Italian
22 | 21 | 21 | $49

Garment District | 310 W. 38th St. (bet. 8th & 9th Aves.) | 212-736-3000 | www.casanonna.com
A "big surprise" in the Garment District, this Italian has its "act together" offering "perfectly fine" Roman-Tuscan standards served with "quick" "professionalism"; it's a "relaxing" option in a "lacking" part of town, with well-spaced tables allowing for "private conversations."

Cascabel Taqueria ❶ Mexican
22 | 15 | 18 | $28

E 80s | 1538 Second Ave. (80th St.) | 212-717-8226
W 100s | 2799 Broadway (108th St.) | 212-665-1500
www.nyctacos.com
"Ay caramba", these "popular" crosstown taquerias are about as "legitimate" as you'll find in these parts, slinging "league-of-their-own" tacos in "funky" quarters; "bargain" tabs and "Downtown" vibes keep them "overwhelmingly busy", so expect service that's "cheerful" but "not very polished."

NEW Catch Seafood
23 | 24 | 20 | $74

Meatpacking | 21 Ninth Ave., 2nd fl. (enter on 13th St., bet. 9th Ave. & Washington St.) | 212-392-5978 | www.catchnewyorkcity.com
"Beautiful people" and random "Kardashians" populate this "trendy" new Meatpacking "scene" where "outstanding" seafood via Top Chef

winner Hung Huynh is dispensed by "Abercrombie model"–like staffers in a sprawling, "pumping" duplex; reservations are "hard" to get
despite the "expensive" tabs.

Ça Va *French*
22 | 21 | 22 | $59

W 40s | InterContinental NY Times Sq. | 310 W. 44th St. (bet. 8th &
9th Aves.) | 212-803-4545 | www.cavatoddenglish.com

Todd English assumes a "straightforward French" accent at this pleasing
Theater District brasserie; though the "nondescript", "hotel-lobby"
decor may be at odds with the "high-end" prices, "thoughtful" service
and a "convenient" address make it a natural "pre-theater."

Caviar Russe *American*
25 | 24 | 26 | $87

E 50s | 538 Madison Ave., 2nd fl. (bet. 54th & 55th Sts.) |
212-980-5908 | www.caviarrusse.com

Roe-mantics "die and go to heaven" at this East Side New American
where "mouthwatering" caviar and crudo is ferried by a "top-notch"
team in "luxe" Romanov digs; "unlimited credit" comes in handy, but
fans say this "unforgettable experience" is "worth saving up for."

Cávo ●Ⓜ *Greek*
21 | 25 | 20 | $45

Astoria | 42-18 31st Ave. (bet. 42nd & 43rd Sts.) | Queens |
718-721-1001 | www.cavoastoria.com

A "cool-looking", "spacious" setting is the lure at this "upscale" Astoria
Greek offering "solid" Hellenica that's upstaged by its "spectacular",
waterfall-equipped garden; just be aware it "can get pricey" and
"loud" – as the evening progresses, it becomes "more of a nightclub."

Cebu ● *Continental*
21 | 19 | 20 | $38

Bay Ridge | 8801 Third Ave. (88th St.) | Brooklyn | 718-492-5095 |
www.cebubrooklyn.com

"Large" and "busy", this "reasonably priced" Continental brings a bit
of "Manhattan chic" to Bay Ridge via an "enjoyable" menu, "on-the-
ball" service and night-owl noshing "till 3 AM"; "younger" folks with
"fake tans" keep the bar scene "buzzing."

Celeste ⊄ *Italian*
24 | 12 | 18 | $33

W 80s | 502 Amsterdam Ave. (bet. 84th & 85th Sts.) | 212-874-4559

"Celestial" Neapolitan cooking, "wonderful" cheese plates and "tough-
to-beat" tabs make for "crammed" conditions at this UWS "winner"
whose engaging owner is "part of the experience"; despite "no rezzies",
"no credit cards" and "little ambiance", "long lines" are the norm here.

Cellini *Italian*
22 | 19 | 22 | $56

E 50s | 65 E. 54th St. (bet. Madison & Park Aves.) | 212-751-1555 |
www.cellinirestaurant.com

A "staple" for "entertaining clients", this "expense-account" Midtowner
draws a "chatty lunch crowd" with "authentic", "sure-bet" Italian standards served in a "not-so-fancy" setting; it's more subdued come suppertime, but you can expect "comfortable, grown-up" dining at any hour.

Centro Vinoteca ● *Italian*
22 | 19 | 21 | $48

W Village | 74 Seventh Ave. S. (Barrow St.) | 212-367-7470 |
www.centrovinoteca.com

"Well-prepared" *piccolini* (small plates) lead off the Italian menu at
this "convenient" West Village duplex, where "motivated" staffers

man the "noisy" ground-floor dining room and "more pleasant" upstairs; fans say it "satisfies every taste bud", though critics counter it has "lost its luster" due to revolving chefs.

Cercle Rouge ● French

`20` `20` `19` `$48`

TriBeCa | 241 W. Broadway (N. Moore St.) | 212-226-6252 | www.cerclerougeresto.com

There's "no need to go to Paris" thanks to this "under-the-radar" TriBeCa bistro purveying "classic" Gallic grub that conjures up a "certain je ne sais quoi"; it's a "comfy" fallback for local boulevardiers who sit outside and "pretend" they're on the Champs-Elysées.

'Cesca Italian

`24` `22` `23` `$60`

W 70s | 164 W. 75th St. (Amsterdam Ave.) | 212-787-6300 | www.cescanyc.com

"Fine-dining" fanciers frequent this 10-year-old "Upper West Side standout" for its "delectable" Italian fare, "stellar" wine list and "warm", "no-rush" service; although it's "as expensive as it is sophisticated", payoffs include a "relaxing" rustic setting, acoustics perfect for "normal conversation" and an open kitchen that's catnip for "armchair chefs."

Chadwick's American

`24` `20` `25` `$44`

Bay Ridge | 8822 Third Ave. (89th St.) | Brooklyn | 718-833-9855 | www.chadwicksny.com

On the Bay Ridge scene since '87, this American "stroll down memory lane" bats out a "solid" menu dispatched by "old-time waiters" who "treat you right"; the decor may "need a little uplift", but the "value" is intact, notably its "early-bird specials" Monday–Thursday.

Chai Home Kitchen ● Thai

`23` `19` `20` `$25`

W 50s | 930 Eighth Ave. (55th St.) | 212-707-8778
Williamsburg | 124 N. Sixth St. (Berry St.) | Brooklyn | 718-599-5889
www.chai-restaurants.com

"Incredibly reasonable prices" keep the trade brisk at these Siamese twins in Williamsburg and Hell's Kitchen vending "spot-on" Thai food ferried by a "prompt" crew; the seating's strictly "sardine"-style in Manhattan, with more room at the Brooklyn original.

Char No. 4 ● Southern

`23` `22` `22` `$39`

Cobble Hill | 196 Smith St. (bet. Baltic & Warren Sts.) | Brooklyn | 718-643-2106 | www.charno4.com

"Brooklyn edge" is everything at this Cobble Hill "pork-and-bourbon paradise" that matches "memorable" Southern eats with a "world-class selection" of brown liquids; "knowledgeable", professional service and "one heck of a weekend brunch" draw flocks of "young, trendy" folk.

NEW Château Cherbuliez ● Ⓜ French

`-` `-` `-` `E`

Flatiron | Limelight Marketplace | 47 W. 20th St. (bet. 5th & 6th Aves.) | 212-203-7088 | www.chateaunyc.com

Nestled in the Limelight Marketplace, this good-looking new St. Tropez–inspired arrival from Todd English serves French fare in a ground-floor wine bar or more exclusive upstairs dining room; still, it's the sprawling outdoor garden that's the real place to be.

	FOOD	DECOR	SERVICE	COST

Chef Ho's
Peking Duck Grill *Chinese*

22 | 15 | 20 | $33

E 80s | 1720 Second Ave. (bet. 89th & 90th Sts.) | 212-348-9444 | www.chefho.com

De-ho-tees say you "won't find better Peking duck" than at this "old-school" Yorkville Chinese, a "neighborhood favorite" also lauded for its "above-average" cooking, "below-average" tabs and "efficient" service; fans say it's so good that there's "no need to go to Chinatown."

Chef Yu *Chinese*

21 | 18 | 19 | $23

Garment District | 520 Eighth Ave. (bet. 36th & 37th Sts.) | 212-736-6150 | www.chefyu-nyc.com

An "easy" option near Penn Station, this "well-located" Garment District Chinese offers "tasty" traditional dishes in "airy", "modern" double-decker digs; the pricing's "reasonable" with lunch specials the "best value", but opinion splits on the service: "friendly" vs. "eat, pay, leave."

Chez Jacqueline ● *French*

20 | 19 | 20 | $50

G Village | 72 MacDougal St. (bet. Bleecker & Houston Sts.) | 212-505-0727 | www.chezjacquelinerestaurant.com

"Unassuming", "been-there-forever" Village bistro that has a "winning way" thanks to "satisfying" traditional French fare served by a "charming" staff that "keeps the *vin rouge* flowing"; critics site "ordinary" decor and feel the "flair is missing" sans Jacqueline.

Chez Josephine ●Ⓜ *French*

21 | 22 | 22 | $54

W 40s | 414 W. 42nd St. (bet. 9th & 10th Aves.) | 212-594-1925 | www.chezjosephine.com

"Josephine Baker lives on" at this "campy" Theater District "tribute" via her "flamboyant", "silk-pajama'd" son Jean-Claude; the "dark", "midnight-in-Paris" setting works well with the "throwback" French food and "energetic" live piano – no wonder it's been "popular" since 1986.

Chez Lucienne *French*

22 | 20 | 22 | $36

Harlem | 308 Lenox Ave. (bet. 125th & 126th Sts.) | 212-289-5555 | www.chezlucienne.com

"Parisian soul" is the thing at this French bistro on a happening stretch of Harlem's Lenox Avenue, where the midpriced Gallic grub is as "genuine" as the "accommodating" service; it's "great alternative" to Red Rooster next door, and sidewalk seats supply people-watching galore.

Chez Napoléon Ⓢ *French*

23 | 16 | 23 | $49

W 50s | 365 W. 50th St. (bet. 8th & 9th Aves.) | 212-265-6980 | www.cheznapoleon.com

"*Vérité*" could be the motto of this circa-1960 Theater District "relic" where an "old-school" crew dispatches "time-stood-still" French bistro classics à la escargot, frogs' legs and calf's brains; the "tiny" setting exudes "faded elegance", but prices are "moderate" and you're "there to eat, not sight-see."

Chez Oskar ● *French*

21 | 19 | 20 | $34

Fort Greene | 211 DeKalb Ave. (Adelphi St.) | Brooklyn | 718-852-6250 | www.chezoskar.com

"Very Brooklyn", this 15-year-old Fort Greene bistro shows its "staying power" with "enjoyable" French plates purveyed in "laid-back" surrounds enhanced by "live music"; its hipster fan base digs its "lack of pretension", not to mention the "reasonable" prices.

Chickpea *Mideastern*
19 | 12 | 16 | $13

E 40s | 45 E. 45th St. (bet. Madison & Vanderbilt Aves.) | 212-697-1666
E 50s | Citigroup Ctr. Atrium Food Court | 601 Lexington Ave. (54th St.) | 212-486-4500
NEW **E 90s** | 1413 Madison Ave. (98th St.) | 212-410-6600
E Village | 210 E. 14th St. (bet. 2nd & 3rd Aves.) | 212-228-3445
Financial District | 110 William St. (John St.) | 212-566-5666
Flatiron | 688 Sixth Ave. (bet. 21st & 22nd Sts.) | 212-243-6275
Garment District | Penn Station | Amtrak Concourse level (8th Ave. & 34th St.) | 212-244-0101 ●
Garment District | Penn Station | LIRR Concourse level (8th Ave. & 34th St.) | 212-697-0001
getchickpea.com

Non-fried falafels are the métier of this Mideastern "quick-bite" chainlet vending baked "balls of goodness" that are "fresh, hot" and "cheap"; "assembly-line" service and "uninspired" decor to the contrary, it's an "easy way to eat healthy."

ChikaLicious *Dessert*
25 | 16 | 21 | $20

E Village | 203 E. 10th St. (bet. 1st & 2nd Aves.) | 212-995-9511 | www.chikalicious.com
E Village | 204 E. 10th St. (bet. 1st & 2nd Aves.) | 212-475-0929 | www.dessertclubnyc.com ●

"Sophisticated sweet tooths" applaud this "blink-and-you-missed-it" East Village "dessert nirvana" for its "scrumptious", three-course prix fixes paired with "perfect" wines; those sour on the "postage stamp"–size layout get takeout from the counter-service satellite across the street.

Chimichurri Grill ● *Argentinean/Steak*
23 | 18 | 21 | $51

W 40s | 609 Ninth Ave. (bet. 43rd & 44th Sts.) | 212-586-8655 | www.chimichurrigrill.com

"Well-cooked" Argentine steaks topped with the namesake sauce thrill carnivores at this "tiny" Hell's Kitchen hideout; "efficient" staffers and "reasonable" pricing make it a natural for the "pre-theater" crowd, who only "wish it had more tables."

China Chalet *Chinese*
20 | 15 | 20 | $27

Financial District | 47 Broadway (bet. Exchange Pl. & Morris St.) | 212-943-4380
Eltingville | Eltingville Shopping Ctr. | 4326 Amboy Rd. (bet. Armstrong & Richmond Aves.) | Staten Island | 718-984-8044
www.chinachalet.com

For "everyday" Chinese chow, this "old-school" FiDi–Staten Island pair does a "solid" job supplying "nostalgia-inducing" standards "quickly" in "spacious" settings; while the "faded" decor "could use some jazzing up", it's cheap enough that few care.

China Grill *Asian*
23 | 22 | 21 | $57

W 50s | 60 W. 53rd St. (bet. 5th & 6th Aves.) | 212-333-7788 | www.chinagrillmgt.com

Long a bastion of "upmarket chic", this Midtown "powerhouse" offers "fancy takes" on Asian cuisine (the "crispy spinach is a must") served in "dark", airy digs with an "'80s James Bond" vibe; it's "deafeningly loud" and "definitely not a bargain", but "business" types still belly up for its "fun bar scene."

Chin Chin ◑ *Chinese*　　24 | 19 | 23 | $54

E 40s | 216 E. 49th St. (bet. 2nd & 3rd Aves.) | 212-888-4555 | www.chinchinny.com

On the scene since 1987, this "fancy" Midtowner is a nexus for "impressive" haute Chinese cuisine (don't miss the "off-the-menu" Grand Marnier shrimp) served by a "crisp" crew led by owner Jimmy "Energizer-bunny" Chin; despite rather "expensive" tabs, the "crowds keep coming."

ChipShop *British*　　21 | 16 | 20 | $22

Brooklyn Heights | 129 Atlantic Ave. (bet. Clinton & Henry Sts.) | Brooklyn | 718-855-7775 ◑
Park Slope | 383 Fifth Ave. (bet. 6th & 7th Sts.) | Brooklyn | 718-832-7701 ⊅
www.chipshopnyc.com

The "British invasion" comes to Brooklyn via this "divey" pub-food duo decorated with "'80s punk memorabilia" and dispensing "cardiologist-disapproved" items like "killer fish 'n' chips" and "seriously deep-fried" candy bars; "homesick Brits" dub it "bloody wonderful."

Chocolate Room *Dessert*　　25 | 20 | 21 | $19

Cobble Hill | 269 Court St. (bet. Butler & Douglass Sts.) | Brooklyn | 718-246-2600
Park Slope | 86 Fifth Ave. (bet. Prospect Pl. & St. Marks Ave.) | Brooklyn | 718-783-2900
www.thechocolateroombrooklyn.com

Dedicated to "all things chocolate", these "brilliant" Brooklyn dessert specialists vend "sinful" homemade desserts best paired with a "glass of vino" to cut the "sugar rush"; the Cobble Hill satellite is roomier, but the staffers are as "sweet" as the goods at both locations.

Cho Dang Gol *Korean*　　23 | 14 | 18 | $30

Garment District | 55 W. 35th St. (bet. 5th & 6th Aves.) | 212-695-8222 | www.chodanggolny.com

"Real-deal" Korean cooking is offered at this "step-above" Garment District joint that's famous for its "luscious" homemade tofu; "low prices", "utilitarian" decor and "typical" service are all part of the package, along with a "full house" at prime times.

Chola *Indian*　　23 | 16 | 20 | $40

E 50s | 232 E. 58th St. (bet. 2nd & 3rd Aves.) | 212-688-4619 | www.cholany.com

"Spices abound" at this "delectable" Indian on East 58th Street's subcontinental strip, supplying a "wide-ranging" roster of "complex" dishes; tariffs are generally "moderate", but for "quality and selection" the $14 buffet lunch provides true "value for the money."

Christos Steak House ◑ *Steak*　　25 | 20 | 23 | $62

Astoria | 41-08 23rd Ave. (41st St.) | Queens | 718-777-8400 | www.christossteakhouse.com

"Manhattan-worthy" steaks provide the sizzle at this "throwback" Astoria chop shop where the "excellent" beef is complemented by "imaginative", "Greek-accented" sides; ok, the decor's "dated" and it's on the "expensive" side for Queens, but at least free "valet parking makes it easier."

Churrascaria Plataforma ● Brazilian/Steak | 24 | 20 | 23 | $78 |

W 40s | 316 W. 49th St. (bet. 8th & 9th Aves.) | 212-245-0505 | www.churrascariaplataforma.com

Churrascaria TriBeCa ● Brazilian/Steak
TriBeCa | 221 W. Broadway (bet. Franklin & White Sts.) | 212-925-6969 | www.churrascariatribeca.com

Brace yourself for a "food coma" after dining at these Brazilian rodizio all-you-can-eat "extravaganzas", where "skewer-bearing" waiters bring on a "nonstop" barrage of "cooked-to-perfection" meats; since it's "kinda expensive", gluttons "try not to fill up" at the "bountiful" salad bar.

Ciano ⊠ Italian | 25 | 22 | 23 | $73 |
Flatiron | 45 E. 22nd St. (bet. B'way & Park Ave. S.) | 212-982-8422 | www.cianonyc.com

"Not just another Italian", this "buzzing" Flatiron destination show-cases chef Shea Gallante's "sublime" cooking; granted, the tables are "close" and the tabs "steep", but payoffs include "attentive" service, "good-looking" patrons and a "charming Tuscan" setting complete with a "romantic" fireplace.

Cibo American/Italian | 21 | 19 | 21 | $47 |
E 40s | 767 Second Ave. (41st St.) | 212-681-1616 | www.cibonyc.com

A "grown-up" favorite in the land of "limited" options around Tudor City, this "comfortable" Tuscan–New American plies "fresh seasonal" fare in a "spacious", "white-tablecloth" milieu; "excellent value" (e.g. the $35 dinner prix fixe) makes it "worth coming back to."

Cilantro Southwestern | 20 | 17 | 19 | $32 |
E 70s | 1321 First Ave. (71st St.) | 212-537-4040 ●
E 80s | 1712 Second Ave. (bet. 88th & 89th Sts.) | 212-722-4242 ●
W 80s | 485 Columbus Ave. (bet. 83rd & 84th Sts.) | 212-712-9090
www.cilantronyc.com

"Ample portions" and "low prices" keep this "serviceable" Southwestern trio enduringly "popular" with twentysomethings on a budget; "gigantic" margaritas help blot out the "excessive noise", "predictable" grub and "fake adobe" decor.

Cipriani Dolci ● Italian | 22 | 22 | 20 | $62 |
E 40s | Grand Central | 89 E. 42nd St. (Vanderbilt Ave.) | 212-973-0999 | www.cipriani.com

It's all about the view from the balcony at this Grand Central Venetian overlooking the "mass of humanity" thronging the Concourse and the new Apple store; the "quality" food and signature Bellinis "warm the heart" and "empty the wallet", but it's still "a treat if you're waiting for a train."

Cipriani Downtown ● Italian | 23 | 22 | 21 | $71 |

SoHo | 376 W. Broadway (bet. Broome & Spring Sts.) | 212-343-0999 | www.cipriani.com

The only thing missing is "Fellini" at this SoHo slice of "la dolce vita", a "ritzy" nexus where "international" types "park their Lamborghinis" out front, then tuck into "*molto bene*" Italian food chased with "delicious"

Bellinis; "astronomical" price tags and "attitude" galore come with the territory.

Cipriani Wall Street ⊠ *Italian* | 23 | 25 | 24 | $72 |
(aka Cipriani Club 55)

Financial District | 55 Wall St., 2nd fl. (bet. Hanover & William Sts.) | 212-699-4099 | www.cipriani.com

"One-percenters" who relish the "high life" "feed their egos" at this FiDi branch of the Cipriani empire, where "excellent" Italiana is dispensed in "posh" environs that include a jaw-dropping columned terrace; "prestige"-wise, it's a "solid" investment "when you have money to burn."

Circo ● *Italian* | 24 | 24 | 24 | $65 |

W 50s | 120 W. 55th St. (bet. 6th & 7th Aves.) | 212-265-3636 | www.osteriadelcirco.com

Exhibiting its "Le Cirque DNA", this "big-top" Midtowner via the Maccioni family purveys "wonderful Tuscan fare" in a "playful" room festooned with fanciful circus decor; given the "high-end" price tags, the "prix fixe deals" draw bargain-hunters, especially "pre- or post–City Center."

Circus ⊠ *Brazilian/Steak* | 23 | 22 | 22 | $53 |

E 60s | 132 E. 61st St. (bet. Lexington & Park Aves.) | 212-223-2965 | www.circusrestaurante.com

There's "no clowning around" in the kitchen at this Brazilian "sleeper" near Bloomie's where a "marvelous", meat-centric menu is served by a "jolly staff" that keeps the "knockout" caipirinhas flowing; "intimate" digs with a "circus motif" add to the "pleasant" vibe.

Citrus Bar & Grill *Asian/Nuevo Latino* | 21 | 19 | 19 | $40 |

W 70s | 320 Amsterdam Ave. (75th St.) | 212-595-0500 | www.citrusnyc.com

"Festive" is putting it mildly at this UWS Latin-Asian fusion specialist where the "interesting" chow takes a backseat to the "awesome" specialty tipples shaken at the "lively bar"; bargain-hunters drawn by "decent-value" pricing "go early" to avoid the "loud" decibels later on.

City Bakery *Bakery* | 22 | 14 | 16 | $19 |

Flatiron | 3 W. 18th St. (bet. 5th & 6th Aves.) | 212-366-1414 | www.thecitybakery.com

Beloved for its "ever-so-rich" hot chocolate and "one-of-a-kind" pretzel croissants, this Flatiron bakery also supplies "scrumptious" sweets, a "wholesome" salad bar and a new juice bar; maybe prices are "out of whack" given the "mess-hall" decor and "unhelpful service", yet that doesn't faze the "crazed" lunch crowds.

City Crab & | 20 | 17 | 19 | $46 |
Seafood Co. *Seafood*

Flatiron | 235 Park Ave. S. (19th St.) | 212-529-3800 | www.citycrabnyc.com

"Casual" and "commercial", this "straightforward" Flatiron fixture offers "no surprises", just a "wide assortment" of "simple", "fresh" seafood dispatched in a "big, boisterous" duplex; "decent" tabs compensate for "spotty" service and "not much character."

	FOOD	DECOR	SERVICE	COST

City Hall ▣ *Seafood/Steak* **22** | **22** | **21** | **$59**
TriBeCa | 131 Duane St. (bet. Church St. & W. B'way) |
212-227-7777 | www.cityhallnyc.com
"Politicos" and "power" players rub elbows at Henry Meer's 15-year-old
TriBeCa "mainstay" where "attentive" staffers ferry "superb" surf 'n' turf
in a "lofty", "sophisticated" setting that feels like "old NY"; bonuses include "space between tables" and "lovely private rooms" downstairs.

City Island Lobster House ● *Seafood* **23** | **19** | **21** | **$46**
City Island | 691 Bridge St. (City Island Ave.) | Bronx | 718-885-1459 |
www.cilobsterhouse.com
Crustacean cravers commend this "basic" City Island "throwback" as a
"fine and dandy" option for "abundant", satisfying seafood; aesthetes
fret about "not much decor", but "budget" pricing and alfresco dining
"overlooking Long Island Sound" give it "staycation" status.

City Lobster & Steak *Seafood* **21** | **19** | **21** | **$51**
W 40s | 121 W. 49th St. (6th Ave.) | 212-354-1717 | www.citylobster.com
For "standard" surf 'n' turf with "no surprises", this "convenient" harbor is a "good all-around" performer in the "touristy" turf around Rock
Center; foes crab about shelling out for "nothing special", but then
again the pre-theater prix fixes are a "best buy."

NEW **The Claw** ● *Seafood* ▽ **20** | **11** | **18** | **$24**
W 50s | 744 Ninth Ave. (bet. 50th & 51st Sts.) | 212-581-8400
It's a "literal lobster bonanza" at this counter-service Hell's Kitchen arrival where "slice-of–New England" seafood classics (notably "heaven-
on-a-bun" lobster rolls) come in minimal digs for minimal price; if the
"kitschy-pink beach decor" doesn't float your boat, hey, "they deliver."

Clinton St. Baking Co. *American* **26** | **15** | **18** | **$26**
LES | 4 Clinton St. (bet. Houston & Stanton Sts.) | 646-602-6263 |
www.clintonstreetbaking.com
"Bring *War and Peace*" to pass the time in the "brunch line" at this "tiny"
LES bakery/cafe where the "ridiculous" waits pay off when homespun
Americana "made with love" (especially those "divine pancakes") ar-
rives; insiders hint "dinner is just as good" – and "you can get in."

Club A Steak House ▣ *Steak* **24** | **23** | **24** | **$67**
E 50s | 240 E. 58th St. (bet. 2nd & 3rd Aves.) | 212-688-4190 |
www.clubasteak.com
Set in the "lesser known" area near the Queensboro Bridge, this bi-
level steakhouse draws "older" locals with "A-1" chops, "top-notch"
service and a "sexy", "bordello"-hued setting; sure, it's on the "pricey"
side, but "live music" and a "relaxed" mood compensate.

NEW **Clyde Frazier's** ▽ **18** | **23** | **20** | **$49**
Wine & Dine ● *American*
Garment District | 485 10th Ave. (37th St.) | 212-842-1110 |
www.clydefraziers.com
Parked in the no-man's-land near the Lincoln Tunnel entrance, this
newcomer from the storied Knicks star serves globe-trotting American
chow in glitzy, arena-size digs; there's a "cool" bar to "watch the
games", but the so-so cooking leads some to contend "Clyde was
better on the court."

	FOOD	DECOR	SERVICE	COST

Co. *Pizza*

| 24 | 17 | 18 | $35 |

Chelsea | 230 Ninth Ave. (24th St.) | 212-243-1105 | www.co-pane.com
It's all about the "love of dough" at this Chelsea pizzeria where "bread guru" Jim Lahey serves "gourmet" pies flaunting "innovative toppings" and crust that "hits the magic spot between crispy and pillowy"; just don't expect much "elbow room" – this baby is "always busy."

Coco Roco *Peruvian*

| 21 | 15 | 19 | $27 |

Cobble Hill | 139 Smith St. (bet. Bergen & Dean Sts.) | Brooklyn | 718-254-9933
Park Slope | 392 Fifth Ave. (bet. 6th & 7th Sts.) | Brooklyn | 718-965-3376
www.cocorocorestaurant.com
"Juicy-crisp" rotisserie chicken is the signature of these Brooklyn Peruvians known for serving "substantial portions" of "hearty", well-marinated grub that "won't empty your wallet"; "no atmosphere" leads aesthetes to fly the coop via "takeout."

Coffee Shop ● *American/Brazilian*

| 17 | 15 | 14 | $31 |

Union Sq | 29 Union Sq. W. (16th St.) | 212-243-7969 | www.thecoffeeshopnyc.com
One of NY's "quintessential" late-night scenes, this longtime Brazilian-American rolls out a "diner-esque menu" delivered by a "leggy" staff that's "more attractive than you" – and "less hardworking" too; since the chow's just "so-so" and the decor "tired", regulars take sidewalk seats to "watch Union Square pass by."

Colbeh *Kosher/Persian*

| 23 | 20 | 20 | $41 |

Garment District | 32 W. 39th St. (bet. 5th & 6th Aves.) | 212-354-8181 | www.colbeh.com
"Authentic Persian recipes" abetted by a selection of sushi are purveyed at this kosher Garment District sleeper where the portions are as "generous" as the flavors are "intense"; "glitzy" new decor divides voters – "stylish" or "tacky Miami" – but you "won't leave hungry."

Colicchio & Sons *American*

| 25 | 25 | 25 | $72 |

Chelsea | 85 10th Ave. (bet. 15th & 16th Sts.) | 212-400-6699 | www.craftrestaurantsinc.com
Top Chef's Tom Colicchio "runs a fine machine" at this "sophisticated" Chelsea American offering "first-rate" cooking, "informed" service and an "airy", "masculine" setting; granted, the pricing is "not for the faint of wallet", but the "relaxing" Tap Room is "less spendy."

Colonie ● *American*

| 26 | 24 | 23 | $52 |

Brooklyn Heights | 127 Atlantic Ave. (bet. Clinton & Henry Sts.) | Brooklyn | 718-855-7500 | www.colonienyc.com
Bringing some oomph to Brooklyn Heights, this "convivial" American "continues to wow" with seasonal "locavore" fare ferried by an "agreeable" crew in wood-lined digs complete with a "live plant wall"; "tight" quarters and a "no-rez" policy keep it "packed, even on weekdays."

Commerce *American*

| 24 | 21 | 21 | $59 |

W Village | 50 Commerce St. (Barrow St.) | 212-524-2301 | www.commercerestaurant.com
The "bread basket alone" merits a visit to this "tucked-away" West Villager that trades in "high-caliber" New Americana served in a "pre-

modern NY" room; it "only takes credit cards" and the decibels "escalate as the night progresses", but in the end the "great bar scene" keeps regulars regular.

Community Food & Juice *American* | 23 | 18 | 19 | $32 |

W 100s | 2893 Broadway (bet. 112th & 113th Sts.) | 212-665-2800 | www.communityrestaurant.com

"Beloved by its own community", this "buzzy" Morningside Heights New American is a "healthy" haven in "Columbialand" for "nourishing" eats with "locavore-ish" leanings; exuding "good vibes" for three meals a day, it's "wildly popular" for brunch, thus there's "always a line."

NEW Cómodo *Pan-Latin* | - | - | - | E |

SoHo | 58 MacDougal St. (bet. Houston & King Sts.) | 646-370-4477 | www.comodonyc.com

From the folks behind pop-up supper club Worth Kitchen, this SoHo newcomer fields a pricey Latin menu that makes stops in Brazil, Mexico, Spain and beyond; the name translates as 'comfortable', an apt description of the rustic, communal-tabled setting.

Congee Bowery ◑ *Chinese* | 21 | 13 | 14 | $24 |

LES | 207 Bowery (bet. Rivington & Spring Sts.) | 212-766-2828

Congee Village ◑ *Chinese*

LES | 100 Allen St. (bet. Broome & Delancey Sts.) | 212-941-1818 www.congeevillagerestaurants.com

Though its namesake "stick-to-your-ribs" porridge is the "main event", this LES duo also "hits the spot" with a "dizzying menu" of "authentic" Cantonese items; "cheesy decor", "communication confusion" and "careless" service are trumped by the "unbelievably low" prices.

Convivium Osteria *Mediterranean* | 25 | 24 | 23 | $54 |

Park Slope | 68 Fifth Ave. (bet. Bergen St. & St. Marks Ave.) | Brooklyn | 718-857-1833 | www.convivium-osteria.com

"Park Slope's Restaurant Row" is home to this "dreamy" Mediterranean "experience" that melds "sumptuous cuisine" with a "serious" vino list and "polite" service; done up in "warm", "rustic" style with "polished wood", "mood lighting" and a "wonderful" garden, it's especially "romantic" in the downstairs wine cellar.

Cookshop ◑ *American* | 23 | 20 | 21 | $49 |

Chelsea | 156 10th Ave. (20th St.) | 212-924-4440 | www.cookshopny.com

Providing "farm-to-hipster dining" in a smart, "High Line–adjacent" address, this "energetic" Chelsea American rolls out an "inspired", "greenmarket-driven" menu served by an "aim-to-please" team; the "cheerful", "sunny" setting attracts "big", "noisy" crowds, especially for its "crazy-popular" brunch.

Coppelia ◑ *Diner/Nuevo Latino* | 23 | 19 | 20 | $30 |

Chelsea | 207 W. 14th St. (bet. 7th & 8th Aves.) | 212-858-5001 | www.coppelianyc.com

An "interesting" spin on a Cuban diner, this "friendly" Chelsea luncheonette slings "accomplished" Pan-Latin comfort chow in "casual", "colorful" confines; the "low tabs", "no-rush atmosphere" and 24/7 open-door policy make it a hit with early-risers and "all-nighters" alike.

	FOOD	DECOR	SERVICE	COST

Coppola's *Italian*
21 17 21 $41

Murray Hill | 378 Third Ave. (bet. 27th & 28th Sts.) | 212-679-0070 ◑
W 70s | 206 W. 79th St. (bet. Amsterdam Ave. & B'way) | 212-877-3840
www.coppolas-nyc.com

"Like an old friend", these longtime Southern Italians are "relaxing", "reliable" fallbacks for "comfort" chow heavy on the "red sauce"; maybe the "homey" settings are becoming "outdated", but "plentiful" portions, "courteous" service and "moderate" prices compensate.

Cornelia Street Cafe ◑ *American/French*
20 17 20 $36

W Village | 29 Cornelia St. (bet. Bleecker & W. 4th Sts.) | 212-989-9319 | www.corneliastreetcafe.com

"Old-school West Village" dining thrives at this circa-1977 "charmer" with a "yoga vibe", offering "perfectly acceptable" Franco-American fare and a "cheap and cheerful" brunch; although "starting to show its age", it gets "bonus" points for the "cool" performance space downstairs.

Corner Bistro ◑ *Burgers*
23 12 15 $20

W Village | 331 W. Fourth St. (Jane St.) | 212-242-9502 ⊞
NEW LIC | 47-18 Vernon Blvd. (47th Rd.) | Queens | 718-606-6500
www.cornerbistrony.com

"Memorable", "messy" burgers dished out on paper plates in "sticky booths" make for classic "slumming" at this "dingy" Village perennial (the atmosphere's "nicer" at the new LIC spin-off); "cheap beer", "long waits" and "student crowds" are all part of the timelessly "cool" experience.

NEW Corner Social ◑ *American*
▽ 21 22 22 $28

Harlem | 321 Lenox Ave. (126th St.) | 212-510-8552 | www.cornersocialnyc.com

A "breath of fresh air" in Harlem, this new "scene" brings even more "potential" to the burgeoning Lenox Avenue corridor that includes Red Rooster and Ginny's Supper Club; look for smart crowds, happening decibels and fairly priced, "better-than-average" American light bites washed down with an extensive beer selection.

Corsino ◑ *Italian*
22 18 21 $45

W Village | 637 Hudson St. (Horatio St.) | 212-242-3093 | www.corsinocantina.com

They "get simplicity right" at this "stylish" West Village Italian where "delectable" small plates are mated with a "vast, affordable" wine list; patronized by "beautiful, thin" types and patrolled by a "thoughtful" team, it's a "vibrant", verging on "boisterous", scene.

◪ Corton ⊠Ⓜ *French*
26 24 26 $133

TriBeCa | 239 W. Broadway (bet. Walker & White Sts.) | 212-219-2777 | www.cortonnyc.com

"Pure magic" awaits at this "exquisite" TriBeCa New French via Drew Nieporent and Paul Liebrandt, where "cerebral", "cutting-edge" cooking (think "chefs with tweezers") is buttressed by "superlative service" and an ultra-"minimalist", white-on-white setting; when the check arrives, the "splurgy" prix fixe–only tabs inspire as much "hushed awe" as the food.

Cotta *Italian*
23 | 23 | 22 | $35

W 80s | 513 Columbus Ave. (bet. 84th & 85th Sts.) | 212-873-8500 | www.cottanyc.com

"Busy and lively" from day one, this "rustic" UWS Italian yearling puts forth "delicious" pizza and "tapas-type" plates in a ground-floor wine bar or "cozy upstairs" (watch out for those "candles on the stairs"); it's "perfect for a casual date", with equally casual tabs to match.

The Counter *Burgers*
21 | 14 | 19 | $20

W 40s | 1451 Broadway (41st St.) | 212-997-6801 | www.thecounterburger.com

"Near-infinite options" are the lure at this Times Square link of the "build-it-yourself" national burger chain, where diners customize their orders "from bun to patty to toppings"; some shrug "nothing stellar", but most can agree it's an "easy, cheap pre-theater bite."

Covo ● *Italian*
23 | 20 | 23 | $35

Harlem | 701 W. 135th St. (12th Ave.) | 212-234-9573 | www.covony.com

"Solid" is the word on this "tucked-away" Harlem Italian supplying "tasty" pizza and pastas for "bang-for-the-buck" tabs in a "spread-out", brick-walled setting; "caring" servers distract from the "ear-ringing" noise, but night owls tout the "upstairs lounge."

Cowgirl *Southwestern*
17 | 19 | 19 | $30

W Village | 519 Hudson St. (W. 10th St.) | 212-633-1133 | www.cowgirlnyc.com

Cowgirl Sea-Horse *Southwestern*

Seaport | 259 Front St. (Dover St.) | 212-608-7873 | www.cowgirlseahorse.com

"Down-to-earth" says it all about this West Village Southwesterner slinging "decent" chow in a "kitschy", "retro rodeo" setting that's "kid-friendly" by day and a "high-octane" margaritaville after dark; the Seaport satellite gets a "fishy spin" with a seafood focus.

Crab Shanty ● *Seafood*
23 | 18 | 21 | $36

City Island | 361 City Island Ave. (Tier St.) | Bronx | 718-885-1810 | www.originalcrabshanty.com

"They pile it on" at this "informal" City Island vet where the "king-size" servings of crab and lobster are "tasty" and "affordable"; though the seafood's "fresh", the "nautical" decor's been out of the water too long.

❷ Craft *American*
26 | 24 | 25 | $77

Flatiron | 43 E. 19th St. (bet. B'way & Park Ave. S.) | 212-780-0880 | www.craftrestaurantsinc.com

"Dining purity" is the goal of this "class-act" Flatiron American from *Top Chef* "rock star" Tom Colicchio, where "perfect ingredients" in "straightforward preparations" make for "eye-openingly complex flavors"; "first-class" service and a "subtly beautiful space" are part of the "upscale" experience – along with tabs that "run up rapidly."

Craftbar *American*
24 | 21 | 22 | $54

Flatiron | 900 Broadway (bet. 19th & 20th Sts.) | 212-461-4300 | www.craftrestaurantsinc.com

Craft's Flatiron "baby brother" is a "more casual" option for "Colicchio fans" seeking the chef's "inventive, seasonal" New Americana at a "lower" price point; "super" staffers oversee the "understated" "loft-like space" that's typically "hopping" with a "noisy" clientele.

⛔️NEW Crave Fishbar *Seafood* | – | – | – | M |

E 50s | 945 Second Ave. (bet. 50th & 51st Sts.) | 646-895-9585 | www.cravefishbar.com

A follow-up to Crave Ceviche Bar, closed after a crane accident, this new Turtle Bay seafooder hooks fans with Asian-accented fresh catch served in a wood-lined, beach-rustic setting; it's an instant hit out of the box, so brace for crowds and noise.

Crema *Mexican* | 23 | 18 | 21 | $44 |

Chelsea | 111 W. 17th St. (bet. 6th & 7th Aves.) | 212-691-4477 | www.cremarestaurante.com

"French techniques" give an "innovative" lift to the modern Mexican cooking at chef Julieta Ballesteros' "tucked-away" Chelsea "sleeper"; it's a "relaxed" enclave for "elevated" eating and "energetic" service, and "affordable" enough for *fanáticos* to "go back again and again."

Creperie ●⇥ *French* | 23 | 13 | 18 | $15 |

G Village | 112 MacDougal St. (bet. Bleecker & W. 3rd Sts.) | 212-253-6705
LES | 135 Ludlow St. (bet. Rivington & Stanton Sts.) | 212-979-5521
www.creperienyc.com

"Savory or sweet", the "comprehensive" roster of "custom-made" crêpes "hits the spot" at this counter-service duo that's a no-brainer for folks "on a budget"; it's one of the "only games in town" for "late-night" noshing, though "tiny", "hole-in-the-wall" settings encourage ordering "to go."

Crif Dogs ● *Hot Dogs* | 23 | 13 | 18 | $12 |

E Village | 113 St. Marks Pl. (bet. Ave. A & 1st Ave.) | 212-614-2728
Williamsburg | 555 Driggs Ave. (N. 7th St.) | Brooklyn | 718-302-3200
www.crifdogs.com

"Spunky", "deep-fried" hot dogs are a "guilty pleasure" at these "gritty" tubesteak twins famed for their "fun toppings" (like bacon, avocado and cream cheese); they're a natural for "cheap", "late-night munchies", and the East Village original features a secret "speakeasy" bar accessed through a "phone booth."

Crispo ● *Italian* | 24 | 19 | 21 | $50 |

W Village | 240 W. 14th St. (bet. 7th & 8th Aves.) | 212-229-1818 | www.crisporestaurant.com

Pastaphiles are "blown away" by this "favorite" West Village trattoria purveying "gratifying" Northern Italian dishes led by a signature spaghetti carbonara that "has no rivals"; its "increasing popularity" results in "loud, cramped" conditions, so insiders head for the "all-seasons garden."

Crown *American* | 21 | 26 | 22 | $86 |

E 80s | 24 E. 81st St. (bet. 5th & Madison Aves.) | 646-559-4880 | www.crown81.com

"Luxurious" is the mind-set at this yearling from chef John DeLucie (Bill's, The Lion), luring "UES billionaires" and "plastic-surgery" practitioners with its "gorgeous" townhouse setting, "upper-class–club" mood and "glass-walled" garden room; "excellent" American fare and "courteous" service round out this "royal treat", best savored when "someone else is paying."

Cuba *Cuban*
24 | 20 | 22 | $41

G Village | 222 Thompson St. (bet. Bleecker & W. 3rd Sts.) | 212-420-7878 | www.cubanyc.com
Everyone's "Havana great time" at this "high-energy" Village supplier of "authentic" Cuban standards and "heavenly" mojitos "charmingly" served in "funky" Latin digs; "live bands", "relatively affordable" tabs and a "cigar-rolling man" lend a "vacation" vibe to the proceedings.

Cubana Café ⇗ *Cuban*
23 | 18 | 20 | $24

Carroll Gardens | 272 Smith St. (bet. Degraw & Sackett Sts.) | Brooklyn | 718-858-3980
Park Slope | 80 Sixth Ave. (St. Marks Pl.) | Brooklyn | 718-398-9818
www.cubanacafenyc.com
"Authenticity" trumps comfort at these "small" Brooklyn Cubans where the "flavorful" food and "decent mojitos" are a "slam dunk" for "satisfaction" and "value"; just be aware the service is "casual" and the payment "cash only."

Da Andrea *Italian*
23 | 17 | 21 | $38

G Village | 35 W. 13th St. (bet. 5th & 6th Aves.) | 212-367-1979 | www.daandreanyc.com
"Hearty", "homestyle" Emilia-Romagna cooking that "doesn't hold back on flavor" is the hallmark of this "congenial" Village "standby"; given the "modest prices", it's no surprise the "casual" space is "a bit too tight" for the crowds of "budget-conscious" fans.

Da Ciro *Italian/Pizza*
23 | 17 | 20 | $47

Murray Hill | 229 Lexington Ave. (bet. 33rd & 34th Sts.) | 212-532-1636
"Mouthwatering" focaccia Robiola is "reason enough" to frequent this Murray Hill duplex that's also a "reliable" source for wood-fired pizza and other "delicious" Italiana; upstairs is quieter than down, but no matter where you wind up, tabs tilt "a bit high."

Dafni Greek Taverna *Greek*
20 | 15 | 19 | $36

W 40s | 325 W. 42nd St. (bet. 8th & 9th Aves.) | 212-315-1010 | www.dafnitaverna.com
Set on a "no-man's-land" block opposite Port Authority, this "genuine" Greek comes across with "decent" renditions of "typical" Hellenica; "convenience to the theater", a short trip to Jersey and "affordability" are its trump cards, though the "nothing-special" decor needs work.

Daisy May's BBQ USA *BBQ*
22 | 8 | 14 | $26

W 40s | 623 11th Ave. (46th St.) | 212-977-1500 | www.daisymaysbbq.com
"Fall-off-the-bone" ribs and other "darn-good" BBQ allow patrons to "get in touch with the caveman within" at Adam Perry Lang's Clinton 'cue hut; despite "cafeteria-style" service, decor "best left undescribed" and a "nearly in-the-Hudson River" address, fans feel "lucky to have it."

Da Nico *Italian*
22 | 17 | 21 | $42

Little Italy | 164 Mulberry St. (bet. Broome & Grand Sts.) | 212-343-1212 | www.danicoristorante.com
A "Mulberry Street staple" for 20 years, this "traditional" Italian rolls out "gargantuan" portions of "tasty" vittles that are "a cut above the

local" norm; "attentive" service, "nominal" prices and a large back garden complete the overall "comfortable" picture.

❷ Daniel ☒ *French* 28 | 28 | 28 | $146

E 60s | 60 E. 65th St. (bet. Madison & Park Aves.) | 212-288-0033 | www.danielnyc.com

"Haute" puts it mildly at chef Daniel Boulud's 20-year-old East Side "classic", where the "exceptional" New French fare arrives in an "elegance personified", jackets-required setting; "carefully choreographed" service distracts from the "lofty", prix fixe–only tabs, making this "sweep-you-off-your-feet" experience an exercise in "pure pleasure"; P.S. there's "less formal", à la carte dining in the lounge.

Danji ●☒ *Korean* 26 | 19 | 21 | $49

W 50s | 346 W. 52nd St. (bet. 8th & 9th Aves.) | 212-586-2880 | www.danjinyc.com

Seoul food gets some "novel" "nouvelle" twists at this "much hyped" Hell's Kitchen Korean offering "complex" small plates; "no reservations" and "shoebox" dimensions make for "out-of-control" waits, but word is this "hot spot" is "definitely worth it."

❷ Danny Brown 26 | 22 | 25 | $51
Wine Bar & Kitchen Ⓜ *European*

Forest Hills | 104-02 Metropolitan Ave. (71st Dr.) | Queens | 718-261-2144 | www.dannybrownwinekitchen.com

"Giving Manhattan a run for the money", this "memorable" boîte brings "serious food" to Forest Hills via an "innovative" European menu paired with "well-chosen wines"; a "casually elegant" milieu, "cheerful" service and "Queens" pricing enhance the "fine-dining" feeling.

Da Noi *Italian* 24 | 20 | 23 | $50

Shore Acres | 138 Fingerboard Rd. (Tompkins Ave.) | Staten Island | 718-720-1650

Travis | 4358 Victory Blvd. (Service Rd.) | Staten Island | 718-982-5040

"Old-world" "red-sauce" Italian cooking "like nonna's" draws fans to this "congenial" Staten Island duo where "generous portions" turn "pricey" tabs into "money well spent"; the crowd's right out of a "scene from *The Godfather*", while the sound level's a bit on "da noisy" side.

🆕 Dans Le Noir ● *Eclectic* - | - | - | E

Garment District | 246 W. 38th St. (bet. 7th & 8th Aves.) | 212-575-1671 | www.danslenoir.com

Importing a dining-in-the-dark concept from same-named eateries across Europe, this Garment District newcomer tests taste buds with three-course Eclectic dinners served in a pitch-black room; the challenge is to identify flavors sans sight cues, though the more immediate challenge may be avoiding spills on your clothing.

Darbar *Indian* 22 | 17 | 21 | $36

E 40s | 152 E. 46th St. (bet. Lexington & 3rd Aves.) | 212-681-4500 | www.darbarny.com

Darbar Grill *Indian*

E 50s | 157 E. 55th St. (bet. Lexington & 3rd Aves.) | 212-751-4600 | www.darbargrill.com

Indian aficionados patronize this Midtown duo for its "standard repertoire" of "solid", "well-prepared" items served by a "gracious" team in "comfortable" confines; even better, there's "no sticker shock", particularly at the "can't-be-beat" $13 lunch buffet.

The Darby *American* 21 | 24 | 20 | $69

W Village | 244 W. 14th St. (bet. 7th & 8th Aves.) | 212-242-4411 | www.thedarbynyc.com

With its "phenomenal" house band and "cool" retro decor, this "trendy" West Village supper club's atmosphere tends to overshadow the "pretty decent" New American eats from Alex Guarnaschelli (Butter); you'll feel you're "in a different era" but for the up-to-date tabs.

Da Silvano ● *Italian* 22 | 18 | 20 | $65

G Village | 260 Sixth Ave. (Bleecker St.) | 212-982-2343 | www.dasilvano.com

The "glitterati" draw the "paparazzi" to this ever-"trendy" Villager where "celeb-spotting" is the "main course", though the Tuscan eats are almost as "delicious"; it costs "wads of cash" and the staff can be "snooty" to outsiders, so for best results, bring "George Clooney" – and get him to pick up the check.

NEW Dassara *Japanese/Noodle Shop* - | - | - | I

Carroll Gardens | 271 Smith St. (bet. Degraw & Sackett Sts.) | Brooklyn | 718-643-0781 | www.dassara.com

Not your typical ramen joint, this new Carroll Gardens noodle shop stirs the pot with some nontraditional versions (i.e. a 'deli' version made with matzo balls and Montreal-style smoked meat); while pricing is in line with the genre, the setting's a tad more upscale.

Da Tommaso ● *Italian* 21 | 16 | 21 | $49

W 50s | 903 Eighth Ave. (bet. 53rd & 54th Sts.) | 212-265-1890 | www.datommasony.com

The "quality never falters" at this 25-year-old Hell's Kitchen Italian purveying "lovely old-school" cooking with "waiters to match"; maybe da "dated" room "could use a face-lift", but "reasonable" rates and a "near-the-Theater District" address keep it "crowded" before a show.

Da Umberto 🆉 *Italian* 25 | 20 | 24 | $67

Chelsea | 107 W. 17th St. (bet. 6th & 7th Aves.) | 212-989-0303 | www.daumbertonyc.com

"Class" remains the hallmark of this "cosmopolitan" Chelsea Northern Italian, an "engaging" stop for "superb" cuisine courtesy of staffers who treat all "like honored guests"; yes, it's "costly", but the "old-world" air and "understated", "white-tablecloth" setting are among its payoffs.

David Burke at Bloomingdale's *American* 20 | 15 | 17 | $36

E 50s | Bloomingdale's | 150 E. 59th St. (bet. Lexington & 3rd Aves.) | 212-705-3800 | www.burkeinthebox.com

Assuage a "shopping hangover" with "high-fashion" New American "quick bites" à la David Burke at this "fast-paced" cafe in Bloomie's (and its grab 'n' go partner); despite "uninspiring" surroundings and "sloppy service", it's "convenient" and thus "continuously crowded."

David Burke Kitchen *American* 24 | 22 | 22 | $59

SoHo | James Hotel | 23 Grand St., downstairs (6th Ave.) | 212-201-9119 | www.davidburkekitchen.com

"Creative" but "casual", this far-from-cheap "farm-to-fork" option from David Burke matches "delightful" New Americana with "on-

| | FOOD | DECOR | SERVICE | COST |

point" service and a "semi-subterranean" setting in SoHo's James Hotel; the Treehouse Bar upstairs adds an extra dimension to the "inviting" package.

David Burke Townhouse *American*
| 25 | 25 | 24 | $69 |

E 60s | 133 E. 61st St. (bet. Lexington & Park Aves.) | 212-813-2121 | www.davidburketownhouse.com

"Upper-crust" Upper Eastsiders indulge in "ritzy" lunches and "transformative" dinners at celeb chef David Burke's "top-end" New American townhouse, where a "kind" staff presents "pretty" plates in a "posh" milieu; 10 years down the road, it remains a "perennial favorite", "sky-high" tabs and "close-fit" seats notwithstanding.

Dawat *Indian*
| 23 | 19 | 21 | $50 |

E 50s | 210 E. 58th St. (bet. 2nd & 3rd Aves.) | 212-355-7555 | www.dawatrestaurant.com

Midtown's Indian "pioneer" (since 1986) "still pleases", thanks to actress/chef Madhur Jaffrey's "sophisticated" cooking, "graciously served" in a "quiet", "contemporary" room that's "conducive to conversation"; it may look "a little worn", but loyalists avow the tabs are "worth the extra cost."

DB Bistro Moderne *French*
| 25 | 22 | 24 | $67 |

W 40s | City Club Hotel | 55 W. 44th St. (bet. 5th & 6th Aves.) | 212-391-2400 | www.danielnyc.com

"Casual" dining, Daniel Boulud–style, comes to the Theater District via this "approachable" though "not inexpensive" French bistro where the "confident" cooking leads off with a signature foie gras–stuffed "Cadillac of burgers"; "responsive" service, "chic" looks and a "value" $45 prix fixe compensate for the "tightly packed" conditions.

DBGB ☻ *French*
| 24 | 23 | 21 | $52 |

E Village | 299 Bowery (bet. 1st & Houston Sts.) | 212-933-5300 | www.danielnyc.com

Daniel Boulud "lets his hair down" at this "exuberant" Bowery bistro rolling out a meat-centric French menu led by "dynamite burgers" and sausages, lubricated with "craft beers"; the "upscale bohemian" setting is "spacious", the service "accommodating", the crowd "youthful" and the acoustics louder than the World Cup finals.

Dee's Ⓜ *Mediterranean/Pizza*
| 22 | 18 | 21 | $30 |

Forest Hills | 107-23 Metropolitan Ave. (74th Ave.) | Queens | 718-793-7553 | www.deesnyc.com

Dee-votees dee-pend on this "homey" Forest Hills outlet for "wonderful" brick-oven pizza along with Mediterranean "comfort" dishes; "fair prices", a "huge" setting and "ample seating" bolster the "amicable", "family-friendly" mood.

Defonte's Sandwich Shop *Sandwiches*
| 24 | 10 | 18 | $15 |

Gramercy | 261 Third Ave. (21st St.) | 212-614-1500
Red Hook | 379 Columbia St. (Luquer St.) | Brooklyn | 718-625-8052

"Don't eat for a week" before attacking the "two-handed" "Dagwood" sandwiches at these "lip-smacking" Italian sub shops; the '20s-era Red Hook prototype "used to feed the longshoremen" and still exudes a whiff of "old-fashioned Brooklyn."

	FOOD	DECOR	SERVICE	COST

DeGrezia ⊠ *Italian*
25 **23** **25** **$65**

E 50s | 231 E. 50th St. (bet. 2nd & 3rd Aves.) | 212-750-5353 |
www.degreziaristorante.com

A "real sleeper" hidden below street level, this Eastsider is a model of
"old-world elegance", offering "first-rate" Italian food, "expert" service and a "civilized" milieu where "one can actually talk"; though "expensive", it's "worth it for special occasions" and "business lunches."

Degustation *French/Spanish*
28 **21** **24** **$79**

E Village | 239 E. Fifth St. (bet. 2nd & 3rd Aves.) | 212-979-1012

East Village "cooler-than-cool" tasting bar from Jack and Grace Lamb
purveying "dazzling" Franco-Spanish small plates assembled by "expert"
chefs; it's "exciting to watch" and the "minuscule" setting lends "intimacy", but be aware that a "big bill" caps the experience.

☒ Del Frisco's ● *Steak*
25 **23** **23** **$76**

W 40s | 1221 Sixth Ave. (bet. 48th & 49th Sts.) | 212-575-5129 |
www.delfriscos.com

☒ Del Frisco's Grille *Steak*

W 50s | 50 Rockefeller Plaza (51st St., bet. 5th & 6th Aves.) |
212-767-0371 | www.delfriscosgrille.com

"Always abuzz", this mahogany-lined Midtown "powerhouse" and its
"less over-the-top" Rock Plaza sibling are "wall-to-wall" with "type-A"
types tucking into "sumptuous" steaks served in a "corporate" setting;
to preserve your "company card", try the $34 prix fixe lunch.

Delicatessen ● *American*
20 **20** **19** **$35**

NoLita | 54 Prince St. (Lafayette St.) | 212-226-0211 |
www.delicatessennyc.com

NoLita is home to this wannabe "trendy" spot slinging "filling"
Americana (e.g. "fantastic" mac 'n' cheese) in "minimalist" digs outfitted with retractable walls; cynics feel it "tries too hard", but concede
that the staff is "pretty" and the downstairs bar "lively."

Dell'anima ● *Italian*
26 **20** **22** **$60**

W Village | 38 Eighth Ave. (Jane St.) | 212-366-6633 | www.dellanima.com

Drawing a "good-looking crowd with money to spend", this West
Village Italian plies a "mind-blowing" menu best savored at its "entertaining" chef's counter; given the "way-small" dimensions, it "fills up
fast" and getting rezzies is "no easy feat", though its "adjacent wine
bar" (Anfora) works as a holding pen.

Delmonico's ⊠ *Steak*
24 **23** **24** **$71**

Financial District | 56 Beaver St. (S. William St.) | 212-509-1144 |
www.delmonicosny.com

Exuding the "charm of a bygone era", this "olde NY" exemplar vends
"decadent" steaks in the FiDi; "pro" service, "timeless" digs and "premium" pricing buttress its "class-all-the-way" approach, and its "Wall
Street" fans like its "quiet" mien.

☒ Del Posto *Italian*
26 **27** **26** **$110**

Chelsea | 85 10th Ave. (bet. 15th & 16th Sts.) | 212-497-8090 |
www.delposto.com

The Batali-Bastianich team "really outdoes themselves" at this "palatial"
Chelsea "production" that "sets the bar" with "superlative" Italian food

and wine, "attention-to-detail" service and a "magnificent", marble-and-mahogany setting replete with balcony seating, private party spaces and "live piano"; granted, the prices are steep, but this "special-occasion" magnet is "worth the splurge."

Delta Grill ● *Cajun/Creole*   20 | 17 | 18 | $33

W 40s | 700 Ninth Ave. (48th St.) | 212-956-0934 | www.thedeltagrill.com
"N'Awlins comes to Ninth Avenue" at this "funky" Hell's Kitchen road-house that channels the "Big Easy" with "reliable" Cajun-Creole grub that "somehow tastes better when a band is playing"; "cheery" vibes and "reasonable" tabs keep the "patrons marching in."

Denino's Pizzeria ⊅ *Pizza*   26 | 13 | 20 | $21

Port Richmond | 524 Port Richmond Ave. (bet. Hooker Pl. & Walker St.) | Staten Island | 718-442-9401 | www.deninos.com
High on the Staten Island food chain, this circa-1937 pizzeria is praised for pies "extraordinaire", served "quick"; the "tavern" setting may be "a bit rough" and the cash-only rule is a drag, but the "packed" house suggests "they're doing something right."

Dervish ● *Mediterranean*   19 | 16 | 20 | $39

W 40s | 146 W. 47th St. (bet. 6th & 7th Aves.) | 212-997-0070 | www.dervishrestaurant.com
"Well established" as a "dependable" curtain-raiser, this Theater District Med specializes in "satisfying" "homestyle" cooking ferried by "expe-ditious" servers who "whirl you in and out"; "modest prices" – i.e. that $28 early-bird prix fixe – make the "tired" decor easy to swallow.

NEW Desi Shack ⊠ *Indian/Pakistani*   ∇ 22 | 14 | 19 | $17

Murray Hill | 331 Lexington Ave. (39th St.) | 212-867-3374 | www.desishack.com
Applying the customizable fast-casual formula to Indian and Pakistani eats, this Murray Hill newcomer dishes up succulent skewers served over rice or a salad, or bundled into a paratha roll; it's "worth a try" for "healthier, simpler" repasts, though the spare, 12-seat space suggests "takeout."

Destino ⊠ *Italian*   20 | 21 | 21 | $60

E 50s | 891 First Ave. (50th St.) | 212-751-0700 | www.destinony.com
Sutton Place "locals" like this "classy" joint for its "well-prepared" Southern Italian cooking via a Rao's alum who knows his way around a meatball; "understated" atmospherics, luxe furnishings and an "occa-sional piano player" make the "high prices" more palatable.

Deux Amis *French*   20 | 19 | 23 | $50

E 50s | 356 E. 51st St. (bet. 1st & 2nd Aves.) | 212-230-1117
The "warm" owner and "agreeable staff" lend a "feel-at-home" air to this East Midtown bistro, an approximation of "side-street-Paris" din-ing serving "solid" French country cuisine; the interior's *plaisant* if "a bit close", so some find it's "best sitting outside."

Dhaba ● *Indian*   23 | 16 | 17 | $31

Murray Hill | 108 Lexington Ave. (bet. 27th & 28th Sts.) | 212-679-1284 | www.dhabanyc.com
"Delicious and different", this "simple" Curry Hill Indian turns out "im-pressive", "pungently spiced" specialties – even "'regular' is hot, hot,

hot" – at "terrific-value" tabs; there's "always a line" at the "sliver" of a space for the "bargain" $11 lunch buffet.

⬧ Di Fara Ⓜ⇄ *Pizza* | 27 | 6 | 11 | $19 |

Midwood | 1424 Ave. J (15th St.) | Brooklyn | 718-258-1367 | www.difara.com
"Mind-boggling" pies emerge from the oven of this circa-1964 Midwood pizzeria where "artisan" pizzaiolo Dom DeMarco demonstrates his "painstaking craft" with "awesome" results; despite "dingy" digs, "lines around the block" and the "most expensive slices in town", devotees declare there "ain't nothing else like it."

Dim Sum Go Go *Chinese* | 21 | 13 | 16 | $24 |

Chinatown | 5 E. Broadway (Chatham Sq.) | 212-732-0797 | www.dimsumgogo.com
"Cheap", "no-frills" dim sum ordered off a menu rather than snagged from a trolley makes this "utilitarian" Chinese "less chaotic" than the typical C-town outfits; traditionalists "miss the ladies schlepping the carts" and report "perfunctory service" and "run-of-the-mill" decor.

Diner ● *American* | 25 | 18 | 21 | $41 |

Williamsburg | 85 Broadway (Berry St.) | Brooklyn | 718-486-3077 | www.dinernyc.com
"Retro" meets "hipster" at this "relaxed" South Williamsburger lodged in a "funky" 1927-vintage dining car; the "inventive" New American bill of fare "changes daily" based on "seasonal" availability, though "recited menus" and somewhat "pricey" tabs are constants.

Dinosaur Bar-B-Que *BBQ* | 23 | 19 | 19 | $31 |

Harlem | 700 W. 125th St. (12th Ave.) | 212-694-1777 | www.dinosaurbarbque.com
West Harlem is home to this "biker-approved" BBQ barn slinging "heaping plates" of "glorious", "five-napkin" 'cue in a "Deep South roadhouse" setting; "working-man's" prices and a "free-for-all" atmosphere suggest it "won't go extinct" anytime soon.

Dirt Candy ⓍⓂ *Vegetarian* | 26 | 18 | 24 | $50 |

E Village | 430 E. Ninth St. (bet. Ave. A & 1st Ave.) | 212-228-7732 | www.dirtcandynyc.com
Chef-owner Amanda Cohen coaxes "big, bold" flavors from nature's bounty at this "super-imaginative" East Village vegetarian, where the "off-the-charts" creations are irresistible even to the most committed carnivores; the "limited" menu is a match for the "shoebox"-size dimensions, so it can be "hard to book a table."

Divino *Italian* | 20 | 17 | 21 | $47 |

E 80s | 1556 Second Ave. (bet. 80th & 81st Sts.) | 212-861-1096
Yorkville denizens "always feel welcome" at this "neighborhood" vet thanks to "gracious" staffers serving "dependable Italian staples" in calm, "comfortable" environs; weekend "live music" lends this "oldie but goodie" a "fun atmosphere."

Docks Oyster Bar *Seafood* | 21 | 18 | 20 | $55 |

E 40s | 633 Third Ave. (40th St.) | 212-986-8080 | www.docksoysterbar.com
"Reliable", "well-prepared" fish and bivalves galore reel in the masses at this "cavernous" seafood standby near Grand Central;

"briskly professional" servers tend to schools of "biz lunchers" and "after-work" revelers who dive in for its "active" happy hour and high-octane "social" scene.

Do Hwa *Korean*

22	18	18	$38

W Village | 55 Carmine St. (Bedford St.) | 212-414-1224 | www.dohwanyc.com

"Authentic" eats packing "lots of spice" chased with "creative" cocktails fuel the "cool vibe" at this "hip" West Village Korean, a slightly "upscale" take on the "traditional" with grill-equipped tables on hand for hands-on types; sure, it may cost "a little more than K-town", but it's a much "sexier" experience.

Dominick's ⊅ *Italian*

24	13	20	$39

Fordham | 2335 Arthur Ave. (bet. Crescent Ave. & E. 187th St.) | Bronx | 718-733-2807

Patrons have been filling the "communal tables" of this "iconic" Arthur Avenue Italian since 1966, despite no decor, "no menus" ("you eat what they're cooking"), "no checks" ("trust the waiter") and no reservations or credit cards; "off-the-charts" food and "cost performance" make the "daunting waits" bearable, but to save time, go early.

NEW Don Antonio *Pizza*

24	17	20	$31

W 50s | 309 W. 50th St. (bet. 8th & 9th Aves.) | 646-719-1043 | www.donantoniopizza.com

Pizza purists praise the "died-and-went-to-Naples" pies purveyed at this "genuine" Hell's Kitchen newcomer vending wood-fired Neapolitan specialties that include vegan, "gluten-free" and lightly fried versions; "noisy", "crowded" conditions are offset by "upscale" atmospherics and "efficient" service.

Donatella *Pizza*

21	19	19	$44

Chelsea | 184 Eighth Ave. (bet. 19th & 20th Sts.) | 212-493-5150 | www.donatellanyc.com

"Glitz" meets garlic at Donatella Arpaia's "cheerful" Chelsea pizzeria, a "jumping" joint turning out "rich, flavorful" Neapolitan pies along with "appetizing" Italian standards; "gracious" staffers patrol the "trattoria"-like setting, dominated by a gold-tiled oven that hints at the "pricey"-for-the-neighborhood tariffs.

NEW Dong Chun Hong M *Chinese/Korean*

▽ 21	18	22	$25

Garment District | 312 Fifth Ave. (bet. 31st & 32nd Sts.) | 212-268-7888 | www.dongchunhongnyc.com

"Quality" Korean-Chinese fusion is the thing at this swanky new K-towner, a Seoul import offering an adventuresome menu that includes delicacies like sea cucumber and jellyfish; slick looks and small tabs add additional value to the "wonderful" equation.

Don Giovanni ◑⊅ *Pizza*

21	15	18	$32

Chelsea | 214 10th Ave. (bet. 22nd & 23rd Sts.) | 212-242-9054
W 40s | 358 W. 44th St. (bet. 8th & 9th Aves.) | 212-581-4939
www.dongiovanni-ny.com

The thin-crust pizza's "a cut above" at this cash-only West Side Italian duo, home of coal-fired pies that are "heavy on the cheese but light on the price"; regulars straying from the slices "stick to the basics" on the "pretty good" Italian menu and opt for "outdoor seating" – there's "not much ambiance" inside.

Donguri  *Japanese* ▽ 25 | 16 | 23 | $65

E 80s | 309 E. 83rd St. (bet. 1st & 2nd Aves.) | 212-737-5656 | www.dongurinyc.com

"Tiny but lovely", this "side-street" Yorkville Japanese specializes in dishes from the Kansai region – think "brilliantly prepared" soba, udon and sashimi (there's "no sushi", however); "hospitable" servers who "don't rush you" make for "relaxing" dining, that is until the "expensive" check arrives.

Donovan's *Pub Food* 21 | 18 | 20 | $28

Bayside | 214-16 41st Ave. (Bell Blvd.) | Queens | 718-423-5178 | www.donovansofbayside.com
Woodside | 57-24 Roosevelt Ave. (58th St.) | Queens | 718-429-9339 | www.donovansny.com ●⽏

"Something-for-everyone" menus lure the "family" trade to these separately owned Queens vets lauded for "perfect" hamburgers along with "solid", "Irish-tinged" pub grub; the Bayside outlet has been "redecorated" and Woodside is "cash only", but both enjoy "bargain" tabs and "pleasant" service.

Don Pedro's *Caribbean* 21 | 16 | 19 | $39

E 90s | 1865 Second Ave. (96th St.) | 212-996-3274 | www.donpedros.net

An Upper East Side "diamond in the rough", this "lively" Latin-Caribbean presents "flavorful" fare served with "flair" and sweetened by fruity cocktails; the split-level dining room is a "classy alternative" to its Uptown competition.

Don Peppe Ⓜ⽏ *Italian* 26 | 13 | 20 | $47

Ozone Park | 135-58 Lefferts Blvd. (bet. 135th & 149th Aves.) | Queens | 718-845-7587

Everything's "floating in garlic" at this 1968 vintage Ozone Park Italian, an "old-school", "cash-only" stop for "top-notch" red-sauce classics plated in "gargantuan" portions; ok, there's "no atmosphere" and "red or white" are the "only wine choices", yet ultimately this one's an "experience" like no other.

Do or Dine ●⽏ *Eclectic* ▽ 25 | 23 | 24 | $30

Bed-Stuy | 1108 Bedford Ave. (bet. Lexington Ave. & Quincy St.) | Brooklyn | 718-684-2290

"Edgy" understates the situation at this "amazing", cash-only Bed-Stuy Eclectic where the menu runs the gamut from "foie gras donuts" to frogs' legs with a Dr. Pepper glaze, and the food's served in ashtrays and cigar boxes; expect "hipsters galore" along with wacky decor including a "disco ball" and a skull-and-bones welcome mat.

Dos Caminos *Mexican* 20 | 20 | 19 | $42

E 50s | 825 Third Ave. (bet. 50th & 51st Sts.) | 212-336-5400
Meatpacking | 675 Hudson St. (14th St.) | 212-699-2400
Murray Hill | 373 Park Ave. S. (bet. 26th & 27th Sts.) | 212-294-1000
SoHo | 475 W. Broadway (bet. Houston & Prince Sts.) | 212-277-4300
www.doscaminos.com

A piquant Mexican menu, highlighted by guacamole made tableside washed down with "serious" margaritas, lures a "young", "keep-'em-coming" crowd to Steve Hanson's "vibrant" quartet; despite "disinterested" service and a "chainy" vibe, nothing dampens the "party."

	FOOD	DECOR	SERVICE	COST

Dos Toros *Mexican*
22 **12** **19** **$14**

NEW **E 70s** | 1111 Lexington Ave. (bet. 77th & 78th Sts.) | 212-535-4658
E Village | 137 Fourth Ave. (13th St.) | 212-677-7300
W Village | 11 Carmine St. (bet. Bleecker St. & 6th Ave.) | 212-627-2051
www.dostorosnyc.com

"Legitimate" Mexican fare by way of the "Bay area" is the specialty of these "cheap, fab" taquerias, "eco-friendly" stops luring both bullish burrito buffs and Cali transplants; there's "always a line and never a table", but the UES and West Village outlets feature "fast delivery."

Dovetail *American*
25 **22** **24** **$81**

W 70s | 103 W. 77th St. (Columbus Ave.) | 212-362-3800 |
www.dovetailnyc.com

John Fraser's "suave" New American is a "memorable" UWS destination, offering an "exquisite symphony" of "original" dishes, "stunningly" presented by a "gracious" staff in a "serene", bi-level setting; such "perfection" is understandably expensive, though the $48 'Sunday suppa' is a "special treat."

Dressler *American*
26 **23** **23** **$59**

Williamsburg | 149 Broadway (bet. Bedford & Driggs Aves.) |
Brooklyn | 718-384-6343 | www.dresslernyc.com

"Special-night-out" dining comes to "hip Williamsburg" via this "brilliant" New American that flaunts its "gastronomic ambition" with an "adventurous", "seasonal" menu; an "on-point" staff and a "retro"-"romantic" room are further reasons to "lure diners from Manhattan", though big-city tabs have crossed the bridge as well.

Duane Park ⊠Ⓜ *American*
22 **21** **21** **$53**

TriBeCa | 157 Duane St. (bet. Hudson St. & W. B'way) |
212-732-5555 | www.duaneparknyc.com

"Wonderfully eccentric", this "class-act" TriBeCa New American aims to please with "solid", Old South–accented cooking and "friendly" hospitality, then ices the cake with live jazz and "naughty" burlesque acts; P.S. a move to new digs on the Bowery is in the works.

Due ● *Italian*
21 **17** **22** **$51**

E 70s | 1396 Third Ave. (bet. 79th & 80th Sts.) | 212-772-3331 |
www.duenyc.com

Locals tout the "simple", "satisfying" Northern Italian cooking and "feel-at-home" atmosphere at this "low-profile" Upper Eastsider, now in its 25th year; "rustic" looks and "warm" service enhance its "unpretentious" air, while fair prices seal the deal.

DuMont *American*
24 **18** **20** **$30**

Williamsburg | 432 Union Ave. (bet. Devoe St. & Metropolitan Ave.) |
Brooklyn | 718-486-7717
DuMont Burger ● *American*
Williamsburg | 314 Bedford Ave. (bet. S. 1st & 2nd Sts.) | Brooklyn |
718-384-6127
www.dumontnyc.com

A "neighborhood mainstay" for "young, hip" types, this "casual" Williamsburg New American offers "mad delicious" grub sourced from the "farmer's markets" and best savored in its "romantic" back garden; the burger-oriented Bedford branch aces the "perfect" patty, but is about as "small" as the bun.

Dumpling Man ●🗷 *Chinese*   21 | 10 | 17 | $13

E Village | 100 St. Marks Pl. (bet. Ave. A & 1st Ave.) | 212-505-2121 | www.dumplingman.com
Steamed or seared, the "scrumptious dumplings" at this East Village Chinese make for a "super-cheap", cash-only snack that's handmade "right in front of you" (a "show in itself"); many prefer to "stuff themselves" on the run since the premises "aren't much to look at."

The Dutch ● *American* 24 | 22 | 21 | $62

SoHo | 131 Sullivan St. (Prince St.) | 212-677-6200 | www.thedutchnyc.com
Andrew Carmellini's "terrific" regional American cooking in "cool" quarters with an "amazing vibe" makes it "hard to get a rez" at this SoHo "standout"; a skeptical few say it "doesn't live up to the hype" or the "steep prices", but its "crowded", "happening", "earplug"-worthy "scene" speaks for itself.

Dylan Prime *Steak* 24 | 23 | 22 | $72

TriBeCa | 62 Laight St. (Greenwich St.) | 212-334-4783 | www.dylanprime.com
Bringing something "sexy" to the steakhouse scene, this "classy" TriBeCan still "hangs with the big boys" via "quality" chops and "personable" service; a "romantic", dimly lit setting makes it a "refreshing change" from the genre's usual "machismo."

E&E Grill House *Steak* 22 | 21 | 23 | $47

W 40s | Pearl Hotel | 233 W. 49th St. (bet. B'way & 8th Ave.) | 212-505-9909 | www.eegrillhouse.com
"Darn-good steaks" and seafood are the headliners at this "heart-of-Times Square" chophouse where a minimalist, "modern" setting and "eager-to-please" staffers set a "delightful" mood; throw in tabs that "won't break the bank", and showgoers say this baby's got star "potential."

East Buffet *Asian/Eclectic* 19 | 15 | 13 | $26

Flushing | 42-07 Main St. (bet. Franklin & Maple Aves.) | Queens | 718-353-6333
It helps to arrive "super-hungry" before facing the "endless" array of "tasty" Asian-Eclectic vittles at this "all-you-can-eat" Flushing buffet, set in a "huge", triple-decker space decked out in an "over-the-top", Vegas-y style; the tabs are as "cheap" as the weekend lines are "long."

East End Kitchen *American* 20 | 20 | 17 | $47

E 80s | 539 E. 81st St. (bet. East End & York Aves.) | 212-879-0450 | www.eastendkitchennyc.com
"Finally", "sleepy" Yorkville has a "neighborhood" haunt all its own in this "promising" spot offering "homey" Americana, "casual" Sunday brunching and even a grab-and-go espresso bar; the "Hamptons"-esque decor is "stylish", but critics wish the servers would "get their act together."

	FOOD	DECOR	SERVICE	COST

East Manor *Chinese*
21 | **15** | **15** | **$24**

Flushing | 46-45 Kissena Blvd. (bet. Kalmia & Laburnum Aves.) |
Queens | 718-888-8998

"Like eating in Grand Central", this "700-seat Flushing Chinese may be
"huge" square footage–wise but is small pricewise; its specialty is
"appetizing" Hong Kong–style dim sum plucked from rolling carts, with
"noise", so-so service and "typical"-for-the-genre decor on the side.

East Pacific *Asian*
22 | **20** | **21** | **$30**

Murray Hill | 120 E. 34th St. (bet. Lexington & Park Aves.) | 212-696-2818
New Springville | Staten Island Mall | 2655 Richmond Ave.
(Richmond Hill Rd.) | Staten Island | 718-370-2225

These "surprisingly good" Pan-Asians in Murray Hill and the Staten
Island Mall offer menus running the gamut from sushi to dim sum and
pad Thai, all "bursting with flavor"; "strive-to-please" service and
"won't-break-the-bank" tabs complete the "palatable" picture.

E.A.T. *American*
20 | **13** | **15** | **$40**

E 80s | 1064 Madison Ave. (bet. 80th & 81st Sts.) | 212-772-0022 |
www.elizabar.com

Before "Museum Mile" or "Madison Avenue shopping", "East Side
ladies" drop by Eli Zabar's "high-style" American for "tastefully prepared" sandwiches and salads; despite "money-is-no-object" tabs,
"rushed" service and "glamorized deli" digs, it's "always busy."

⌿ Eataly *Italian*
24 | **20** | **18** | **$40**

Flatiron | 200 Fifth Ave. (bet. 23rd & 24th Sts.) | 212-229-2560 |
www.eataly.com

"Disneyland for foodies", this "larger-than-life" Flatiron food hall via
the Batali-Bastianich team celebrates "everything Italian", offering
noshing at counters vending cheese, coffee, fish, gelato, pasta, pizza,
vegetables and wine, all in the "middle of a grocery store" the size of
"Grand Central Station"; the "price of success" includes "extreme
crowds", "no available seats" and "sensory overload", but then again,
there's "nothing else like it anywhere."

Eatery ◑ *American*
22 | **17** | **19** | **$34**

W 50s | 798 Ninth Ave. (53rd St.) | 212-765-7080 | www.eaterynyc.com

"Comfort food with a trendy twist" is the calling card of this Hell's
Kitchen American where the midpriced chow arrives in "minimalist",
"diner-chic" digs; "be-seen" types like the "gay-friendly" people-
watching and tolerate the high-volume "hustle and bustle."

Ecco ☒ *Italian*
23 | **20** | **23** | **$56**

TriBeCa | 124 Chambers St. (bet. Church St. & W. B'way) |
212-227-7074 | www.eccorestaurantny.com

"Still going strong", this "old-school" TriBeCan turns out "true-to-its-
roots" Italian fare to the tune of a weekend "piano player"; "formal"
staffers are also on key, leaving "Uptown prices" as the only off-notes.

Edi & the Wolf ◑ *Austrian*
23 | **22** | **20** | **$48**

E Village | 102 Ave. C (bet. 6th & 7th Sts.) | 212-598-1040 |
www.ediandthewolf.com

"Unique" is the word on this "funky" East Village Austrian offering
"rich", "authentic" fare paired with super suds and wines; the hipster

"cozy-cottage" design seems straight out of a fractured fairytale, while the "cute" garden is a quiet alternative to the "loud" goings-on inside.

Ed's Chowder House *Seafood*   20 | 21 | 20 | $57

W 60s | Empire Hotel | 44 W. 63rd St., mezzanine (bet. B'way & Columbus Ave.) | 212-956-1288 | www.chinagrillmgt.com

Perched in "classy digs" in the Empire Hotel, this "spiffy" seafooder is a catch for landlubbers seeking "expertly cooked" fish served "fast"; the "dopey", "Cape Cod"–sounding moniker may be at odds with its "fancy", "pricey" identity, but fans like its "easy access to Lincoln Center."

Ed's Lobster Bar   *Seafood*   24 | 16 | 20 | $42

NoLita | 222 Lafayette St. (bet. Kenmare & Spring Sts.) | 212-343-3236

Ed's Lobster Bar Annex Ⓜ *Seafood*

LES | 25 Clinton St. (bet. Houston & Stanton Sts.) | 212-777-7370 www.lobsterbarnyc.com

"Simple, whitewashed" settings give these "upbeat" fish houses a "New England" mood that goes well with its "pricey", "near-perfection" lobster rolls and bivalves; given the "cramped" table seating, regulars "eat at the bar" for "more attentive" service and added wiggle room.

Egg ⊄ *Southern*   24 | 15 | 17 | $23

Williamsburg | 135 N. Fifth St. (bet. Bedford Ave. & Berry St.) | Brooklyn | 718-302-5151 | www.pigandegg.com

"Heavenly" "country cooking" lures "hordes of hipsters" to this egg-ceptional Williamsburg Southerner where the "organic", "farm"-fresh bounty is as "astonishing" as the lines often are; "tiny" digs, "rushed service" and a cash-only policy are the downsides.

Eisenberg's Sandwich Shop   *Sandwiches*   18 | 11 | 17 | $17

Flatiron | 174 Fifth Ave. (bet. 22nd & 23rd Sts.) | 212-675-5096 | www.eisenbergsnyc.com

A "bygone" ode to the "greasy spoon", this circa-1929 Flatiron luncheonette is known for "basics" like tuna sandwiches and "old-style" egg creams; modernists may moan about "shabby" decor and "rickety" service, but for many, this remains a "sentimental" favorite.

El Centro ● *Mexican*   21 | 18 | 20 | $27

W 50s | 824 Ninth Ave. (54th St.) | 646-763-6585 | www.elcentro-nyc.com

This "upbeat" Hell's Kitchen Mexican throws a "hip", "loud" fiesta ramped up by "awesome" margaritas and, oh yeah, "decently priced" south-of-the-border bites; the "quirky", "kitschy" setting is "always packed", though regulars wish the "music could be lowered a few decibels."

🅩 Eleven Madison Park ⓧ *French*   28 | 28 | 28 | $254

Flatiron | 11 Madison Ave. (24th St.) | 212-889-0905 | www.elevenmadisonpark.com

For years now, chef-owner Daniel Humm has been producing "flawless" New French cooking at this Madison Square Park "temple of fine dining", where "stunning", "deceptively simple" dishes are served with "Swiss precision" in a "gorgeous", high-ceilinged setting; a recent menu change will add elements of showmanship like card tricks and glass domes filled with smoke.

El Faro ●Ⓜ *Spanish*

	23	13	19	$43

W Village | 823 Greenwich St. (bet. Horatio & Jane Sts.) |
212-929-8210 | www.elfaronyc.com

"Old as the hills", this circa-1927 West Village Spaniard is renowned for "can't-be-beat", garlic-laden paella, backed up by "succulent" seafood and "top-notch" tapas; seemingly "unchanged" for decades, the "worn" room gets more "charming" with each "jumbo pitcher" of sangria.

Eliá Ⓜ *Greek*

	26	21	23	$50

Bay Ridge | 8611 Third Ave. (bet. 86th & 87th Sts.) | Brooklyn |
718-748-9891 | www.eliarestaurant.com

Bringing Bay Ridge an "exceptional" "taste of the Mediterranean", this Greek "neighborhood" fixture produces "perfectly cooked" whole fish and other "innovative" specials; sure, it's a "splurge", but the staff is "hospitable" and there are bonus "outdoor seats" on the garden deck.

Elias Corner ●♄ *Greek/Seafood*

	23	10	15	$40

Astoria | 24-02 31st St. (24th Ave.) | Queens | 718-932-1510 |
www.eliascorner.com

Grilled fish so fresh it tastes like it was "caught an hour ago" is the specialty of this "no-frills" Astoria Greek with not much decor and "no menus" (just check out the "cold case" and point); though it only accepts cash and service is "so-so", the tabs are sure "hard to beat."

Elio's ● *Italian*

	24	19	20	$68

E 80s | 1621 Second Ave. (bet. 84th & 85th Sts.) | 212-772-2242

A magnet for "media" moguls, "Page Six regulars" and "monied" UES types, this "old-school" Italian dispenses food "delectable" enough to justify the "through-the-nose" tabs; expect the "cold shoulder" if you're not a "member of the club", but at least the "cheek-to-jowl" seating bolsters the chance of rubbing elbows with "Matt Lauer."

El Malecon ● *Dominican*

	22	12	17	$20

Washington Heights | 4141 Broadway (bet. 175th & 176th Sts.) |
212-927-3812
W 90s | 764 Amsterdam Ave. (bet. 97th & 98th Sts.) | 212-864-5648
Kingsbridge | 5592 Broadway (bet. 231st & 233rd Sts.) | Bronx |
718-432-5155

Churning out "super-good" Dominican chow, this trio is famed for "finger-lickin' chicken" slathered in so much "garlicky goodness" it's best to "wear a bib"; given the mega-portions and mini-prices, fans excuse "hole-in-the-wall" looks and service as "slow" as the rotisserie.

El Parador Cafe *Mexican*

	23	17	22	$46

Murray Hill | 325 E. 34th St. (bet. 1st & 2nd Aves.) | 212-679-6812 |
www.elparadorcafe.com

A "devoted clientele" gets its "paella fix" at this '59-vintage Murray Hill vet that's known for "true-to-its-roots", "old-world" Mexican cooking; obscured by Midtown Tunnel traffic, it's a "hidden gem" – polished by "cordial" servers – that insiders want to keep "secret."

El Paso Taqueria *Mexican*

	24	17	20	$29

E 100s | 1643 Lexington Ave. (bet. 103rd & 104th Sts.) |
212-831-9831
E 90s | 64 E. 97th St. (bet. Madison & Park Aves.) | 212-996-1739

(continued)

(continued)

El Paso Taqueria

Harlem | 237 E. 116th St. (bet. 2nd & 3rd Aves.) | 212-860-4875
Mole mavens hail the "must-have" tacos, "fresh guacamole" and "friendly" service at these "*muy bueno*" Uptown Mexicans; devotees "don't come for the decor", but rather for "lots of flavor" at little cost.

El Porrón *Spanish*

23 | 19 | 22 | $48

E 60s | 1123 First Ave. (bet. 61st & 62nd Sts.) | 212-207-8349 | www.elporronnyc.com
Tapas "like you'd find in Barcelona" make for "real-thing" dining at this UES Spaniard sporting a "something-for-everyone" menu; "winning wine" arrives in the namesake pitcher, and the crowd's a mix of "lively" types who "come hungry, thirsty and often."

El Pote ⊠ *Spanish*

23 | 15 | 22 | $44

Murray Hill | 718 Second Ave. (bet. 38th & 39th Sts.) | 212-889-6680 | www.elpote.com
"Home away from home" for Murray Hill amigos since '77, this Spanish stalwart keeps business brisk with "fantastic paella" and other "first-rate" Iberian standards; maybe it's looking a bit "shabby", but locals count themselves "lucky" to have it, especially for the price.

El Quijote ● *Spanish*

22 | 16 | 20 | $44

Chelsea | 226 W. 23rd St. (bet. 7th & 8th Aves.) | 212-929-1855
"Old-school to the hilt", this "colorful" Chelsea octogenarian may be "faded" but is still "memorable" for Spanish food plated in "gut-buster portions"; the decor lies somewhere between "tacky" and "kitschy", but the prices are "decent" and that "lobster deal can't be beat."

El Quinto Pino ● *Spanish*

∇ 24 | 19 | 21 | $40

Chelsea | 401 W. 24th St. (bet. 9th & 10th Aves.) | 212-206-6900 | www.elquintopinonyc.com
"Big things come in little spaces" at this "transporting" Chelsea Spaniard from the Txikito team, purveying an "ever-changing" tapas menu – highlighted by "amazing" uni panini – matched with a "well-curated" wine list; the "intimate" vibe clinches plenty of second dates, despite bar-style seating (and standing).

Ember Room *Asian*

22 | 22 | 21 | $43

W 40s | 647 Ninth Ave. (bet. 45th & 46th Sts.) | 212-245-8880 | www.emberroom.com
From consulting chef Ian Kittichai comes this "sleek" Hell's Kitchen yearling specializing in "exceptional" Asian fusion BBQ plus a plethora of small plates, all served in a "dark", nightclub-ish setting; moderate pricing and service with "panache" complete the promising picture.

Embers *Steak*

23 | 16 | 20 | $47

Bay Ridge | 9519 Third Ave. (bet. 95th & 96th Sts.) | Brooklyn | 718-745-3700 | www.embersbayridge.com
A "working-class" Bay Ridge chophouse primed to "fill that steak craving", this area "institution" sears tender, "juicy" cuts at nearly "half the price" of the Midtown big boys; it remains "reliable" under "new ownership", but when it's "too crowded", there's always the "next-door meat store."

	FOOD	DECOR	SERVICE	COST

Empanada Mama ● *S American* | 24 | 13 | 17 | $17

W 50s | 763 Ninth Ave. (bet. 51st & 52nd Sts.) | 212-698-9008 | www.empmamanyc.com

Stuffing its "huge following" with "amazing" empanadas and arepas, this 24/7 Hell's Kitchen "hole-in-the-wall" is the mother of all "cheap" South American "pocket"-food purveyors; undersized, "overcrowded" and at times "disorganized", it "lends itself to takeout"; P.S. a spin-off at 189 Houston Street is in the works.

Empellón Cocina *Mexican* | 23 | 19 | 19 | $53

NEW E Village | 105 First Ave. (bet. 6th & 7th Sts.) | 212-780-0999
Empellón Taqueria ● *Mexican*
W Village | 230 W. Fourth St. (W. 10th St.) | 212-367-0999
www.empellon.com

Chef Alex Stupak's "bold" detour from desserts at WD-50 to "high-minded" Mexicana pays off at this "trendy" twosome; the original West Village outlet "redefines the taco", while the "more upscale" East Village spin-off aces "super-imaginative" small plates; between the "killer" drinks and "fashionable" following, both enjoy crazy "buzz."

Empire Steakhouse *Steak* | 25 | 21 | 24 | $66

E 50s | 36 W. 52nd St. (bet. 5th & 6th Aves.) | 212-582-6900 | www.empiresteakhousenyc.com

Porterhouse partisans praise the "tender" steaks at this "busy" Midtown chop shop steered by the owners of Ben & Jack's; a "welcoming" staff fosters a "feel-at-home" vibe that's rare for the genre, though holy-cow pricing is in line with the norm.

Emporio ● *Italian* | ▽ 24 | 21 | 20 | $41

NoLita | 231 Mott St. (bet. Prince & Spring Sts.) | 212-966-1234 | www.emporiony.com

Aurora alums are behind this *"bellissimo"* NoLita trattoria, a "sublime" option for "authentic" Neapolitan pizzas and "homemade pastas" served in a rustic industrial setting; when the front room gets too "tight", regulars head for the "greenhouse"-like back room.

⌷ EN Japanese Brasserie *Japanese* | 26 | 26 | 23 | $66

W Village | 435 Hudson St. (Leroy St.) | 212-647-9196 | www.enjb.com

From the "stunning" yet "serene" setting to its "fabulous" homemade tofu, this "upper-tier" Village Japanese appeals to all the senses; the interior's "sexy" "minimalism" doesn't extend to the prices, but the "impeccable sake selection" and "wonderful" staff put patrons in a "Zen-like" state.

Enzo's *Italian* | 24 | 19 | 22 | $40

Fordham | 2339 Arthur Ave. (bet. Crescent Ave. & E. 186th St.) | Bronx | 718-733-4455
Morris Park | 1998 Williamsbridge Rd. (Neill Ave.) | Bronx | 718-409-3828 Ⓜ
www.enzosofthebronx.com

These "blue-ribbon" "red-sauce palaces" in the Bronx dish out "down-home" Italian standards in mammoth portions, and toss in some "old-school charm" on the side; the "unpretentious" staff "treats you like family", so embrace the "time warp" – and "don't fill up on the bread."

	FOOD	DECOR	SERVICE	COST

Eolo *Italian*
▽ 22 | 14 | 20 | $49

Chelsea | 190 Seventh Ave. (bet. 21st & 22nd Sts.) | 646-225-6606 |
www.eolonyc.com

There's "intelligent life in the kitchen" of this Sicilian "contender" of
fering "off-the-beaten-recipe-path" dishes paired with "exceptional
wines"; the "nondescript" trattoria setting may be at odds with the
"Chelsea prices", perhaps why there are "no struggles to get a table."

Epices du Traiteur *Mediterranean/Tunisian*
20 | 17 | 19 | $42

W 70s | 103 W. 70th St. (Columbus Ave.) | 212-579-5904

The "fragrance of Mediterranean spices" greets you at this "different"
UWS nook applauded for its "unique" North African cooking with a
"Tunisian bent"; the "narrow" digs get "cramped" during the "pre-
Lincoln Center" rush, so regulars head for the "hidden-away garden."

Erawan *Thai*
24 | 21 | 21 | $35

Bayside | 42-31 Bell Blvd. (bet. 42nd & 43rd Aves.) | Queens |
718-428-2112 | www.erawanthaibayside.com

Bayside locals tout this "go-to Thai" for its "aromatic" offerings with
"interesting modern twists", abetted by "gentle" service and a "fancy"
"Manhattan atmosphere"; though prices lie on the "premium" side,
it's ever "crowded" at prime times.

Erminia ☒ *Italian*
25 | 23 | 24 | $68

E 80s | 250 E. 83rd St. (bet. 2nd & 3rd Aves.) | 212-879-4284 |
www.erminiaristorante.com

If you're looking for "romance", try this "transporting" UES Roman
boîte where a "cavelike", candlelit setting sets the mood for "knockout" cooking, while "attentive" service and a "leisurely" pace do the
rest; sure, it's "expensive", but there are "only a few tables", lending
exclusivity to this "special experience."

Esca ● *Italian/Seafood*
25 | 21 | 23 | $73

W 40s | 402 W. 43rd St. (bet. 9th & 10th Aves.) | 212-564-7272 |
www.esca-nyc.com

"Like eating at Neptune's table", this Batali-Bastianich-Pasternack
Italian seafooder in Hell's Kitchen purveys "delectable" catch – along
with "unbelievable" crudo and pastas – in a location perfect for "pre-
or post-theater"; "smooth-as-silk" servers ensure there's "not a wrong
note" to be found in the "pricey" experience.

Etcetera Etcetera *Italian*
23 | 20 | 23 | $51

W 40s | 352 W. 44th St. (bet. 8th & 9th Aves.) | 212-399-4141 |
www.etcetcnyc.com

"More casual" than sibling ViceVersa, this "lively" Hell's Kitchen Italian
features a "modern" menu that's a match for its "contemporary" looks;
"splendid", "get-you-to-the-theater-on-time" service makes up for
"noisy" acoustics, though regulars say it's "quieter upstairs."

Ethos *Greek*
22 | 18 | 19 | $45

E 50s | 905 First Ave. (51st St.) | 212-888-4060
Murray Hill | 495 Third Ave. (bet. 33rd & 34th Sts.) | 212-252-1972
www.ethosrestaurants.com

"Fish is the star" at these "cheerful" Greek tavernas where the "always-
fresh" catch arrives in "abundant portions" and is dispensed "with fi-

nesse" by a "friendly" crew; Sutton Place may be "much better" than Murray Hill lookswise, but both share "affordability."

Excellent Dumpling House ⊅ Chinese — 23 | 8 | 14 | $18

Chinatown | 111 Lafayette St. (bet. Canal & Walker Sts.) | 212-219-0212 | www.excellentdumplinghouse.com

There's "no false advertising" at this cash-only Chinatown spot where the "name-says-it-all" dumplings are served with equally "excellent" Shanghainese plates; true, there's "no atmosphere" and service is of the "rush-you-out" variety, but "at these prices, who cares?"

NEW The Exchange ⊠ American — – | – | – | E

Financial District | Setai Wall Street | 40 Broad St., 2nd fl. (bet. Beaver St. & Exchange Pl.) | 212-809-3993

Ensconced in the former SHO Shaun Hergatt digs in the Setai Wall Street, this newcomer stays the course serving similarly sophisticated Americana at a more approachable price; the sprawling setting complete with a wine corridor is unchanged from its prior incarnation.

NEW Extra Fancy ● Seafood — – | – | – | M

Williamsburg | 302 Metropolitan Ave. (Roebling St.) | Brooklyn | 347-422-0939 | www.extrafancybklyn.com

Ironic moniker to the contrary, this Williamsburg seafooder is relatively down-to-earth, both in its moderately priced, New England–inspired eats and clam-shack looks; its impressive array of craft beers and fancy cocktails is best enjoyed in its great big backyard.

Extra Virgin Mediterranean — 23 | 20 | 19 | $43

W Village | 259 W. Fourth St. (Perry St.) | 212-691-9359 | www.extravirginrestaurant.com

The "young" and "glamorous" hobnob at this "fashionable" West Villager over "seasonal" Med fare that "won't break the bank"; although the place is usually "crowded" and the no-rez policy leads to "waits", amusing "people-watching" helps pass the time.

Fabio Piccolo Fiore Italian — 24 | 20 | 23 | $55

E 40s | 230 E. 44th St. (bet. 2nd & 3rd Aves.) | 212-922-0581 | www.fabiopiccolofiore.com

"Fab-u-lous" chef Fabio "works the room" (and even "cooks off the menu") at this "enjoyable" Italian situated between Grand Central and the U.N.; the "reliable" food arrives in a "serene" setting enhanced by "welcoming" service, "well-spaced tables" and "quiet" acoustics.

Fairway Cafe American — 19 | 11 | 14 | $25

E 80s | 240 E. 86th St. (2nd Ave.) | 212-327-2008
W 70s | 2127 Broadway, 2nd fl. (74th St.) | 212-595-1888
Red Hook | 480-500 Van Brunt St. (Reed St.) | Brooklyn | 718-694-6868
NEW Douglaston | 24-002 61st Ave. (Long Island Expy.) | Queens | 718-423-2100
www.fairwaymarket.com

"Hungry shoppers" head for these "convenient" in-store cafes for "reliable" American basics (and steaks on the UWS) at "decent" tabs; sure, service "needs to improve" and the decor's strictly "grocery store", but Red Hook's "million-dollar view" of Lady Liberty is pretty darn "fabulous."

	FOOD	DECOR	SERVICE	COST

F & J Pine Restaurant *Italian*   23 | 21 | 21 | $38

Morris Park | 1913 Bronxdale Ave. (bet. Matthews & Muliner Aves.) | Bronx | 718-792-5956 | www.fjpine.com

"Gigantic portions" are the name of the game at this "doggy bag"–guaranteed Bronx Italian ladling out "loads of red sauce" for fans of "old-time" carbo-loading; "checkered" tablecloths, sports "memorabilia" decor and Yankee sightings are all part of the "colorful" proceedings.

Farm on Adderley ❶ *American*   24 | 21 | 22 | $37

Ditmas Park | 1108 Cortelyou Rd. (bet. Stratford & Westminster Rds.) | Brooklyn | 718-287-3101 | www.thefarmonadderley.com

Ditmas Park denizens feel "lucky" to have this "worthwhile" New American raising the neighborhood bar with "ambitious" meals composed from "super-fresh" ingredients; a harvest like this could "cost twice as much in Manhattan", and insiders hint the food tastes even better from a "garden" seat.

Fat Radish ❶ *British*   24 | 23 | 19 | $48

LES | 17 Orchard St. (bet. Canal & Hester Sts.) | 212-300-4053 | www.thefatradishnyc.com

"Veggie fanatics" get the royal treatment at this "trendy" Lower Eastsider that "oozes cool" with its "creative" Modern British cooking and "hip-tastic" "art-crowd" following; allow extra time since the "slacker" servers are in no hurry to mete out the "pricey but princely" fare.

Fatty Crab ❶ *Malaysian*   21 | 14 | 17 | $45

W Village | 643 Hudson St. (bet. Gansevoort & Horatio Sts.) | 212-352-3590 | www.fattycrab.com

"Sticky-salty-sweet" Malaysian street eats make for "delectable" dining at Zak Pelaccio's "buzzy" West Villager that's a magnet for "adventurous" "heat"-seekers; however, it's "not for the faint of heart" given the "doing-you-a-favor" service, "pounding music" and "steadily climbing bills."

Fatty 'Cue ❶ *BBQ/SE Asian*   23 | 18 | 21 | $46

W Village | 50 Carmine St. (bet. Bedford & Bleecker Sts.) | 212-929-5050 | www.fattycue.com

SE Asian spices and "American smoke" bond with "spectacular" results at this fusion BBQ joint from chef Zak Pelaccio; the Williamsburg flagship is currently on hiatus, but the Village spin-off is "just as exciting and delicious" as the original and not that expensive.

Fatty Fish *Asian*   24 | 17 | 21 | $39

E 60s | 406 E. 64th St. (bet. 1st & York Aves.) | 212-813-9338 | www.fattyfishnyc.com

Upper Eastsiders are hooked on this Asian fusion practitioner boasting "surprisingly creative" cooking (and sushi) served by "solicitous" staffers who just "keep smiling"; a "Zen-like" mood and "beautiful outdoor patio" distract from the "small" dimensions.

Fedora ❶ *American/French*   23 | 20 | 21 | $54

W Village | 239 W. Fourth St., downstairs (bet. Charles & W. 10th Sts.) | 646-449-9336 | www.fedoranyc.com

Gabe Stulman's "low-key chic" relaunch of a longtime West Village basement earns a tip of the cap for its "interesting" Franco-American

	FOOD	DECOR	SERVICE	COST

menu and "beautiful neon sign"; retaining the "speakeasy vibe" of the old haunt and tossing in some "Wisconsin hospitality", it's now "better than ever", except perhaps for the cost.

Felice *Italian*

21	20	21	$46

E 60s | 1166 First Ave. (64th St.) | 212-593-2223
E 80s | 1593 First Ave. (83rd St.) | 212-249-4080 ◗
www.felicenyc.com

These "moderately hip" UES wine bars spice up "date nights" with "affordable", "well-chosen" vinos paired with "tasty" Italian small plates; the "gracious" service and "sexy" "Downtown" ambiance "appeal to multiple generations", though they mainly draw "younger" folks.

✓ Felidia *Italian*

26	22	24	$80

E 50s | 243 E. 58th St. (bet. 2nd & 3rd Aves.) | 212-758-1479 |
www.felidia-nyc.com

"Italian cuisine queen" Lidia Bastianich "still reigns" at this circa-1981 East Side "grande dame" where "superb" meals are dispatched in a "lovely" townhouse by an "enthusiastic" staff; "cramped" seating and "dated" decor to the contrary, it's ever an "exceptional experience" . . . "if your bank account permits."

Ferrara ◗ *Bakery*

24	18	19	$22

Little Italy | 195 Grand St. (bet. Mott & Mulberry Sts.) |
212-226-6150 | www.terraracafe.com

It's "120 years and counting" for this Little Italy bakery "legend" famed for its "heaven-on-a-plate" cannoli and "pick-me-up" espresso; "crowds of tourists" and "expensive"-for-what-it-is tabs draw brickbats, yet most agree this NYC relic "still has charm."

Fette Sau *BBQ*

26	17	16	$31

Williamsburg | 354 Metropolitan Ave. (bet. Havemeyer & Roebling Sts.) |
Brooklyn | 718-963-3404 | www.fettesaubbq.com

Voted NYC's Top BBQ for the fifth year running, this Williamsburg "meatfest" staged in a "converted garage" is lauded for "sinfully succulent" 'cue priced by the pound and washed down with "craft beers and bourbon"; "cafeteria-style" service and "picnic-bench" seating lend some down-home authenticity, but no reservations make for "interminable lines."

15 East ✄ *Japanese*

26	22	24	$77

Union Sq | 15 E. 15th St. (bet. 5th Ave. & Union Sq. W.) |
212-647-0015 | www.15eastrestaurant.com

"Master" sushi chef Masato Shimizu's "elemental" preparations of "amazingly fresh" fish are the "sublime" stars at this "minimalist-chic" Union Square Japanese whose "first-class kitchen" also assembles "excellent" cooked dishes; the "refined" experience is overseen by an "attentive" "pro" staff, and though the experience concludes with an "astonishing" bill, to most "it's totally worth it."

57 Napoli Pizza e Vino *Pizza*

23	19	21	$29

E 50s | 120 E. 57th St., upstairs (bet. Lexington & Park Aves.) |
212-750-4586 | www.57napoli.com

Ok, the obscure second-floor address may be "easy to miss", but this East Midtown pizzeria is worth seeking out for "tasty" Neapolitan pies fired in a "wood-burning oven"; there's not much decor save for a floor-to-ceiling window overlooking 57th Street, but service is "friendly" and the tabs "affordable."

Fig & Olive *Mediterranean*

E 50s | 10 E. 52nd St. (bet. 5th & Madison Aves.) | 212-319-2002
E 60s | 808 Lexington Ave. (bet. 62nd & 63rd Sts.) | 212-207-4555
Meatpacking | 420 W. 13th St. (bet. 9th Ave. & Washington St.) | 212-924-1200
www.figandolive.com

A "vast" array of "fragrant" olive oils lends pizzazz to the "terrific" Mediterranean offerings at this "high-energy" trio; the East Side outlets are a natural "after shopping", while the "way sexier" Meatpacking edition draws "noise"-makers, "High Line" strollers and "*Sex and the City*" types.

Fiorentino's Ⓜ *Italian* 22 | 16 | 21 | $35

Gravesend | 311 Ave. U (bet. McDonald Ave. & West St.) | Brooklyn | 718-372-1445

"Old-school Brooklyn" endures at this "bustling", 30-year-old Gravesend Italian best known for "grandma"-style Neapolitan food plated in "tremendous" portions; its "*Goodfellas*"-esque crowd doesn't mind the "no-frills" decor, "noisy" decibels and "no-rez" rule given the "astonishingly cheap" tabs.

Fiorini Ⓩ *Italian* 21 | 20 | 21 | $56

E 50s | 209 E. 56th St. (bet. 2nd & 3rd Aves.) | 212-308-0830 | www.fiorinirestaurantnyc.com

Somewhat "off the beaten path" in East Midtown, Lello Arpaia's "neighborhood" Neapolitan offers "hearty", "traditional" fare in a "comfortable" milieu; "spacious" dimensions and "never-too-noisy" acoustics please its mature following, the "steep" tabs not so much.

Ⓩ FireBird *Russian* 20 | 26 | 22 | $66

W 40s | 365 W. 46th St. (bet. 8th & 9th Aves.) | 212-586-0244 | www.firebirdrestaurant.com

"Dining with the tsars" comes to Restaurant Row via this "ornate" townhouse celebrating "imperial Russia" in an "antiques"-laden du-plex that outsparkles the "tasty" mother-country cuisine; "excellent" infused vodkas and "first-class" service burnish the "schmaltzy" mood that ends with bills "too rich for peasant blood."

Firenze ◗ *Italian* 21 | 21 | 23 | $53

E 80s | 1594 Second Ave. (bet. 82nd & 83rd Sts.) | 212-861-9368 | www.firenzeny.com

"Candlelight and exposed-brick walls" set a "romantic" groove at this longtime UES Italian that manages to evoke "Florence" with "solid" Tuscan cooking delivered by a "couldn't-be-nicer" crew; neighborly prices complete the "charming" picture.

Fish *Seafood* 23 | 15 | 20 | $37

W Village | 280 Bleecker St. (Jones St.) | 212-727-2879 | www.fishrestaurantnyc.com

Like the "simpleton name" implies, there's "nothing fancy" going on at this West Village seafood shack, just "truly good" catch proffered with great shuck for your buck (check out the $8 oyster special); trade-offs include "funky" looks and "tight-squeeze" seating.

	FOOD	DECOR	SERVICE	COST

FishTag *Greek/Seafood*

23 | **20** | **21** | **$50**

W 70s | 222 W. 79th St. (bet. Amsterdam Ave. & B'way) |
212-362-7470 | www.fishtagrestaurant.com

Bringing a "Downtown" vibe to the UWS, Michael Psilakis' "relaxed" Greek seafooder is a "breath of fresh air" for "delectable" fish dispatched in "nice-looking" digs by "enthusiastic" staffers; "decoding the menu" may require repeat visits, provided you can abide the "din" and the expense.

Fishtail by David Burke *Seafood*

24 | **24** | **23** | **$67**

E 60s | 135 E. 62nd St. (bet. Lexington & Park Aves.) | 212-754-1300 |
www.fishtaildb.com

"Whimsy abounds" on the walls (and plates) at David Burke's UES seafooder where "fantabulous" fish is served in a "beautiful" duplex with a sushi bar downstairs and more "formal" dining above; "unobtrusive" service and an outdoor terrace distract its "ritzy" clientele from the "inflated prices."

5 & Diamond *American*

23 | **20** | **21** | **$37**

Harlem | 2072 Frederick Douglass Blvd. (112th St.) | 646-684-4662 |
www.5anddiamondrestaurant.com

Exemplifying Harlem's "burgeoning restaurant scene", this "itty-bitty" New American lures an "eclectic crowd" with "fine", moderately priced takes on familiar classics, including "luscious mac 'n' cheese"; "friendly" service enhances the overall "unrushed affair."

Five Guys *Burgers*

21 | **11** | **16** | **$14**

E 40s | 690 Third Ave. (bet. 43rd & 44th Sts.) | 646-783-5060
G Village | 496 La Guardia Pl. (bet. Bleecker & Houston Sts.) |
212-228-6008
NEW W 40s | 253 W. 42nd St. (bet. 7th & 8th Aves.) | 212-398-2600 ●
W 40s | 36 W. 48th St. (bet. 5th & 6th Aves.) | 212-997-1270
W 50s | 43 W. 55th St. (bet. 5th & 6th Aves.) | 212-459-9600
W Village | 296 Bleecker St. (Barrow St.) | 212-367-9200 ●
Bay Ridge | 8510 Fifth Ave. (bet. 85th & 86th Sts.) | Brooklyn |
718-921-9380
Brooklyn Heights | 138 Montague St. (bet. Clinton & Henry Sts.) |
Brooklyn | 718-797-9380
Downtown Bklyn | 2 Metrotech Ctr. (bet. Bridge & Lawrence Sts.) |
Brooklyn | 718-852-9380
Park Slope | 284 Seventh Ave. (bet. 6th & 7th Sts.) | Brooklyn |
718-499-9380
www.fiveguys.com
Additional locations throughout the NY area

"Customizable burgers" with the "flavor of a backyard cookout" plus "enough fries to feed a small country" equal "sloppy goodness" at this fast-growing chain; there's "too much lighting" and "no ambiance" (save for "peanut shells on the floor"), but "you're not there for the decor."

Five Leaves ● *American*

26 | **22** | **19** | **$32**

Greenpoint | 18 Bedford Ave. (bet. Lorimer St. & Manhattan Ave.) |
Brooklyn | 718-383-5345 | www.fiveleavesny.com

"Low-fuss", high-cool, all-day Greenpoint bistro offering "indulgent" New American comfort cooking with Aussie twists in tiny, rustic digs; "always packed" with "hipsters" (especially during the "seriously perfect" brunch), it's usually accessed after a "long wait."

	FOOD	DECOR	SERVICE	COST

⚡ 5 Napkin Burger *Burgers*   22 | 18 | 19 | $27

NEW E Village | 150 E. 14th St. (bet. 3rd & 4th Aves.) | 212-228-5500 ●
W 40s | 630 Ninth Ave. (bet. 44th & 45th Sts.) | 212-757-2277 ●
W 80s | 2315 Broadway (84th St.) | 212-333-4488 ●
Astoria | 35-01 36th St. (35th Ave.) | Queens | 718-433-2727
www.5napkinburger.com

"Drop cloths" might be more appropriate at this "higher-end" burger chainlet where the "big", "drippy" patties are dispatched in "butcher shop"–esque settings complete with "dangling meat hooks"; "deafening dins" and prime-time "mob scenes" to the contrary, these "family-oriented" joints are still touted for "easy-breezy" dining.

5 Ninth *American*   20 | 22 | 20 | $46

Meatpacking | 5 Ninth Ave. (bet. Gansevoort & Little W. 12th Sts.) | 212-929-9460 | www.5ninth.com

At this "romantic Meatpacking retreat", the "lovely" tri-level brownstone setting complete with "fantastic" outdoor patio supplies ample room for bonding with "that special someone"; fans credit the "well-made" drinks for keeping the action "lively", but are less enthusiastic about the "just-ok" eats.

508 ● *Italian/Mediterranean*   22 | 20 | 20 | $44

Hudson Square | 508 Greenwich St. (bet. Canal & Spring Sts.) | 212-219-2444 | www.508nyc.com

"Better-than-expected" Italian-Med dishes are paired with a "nice assortment" of beers "brewed on the premises" at this Hudson Square boîte; though the "out-of-the-way" address makes the crowd "mostly locals", the "cozy", candlelit ambiance charms whoever drops in.

Five Points *American/Mediterranean*   22 | 20 | 20 | $48

NoHo | 31 Great Jones St. (bet. Bowery & Lafayette St.) | 212-253-5700 | www.fivepointsrestaurant.com

"Simple yet sophisticated" Mediterranean–New Americana draws diners to this "off-the-beaten-track" NoHo "oasis of calm" where "helpful" staffers and a "hypnotic" babbling brook supply the "feng shui"; it's famed for an "out-of-this-world" brunch, when "reservations are an absolute must."

Flatbush Farm ● *American*   21 | 19 | 18 | $38

Park Slope | 76 St. Marks Ave. (Flatbush Ave.) | Brooklyn | 718-622-3276 | www.flatbushfarm.com

"Farm-to-table" bounties are the draw at this affordable Park Slope American where the "solid" menu is assembled from "local ingredients"; cynics nix "uneven" service and overblown "hype", but it wins kudos for a "super brunch" and a "little-piece-of-heaven" garden.

Flex Mussels *Seafood*   23 | 18 | 20 | $44

E 80s | 174 E. 82nd St. (bet. Lexington & 3rd Aves.) | 212-717-7772
W Village | 154 W. 13th St. (bet. 6th & 7th Aves.) | 212-229-0222
www.flexmussels.com

Fans "flex their taste buds" at these "bustling" bivalve bastions imported from Prince Edward Island that "exceed expectations" with "plump" moules and "unusual" desserts (e.g. "boozy donuts", "deep-fried whoopie pies"); "price-is-right" tabs seal the deal, though the "cost of popularity" is a "maddening din."

	FOOD	DECOR	SERVICE	COST

Flor de Mayo ❷ *Chinese/Peruvian* | 21 | 11 | 18 | $25 |

W 80s | 484 Amsterdam Ave. (bet. 83rd & 84th Sts.) | 212-787-3388
W 100s | 2651 Broadway (bet. 100th & 101st Sts.) | 212-663-5520
www.flordemayo.com

"Widen your belt a notch" before approaching these UWS Chinese-Peruvian "perennial favorites" where "flavorful" rotisserie chicken and other "bracing" eats are slung in "huge" portions for "bargain" sums; "zero" decor, "minimal" service and "hectic" quarters make a strong case for "takeout."

Flor de Sol *Spanish* | 22 | 20 | 20 | $49 |

TriBeCa | 361 Greenwich St. (bet. Franklin & Harrison Sts.) | 212-366-1640 | www.flordesolnyc.com

"Dim" lighting, cheek-by-jowl seating and enough exposed brick to build a Catalonian "castle" set the mood for "sultry romance" at this TriBeCa Spaniard that further seduces with "top-notch" tapas and "killer sangria"; "sweet" servers, "fabulous bands" and live flamenco ratchet up the "enjoyable" vibe.

Fonda *Mexican* | 23 | 19 | 21 | $36 |

NEW E Village | 40 Ave. B (3rd St.) | 212-677-4069
Park Slope | 434 Seventh Ave. (bet. 14th & 15th Sts.) | Brooklyn | 718-369-3144 **M**
www.fondarestaurant.com

"Real Mexican cooking" gets the "haute" treatment at this "classier"-than-the-norm duo where the price tags are a "bargain" given the quality; the Park Slope original is "rather small", the newcomer across the *rio* a tad larger, but both feel like a "party."

NEW Foragers | ▽ 20 | 21 | 22 | $27 |

City Table *American/Asian*

Chelsea | Gem Hotel | 300 W. 22nd St. (8th Ave.) | 212-243-8888 | www.foragerscitygrocer.com

This "welcome" Chelsea newcomer vends a variety of Asian-accented American small plates made from "fresh ingredients" from an adjacent gourmet market; the industrial-chic interior is workmanlike, the pricing on par for greenmarket-sourced vittles.

Forcella *Pizza* | 23 | 17 | 20 | $28 |

NEW NoHo | 334 Bowery (bet. Bond & Great Jones Sts.) | 212-466-3300
Williamsburg | 485 Lorimer St. (bet. Grand & Powers Sts.) | Brooklyn | 718-388-8820
www.forcellaeatery.com

An "experience straight from Italy", these "real-deal" pizzerias feature "light-as-air" Neapolitan pies, many of which are "flash-fried", then oven-finished in brightly tiled stoves; the digs are plain and the staff "could be more attentive", but at least they're "lively" and "affordable."

Forlini's ❷ *Italian* | 20 | 15 | 20 | $44 |

Chinatown | 93 Baxter St. (Walker St.) | 212-349-6779

Whether you're on "jury duty" or "just got out of the Tombs", this circa-1943, courthouse-convenient Italian remains a "workmanlike" source for "red-sauce" cooking; some hold it in contempt for "tired" looks, but the final verdict is "satisfying" enough.

	FOOD	DECOR	SERVICE	COST

Fornino *Pizza*   22 | 18 | 19 | $34

Park Slope | 256 Fifth Ave. (bet. Carroll St. & Garfield Pl.) | Brooklyn | 718-399-8600 | www.forninoparkslope.com
Williamsburg | 187 Bedford Ave. (bet. 6th & 7th Sts.) | Brooklyn | 718-384-6004 | www.forninopizza.com

In the eternal "NY pizza wars", these separately owned Brooklyn pie palaces are "strong players" thanks to "decadent" toppings and "perfectly done" wood-fired crusts; the Park Slope outpost provides "more elbow room", a wider Italian menu and grilled pies.

44 *American*   21 | 23 | 21 | $57

W 40s | Royalton Hotel | 44 W. 44th St. (bet. 5th & 6th Aves.) | 212-944-8844 | www.royaltonhotel.com

This "swanky" New American has long been a favored "media" "power" player due to its "quiet" hotel location, "excellent cocktails" and "solid" cooking (especially at breakfast), which arrives via "very good" servers; it'll "cost a lot" to hang with the "Condé Nast" folks, but playing like an "insider" could be worth the "indulgence."

44 & X ◐ *American*   22 | 21 | 21 | $44

W 40s | 622 10th Ave. (44th St.) | 212-977-1170
44½ ◐ *American*
W 40s | 626 10th Ave. (bet. 44th & 45th Sts.) | 212-399-4450
www.heaveninhellskitchen.com

"Tasty" American comfort chow plays second fiddle to the "entertaining", "aspiring-actor" waiters clad in "double entendre" T-shirts at this "gay-friendly" Hell's Kitchen duo; they're "uplifting" options in an otherwise "dreary part of town", earning bonus points for proximity to the "Signature Theatre complex."

Z Four Seasons ⊠ *American*   27 | 28 | 27 | $102

E 50s | 99 E. 52nd St. (bet. Lexington & Park Aves.) | 212-754-9494 | www.fourseasonsrestaurant.com

A "calm oasis" in "throbbing Manhattan", this Midtown "icon" draws "one-percenters" and "seriously famous" folk with "outstanding" New Americana ferried by a "meticulous" team overseen by owners Alex von Bidder and Julian Niccolini; the "chic-in-a-'50s-way" setting includes the "luminous" Pool Room (best for romance) and the more power lunch-appropriate Grill Room, but no matter where you sit, wear a jacket and bring your checkbook: this "time-honored tradition" is "predictably expensive."

1492 Food *Spanish*   23 | 21 | 22 | $45

LES | 60 Clinton St. (bet. Rivington & Stanton Sts.) | 646-654-1114 | www.1492food.com

Chart a course for this Lower East Side Spaniard when seeking "well-executed" (if "not overly imaginative") tapas washed down with "heaven-in-a-glass" sangria; a "super-nice" crew and "surprisingly cute" back patio round out the "enjoyable evenings" here.

Fragole *Italian*   25 | 18 | 22 | $34

Carroll Gardens | 394 Court St. (bet. Carroll & 1st Pl.) | Brooklyn | 718-522-7133 | www.fragoleny.com

This 10-year-old Carroll Gardens Italian remains a "neighborhood favorite" thanks to "solid" cooking "with an eye toward authenticity", a "quality wine list" and "charming" environs; "friendly" staffers and "affordable" tabs keep it filled with "happy" customers.

NEW Francesca ☻ *Spanish* | - | - | - | M |

LES | 17 Clinton St. (bet. Houston & Stanton Sts.) | 212-253-2303 | www.francescanyc.com

The Frankies team has retooled its former LES Spuntino space into this new Spaniard specializing in Basque-style tapas paired with wines from the region; the interior remains as dark and cozy as ever, and now there's a spacious garden too.

Francisco's Centro Vasco *Seafood/Spanish* | 24 | 14 | 21 | $52 |

Chelsea | 159 W. 23rd St. (bet. 6th & 7th Aves.) | 212-645-6224 | www.franciscoscentrovasco.com

"Monster-size" lobsters at "fair prices" are the highlight of this long-time Chelsea Spaniard that also offers "wonderful paella" and "potent sangria"; "dumpy digs" and "noisy, crowded" conditions don't deter fans who feel it's "cheaper to come here than to cook your own."

Frank ☻⊟ *Italian* | 23 | 15 | 18 | $36 |

E Village | 88 Second Ave. (bet. 5th & 6th Sts.) | 212-420-0202 | www.frankrestaurant.com

"Essential East Village dining" is yours at this "funky" Italian where the "not-fancy" setting is as "rustic" as the "amazing" cooking is "comforting"; "teeny-tiny" dimensions, "perpetual crowds" and no-rezzie, no-credit-card rules detract, but ultimately "inexpensive" pricing carries the day.

Frankie & Johnnie's Steakhouse ⊠ *Steak* | 23 | 17 | 21 | $67 |

Garment District | 32 W. 37th St. (bet. 5th & 6th Aves.) | 212-947-8940
W 40s | 269 W. 45th St., 2nd fl. (bet. B'way & 8th Ave.) | 212-997-9494 ☻ www.frankieandjohnnies.com

To experience "days long past", try this circa-1926 Theater District "throwback" accessed via "rickety stairs" and known for "delectable" steaks, "career" waiters and "rough-around-the-edges" decor; its Garment District sibling (set in John Barrymore's former townhouse) is similarly "old-fashioned", though prices are decidedly up to date.

Frankies Spuntino *Italian* | 24 | 19 | 20 | $42 |

NEW W Village | 570 Hudson St. (11th St.) | 212-924-0818 ☻
Carroll Gardens | 457 Court St. (bet. 4th Pl. & Luquer St.) | Brooklyn | 718-403-0033
www.frankiesspuntino.com

"Pleasant vibes" make for "huge buzz" at this Italian twosome touted for "impressive" Tuscan cooking and "charming" settings; the Carroll Gardens original boasts a "beautiful garden", but both share "decent" prices, "noise" and no-rez rules.

Franny's *Italian/Pizza* | 25 | 18 | 20 | $40 |

Prospect Heights | 295 Flatbush Ave. (bet. Prospect Pl. & St. Marks Ave.) | Brooklyn | 718-230-0221 | www.frannysbrooklyn.com

Pie-eyed patrons praise the "second-to-none" artisanal pizzas and "exquisite" appetizers served at this Prospect Heights Italian; given no rezzies and "long waits", fans welcome its imminent move to larger digs at 348 Flatbush Avenue.

Fratelli   *Italian*   21 | 17 | 19 | $43

Pelham Gardens | 2507 Eastchester Rd. (Mace Ave.) | Bronx |
718-547-2489 | www.fratellinewyork.com
"Where all the locals go", this "neighborhood" Pelham Gardens
Italian has been plating "large portions" of "tasty" red-sauce chow
for nearly two decades; "friendly" service and "decent" pricing trump
the "nondescript" environs.

Fraunces Tavern ◐ *Pub Food*   18 | 22 | 19 | $43

(aka The Porterhouse Brewing Co. at Fraunces Tavern)
Financial District | 54 Pearl St. (Broad St.) | 212-968-1776 |
www.frauncestavern.com
Have a side of "history" with dinner at this FiDi "landmark" where
"George Washington bid farewell to his troups" in 1783; today, it's a
"refurbished" pub serving "decent" Irish-American grub and "diverse"
beers in a "faux Revolutionary" setting; cynics snipe it's "all about the
building – not the food."

Fred's at Barneys NY   *American/Italian*   21 | 19 | 20 | $49

E 60s | Barneys NY | 660 Madison Ave., 9th fl. (60th St.) |
212-833-2200 | www.barneys.com
"Shopping is hard work" and "sustenance is necessary", so "well-
Botoxed" types unwind and "pick at a salad" at this "chichi" department-
store canteen in Barneys; the "consistently good" Italian-American
fare may be "pricey for what it is", but no one cares – it's "fun to
be chic" here.

Freemans ◐ *American*   22 | 24 | 19 | $47

LES | Freeman Alley (off Rivington St., bet. Bowery & Chrystie St.) |
212-420-0012 | www.freemansrestaurant.com
"Tucked away" down a Lower East Side alley, this "hipster" magnet
feels "miles from NY" given the "kooky", Colonial tavern decor replete
with "taxidermy" and "creaky wooden floors"; "solid" American cookery offsets the "hit-or-miss" service and "killer waits", but mostly, it's
about the "scene."

Fresco by Scotto ⊠ *Italian*   23 | 19 | 21 | $53

E 50s | 34 E. 52nd St. (bet. Madison & Park Aves.) | 212-935-3434 |
www.frescobyscotto.com

Fresco on the Go   *Italian*

E 50s | 40 E. 52nd St. (bet. Madison & Park Aves.) | 212-754-2700
Financial District | 114 Pearl St. (Hanover Sq.) | 212-635-5000 ⊠
www.frescoonthego.com
For "delicious", "dependable" Tuscan fare with "*Today Show*" people-
watching on the side, try this "friendly" 20-year-old Midtowner via the
"dedicated" Scotto family; it's "pricey", and "always packed" for lunch,
so many opt for "super-fast" takeout from the to-go outlets.

Friedman's Lunch   *American*   22 | 16 | 18 | $23

Chelsea | Chelsea Mkt. | 75 Ninth Ave. (bet. 15th & 16th Sts.) |
212-929-7100 | www.friedmanslunch.com
Name notwithstanding, they also whip up breakfast and dinner at this
"upscale" Chelsea Market American where the "gourmet comfort
food" includes some "terrific gluten-free options"; "slow service" and
"not much seating" explain the typical "waits" for a table.

	FOOD	DECOR	SERVICE	COST

Friend of a Farmer *American* | 19 | 19 | 18 | $32 |

Gramercy | 77 Irving Pl. (bet. 18th & 19th Sts.) | 212-477-2188 | www.friendofafarmerny.com

Bringing the flavor of "Vermont" to Gramercy Park, this "quaint" American "country kitchen" has crowds crowing about its "farm-fresh" vittles and "hippie" air; citified pricing, "slow service" and weekend brunch "lines down the block" come with the territory.

Fuleen Seafood ● *Chinese/Seafood* | ▽ 23 | 12 | 19 | $34 |

Chinatown | 11 Division St. (Bowery) | 212-941-6888

"Squirmingly fresh", Hong Kong–style fish straight from a "saltwater tank" reels folks into this "cheap" Chinatown seafooder; despite a "boisterous", "fluorescent" setting, it remains a "dive worth diving into" whether on jury duty or painting the town red (it's open till 2 AM).

Fulton *Seafood* | 23 | 18 | 21 | $55 |

E 70s | 205 E. 75th St. (bet. 2nd & 3rd Aves.) | 212-288-6600 | www.fultonnyc.com

It's from the "Citarella folks", so it's no surprise the fish is simply "delish" at this "memorable" Upper East Side dock – and so "fresh" it "just may jump off your plate"; "gracious service", a "charming", brick-walled setting and a "never-too-busy" atmosphere make the prices more palatable.

Fushimi *Japanese* | 23 | 24 | 20 | $44 |

Bay Ridge | 9316 Fourth Ave. (bet. 93rd & 94th Sts.) | Brooklyn | 718-833-7788

NEW Williamsburg | 475 Driggs Ave. (bet. N. 10th & 11th Sts.) | Brooklyn | 718-963-2555

Grant City | 2110 Richmond Rd. (Lincoln Ave.) | Staten Island | 718-980-5300

www.fushimi-us.com

"Airlifted-from-Las-Vegas" decor makes this "fancy" Japanese trio catnip for "twentysomethings", and it follows through with "delectable" sushi served by "friendly" folks; ok, it's "a bit pricey" and a lot "loud" late-night, but admirers say it brings some "cool" to "underserved" parts of town.

Gabriel's 🗷 *Italian* | 23 | 19 | 23 | $62 |

W 60s | 11 W. 60th St. (bet. B'way & Columbus Ave.) | 212-956-4600 | www.gabrielsbarandrest.com

"Polished service" overseen by "natural host" Gabriel Aiello sets the "classy" tone at this "even-keeled" Columbus Circle Italian known for "delicious" cooking, a "comfortable" setting and proximity to Lincoln Center; given the rather "hefty" tabs, "media" types from nearby CBS and CNN prefer it for lunch.

Gahm Mi Oak ● *Korean* | 22 | 15 | 16 | $25 |

Garment District | 43 W. 32nd St. (bet. B'way & 5th Ave.) | 212-695-4113 | www.gahmmioak.com

Renowned for its "lifesaving" *sollongtang* beef soup – especially "good when hung over" – this K-town Korean is also commended for its "delectable" kimchi; "rushed" service and a "hectic" atmosphere are counterbalanced by "cheap" tabs and 24/7 availability.

| | FOOD | DECOR | SERVICE | COST |

Gallagher's Steak House ● *Steak* — 22 | 19 | 20 | $72

W 50s | 228 W. 52nd St. (bet. B'way & 8th Ave.) | 212-245-5336 |
www.gallaghersnysteakhouse.com

Exuding "old-time flair", this circa-1927 Theater District chop shop is
known for first-rate house-aged steaks flaunted in a glass-enclosed
"meat locker" and a "throwback" look that's a mix of "red-checkered
tablecloths" and "sports memorabilia"; service is "old school", but the
prices are more up-to-date.

Garden Café *American* — 21 | 19 | 21 | $27

Inwood | 4961 Broadway (bet. Isham & 207th Sts.) | 212-544-9480 |
www.gardencafenyc.com

"Solid" New Americana turns up at this "cozy" Inwood spot near the
Cloisters that "feels like Downtown without the Downtown prices";
some shrug "nothing special", but all agree on the "friendly" service
and "cute" back garden.

Gargiulo's *Italian* — 24 | 20 | 23 | $49

Coney Island | 2911 W. 15th St. (bet. Mermaid & Surf Aves.) |
Brooklyn | 718-266-4891 | www.gargiulos.com

After a "swim at the beach", have a "swim in red sauce" at this circa-
1907 Coney Island "time warp", a "catering hall"–size arena for good
"old-fashioned" Neapolitan cooking ferried by "tuxedo-clad" waiters;
the "colorful" crowd feels its "reputation is deserved", while a nightly
raffle means "you could eat for free."

🛂 Gari ● *Japanese* — 27 | 16 | 22 | $82

W 70s | 370 Columbus Ave. (bet. 77th & 78th Sts.) | 212-362-4816
Sushi of Gari *Japanese*

E 70s | 402 E. 78th St. (bet. 1st & York Aves.) | 212-517-5340
NEW **W 50s** | Plaza Food Hall | 1 W. 59th St., lower level (5th Ave.) |
646-755-3230
Sushi of Gari 46 ● *Japanese*

W 40s | 347 W. 46th St. (bet. 8th & 9th Aves.) | 212-957-0046
www.sushiofgari.com

The "omakase is off the hook" at this "innovative" Japanese quartet from
chef Gari Sugio, whose "buttery", "ethereal" sushi amounts to "bite-
size works of art"; though the settings are austere and the morsels "expensive", purists pronounce the experience "worth every last penny";
P.S. the new takeout-oriented Plaza Food Hall satellite is cheaper.

Gascogne *French* — 22 | 21 | 22 | $55

Chelsea | 158 Eighth Ave. (bet. 17th & 18th Sts.) | 212-675-6564 |
www.gascognenyc.com

For a "taste of Gascony" in Chelsea, check out this *"très authentique"*
French bistro offering "classic", "old-fashioned" dishes shuttled by
"welcoming" staffers; "moderate" prices, a "civilized" atmosphere
and a "gem of a garden" seal its neighborhood "favorite" status.

Gastroarte ● *Spanish* — 23 | 23 | 23 | $60

W 60s | 141 W. 69th St. (bet. B'way & Columbus Ave.) |
646-692-8762 | www.gastroartenyc.com

"Food as art" is the concept at chef Jesús Núñez's "innovative" Spanish
yearling near Lincoln Center, where the "elevated" offerings are "so
beautiful" you don't know "whether to eat them or hang them on the

wall"; some say it's "pricey", but payoffs include "sleek" looks, caring service and "over-the-top" desserts.

Gazala's *Mideastern*

21 | **15** | **18** | **$32**

W 40s | 709 Ninth Ave. (bet. 48th & 49th Sts.) | 212-245-0709
W 70s | 380 Columbus Ave., upstairs (78th St.) | 212-873-8880
www.gazalaplace.com

"Delectable" Druze dishes are delivered by this Mideastern duo where the "solid" cooking and "inexpensive", BYO-friendly tabs offset "modest" decor and "hit-or-miss" service; the UWS spin-off is "more spacious" than the "cramped" Hell's Kitchen original.

Gemma ● *Italian*

21 | **23** | **21** | **$44**

E Village | Bowery Hotel | 335 Bowery (bet. 2nd & 3rd Sts.) |
212-505-7300 | www.theboweryhotel.com

Primo "people-watching" abounds at this "fun", all-day Bowery Hotel Italian that lures "scenesters" with a "romantic", "country-chic" setting festooned with "hundreds of candles"; "tasty" vittles, "attentive service" and "fair prices" make the "no-rez" policy less of a drag.

General Greene *American*

20 | **18** | **20** | **$30**

Fort Greene | 229 DeKalb Ave. (Clermont Ave.) | Brooklyn |
718-222-1510 | www.thegeneralgreene.com

"Small plates win big" at this "casual" Fort Greene New American, where the grub's "local", "seasonal" and "affordable"; it's a natural for a "hipster" brunch or "before the Brooklyn Flea", and the "very Brooklyn" vibe extends to the "simple" decor and pleasant "outdoor seating."

Gennaro ⊘ *Italian*

24 | **15** | **19** | **$43**

W 90s | 665 Amsterdam Ave. (bet. 92nd & 93rd Sts.) |
212-665-5348 | www.gennaronyc.com

Be ready for a "long line" at this "durable" UWS Italian that takes "no reservations" and no plastic but does provide "hearty", "consistently delicious" chow for "non-gourmet prices"; even after a "third expansion", it's still "difficult to get a table after 7 PM."

Gigino Trattoria *Italian*

21 | **20** | **19** | **$45**

TriBeCa | 323 Greenwich St. (bet. Duane & Reade Sts.) |
212-431-1112 | www.gigino-trattoria.com

Gigino at Wagner Park *Italian*

Financial District | 20 Battery Pl. (West St.) | 212-528-2228 |
www.gigino-wagnerpark.com

It almost "feels like Florence" at this "affordable" TriBeCa Tuscan featuring "above-average" food, "friendly" service and a "high-ceilinged", "farmhouselike" milieu; its "off-the-beaten-path" sibling in Wagner Park boasts "can't-get-any-closer" views of the harbor and Statue of Liberty.

Gilt ⊠Ⓜ *American*

26 | **28** | **26** | **$124**

E 50s | NY Palace Hotel | 455 Madison Ave. (bet. 50th & 51st Sts.) |
212-891-8100 | www.giltnewyork.com

Everything's pretty "fancy" at this New American "jewel box" in the Palace Hotel, where the "beautifully presented" prix fixe–only menus are shuttled by "on-point" staffers in a "remarkable", "Versailles"-like room; naturally, all of this "over-the-top" refinement comes at "not-everyday" tabs, thus it's best for "special occasions."

The table headers (top right): FOOD, DECOR, SERVICE, COST

NEW Ginny's Supper Club ●Ⓜ *American* — | — | — | E

Harlem | 310 Lenox Ave., downstairs (bet. 125th & 126th Sts.) | 212-421-3821 | www.ginnyssupperclub.com

A riff on legendary Harlem nightspots like the Cotton Club, this moody new supper club in the basement of Marcus Samuelsson's Red Rooster serves New Americana with Asian and soul-food accents, along with updated classic cocktails; live music and a Sunday gospel brunch add zip to the proceedings.

Giorgio's of Gramercy *Italian* 21 | 19 | 22 | $47

Flatiron | 27 E. 21st St. (bet. B'way & Park Ave. S.) | 212-477-0007 | www.giorgiosofgramercy.com

The epitome of a "true sleeper", this 20-year-old Flatiron Italian "class act" features "consistently good" cooking that suggests "unsung talent in the kitchen"; "reasonable" rates, "gracious" service and "early brothel" decor are other incentives.

Giovanni Venticinque *Italian* 25 | 20 | 25 | $65

E 80s | 25 E. 83rd St. (bet. 5th & Madison Aves.) | 212-988-7300 | www.giovanniventicinque.com

A "gem" in an "expensive neighborhood", this "civilized" Italian "steps from the Met" caters to "aging UES swells" with "terrific" Tuscan food delivered by a "cosseting" crew; all that "old-world charm" comes at a steep price, but at least the $25 prix fixe lunch is a "bargain."

Girasole *Italian* 22 | 17 | 20 | $63

E 80s | 151 E. 82nd St. (bet. Lexington & 3rd Aves.) | 212-772-6690 | www.girasolerestaurantnyc.com

"Above-average" UES "neighborhood" Italian that's been hosting an "older crowd" since 1989; "reliably good" cooking and "efficient" service compensate for the somewhat "stodgy" air, though it earns bonus points since "you can actually hear your dining companion."

Glass House Tavern ● *American* 20 | 19 | 21 | $46

W 40s | 252 W. 47th St. (bet. B'way & 8th Ave.) | 212-730-4800 | www.glasshousetavern.com

Something "calming" in the "hectic Theater District", this "solid performer" fields New Americana that tastes even better when Broadway "stars" are seated alongside you; "reasonable" rates and "cordial" service also draw applause, though insiders advise "eat upstairs."

Gnocco *Italian* 23 | 18 | 20 | $37

E Village | 337 E. 10th St. (bet. Aves. A & B) | 212-677-1913 | www.gnocco.com

"Authentic Emilian fare" is the focus of this East Village Italian praised for its "tasty pizza", "lengthy wine list" and "excellent" namesake dish; the "most prized tables" are in its "lovely", all-seasons garden, though "modest" pricing and "helpful" service are available throughout.

Gobo *Vegan/Vegetarian* 24 | 20 | 21 | $36

E 80s | 1426 Third Ave. (81st St.) | 212-288-5099
W Village | 401 Sixth Ave. (bet. 8th St. & Waverly Pl.) | 212-255-3242 | www.goborestaurant.com

Vegan food gets some "fancy" twists at this "non-preachy" duo offering an "unusually varied" menu of Asian-accented vittles that are "wonderfully healthy"; the UES outpost may be more "upscale" than its "earthy" Village cousin, but both share good, "down-to-earth" service.

Go Burger *Burgers*

19 | 15 | 17 | $23

E 70s | 1448 Second Ave. (bet. 75th & 76th Sts.) | 212-988-9822
Garment District | 310 W. 38th St. (bet. 8th & 9th Aves) | 212-290-8000 ●
www.goburger.com

"Gourmet burgers" and "spiked shakes" are the specialty of these satellites of a national chain via the BLT Burger team; service may "need improvement", but "massive crowds" suggest it's doing something right; P.S. the Garment District outlet is a kiosk inside restaurant Casa Nonna.

Golden Unicorn *Chinese*

21 | 14 | 15 | $27

Chinatown | 18 E. Broadway, 2nd fl. (Catherine St.) | 212-941-0911 |
www.goldenunicornrestaurant.com

"Mobbed and noisy" is a given at this "huge" C-town Cantonese featuring "endless carts" stocked with "heavenly dim sum"; "hurried", "English"-challenged service and "basic Chinatown wedding party decor" are forgiven since it's a lot "cheaper than flying to Hong Kong."

Good *American*

21 | 17 | 19 | $43

W Village | 89 Greenwich Ave. (bet. Bank & W. 12th Sts.) |
212-691-8080 | www.goodrestaurantnyc.com

"Should be named great" say die-hard supporters of this West Village American "respite" that's still something of a "hidden gem" despite "simple", "hearty" cooking and "kind service"; aesthetes may find the decor "boring", but there's always a "weekend line" for its "amazing brunch."

Goodburger *Burgers*

19 | 12 | 16 | $15

E 40s | 800 Second Ave. (42nd St.) | 212-922-1700
E 50s | 636 Lexington Ave. (54th St.) | 212-838-6000
Financial District | 101 Maiden Ln. (Pearl St.) | 212-797-1700
Flatiron | 870 Broadway (bet. 17th & 18th Sts.) | 212-529-9100
W 50s | 977 Eighth Ave. (bet. 57th & 58th Sts.) | 212-245-2200
www.goodburgerny.com

Maybe it "could be better", but this "messy burger" mini-chain does dispatch "above-average" patties and fries for "decent" dough; "non-existent decor", "disorganized" service and "long wait times" are the trade-offs.

Good Enough to Eat *American*

22 | 16 | 18 | $27

W 80s | 483 Amsterdam Ave. (bet. 83rd & 84th Sts.) | 212-496-0163 |
www.goodenoughtoeat.com

Starting with the "white picket fence" outside, this "longtime", "great-value" UWS American offers all-day dining à la "Vermont" with "simple" comfort items served in a "cute", farmhousey setting; "painful waits" for weekend brunch are forgiven when the food arrives.

Good Fork Ⓜ *Eclectic*

25 | 18 | 23 | $44

Red Hook | 391 Van Brunt St. (bet. Coffey & Van Dyke Sts.) | Brooklyn |
718-643-6636 | www.goodfork.com

"Rough Red Hook" gets its own "culinary outpost" via this "small" Eclectic where the "seriously good" Asian-accented menu is dispatched at a "fair price" point; "attractive" rustic looks, a back garden and "actually friendly hipster waiters" are further incentives.

	FOOD	DECOR	SERVICE	COST

NEW The Goodwin ❶ *American* — | — | — | M

W Village | 430 Hudson St. (bet. Leroy & Morton Sts.) | 212-929-6181 | www.thegoodwinnyc.com

This charming West Village wine bar's exposed brick and rustic wood-work are enhanced by views of lush greenery in the backyard garden; it specializes in midpriced New American small plates meant for sharing, but a limited selection of larger entrees is rolled out after 5 PM.

Z The Grocery 🈂🅜 *American* 28 | 18 | 27 | $65

Carroll Gardens | 288 Smith St. (bet. Sackett & Union Sts.) | Brooklyn | 718-596-3335 | www.thegroceryrestaurant.com

"Exquisite", "market-driven" fare "imaginatively" rendered has made this "pricey" Carroll Gardens New American a Smith Street standby, as has the "exceptional" service that makes "every diner feel like a VIP"; ok, the "no-frills", "matchbox"-size interior can get "a little claustrophobic", but the "beautiful backyard" offers more elbow room.

Gordon Ramsay 🈂🅜 *French* 24 | 23 | 23 | $104

W 50s | London NYC Hotel | 151 W. 54th St. (bet. 6th & 7th Aves.) | 212-468-8888 | www.gordonramsay.com

Though he's just a consultant now, Gordon Ramsay's "spirit" lives on at his namesake Midtown hotel dining room where the "first-rate", prix fixe–only French menu is "expertly crafted" and delivered by a "charming" crew; the "modern" setting is "elegantly decorated", but some feel the "high tariffs" could use "fine tuning" absent the star of the show.

Z Gotham Bar & Grill *American* 28 | 26 | 26 | $84

G Village | 12 E. 12th St. (bet. 5th Ave. & University Pl.) | 212-620-4020 | www.gothambarandgrill.com

A "ritual" for many Gothamites, Alfred Portale's "iconic" Village New American offers "standout" dining via "towering plates" of "glorious food", "stellar" service and a "beautiful", "white-linen" setting; nearly 30 years along, "this star shows no sign of dimming", but if the price tags are too "extravagant", there's always the $25 greenmarket lunch.

Gottino ❶ *Italian* ∇ 21 | 20 | 22 | $41

W Village | 52 Greenwich Ave. (bet. Charles & Perry Sts.) | 212-633-2590 | www.ilmiogottino.com

Fans love "getting into small-plate trouble" at this itty-bitty West Village enoteca where the food is "delicious" and the mood "hip"; if "courteous" service and moderate pricing aren't enough, there's also an "absolute-heaven" back garden.

NEW Governor ❶ *American* — | — | — | M

Dumbo | 15 Main St. (bet. Plymouth & Water Sts.) | Brooklyn | 718-858-4756 | www.governordumbo.com

From the Colonie and Gran Electrica folks comes this Dumbo newcomer fielding a frequently changing, forager-friendly American menu; its double-decker, mezzanine-equipped setting reeks of industrial cool, with soaring ceilings, arched windows and a live garden wall.

Grace's Trattoria *Italian* 21 | 17 | 21 | $46

E 70s | 201 E. 71st St. (bet. 2nd & 3rd Aves.) | 212-452-2323

For "no-nonsense", "well-prepared" Italiana, this longtime UES trattoria offers the same "great quality" as Grace's Marketplace next door;

maybe the decor's a bit dull, but the "prompt service" and "fair prices" make for such an "easy night out" that its "graying crowd" doesn't mind.

Gradisca *Italian*

| 26 | 20 | 23 | $55 |

W Village | 126 W. 13th St. (bet. 6th Ave. & 7th Ave. S.) | 212-691-4886 | www.gradiscanyc.com

"Spectacular pastas" hand-rolled up front by the owner's mama are the thing to order at this "first-rate" Village Italian study in "old-world charm"; "intimate" digs and "helpful" service mute tabs that are on the "pricey" side.

Graffiti Ⓜ *Eclectic*

| 25 | 18 | 23 | $45 |

E Village | 224 E. 10th St. (bet. 1st & 2nd Aves.) | 212-677-0695 | www.graffitinyc.com

"Surprising flavor combinations" are the forte of this "super-inventive" East Village Eclectic showcasing chef Jehangir Mehta's "delectable" Indian-accented small plates; though the "communal"-tabled space is beyond "minuscule", the "value is big", the service "good-humored" and the mood "friendly."

⒉ Gramercy Tavern *American*

| 28 | 26 | 27 | $114 |

Flatiron | 42 E. 20th St. (bet. B'way & Park Ave. S.) | 212-477-0777 | www.gramercytavern.com

"About as perfect as a restaurant can get", Danny Meyer's Flatiron "standard bearer" remains a "great NY institution" thanks to chef Michael Anthony's "exceptional farm-to-fork" New American cuisine coupled with a "soothing", "elegantly rustic" setting and "superior" service that "runs like a well-oiled machine"; granted, the tabs are "quite dear" in the prix fixe–only main dining room, but the non-reserving front tavern offers "cheaper" à la carte options.

Grand Sichuan *Chinese*

| 21 | 10 | 15 | $28 |

Chelsea | 172 Eighth Ave. (bet. 18th & 19th Sts.) | 212-243-1688
Chelsea | 229 Ninth Ave. (24th St.) | 212-620-5200 ◗
E 50s | 1049 Second Ave. (bet. 55th & 56th Sts.) | 212-355-5855
E Village | 19-23 St. Marks Pl. (bet. 2nd & 3rd Aves.) | 212-529-4800
Murray Hill | 227 Lexington Ave. (bet. 33rd & 34th Sts.) | 212-679-9770
W 40s | 368 W. 46th St. (bet. 8th & 9th Aves.) | 212-969-9001
W 70s | 307 Amsterdam Ave. (bet. 74th & 75th Sts.) | 212-580-0277
W Village | 15 Seventh Ave. S. (bet. Carmine & Leroy Sts.) | 212-645-0222
Rego Park | 98-108 Queens Blvd. (bet. 66th Rd. & 67th Ave.) | Queens | 718-268-8833
www.thegrandsichuan.com

"Super-hot" Sichuan meals for "cheap" money draw throngs to this "Maalox"-worthy Chinese chain where the "extensive menu" can be as "overwhelming" as the "sizzle on the tongue"; "perfunctory" service and "grubby" decor lead many to opt for takeout or "zippy" delivery.

Grand Tier Ⓢ *Italian*

| 21 | 25 | 24 | $84 |

W 60s | Metropolitan Opera House, 2nd fl. | Lincoln Center Plaza (bet. 63rd & 65th Sts.) | 212-799-3400 | www.patinagroup.com

"Those long opera nights" have a "delightful" prelude at this Lincoln Center Italian where the "tasty" if "limited" menu is served in a "dramatic", "chandeliered" setting overlooking the Met foyer; not surprisingly, the crowd's "well dressed" and the tabs "expensive", but payoffs include "efficiency" and "dessert at intermission."

	FOOD	DECOR	SERVICE	COST

NEW Gran Electrica ● *Mexican*

- | - | - | M

Dumbo | 5 Front St. (Old Fulton St.) | Brooklyn | 718-852-2789 | www.granelectrica.com

The owners of Brooklyn Heights' Colonie come to "underserved" Dumbo via this new taqueria offering "authentic", midpriced Mexicana washed down with a variety of exotic mescals; the rustic-chic space features exposed brick galore, the "best wallpaper this side of Oaxaca" and a "perfect", beneath-the-Brooklyn-Bridge patio.

Gray's Papaya ●⇔ *Hot Dogs*

20 | 7 | 15 | $7

G Village | 402 Sixth Ave. (8th St.) | 212-260-3532
W 70s | 2090 Broadway (72nd St.) | 212-799-0243

These 24/7 hot dog stands vend "surprisingly good" wieners washed down with "frothy" papaya drinks; "quick" turnaround and "chump-change" tabs offset the "gruff" service, "what-a-dump" decor and lack of seats that make them "quintessential" NY "institutions."

Great Jones Cafe ● *Cajun*

21 | 15 | 19 | $29

NoHo | 54 Great Jones St. (bet. Bowery & Lafayette St.) | 212-674-9304 | www.greatjones.com

"No-frills" says it all about this "friendly" NoHo Cajun where the "solid" vittles arrive in a "dumpy" verging on "campy" setting; 30 years on, the crowd's still "local", the vibe "Downtown" and the jukebox as "great" as ever.

Great NY Noodle Town ●⇔ *Noodle Shop*

23 | 7 | 12 | $18

Chinatown | 28½ Bowery (Bayard St.) | 212-349-0923

"Surrender to the crowd experience" and "sit with strangers" at this "chaotic" C-town noodle shop known for "dirt-cheap" Cantonese chow (and notable salt-baked seafood) served into the wee hours; not so great is "no decor", "no credit cards" and "difficult" service.

Greek Kitchen *Greek*

21 | 15 | 19 | $30

W 50s | 889 10th Ave. (58th St.) | 212-581-4300 | www.greekkitchennyc.com

Set on the "fringes of Hell's Kitchen", this "spacious" Greek rolls out "solid" cooking at "moderate" tabs, then ups the ante with "convenience" to Fordham, John Jay College and Lincoln Center; it's more than "welcome" in an "area of limited culinary resources", though "nothing to write home about."

Greenhouse Café *American*

21 | 20 | 22 | $36

Bay Ridge | 7717 Third Ave. (bet. 77th & 78th Sts.) | Brooklyn | 718-833-8200 | www.greenhousecafe.com

This circa-1979 Bay Ridge American fields a "reliable" American menu that's best savored in its "lovely" greenhouse room; "family-friendly" atmospherics, "moderate prices" and "rapid" service tell the rest of the appealing story.

NEW Grey Lady ● *Seafood*

- | - | - | M

LES | 77 Delancey St. (Allen St.) | 646-580-5239 | www.greyladynyc.com

Annexing the former White Slab Palace digs, this new Lower Eastsider retains the shabby-chic vibe and long white marble bar of its predecessor; the limited eats include seafood items like steamers and lobster rolls, but most patrons are more interested in the cocktail list.

	FOOD	DECOR	SERVICE	COST

Grifone ⌧ *Italian*
25 | 18 | 24 | $65

E 40s | 244 E. 46th St. (bet. 2nd & 3rd Aves.) | 212-490-7275
A "tried-and-true" East Side option since '85, this "old-line" Northern
Italian near the U.N. fields an "extensive" menu of "outstanding" dishes;
"dated" decor and "captains-of-industry" price tags detract, but its
mature following digs the "discreet" service and "calm, quiet" mien.

Grimaldi's ⌻ *Pizza*
24 | 14 | 17 | $23

Flatiron | Limelight Marketplace | 656 Sixth Ave. (bet. 20th & 21st Sts.) |
646-484-5665
NEW Coney Island | Surf Ave. (Stillwell Ave.) | Brooklyn | 718-676-2630
Dumbo | 1 Front St. (Old Fulton St.) | Brooklyn | 718-858-4300
Douglaston | Douglaston Plaza | 242-02 61st Ave. (bet. Douglaston Pkwy. &
244th St.) | Queens | 718-819-2133
www.grimaldis.com
"Long lines" are the norm at this iconic Dumbo pizzeria, recently
relocated to a "bigger" Front Street address but still slinging the same
"killer" pies; the spin-offs in Coney Island, Douglaston and the Flatiron
enjoy easier access while sharing the mother ship's "cash-only" policy.

Guantanamera ● *Cuban*
21 | 17 | 20 | $35

W 50s | 939 Eighth Ave. (bet. 55th & 56th Sts.) | 212-262-5354 |
www.guantanamerany.com
"Jumping" is the word on this "fun" Midtown Cuban where the "tasty",
"authentic" chow is nearly overwhelmed by the "amazing mojitos" and
"ridiculously loud live music"; "reasonable" rates and hand-rolled ci-
gars on weekend nights supply extra "oomph."

NEW Gwynnett St. *American*
∇ 28 | 22 | 23 | $42

Williamsburg | 312 Graham Ave. (bet. Ainslie & Devoe Sts.) |
Brooklyn | 347-889-7002 | www.gwynnettst.com
A former WD-50 chef mans the stove at this "unique" new Williamsburg
American whose "high aspirations" are realized in "exceptional",
"avant-garde" cooking; the basic but "comfortable" setting seems
designed not to upstage the food, ditto the "first-rate" service and
"Brooklyn" price point.

Gyu-Kaku *Japanese*
22 | 19 | 20 | $42

E 40s | 805 Third Ave., 2nd fl. (bet. 49th & 50th Sts.) | 212-702-8816
E Village | 34 Cooper Sq. (bet. Astor Pl. & 4th St.) | 212-475-2989
NEW W 40s | 321 W. 44th St. (bet. 8th & 9th Aves.) | 646-692-9115
www.gyu-kaku.com
"Novelty"-seekers hype this "delicious, do-it-yourself" Japanese franchise where you "cook your own" BBQ on tabletop charcoal braziers;
since the "small portions" can add up to "pricey" tabs, bargain-hunters
show up for the "happy-hour specials."

NEW Hakkasan *Chinese*
∇ 23 | 26 | 20 | $95

W 40s | 311 W. 43rd St. (bet. 8th & 9th Aves.) | 212-776-1818 |
www.hakkasan.com
"Handsome", Shanghai-chic decor sets the swank mood at this new
Theater District outpost of the London-based chain, fielding "fancy"
Cantonese-inspired dishes with Western accents; ornate latticework
partitions make the "massive" space feel more intimate, but the super-
"expensive" tabs are harder to disguise.

	FOOD	DECOR	SERVICE	COST

Hampton Chutney Co. *Indian* 22 | 10 | 16 | $17

SoHo | 68 Prince St. (bet. Crosby & Lafayette Sts.) | 212-226-9996
W 80s | 464 Amsterdam Ave. (bet. 82nd & 83rd Sts.) |
212-362-5050
www.hamptonchutney.com

Both "light and filling", "delicious" dosas with "nonconventional" fillings add up to "exotic", "affordable" dining at this toothsome Indian twosome; although it's a "cool concept", "poor service" and "unkempt" looks make them better to-go options.

Hanci Turkish Cuisine *Turkish* 22 | 14 | 20 | $34

W 50s | 854 10th Ave. (bet. 56th & 57th Sts.) | 212-707-8144 |
www.hanciturkishnyc.com

"Worth the walk" to way west 10th Avenue, this "low-key" Turk proffers "simple", "nicely prepared" plates for a modest price; not much decor is offset by "good service" and convenience to "John Jay College and Lincoln Center."

Hanco's *Vietnamese* 20 | 9 | 15 | $12

Boerum Hill | 85 Bergen St. (bet. Hoyt & Smith Sts.) | Brooklyn |
718-858-6818 | www.hancosny.com
Brooklyn Heights | 147 Montague St. (bet. Clinton & Henry Sts.) |
Brooklyn | 347-529-5054
Park Slope | 350 Seventh Ave. (10th St.) | Brooklyn | 718-499-8081 |
www.hancosny.com

"Addictive", "drool"-inducing banh mi sandwiches washed down with "excellent" bubble teas are the draw at these "always busy" Vietnamese storefronts; "no frills" sums up both the decor and service, but few mind given the price.

HanGawi *Korean/Vegetarian* 25 | 24 | 23 | $51

Murray Hill | 12 E. 32nd St. (bet. 5th & Madison Aves.) |
212-213-0077 | www.hangawirestaurant.com

An "experience to be savored", this K-town vegetarian "revelation" offers "sublime" Korean food, "attention-to-detail" service and a "tranquil", "templelike" setting where "shoes come off at the door"; perhaps "you won't believe you spent so much for vegetables", but most feel it's "worth every penny."

The Harrison *American* 23 | 22 | 23 | $62

TriBeCa | 355 Greenwich St. (Harrison St.) | 212-274-9310 |
www.theharrison.com

Even "after all these years", "they get it all right" at Jimmy Bradley's "cozy, warm" TriBeCan where "delicious", "seasonal" New American cooking is matched by "gracious", "quietly attentive" service; it's "pricey", but the locals don't mind 'cause "you can't go wrong."

Harry Cipriani *Italian* 22 | 22 | 24 | $89

E 50s | Sherry-Netherland Hotel | 781 Fifth Ave. (bet. 59th & 60th Sts.) |
212-753-5566 | www.cipriani.com

"Billionaires" and "divorcées" nibble on "upscale" Venetian victuals at this Sherry-Netherland "one-percenter" refuge known for serving the "best Bellinis in town"; the "eye-popping" tabs may cause more of a stir than the food, but then again, "you're paying to see who's sitting next to you."

	FOOD	DECOR	SERVICE	COST

Harry's Cafe & Steak ◑⊠ *Steak*   24 | 21 | 23 | $54

Financial District | 1 Hanover Sq. (bet. Pearl & Stone Sts.) |
212-785-9200 | www.harrysnyc.com

Long "Wall Street's go-to eatery", this FiDi "throwback" in the historic
India House attracts "captains of industry" with "mouthwatering"
steaks and one of the best wine cellars in the city, plus Eclectic eats in
an adjoining cafe; it's "busy" for lunch, quieter at dinner and "expense
account"–worthy all the time.

Harry's Italian *Italian*   22 | 18 | 21 | $34

Financial District | 2 Gold St. (bet. Maiden Ln. & Platt St.) | 212-747-0797 ◑
NEW **Financial District** | 225 Murray St. (West St.) | 212-608-1007
W 40s | 30 Rockefeller Plaza, Concourse Level (on 6th Ave., bet. 49th &
50th Sts.) | 212-218-1450
www.harrysitalian.com

"Delicious" pizzas and "family-style" pastas are doled out at this "casual" Italian trio from the Harry's Cafe team that's touted for "affordability"; the FiDi sites are better for "groups" than the takeout-only
Rock Center outlet.

Haru *Japanese*   21 | 18 | 19 | $42

E 70s | 1327 Third Ave. (76th St.) | 212-452-1028 ◑
E 70s | 1329 Third Ave. (76th St.) | 212-452-2230 ◑
Financial District | 1 Wall Street Ct. (bet. Beaver & Pearl Sts.) | 212-785-6850
Flatiron | 220 Park Ave. S. (18th St.) | 646-428-0989 ◑
W 40s | 205 W. 43rd St. (bet. B'way & 8th Ave.) | 212-398-9810
W 80s | 433 Amsterdam Ave. (bet. 80th & 81st Sts.) | 212-579-5655 ◑
www.harusushi.com

"Delish fish" sliced in "large" pieces is the hook at this stylish Japanese
mini-chain where the "premium" sushi "won't break the budget"; it
may be "a bit of a factory" and "blasting music" puts it high on the
"decibel meter", but its "young, vibrant" following doesn't care.

Hasaki *Japanese*   24 | 17 | 19 | $45

E Village | 210 E. Ninth St. (bet. 2nd & 3rd Aves.) | 212-473-3327 |
www.hasakinyc.com

"Gourmet" sushi and "authentic" Japanese dishes are served for "reasonable" rates at this compact, '84-vintage East Villager; a no-rez rule
makes for "long lines" at prime time, so regulars show up for the "can't-
go-wrong" lunch specials.

Hatsuhana ⊠ *Japanese*   24 | 17 | 22 | $58

E 40s | 17 E. 48th St. (bet. 5th & Madison Aves.) | 212-355-3345
E 40s | 237 Park Ave. (46th St.) | 212-661-3400
www.hatsuhana.com

"Serious", "old-school sushi" is the lure at this "long-established"
Midtown Japanese duo where the "artful presentation" begins with
"aim-to-please" service; "bland decor" that "needs refreshing" seems
at odds with the rather "pricey" tabs, but you don't last this long without doing something right.

Havana Alma de Cuba *Cuban*   22 | 18 | 21 | $40

W Village | 94 Christopher St. (bet. Bedford & Bleecker Sts.) |
212-242-3800 | www.havananyc.com

"Good-humored" servers pass "pitchers of mojitos" and "substantial"
portions of appealing Cuban comfort chow at this "festive" West

Villager; "live music", "reasonable" rates and a "lovely rear garden" keep things "bustling" here, so be prepared for "noise" and "chair-bumping."

Havana Central *Cuban*   20 | 19 | 19 | $35

W 40s | 151 W. 46th St. (bet. 6th & 7th Aves.) | 212-398-7440
W 100s | 2911 Broadway (bet. 113th & 114th Sts.) | 212-662-8830
www.havanacentral.com

"Always a blast", this "lush-bordering-on-tacky" West Side twosome conjures up "Havana in a bygone era" via "satisfying" Cuban comestibles and "kick-butt" cocktails; both share "uneven" service, "reasonable" tabs and "noisy-as-all-get-out" decibels, though Midtown's "touristy" and Uptown more "collegiate."

Haveli ❶ *Indian*   22 | 17 | 21 | $33

E Village | 100 Second Ave. (bet. 5th & 6th Sts.) | 212-982-0533 | www.havelinyc.com

Offering "higher quality" than its nearby Sixth Street competitors, this "respectable" East Village Indian features "tasty, well-presented" dishes dispensed by "caring" staffers; its "grown-up atmosphere" and "white-tablecloth", double-decker setting explain the "bit pricier" tabs.

Hearth *American/Italian*   25 | 21 | 24 | $66

E Village | 403 E. 12th St. (1st Ave.) | 646-602-1300 | www.restauranthearth.com

Chef Marco Canora's "classy" East Village "foodie heaven" provides a "warm setting" in which to savor his "elegant" Tuscan-American cooking, paired with an "appealing wine list"; "professional, nonintrusive" service and a "great show" at the "kitchen bar" blunt "hedge fund–hot spot" pricing.

Hecho en Dumbo ❶ *Mexican*   23 | 17 | 19 | $41

NoHo | 354 Bowery (bet. 4th & Great Jones Sts.) | 212-937-4245 | www.hechoendumbo.com

"Inventive" Mexican small plates are "served with a side of hipster" at this "sceney", "sex-Mex" cantina that's a prime example of the "Bowery renaissance"; sure, "service could be better", but tabs are "pretty reasonable" and insiders say the tasting menu–only "chef's table is the way to go."

Heidelberg *German*   19 | 17 | 19 | $41

E 80s | 1648 Second Ave. (bet. 85th & 86th Sts.) | 212-628-2332 | www.heidelbergrestaurant.com

When it comes to "classic", "stick-to-your-ribs" Germanica, this 75-year-old Yorkville "time capsule" fields a "heavy", "no-apologies" menu washed down with "boots of beer"; "costumed" staffers and a "kitschy", "oompah-pah" setting are part of the "fun" package.

Hell's Kitchen *Mexican*   24 | 19 | 21 | $44

W 40s | 679 Ninth Ave. (bet. 46th & 47th Sts.) | 212-977-1588 | www.hellskitchen-nyc.com

"Tasty modern" Mexican food draws "big crowds" to this "high-concept" Clinton cantina where the "margaritas keep flowing" as the "noise" levels rise; even "thoughtful service" can't ease the "pre-theater crush", yet the overall experience is "closer to heaven" than the name suggests.

	FOOD	DECOR	SERVICE	COST

Henry Public ◐⌀ *Pub Food* — 22 | 21 | 19 | $32

Cobble Hill | 329 Henry St. (bet. Atlantic & Pacific Sts.) | Brooklyn | 718-852-8630 | www.henrypublic.com

"Trendy in a late-1800s sort of way", this "olde-timey" Cobble Hill pub serves a "limited" menu anchored by an "off-the-charts" turkey-leg sandwich; bartenders with "waxed mustaches" shake "sophisticated" cocktails, leaving the "cash-only", no-rez rules as the only downsides.

Henry's *American* — 20 | 20 | 21 | $40

W 100s | 2745 Broadway (105th St.) | 212-866-0600 | www.henrysnyc.com

"Widely spaced tables", "high ceilings" and "conversation"-enabling alfresco seating are among the appeals at this Columbia-area bistro; the New American cooking is as "reliable" as the "good-value" tabs and "aim-to-please" service, hence its popularity with everyone from "families" to local "literati."

Henry's End *American* — 25 | 17 | 24 | $48

Brooklyn Heights | 44 Henry St. (bet. Cranberry & Middagh Sts.) | Brooklyn | 718-834-1776 | www.henrysend.com

"As good as the day it opened" in 1973, this "distinctive" Brooklyn Heights destination remains a "sentimental favorite" due to "inventive" New American cooking, à la its seasonal "wild-game festival" bringing "exotic critters" to the table; a "small-town" atmosphere and "efficient" service make the "sardine seating" feel almost "cozy."

Hibino *Japanese* — ▽ 25 | 19 | 23 | $38

Cobble Hill | 333 Henry St. (Pacific St.) | Brooklyn | 718-260-8052 | www.hibino-brooklyn.com

"Fresh-as-one-can-get" sushi vies for the spotlight with the "daily changing" *obanzai* (small plates) and "amazing" housemade tofu at this "quirky" Cobble Hill Japanese; "budget-friendly" tabs and "unobtrusive" service embellish its "subdued", "unique" ambiance.

Hide-Chan *Japanese/Noodle Shop* — ▽ 21 | 15 | 17 | $20

E 50s | 248 E. 52nd St., 2nd fl. (bet. 2nd & 3rd Aves.) | 212-813-1800 | www.hidechanramen.com

The sound of diners "noisily slurping" "cooked-to-perfection" noodles swimming in "flavorful" broth provides the background music at this "authentic" East Midtown Japanese ramen joint; alright, the service is "a bit rushed" and the setting "cramped", but "low costs" keep the trade brisk.

NEW High Heat ◑ *Burgers/Pizza* — - | - | - | I

G Village | 154 Bleecker St. (bet. La Guardia Pl. & Thompson St.) | 212-300-4446 | www.highheatnyc.com

High-quality ingredients are used in the grilled burgers and thin-crust wood-oven pizzas at this new Village hybrid from chef Waldy Malouf (Beacon); low tabs and tap wine and beer round out the casual picture.

Hill Country *BBQ* — 23 | 16 | 16 | $34

Flatiron | 30 W. 26th St. (bet. B'way & 6th Ave.) | 212-255-4544 | www.hillcountryny.com

You have to "schlep your own food to the table" at this Flatiron roadhouse, but fans endure "long" counter lines for "bold", "Lone Star state"–worthy BBQ and "real-deal" sides; though the "cavernous", bi-level setting can get "raucous", that's because it's so popular.

Hill Country Chicken *Southern*
`20` `13` `16` `$20`

Flatiron | 1123 Broadway (25th St.) | 212-257-6446 | www.hillcountrychicken.com

"Crispy-crunchy" fried chicken (including a "fabulous" skinless version) and "decent sides" make it hard to "save room for pie" at this low-budget Flatiron Southerner; regulars ignore the "service hiccups" and "groan-inducing", "rec-room" decor, reporting it's "quieter" downstairs.

Hillstone *American*
`23` `22` `22` `$42`
(fka Houston's)

E 50s | Citicorp Bldg. | 153 E. 53rd St. (enter on 3rd Ave. & 54th St.) | 212-888-3828
Murray Hill | NY Life Bldg. | 378 Park Ave. S. (27th St.) | 212-689-1090
www.hillstone.com

Young "corporate" guns frequent these "surprisingly good", surprisingly affordable outlets of the national chain for "easy" American comfort items (i.e. its "famous" spinach-artichoke dip) served in "dark", "roomy" environs; "lively bar scenes" distract from the perennial "waits" at prime times.

Home *American*
`23` `19` `21` `$45`

W Village | 20 Cornelia St. (bet. Bleecker & W. 4th Sts.) | 212-243-9579 | www.homerestaurantnyc.com

"Not widely known" despite 20 years on the scene, this "solid" West Village "nook" offers "dressed-up" Americana assembled from "local, seasonal" ingredients; the "rustic" interior is appropriately "homey", but the "small" verging on "cramped" setup leads regulars to "ask for garden seating."

Hop Kee ●▱ *Chinese*
`22` `8` `15` `$21`

Chinatown | 21 Mott St., downstairs (bet. Chatham Sq. & Mosco St.) | 212-964-8365 | www.hopkeenyc.com

"Old-guard", cash-only Chinatown cellar that's been slinging "traditional" Cantonese food – "and plenty of it" – since 1968; "dank" decor and "zombie" service are offset by "late"-night hours, "rock-bottom" tabs and an "Anthony Bourdain" endorsement.

Hospoda *Czech*
`23` `24` `24` `$56`

E 70s | Bohemian National Hall | 321 E. 73rd St. (bet. 1st & 2nd Aves.) | 212-861-1038 | www.hospodanyc.com

Ensconced in the UES Bohemian National Hall, this "upscale" yearling incorporates "striking" modern decor and "accommodating" service to buttress its "new turns on old Czech dishes"; "Pilsner Urquell on tap" pleases patrons, "tiny portions" and "pricey" tabs less so, but the general "prague-nosis is it's worth czeching out."

The House ● *American*
`21` `24` `21` `$55`

Gramercy | 121 E. 17th St. (bet. Irving Pl. & Park Ave. S.) | 212-353-2121 | www.thehousenyc.com

This tri-level Gramercy standout proffers "solid" New American cooking but "even better ambiance" given its "romantic", "candlelit" setting in a "gorgeous" 1854 carriage house; factor in "attentive" service, and obviously it's a "perfect" "date place", though you pay to "impress" here.

Hudson Clearwater *American*
24 | 22 | 23 | $55

W Village | 447 Hudson St. (enter on Morton St. bet. Greenwich & Hudson Sts.) | 212-989-3255 | www.hudsonclearwater.com

A "hidden entrance" on Morton Street isn't deterring the crowds from this West Village "total scene", incidentally offering "first-rate" New American food backed up by "exceptional" cocktails; its "hip young" following doesn't mind the "lively" acoustics and "tables on top of one another."

Hudson River Café *American*
21 | 21 | 19 | $41

Harlem | 697 W. 133rd St. (12th Ave.) | 212-491-9111 | www.hudsonrivercafe.com

There's "a lot going on" at this "indoor-outdoor" West Harlem venue, starting with its "outstanding views of the Hudson" and "delicious", Latin-accented Americana; as the evening progresses, it "turns into a club" complete with "live music" and "weekend pat-downs."

Hummus Kitchen *Kosher/Mediterranean*
21 | 16 | 18 | $21

E 80s | 1613 Second Ave. (bet. 83rd & 84th Sts.) | 212-988-0090
Murray Hill | 444 Third Ave. (bet. 30th & 31st Sts.) | 212-696-0055
W 50s | 768 Ninth Ave. (bet. 51st & 52nd Sts.) | 212-333-3009 ◗
NEW **W 80s** | 416 Amsterdam Ave. (80th St.) | 212-799-0003
www.hummuskitchen.com

This "casual" Med quartet whips up "quality" hummus with a "special zing" along with a raft of vegetarian options; despite "smallish" settings and "disorganized" service, it's an "affordable" "fast-food alternative", especially for those who need it "kosher."

Hummus Place *Israeli/Kosher/Vegetarian*
23 | 14 | 18 | $18

E Village | 109 St. Marks Pl. (bet. Ave. A & 1st Ave.) | 212-529-9198 ◗
W 70s | 305 Amsterdam Ave. (bet. 74th & 75th Sts.) | 212-799-3335 ◗
W 90s | 2608 Broadway (bet. 98th & 99th Sts.) | 212-222-1554
W Village | 71 Seventh Ave. S. (bet. Barrow & Bleecker Sts.) | 212-924-2022
www.hummusplace.com

Those who like their hummus "silky" and their pita bread "warm" kvell over the kosher vegetarian offerings at this "popular" Israeli quartet; though decor is nearly "nonexistent", service is "pleasant", the grub filling and the tabs "terrific."

NEW Humphrey *American*
- | - | - | M

Chelsea | Eventi Hotel | 839 Sixth Ave., 2nd fl. (29th St.) | 212-201-4065

A scaled-down version of predecessor Bar Basque, this simple American newcomer in Chelsea's Eventi Hotel features a menu that's as abbreviated as its dimensions; there's all-seasons dining on its open-air breezeway setting (equipped with a retractable roof), while an indoor piano bar and lounge area lend festive notes.

Hundred Acres *American*
21 | 21 | 20 | $50

SoHo | 38 MacDougal St. (Prince St.) | 212-475-7500 | www.hundredacresnyc.com

"Farm-fresh" New American "home cooking" arrives in an appropriately "country-road" setting at this SoHo charmer that's kin to Cookshop and Five Points; its "cult following" commends its "delicious brunch" and "awesome garden", only wishing there were "more menu options."

	FOOD	DECOR	SERVICE	COST

☑ Hurricane Club *Polynesian* | 21 | 26 | 21 | $58 |

Flatiron | 360 Park Ave. S. (26th St.) | 212-951-7111 |
www.thehurricaneclub.com

"Dressed-to-impress" young folks channel their "inner beachcomber" at
this Flatiron Polynesian "whirlwind" where the "tasty" pupu platters are
chased with "clever cocktails" served in "giant fishbowls"; the big, "exotic" room may be "less a restaurant" and more of a "club scene", but
despite "loud" acoustics and "pricey" tabs, it's immensely popular.

I Coppi   *Italian* | 23 | 23 | 23 | $47 |

E Village | 432 E. Ninth St. (bet. Ave. A & 1st Ave.) | 212-254-2263 |
www.icoppinyc.com

"Calming" is the word on this "pretty" East Village Italian "oasis"
that's as much praised for its "unequaled, all-seasons" garden as
its "delicious" Tuscan fare straight from a "wood-burning" oven;
"personable" service, "reasonable" tabs and the promise of "romance" keep the trade brisk.

Il Bagatto ●Ⓜ *Italian* | 25 | 17 | 20 | $45 |

E Village | 192 E. Second St. (bet. Aves. A & B) | 212-228-0977 |
www.ilbagattonyc.com

A "diamond in the rough", this "no-frills" East Village Italian is known
for its "top-notch" "homestyle" cooking, especially its "scrumptious"
pastas; fair pricing and "warm" service make it "hard to get reservations" at prime times, so it's good that the holding-pen next-door
wine bar "rocks."

Il Bambino *Italian* | 27 | 20 | 22 | $23 |

Astoria | 34-08 31st Ave. (bet. 34th & 35th Sts.) | Queens |
718-626-0087 | www.ilbambinonyc.com

"Fantastic" panini fashioned from "unbeatable" breads and "quality
ingredients" plus lots of "affordable wines" are the focus of this "relaxing" Astoria Italian; a "nice" garden, modest prices and "fast, friendly"
service seal the deal.

Il Buco ● *Italian/Mediterranean* | 26 | 23 | 22 | $60 |

NoHo | 47 Bond St. (bet. Bowery & Lafayette St.) | 212-533-1932 |
www.ilbuco.com

Il Buco Alimentari e Vineria ● *Italian/Mediterranean*

NoHo | 53 Great Jones St. (bet. Bowery & Lafayette St.) |
212-837-2622 | www.ilbucovineria.com

"Robust", "ingredient-driven" Med-Italian cuisine is presented in a
transporting farmhouse setting at this longtime NoHo exercise in "la
dolce vita", where everything is done well; its nearby market/bakery/
wine bar spin-off is a more "casual" affair with "communal tables" and
an "open kitchen", but "just as charming."

Il Cantinori *Italian* | 23 | 23 | 22 | $70 |

G Village | 32 E. 10th St. (bet. B'way & University Pl.) | 212-673-6044 |
www.ilcantinori.com

"Thankfully reopened following a fire", this 20-year-old Northern Italian
remains a "lovable" Village option thanks to "terrific" Tuscan food
served in a "simply beautiful" space bedecked with "fresh flowers";
though renowned for "celeb-watching", admirers aver it "treats all
diners like stars" – as it should, given the prices.

	FOOD	DECOR	SERVICE	COST

Il Cortile *Italian*
23 | 21 | 21 | $53

Little Italy | 125 Mulberry St. (bet. Canal & Hester Sts.) | 212-226-6060 | www.ilcortile.com

"*Buongusto* is an understatement" at this "memory-lane" Italian, a "good bet on Mulberry" since 1975 owing to "hearty" food served by waiters who have "been there forever"; though it's "a bit pricey" for the area, regulars report a seat in the "delightful" garden atrium is "worth the trip" alone.

Il Fornaio *Italian*
23 | 17 | 20 | $36

Little Italy | 132 Mulberry St. (bet. Grand & Hester Sts.) | 212-226-8306

"Basic" Italian cooking that's "better than much in the neighborhood" is the métier of this "pleasant" Little Italy vet whose "generous" portions are "presented without pretense"; since the "simple" decor is just that, insiders opt for sidewalk seats overlooking the passing parade.

Il Gattopardo ● *Italian*
24 | 21 | 23 | $71

W 50s | 33 W. 54th St. (bet. 5th & 6th Aves.) | 212-246-0412 | www.ilgattopardonyc.com

Across from MoMA, this "art-world canteen" purveys "big-flavored" Neapolitan cuisine in a "stylish" townhouse tended by "pro" staffers with "thick accents"; it's popular for "power lunches" or "romantic" interludes, but most enjoyable "if someone else is paying."

Il Giglio 🔲 *Italian*
25 | 20 | 24 | $73

TriBeCa | 81 Warren St. (bet. Greenwich St. & W. B'way) | 212-571-5555 | www.ilgigliorestaurant.com

An "empty stomach and a full wallet" are necessities at this "longtime" TriBeCa Italian where a meal begins with "complimentary" antipasti followed by a "luxurious" array of "old-world classics"; "outdated" decor, "tight quarters" and high prices are offset by "attentive" service and "generous portions."

Ilili *Lebanese*
25 | 22 | 22 | $56

Chelsea | 236 Fifth Ave. (bet. 27th & 28th Sts.) | 212-683-2929 | www.ililinyc.com

"Twentysomething" types are "blown away" by this "palindromic" Lebanese near Madison Square Park, where the "original" small plates (including some "must-try Brussels sprouts") arrive in a "vast", "modernist" setting; it's a "hopping" scene complete with plenty of "noise", "patient" servers and rather "pricey" tariffs.

🔳 Il Mulino *Italian*
27 | 20 | 24 | $94

G Village | 86 W. Third St. (bet. Sullivan & Thompson Sts.) | 212-673-3783

Il Mulino Uptown 🔲 *Italian*

NEW **E 60s** | 37 E. 60th St. (bet. Madison & Park Aves.) | 212-750-3270 | www.ilmulino.com

"CEOs", "politicians" and "expense-account"–bearing "suits" pile into this "exceptional" Village Italian that's renowned for its "freebie" appetizer "bacchanalia", followed by mega-portioned, "gold-standard" Abruzzi cooking; "old-school" waiters in "black tie", "outdated" decor, "high prices" and "tough" reservations come with the territory; P.S. an UES satellite near Barney's promises more of the same.

		FOOD	DECOR	SERVICE	COST

Il Postino ◐ *Italian*

23 | 20 | 23 | $68

E 40s | 337 E. 49th St. (bet. 1st & 2nd Aves.) | 212-688-0033 | www.ilpostinony.com

Waiters inhale, then recite a "huge list of daily specials" – sans prices – at this "old-world" U.N.-area Italian that will also "cook anything you want"; aesthetes applaud the recent "spruce up", but value-seekers avoid the "reliably expensive" tabs by opting for the lunchtime "prix fixe."

Il Riccio ◐ *Italian*

20 | 16 | 20 | $56

E 70s | 152 E. 79th St. (bet. Lexington & 3rd Aves.) | 212-639-9111 | www.ilriccioblu.com

UES denizens "of a certain age" (hello Mayor Bloomberg!) patronize this "clubby" Italian for its "above-average" Amalfi Coast food served in a "friendly", "white-tablecloth" room; if the compact interior gets too "tight", there's a "lovely garden" out back.

◪ Il Tinello ◪ *Italian*

25 | 21 | 26 | $77

W 50s | 16 W. 56th St. (bet. 5th & 6th Aves.) | 212-245-4388 | www.iltinellony.com

"Serenity" reigns at this Midtown "grande dame" exuding "senior appeal" and patrolled by "conscientious" waiters in "black tie"; everyone agrees that the Northern Italian cooking is "superb", but given the "corporate-checkbook" tabs, many save it for "special occasions."

Il Vagabondo *Italian*

20 | 18 | 20 | $50

E 60s | 351 E. 62nd St. (bet. 1st & 2nd Aves.) | 212-832-9221 | www.ilvagabondo.com

"Old-school" Italian fans find "all the favorites" at this 1965-vintage Upper Eastsider, where the food "sticks to your ribs" and the waiters have "been there for centuries"; the decor may be "nothing to write home about", but the "unique" indoor bocce court is.

Inakaya *Japanese*

22 | 22 | 23 | $58

W 40s | NY Times Bldg. | 231 W. 40th St. (bet. 7th & 8th Aves.) | 212-354-2195 | www.inakayany.com

It's always "showtime" at this "high-drama" Japanese in the NY Times building, where "friendly" staffers dish out "grilled delights" (plus "swanky sushi") while engaging in ritualized "yelling and screaming"; however, all the "fun" – which is most intense at the robata counter – can add up to "big bucks."

Indochine ◑ *French/Vietnamese*

22 | 22 | 20 | $55

E Village | 430 Lafayette St. (bet. Astor Pl. & 4th St.) | 212-505-5111 | www.indochinenyc.com

Ever "sexy" – even "timeless" – this "'80s hot spot" opposite the Public Theater still lures "attractive thin" folk with "on-target" French-Vietnamese fare served in "exotic" digs à la 1930s Saigon; perhaps its "elegance is slightly worn", but the "people-watching" is as stellar as ever.

Indus Valley *Indian*

22 | 16 | 20 | $33

W 100s | 2636 Broadway (100th St.) | 212-222-9222 | www.indusvalleyus.com

Though the ambiance may be "average", the "intensely flavorful" eats at this UWS Indian are "a cut above", ditto the "solicitous" service;

penny-pinchers find the $14 weekend lunch buffet "awesome", and allow it's "worth the few extra bucks" at dinner.

'Ino ◐ *Italian*

| 25 | 16 | 21 | $31 |

W Village | 21 Bedford St. (bet. Downing St. & 6th Ave.) | 212-989-5769 | www.cafeino.com

"Small is an understatement" at this "dollhouse"-size Village Italian wine bar that's a big hit thanks to "spectacular" panini, bruschetta and truffled egg toast; the "no-fuss" mood extends to the "couldn't-be-nicer" staff, "affordable" tabs and "late-night" hours (till 2 AM).

'Inoteca ◐ *Italian*

| 22 | 18 | 19 | $41 |

LES | 98 Rivington St. (Ludlow St.) | 212-614-0473
Murray Hill | 323 Third Ave. (24th St.) | 212-683-3035
www.inotecanyc.com

It's "easy to get carried away" at these "lively" Italian enotecas given the "right-on" small plates and "dizzying" wine selection; "hit-or-miss" service, "over-the-top" decibels and "challenging" non-English menus don't faze its "twentysomething" clientele.

Ipanema *Brazilian/Portuguese*

| ∇ 26 | 19 | 22 | $40 |

W 40s | 13 W. 46th St. (bet. 5th & 6th Aves.) | 212-730-5848 | www.ipanemanyc.com

Under the radar "in the middle of Little Brazil", this "friendly" joint in the West 40s has been churning out "authentic" Brazilian-Portuguese dishes for two decades; the kitschy "samba decor" may be "less spectacular" than the "tasty" grub, but the vibe's "relaxed" and the prices "better than fair."

Ippudo ◐ *Japanese/Noodle Shop*

| 26 | 21 | 20 | $30 |

E Village | 65 Fourth Ave. (bet. 9th & 10th Sts.) | 212-388-0088 | www.ippudony.com

"Hipster" East Village Japanese "ramen king" ladling out "serious" noodles in the "richest, most complex" broth along with "succulent pork buns"; slick looks and "speedy" staffers who "cheer when you enter" distract from the "famously long waits."

Isa *Mediterranean*

| ∇ 22 | 24 | 24 | $56 |

Williamsburg | 348 Wythe Ave. (S. 2nd St.) | Brooklyn | 347-689-3594 | www.isa.gg

"Quirky" is the mindset at this "instant hit" Williamsburg yearling where the industrial "log cabin" decor and "psychedelic menu" art seem inspired by "Jerry Garcia"; following a chef change, it now features a 'born again' Mediterranean menu that's less of a "head-scratcher" than before.

Isabella's *American/Mediterranean*

| 21 | 20 | 20 | $44 |

W 70s | 359 Columbus Ave. (77th St.) | 212-724-2100 | www.isabellas.com

"Convenience" to the Museum of Natural History and the New-York Historical Society is a draw at this 25-year-old Steve Hanson "standby", where "reliable" Mediterranean-American meals are ferried by "friendly" folks; during its "mobbed" weekend brunch, regulars request sidewalk seats – the "traffic on Columbus Avenue is quieter than the noise inside."

	FOOD	DECOR	SERVICE	COST

Ise *Japanese*
22 | 13 | 19 | $40

E 40s | 151 E. 49th St. (bet. Lexington & 3rd Aves.) | 212-319-6876
Financial District | 56 Pine St. (bet. Pearl & William Sts.) |
212-785-1600 ⓢ
W 50s | 58 W. 56th St. (bet. 5th & 6th Aves.) | 212-707-8702
www.iserestaurant.com

Authentically Japanese with a "clientele to match", this "solid" iza-kaya trio provides "real-deal" sushi and "legit" cooked items that re-sult in "crowded" lunch hours; "spare" digs and "perfunctory" service are offset by a "reasonable" bottom line.

Island Burgers & Shakes *Burgers*
22 | 14 | 19 | $19

W 50s | 766 Ninth Ave. (bet. 51st & 52nd Sts.) | 212-307-7934 ◑
W 80s | 422 Amsterdam Ave. (80th St.) | 212-877-7934 |
www.islandburgersandshakesnyc.com Ⓜ

"Huge burgers" on "big buns" accessorized with "every topping known to man" are the raisons d'être of these "retro" West Side patty palaces that, thank God, "finally sell fries"; "spoon-licking shakes" sweeten the sour taste left by "sparse seating and service."

I Sodi ◑ *Italian*
25 | 18 | 22 | $59

W Village | 105 Christopher St. (bet. Bleecker & Hudson Sts.) |
212-414-5774 | www.isodinyc.com

A "little bit of Florence" in the West Village, this "small" Italian supplies "generously sized" portions of "first-tier" Tuscan fare lubricated by a "substantial wine list" and signature Negronis; "charming" service makes the "tight squeeze" seem delightfully "intimate," even "romantic."

NEW Isola ◑ *Italian*
- | - | - | E

SoHo | Mondrian SoHo | 9 Crosby St. (bet. Grand & Howard Sts.) |
212-389-0000 | www.mondriansoho.com

A reboot of the Mondrian SoHo Hotel's Imperial No. 9, this new iteration serves coastal Italian dishes (with a focus on crudo) in a striking, glass-lined greenhouse; no reservations are accepted, save for guests of the hotel, and the upscale pricing is in keeping with the tony mood.

Italianissimo *Italian*
23 | 19 | 23 | $54

E 80s | 307 E. 84th St. (bet. 1st & 2nd Aves.) | 212-628-8603 |
www.italianissimonyc.net

Its "jewel box" size reflects the neighborhood-"gem" status of this "*bellissimo*" UES Italian where the "just-like-mama" cooking and "brick-walled" setting seem right out of a "Woody Allen" movie; "solicitous" service and an "excellent" $27 early-bird make this one a "great find."

Ithaka *Greek/Seafood*
20 | 17 | 20 | $47

E 80s | 308 E. 86th St. (bet. 1st & 2nd Aves.) | 212-628-9100 |
www.ithakarestaurant.com

"Neighborhood tavernas" don't get much more "relaxed" than this "quiet" Yorkville Greek where the "honest" food and "wonderful grilled fish" channel Santorini – or at least "Astoria"; maybe the white-washed setting could be "spiffed up", but thankfully the tables are "far enough apart" and service is "attentive."

	FOOD	DECOR	SERVICE	COST

I Trulli *Italian* ⬛ 22 | 21 | 21 | $61

Murray Hill | 122 E. 27th St. (bet. Lexington Ave. & Park Ave. S.) | 212-481-7372 | www.itrulli.com

"Rustic but sophisticated", this Murray Hill Southern Italian purveys a trulli "special" Puglian menu paired with "outstanding" wines via its adjoining enoteca; an "expansive" garden and "roaring" fireplace are seasonal draws, though "helpful" service and "costly" tabs are available year-round.

Jack's Luxury ▽ 28 | 18 | 25 | $62
Oyster Bar ⊠ *Continental/French*

E Village | 101 Second Ave. (bet. 5th & 6th Sts.) | 212-979-1012

At Jack Lamb's super-"tiny" East Villager, the "chef's in constant motion", whipping up a "memorable" French-Continental menu focused on "wonderful seafood"; a "hip" mood and "excellent" service mute the "spartan" setting and "expensive" tariffs.

Jackson Diner *Indian* 21 | 13 | 17 | $25

G Village | 72 University Pl. (bet. 10th & 11th Sts.) | 212-466-0820 | www.jacksondinernyc.com
Jackson Heights | 37-47 74th St. (bet. Roosevelt & 37th Aves.) | Queens | 718-672-1232 | www.jacksondiner.com

Jackson Heights' Little India is home to this 30-year-old super subcontinental that's recently spun off a Village satellite; though they're not much to look at, both outlets feature "satisfying" grub, "low prices" and "laid-back" service, and regulars say the lunchtime "buffet is the way to go."

Jackson Hole *Burgers* 19 | 13 | 17 | $24

E 60s | 232 E. 64th St. (bet. 2nd & 3rd Aves.) | 212-371-7187 ☾
E 80s | 1611 Second Ave. (bet. 83rd & 84th Sts.) | 212-737-8788 ☾
E 90s | 1270 Madison Ave. (91st St.) | 212-427-2820
Murray Hill | 521 Third Ave. (35th St.) | 212-679-3264 ☾
W 80s | 517 Columbus Ave. (85th St.) | 212-362-5177
Bayside | 35-01 Bell Blvd. (35th Ave.) | Queens | 718-281-0330 ☾
Jackson Heights | 69-35 Astoria Blvd. (70th St.) | Queens | 718-204-7070 ☾
www.jacksonholeburgers.com

"Immense" burgers ("share or explode") and moderate prices are the calling cards of this longtime mini-chain; though the patties are "juicy" enough, "amateur" service and "jackson-hole-in-the-wall" decor make it an "average experience" for many.

NEW Jack's Wife Freda ☾ *American* ▽ 20 | 17 | 25 | $34

SoHo | 224 Lafayette St. (bet. Kenmare & Spring Sts.) | 212-510-8550 | www.jackswifefreda.com

"Solid", homey Americana with kosher flair draws SoHo locals to this "inviting", new all-day cafe whose name references the owner's grandparents; some find the going "just ok", though there's agreement on the "superb" service and low price point.

Jack the Horse Tavern *American* 24 | 21 | 22 | $44

Brooklyn Heights | 66 Hicks St. (Cranberry St.) | Brooklyn | 718-852-5084 | www.jackthehorse.com

"Cozy, taverny" vibes prevail at this Brooklyn Heights "hideaway" where "upscale" American food (including "amazing mac 'n' cheese") is dispatched in a room conducive to "relaxed conversation"; "cheerful" service offsets the "small portions" and "slightly pricey" tabs.

NEW Jacob's Pickles ❶ *American*   ▽ 21 | 21 | 21 | $31

W 80s | 509 Amsterdam Ave. (bet. 84th & 85th Sts.) | 212-392-5407 | www.jacobspickles.com

Beer, biscuits and pickles are the backbone of the Southern-accented menu at this new, "Brooklyn-esque" Upper West Side tavern; expect "comforting" American dishes – many slathered in gravy – served in a "handsome" wood- and brick-lined room that includes an upfront retail area for takeaway.

Jaiya New York *Thai*   22 | 16 | 17 | $32

NEW E 80s | 1553 Second Ave. (bet. 80th & 81st Sts.) | 212-717-8877

Jaiya Thai *Thai*

Murray Hill | 396 Third Ave. (28th St.) | 212-889-1330
www.jaiya.com

Whether you prefer "spicy" or "incendiary", these East Side Thais offer "authentic" Siamese food running the gamut from standard classics to "challenging, take-no-hostages" items; "decent" price points trump the "noisy" settings and less than stellar service.

Jake's Steakhouse *Steak*   24 | 20 | 22 | $54

Riverdale | 6031 Broadway (242nd St.) | Bronx | 718-581-0182 | www.jakessteakhouse.com

"Scenic views of Van Cortlandt Park" make the "Manhattan-quality" steaks taste even juicier at this "neighborhood" Riverdale chophouse where the service is "professional" and the beer selection "vast"; although "expensive", it's "cheaper than the city", and there's "valet parking" to boot.

James *American*   25 | 23 | 23 | $44

Prospect Heights | 605 Carlton Ave. (St. Marks Ave.) | Brooklyn | 718-942-4255 | www.jamesrestaurantny.com

"Seriously good" American cooking gets a "classy" home at this Prospect Heights "hipster hideaway" where "cool cocktails" and "delightful service" burnish the "welcoming" mien; a modern, whitewashed-brick setting with "cozy" lighting makes it a no-brainer for "date night."

Jane *American*   22 | 17 | 20 | $41

G Village | 100 W. Houston St. (bet. La Guardia Pl. & Thompson St.) | 212-254-7000 | www.janerestaurant.com

"Young, trendy" folk flock to this "upbeat" Village American for "quite tasty" cooking, with "moderate" tabs, "austere" decor and "generally good service" on the side; though "insanely busy", the weekend brunch is the scene to make, provided you can stomach "loud" decibels on top of your "hangover."

Japonica *Japanese*   23 | 15 | 21 | $47

G Village | 100 University Pl. (12th St.) | 212-243-7752 | www.japonicanyc.com

An "old friend" in the Village since '78, this Japanese vet "never gets old" thanks to "enormous portions" of "delicate", "fresh" sushi that "tastes expensive"; the decor may be "long in the tooth", but service is "attentive" and the overall dining experience "solid."

	FOOD	DECOR	SERVICE	COST

Z Jean Georges *French* **28 27 28 $140**

W 60s | Trump Int'l Hotel | 1 Central Park W. (bet. 60th & 61st Sts.) | 212-299-3900 | www.jean-georges.com

"Special event" dining is alive and well at this "hub" of the Jean-Georges Vongerichten "empire", a "well-oiled" CPW machine where "heavenly" New French "art on a plate" is dispatched by a team that has service "down to a science"; the "lovely", "light-filled" setting burnishes its "gold-standard" aura, but keep in mind that both jackets and deep pockets are "mandatory" here; P.S. the "superb" $38 prix fixe lunch is a NYC "best bet."

Z Jean Georges' **27 24 26 $67**
Nougatine *French*

W 60s | Trump Int'l Hotel | 1 Central Park W. (bet. 60th & 61st Sts.) | 212-299-3900 | www.jean-georges.com

More "approachable" than Jean Georges, this front-room "alternative" features the same "high-standards" New French fare served in an attractively renovated space for "lighter-on-the-checkbook" tabs; the "peaceful" ambiance is especially good for breakfast and after-work cocktails, while the three-course, $32 prix fixe lunch provides "perfection for a pittance."

Jeffrey's Grocery ● *American* **▽ 22 20 21 $50**

W Village | 172 Waverly Pl. (Christopher St.) | 646-398-7630 | www.jeffreysgrocery.com

There's "Wisconsin" in the air at Gabe Stulman's "hip" Village American, a tiny, "homey" thing where the "tasty" menu is as limited as the square footage; "divine oysters" and "attention to detail" offset the "not-Midwestern prices", though a few feel it's "more scene than place to eat."

Jewel Bako 図 *Japanese* **26 23 23 $78**

E Village | 239 E. Fifth St. (bet. 2nd & 3rd Aves.) | 212-979-1012

"Casually elegant" and "expensively" priced, this bamboo-lined East Village Japanese slices a "flawless symphony" of "incredibly fresh fish"; for best results, aficionados "sit at the sushi bar" and go the "omakase" route, though no matter where you land, owners Jack and Grace Lamb "really take care of you."

NEW Jezebel *American/Kosher* **- - - E**

SoHo | 323 W. Broadway (bet. Canal & Grand Sts.) | 646-410-0717 | www.jezebelsoho.com

Glatt kosher cooking lands Downtown at this new SoHo duplex offering New American dishes geared toward swinging young observant types; the tabs are pricey and the gaudily elegant setting is done up with cheeky artwork – i.e. a version of 'The Last Supper' with Woody Allen as Jesus.

J.G. Melon ●⇄ *Pub Food* **21 13 16 $29**

E 70s | 1291 Third Ave. (74th St.) | 212-744-0585

"Prep school" alumni and assorted "J. Crew" types populate this "no-fuss, no-muss" Upper East Side pub celebrated for "killer burgers" washed down with "old-school" cottage fries; despite "rushed" service, a "cash-only" rule and digs in need of "freshening", it's "always mobbed."

	FOOD	DECOR	SERVICE	COST

Jing Fong *Chinese* | 21 | 14 | 13 | $22 |

Chinatown | 20 Elizabeth St. (bet. Bayard & Canal Sts.) | 212-964-5256 | www.jingfongny.com

Set in a "football field–size" hall, this "bustling" C-town Cantonese rolls out "delectable" dim sum "à la Hong Kong" on "quickly moving carts" propelled by "brusque" staffers; it's "crowded at peak hours", a "hectic madhouse" on weekends and "affordable" all the time.

NEW Joanne *American/Italian* | ∇ 18 | 20 | 20 | $49 |

W 60s | 70 W. 68th St. (bet. Columbus Ave. & CPW) | 212-721-0068 | www.joannenyc.com

Lady Gaga's folks and chef/cookbook author Art Smith are behind this new UWS Italian-American that early visitors say needs "a bit of tweaking" in the kitchen; the "perfect" patio, rustic fireplaces and "amiable" service are fine as is, ditto the moderate price tags.

Joe Allen ● *American* | 19 | 18 | 20 | $45 |

W 40s | 326 W. 46th St. (bet. 8th & 9th Aves.) | 212-581-6464 | www.joeallenrestaurant.com

Known for its "posters of Broadway bombs" and "serviceable" American grub, this "timeless" Theater District joint is still a magnet for "show-biz" types and those who love them; après-theater "stargazing" – "yes, that's who you think it is in that dark corner" – lends "glamour" to the proceedings.

Joe & Pat's *Italian/Pizza* | 24 | 15 | 19 | $23 |

Castleton Corners | 1758 Victory Blvd. (Manor Rd.) | Staten Island | 718-981-0887 | www.joeandpatspizzany.com

There's "a lot to choose from" on the menu of this circa-1960 Italian, but "generations of Staten Islanders" mainly show up for its "outstanding" thin-crust pizza; not much decor and "unmotivated" service detract, but at least Joe is "still present to greet you as you enter."

JoeDoe *American* | ∇ 26 | 20 | 21 | $51 |

E Village | 45 E. First St. (bet. 1st & 2nd Aves.) | 212-780-0262 | www.chefjoedoe.com

Parlaying "big ideas in a small space", this East Village American offers "distinctive", Jewish-accented dishes assembled from "quality ingredients"; the overall vibe is "cool-comfortable" and the staff "just the right amount of helpful" – only "Uptown prices" give any pause.

Joe's Ginger ⑁ *Chinese* | 21 | 11 | 14 | $23 |

Chinatown | 25 Pell St. (Doyers St.) | 212-285-0999 | www.joeginger.com

"Slightly slicker" and "less crazy" than its nearby sibling, Joe's Shanghai, this C-town contender features the "same great soup dumplings", "rushed service" and lack of decor; "individual tables" and "less waiting on line" are additional benefits.

Joe's Pizza ● *Pizza* | 23 | 8 | 15 | $12 |

W Village | 7 Carmine St. (bet. Bleecker St. & 6th Ave.) | 212-366-1182 | www.joespizzanyc.com

"Legendary to locals", this "grab-and-go" West Village pizzeria has been slinging "hot-out-of-the-oven" slices since 1975; "hole-in-the-wall" looks and "stand-up counter service" are part of this "quintessential NY" experience, but explain why some are "not impressed."

	FOOD	DECOR	SERVICE	COST

Joe's Shanghai *Chinese*
22 | 10 | 14 | $26

Chinatown | 9 Pell St. (bet. Bowery & Mott St.) | 212-233-8888 ⊄
W 50s | 24 W. 56th St. (bet. 5th & 6th Aves.) | 212-333-3868
Flushing | 136-21 37th Ave. (bet. Main & Union Sts.) | Queens |
718-539-3838 ⊄
www.joeshanghairestaurants.com

"Believe the hype": the "scrumptious", "savory" soup dumplings at this
"highly popular", "no-frills" Shanghainese trio trump complaints about
"zero decor", "curt service" and "awkward" communal tables; since
they try to "get you in and out quickly", it's "not for leisurely dining."

John Dory Oyster Bar ● *Seafood*
24 | 20 | 19 | $55

Chelsea | Ace Hotel | 1196 Broadway (29th St.) | 212-792-9000 |
www.thejohndory.com

Berthed in Chelsea's Ace Hotel, this "airy" seafooder via April Bloomfield
and Ken Friedman offers everything from "succulent oysters" to "inspired" small plates; "guppy-size portions", "hefty" tabs and "disinterested" service are offset by a "happening vibe", kitschy-"cool" digs
and "sublime" Parker House rolls.

John's of 12th Street ⊄ *Italian*
22 | 16 | 20 | $36

E Village | 302 E. 12th St. (2nd Ave.) | 212-475-9531 |
www.johnsof12thstreet.com

"Upholding the art of Italian cooking" since 1908, this East Village "institution" endures thanks to "no-nonsense" red-sauce meals (plus recently added "vegan selections"), all at "fair prices"; "no credit cards"
and "nothing-fancy" decor (think "Chianti bottles" and "melted candle
wax") add to the "time-warp" vibe.

John's Pizzeria *Pizza*
23 | 15 | 17 | $25

E 60s | 408 E. 64th St. (bet. 1st & York Aves.) | 212-935-2895
W 40s | 260 W. 44th St. (bet. B'way & 8th Ave.) | 212-391-7560 |
www.johnspizzerianyc.com ●
W Village | 278 Bleecker St. (bet. 6th Ave. & 7th Ave. S.) |
212-243-1680 | www.johnsbrickovenpizza.com ●⊄

"Heavenly" brick-oven thin-crust pies – but "no slices" – are dispensed
at this "greasy, gooey" pizzeria trio; the "FDR-era" Village original with
its wooden booths is a bona fide "landmark", while the "convenient"
Theater District outpost in a "converted church" may soon become one.

JoJo *French*
24 | 22 | 23 | $69

E 60s | 160 E. 64th St. (bet. Lexington & 3rd Aves.) | 212-223-5656 |
www.jean-georges.com

The "intimate rooms" at this Jean-Georges Vongerichten French bistro
lure "plutocrats" in the mood for "romance"; the cooking is "excellent",
the service "courteous" and though the pricing's geared toward "one-
percenters", prix fixe deals carry the day.

Jones Wood Foundry ● *British*
20 | 21 | 19 | $40

E 70s | 401 E. 76th St. (bet. 1st & York Aves.) | 212-249-2700 |
www.joneswoodfoundry.com

Bringing a bit of "jolly old England" to Yorkville, this wood-paneled
British pub dispenses "wonderful fish 'n' chips" and other "simple"
classics washed down with an "impressive" suds selection; "ambiance is
what sells this place", along with "helpful" service and a "lovely garden."

	FOOD	DECOR	SERVICE	COST

Jordan's Lobster Dock *Seafood*
| | 22 | 11 | 17 | $31 |

Sheepshead Bay | 3165 Harkness Ave. (bet. Plumb 2nd & 3rd Sts.) | Brooklyn | 718-934-6300 | www.jordanslobster.com

Locals "pretend they're in Maine" at this "salty" Sheepshead Bay seafooder where live lobsters in "big tanks" make for ultra-"fresh" eating; sure, the "decor's as minimal as the service", but tabs are "dirt cheap" and an on-site retail market means you can "eat your goodies at home."

Joseph Leonard ● *American*
| | 24 | 20 | 23 | $47 |

W Village | 170 Waverly Pl. (Grove St.) | 646-429-8383 | www.josephleonard.com

"Original", "deeply satisfying" takes on New American standards draw "super-cool" folks to Gabe Stulman's West Village "hot spot" that ups the ante with "reasonable" tariffs and open-all-day hours; the "hiply rustic", "lumberjacky" setting is so "tiny" that "crowded" conditions and long "waits" are a given.

Josie's *Eclectic*
| | 20 | 15 | 18 | $35 |

Murray Hill | 565 Third Ave. (37th St.) | 212-490-1558
W 70s | 300 Amsterdam Ave. (74th St.) | 212-769-1212
www.josiesnyc.com

They "do healthy right" at these "mostly organic" Eclectics where the "meats are free-range", the pricing "midrange" and the overall experience "guilt-free"; too bad about the "diner" looks and "hit-or-miss" service, but the "upbeat" mood still draws lots of "chicks" and "children."

Joya ✈ *Thai*
| | 23 | 18 | 19 | $22 |

Cobble Hill | 215 Court St. (bet. Warren & Wyckoff Sts.) | Brooklyn | 718-222-3484 | www.joyanyc.com

Scenes don't get much more "boisterous" or "fun" than at this Cobble Hill Thai where a mix of "awesome" food, "cheap" tabs and "sleek" design attracts "young, hip" throngs; "dance-club" acoustics send regulars to the "more peaceful" back garden, but there's no sidestepping the "so-so service" and "cash-only" rule.

NEW Jungsik ⊠ *Korean*
| | ▽ 26 | 25 | 28 | $122 |

TriBeCa | 2 Harrison St. (Hudson St.) | 212-219-0900 | www.jungsik.kr

"Haute Korean" dining lands in TriBeCa via this "sublime" newcomer offering "innovative", meticulously rendered dishes for an "expensive" price tag; further assets include "flawless service" and the "calming" mien offered by the former Chanterelle space.

Junior's *Diner*
| | 20 | 15 | 18 | $27 |

E 40s | Grand Central | Lower Level (42nd St. & Vanderbilt Ave.) | 212-983-5257
W 40s | Shubert Alley | 1515 Broadway (Enter on 45th St., bet. B'way & 8th Ave.) | 212-302-2000 ●
Downtown Bklyn | 386 Flatbush Ave. Ext. (DeKalb Ave.) | Brooklyn | 718-852-5257 ●
www.juniorscheesecake.com

"You can't get more Brooklyn" than this diner trio famed for its "heavenly cheesecake", though the rest of the standard menu is less ethereal; all branches share "downscale" decor and typically "curt" service, but purists say the Flatbush Avenue original is the "real thing."

	FOOD	DECOR	SERVICE	COST

Junoon *Indian* | 24 | 25 | 24 | $69

Flatiron | 27 W. 24th St. (bet. 5th & 6th Aves.) | 212-490-2100 | www.junoonnyc.com

"Fit for a maharaja", this Flatiron yearling features an appropriately "lavish" setting in which to savor Vikas Khanna's "intriguing" Indian cuisine dispatched by a "sophisticated" crew; be prepared to "drop a bundle" for the privilege, though the $24 prix fixe lunch is a princely "bargain."

Juventino *Eclectic* | ▽ 26 | 23 | 24 | $38

Park Slope | 370 Fifth Ave. (bet. 5th & 6th Sts.) | Brooklyn | 718-360-8469 | www.juventinonyc.com

"Talk about fresh ingredients", you can "almost taste the soil" at this "exceptional" Park Slope Eclectic that's "come out of nowhere to become one of the best restaurants in Brooklyn"; modest prices, "warm" service and a "farmhouse-chic" setting with a "pretty" patio are among the reasons why, though habitués go late to "avoid the strollers."

Kajitsu Ⓜ *Japanese/Vegetarian* | 28 | 23 | 27 | $91

E Village | 414 E. Ninth St. (bet. Ave. A & 1st Ave.) | 212-228-4873 | www.kajitsunyc.com

The atmosphere is "hushed" at this East Village Japanese vegetarian where ancient Buddhist *shojin* cuisine is served kaiseki-style and priced "as if it were Harry Winston jewels"; a "Zen" mood and "phenomenal" service round out the "alternate-universe" experience.

Kang Suh ◑ *Korean* | 23 | 12 | 17 | $36

Garment District | 1250 Broadway (32nd St.) | 212-564-6845

"After-hours" types tout this 30-year-old Garment Center Korean for its "authentic" BBQ, low tabs and "24/7" open-door policy; since it's "not much to look at" and "you'll smell like it when you leave", maybe it's good that the staff "rushes you through your meal."

Kanoyama ◑ *Japanese* | 26 | 16 | 19 | $54

E Village | 175 Second Ave. (bet. 11th & 12th Sts.) | 212-777-5266 | www.kanoyama.com

"Artfully arranged" sushi, including "varieties you don't often see", is the hook at this East Village Japanese "adventure" that seals the deal with tabs that are "reasonable" vis-a-vis the "high quality"; maybe the place "doesn't look like much", but an adjacent sake/oyster bar allows room to spread out.

Kashkaval *Mediterranean* | 23 | 16 | 18 | $28

W 50s | 856 Ninth Ave. (56th St.) | 212-581-8282 | www.kashkavalfoods.com

Despite "small" dimensions, this Hell's Kitchen Med features a "gourmet cheese market" up front plus a "secret" rear wine bar dispensing "quality" fondues and small plates; "cheap" tabs and "candelight" distract from "hole-in-the-wall" looks and iffy service.

Kati Roll Co. *Indian* | 23 | 10 | 15 | $12

🆕 **E 50s** | 229 E. 53rd St. (bet. 2nd & 3rd Aves.) | 212-888-1700
Garment District | 49 W. 39th St. (bet. 5th & 6th Aves.) | 212-730-4280
G Village | 99 MacDougal St. (bet. Bleecker & W. 3rd Sts.) | 212-420-6517 ◑
www.thekatirollcompany.com

"Grab-and-go" Indian street food is the concept at this trio rolling out "mouthwatering" kati wraps assembled from "fragrant ingredients";

"exceptional value" keeps them as "busy as Bombay" at lunchtime, "tacky" settings and "slow" service to the contrary.

Katsu-Hama *Japanese*

FOOD	DECOR	SERVICE	COST
22	13	17	$31

E 40s | 11 E. 47th St. (bet. 5th & Madison Aves.) | 212-758-5909
W 50s | 45 W. 55th St., 2nd fl. (bet. 5th & 6th Aves.) | 212-541-7145
www.katsuhama.com

"Deep-fried comfort food" in pork-cutlet form is the specialty of these Midtown Japanese tonkatsu parlors where the goods are "tender and juicy" and "most of the customers speak the language"; "easy-on-the-pocketbook" tabs trump "not much decor" and "indifferent" service.

☒ Katz's Delicatessen ⌀ *Deli*

25	11	14	$25

LES | 205 E. Houston St. (Ludlow St.) | 212-254-2246 |
www.katzdeli.com

"Borscht Belt" dining doesn't get more "authentic" than at this LES Jewish deli that's been supplying "skyscraping" pastrami and corned beef sandwiches since 1888; true, it's "cash only" with "low-frills" decor and service, but ultimately it's a "completely NY experience", best known for the immortal line 'I'll have what she's having' from *When Harry Met Sally*.

Keens Steakhouse *Steak*

26	25	24	$74

Garment District | 72 W. 36th St. (bet. 5th & 6th Aves.) |
212-947-3636 | www.keens.com

Representing "old NY at its finest", this Garment District "time-traveler's delight" rolls out "superlative" steaks and "brontosaurus-size" mutton chops in a "historic", circa-1885 setting where "Teddy Roosevelt" would feel at home; a "top-flight" single-malt selection and – count 'em – 88,000 clay pipes on the ceiling add to the "unforgettable" feeling; P.S. it also features notable private party rooms.

Kefi *Greek*

23	17	19	$36

W 80s | 505 Columbus Ave. (bet. 84th & 85th Sts.) | 212-873-0200 |
www.kefirestaurant.com

"Pure pleasure" of the "down-home Greek" variety is yours at Michael Psilakis' "big", "boisterous" UWS taverna celebrated for "confident" cooking that's particularly "light on the wallet"; the decor's "simple" and the service "spotty", but most everyone leaves "happy."

Kellari Taverna ● *Greek*

23	22	21	$55

W 40s | 19 W. 44th St. (bet. 5th & 6th Aves.) | 212-221-0144 |
www.kellari.us

"No Greek austerity measures" are in evidence at this "classy" Midtown Hellenic where the "delicious" menu built around "superb fresh fish" is "expensive but not outrageous"; an "airy", flower-filled setting, "perfect lighting" and "hospitable" service round out the "vibrant" picture.

NEW Ken & Cook ● *American*

–	–	–	E

NoLita | 19 Kenmare St. (bet. Bowery & Elizabeth Sts.) |
212-966-3058 | www.kenandcook.com

A Keith McNally–esque, 'industrial brasserie' setting (think subway tiles, bottles galore) sets the hep tone at this NoLita newcomer offering luxe American eats along with a raw bar; French doors opening onto the street lend airiness, while a basement lounge dubbed Li'l Charlie's seals the deal.

	FOOD	DECOR	SERVICE	COST

Keste Pizza e Vino *Pizza*   `25` `15` `20` `$26`

W Village | 271 Bleecker St. (Morton St.) | 212-243-1500 |
www.kestepizzeria.com

Baked "fast and furiously" in a brick oven, the Neapolitan pies at this
West Village pizzeria become "works of art" once the "unusual toppings" are applied; "bare-bones", "phone booth"–size quarters and
some serious "hustle and bustle" make some want to "linger elsewhere."

Kings' Carriage House   *American*   `22` `25` `23` `$64`

E 80s | 251 E. 82nd St. (bet. 2nd & 3rd Aves.) | 212-734-5490 |
www.kingscarriagehouse.com

Best known for its "lovely setting", this UES "hidden treasure" is nestled
in a "romantic" duplex suggesting an "English country house"; the prix
fixe–only New American menu is also "top-drawer", with "gracious"
service, "quiet" decibels and "dainty" afternoon tea as bonuses.

King Yum *Chinese/Polynesian*   `21` `17` `21` `$27`

Fresh Meadows | 181-08 Union Tpke. (181st St.) | Queens |
718-380-1918 | www.kingyumrestaurant.com

At this 1953-vintage Fresh Meadows "institution", "standard suburban" Chinese-Polynesian chow is dispatched in a "hokey", tiki-fied
setting replete with "bamboo walls" and "umbrella drinks"; other winning features include "friendly service" and "old-timey" tabs.

Kin Shop *Thai*   `25` `18` `21` `$49`

W Village | 469 Sixth Ave. (bet. 11th & 12th Sts.) | 212-675-4295 |
www.kinshopnyc.com

"Sophisticated" takes on Thai cuisine turn up at this "aromatic" West
Villager via *Top Chef* star Harold Dieterle, whose cooking is "better
than authentic" and delivered by a "knowledgeable" team; weak spots
include "minimalist" decor and not so minimalist tabs.

Ki Sushi *Japanese*   `25` `20` `21` `$38`

Boerum Hill | 122 Smith St. (bet. Dean & Pacific Sts.) | Brooklyn |
718-935-0575

"Pristine sushi", "innovative rolls" and "clean", minimal looks keep
business booming at this Boerum Hill Japanese that clinches the deal
with "reasonable" prices; throw in "pleasant" service and it's "pretty
much what you want in a neighborhood restaurant."

Kitchenette *Southern*   `20` `16` `17` `$24`

TriBeCa | 156 Chambers St. (bet. Greenwich St. & W. B'way) | 212-267-6740
W 100s | 1272 Amsterdam Ave. (bet. 122nd & 123rd Sts.) | 212-531-7600
www.kitchenetterestaurant.com

"Kitschy" Southern cooking is the specialty of this duo where both the
menus and the portions are "big"; the "cutesy", "small-town" decor
earns mixed response, but all agree on the "rushed" service and low tabs.

🅩 Kittichai *Thai*   `24` `26` `21` `$61`

SoHo | 60 Thompson Hotel | 60 Thompson St. (bet. Broome & Spring Sts.) |
212-219-2000 | www.kittichairestaurant.com

"Stunningly gorgeous", this "dark", "orchid"-laden Siamese in SoHo's
60 Thompson Hotel exudes "movie-set cool" and follows through with
"superior" Thai cooking that "befits the premium pricing"; "killer mixed
drinks" and "trendy" vibes come with the territory.

Knickerbocker Bar & Grill ● *American* `21` `19` `21` `$50`

G Village | 33 University Pl. (9th St.) | 212-228-8490 |
www.knickerbockerbarandgrill.com

"Time warps" don't get more "lovable" than this 1977-vintage Villager,
an "old-school" source of "no-surprises" Americana that's "solid" but
"won't knock your socks off"; though the room's a tad "tattered", "warm"
service and "surprisingly good" weekend jazz make this one a keeper.

Koi *Japanese* `25` `24` `22` `$63`

W 40s | Bryant Park Hotel | 40 W. 40th St. (bet. 5th & 6th Aves.) |
212-921-3330 | www.koirestaurant.com

Fashionable folk feast on "designer" sushi and other "Japanese delicacies" at this "plush" retreat in the Bryant Park Hotel; the "LA vibe" and
"wonderfully snooty" service are a "bit too Beverly Hills" for some, but
all agree it's best to "avoid getting stuck with the bill."

Ko Sushi *Japanese* `22` `16` `20` `$33`

E 70s | 1329 Second Ave. (70th St.) | 212-439-1678 | www.newkosushi.com
E 80s | 1619 York Ave. (85th St.) | 212-772-8838 | www.newkosushi.com
Gramercy | 208 Third Ave. | 212-677-6921 | www.kosushinyc.com 🅢 🅜

"No-frills", separately owned Japanese trio bringing Eastsiders
"tasty" raw fish that's "priced right"; "quick" service makes the
"cafeteria"-like settings more palatable, though aesthetes recom-
mend its "reliable delivery."

Kouzan ● *Japanese* `20` `19` `21` `$35`

W 90s | 685 Amsterdam Ave. (93rd St.) | 212-280-8099 |
www.kouzanny.com

Starting with its "dim lighting" and "serene" feeling, this "pretty"
Upper West Side Japanese "raises expectations" that are met by
"quality" sushi and cooked items, all delivered by a "bend-over-
backwards" team; throw in tabs geared to the "99%" and no wonder it's
such a "neighborhood asset."

🆕 Kristalbelli *Korean* `-` `-` `-` `E`

Garment District | 8 W. 36th St. (bet. 5th & 6th Aves.) |
212-290-2211 | www.kristalbelli.com

K-town goes upscale-trendy via this new haute Korean BBQ duplex
bringing a new twist to the genre with crystal grills employing smoke-
free infrared cooking technology; quality grillables, high-end cocktails
and slick, loungelike looks help explain steep-for-the-zip-code pricing.

🆕 Ktchn *American* `-` `-` `-` `M`

W 40s | The Out NYC | 508 W. 42nd St. (bet. 10th & 11th Aves.) |
212-868-2999 | www.ktchnnyc.com

Set in Way West Hell's Kitchen, this straight-friendly eatery in the
city's first gay hotel serves midpriced, no-surprises New Americana
shuttled by a flirty crew; the oh-so-sleek, white-on-white setting is
nearly as stylish as the crowd.

Kuma Inn ⌘ *Filipino/Thai* `25` `14` `19` `$34`

LES | 113 Ludlow St., 2nd fl. (bet. Delancey & Rivington Sts.) |
212-353-8866 | www.kumainn.com

One of NYC's "best hidden gems", this "obscure" Filipino-Thai accessed
up a flight of LES stairs puts out an "avant-garde" small-plates menu

"exploding with flavor"; the "hole-in-the-wall" digs are "tight", but the "price is right" and "BYO makes it even better."

Kum Gang San ❶ *Korean* | 22 | 16 | 18 | $34 |

Garment District | 49 W. 32nd St. (bet. B'way & 5th Ave.) | 212-967-0909
Flushing | 138-28 Northern Blvd. (bet. Bowne & Union Sts.) | Queens | 718-461-0909
www.kumgangsan.net

These 24/7 "kitsch" palaces sling Korean BBQ in "cavernous" settings equipped with waterfalls and pianos; the "traditional" food is "solid", the decor "age worn" and the service "rush-rush", but it's still "good for first-timers" and "out-of-towners."

Kuruma Zushi ⓈⒷ *Japanese* | ∇ 28 | 16 | 24 | $159 |

E 40s | 7 E. 47th St., 2nd fl. (bet. 5th & Madison Aves.) | 212-317-2802 | www.kurumazushi.com

For an "unparalleled" omakase experience, sit at the bar of this Midtown sushi pioneer and savor chef Toshihiro Uezu's "no-holds-barred" preparations; a "hidden", second-floor address and "understated" mien enhance the mood, but bring your "trust fund" since the prices here are "astronomical."

🆕 Kutsher's *American/Jewish* | 21 | 21 | 21 | $50 |

TriBeCa | 186 Franklin St. (bet. Greenwich & Hudson Sts.) | 212-431-0606 | www.kutsherstribeca.com

"TriBeCa meets the Borscht Belt" at this "Catskills-inspired" newcomer from Jeffrey Chodorow, purveying "upscale versions" of "heartburn-worthy" Jewish-American soul food in "hip", "modern" digs; although it's "noisy" and "not kosher", even traditionalists call it a "nice try."

Kyochon Chicken ❶ *Chicken* | 21 | 16 | 15 | $19 |

Murray Hill | 319 Fifth Ave. (bet. 32nd & 33rd Sts.) | 212-725-9292
Flushing | 156-50 Northern Blvd. (bet. 156th & 157th Sts.) | Queens | 718-939-9292
www.kyochon.com

Fried chicken gets an "oh-so-spicy" Korean spin – and some "soy-garlic" inflections – at these "addictive" Murray Hill–Flushing satellites of the global poultry chain; "modern" food-court design distracts from the "small portions" and tabs that are "a bit pricey for wings."

Kyotofu ❶ *Dessert/Japanese* | 24 | 19 | 20 | $28 |

W 40s | 705 Ninth Ave. (bet. 48th & 49th Sts.) | 212-974-6012 | www.kyotofu-nyc.com

"Most everything is made from tofu" at this Hell's Kitchen Japanese dessert dealer where the "unique", soy-based specialties are both "delicious" and "healthy"; the "creative goings-on" extend to the "contemporary" digs where "tiny" dimensions make for "crowded" conditions.

Kyo Ya ❶ *Japanese* | 27 | 24 | 25 | $97 |

E Village | 94 E. Seventh St., downstairs (1st Ave.) | 212-982-4140 | www.kyoyarestaurant.com

"Keep your mind open" at this subterranean East Village Japanese known for "transcendent", Kyoto-style kaiseki dinners, though à la carte dining is equally "spectacular"; "curvaceous wooden walls" and "hidden doors" bring on the "Zen" vibrations, but be ready to spend a "pretty penny" for the privilege.

	FOOD	DECOR	SERVICE	COST

La Baraka *French* | 24 | 19 | 26 | $45 |

Little Neck | 255-09 Northern Blvd. (2 blocks east of Little Neck Pkwy.) | Queens | 718-428-1461 | www.labarakarest.com

Renowned for the "hospitality" of "lovely hostess" Lucette, this long-standing Little Neck venue follows through with "terrific" Tunisian-accented French fare; though the "cheesy" decor "needs an update", tabs are "reasonable" and the overall mood definitely "enjoyable."

La Bergamote *Bakery/French* | 25 | 17 | 17 | $21 |

Chelsea | 177 Ninth Ave. (20th St.) | 212-627-9010
W 50s | 515 W. 52nd St. (bet. 10th & 11th Aves.) | 212-586-2429
www.labergamotenyc.com

These "buttery" patisserie/cafes supply "high-quality" French pastries that are "gorgeous to look at and just as delicious to taste", plus other savory "light meals"; granted, the service "could use a little help", but "more seating" at the casual Chelsea original draws applause.

La Boîte en Bois *French* | 22 | 15 | 21 | $55 |

W 60s | 75 W. 68th St. (bet. Columbus Ave. & CPW) | 212-874-2705 | www.laboitenyc.com

A longtime "pre-theater favorite" near Lincoln Center, this tiny French boîte turns out "classic" bistro dishes in a "congenial" setting overseen by "fast-moving", curtain time-sensitive staffers; "sardine"-can dimensions, "old-fashioned" decor and steep prices are downsides.

La Bonne Soupe *French* | 19 | 14 | 17 | $33 |

W 50s | 48 W. 55th St. (bet. 5th & 6th Aves.) | 212-586-7650 | www.labonnesoupe.com

"Serviceable" enough for a "quick bite", this 40-year-old Midtown "pinch hitter" is best known for its "divine onion soup", though the rest of its French bistro menu is certainly "reliable"; "brusque" service, "crowded" conditions and "no-frills" looks are blunted by good "value."

La Bottega ● *Italian/Pizza* | 22 | 21 | 19 | $41 |

Chelsea | Maritime Hotel | 88 Ninth Ave. (17th St.) | 212-243-8400 | www.themaritimehotel.com

It's all about the "amazing outdoor terrace" at this lazy-day Italian in the Maritime Hotel where the "simple but delicious" offerings take a backseat to the "trendy" people–watching and "happening" scene; "loud" acoustics and "slow" service are the price of its popularity.

L'Absinthe *French* | 22 | 22 | 21 | $67 |

E 60s | 227 E. 67th St. (bet. 2nd & 3rd Aves.) | 212-794-4950 | www.labsinthe.com

"Toulouse-Lautrec" would feel at home in this "classic" UES brasserie where the "fine food", "attentive service" and *très Gallic* ambiance evoke a "midnight-in-Paris" mood; *bien sûr,* it's "expensive" to "pretend you're in France", but its "upscale crowd" doesn't seem to care.

Lady Mendl's *Teahouse* | 21 | 26 | 23 | $45 |

Gramercy | Inn at Irving Pl. | 56 Irving Pl. (bet. 17th & 18th Sts.) | 212-533-4466 | www.ladymendls.com

Ladies like to live it up à la *Downton Abbey* at this "mahvelous" Gramercy tearoom where "excellent" servers present "tasty" sandwiches and sweets along with "wonderful" brews in an "elegant"

| | FOOD | DECOR | SERVICE | COST |

"Victorian setting"; it's "pricey" whether "your boyfriend" comes or not, but a "pampered afternoon" is the reward.

La Esquina ● *Mexican*   23 | 22 | 18 | $40

Little Italy | 114 Kenmare St. (bet. Cleveland Pl. & Lafayette St.) | 646-613-7100 | www.esquinanyc.com

Café de la Esquina ●Ⓜ *Mexican*

Williamsburg | 225 Wythe Ave. (bet. Metropolitan Ave. & N. 3rd St.) | Brooklyn | 718-393-5500 | www.esquinabk.com

"Straight-up *delicioso*" describes both the food and the scene at this ever-"trendy" Little Italy Mexican comprised of a "dive"-like taqueria, casual indoor/outdoor cafe and "ultracool", hard-to-access underground grotto; the newer Williamsburg spin-off set in a "futuristic retro diner" comes equipped with a "huge outdoor patio."

La Follia *Italian*   22 | 19 | 22 | $40

Gramercy | 226 Third Ave. (19th St.) | 212-477-4100 | www.lafollianyc.com
Whether you land in the up-front enoteca or the rear dining room, the same "terrific" Italian small plates and pastas are available at this "casual" Gramercy "neighborhood place"; fans like the "sincere" service and "affordable" rates, the "no-reservations policy" not so much.

La Fonda del Sol Ⓩ *Spanish*   23 | 21 | 21 | $56

E 40s | MetLife Bldg. | 200 Park Ave. (enter on 44th St. & Vanderbilt Ave.) | 212-867-6767 | www.patinagroup.com
Conveniently sited above Grand Central, this reincarnation of a "classic" '60s Spaniard offers both a "lively after-work bar" serving "upscale tapas" and a "soothing", more "sophisticated" back room; it's "a bit high-priced", but at least the service is "professional."

La Gioconda *Italian*   23 | 18 | 22 | $40

E 50s | 226 E. 53rd St. (bet. 2nd & 3rd Aves.) | 212-371-3536 | www.lagiocondany.com
"Neighborhood" cognoscenti claim this "tiny" Turtle Bay "hideaway" is worth a visit for "fine Italian" fare at moderate tabs served up by a "warm", "attentive" team; it's rather "undiscovered" despite many years in business, and regulars relish the "unrushed" pace.

Ⓩ La Grenouille Ⓩ Ⓜ *French*   28 | 28 | 28 | $114

E 50s | 3 E. 52nd St. (bet. 5th & Madison Aves.) | 212-752-1495 | www.la-grenouille.com
Offering "crème de la crème" haute French dining since 1962, Charles Masson's "unsurpassed" Midtown "bastion" of "indulgence" still provides "ethereal" cuisine served by "flawless" staffers amid "exquisite" surroundings with flowers galore; jackets are de rigueur and, naturally, all this "perfection" commands high prices, but the $40 upstairs lunch deal is a steal; P.S. it also features some of NYC's best private-party rooms.

La Lanterna di Vittorio ● *Italian*   21 | 23 | 20 | $28

G Village | 129 MacDougal St. (bet. W. 3rd & 4th Sts.) | 212-529-5945 | www.lalanternacaffe.com
It's all about the "romantic feel" at this Village Italian "slice of heaven" purveying "enjoyable", "affordable" light bites in "quaint" quarters lit by a fireplace and "lantern-filled" garden; "live jazz" in the adjoining bar adds "first-date" appeal.

	FOOD	DECOR	SERVICE	COST

La Lunchonette *French*　　22　15　20　$43
Chelsea | 130 10th Ave. (18th St.) | 212-675-0342
"It hasn't changed much in all these years, and that's a good thing" say supporters of this "low-key", "fair-priced" West Chelsea bistro; its "divey charm" is just the thing post–"High Line" – and on Sunday night there's a "chanteuse/accordionist."

La Mangeoire *French*　　23　21　22　$55
E 50s | 1008 Second Ave. (bet. 53rd & 54th Sts.) | 212-759-7086 | www.lamangeoire.com
If you "can't get to Provence", check out this next-best-thing Midtowner where chef Christian Delouvrier whips up "imaginative takes on traditional country French dishes"; its "amazing longevity" (since 1975) may be due to the "warm" service and "refreshed" decor.

NEW La Mar Cebicheria *Peruvian*　　24　21　21　$69
Flatiron | 11 Madison Ave. (25th St.) | 212-612-3388 | www.lamarcebicheria.com
The latest link of an international chain, this new Madison Square Park Peruvian offers "excellent" sustainably sourced seafood, with an emphasis on "complex", "blow-your-mind" ceviche; the stylish, bi-level setting (formerly Tabla) includes a "serene" upstairs dining room and more "noisy" ground floor, but expect to drop some "serious cash" wherever you land.

La Masseria ● *Italian*　　23　21　22　$57
W 40s | 235 W. 48th St. (bet. B'way & 8th Ave.) | 212-582-2111 | www.lamasserianyc.com
Showgoers tout this "quick-pace" Hell's Kitchen Southern Italian for its "hearty" cooking, "sweet farmhouse" setting and "fast" service that "gets you to the theater on time"; "crowded" conditions and "pricey-but-worth-the-money" tabs complete the overall appealing picture.

☑ Lambs Club *American*　　24　26　24　$71
W 40s | Chatwal Hotel | 132 W. 44th St. (bet. 6th & 7th Aves.) | 212-997-5262 | www.thelambsclub.com
Slip into a "swanky red leather" booth by the fireplace and savor the "retro-cool" mood at Geoffrey Zakarian's "top-notch" New American in the Theater District's Chatwal Hotel; "crisp" service, "gorgeous deco" decor and a "beautiful upstairs bar" make the expensive tabs easier to digest.

La Méditerranée *French*　　21　17　20　$50
E 50s | 947 Second Ave. (bet. 50th & 51st Sts.) | 212-755-4155 | www.lamediterraneeny.com
"Delicious", "no-surprises" cooking, "friendly service" and "fair prices" have kept this "old-fashioned" Midtown Provençal a "neighborhood favorite" for more than 30 years; few notice the "dated" decor when the nightly pianist is "taking requests."

La Mela ● *Italian*　　22　15　20　$39
Little Italy | 167 Mulberry St. (bet. Broome & Grand Sts.) | 212-431-9493 | www.lamelarestaurant.com
"Belly-busting, multicourse" meals are the backbone of this "old-school Little Italy" vet where the "solid" Southern Italian cooking can be ordered

either à la carte or in family-style prix fixes; maybe the decor "leaves much to be desired", but "service is "prompt" and the pricing "fair."

La Mirabelle *French* | 23 | 19 | 23 | $55

W 80s | 102 W. 86th St. (bet. Amsterdam & Columbus Aves.) | 212-496-0458 | www.lamirabellenyc.com

"True French" cooking endures at this "steady" UWS "favorite" where the "lovely waitresses" sometimes enliven the "quiet" room with an "Edith Piaf" impression; prices are "appropriate", and since it's "not the hippest place in town", expect an "older crowd."

Land *Thai* | 23 | 15 | 19 | $30

E 80s | 1565 Second Ave. (bet. 81st & 82nd Sts.) | 212-439-1847
W 80s | 450 Amsterdam Ave. (bet. 81st & 82nd Sts.) | 212-501-8121
www.landthaikitchen.com

"Big on flavor" but not in decor or size, these crosstown "neighborhood Thais" dispense "top-notch" standards "quick" at "wallet-friendly" rates; since "waits" are the norm at peak times, many elect for "takeout/delivery."

L & B Spumoni Gardens *Dessert/Pizza* | 25 | 13 | 18 | $23

Bensonhurst | 2725 86th St. (bet. W. 10th & 11th Sts.) | Brooklyn | 718-449-6921 | www.spumonigardens.com

"Legendary" Sicilian square pizzas and "spectacular" spumoni deliver the "one-two knockout punch" at this circa-1939 Bensonhurst trip down "memory lane"; despite "long waits", "no decor" and "lackadaisical" service, it remains a "true taste" of old Brooklyn.

Landmarc ◑ *French* | 21 | 21 | 20 | $47

TriBeCa | 179 W. Broadway (bet. Leonard & Worth Sts.) | 212-343-3883
W 60s | Time Warner Ctr. | 10 Columbus Circle, 3rd fl. (60th St. at B'way) | 212-823-6123
www.landmarc-restaurant.com

Relatively "upscale" yet "easygoing", Marc Murphy's "bustling", no-rez, open-till-2-AM French standbys are "landmarks" for "well-done" basics, "extensive" kids' choices and "low-markup" wines; the "understated" TriBeCa original is outshined by the "spacious" TWC spin-off and its "surprisingly affordable" (for the location) tabs and "family-friendly" appeal.

Landmark Tavern ◑ *Pub Food* | 19 | 21 | 19 | $40

W 40s | 626 11th Ave. (46th St.) | 212-247-2562 | www.thelandmarktavern.org

"Around for 140-plus years", this "off-the-beaten-path" Hell's Kitchen tavern is deemed "worth the detour" for the "wonderful" "cozy olde NY" atmosphere alone; "grab a pint" and some "standard" pub grub delivered by a "caring" crew – "they don't make 'em like this anymore."

La Palapa ◑ *Mexican* | 22 | 20 | 22 | $35

E Village | 77 St. Marks Pl. (bet. 1st & 2nd Aves.) | 212-777-2537 | www.lapalapa.com

"High-class Mexican" cuisine "cooked with love" is offered "cheap" and served with "courtesy" at this East Village cantina; the "luscious margaritas" that pack "plenty of punch" take your mind off "scrunched" seating, but "bring ear protection" at peak times.

| | FOOD | DECOR | SERVICE | COST |

La Piazzetta *Italian* ▽ 23 | 20 | 22 | $39
Williamsburg | 442 Graham Ave. (bet. Frost & Richardson Sts.) |
Brooklyn | 718-349-1627 | www.lapiazzettany.com
This "charm"-filled trattoria transports diners away from the "crazi-
ness of Williamsburg" and "back to Italy" with "old-world" comfort
dishes so "authentic" that locals worry the "secret will get out"; it's a
natural for "date night", with "pre-hip prices" heightening the appeal.

La Pizza Fresca Ristorante *Italian/Pizza* ▽ 23 | 18 | 19 | $40
Flatiron | 31 E. 20th St. (bet. B'way & Park Ave. S.) | 212-598-0141 |
www.lapizzafrescaristorante.com
A "granddaddy of the artisan pizza trend", this Flatiron "favorite" turns
out "superior" Neapolitan pies along with "terrific pasta"; "attentive"
staffers with "smiles on all faces" help maintain the "relaxed" mood.

NEW La Promenade 25 | 23 | 22 | $60
des Anglais *French/Italian*
Chelsea | 461 W. 23rd St. (bet. 9th & 10th Aves.) | 212-255-7400 |
www.lapromenadenyc.com
Chef Alain Allegretti brings the French Riviera to Chelsea's London
Terrace at this "haute" new arrival proffering "sumptuous" contemporary niçoise cooking with a seafood focus; "stylish" decor,
"courteous" service and a "high-energy" mood make the "expensive"
tabs easier to swallow.

Z L'Artusi *Italian* 27 | 23 | 24 | $59
W Village | 228 W. 10th St. (bet. Bleecker & Hudson Sts.) |
212-255-5757 | www.lartusi.com
Having mastered *l'art* of being "trendy but welcoming", this "beautiful", "lively" bi-level Village Italian from the Dell'anima folks "packs
'em in" for "delectable" small plates and wines conveyed by "delightful" staffers; despite "high prices" and "off-the-charts" noise, most
find it "totally satisfying."

La Silhouette *French* 25 | 20 | 25 | $74
W 50s | 362 W. 53rd St. (bet. 8th & 9th Aves.) | 212-581-2400 |
www.la-silhouettenyc.com
"Off the beaten path" in Hell's Kitchen, this "serious" French "destination restaurant" wins raves thanks to "terrific" food and an "able" staff;
critics cite "stark" decor, a "labyrinthine" layout and "Le Bernardin
prices", but still like that it's "close to the theaters."

La Sirène ⊅ *French* ▽ 23 | 15 | 22 | $50
Hudson Square | 558½ Broome St. (Varick St.) | 212-925-3061 |
www.lasirenenyc.com
"Decadent" preparations of "traditional" French cuisine shuttled by
"charming" staffers are the lures at this "cozy" (read: "small") Hudson
Square bistro; "tight" seating and a no-plastic policy are offset by a no-
corkage-fee BYO policy that helps keep the tabs more bearable.

Las Ramblas ◑ *Spanish* ▽ 23 | 19 | 21 | $36
W Village | 170 W. Fourth St. (bet. Cornelia & Jones Sts.) |
646-415-7924 | www.lasramblasnyc.com
Like "spending a couple of hours in Barcelona" without the airfare, this
"tiny" Village tapas joint offers "fantastic" tidbits and "delicious san-

"gria" for little *dinero*; staffers "make sure everyone's happy" despite "noisy", crowded conditions, so just "grab a table and start ordering."

La Superior ●⊘⇗ *Mexican* ▽ 25 | 14 | 15 | $22

Williamsburg | 295 Berry St. (bet. S. 2nd & 3rd Sts.) | Brooklyn | 718-388-5988 | www.lasuperiornyc.com

"Fantastic tiny tacos" and offbeat takes on Mexican street food hit the trifecta for "tasty, authentic, cheap" satisfaction at this Williamsburg "standout"; the "cramped", undistinguished setting and cash-only policy don't deter the "hipster" masses from queuing up.

La Taza de Oro ⊠⇗ *Puerto Rican* ▽ 22 | 11 | 19 | $17

Chelsea | 96 Eighth Ave. (bet. 14th & 15th Sts.) | 212-243-9946

"Stick-to-your-ribs" Puerto Rican chow washed down with signature cafe con leche comes at an "unbeatable price" at this Chelsea "old-timer"; the neighborhood may have gone "fancy", but there's been "no decor" here since it opened in 1957.

Lattanzi ● *Italian* 22 | 19 | 21 | $59

W 40s | 361 W. 46th St. (bet. 8th & 9th Aves.) | 212-315-0980 | www.lattanzinyc.com

"A little different from other Italians" on Restaurant Row, this "long-time favorite" serves up "reliable" "standards" in the pre-theater hours, but after 8 PM rolls out an "unusual" menu of "Roman Jewish" dishes; in either mode, its "warm" townhouse setting and "courteous" service help balance "pricey" tabs.

Laut *Malaysian/Thai* 22 | 15 | 19 | $32

Union Sq | 15 E. 17th St. (bet. B'way & 5th Ave.) | 212-206-8989 | www.lautnyc.com

Southeast Asia's "vast variety of flavors" get their due at this Union Square purveyor of "authentic", "crazy-good" dishes from Malaysia, Thailand and beyond; there's "no ambiance" to speak of, but "affordable" tabs and "friendly" service keep things copacetic.

Lavagna *Italian* 24 | 18 | 21 | $47

E Village | 545 E. Fifth St. (bet. Aves. A & B) | 212-979-1005 | www.lavagnanyc.com

At this "unassuming" yet "polished" Alphabet City "gem", "terrific" Tuscan cooking, "attentive" staffers and "cozy, brick-walled" digs work "romantic" wonders; factor in "affordable" prices, and it's no wonder the "tight" digs are "always crowded."

NEW La Vara *Spanish* - | - | - | M

Cobble Hill | 268 Clinton St. (bet. Verandah Pl. & Warren St.) | Brooklyn | 718-422-0065

The folks behind Txikito and El Quinto Pino expand their tapas portfolio into Brooklyn via this cozy Cobble Hill entry whose "delicious" menu highlights the Moorish and Jewish heritage of Southern Spain; while its small plates can run up a *grande* tally, the early word is it's a "must try."

La Vigna *Italian* ▽ 23 | 18 | 21 | $39

Forest Hills | 100-11 Metropolitan Ave. (70th Ave.) | Queens | 718-268-4264 | www.lavignany.com

Merging "local charm" and "big-city quality", this Forest Hills "stand-out" rolls out "excellent" Italian food conveyed by "nice-to-see-you-again" staffers; the "simple" setting is similarly in keeping with the "down-home" neighborhood feel.

La Villa Pizzeria *Pizza* | 23 | 18 | 21 | $27 |

Mill Basin | Key Food Shopping Ctr. | 6610 Ave. U (bet. 66th & 67th Sts.) | Brooklyn | 718-251-8030
Park Slope | 261 Fifth Ave. (bet. 1st St. & Garfield Pl.) | Brooklyn | 718-499-9888
Howard Bch | Lindenwood Shopping Ctr. | 82-07 153rd Ave. (82nd St.) | Queens | 718-641-8259
www.lavillaparkslope.com

These "basic neighborhood red-sauce" joints dish out "first-rate" pizzas along with a "lengthy" roster of "comfort" Italian items; nondescript settings and "loud" acoustics are offset by "modest" tabs.

Lavo ❶ *Italian* | 22 | 22 | 20 | $64 |

E 50s | 39 E. 58th St. (bet. Madison & Park Aves.) | 212-750-5588 | www.lavony.com

It's one "crazy" "scene" at this "pricey" Midtown Italian that rivals nearby sibling Tao as a "meet-and-mingle" hub for "Botox-and-high-heels" types and the "expense-account suits" who love them; just bring "earplugs" and an appetite – the "garlicky" fare is "surprisingly good" – and then "go party" in the "thumping" downstairs club.

Lazzara's 🆇 *Pizza*   ▽ | 23 | 11 | 15 | $20 |

Garment District | 221 W. 38th St., 2nd fl. (bet. 7th & 8th Aves.) | 212-944-7792 | www.lazzaraspizza.com

"Square and superb" sums up the thin-crust pies produced by this "under-the-radar" Garment Distict "staple"; its second-floor "hole-in-the-wall" setting is a "busy" scene at lunch, so plenty procure pies to go.

🆉 Le Bernardin 🆇 *French/Seafood* | 29 | 28 | 29 | $163 |

W 50s | 155 W. 51st St. (bet. 6th & 7th Aves.) | 212-554-1515 | www.le-bernardin.com

Maguy Le Coze and chef Eric Ripert's "best-in-class" Midtown French "seafood shrine" is once again voted NYC's Most Popular and No. 1 for Food because it embodies a "commitment to excellence" across the board, e.g. "delicate", "impossibly fresh" fish dishes, "efficient-beyond-belief" staffers and a "glorious", "soothing" setting (including the non-reserving "godsend" of a lounge); the prix fixe–only dinner starts at $125, but "you pay for the extraordinary – and you get it."

Le Bilboquet *French* | 22 | 19 | 17 | $67 |

E 60s | 25 E. 63rd St. (bet. Madison & Park Aves.) | 212-751-3036

"If you're lucky enough" to get by the "typical French attitude" at the door at this "tiny" UES bistro, you'll be rewarded with "solid", "pricey" cooking and a "trendy" "Euro"-soaked atmosphere; there's prime "people-watching" from lunchtime till late, when "dinner turns to dance party."

🆉 Le Cirque 🆇 *French* | 25 | 26 | 25 | $99 |

E 50s | One Beacon Court | 151 E. 58th St. (bet. Lexington & 3rd Aves.) | 212-644-0202 | www.lecirque.com

To "rub elbows with the upper echelon" there's always Sirio Maccioni's Midtown "landmark", where the "lavish" experience includes "delicious" "haute" French cuisine, "excellent service" and a "playful" yet "elegant" "circus"-themed setting; you'll "need deep pockets" and dapper duds ("jackets required"), but the non-reserving, "more casual" adjunct cafe is lots of fun for a lot less.

L'Ecole *French* | 24 | 20 | 24 | $57 |

SoHo | Intl. Culinary Ctr. | 462 Broadway (Grand St.) | 212-219-3300 | www.lecolenyc.com

"Eager students" "cook for you" at this "charming" International Culinary Center trainer restaurant in SoHo; with "delicious" execution that's "often as good as the pros" and prix fixe menus proffering "excellent value", its "occasional slip-ups" are easy to overlook.

Le Colonial *French/Vietnamese* | 22 | 23 | 21 | $63 |

E 50s | 149 E. 57th St. (bet. Lexington & 3rd Aves.) | 212-752-0808 | www.lecolonialnyc.com

At this "gorgeous" Midtowner you'll be "transported to an exotic place" where the spirit of 1920s "colonial" "Indochine" is in the air and on the plate in the form of "terrific" French-Vietnamese fare; the "old Saigon" sensibility extends to a "comfortable upstairs lounge", though prices are strictly modern-day.

Le Comptoir ●▱ *American/French* | ▽ 23 | 16 | 22 | $44 |

Williamsburg | 251 Grand St. (bet. Driggs Ave. & Roebling St.) | Brooklyn | 718-486-3300 | www.lecomptoirny.com

"Creative" American-French eats delivered by "personable" staffers put the "hipster" crowd in "feel-good" mode at this "funky" Williamsburg bistro; it's cash only and "very small", but pluses like a backyard garden and "all-you-can-drink" brunch help keep the "relaxed" vibes flowing.

Legend *Chinese* | ▽ 22 | 16 | 17 | $33 |

Chelsea | 88 Seventh Ave. (bet. 15th & 16th Sts.) | 212-929-1778 | www.legendrestaurant88.com

"Your mouth won't feel the same" after sampling the "super-hot", "super-good" Sichuan fare at this "spacious", affordable Chelsea Chinese; happy-hour deals at the "A-1 bar" draw a "vibrant crowd", and timid palates should know that it also offers less-fiery food options.

⧆ Le Gigot Ⓜ *French* | 25 | 20 | 25 | $58 |

W Village | 18 Cornelia St. (bet. Bleecker & W. 4th Sts.) | 212-627-3737 | www.legigotrestaurant.com

"Everything's right" at this "petite" West Village "Francophile's dream" bistro where "meticulously prepared" Provençal dishes come via a "superb" staff; granted, seating's "tight" and tabs are "pricey", but it's hard to beat when you seek a "romantic dinner for two."

Le Grainne Cafe ● *French* | ▽ 21 | 18 | 18 | $27 |

Chelsea | 183 Ninth Ave. (21st St.) | 646-486-3000 | www.legrainnecafe.com

A "charming breath of France" blows your way at this "cozy" Chelsea French cafe where "delightful vittles"and birdbath-size café au laits supply "simple" comfort; habitués say the "crowded" digs and "occasionally distracted" service are the trade-off for "feeling transported."

Le Marais *French/Kosher/Steak* | 21 | 16 | 19 | $54 |

W 40s | 150 W. 46th St. (bet. 6th & 7th Aves.) | 212-869-0900 | www.lemarais.net

"If you're a kosher carnivore", this Theater District French "staple" comes through with "excellent steaks" that pass muster with the highest authority; though the service "doesn't match" the food quality and the surrounds are "forgettable", it's generally "packed" all the same.

Lemongrass Grill *Thai* | 20 | 16 | 18 | $26

Murray Hill | 138 E. 34th St. (bet. Lexington & 3rd Aves.) | 212-213-3317
Cobble Hill | 156 Court St. (bet. Dean & Pacific Sts.) | Brooklyn | 718-522-9728

"Pretty standard" is the word on these "acceptable" if "predictable" Thais turning out "consistently ok" chow at "affordable" rates; maybe the interiors "could use refurbishing", but who cares when you can get so much for so little?

☑ Leopard at des Artistes ● *Italian* | 22 | 26 | 23 | $78

W 60s | 1 W. 67th St. (bet. Columbus Ave. & CPW) | 212-787-8767 | www.theleopardnyc.com

The UWS space that once housed Cafe des Artistes has been "beautifully updated" and "reenergized" with the "beloved" Howard Chandler Christy murals "looking brighter than ever" and "honest" Italiana delivered by "skilled" staffers; no wonder "well-heeled" locals and the "Lincoln Center" crowd have returned in droves.

Leo's Latticini 🅂🅼 *Deli/Italian* | 26 | 12 | 23 | $14
(aka Mama's of Corona)

Corona | 46-02 104th St. (46th Ave.) | Queens | 718-898-6069
Mama's of Corona 🅂🅼 *Deli/Italian*
Flushing | Citi Field | 126th St. & Roosevelt Ave. | Queens | No phone

"Nobody makes a sandwich" like this "family-run" Corona "old-school Italian deli" dating to 1920, where the subs are "fit for royalty" and the mozz is among the "best in the boroughs"; its Citi Field stand services "Mets fans" on game day, but unfortunately without those "adorable ladies" behind the counter.

Le Pain Quotidien *Bakery/Belgian* | 20 | 16 | 16 | $23

E 60s | 833 Lexington Ave. (bet. 63rd & 64th Sts.) | 212-755-5810
E 70s | 252 E. 77th St. (bet. 2nd & 3rd Aves.) | 212-249-8600
E 80s | 1131 Madison Ave. (bet. 84th & 85th Sts.) | 212-327-4900
Flatiron | ABC Carpet & Home | 38 E. 19th St. (bet. B'way & Park Ave. S.) | 212-673-7900
G Village | 10 Fifth Ave. (8th St.) | 212-253-2324
G Village | 801 Broadway (11th St.) | 212-677-5277
SoHo | 100 Grand St. (bet. Greene & Mercer Sts.) | 212-625-9009
W 50s | 922 Seventh Ave. (58th St.) | 212-757-0775
W 60s | 60 W. 65th St. (bet. B'way & CPW) | 212-721-4001
W 70s | 50 W. 72nd St. (bet. Columbus Ave. & CPW) | 212-712-9700
www.lepainquotidien.com

For a "fresh", "healthy, organic" "light bite", this Belgian bakery/cafe mini-empire can be depended on for its "fabulous" breads (and "terrific tartine" sandwiches), "wake-you-up" coffee and other "feel-good" basics; communal tables bolster the "rustic" "Euro" vibe, and if service is "slow", there's a location "wherever you turn."

Le Parisien *French* | ∇ 24 | 18 | 24 | $39

Murray Hill | 163 E. 33rd St. (bet. Lexington & 3rd Aves.) | 212-889-5489 | www.leparisiennyc.com

"Teleport" to the "banks of the Seine" via this "cozy", "well-priced" "Paris-in-Murray Hill" French bistro offering "excellent" renditions of "all the classics"; "charming" staffers compensate for "tiny" dimensions and help seal its standing as a local "winner."

Le Perigord *French* `25` `21` `25` `$83`

E 50s | 405 E. 52nd St. (bet. FDR Dr. & 1st Ave.) | 212-755-6244 | www.leperigord.com

"Formidable", this circa-1964 Sutton Place "bastion of formal French dining" feeds your "taste for nostalgia" with classic cuisine "seamlessly" presented under the watch of "host par excellence" Georges Briguet; it's "old school" "down to the last detail" – including the clientele.

Le Pescadeux ◐ Ⓜ *Seafood* `22` `18` `21` `$51`

SoHo | 90 Thompson St. (bet. Prince & Spring Sts.) | 212-966-0021 | www.lepescadeux.com

A slice of Quebec in SoHo, this "relaxed" French-Canadian seafood specialist offers "delicious" midpriced dishes in pairable half-orders, a "catchy" hook that diversifies your meal; "congenial" hospitality and live music some nights enhance the "inviting" ambiance.

Le Relais de Venise L'Entrecôte *French/Steak* `21` `18` `19` `$43`

E 50s | 590 Lexington Ave. (52nd St.) | 212-758-3989 | www.relaisdevenise.com

"Steak frites and salad" are what you'll have at this no-rez Midtown Paris import, because that's basically "all there is" on its "couldn't-be-simpler" $26 set menu; the "tasty" goods arrive with "assembly-line efficiency" via waitresses in "traditional French getups."

Le Rivage *French* `22` `19` `22` `$49`

W 40s | 340 W. 46th St. (bet. 8th & 9th Aves.) | 212-765-7374 | www.lerivagenyc.com

"Good value" abounds at this "old-reliable" (since 1958) Restaurant Row French bistro whose "well-executed" "classics" come in a "pre-theater" package with value rates and an "even better" $25 prix fixe after 8 PM; "warm welcomes" and "dated" digs are part of the deal.

Les Halles *French/Steak* `21` `18` `19` `$48`

Financial District | 15 John St. (bet. B'way & Nassau St.) | 212-285-8585
Murray Hill | 411 Park Ave. S. (bet. 28th & 29th Sts.) | 212-679-4111 ◐
www.leshalles.net

The halles-mark of these "bustling", "unpretentious" French twins are *très bon* steak frites and "reasonable prices"; they're dubbed "Les Yell" for their "noisy" acoustics, but they generally "hit the spot" despite the fact that "you won't see Anthony Bourdain in the kitchen."

Le Veau d'Or Ⓩ *French* `21` `17` `22` `$57`

E 60s | 129 E. 60th St. (bet. Lexington & Park Aves.) | 212-838-8133

"Forgotten classics" of French bistro cuisine work their "throwback" magic on a "clientele that has been coming for decades" to this circa-1937 East Side "charmer"; though it's "had a full life", and it shows, here's hoping it may "continue forever."

🆕 Lexington Brass ◐ *American* ▽ `21` `19` `21` `$44`

E 40s | Hyatt 48 Lex Hotel | 517 Lexington Ave. (48th St.) | 212-392-5976 | www.lexingtonbrass.com

Just north of Grand Central, this big, "casual" brasserie from the EMM Group (Abe & Arthur's, Catch) vends midpriced New American standards to a "business"-oriented crowd from morning till late; its "cool bar" is a magnet for "after-work" sorts and "tourists" resting their feet.

Le Zie 2000 *Italian*   22 | 16 | 20 | $44

Chelsea | 172 Seventh Ave. (bet. 20th & 21st Sts.) | 212-206-8686 | www.lezie.com

"High-end in quality but not in price" sums up the Venetian cuisine at this "lively" Chelsea Italian; regulars suggest the "back room" if "quiet" dining is preferred, and say "beware" the "daily specials" that sell for "much more" than the regular fare.

Lido *Italian*   23 | 21 | 20 | $38

Harlem | 2168 Frederick Douglass Blvd. (117th St.) | 646-490-8575 | www.lidoharlem.com

Harlem denizens declare you "don't need to go Downtown for first-rate Italian food" thanks to this "solid" Uptown player; its "skillfully prepared" dishes are served in "relaxed" environs by "friendly" staffers, with no letup in "quality" during the popular "bottomless-mimosa" brunch.

Liebman's Delicatessen *Deli/Kosher*   22 | 12 | 19 | $24

Riverdale | 552 W. 235th St. (Johnson Ave.) | Bronx | 718-548-4534 | www.liebmansdeli.com

Classic "stacked" sandwiches, matzo ball soup and plenty of "nostalgia" for "a simpler time" are what you'll find at this circa-1953 Bronx kosher Jewish deli; it's "one of the last around", so most don't kvetch about the "worn" setting and variable service from "been-there-forever" staffers.

Lil' Frankie'sPizza *Pizza*   24 | 18 | 19 | $31

E Village | 19 First Ave. (bet. 1st & 2nd Sts.) | 212-420-4900 | www.lilfrankies.com

Really "solid" Italian fare "without frills" at an "affordable price" is the signature of this "casual", cash-only East Villager (sibling of Frank and Supper); it offers "standout" Neapolitan pizzas, late hours and a "garden room", with way-"crowded" peak times as the main detraction.

Lime Jungle *Mexican*   20 | 16 | 17 | $21

W 50s | 741 Ninth Ave. (50th St.) | 212-582-5599
W 50s | 803 Ninth Ave. (bet. 53rd & 54th Sts.) | 212-586-6032
www.limejunglenyc.com

"Standard" Mexican fare and even "better drinks" for an "affordable" price are the attractions at this Hell's Kitchen twosome; they're strictly "no-frills" affairs, but "none are needed" when the tequila starts flowing.

ⓩ Lincoln *Italian*   25 | 26 | 25 | $83

W 60s | Lincoln Ctr. | 142 W. 65th St. (bet. Amsterdam Ave. & B'way) | 212-359-6500 | www.lincolnristorante.com

Its "off-tune opening" long past, this "classy" place housed in a "dramatic" glass wedge on Lincoln Center's campus has "hit its stride", with Jonathan Benno's "first-rate" Modern Italian cuisine – assembled in an "open kitchen" and delivered by "informed" servers – leading the way; despite the "super-size" tabs, there's usually a full house here for "special-occasion" visits.

	FOOD	DECOR	SERVICE	COST

The Lion ❶ *American*   22 | 24 | 21 | $67

G Village | 62 W. Ninth St. (bet. 5th & 6th Aves.) | 212-353-8400 |
www.thelionnyc.com

Chef-owner John DeLucie conjures "old-school" NY at his "swanky"
Village American where a "huge skylight, eclectic art and photos" provide the backdrop for a "happening", "celeb"-centric "scene"; the
"homey-yet-upscale" fare takes a backseat to the "exciting" "buzz",
but it's "delicious" all the same.

NEW Littleneck ⊄ *Seafood*   ▽ 24 | 18 | 21 | $38

Gowanus | 288 Third Ave. (bet. Carroll & President Sts.) | Brooklyn |
718-522-1921 | www.littleneckbrooklyn.com

Who knew a "clam shack could thrive" a block from the Gowanus, but
this New England–style seafooder has already gained a loyal local following for its well-priced shore classics; "friendly" service and a "cute"
rough-hewn setting balance "lack-of-reservations" and cash-only
"pains" in the neck.

Little Owl *American/Mediterranean*   26 | 20 | 23 | $57

W Village | 90 Bedford St. (Grove St.) | 212-741-4695 |
www.thelittleowlnyc.com

Chef-owner Joey Campanaro's "expertly prepared" Med–New American
dishes and his staff's "personalized touches" explain why this West
Villager in a "phone booth"–size space is so "very popular"; with 28
seats and a following that would "happily eat here every night", you'd
better "start dialing now" for a rez.

Little Poland *Diner/Polish*   21 | 9 | 19 | $19

E Village | 200 Second Ave. (bet. 12th & 13th Sts.) | 212-777-9728

"Heaping portions" of "filling" Polish "diner food" comes "cheap as
can be" at this "old-time" cash-only East Village "greasy spoon"; "drab"
the interior may be, but wait till you taste those "perfect pierogis" –
you couldn't do better in Gdansk.

Lobster Box ❶ *Seafood*   20 | 16 | 19 | $47

City Island | 34 City Island Ave. (bet. Belden & Rochelle Sts.) | Bronx |
718-885-1952 | www.lobsterboxrestaurant.com

City Island's veteran dockside seafooder supplies a "super view" of
Long Island Sound as a backdrop for the shore meals that are "decent"
but not fine dining"; prepare to "wait on line" because both "tourists"
and locals like being netted here.

Locale *Italian*   ▽ 21 | 22 | 21 | $38

Astoria | 33-02 34th Ave. (33rd St.) | Queens | 718-729-9080 |
www.localeastoria.com

As its moniker suggests, this midpriced Astoria Italian "neighborhood"
spot serves "cut-above-normal" fare in a "pleasant", "SoHo"-like
space; its "friendly" staff, enticing bar and weekend brunch are additional assets rendering it "worth a try."

Locanda Verde *Italian*   25 | 23 | 21 | $63

TriBeCa | Greenwich Hotel | 377 Greenwich St. (N. Moore St.) |
212-925-3797 | www.locandaverdenyc.com

"Vibrant" and "celeb"-studded, this "sceney" TriBeCan is also home to
"seriously good" eating thanks to Andrew Carmellini's "terrific riffs"

on classic Italian cuisine, delivered by "helpful" servers; its rep as a "difficult reservation", "way-loud" acoustics and "pricey" tabs deter few.

Locanda Vini & Olii ⓜ *Italian* | 26 | 26 | 25 | $53 |

Clinton Hill | 129 Gates Ave. (bet. Cambridge Pl. & Grand Ave.) | Brooklyn | 718-622-9202 | www.locandany.com

"Marvelous" Northern Italian food comes in "converted-old-drugstore" digs at this Clinton Hill "find" run by a "knowledgeable" team that "takes pride" in its work; in short, the "lovely" "vintage" setting, "really friendly" staff and "eclectic" eats are a prescription for "top-notch" dining.

NEW Loi *Greek* | 22 | 23 | 22 | $59 |

W 70s | 208 W. 70th St. (bet. Amsterdam & West End Aves.) | 212-875-8600 | www.restaurantloi.com

"High-quality", "high-priced" Greek cuisine with a "healthy" spin and "gracious" chef-owner Maria Loi's signature "personal touch" are the hook at this "classy addition" to the UWS dining scene; "spacious", "comfortable" quarters "close to Lincoln Center" seal the deal.

Lombardi's ⊘ *Pizza* | 25 | 16 | 18 | $25 |

NoLita | 32 Spring St. (bet. Mott & Mulberry Sts.) | 212-941-7994 | www.firstpizza.com

Pie mavens say this NoLita "landmark" for "coal-fired", "thin-crust" pizzas still cranks out the "real McCoy", "end of story"; the epilogue, then, is that it's cash-only with "ridiculous waits" because "tourists" "can't say they were in NYC" without dropping by.

Lomzynianka ⊘ *Polish* | ▽ 24 | 13 | 18 | $20 |

Greenpoint | 646 Manhattan Ave. (bet. Nassau & Norman Aves.) | Brooklyn | 718-389-9439 | www.lomzynianka.com

It's "classic Greenpoint" at this local "treasure" dishing up "wonderful" Polish home cooking that "rises above" the "modest" decor; the BYO policy and "astonishingly reasonable prices" mean "you can't go wrong" here – except when you try to pronounce the name.

London Lennie's *Seafood* | 24 | 18 | 21 | $45 |

Rego Park | 63-88 Woodhaven Blvd. (bet. Fleet Ct. & Penelope Ave.) | Queens | 718-894-8084 | www.londonlennies.com

"You don't survive in NYC for 50 years unless you're really good", and this circa-1959 Rego Park fish "favorite" sticks to its winning combo of the "freshest seafood", "fair prices" and genuine hospitality; maybe it's "showing its age" a bit, but "there's a reason it's always crowded."

Lorenzo's *Italian* | ▽ 22 | 23 | 21 | $49 |

Bloomfield | Hilton Garden Inn | 1100 South Ave. (Lois Ln.) | Staten Island | 718-477-2400 | www.lorenzosdining.com

"Food and entertainment" go hand in hand at this SI Italian in Bloomfield, whose "weekend cabarets" and "jazz brunch" are big hits with "locals" looking for a "classy" outing "without city hassles"; its hosts also rate high, but grumbles about "uneven" cuisine persist.

Loukoumi Taverna *Greek* | ▽ 24 | 20 | 23 | $32 |

Astoria | 45-07 Ditmars Blvd. (bet. 45th & 46th Sts.) | Queens | 718-626-3200 | www.loukoumitaverna.com

"Excellent", "authentic" taverna fare leads the charge at this "warm and inviting" Astoria Greek; it's located "a bit away" from the main neighborhood action, but "affordable" tabs and a back garden clinch the "good-on-all-counts" endorsement.

	FOOD	DECOR	SERVICE	COST

Z Lucali ℗ *Pizza* 27 | 19 | 20 | $27

Carroll Gardens | 575 Henry St. (bet. Carroll St. & 1st Pl.) | Brooklyn | 718-858-4086

An "unwavering focus on creating the perfect pie" pays off at this "big-league" BYO Carroll Gardens joint that nabs this year's No. 1 Pizza in NYC crown; devotees gladly endure no rez–induced "long waits" and a cash-only policy, 'cause these "brick-oven" beauties are "all they're cracked up to be."

Lucien ⦿ *French* 23 | 17 | 21 | $49

E Village | 14 First Ave. (1st St.) | 212-260-6481 | www.luciennyc.com

"Charming" owner Lucien Bahaj's East Village French "favorite" "still delivers" with "first-rate bistro" classics and a "convivial" vibe that "take you to Paris in a flash"; ok, it's on the "cramped" side, but tell that to its regulars who "leave with a smile every time."

Lucky's Famous Burgers ⦿ *Burgers* 22 | 12 | 18 | $15

Chelsea | 264 W. 23rd St. (bet. 7th & 8th Aves.) | 212-242-4900
LES | 147 E. Houston St. (bet. Eldridge & Forsyth Sts.) | 212-254-4900
W 50s | 370 W. 52nd St. (bet. 8th & 9th Aves.) | 212-247-6717
www.luckysfamousburgers.com

For a "decent" burger that'll "fill you up" on a "budget" at just about any hour, this "fast-food-type" franchise "does the trick"; most say "takeout" is the way to go, unless "tacky" "bright-red-and-yellow" interiors are your thing.

Luke's Lobster *Seafood* 24 | 11 | 17 | $24

E 80s | 242 E. 81st St. (bet. 2nd & 3rd Aves.) | 212-249-4241
E Village | 93 E. Seventh St. (bet. Ave. A & 1st Ave.) | 212-387-8487
Financial District | 26 S. William St. (Stone St.) | 212-747-1700
NEW W 50s | Plaza Food Hall | 1 W. 59th St., lower level (5th Ave.) | 646-755-3227
W 80s | 426 Amsterdam Ave. (bet. 80th & 81st Sts.) | 212-877-8800
www.lukeslobster.com

"The simpler the better" is the ethos at these "bare-bones" New England–style seafood "shacks" dispensing "luscious" lobster rolls that showcase "fresh-off-the-boat" catch "unadulterated" by "fillers"; given the "minimal seating", "Maine-iacs" in the know often "take it to go."

Luna Piena *Italian* 23 | 19 | 23 | $52

E 50s | 243 E. 53rd St. (bet. 2nd & 3rd Aves.) | 212-308-8882 | www.lunapienanyc.com

Midtown "office" folk and "locals" alike say "you can't go wrong" at this midpriced Italian "gem" where "winning" dishes arrive via "attentive" staffers who "go out of their way" to please; maybe the garden-equipped setting's a bit "unprepossessing", but most call the overall experience "genuinely nice."

Lunetta Ⓜ *Italian* ▽ 22 | 17 | 20 | $38

Boerum Hill | 116 Smith St. (bet. Dean & Pacific Sts.) | Brooklyn | 718-488-6269 | www.lunetta-ny.com

This "cozy" Boerum Hill Italian "keeps things interesting" with a menu of "seasonal" midpriced small plates that are "crafted with care"; the accommodations feature a "kitchen bar" where you can "watch the chef" work, as well as a garden in back.

Lupa ● *Italian*   25 | 18 | 21 | $56

G Village | 170 Thompson St. (bet. Bleecker & Houston Sts.) | 212-982-5089 | www.luparestaurant.com

The "unpretentious" "workhorse of the Batali restaurant empire", this "convivial" Village Italian "gets it right" with "so simple, so delicious" Roman cuisine and "excellent wines" served by a "friendly" crew; the "small" space is way "overcrowded", though, so "make a reservation" to avoid a "long wait" – or go at "not-nearly-as-crazy" lunch.

Lure Fishbar *Seafood*   23 | 23 | 21 | $57

SoHo | 142 Mercer St., downstairs (Prince St.) | 212-431-7676 | www.lurefishbar.com

This "yacht"-themed SoHo fish joint is popular with "sceney" types who dig the "bumpin'" atmosphere as much as the "top-quality" fin fare; "intense noise" levels make it a "no-go for quiet conversation", and while it's surely "cheaper than going on a cruise", a bargain it ain't.

Lusardi's ● *Italian*   24 | 20 | 23 | $64

E 70s | 1494 Second Ave. (bet. 77th & 78th Sts.) | 212-249-2020 | www.lusardis.com

With "top-notch" fare and a staff whose "first priority is the customer", Mario Lusardi's "well-run" UES Italian is "still a champ" "after all these years"; factor in the "old-world ambiance" and no wonder it's a favorite among "locals" who've "got a few bucks" to throw down.

Luz *Nuevo Latino*   ▽ 23 | 19 | 21 | $36

Fort Greene | 177 Vanderbilt Ave. (bet. Myrtle Ave. & Willoughby St.) | Brooklyn | 718-246-4000 | www.luzrestaurant.com

Nuevo Latino dishes sporting "interesting flavor combos" team up with "great" cocktails to deliver "reasonably priced" good times at this Fort Greene find; granted, it's "slightly out of the way", but fans say it's "worth the trip" for a "zesty" meal in "cool", "unpretentious" environs.

Luzzo's *Pizza*   27 | 16 | 19 | $30

E Village | 211 First Ave. (bet. 12th & 13th Sts.) | 212-473-7447

Thin-crust pies pulled from "one of the few coal-burning ovens" still operating in NYC make this East Villager a "leading" contender in the city's "ongoing pizza war"; if it weren't for the "not-very-comfortable" digs and "harried" scene, groupies might just "live in this place."

Lychee House *Chinese*   23 | 18 | 21 | $39

E 50s | 141 E. 55th St. (bet. Lexington & 3rd Aves.) | 212-753-3900 | www.lycheehouse.com

Ranking a "notch above most", this Midtown Chinese BYO offers a "wide variety" of "well-prepared", well-priced chow including "fine Shanghainese and Malaysian" dishes as well as "inventive dim sum"; aside from "waiters in tuxes", ambiance ain't the focus here.

Lyon *French*   19 | 18 | 18 | $50

W Village | 118 Greenwich Ave. (13th St.) | 212-242-5966 | www.lyonnyc.com

Francophiles weary of Parisian-style bistros turn to this "casual" West Village wedge modeled after a "classic" Lyonnaise bouchon serving

| | FOOD | DECOR | SERVICE | COST |

"hearty" classic dishes; while some call it "*charmant*", others find it "uneven" and "oh-so-noisy."

Mable's Smoke House *BBQ*
▽ 24 | 18 | 19 | $27

Williamsburg | 44 Berry St. (enter on N. 11th St. bet. Berry St. & Wythe Ave.) | Brooklyn | 718-218-6655 | www.mablessmokehouse.com

Get your "BBQ fix" at this "spacious", "laid-back" West Williamsburg joint where the "plentiful" ribs, brisket and pulled pork pack "bold and robust flavor" and are "priced just right"; "cafeteria-style ordering" and "shared tables" bolster the "transports-you-to-Tennessee" vibe.

Macao Trading Co. ❶ *Chinese/Portuguese*
20 | 24 | 19 | $54

TriBeCa | 311 Church St. (bet. Lispenard & Walker Sts.) | 212-431-8750 | www.macaonyc.com

Channeling a "1940s" "Macao gambling parlor", this "dazzling" bi-level TriBeCan offers plentiful "eye candy" to go with its "well-crafted cocktails" and Chinese-Portuguese small plates; in later hours it turns "club"-like – "loud and crowded" with uneven service – but most are having too much "fun" to care.

Macelleria ❶ *Italian/Steak*
23 | 21 | 21 | $56

Meatpacking | 48 Gansevoort St. (bet. Greenwich & Washington Sts.) | 212-741-2555 | www.macelleria.com

"When you want some pasta with your steak" there's this "buzzy" Meatpacking District Italian chophouse whose "unadorned" fare "doesn't disappoint" but also "doesn't come cheap"; it boasts a "witty butcher theme" indoors, and the alfresco seating affords prime "MPD crowd" watching.

Macondo ❶ *Pan-Latin*
▽ 23 | 20 | 22 | $41

LES | 157 E. Houston St. (bet. Allen & Eldridge Sts.) | 212-473-9900 | www.macondonyc.com

Pan-Latin "street food at its best" comes in "lively" environs at this "friendly" Lower Eastsider where small plates "packed with flavor" meet "tropical" cocktails "made to perfection"; it hosts a *muy* "happening bar scene", so be ready for "crowds and noise."

Mad Dog & Beans ❶ *Mexican*
20 | 18 | 17 | $31

Financial District | 83 Pearl St. (bet. Coenties Slip & Hanover Sq.) | 212-269-1177 | www.maddogandbeans.com

Among the Financial District's "only Mexican" options, this "festive after-work scene" serves up "fab guac" and "even better margaritas", plus other "decent" standards; it's "dark and noisy" with "so-so service", but all's forgiven "during summer" when you sit out on "the Stone Street strip."

Madiba ❶ *S African*
24 | 24 | 21 | $30

Fort Greene | 195 DeKalb Ave. (Carlton Ave.) | Brooklyn | 718-855-9190 | www.madibarestaurant.com

For a rare "real taste of South Africa", hit this "unassuming, relaxed" Fort Greene "hangout" that feels "like a vacation" thanks to its "cool" eclectic look, "comforting", "affordable" fare and "warm" service (just "don't be in a rush"); regulars note it's "*the* place to watch futbol/World Cup games."

Madison Bistro *French*

| 20 | 17 | 20 | $50 |

Murray Hill | 238 Madison Ave. (bet. 37th & 38th Sts.) |
212-447-1919 | www.madisonbistro.com

"Every neighborhood should have" a "local bistro" like this Murray Hill
"sleeper" that's appreciated for its "quality" French classics and prix
fixe deals; "well-behaved" locals are drawn to its "friendly" vibe and
"relaxing" (if "generic") room "conducive to conversation."

Madison's *Italian*

| 20 | 18 | 20 | $40 |

Riverdale | 5686 Riverdale Ave. (259th St.) | Bronx | 718-543-3850

"One of the more upscale" options on Riverdale's "main drag", this
"popular" Italian fallback features "fresh, well-prepared" fare delivered by an "attentive" crew, justifying the "slightly pricey" tab; those
who "don't want to go" to Manhattan call it a "safe" bet.

Maggie Brown ⊐ *American*

| ∇ 23 | 19 | 20 | $25 |

Clinton Hill | 455 Myrtle Ave. (bet. Washington & Waverly Aves.) |
Brooklyn | 718-643-7001 | www.maggiebrownrestaurant.com

"Dinner's not bad", but it's the "brunch done right" – "comfort"-oriented
Americana "recalling mom, if she went to culinary school" – that draws
the "mobs" to this "relaxed", "cash-only" Clinton Hill "hangout"; the
"clever package" includes "spot-on" prices, "funky" "retro-homey"
digs with a "lovely garden" and "friendly" "bohemian" service.

NEW Maharlika ⊐ *Filipino*

| ∇ 26 | 23 | 23 | $34 |

E Village | 111 First Ave. (bet. 6th & 7th Sts.) | 646-392-7880 |
www.maharlikanyc.com

"Beautiful, tasty", porkalicious Filipino classics "with modern flair"
plus "strong" cocktails add up to a "hopping" scene at this "somewhat
upscale" East Village storefront; factor in "enthusiastic" service and
low prices, and "you can't go wrong."

Ⓩ Maialino *Italian*

| 26 | 23 | 25 | $66 |

Gramercy | Gramercy Park Hotel | 2 Lexington Ave. (21st St.) |
212-777-2410 | www.maialinonyc.com

"Maestro" Danny Meyer "hits all the right notes" at this "energetic"
take on the Roman trattoria, where "soul-satisfying" Italiana (including the eponymous roast baby pig) and trademark "informed, caring"
service come in "comfortable" environs that "strike the right balance
between casual and formal"; yes, the "check's a little steep" and it's
"tough to get a rez", but it's an NYC "must."

Malagueta Ⓜ *Brazilian*

| ∇ 24 | 16 | 21 | $36 |

Astoria | 25-35 36th Ave. (28th St.) | Queens | 718-937-4821 |
www.malaguetany.com

"You'll have to search" to find this "family-owned" "little gem" in
"residential" Astoria, but its "delicious" "real-deal" Brazilian fare is
deemed "well worth the effort"; the "small storefront" digs are "nothing fancy", but "friendly" service and "reasonable" prices add value.

Malatesta Trattoria ◑⊐ *Italian*

| 25 | 18 | 20 | $37 |

W Village | 649 Washington St. (Christopher St.) | 212-741-1207 |
www.malatestatrattoria.com

"Wonderful", "honest trattoria-style" staples at "reasonable" cash-
only rates mean this "friendly" "far West Village" Italian remains

"popular" enough to justify "long waits"; the "simple" interior gets "crowded and noisy", but in summer there's "sidewalk dining."

Maloney & Porcelli *Steak* | 24 | 20 | 23 | $70 |

E 50s | 37 E. 50th St. (bet. Madison & Park Aves.) | 212-750-2233 | www.maloneyandporcelli.com
Alan Stillman's circa-1996 East Midtown steakhouse recently got a "fantastic" top-to-tail overhaul, ushering in a retro "old-school chophouse" vibe worthy of a "scene from *Mad Men*"; the "superb pork shank" remains, as do "business-class prices", but a roaming martini cart, tableside presentations and a parade of desserts add new excitement.

Mamajuana Cafe *Dominican/Nuevo Latino* | 21 | 21 | 19 | $39 |

NEW E 40s | 134 E. 48th St. (bet. Lexington & 3rd Aves.) | 212-421-1116 ●
Inwood | 247 Dyckman St. (bet. Payson & Seaman Aves.) | 212-304-0140 ●
NEW W 80s | 570 Amsterdam Ave. (bet. 87th & 88th Sts.) | 212-362-1514
NEW Woodside | 33-15 56th St. (bet. B'way & Northern Blvd.) | Queens | 718-565-6454 ●
www.mamajuana-cafe.com
Admirers advise "go hungry" to these "inviting" Dominican-Nuevo Latino cafes since they serve "delish" fare with "modern flair"; a "lively" scene fueled by "fantastic" sangria makes for "fun times", especially in summer in the Inwood original's sidewalk seating area.

Mandoo Bar *Korean* | 20 | 11 | 16 | $21 |

Garment District | 2 W. 32nd St. (bet. B'way & 5th Ave.) | 212-279-3075
"Man oh mandoo" - the "freshest" "fast and fab" dumplings "made in front of you" are the main event at this "reliable" Garment District Korean; its "no-decor" digs are "small" and "often crowded", but "cheap" prices compensate.

Manducatis *Italian* | 23 | 16 | 21 | $44 |

LIC | 13-27 Jackson Ave. (47th Ave.) | Queens | 718-729-4602 | www.manducatis.com

Manducatis Rustica *Italian*

LIC | 46-33 Vernon Blvd. (bet. 46th & 47th Sts.) | Queens | 718-937-1312 | www.manducatisrustica.com
Like a "visit to the old country", this "warm", "family-run" LIC Italian supplies "wonderful" "homestyle" fare and wines from a "very deep" list; yes, the look may be "dated", but loyalists say that only "adds to the charm"; pizza and gelato highlight the "scaled-down" Rustica offshoot.

Manetta's 🛇 *Italian* | 23 | 18 | 21 | $38 |

LIC | 10-76 Jackson Ave. (49th Ave.) | Queens | 718-786-6171
"Delish" Italiana "straight out of nonna's kitchen" - including "fantastic" "wood-fired" pizza - and service that's "all smiles" have locals calling this LIC "mainstay" the "perfect neighborhood restaurant"; "family-run" and kid-friendly, it "exudes a comfort factor", especially in winter before the fireplace.

Manzo *Italian/Steak* | 26 | 16 | 22 | $72 |

Flatiron | Eataly | 200 Fifth Ave. (bet. 23rd & 24th Sts.) | 212-229-2180 | www.eataly.com
The sole "white-tablecloth" option within the Batali-Bastianich team's Flatiron "foodie mecca", Eataly, this "carnivore heaven" presents a

"*delizioso*" beef-centric Italian menu that also features "wonderful fresh pastas"; being located in a "bustling", "noisy" market is "not the sexiest", and "you pay for the privilege" – but to most it's "worth every hard-earned penny."

Maoz Vegetarian   *Mideastern/Vegetarian*

22 | 11 | 16 | $12

NEW **E 100s** | Central Park | Harlem Meer, 5th Ave. & 106th St. | No phone
G Village | 59 E. Eighth St. (Mercer St.) | 212-420-5999
Union Sq | 38 Union Sq. E. (bet. 16th & 17th Sts.) | 212-260-1988
W 40s | 558 Seventh Ave. (40th St.) | 212-777-0820 ◗
W 40s | 683 Eighth Ave. (bet. 43rd & 44th Sts.) | 212-265-2315 ◗
W 70s | 2047 Broadway (enter on Amsterdam Ave., bet. 70th & 71st Sts.) | 212-362-2622 ◗
W 100s | 2857 Broadway (bet. 110th & 111th Sts.) | 212-222-6464
www.maozusa.com

A welcome "upgrade" to the "fast-food" genre, this "efficient" Mideastern-vegetarian mini-chain specializes in "absolutely delicious" falafels and salads customized at an "all-you-can-fit-in-the-pita" toppings bar; seating is "limited" and the surroundings "spartan", but maoz don't mind given the "dirt-cheap" prices.

Má Pêche   *American*

24 | 19 | 20 | $61

W 50s | Chambers Hotel | 15 W. 56th St. (bet. 5th & 6th Aves.) | 212-757-5878 | www.momofuku.com

Momofuku magnate David Chang's "civilized", pricey Midtowner has a new chef and a revamped New American menu, but its promise of a "top-shelf" "gastronomic adventure" remains; opinions split over the "cavernous" space ("lovely, dramatic" vs. "spartan", "odd"), ditto the "interesting play list", but all approve of the Milk Bar's "guilty pleasures" available "on the way out."

Marble Lane ◗   *Steak*

▽ 23 | 27 | 20 | $66

Chelsea | Dream Downtown Hotel | 355 W. 16th St. (bet. 8th & 9th Aves.) | 212-229-2559 | www.dreamdowntown.com

"Gorgeous", "chic" nightclub-esque digs and *Top Chef* alum Manuel Treviño's "fine aged" meat draw "models and scenesters" to this under-the-radar steakhouse in Chelsea's Dream Downtown Hotel; the only beefs are variable service and "high prices."

Marc Forgione   *American*

25 | 23 | 24 | $71

TriBeCa | 134 Reade St. (bet. Greenwich & Hudson Sts.) | 212-941-9401 | www.marcforgione.com

"Iron Chef" Marc Forgione "takes comfort food to a new level" at this "candlelit, characterful" TriBeCa New American with an "upscale lodge" feel, overseen by a "thoughtful" staff; it's a "perfect date" place – just book far ahead and plan on a "pricey" tab, and know that the "crowded bar" can be "noisy."

Marcony   *Italian*

26 | 23 | 26 | $67

Murray Hill | 184 Lexington Ave. (bet. 31st & 32nd Sts.) | 646-837-6020 | www.marconyusa.com

When an "Italian vacation" isn't in the cards, there's this "Murray Hill standout" whose "fantastic" classic dishes and "service to match" come in "transporting" "Capri-comes-to-NY" quarters; it's an "all-around wonderful dining experience" that justifies the "pricey" tab and the trip to an out-of-the-way block.

			FOOD	DECOR	SERVICE	COST

Marco Polo Ristorante Ⓜ *Italian* ▽ 22 | 19 | 22 | $44

Carroll Gardens | 345 Court St. (Union St.) | Brooklyn |
718-852-5015 | www.marcopoloristorante.com

A Carroll Gardens "tradition" for 30 years, this "throwback" specializes in "old-school Sunday dinner"–type Italiana served in "comfortable", fireplace-equipped digs with a pianist on weekends; "gracious"
servers cement the "great old Brooklyn feel."

❷ Marea *Italian/Seafood* 28 | 26 | 26 | $103

W 50s | 240 Central Park S. (bet. B'way & 7th Ave.) | 212-582-5100 |
www.marea-nyc.com

Chef Michael White presents an "unforgettable fine-dining experience" at this "world-class" CPS "treasure", once again voted NYC's
No. 1 Italian thanks to its "incomparable" seafood and housemade
pastas, seamless service and "chic", "modern" environs; it's a "definite splurge" – though it's "equally superb and less costly" at lunch,
brunch or at the "gorgeous bar", with "celeb" spottings as a bonus.

Maria Pia *Italian* 20 | 17 | 20 | $40

W 50s | 319 W. 51st St. (bet. 8th & 9th Aves.) | 212-765-6463 |
www.mariapianyc.com

"Geared to the pre-theater crowd", this "reliable" Hell's Kitchen "red-
sauce joint" keeps 'em coming back with "quick" service, "reasonable"
rates (especially the $25 dinner prix fixe) and a "charming garden";
non-showgoers hit it "off-hours" to avoid the "noisy" crush.

Marina Cafe *Seafood* 21 | 22 | 20 | $44

Great Kills | 154 Mansion Ave. (Hillside Terr.) | Staten Island |
718-967-3077 | www.marinacafegrand.com

"Beautiful" water views and "delicious" catch are the main draws at
this "charming" seafooder on SI's Great Kills Harbor; "hot summer
evenings" are "best on the deck" where there's a tiki bar and live music,
but the $24 weeknight early-bird "can't be beat" at any time of year.

Marinella *Italian* 21 | 15 | 21 | $46

W Village | 49 Carmine St. (Bedford St.) | 212-807-7472

"Stands the test of time" say loyalists of this West Village vet serving up
"consistent, comforting", "value"-priced Italian staples via "welcoming" waiters; "cozy and old-fashioned", it's "like having Sunday dinner
at grandma's" – but with a "rolling blackboard listing the specials."

Mario's Ⓜ *Italian* 23 | 17 | 22 | $41

Fordham | 2342 Arthur Ave. (bet. 184th & 186th Sts.) | Bronx |
718-584-1188 | www.mariosrestarthurave.com

An "iconic red-sauce" Bronx "experience", this "family-run" Neapolitan
along the "bustling" Arthur Avenue "tourist strip" "never steers you
wrong"; "old-time waiters" working the "no-pretense" digs ensure
regulars remain in their "comfort zone."

Mari Vanna ◑ *Russian* 21 | 25 | 22 | $60

Flatiron | 41 E. 20th St. (bet. B'way & Park Ave. S.) | 212-777-1955 |
www.marivanna.ru

Like "stepping into your grandmother's house in Moscow" – but with a
"party vibe fueled by "flowing vodka" – this "fabulous" Flatiron
magnet for "expats" and "beautiful young things" serves up "hearty",

"babushka"-worthy Russian staples; "attentive" service and a "unique-in-NY" experience help justify the "pricey" tab.

Market Table *American*

W Village | 54 Carmine St. (Bedford St.) | 212-255-2100 | www.markettablenyc.com

As the name implies, this West Villager spotlights "farmer's market-fresh" ingredients on its "up-to-date" New American menu; the "bustling" room with "huge windows" overlooking the passing scene is on the "tight" and "noisy" side, but "friendly" staffers help keep things "comfy."

MarkJoseph Steakhouse *Steak*
24 | 19 | 22 | $73
Financial District | 261 Water St. (bet. Dover St. & Peck Slip) | 212-277-0020 | www.markjosephsteakhouse.com

Pack a "huuuge appetite" and "corporate card" to best enjoy this "out-of-the-way" FiDi meatery; "no-frills", "standard steakhouse" digs put the focus on the "outstanding" beef (and "even better" bacon appetizer) delivered by "knowledgeable" staffers; P.S. "lunch is a better value."

The Mark Restaurant 🌑 *American*
23 | 25 | 23 | $77
E 70s | Mark Hotel | 25 E. 77th St. (bet. 5th & Madison Aves.) | 212-606-3030 | www.jean-georges.com

Catering to the "UES upper crust", this "posh" hoteler from Jean-Georges Vongerichten keeps its "see-and-be-seen" crowd content with "excellent", "pricey" New American cuisine well served in "quiet" confines; still, some say the "hopping" bar crowd is "having more fun."

Markt *Belgian*
20 | 17 | 18 | $43
Flatiron | 676 Sixth Ave. (21st St.) | 212-727-3314 | www.marktrestaurant.com

There's "nothing fishy" about this "thriving" Flatiron brasserie, just "mussels in excelsis" and other "simple", "tasty" Belgian staples backed by a "gazillion excellent beers"; it's a "busy, loud" room and service can be "hurried", but that's just part of the "fun" package.

Marlow & Sons 🌑 *American*
25 | 19 | 21 | $43
Williamsburg | 81 Broadway (bet. Berry St. & Wythe Ave.) | Brooklyn | 718-384-1441 | www.marlowandsons.com

"Pitch-perfect", "farm-fresh" New Americana from a "limited", "daily changing" lineup is the lure at this "welcoming" Williamsburg pioneer that still packs plenty of "hipster" cred; the "rustic", micro-size confines can be "cramped", so many angle to "sit outside."

Marseille *French/Mediterranean*
21 | 20 | 20 | $48
W 40s | 630 Ninth Ave. (bet. 44th & 45th Sts.) | 212-333-2323 | www.marseillenyc.com

"Solid", relatively "affordable" French-Med brasserie classics delivered "quickly" make this "dependable" Hell's Kitchen vet a "wonderful pre-theater" pick; its "roomy" "you're-in-Paris" quarters get "busy and noisy", but fans consider that a "lively" "plus."

Maruzzella 🌑 *Italian*

E 70s | 1483 First Ave. (bet. 77th & 78th Sts.) | 212-988-8877 | www.maruzzellanyc.com

There's "nothing fancy" about this UES "quintessential neighborhood Italian", just "surprisingly good, authentic" cooking brought to table by "old-school" servers; "friendly owners" on the scene and "reasonable"-for-the-zip-code rates make the "modest" decor easy to overlook.

Mary's Fish Camp ☒ *Seafood*
25 | **16** | **20** | **$43**

W Village | 64 Charles St. (W. 4th St.) | 646-486-2185 | www.marysfishcamp.com

"Forget about Maine" – this perennial West Village "hot spot" presents a lobster roll that's "one of life's treats", along with other "fish-shack" classics served up by a "cool staff"; true, its "no-reservations" policy and "tiny" "dive" digs result in "long lines."

☒ Mas (Farmhouse) ● *American*
28 | **25** | **27** | **$92**

W Village | 39 Downing St. (bet. Bedford & Varick Sts.) | 212-255-1790 | www.masfarmhouse.com

"Just gets better and better" say fans of chef Galen Zamarra's near-"flawless" Villager where "simple, fresh, satisfying" New American cuisine and a "polished" yet "warm" staff make you "feel like nobility"; factor in moodily lit digs "quiet" enough for "intimate conversation", and it makes the "perfect" date place – "if you're in the mood to splurge."

NEW Mas (La Grillade) ● *American*
24 | **23** | **24** | **$80**

W Village | 28 Seventh Ave. S. (bet. Bedford & Leroy Sts.) | 212-255-1795 | www.maslagrillade.com

Chef Galen Zamarra "hits the mark again" with this "slightly more casual" spin-off of his "beloved" nearby Villager Mas (Farmhouse); besides the "excellent", "expensive" Americana from a wood-fired grill, it provides an "applewood-and-hickory"–scented atmosphere, and "outstanding" service overcomes its somewhat "awkward" bi-level layout.

☒ Masa ☒ *Japanese*
27 | **24** | **25** | **$585**

W 60s | Time Warner Ctr. | 10 Columbus Circle, 4th fl. (60th St. at B'way) | 212-823-9800

Bar Masa ☒ *Japanese*

W 60s | Time Warner Ctr. | 10 Columbus Circle, 4th fl. (60th St. at B'way) | 212-823-9800
www.masanyc.com

Sushi sticklers pay "homage to grand master" Masayoshi Takayama at his "special-occasion" Time Warner Center Japanese, famed for its "exquisite" fish and "business-class-ticket-to-Tokyo" tabs (prix fixes *start* at $450); the "less expensive" next-door bar offers "mere mortals" a hint of the experience "without the mortgage" payment.

Max *Italian*
22 | **17** | **20** | **$32**

E Village | 51 Ave. B (bet. 3rd & 4th Sts.) | 212-539-0111
TriBeCa | 181 Duane St. (bet. Greenwich & Hudson Sts.) | 212-966-5939
www.max-ny.com

"Amazing housemade pastas" and other "hearty" Italian basics offered at some of the "best prices in Manhattan" keep the locals coming to this "friendly" twosome; they're "low-key" decorwise, but the East Villager boasts an "adorable outdoor patio" – "what's not to like?"

Max Brenner ● *Dessert*
22 | **21** | **19** | **$29**

G Village | 841 Broadway (bet. 13th & 14th Sts.) | 212-388-0030 | www.maxbrenner.com

You almost expect "Willy Wonka to stop by" this "chocolate factory"-esque Village "tourist" favorite where the American savories are "surprisingly good", but it's the "to-die-for" desserts that "draw the crowds"; "packed" and "noisy" it is, but you "can't beat it" for a "one-time experience" with the "kids."

Max SoHa ●🍴 *Italian*   24 | 18 | 18 | $27
W 100s | 1274 Amsterdam Ave. (123rd St.) | 212-531-2221
Max Caffe ● *Italian*
W 100s | 1262 Amsterdam Ave. (bet. 122nd & 123rd Sts.) | 212-531-1210
www.maxsoha.com

"Popular with the Columbia crowd", these "friendly", low-cost UWSers have two distinct personalities: "cash-only" SoHa offers "rustic" Italian staples in a "cozy" space with the option to "eat outside", while the Caffe features "comfy couches and chairs for relaxing and eating."

Maya *Mexican*   24 | 20 | 21 | $52
E 60s | 1191 First Ave. (bet. 64th & 65th Sts.) | 212-585-1818 | www.richardsandoval.com

"Not your typical taco place", this "classy" Upper Eastsider specializes in "excellent upscale Mexican" cuisine "courteously" served in a "pretty" setting; the "party" atmosphere gets "noisy" when the "crowds" come in and the "killer margaritas" flow, but "you'll go away happy."

Maze *French*   25 | 22 | 21 | $71
W 50s | London NYC Hotel | 151 W. 54th St. (bet. 6th & 7th Aves.) | 212-468-8889 | www.gordonramsay.com

This New French eatery proffers "simple, elegant" small plates in a "bustling" space off the lobby of the "fashionable" London Hotel; those who find it "too noisy" and "pricey" at dinner note it's "terrific" for a quieter lunch, when there's a "wonderful" $27 prix fixe.

Maz Mezcal *Mexican*   21 | 19 | 22 | $40
E 80s | 316 E. 86th St. (bet. 1st & 2nd Aves.) | 212-472-1599 | www.mazmezcal.com

"Hits all the right spots" say Yorkville locals of this "family owned" Mexican "standby" where a "lively neighborhood crowd" assembles for "tasty" classics; "reasonable prices" and "friendly" service are two more reasons it's "still packed after all these years."

McCormick & Schmick's *Seafood/Steak*   21 | 20 | 21 | $54
W 50s | 1285 Sixth Ave. (enter on 52nd St., bet. 6th & 7th Aves.) | 212-459-1222 | www.mccormickandschmicks.com

There are "no surprises" at this Rock Center–area "corporate" surf 'n' turf house – and "sometimes that's exactly what you want"; "reliable" fresh fare and "solid" service in "publike" environs are what's on offer – along with one of the "best happy hours ever."

Meatball Shop ● *Sandwiches*   24 | 17 | 19 | $23
LES | 84 Stanton St. (bet. Allen & Orchard Sts.) | 212-982-8895
NEW **W Village** | 64 Greenwich Ave. (Perry St.) | 212-982-7815
Williamsburg | 170 Bedford Ave. (bet. N. 7th & 8th Sts.) | Brooklyn | 718-551-0520
www.themeatballshop.com

An "original concept" that "works", this "rapidly expanding" meatball specialist offers "mouthwatering" orbs "served in a variety of ways" plus "even better" "make-your-own ice cream sandwiches"; "can't-go-wrong" pricing ensures the "no-frills" setups are "always packed."

	FOOD	DECOR	SERVICE	COST

⊠ Megu *Japanese* — **24 | 26 | 23 | $88**
TriBeCa | 62 Thomas St. (bet. Church St. & W. B'way) | 212-964-7777
Megu Midtown *Japanese*
E 40s | Trump World Tower | 845 United Nations Plaza (1st Ave. & 47th St.) | 212-964-7777
www.megurestaurants.com
"Over-the-top" "impressive" decor centered around a "giant Buddha" ice sculpture sets the stage for "delectable" "modern Japanese fine dining" at these TriBeCa–Midtown East "stunners", where "meticulous" service takes the edge off "steep" tabs; they're "perfect for a "power meal", "date" or any time "someone else is paying."

Mehtaphor ⊠ *Eclectic* — **▽ 24 | 18 | 22 | $57**
TriBeCa | Duane Street Hotel | 130 Duane St. (Church St.) | 212-542-9440 | www.mehtaphornyc.com
"Super-talented" chef Jehangir Mehta turns out "terrific, original" Eclectic small plates at his "cool, funky" TriBeCan in the Duane Street Hotel; "accommodating" service is another reason to "love this place" despite "shoeboxlike" dimensions.

Melba's *American/Southern* — **24 | 22 | 22 | $32**
Harlem | 300 W. 114th St. (Frederick Douglass Blvd.) | 212-864-7777 | www.melbasrestaurant.com
"Divine chicken 'n' waffles" and other "Southern"-accented American "comfort" classics "done right" are the thing at this "warm, wonderful" Harlem highlight; its "stylish", retro digs are "chill and homey" by day, "hopping and grooving" come evening (especially on Tuesdays when there's live music).

Mémé *Mediterranean/Moroccan* — **▽ 23 | 17 | 22 | $38**
W Village | 581 Hudson St. (Bank St.) | 646-692-8450 | www.memeonhudson.com
It's the "Mediterranean on Hudson Street" at this "affordable" West Villager dispensing "wonderful" small plates and entrees with "Moroccan flair"; "friendly" service and an appealing "bohemian Paris" vibe will "keep you returning" unless the "tight-packed tables" make you feel like you're "flying coach."

Menchanko-tei *Japanese/Noodle Shop* — **20 | 11 | 16 | $23**
E 40s | 131 E. 45th St. (bet. Lexington & 3rd Aves.) | 212-986-6805 | www.menchankotei.com
"Big bowls" brimming with "delicious broth and lots of slurpy noodles" come out "lightning fast" at this "no-frills" Midtown ramen joint that's "packed during lunch"; it's a "tiny, cramped" "hole-in-the-wall" with "brusque" service, but "the price is right" and "on a cold winter day" it's perfect.

Menkui Tei ⊭ *Japanese/Noodle Shop* — **21 | 10 | 17 | $18**
E Village | 63 Cooper Sq. (bet. 7th St. & St. Marks Pl.) | 212-228-4152 ◗
W 50s | 60 W. 56th St. (bet. 5th & 6th Aves.) | 212-757-1642
You "hang out with Japanese salarymen" at these low-budget East Village–Midtown "real ramen bars" ladling out "slurp-worthy noodles" and other "quick", "delicious" classics; despite decidedly "unpretentious" environs and cash-only policies, they're on the "regular rotation" for many surveyors.

	FOOD	DECOR	SERVICE	COST

Mercadito *Mexican* — 24 | 17 | 18 | $33
E Village | 179 Ave. B (bet. 11th & 12th Sts.) | 212-529-6490
Mercadito Grove ◐ *Mexican*
W Village | 100 Seventh Ave. S. (bet. Bleecker & Grove Sts.) |
212-647-0830
www.mercaditorestaurants.com
To "quench taco cravings", hit these crosstown Mexican "favorites"
where the "fair-priced", "authentic tastes" are best washed down with
a "terrific margarita" or two; both the service and the "tight" quarters
are "undistinguished", but in "warm weather" the West Villager's patio is the "spot to be."

Mercato ◐ *Italian* — 24 | 19 | 21 | $42
Garment District | 352 W. 39th St. (bet. 8th & 9th Aves.) |
212-643-2000 | www.mercatonyc.com
"A pleasant surprise" in the restaurant-"barren" zone near Port
Authority, this "charming" "find" slings "genuine homestyle" Italian
cooking at "reasonable" rates; its "cozy" "brick-walled" room tended
by a "warm" staff is "worth seeking out" if you're in the area.

Mercer Kitchen ◐ *American/French* — 22 | 22 | 19 | $54
SoHo | Mercer Hotel | 99 Prince St. (Mercer St.) | 212-966-5454 |
www.jean-georges.com
"After all these years", this "sleek" SoHo member of the "Jean-Georges
empire" remains a "cool" pick for "consistently very good" French-
American fare; its "underground cave" space offers prime "people-
watching", and service "on the slow side" allows more time to take in
the "lively" scene.

Mermaid Inn *Seafood* — 22 | 18 | 20 | $45
E Village | 96 Second Ave. (bet. 5th & 6th Sts.) | 212-674-5870
W 80s | 568 Amsterdam Ave. (bet. 87th & 88th Sts.) | 212-799-7400
Mermaid Oyster Bar *Seafood*
G Village | 79 MacDougal St. (bet. Bleecker & Houston Sts.) | 212-260-0100
www.themermaidnyc.com
They have the "Cape Cod-ish" formula down at these "convivial", perpetually "packed" seafooders where the "fresh" catch includes a "terrific
lobster roll" and "amazing $1 oysters" at the "happy hour-and-a-half";
"simple" "fish shack" decor and "friendly" service complete the picture.

Mesa Coyoacan ◐ *Mexican* — ▽ 23 | 21 | 20 | $36
Williamsburg | 372 Graham Ave. (bet. Conselyea St. & Skillman Ave.) |
Brooklyn | 718-782-8171 | www.mesacoyoacan.com
"Why fly to Mexico City" when there's this Williamsburg standout
proffering "incredible tacos" and other "damn-fine", "authentic" dishes
in "hip, fun", modern digs; "amazing margaritas" and "inexpensive" tabs
are additional reasons why locals declare "you will not be disappointed."

Mesa Grill *Southwestern* — 24 | 21 | 22 | $60
Flatiron | 102 Fifth Ave. (bet. 15th & 16th Sts.) | 212-807-7400 |
www.mesagrill.com
"It was Bobby Flay's first, and is still the best" declare devotees of the
"TV" champ's "buzzing" Flatiron "flagship" that's been turning out
"fabulous" SW fare since 1991; maybe the room "needs an update", but
it's a "safe bet" for a "top-notch" meal (especially "don't miss" brunch).

| | FOOD | DECOR | SERVICE | COST |

Meskerem *Ethiopian*
▽ 23 | 12 | 16 | $28

G Village | 124 MacDougal St. (bet. Bleecker & W. 3rd Sts.) | 212-777-8111
W 40s | 468 W. 47th St. (bet. 9th & 10th Aves.) | 212-664-0520

If you're "looking for something different", there's these "hole-in-the-wall", "no-fork-necessary" Ethiopians offering "delicious" traditional dishes "eaten with the hands" using "spongy" injera bread; wallet-friendly rates are another reason people "come often" despite "no decor" and "lackadaisical" service.

Meson Sevilla *Spanish*
21 | 16 | 21 | $41

W 40s | 344 W. 46th St. (bet. 8th & 9th Aves.) | 212-262-5890 | www.mesonsevilla.com

Theater ticket–holders seeking a paella fix turn to this "popular" Restaurant Row Spaniard (with Italian dishes too) for "pleasant" provender and sangria; the room's "a bit tatty" and gets "elbow-to-elbow" pre-curtain, but it's hard to beat the rates or location.

MexiBBQ ● *BBQ/Mexican*
21 | 21 | 19 | $26

Astoria | 37-11 30th Ave. (bet. 37th & 38th Sts.) | Queens | 718-626-0333 | www.mexiqny.com

"Dozens of beers on tap" are the claim to fame of this "high-energy" Astorian, which also earns *olés* for its *"muy bueno"* low-cost Mexican BBQ; "friendly" servers work the "industrial-chic" interior – "now if they would just take reservations."

Mexicana Mama Ⓜ *Mexican*
23 | 15 | 19 | $33

G Village | 47 E. 12th St. (bet. B'way & University Pl.) | 212-253-7594
W Village | 525 Hudson St. (bet. Charles & W. 10th Sts.) | 212-924-4119

"Pequeño place", *grande* taste sums up these "miniscule" Village Mexicans doling out "addictive" eats at more than "fair prices"; they're "always packed" and "waits can be long", so amigos advise go "early" or do delivery; P.S. Hudson Street is open for lunch.

Mexican Radio ● *Mexican*
23 | 17 | 20 | $32

NoLita | 19 Cleveland Pl. (bet. Kenmare & Spring Sts.) | 212-343-0140 | www.mexrad.com

"Comes in loud and clear" say supporters of this "friendly, casual" NoLita "favorite", a provider of "way better-than-average" Mexican "standards" and the "best margaritas"; the decor's "not very impressive", but the "party" people don't seem to mind.

Mexico Lindo *Mexican*
▽ 23 | 19 | 23 | $34

Gramercy | 459 Second Ave. (26th St.) | 212-679-3665 | www.mexicolindonyc.com

A Gramercy Park "fixture", this "family-owned", "brightly colored" Mexican keeps 'em "coming back" for "truly authentic" "homestyle food"; "very friendly" service and "best-buy" prices are other endearments – it's "been around for 40 years, and for good reason."

Mexicue *BBQ/Mexican*
22 | 15 | 20 | $13

Chelsea | 345 Seventh Ave. (bet. 29th & 30th Sts.) | 212-244-0002 ⊠
LES | 106 Forsyth St. (bet. Broome & Grand Sts.) | 646-559-4100 ●
www.mexicue.com

It's the "popular food truck" gone "brick-and-mortar" at these LES-Chelsea spin-offs offering the same "fresh", Mexican-meets-BBQ fare ("from brisket tacos to pulled pork") served up "quick" in "small", colorful settings; "very reasonable prices" seal the deal.

Mezzaluna ● *Italian* 22 | 15 | 19 | $44

E 70s | 1295 Third Ave. (bet. 74th & 75th Sts.) | 212-535-9600 |
www.mezzalunany.com

Pizza Mezzaluna *Pizza*

G Village | 146 W. Houston St. (MacDougal St.) | 212-533-1242 |
www.pizzamezzalunanyc.com

Despite the "tiniest" of dimensions, this "friendly" Upper East Side Italian boasts a "strong" track record of "many years'" standing, "swiftly" sending out wood-oven pizzas ("the highlight") and other "soulful" standards; they "could update the decor", but it's "usually packed" all the same; P.S. the takeout-oriented Greenwich Villager supplies mostly pies.

Mezzogiorno *Italian* ▽ 21 | 18 | 20 | $45

SoHo | 195 Spring St. (Sullivan St.) | 212-334-2112 |
www.mezzogiorno.com

"Authentic and ample" Italiana is the forte of this "cute little" SoHo stalwart, an "old reliable" whose "cheerful" atmosphere and "attentive" service keep the "locals and tourists" coming back for more; "on a nice night", insiders try to nab a table outside or by the "open French doors."

Michael Jordan's
The Steak House NYC *Steak* 21 | 21 | 20 | $66

E 40s | Grand Central | Northwest Balcony (43rd St. & Vanderbilt Ave.) |
212-655-2300 | www.michaeljordansnyc.com

Set on Grand Central's mezzanine "with the night sky constellations above" and "all the bustle" below, this "classy" chophouse "scores points" for its "can't-be-beat setting" and "high-quality" beef; yes, prices are "over the top", but "you're paying" to dine – and dine well – in an "NYC landmark."

Michael's ▨ *Californian* 22 | 23 | 23 | $68

W 50s | 24 W. 55th St. (bet. 5th & 6th Aves.) | 212-767-0555 |
www.michaelsnewyork.com

"Media titans" ("did Diane really just say that?") collect at this "classy" Midtowner that's known more for its breakfast and lunch "power" scenes than its "fresh", "premium-priced" Californian fare and "pro" service; "relaxed" dinner comes "without the hot crowd", but the food is as good as ever and there's always the "lovely" room's "fresh flowers and art" to look at.

Mike's Bistro *American/Kosher* ▽ 25 | 20 | 23 | $53

W 70s | 228 W. 72nd St. (bet. B'way & West End Ave.) |
212-799-3911 | www.mikesbistro.com

Kosher food gets the "gourmet" treatment at this Upper Westsider where the eponymous chef-owner turns out "delicious" New American dishes; yes, "you pay", but "wonderful service" and "Mike going from table to table" add value – "his mother must be kvelling."

Mile End *Deli* 25 | 15 | 19 | $25

Boerum Hill | 97 Hoyt St. (bet. Atlantic & Pacific Sts.) | Brooklyn |
718-852-7510 | www.mileendbrooklyn.com

(continued)

Mile End Sandwich *Sandwiches*

NEW **NoHo** | 53 Bond St. (bet. Bowery & Lafayette St.) |
212-529-2990 | www.mileenddeli.com

Again rated NYC's No. 1 deli, this Montreal-style "meat temple" brings
"hipster love" to the Jewish "classics", including "moist", "house-
smoked" pastrami that stacks up as one "incredible sandwich"; at
prime times the "line out front" its "microscopic" Boerum Hill digs
"seems a mile" long, but the stripped-down NoHo offshoot is roomier.

Mill Basin Kosher Deli *Deli/Kosher*

| 23 | 16 | 19 | $27 |

Mill Basin | 5823 Ave. T (59th St.) | Brooklyn | 718-241-4910 |
www.millbasindeli.com

"Memories of delis past come alive" when noshing on a "what-could-
be-better pastrami on rye" at this Mill Basin vet; given such "rich Jewish
delicacies" "done right", mavens "tolerate" the no-frills service and
setting dressed up with "gallery"-worthy fine art.

Millesime *Seafood*

| 20 | 21 | 19 | $66 |

Murray Hill | Carlton Hotel | 92 Madison Ave., 2nd fl. (29th St.) |
212-889-7100 | www.millesimerestaurant.com

"Tucked away" on the Carlton Hotel's mezzanine, this "pretty" Murray
Hill seafooder is appreciated as much for its "enchanting" stained-
glass skylight as for its "fresh", pricey fin fare; a "quiet oasis" by day,
it "comes alive" at happy hour when there's live jazz.

☒ Milos, Estiatorio ● *Greek/Seafood*

| 27 | 24 | 24 | $87 |

W 50s | 125 W. 55th St. (bet. 6th & 7th Aves.) | 212-245-7400 |
www.estiatoriomilos.com

"The freshest, most superbly prepared" seafood is the lure at this
Midtown Greek whose "gorgeous" whitewashed setting "brings
Santorini to NYC"; unless you stick with the "wonderful" appetizers,
you'd best plan on paying "stratospheric" "by-the-pound" pricing – still,
you "can't go wrong" with the lunch and pre-theater prix fixe "bargains."

Mimi's Hummus *Mideastern*

| ▽ 26 | 16 | 22 | $23 |

Ditmas Park | 1209 Cortelyou Rd. (Westminster Rd.) | Brooklyn |
718-284-4444 | www.mimishummus.com

"Phenomenal housemade hummus" and "the fluffiest pita" star on the
"limited menu" of "delicious" Middle Eastern eats at this "tiny", "modest" Ditmas Park standout; "inexpensive" prices and "incredibly friendly"
service have locals declaring it "never disappoints."

Minca ●⊟ *Japanese/Noodle Shop*

| ▽ 24 | 10 | 19 | $21 |

E Village | 536 E. Fifth St. (bet. Aves. A & B) | 212-505-8001 |
www.newyorkramen.com

There are "no pretenses" at this "tiny", "basic" East Village noodle
shop, just the "charming simplicity" of "excellent" ramen with "the
most slurp-worthy broth"; it's "perpetually packed", but "service is
fast" and prices low, so most "would come back anytime."

Minetta Tavern ● *French*

| 24 | 22 | 21 | $67 |

G Village | 113 MacDougal St. (bet. Bleecker & W. 3rd Sts.) |
212-475-3850 | www.minettatavernny.com

"Old NY shines" at Keith McNally's circa-1937 Villager redone as a
"fantastic" French bistro, where the food's "wonderful" – especially

the côte de boeuf for two; it practically "takes an act of Congress to get a reservation", especially for the "coveted back room" where you "may rub elbows with celebs", but it's also fun to "muscle up to the bar" given the company there.

Miranda *Italian/Pan-Latin* ▽ | 24 | 21 | 24 | $46 |

Williamsburg | 80 Berry St. (N. 9th St.) | Brooklyn | 718-387-0711 | www.mirandarestaurant.com

"The food is full of love, as is the service" at this Williamsburg "neighborhood gem" dishing up an "inspired" mix of Italian and Pan-Latin dishes; "hidden in an old saloon" space, it offers a rare-for-the-area "minimal noise level", further inspiring newbies to "become regulars."

Miriam *Israeli/Mediterranean* | 22 | 19 | 20 | $32 |

Park Slope | 79 Fifth Ave. (Prospect Pl.) | Brooklyn | 718-622-2250 | www.miriamrestaurant.com

"Dinner is a pleasure" but "brunch is the meal" that has Park Slopers "flocking" to this "affordable" Israeli-Med, whose narrow space is a "mob scene" on weekends, but happily service remains "prompt"; "go at off times" for a calmer taste of its "fabulous" fare.

NEW Mission Chinese Food *Chinese* | - | - | - | M |

LES | 154 Orchard St. (bet. Rivington & Stanton Sts.) | 212-529-8800 | www.missionchinesefood.com

The LES outpost of Danny Bowien's well-loved San Francisco eatery is housed in what looks like a dilapidated take-out joint, but its superspicy, creatively crafted Sichuan cooking is way more innovative than what you'll find at your average wok shop; the cramped space bedecked with a paper dragon and festive red lights fills up early, so come prepared to wait.

Miss Korea BBQ ●◪Ⓜ *Korean* ▽ | 22 | 20 | 21 | $34 |

Garment District | 10 W. 32nd St. (bet. B'way & 5th Ave.) | 212-594-4963 | www.misskoreabbq.com

Ok, the "name is odd", but the food's "delicious" at this "busy" Korean BBQ specialist; its Zen-like quarters are "lovely" and "spacious compared to others" in K-town, and the prices are "competitive", so no surprise it's "always packed."

Miss Lily's *Jamaican* | 21 | 22 | 20 | $38 |

G Village | 132 W. Houston St. (Sullivan St.) | 646-588-5375 | www.misslilysnyc.com

"The place to be" for the "cool" crowd, Serge Becker's "sexy" Village Jamaican features a clever "diner"-like interior pulsing with "hip" island tunes and overseen by an "utterly beautiful" staff; the well-priced Caribbean food is "delicious" (especially at "killer brunch"), but that's almost beside the point.

Miss Mamie's *Soul Food/Southern* | 23 | 14 | 19 | $25 |

Harlem | 366 W. 110th St. (bet. Columbus & Manhattan Aves.) | 212-865-6744

Miss Maude's *Soul Food/Southern*

Harlem | 547 Lenox Ave. (bet. 137th & 138th Sts.) | 212-690-3100 | www.spoonbreadinc.com

"Real Southern comfort food" in "tremendous portions" keeps the "crowds" coming to these Harlem soul fooders; their "luncheonette"-in-

Carolina looks are "kind of plain" and the "friendly" servers "can be slow", but with "such fantastic" eats at "fair prices", "who cares?"

The Modern ⊠ *American/French* | 26 | 26 | 25 | $127 |

W 50s | Museum of Modern Art | 9 W. 53rd St. (bet. 5th & 6th Aves.) | 212-333-1220 | www.themodernnyc.com

Danny Meyer's MoMA "marvel" presents the "ultimate" in museum dining, with chef Gabriel Kreuther's "work-of-art" French–New American cuisine arriving at table via a "terrific" "pro" staff in "beautiful" Bauhaus-influenced confines; it's divided between a "lively", "casual" front barroom offering "less expensive" à la carte small plates, and a "formal" prix fixe–only back room where the "impressive sculpture garden view" is factored into the bill.

Moim ⓜ *Korean* | ▽ 24 | 23 | 21 | $40 |

Park Slope | 206 Garfield Pl. (bet. 7th & 8th Aves.) | Brooklyn | 718-499-8092 | www.moimrestaurant.com

"Wonderful, modern" spins on classic dishes have earned a loyal local following for this "sleek" Park Slope Korean, a "chill" choice for "creative" dining; "efficient, pleasant" service and "reasonable"-for-the-"refined"-repast prices lead to occasional "waits."

Mojave *Southwestern* | 23 | 23 | 21 | $31 |

Astoria | 22-36 31st St. (bet. Ditmars Blvd. & 23rd Ave.) | Queens | 718-545-4100 | www.mojaveny.com

A place for "good times with friends" or family, this spacious Astorian plies "flavorful" SW food and "fabulous margaritas" in "beautiful" adobe hacienda digs with a pleasant patio out back; low prices and "welcoming" service cement its standing as a solid "neighborhood spot."

Móle *Mexican* | 22 | 17 | 19 | $35 |

NEW E 80s | 1735 Second Ave. (bet. 89th & 90th Sts.) | 212-289-8226
LES | 205 Allen St. (Houston St.) | 212-777-3200 ⊄
W Village | 57 Jane St. (Hudson St.) | 212-206-7559
Williamsburg | 178 Kent Ave. (N. 4th St.) | Brooklyn | 347-384-2300
www.molenyc.com

"Olé Móle!" cheer amigos who "can't get enough" of this "everyday" mini-chain's "tasty" Mexican staples and "even better" margaritas; the setups are "tight and noisy" and service variable, but bite into an "awesome taco" and "you soon forget" all that.

Molly's ❶ *Pub Food* | 23 | 19 | 22 | $28 |

Gramercy | 287 Third Ave. (bet. 22nd & 23rd Sts.) | 212-889-3361 | www.mollysshebeen.com

A burger that "could vie for best in town", the "freshest pints" and "lovely Colleens waiting on you" make this "step-back-in-time" Irish pub a Gramercy "favorite"; it's the "real deal" with a "sawdust-covered floor", "wood-burning fireplace" and "like-in-Dublin" feel.

Molyvos ❶ *Greek* | 23 | 21 | 21 | $58 |

W 50s | 871 Seventh Ave. (bet. 55th & 56th Sts.) | 212-582-7500 | www.molyvos.com

Ever popular for "simply and elegantly prepared" seafood, this "upscale" Midtown Greek is also "well located" a stone's throw from Carnegie Hall and City Center; "bright", "spiffy" new decor, "solid" service and a "bargain" $35 pre-theater prix fixe shore up its standing as a "winner."

| | FOOD | DECOR | SERVICE | COST |

Momofuku Ko ◐ *American*   26 | 19 | 23 | $163

E Village | 163 First Ave. (bet. 10th & 11th Sts.) | 212-500-0831 |
www.momofuku.com

"Quite the experience", David Chang's East Village "temple of gastronomy" is an Asian-accented American 12-seater where you "sit at
the counter" on "hard wooden stools" and "watch the chefs" prepare
your "sublime" muliticourse meal; sure, paying $125 for dinner
"hurts", but the real "pain" is "scoring a rez" – but "if you can get in, go!"

Momofuku Milk Bar *Bakery/Dessert*   22 | 14 | 18 | $18

E Village | 251 E. 13th St. (bet. 2nd & 3rd Aves.) | 347-577-9504 ◐
W 50s | Chambers Hotel | 15 W. 56th St. (bet. 5th & 6th Aves.) |
347-577-9504
NEW **W 80s** | 561 Columbus Ave. (87th St.) | 347-577-9504
NEW **Carroll Gardens** | 360 Smith St. (2nd Pl.) | Brooklyn | 347-577-9504
Williamsburg | 382 Metropolitan Ave. (bet. Havemeyer St. & Marcy Ave.) |
Brooklyn | 347-577-9504
www.momofuku.com

"Park your diet on the street" when entering these "quirky" David
Chang bakeries, where pastry chef Christina Tosi "always has a surprise in store" with her "so-sweet" "off-beat" dessert "experiments"
("try the crack pie") and "addictive" "savory bites"; there's "no seating" and "no decor", but "everyone needs to try it" at least once.

Momofuku Noodle Bar *American*   25 | 17 | 19 | $34

E Village | 171 First Ave. (bet. 10th & 11th Sts.) | 212-777-7773 |
www.momofuku.com

Where David Chang's "famous pork buns" originated, this affordable
East Villager remains a "hip, happening" source for "crave-worthy" ramen and other "flavorful" Asian-accented American fare in "sparse"
digs; an "inevitable wait", "raucous noise" and "hit-or-miss" service
come with the territory, unless you go for more "relaxed" lunch.

Momofuku Ssäm Bar ◐ *American*   26 | 18 | 20 | $60

E Village | 207 Second Ave. (13th St.) | 212-254-3500 | www.momofuku.com

"Legions wait outside for a seat" at David Chang's "simple" East
Villager where the reward is "phenomenal" Asian-accented New
American fare that's "worth much more than you'll pay"; it's a "noisy,
crowded, rushed" scene – but that's just part of the "adventure";
P.S. reserve ahead for the bo ssäm feast, it's "fantastic."

Momo Sushi Shack ∅ *Japanese*   ∇ 26 | 23 | 25 | $30

Bushwick | 43 Bogart St. (Moore St.) | Brooklyn | 718-418-6666 |
www.momosushishack.com

"Definitely not a shack", this "trendy", cash-only Bushwick Japanese
serves "amazing, creative" small plates and sushi at "wooden communal tables" where "the owner stops by and talks to you about the food";
it "fills up fast" despite the "unexpected location", so "get there early."

Momoya *Japanese*   24 | 20 | 20 | $44

Chelsea | 185 Seventh Ave. (21st St.) | 212-989-4466
W 80s | 427 Amsterdam Ave. (bet. 80th & 81st Sts.) | 212-580-0007 ◐
www.themomoya.com

Sushi sophisticates head to this "unassuming" Chelsea-UWS Japanese
duo for "generous portions" of "amazingly fresh" fish plus "top-notch

	FOOD	DECOR	SERVICE	COST

entrees" at "won't-break-the-bank" prices; it's "always bustling" but the staff keeps pace, and "they know how to manage a wait list."

Monkey Bar ●☒ *American* | 21 | 24 | 21 | $67 |

E 50s | Elysée Hotel | 60 E. 54th St. (bet. Madison & Park Aves.) | 212-308-2950 | www.monkeybarnewyork.com

Graydon Carter's "revamp" of a Midtown "classic" is like "a trip back to old NY" complete with "clubby" milieu and "clever murals" depicting Jazz Age icons – but the "celeb" sightings are strictly up to date; the "perfectly fine" American food may be "pricey", but not so much when you consider the "convivial" "scene."

Mon Petit Cafe *French* | 21 | 17 | 21 | $43 |

E 60s | 801 Lexington Ave. (62nd St.) | 212-355-2233 | www.monpetitcafe.com

A "little bit of Paris in the shadow of Bloomingdale's", this tearoom-style vet offers well-priced "homey French" staples that are a great break "in the middle of an intense shopping day"; the room "may not meet the standards of the Designers Guild", but it possesses a "warm, cozy" vibe bolstered by "sweet" service.

Mont Blanc ● *Austrian/Swiss* | ▽ 24 | 16 | 23 | $42 |

W 40s | 315 W. 48th St. (bet. 8th & 9th Aves.) | 212-582-9648 | www.montblancrestaurant.com

Fondue freaks "love" this "cozy" Theater District "time capsule" that's been dishing up "delicious" Swiss-Austrian staples since 1982; "gracious" staffers overseen by a "charming" owner "get you to the show on time", so it's a "win-win all around" – even if it "could use a face-lift."

Montebello ☒ *Italian* | ▽ 23 | 20 | 24 | $55 |

E 50s | 120 E. 56th St. (bet. Lexington & Park Aves.) | 212-753-1447 | www.montebellonyc.com

One of the "best-kept secrets in Midtown" is this "oasis of peace and quiet" where "personalized" service and "fantastic" Northern Italian fare keep the "white-haired ladies and their husbands" coming; it's "a bit on the expensive side", but hey, at least "you can linger."

Monte's ⓜ *Italian* | ▽ 22 | 18 | 23 | $40 |

Gowanus | 451 Carroll St. (bet. Nevins St. & 3rd Ave.) | Brooklyn | 718-852-7800 | www.montesnyc.com

Dating back to 1906, this Gowanus "neighborhood Italian" reopened last year following a makeover; given "terrific brick-oven pizzas" and other "freshly made", "reasonably priced" classics delivered by staffers who "take good care" of you, locals say "welcome back!"

Mooncake Foods ☒🥡 *Asian* | 21 | 11 | 19 | $22 |

Chelsea | 263 W. 30th St. (8th Ave.) | 212-268-2888
SoHo | 28 Watts St. (bet. 6th Ave. & Thompson St.) | 212-219-8888
W 50s | 359 W. 54th St. (bet. 8th & 9th Aves.) | 212-262-9888
www.mooncakefoods.com

"The best healthy cheap eats" come "quickly and without fuss" at this "cool", "cash-only" Pan-Asian trio; it's "loud" and "crowded" with "nonexistent decor", but "fabulous" "for the price", inspiring many to "keep it in the rotation" – especially for delivery and takeout.

| | FOOD | DECOR | SERVICE | COST |

Morandi ● *Italian*   23 | 22 | 21 | $53

W Village | 211 Waverly Pl. (Charles St.) | 212-627-7575 |
www.morandiny.com

A somewhat under-the-radar "jewel in Keith McNally's crown", this
"welcoming" West Village trattoria "never fails" with its "off-the-
hook" Italiana dished up in "rustic", "perennially buzzy" confines; the
"energy is contagious" – but if the "noise overwhelms", "sit out on the
sidewalk and people-watch."

The Morgan *American*   19 | 23 | 20 | $40

Murray Hill | The Morgan Library & Museum | 225 Madison Ave.
(bet. 36th & 37th Sts.) | 212-683-2130 | www.themorgan.org

For a "civilized" repast while taking in "the wonders of the Morgan
Library", this lunch-only Murray Hill musuem cafe offers "limited"
but quite "good" American bites served in the "light-filled" atrium or J.
Pierpont's "elegant" former dining room; it's all very "genteel" – with
"prices to match."

☒ Morimoto *Japanese*   26 | 27 | 24 | $86

Chelsea | 88 10th Ave. (bet. 15th & 16th Sts.) | 212-989-8883 |
www.morimotonyc.com

Iron Chef Masaharu Morimoto's "phenomenal" Japanese cuisine at
this Chelsea destination is as "beautiful and creative" as the "must-
see" "modern" duplex space; "excellent", "almost-psychic" service is
part of the "unforgettable" experience, as are "eye-popping prices" –
especially for the "oh my" omakase; P.S. don't miss the "cool" downstairs bar and "ultra-high-tech bathrooms."

Morton's The Steakhouse *Steak*   25 | 22 | 24 | $79

E 40s | 551 Fifth Ave. (45th St.) | 212-972-3315 |
www.mortons.com

"You can't go wrong" at this "wood-paneled", perpetually "packed"
Midtown "carnivorium" that "can be counted on" for "fantastic",
"huge" slabs tendered by "efficient" "pro" waiters; yes, it's
"pricey" – "so are all the big-time steakhouses" – but "power hour
at the bar is a steal."

Motorino ● *Pizza*   25 | 14 | 18 | $27

E Village | 349 E. 12th St. (bet. 1st & 2nd Aves.) | 212-777-2644 |
www.motorinopizza.com

The "gold standard" for "artsy pizza" (think "Sunday egg, Brussels
sprouts"), this "tiny", "spartan" East Villager builds Neapolitan-
style pies with "superb ingredients" on "sublime thin crusts" that'll
"haunt your dreams"; it's "crowded", "cramped", "crazy" – and "totally worth the wait."

Moustache ●⌀ *Mideastern*   23 | 15 | 18 | $28

E 100s | 1621 Lexington Ave. (102nd St.) | 212-828-0030
E Village | 265 E. 10th St. (bet. Ave. A & 1st Ave.) | 212-228-2022
W Village | 90 Bedford St. (Grove St.) | 212-229-2220
www.moustachepitza.com

"Straightforward", "delicious" Middle Eastern staples come at a "low
price" at this "popular" "cash-only" trio; the "no-decor" setups tilt
"tiny and cramped" and service is "nonchalant", but the minute that
"just-baked pita" arrives, "all is forgiven."

	FOOD	DECOR	SERVICE	COST

Mr. Chow ◑ *Chinese* — 22 | 22 | 22 | $75
E 50s | 324 E. 57th St. (bet. 1st & 2nd Aves.) | 212-751-9030
Mr. Chow Tribeca ◑ *Chinese*
TriBeCa | 121 Hudson St. (N. Moore St.) | 212-965-9500
www.mrchow.com
"Upscale" Chinese served on "fine china" by "white-jacketed" waiters is
the signature of this "glamorous" East Side–TriBeCa duo that's "still a
scene" "after all these years"; most find the food "outstanding", but
some take issue with the "expensive" tab and "salesman"-like tactics.

Mr. K's *Chinese* — 23 | 24 | 23 | $62
E 50s | 570 Lexington Ave. (51st St.) | 212-583-1668 | www.mrksny.com
An "opulent" "pink" art deco interior is the backdrop for "sumptuous"
Chinese cuisine at this "high-class" Eastside "throwback" overseen by
a "ritzy, tuxedoed" staff; yes, prices run "high", but there's always the
$28 prix fixe lunch.

Mughlai *Indian* — 21 | 15 | 18 | $35
W 70s | 320 Columbus Ave. (75th St.) | 212-724-6363 |
www.mughlainyc.com
"Save yourself a trip to Sixth Street" at this "quiet mainstay" supplying
the Upper West Side with "delish" Indian standards for more than
three decades; "slightly more-than-average prices" for the genre and
"often-disinterested" service don't deter devotees.

Mundo *Argentinean/Turkish* — ▽ 23 | 19 | 25 | $28
Astoria | 31-18 Broadway (32nd St.) | Queens | 718-777-2829 |
www.mundoastoria.com
Locals return to this "teeny" Astorian "again and again" for its "ingenious combination" of Argentine and Turkish that "delights" "omni-
vores and veggies" at wallet-pleasing prices; a "wonderfully attentive"
staff that's "full of life" helps make it "an experience to remember."

Nanni ⊠ *Italian* — 25 | 14 | 23 | $65
E 40s | 146 E. 46th St. (bet. Lexington & 3rd Aves.) | 212-697-4161
"Loyal regulars" populate this "old-world" Northern Italian near Grand
Central, where the "fabulous" classics "like grandma's" are ferried by
beloved, "been there forever" waiters; yes, it's "expensive" given the
"ancient surroundings", but you'll "not leave disappointed."

Naples 45 ⊠ *Italian/Pizza* — 20 | 17 | 18 | $37
E 40s | MetLife Bldg. | 200 Park Ave. (45th St.) | 212-972-7001 |
www.naples45.com
"You can't beat" the location – or the "authentic" Neapolitan pizza – at
this "cavernous" Italian that's "oh-so-convenient" to Grand Central;
"efficient" service makes it a popular (and "loud") lunch pick, and it's
"packed" with "corporate" types at happy hour; P.S. closed weekends.

Naruto Ramen ⊅ *Japanese/Noodle Shop* — ▽ 23 | 14 | 19 | $16
E 80s | 1596 Third Ave. (bet. 89th & 90th Sts.) | 212-289-7803 |
www.narutoterakawa.com
Slurpaholics "line up outside" this low-cost, cash-only UES noodle
shop "before it opens" to snag one of its "14 bar seats" and watch the
cooks concoct "delicious", "traditional" ramen soups "right in front of
you"; "not the most comfortable", it's "hard to beat on a cold day."

	FOOD	DECOR	SERVICE	COST

NEW Nasha Rasha 🌙 *Russian* — | - | - | - | E

Flatiron | 4 W. 19th St. (bet. 5th & 6th Aves.) | 212-929-4444 |
www.nasharashanyc.com
"They took the Soviet theme and ran with it" at this "friendly" Flatiron
Russian where red walls and star lighting fixtures make a kitschy backdrop for hearty classics (beef stroganoff, borscht, etc.) and a mega
vodka selection; it's a bit on the "expensive" side, but the happy-hour
specials are a steal.

The National 🌙 *American* — | 21 | 20 | 18 | $53

E 50s | Benjamin Hotel | 557 Lexington Ave. (50th St.) |
212-715-2400 | www.thenationalnyc.com
"Crazy-busy for lunch, quieter and more relaxed at dinner", Geoffrey
Zakarian's "business" nexus in Midtown's Benjamin Hotel presents a
"sophisticated" setting for "solid", "simple" American cooking; noise
levels are "loud" and service "spotty", but the crowds keep coming.

Natsumi 🌙 *Japanese* — | 23 | 20 | 22 | $45

W 50s | Amsterdam Court Hotel | 226 W. 50th St. (bet. B'way & 8th Ave.) |
212-258-2988 | www.natsuminyc.com
Amid the Theater District "madness" is this Japanese "sleeper" that
"exceeds expectations" with its "delectable sushi" and "helpful" service
at "reasonable" rates; that its "sleek" room has a "tolerable noise level"
and is "not filled to the brim with tourists" are other endearments.

Naya *Lebanese* — | 23 | 18 | 20 | $36

E 50s | 1057 Second Ave. (bet. 55th & 56th Sts.) | 212-319-7777
Naya Express 🗷 *Lebanese*
E 40s | 688 Third Ave. (43rd St.) | 212-557-0007
www.nayarestaurants.com
Meze mavens "fill up" on "marvelous" Lebanese dishes at this "classy"
Eastsider where the "staff treats you like family", but the "striking"
"all-white" interior feels more "futuristic railway car" than homey taverna; the "line at lunchtime" at the counter-service Grand Central-
area offshoot "says it all."

Neary's 🌙 *Pub Food* — | 18 | 16 | 23 | $47

E 50s | 358 E. 57th St. (1st Ave.) | 212-751-1434 | www.nearys.com
"Consummate host" Jimmy Neary and his "welcoming" "old-school
staff" are what keep "loyal" "seniors" coming back to this "frozen-in-
time" Midtown "watering hole"; it's a "cozy place" to "relax and have
a drink", with "dependable" "Irish bar food" in a supporting role.

Negril 🌙 *Caribbean/Jamaican* — | 23 | 21 | 20 | $36

G Village | 70 W. Third St. (bet. La Guardia Pl. & Thompson St.) |
212-477-2804 | www.negrilvillage.com
"Hot food, hot crowd" sums up this "modern" Village Jamaican where
the "lively" scene is fueled by "phenomenal" cocktails and "flavorful",
"dressed-up" Caribbean fare; sure, there are "West Indian restaurants
that are less expensive", but you're paying for the "upscale" milieu.

Nello 🌙 *Italian* — | 18 | 18 | 16 | $116

E 60s | 696 Madison Ave. (bet. 62nd & 63rd Sts.) | 212-980-9099
Yes, it's "absurdly expensive" with just "fair" food and "haughty" service,
but that's beside the point for the "wannabe socialites" and "Eurotrash"

who gravitate to this UES Italian playground; "rob a bank" and go "enjoy the crazy scene."

NEW Neta ⑤ *Japanese* — | — | — | VE

G Village | 61 W. Eighth St. (6th Ave.) | 212-505-2610 | www.netanyc.com
Early-goers to this new Village Japanese from Masa alums rave "this is the good stuff" citing "fantastic" sushi and small plates that put the focus on "fresh ingredients", not the minimalist digs; insiders say "order the omakase" and "let the chefs give you what's best" – though as it's "not cheap", some may prefer à la carte.

New Hawaii Sea ❶ *Chinese* ∇ 24 | 22 | 24 | $28

Westchester Heights | 1475 Williamsbridge Rd. (bet. Silver St. & St. Raymonds Ave.) | Bronx | 718-863-7900 | www.hawaiiseanyc.com
"Well-flavored", "typical Chinese" fare, "always-fresh" sushi, plus plentiful Polynesian potables have kept this Bronx spot afloat for decades; the setting's "quiet" and service "quick", but those who don't want to venture out find delivery is equally "speedy."

New Leaf Ⓜ *American* 21 | 24 | 21 | $43

Washington Heights | Fort Tryon Park | 1 Margaret Corbin Dr. (190th St.) | 212-568-5323 | www.newleafrestaurant.com
Almost "like a country inn", this "charming" American "getaway" in "lovely" Fort Tryon Park offers "appealing" locavore-friendly fare matched with equally "pleasant" service; profits go to Bette Midler's NY Restoration Project, so few mind if it's "a bit pricey" – especially if they're dining on the "magical" terrace.

New Malaysia *Malaysian* ∇ 23 | 13 | 16 | $20

Chinatown | Chinatown Arcade | 46-48 Bowery (Canal St.) | 212-964-0284
Despite its "awkward location" in a "Chinatown alley", this Malaysian mainstay has been "packing in the locals" for 30-plus years; given its "huge menu" of "delicious", seriously "inexpensive" dishes, "flavor" junkies overlook its "cramped" digs and "not-up-to-snuff" service.

New WonJo ❶ *Korean* ∇ 24 | 15 | 19 | $35

Garment District | 23 W. 32nd St. (bet. B'way & 5th Ave.) | 212-695-5815 | www.newwonjo.com
"Korean awesomeness, 24 hours a day" is the deal at this K-town vet whose low-cost, "crave"-worthy specialties include tableside BBQ; "service can be harried", but the room's recent "update" wins "bonus points" because now "you won't smell like the grill."

NEW Ngam ❶ *Thai* ∇ 21 | 15 | 19 | $38

E Village | 99 Third Ave. (bet. 12th & 13th Sts.) | 212-777-8424 | www.ngamnyc.com
"Worth a try" for its "imaginative" "twists" on Thai comfort fare, this "bright" East Villager is also favored for its "value" pricing and "personable" service; while "giant plates" on "small tables" add to the "tight" feel of its rough-hewn space, sidewalk seating eases the crush.

Nha Trang *Vietnamese* 23 | 8 | 17 | $20

Chinatown | 148 Centre St. (bet. Walker & White Sts.) | 212-941-9292
Chinatown | 87 Baxter St. (bet. Bayard & Canal Sts.) | 212-233-5948
The "wonderful pho" and other "honest" Vietnamese fare dished up at this Chinatown twosome is "so good", it's almost a "reason to love jury

duty"; sure, service is "get-'em-in-and-out" and the settings "totally charmless", but "who cares" – "it's so cheap, you could treat 10 friends."

Nice Green Bo ⌀ *Chinese*   23 | 6 | 12 | $19

Chinatown | 66 Bayard St. (bet. Elizabeth & Mott Sts.) | 212-625-2359
"Hungry hordes" hit this Chinatown "hole-in-the-wall" to nosh on "some of NY's best soup dumplings" and other "first-rate, bargain-priced" Shanghai specialties; "dumpy" digs and "grumpy" staffers are part of the "experience."

Nice Matin ● *French/Mediterranean*   20 | 19 | 19 | $45

W 70s | 201 W. 79th St. (Amsterdam Ave.) | 212-873-6423 | www.nicematinnyc.com
An "ol' reliable" for "every meal", this "smart" UWS "crowd-pleaser" combines a "Riviera vibe" with "well-prepared" French-Med fare and "impressive" wines at "reasonable prices"; "alfresco dining" is another "draw", especially when the "pretty" interior gets "busy" and the "din" goes "over the top."

Nick & Toni's Cafe *Mediterranean*   20 | 17 | 19 | $48

W 60s | 100 W. 67th St. (bet. B'way & Columbus Ave.) | 212-496-4000 | www.nickandtoniscafe.com
Just a "short walk" from Lincoln Center, this "low-key" offshoot of the "popular" East Hampton standby plies "enjoyable", "straightforward" Mediterranean fare with "quick" service; "reasonable" prices make it a good bet "pre-movie or -show", with the chance of spotting "journalists from nearby ABC."

Nick's ⌀ *Pizza*   24 | 15 | 19 | $25

E 90s | 1814 Second Ave. (94th St.) | 212-987-5700 | www.nicksnyc.com
Forest Hills | 108-26 Ascan Ave. (bet. Austin & Burns Sts.) | Queens | 718-263-1126
"Outta-this-world", "charred", thin-crust pizzas "still rock" at this "cash-only" Forest Hills pie purveyor and its UES sibling, which offer "good, old-fashioned" Italian basics; "prickly" service and "no-frills" decor deter few – those "lines are out the door for good reason."

Nicky's Vietnamese Sandwiches ⌀ *Sandwiches*   22 | 8 | 17 | $12

Financial District | 99-C Nassau St. (bet. Ann & Fulton Sts.) | 212-766-3388
Boerum Hill | 311 Atlantic Ave. (bet. Hoyt & Smith Sts.) | Brooklyn | 718-855-8838
"Crusty baguettes" and "tasty" fillings make for "the best banh mi outside of Vietnam" at this "cheap", cash-only, "bare-bones" Boerum Hill storefront, which also ladles out "fantastic" pho; the FiDi offshoot is roomier but equally "plain-Jane", so many "grab and go."

Nicola's ● *Italian*   22 | 18 | 21 | $61

E 80s | 146 E. 84th St. (bet. Lexington & 3rd Aves.) | 212-249-9850 | www.nicolasnyc.com
"Yes, it is like a private club" admit the "well-heeled" "regulars" who are drawn to this "unhurried" Upper Eastsider by its "scrumptious", "old-time" Italian cooking and its "warm welcomes"; despite being "expensive" and "a wee bit dated", it's good to know that you can "develop membership status" with return visits.

NEW Nicoletta ● *Italian/Pizza*

— | — | — | M

E Village | 160 Second Ave. (10th St.) | 212-432-1600 |
www.nicolettanyc.com

Michael White (Marea, Osteria Morini) unveils his most casual venture to date with this East Village Italian, a buzzy, moderately priced pizzeria whose pies sport thick Midwestern-style crusts and traditional toppings; the flashy, roller derby–esque decor includes branded tableware and shiny silver light fixtures, offset by exposed-brick walls that do little to buffer the din.

99 Miles to Philly ●⍧ *Cheesesteaks*

22 | 12 | 18 | $15

E Village | 94 Third Ave. (bet. 12th & 13th Sts.) | 212-253-2700 |
www.99milestophilly.com

The closest you'll get to Philly that "doesn't involve a Chinatown bus", this cash-only East Village cheesesteak palace offers a marquee sandwich that's a "solid", "satisfying", "gooey mess"; "late-night" availability trumps "grungy" looks and minimal seats, but aesthetes advise "get it to go"; P.S. a Midtown spin-off at 300 East 45th Street is in the works.

Ninja *Japanese*

19 | 26 | 24 | $60

TriBeCa | 25 Hudson St. (bet. Duane & Reade Sts.) | 212-274-8500 |
www.ninjanewyork.com

With "jumping ninjas and a roaming magic act", they really "go all out" at this "gimmicky" TriBeCa theme joint done up "like a Japanese village" in feudal times; it's "fun for kids", but grown-ups' opinions vary ("naff" vs. "a blast") – most agree you'll "shell out" for only "so-so" eats.

Nino's *Italian*

21 | 19 | 22 | $56

E 70s | 1354 First Ave. (bet. 72nd & 73rd Sts.) | 212-988-0002

Nino's Bellissima Pizza *Pizza*

E 40s | 890 Second Ave. (bet. 47th & 48th Sts.) | 212-355-5540

Nino's Positano *Italian*

E 40s | 890 Second Ave. (bet. 47th & 48th Sts.) | 212-355-5540

Nino's Tuscany Steak House *Italian/Steak*

W 50s | 117 W. 58th St. (bet. 6th & 7th Aves.) | 212-757-8630
www.ninony.com

"Terrific host" Nino himself oversees the "gracious" service at his mini-empire dishing up "truly good", pleasingly "familiar" fare, including steakhouse classics at the Tuscany outpost and pies at the more casual Bellissima Pizza; besides the "old-world" settings, you can expect "comfortable" "hospitality."

Nippon ⌧ *Japanese*

▽ 23 | 18 | 23 | $66

E 50s | 155 E. 52nd St. (bet. Lexington & 3rd Aves.) | 212-758-0226 |
www.restaurantnippon.com

"One of NYC's oldest", this circa-1963 Japanese "favorite" still turns out "delicious", "traditional" fare – including sushi – with "no glitz, no glam", just "gracious" attention; maybe it's a tad "pricey" and the decor "hasn't been updated" of late, but overall it's "a treat."

Nirvana *Indian*

▽ 22 | 20 | 21 | $39

Murray Hill | 346 Lexington Ave. (bet. 39th & 40th Sts.) |
212-983-0000 | www.nirvanany.com

"Perfectly seasoned" classics at moderate rates draw curryphiles to this "upscale", lesser-known Murray Hill Indian where they "tailor the spice to taste"; "attentive" staffers tend the "contemporary", brick-walled setting featuring a livelier lounge and "inviting" upstairs dining room.

Nizza ● French/Italian

20 | 17 | 19 | $38

W 40s | 630 Ninth Ave. (bet. 44th & 45th Sts.) | 212-956-1800 | www.nizzanyc.com

"Won't-break-the-bank" prices for "solid" classics ensure this "casual" Hell's Kitchen French-Italian is plenty "popular" pre- or post-theater; the noise level can be "a bit much", but "cheerful" staffers and sidewalk seating take the edge off; P.S. the "gluten-free options are a godsend."

☑ Nobu Japanese

27 | 23 | 24 | $83

TriBeCa | 105 Hudson St. (Franklin St.) | 212-219-0500

Nobu 57 ● Japanese

W 50s | 40 W. 57th St. (bet. 5th & 6th Aves.) | 212-757-3000

Nobu, Next Door Japanese

TriBeCa | 105 Hudson St. (bet. Franklin & N. Moore Sts.) | 212-334-4445 www.noburestaurants.com

"Still going strong", Nobu Matsuhisa's "groundbreaking" 1994 TriBeCa flagship draws a "glitzy crowd" to feast on "delectable" Japanese-Peruvian fare in a "stunning" space designed by David Rockwell with a "cool little brother" next door; at any of the three you're likely to "bump into someone famous", especially at the "sleek", "sexy" (if "more touristy") Midtown outpost – you can also expect tabs that run "a pretty penny."

Nocello Italian

24 | 19 | 22 | $51

W 50s | 257 W. 55th St. (bet. B'way & 8th Ave.) | 212-713-0224 | www.nocello.net

"Enduring and endearing" – not to mention "convenient" if you're bound for Carnegie Hall or City Center – this "cozy" Tuscan turns out "plentiful" platefuls of "fine" fare; "charming owners" who "take pride" add an "intimate" feel to the "unassuming" digs.

Noche Mexicana Mexican

∇ 23 | 13 | 19 | $21

W 100s | 842 Amsterdam Ave. (bet. 101st & 102nd Sts.) | 212-662-6900 | www.noche-mexicana.com

"Come hungry" to this Upper Westsider dishing up "*muy autentico*" "homestyle" Mexican cooking; it's in new down-the-block quarters but boasts the same "unbeatable prices", and as for service, it "improves if you speak Spanish (even just a little)."

NoHo Star ● American/Asian

20 | 17 | 19 | $36

NoHo | 330 Lafayette St. (Bleecker St.) | 212-925-0070 | www.nohostar.com

The "offbeat" menu "should just say 'everything, plus Chinese'" at this "longstanding" NoHo "favorite" that "cheerfully" offers Asian specialties "side by side" with "kicked-up" New American eats; tabs "priced right" and a "bright", "comfy" setting are other reasons this "star keeps shining."

Noi Due Italian/Kosher

∇ 21 | 17 | 20 | $34

W 60s | 143 W. 69th St., downstairs (bet. B'way & Columbus Ave.) | 212-712-2222 | www.noiduecafe.com

Italian fare so "surprisingly good" you "wouldn't know it's kosher" is the lure at this "casual" Lincoln Center–area eatery specializing in brick-oven pizzas; "affordable" rates compensate for a no-rez policy that spells "long" waits, while a "friendly", "handsome" owner dresses up the "tight", "bare-bones" basement digs.

NEW Noir ●☒ *American* | - | - | - | E |

E 50s | 151 E. 50th St. (bet. Lexington & 3rd Aves.) | 212-753-1144 | www.noir-ny.com

This bi-level American brasserie is a flashy new addition to the East 50s, serving upscale, updated comfort favorites and complicated cocktails in a clubby room accented by old Hollywood portraits, plush banquettes and a swooping spiral staircase separating the dining area from a swanky upstairs lounge.

Z NEW NoMad *American/European*   ▽ 26 | 27 | 25 | $84 |

Chelsea | NoMad Hotel | 1170 Broadway (28th St.) | 347-472-5660 | www.thenomadhotel.com

Devotees of Eleven Madison's Daniel Humm and Will Guidara declare "they've done it again" with this "less expensive" (though certainly not cheap) "chill new spot" in the happening NoMad Hotel; the "sublime" à la carte American-European cuisine showcases seasonal produce and comes via an "on-point" team in a variety of "lovely" rooms; fans say it should be renamed "YesMad."

Nom Wah Tea Parlor *Chinese*   22 | 13 | 18 | $22 |

Chinatown | 13 Doyers St. (bet. Bowery & Pell St.) | 212-962-6047 | www.nomwah.com

You may "need Google Maps" to find it, but it's worth seeking out this "quintessential" Chinatown parlor for its "dazzling array" of "real-deal", "made-to-order" dim sum; around since 1920 but recently "re-vitalized", it gets a "bravo" for its "fire-sale prices" and newly added wines and beers.

Noodle Bar ⊄ *Asian/Noodle Shop*   22 | 13 | 18 | $20 |

LES | 172 Orchard St. (Stanton St.) | 212-228-9833
W Village | 26 Carmine St. (bet. Bedford & Bleecker Sts.) | 212-524-6800 | www.noodlebarnyc.com

"Fast and satisfying" noodle soups and wok dishes are what's on offer at this "unassuming" LES-West Village Pan-Asian duo; they "warm you up" and "fill you up" for "cheap", so most don't mind the "no-frills" settings and service with some "rough" edges.

Noodle Pudding Ⓜ⊄ *Italian*   25 | 18 | 21 | $39 |

Brooklyn Heights | 38 Henry St. (bet. Cranberry & Middagh Sts.) | Brooklyn | 718-625-3737

A "beacon" in Brooklyn Heights, this "boisterous", "noisy" Italian is usually "hopping by 6:30" thanks to a "loyal local following" that "loves" its "fantastic food" and "delightful" staff; cash-only, no-rez" hassles are offset by the "convivial" mood and "more-than-fair" prices.

Nook ⊄ *Eclectic*   23 | 13 | 19 | $30 |

W 50s | 746 Ninth Ave. (bet. 50th & 51st Sts.) | 212-247-5500

Only "slightly bigger than a walk-in closet", this "aptly named" Hell's Kitchen "neighborhood hangout" compensates for its "cramped setting" and "sometimes gruff" service with "well-prepared" Eclectic eats; the "cash-only" policy hardly matters since "BYO makes it a super bargain."

	FOOD	DECOR	SERVICE	COST

Norma's *American*
25 | 20 | 21 | $44

W 50s | Le Parker Meridien | 119 W. 56th St. (bet. 6th & 7th Aves.) |
212-708-7460 | www.normasnyc.com

"Even the OJ is amazing" at this Parker Meridien American that's a
"legend" for "over-the-top" breakfast and brunch; it's a "star-spotting"
"mob scene" (reserve ahead or face "long queues"), and you'll "pay
handsomely" – but then it "may be the only meal you need that day."

☑NEW North End Grill *American/Seafood*
25 | 23 | 26 | $71

Financial District | 104 North End Ave. (bet. Murray & Vesey Sts.) |
646-747-1600 | www.northendgrillnyc.com

"Danny Meyer hits another home run" with this "pricey" New American
arrival to Battery Park City, where ex-Tabla toque Floyd Cardoz per-
forms "subtle" "magic" with a "remarkable" seafood-centric menu;
beyond the "Goldman Sachsers letting off steam" in the bar lies a
"quiet", "modern" dining room tended by an "exceptional" crew, with
a chef's counter overlooking the "kitchen action."

Northern Spy Food Co. *American*
24 | 18 | 21 | $43

E Village | 511 E. 12th St. (bet. Aves. A & B) | 212-228-5100 |
www.northernspyfoodco.com

A "wizard" must man the burners at this "wonderfully eccentric" East
Village "destination for locavores" given its "savory" "farm-to-table"
American fare offered at "moderate" rates; service from "warm, fuzzy
folks" makes up for "little" digs that are "crammed" at prime times.

North Square *American*
23 | 19 | 22 | $48

G Village | Washington Sq. Hotel | 103 Waverly Pl. (MacDougal St.) |
212-254-1200 | www.northsquareny.com

Apart from the "Washington Square regulars" and "half of NYU", "no
one knows" about this "swell little neighborhood place", a "favorite"
of "grown-ups" who "count on" its "superior", "value"-priced New
American cuisine and "cordial, pro" service; an "easy" vibe – i.e. you
"can talk without going hoarse" – seals the deal.

No. 7 ●Ⓜ *American*
23 | 17 | 18 | $26

Fort Greene | 7 Greene Ave. (bet. Cumberland & Fulton Sts.) |
Brooklyn | 718-522-6370 | www.no7restaurant.com

No. 7 Sub *Sandwiches*

Chelsea | Ace Hotel | 1188 Broadway (bet. 28th & 29th Sts.) |
212-532-1680 Ⓢ

NEW **W 50s** | Plaza Food Hall | 1 W. 59th St., lower level (5th Ave.) |
646-755-3228

NEW **Greenpoint** | 931 Manhattan Ave. (bet. Java & Kent Sts.) |
Brooklyn | 718-389-7775
www.no7sub.com

Fort Greene locals and BAM-goers seeking something "original" hit
this "relaxed", "hipster"-friendly New American known for "inventive"
combos that sound "bizarre" but generally "hit the flavor Lotto"; similarly "odd pairings work magic" in sandwich form at the "laid-back"
Ace Hotel, Greenpoint and Plaza Food Hall take-out spin-offs.

Numero 28 ⊘ *Pizza*
24 | 14 | 19 | $27

NEW **E 70s** | 1431 First Ave. (bet. 74th & 75th Sts.) | 212-772-8200
E Village | 176 Second Ave. (bet. 11th & 12th Sts.) | 212-777-1555 ●

(continued)

Numero 28

SoHo | 196 Spring St. (bet. Sullivan & Thompson Sts.) | 212-219-9020
W Village | 28 Carmine St. (bet. Bedford & Bleecker Sts.) | 212-463-9653
www.numero28.com

"Real Italians" are responsible for the "perfectly crisp"–crusted "rect-
angular" pies from wood-fired brick ovens at this pizzeria mini-chain;
the "reasonable cost" pleases the wallet-consicous, while a general
"nonchalant" attitude boosts the "authentic" dolce vita vibe;
P.S. SoHo's mostly takeout.

Nove Ⓜ *Italian*

∇ 26 | 24 | 25 | $52

Eltingville | 3900 Richmond Ave. (Amboy Rd.) | Staten Island |
718-227-3286 | www.noveitalianbistro.com

"Not your typical SI Italian", this "trendy" trattoria "fills a void" with its
"excellent" cuisine served in "fancy" environs by staffers who treat you
"really well"; yes, it's "high-priced" for the borough, but it's "crowded"
nonetheless – be sure to "make a reservation."

Novitá ⬤ *Italian*

25 | 19 | 23 | $60

Gramercy | 102 E. 22nd St. (bet. Lexington Ave. & Park Ave. S.) |
212-677-2222 | www.novitanyc.com

"The definition of 'neighborhood gem'", this "unpretentious" Gramercy
vet serves Northern Italian fare "so scrumptious", "no one seems to
mind" "cheek-to-jowl" seating and "concomitant noise levels"; "highly
efficient" service and "modestly priced wines" are other reasons regulars plead "please keep this a secret."

Num Pang *Cambodian/Sandwiches*

25 | 7 | 16 | $13

E 40s | 140 E. 41st St. (bet. Lexington & 3rd Aves.) | 212-867-8889
G Village | 21 E. 12th St. (bet. 5th Ave. & University Pl.) | 212-255-3271 ⊅
www.numpangnyc.com

"Cambodia's answer" to the banh mi "craze", this duo dispenses
"damn-good" sandwiches "worth standing in line" for, with "more-
than-fair" prices and "speedy service" sweetening the deal; the newer
East 41st Street branch offers more seating than the Village original,
but "no-frills" describes both locations.

Nurnberger Bierhaus *German*

∇ 23 | 21 | 22 | $32

New Brighton | 817 Castleton Ave. (bet. Davis & Pelton Aves.) |
Staten Island | 718-816-7461 | www.nurnbergerbierhaus.com

Staten Islanders in the mood for "Wiener schnitzel and beer" "meet
the gang" at New Brighton's "fun" take on Bavaria, where the German
grub is matched with "wonderful" brews on tap; it's "authentic" down
to the "hokey decor", dirndl-clad staff and biergarten in back.

Nyonya ⊅ *Malaysian*

23 | 15 | 16 | $24

Little Italy | 199 Grand St. (bet. Mott & Mulberry Sts.) |
212-334-3669 ⬤
Bensonhurst | 2322 86th St. (bet. 23rd & 24th Aves.) | Brooklyn |
718-265-0888
Borough Park | 5323 Eighth Ave. (bet. 53rd & 54th Sts.) | Brooklyn |
718-633-0808 ⬤
www.ilovenyonya.com

When you crave "spice and exotic flavors", this "amazing" Malaysian
trio fills the bill with "generous" servings of "fresh", "delicious" dishes

at "ridiculously good" rates (just "bring cash"); "assembly-line" service and "packed", basic quarters only "add to the experience."

NYY Steak *Steak* | 23 | 22 | 21 | $66 |

Yankee Stadium | Yankee Stadium | 1 E. 161st St., Gate 6 (River Ave.) | Bronx | 646-977-8325 | www.nyysteak.com

"Heaven" for Bronx Bombers fans, this year-round steakhouse inside Yankee Stadium is a carnivore's "home run" given its "surprisingly good" beef served up in "baseball-themed" digs; "you'll pay" for sure, but "you can't beat the atmosphere" – especially when the team "just won."

Oaxaca 🖘 *Mexican* | 21 | 12 | 18 | $15 |

E Village | 16 Extra Pl. (bet. Bowery & 2nd Ave.) | 212-677-3340
NEW W Village | 48 Greenwich Ave. (bet. Charles & Perry Sts.) | 212-366-4488
Cobble Hill | 251 Smith St. (bet. Degraw & Douglass Sts.) | Brooklyn | 718-643-9630
Park Slope | 250 Fourth Ave. (bet. Carroll & President Sts.) | Brooklyn | 718-222-1122 ☻
www.oaxacatacos.com

"Addictive", "legit" tacos keep 'em coming to these "casual" Mexicans where "unbeatable prices" also "hit the mark"; service of the "don't-hold-your-breath" variety and "small", "no-frills" settings mean many suggest "skip eating in" and get it to go.

Oceana *American/Seafood* | 24 | 23 | 24 | $76 |

W 40s | McGraw Hill Bldg. | 120 W. 49th St. (bet. 6th & 7th Aves.) | 212-759-5941 | www.oceanarestaurant.com

"*Mad Men*" types and other "Midtown suits" mosey into this "vast" Rock Center American "temple of seafood" to feast on marine cuisine ferried by a "smooth, efficient" crew; some complain the "posh" setting is a cross between "boardroom" and "fishbowl", with tariffs at "corporate-card" level, but the hooked maintain they'd "even spend" their "own money" to go.

Ocean Grill *Seafood* | 24 | 21 | 22 | $56 |

W 70s | 384 Columbus Ave. (bet. 78th & 79th Sts.) | 212-579-2300 | www.oceangrill.com

"King Neptune would approve" of Steve Hanson's "stylish" UWS piscatorium where "swimmingly good" fin fare comes via a "sweet", "well-trained" staff; the "nautical, white-linen" interior can get "loud and boisterous", but if you're "lucky" you'll land a quieter "outside" seat.

The Odeon ☻ *American/French* | 20 | 18 | 19 | $51 |

TriBeCa | 145 W. Broadway (bet. Duane & Thomas Sts.) | 212-233-0507 | www.theodeonrestaurant.com

Its '80s heyday is long past, but this TriBeCa "institution" "still has a bit of buzz" thanks to its "reliable" Franco-American fare "promptly" served in "pleasant" bistro digs; it's perfect for a "casual" meal with the "kids" ("all on their iPads"), brunch or a "lively" late-night bite.

Ofrenda *Mexican* | ▽ 23 | 17 | 22 | $38 |

W Village | 113 Seventh Ave. S. (bet. Christopher & W. 10th Sts.) | 212-924-2305 | www.ofrendanyc.com

A "cut above" your corner Mexican joint – "make that two cuts" – this "informal" Village cantina cooks up "innovative", "*fabuloso*" fare delivered by a "terrific" staff; yes, the "cute, cozy" space is a tad "tight", but given "affordable" tabs and "creative drinks", most hardly notice.

Okeanos *Greek* | 20 | 18 | 21 | $39 |

Park Slope | 314 Seventh Ave. (8th St.) | Brooklyn | 347-725-4162 | www.okeanosnyc.com

Ok, it may look like a "glorified diner", but this "welcoming" Park Slope Hellenic produces relatively "upscale" takes on Greek staples, including flapping "fresh seafood"; an "eager-to-please" staff and "reasonable" prices are other reasons neighbors call it "a keeper."

Old Homestead *Steak* | 25 | 19 | 22 | $80 |

Meatpacking | 56 Ninth Ave. (bet. 14th & 15th Sts.) | 212-242-9040 | www.theoldhomesteadsteakhouse.com

Forget the "trendy" zip code, this "true relic" of the "old Meatpacking District" has held steady with "first-rate" steaks since "forever" (actually 1868), with "historic" chophouse decor "as evidence"; "pro" service is a given, while portions sized "to feed a family of six" help make the "high-roller" prices "worth it."

Olea *Mediterranean* | ∇ 22 | 21 | 20 | $32 |

Fort Greene | 171 Lafayette Ave. (Adelphi St.) | Brooklyn | 718-643-7003 | www.oleabrooklyn.com

"Delicious", "ambitious" tapas and a "dream"-worthy brunch "bring the Mediterranean" – and "the masses" – to this "inviting" Fort Greene "mainstay"; it boasts a "BAM-convenient" location, "charming" service, "gentle" live music – but just go "off peak" to avoid a "wait."

Olives *Mediterranean* | 23 | 22 | 22 | $56 |

Union Sq | W Hotel Union Sq. | 201 Park Ave. S. (17th St.) | 212-353-8345 | www.toddenglish.com

"Singles" "mingle" at Todd English's "fun" W Union Square Med plying an "inventive" (if "pricey") menu spotlighting "marvelous" flatbreads; an "attentive staff" tends the newly made-over "modern" digs, but the "noise" issuing from the "vibrant bar scene" can be "the pits."

Omai *Vietnamese* | 24 | 17 | 20 | $40 |

Chelsea | 158 Ninth Ave. (bet. 19th & 20th Sts.) | 212-633-0550 | www.omainyc.com

"For a change of pace", this "pleasant" Chelsea Vietnamese fills the bill with "delicious", "delicate" fare, "spiced just right"; "pleasant prices" are a plus, but since they "added the sign" outside, insiders lament that the "tight", "low-key" space has become "crowded."

Omen ● *Japanese* | ∇ 26 | 22 | 24 | $60 |

SoHo | 113 Thompson St. (bet. Prince & Spring Sts.) | 212-925-8923

"Outstanding" Kyoto-style fare is the hallmark of this "classic SoHo" Japanese veteran offering "excellent" cooked dishes plus sashimi (but no sushi); "efficient" staffers oversee the "serene setting" where "celeb sightings" are a "good omen" – if also a prediction of "expensive" tabs.

Omonia Cafe ● *Coffeehouse/Greek* | 20 | 17 | 17 | $21 |

Astoria | 32-20 Broadway (33rd St.) | Queens | 718-274-6650 | www.omoniacafe.com

A "mind-boggling array" of "heavenly" sweets awaits at this Astoria Greek coffeehouse also serving savory "comfort food"; the "neon "lights" and "disco vibe" suit "teenagers" who "hang out and socialize", but everyone appreciates prices that don't "break your piggy bank."

NEW 1 Bite Mediterranean *Mediterranean*   22 | 21 | 22 | $35
E 50s | 1071 First Ave. (bet. 58th & 59th Sts.) | 212-888-0809 | www.1bitenyc.com
Plan on consuming more than the name suggests at this new East Side Med, because the kitchen's "authentic" small plates are "very tasty" and "healthy" to boot; a "friendly" staff, affordable tabs and "pleasing" ambiance round out the "enjoyable" package.

☒ One if by Land, Two if by Sea *American*   24 | 27 | 25 | $104
W Village | 17 Barrow St. (bet. 7th Ave. S. & W. 4th St.) | 212-228-0822 | www.oneifbyland.com
"Prepare to be swept away" by this "gorgeous" Village American that was "once the carriage house of Aaron Burr" and now "oozes" "romance" with ambiance as "seductively delicious" as the beef Wellington on its "stellar" prix fixe–only menu; add "classy service" and it "makes for a magical evening", though you'd best be "feeling splurgey."

101 *American/Italian*   22 | 21 | 21 | $43
Bay Ridge | 10018 Fourth Ave. (101st St.) | Brooklyn | 718-833-1313
It's "still tough to find a table" on prime nights at this longtime Bay Ridge "local joint" whose solid, midpriced Italian-American fare, "wonderful location overlooking the Verrazano" and convenient valet parking keep 'em coming; "busy, loud" atmosphere is part of the package.

1 or 8 Ⓜ *Japanese*   24 | 22 | 24 | $48
Williamsburg | 66 S. Second St. (bet. Kent & Wythe Aves.) | Brooklyn | 718-384-2152 | www.oneoreightbk.com
"Unique style" permeates this "off-the-beaten-path" Williamsburg sushi standout spinning "unconventional" takes on Japanese fare in a "sleek white" setting that's a "minimalist's" "heaven"; along with the "high quality" fare, regulars single out the "delightful staff" as key to the "consistently solid" experience.

107 West *Eclectic*   21 | 19 | 20 | $35
W 100s | 2787 Broadway (bet. 107th & 108th Sts.) | 212-864-1555 | www.107west.com
A "longtime haunt" near Columbia, this no-frills "favorite" plies a "decent" "do-all" Eclectic menu spanning the gamut from Cajun and Tex-Mex "basics" to pastas and sushi; maybe it's "nothing too exciting", but the "happy-to-have you" service and "fair prices" keep the seats full.

Oriental Garden *Chinese/Seafood*   23 | 13 | 15 | $35
Chinatown | 14 Elizabeth St. (bet. Bayard & Canal Sts.) | 212-619-0085
"Don't let the drab decor fool you" at this vintage C-town Cantonese, because the fresh seafood, straight from the tanks in front, will likely "knock your socks off", as will the "wonderful dim sum"; the mood may be "manic", but the "banquet" comes "without an insane price."

Orsay ◗ *French*   19 | 21 | 18 | $56
E 70s | 1057 Lexington Ave. (75th St.) | 212-517-6400 | www.orsayrestaurant.com
"*Une petite pièce de Paris*", this "boffo" brasserie draws "expats" and "the UES crowd" for "true French" fare in a "chic" art nouveau setting –

| | FOOD | DECOR | SERVICE | COST |

once you "attract a waiter", that is; despite being "expensive as sin", with decibels reaching "cacophony" at times, it's a "loved" "local haunt."

Orso ● *Italian*   24 | 19 | 22 | $57

W 40s | 322 W. 46th St. (bet. 8th & 9th Aves.) | 212-489-7212 | www.orsorestaurant.com

For 30 years "ingenues and the famous" have "schmoozed" alongside regular "hoi polloi" at this "clubby" Theater District "charmer" that still earns raves for its "phenomenal" Tuscan fare and "never-miss-the-curtain" service; even though it's a tad "spendy", "the worst problem is getting a reservation" – it's "packed for a reason."

Osso Buco *Italian*   22 | 18 | 21 | $44

E 90s | 1662 Third Ave. (93rd St.) | 212-426-5422 | www.ossobuco2010.com

It's "not adventurous" and the digs are "nothing special", but this "trusty" Italian is "a satisfying option" for Upper Eastsiders and 92nd Street Y visitors, thanks to its "tasty" "red-sauce" fare served "family-style"; "accommodating" service, a "relaxed" vibe and "easy prices" seal the deal.

Osteria al Doge ● *Italian*   21 | 18 | 20 | $48

W 40s | 142 W. 44th St. (bet. B'way & 6th Ave.) | 212-944-3643 | www.osteria-doge.com

"Handy" for showgoers, this "pleasant" Theater District Italian vends "well-executed", "well-priced" Venetian cooking ferried by "prompt" staffers who "get you in and out" for the curtain; the "busy" main room becomes "deafening" at prime times, but "the balcony is quieter."

Osteria Laguna ● *Italian*   22 | 18 | 19 | $46

E 40s | 209 E. 42nd St. (bet. 2nd & 3rd Aves.) | 212-557-0001 | www.osteria-laguna.com

Offering a "welcome" "neighborhood feel in a non-neighborhood area", this "busy" Italian between Grand Central and the U.N. serves "straight-ahead" Venetian eats at fair rates; it's a "perfect lunch spot for on-the-go execs", with a "people-watching" bonus when the French doors are open.

Osteria Morini *Italian*   24 | 20 | 21 | $57

SoHo | 218 Lafayette St. (bet. Kenmare & Spring Sts.) | 212-965-8777 | www.osteriamorini.com

"Another winner for Michael White" (Marea), this "more casual", more "affordable" SoHo Italian "hot spot" offers "fantastic" pastas and other fare from the Emilia-Romagna region; service is "efficient", and even though the "cute, rustic" quarters can get "crammed" and "raucous", you're likely to "leave happy."

Otto ● *Italian/Pizza*   24 | 20 | 20 | $40

G Village | 1 Fifth Ave. (enter on 8th St., bet. 5th Ave. & University Pl.) | 212-995-9559 | www.ottopizzeria.com

"All age groups" "enjoy the ride" at the Village's "upbeat" Batali-Bastianich enoteca/pizzeria done up like an "old railway station" and dispensing "brilliant" pizzas backed by a "mile-long" wine list; "pro" service and "low prices" are on track, so the only downside is there's so much "good energy" that you may "think the train's arriving."

Ouest *American*
`25` `22` `23` `$67`

W 80s | 2315 Broadway (84th St.) | 212-580-8700 | www.ouestny.com
"Still bringing it" on the UWS, Tom Valenti's "high-end hangout" supplies "scrumptious", "feel-good" New American fare in a "classy" setting straight off an "old movie" set; "gracious" service and "blissfully subdued" decibels are added reasons for the crowd to say 'go Ouest young man' – especially for the "easy-on-the-wallet" $34 early-bird.

Our Place *Chinese*
`20` `16` `19` `$37`

E 70s | 242 E. 79th St. (bet. 2nd & 3rd Aves.) | 212-288-4888 | www.ourplace79.com
At this "white-tablecloth" UES Chinese "standby", "above-par" Cantonese standards – plus dim sum on weekends – please locals who "don't want to travel" Downtown; "usually smooth service" and slightly "nicer digs" since a recent move help make it "worth the few extra yuan."

Ovelia *Greek*
▽ `23` `20` `21` `$35`

Astoria | 34-01 30th Ave. (34th St.) | Queens | 718-721-7217 | www.ovelia-ny.com
A "go-to" for Astorians seeking "Greek chic", this bar/eatery offers "fresh" Hellenic specialties with "a modern twist", including housemade sausages; "hospitable" owners, modest tabs and a "casual", "pleasant" setting that opens to "outdoor seating" help keep it "popular."

Oyster Bar 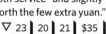 *Seafood*
`23` `18` `18` `$49`

E 40s | Grand Central | Lower level (42nd St. & Vanderbilt Ave.) | 212-490-6650 | www.oysterbarny.com
You can imagine "the ghosts of commuters past" at this "brassy" seafooder "in the belly of Grand Central", celebrating 100 years and still serving an "amazing" array of "plump, fresh" bivalves, "succulent" pan roasts and chowders; its "gruff service" is "legendary", as is the general "roar" in the "great vaulted room", though the Saloon in back is "quieter"; in case you wonder, this is New York.

Pachanga Patterson *Mexican*
▽ `23` `21` `21` `$28`

Astoria | 33-17 31st Ave. (bet. 33rd & 34th Sts.) | Queens | 718-554-0525 | www.pachangapatterson.com
Putting a "cool spin" on Mexican classics, this "hip" new Astorian from the Vesta folks offers "reasonably priced" tacos, small plates and a few mains; the colorful quarters serve as a "low-key" "hangout", while the "sunny" backyard is another reason it's a "wonderful find."

Pacificana *Chinese*
`24` `17` `19` `$28`

Sunset Park | 813 55th St., 2nd fl. (8th Ave.) | Brooklyn | 718-871-2880
"Delicious dim sum" at "pleasing" prices draws "throngs" to this Hong Kong–style "palace" in Sunset Park, where a roster of Cantonese classics backs up what's on the "carts rolling by"; although the "helpful" staff is "quick", the "huge" digs are often a "madhouse", so "be patient" – it's "worth the wait."

Padre Figlio 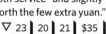 *Italian*
▽ `25` `20` `24` `$59`

E 40s | 310 E. 44th St. (bet. 1st & 2nd Aves.) | 212-286-4310 | www.padrefiglio.com
A "welcoming" vibe prevails at this "unheralded" Midtown Italian steakhouse, where a "father-and-son team" "makes you feel at home"

as you dine on "simply scrumptious" fare; live jazz on weekends is a bonus, as is the $39 prix fixe.

�"2 The Palm *Steak*

FOOD	DECOR	SERVICE	COST
25	19	23	$77

E 40s | 837 Second Ave. (bet. 44th & 45th Sts.) | 212-687-2953 🖪
E 40s | 840 Second Ave. (bet. 44th & 45th Sts.) | 212-697-5198
TriBeCa | 206 West St. (bet. Chambers & Warren Sts.) | 646-395-6393
W 50s | 250 W. 50th St. (bet. B'way & 8th Ave.) | 212-333-7256
www.thepalm.com

Epitomizing "everything you expect" from a great steakhouse, these meateries serve up "big, fat steaks" and "humongous" lobsters in a "masculine" milieu with "sawdust on the floor" and "caricatures of famous customers" on the walls; they're "perennial favorites" for "business lunches" and "guys' nights out", complete with "expense account"-ready prices, and insiders say the circa-1926 flagship at 837 Second Avenue is "the best" of the bunch.

Palma *Italian*

▽ 23	19	22	$55

W Village | 28 Cornelia St. (bet. Bleecker & W. 4th Sts.) | 212-691-2223 | www.palmanyc.com

Sicilian cooking made with "loving care" tastes "like nonna's homemade" at this "charming" West Villager, where "friendly attention" from the staff boosts the "true neighborhood" feel; the "lovely garden" adds appeal, while the back carriage house is "perfect for a special occasion."

🖪 Palm Court *American*

21	27	22	$66

W 50s | Plaza Hotel | 768 Fifth Ave. (59th St.) | 212-546-5300 | www.theplaza.com

It doesn't "come much more elegant" than this NYC "icon" within the Plaza, where a "gracious" staff glides through the "gorgeous", "gilded, marble"-and-palm-lined setting to offer the American "royal" treatment at lunch, brunch and afternoon tea; it's a "splurge", yes, but "not just for tourists."

Palo Santo *Pan-Latin*

▽ 22	21	22	$40

Park Slope | 652 Union St. (bet. 4th & 5th Aves.) | Brooklyn | 718-636-6311 | www.palosanto.us

Park Slopers seeking a "change from the usual" head to this "intimate", midpriced "favorite" supplying "surprising", "*delicioso*" Pan-Latin dishes centered around "seasonal" ingredients; a "super-casual" setting manned by the "sweetest" staffers makes it a favorite for "repeat" visits.

Pampano *Mexican/Seafood*

24	21	21	$54

E 40s | 209 E. 49th St., 2nd fl. (bet. 2nd & 3rd Aves.) | 212-751-4545
Pampano Botaneria 🖪 *Mexican*
NEW **E 40s** | 209 E. 49th St. (bet. 2nd & 3rd Aves.) | 212-751-4545
Pampano Taqueria *Mexican*
E 40s | Crystal Pavilion | 805 Third Ave. (bet. 49th & 50th Sts.) | 212-751-5257
www.modernmexican.com

Mexican "hits the high notes" at this "top-drawer" seafooder from chef Richard Sandoval and tenor Placido Domingo, where "unobtrusive" servers tend the "upstairs dining room" and "lovely" "rooftop" terrace; the new ground-floor Botaneria earns "kudos" for its "interesting tapas", while Taqueria around the corner continues to do "gangbuster business."

	FOOD	DECOR	SERVICE	COST

Pam Real Thai Food ⊅ *Thai*

22 | 10 | 18 | $23

W 40s | 402 W. 47th St. (bet. 9th & 10th Aves.) | 212-315-4441
W 40s | 404 W. 49th St. (bet. 9th & 10th Aves.) | 212-333-7500
www.pamrealthaifood.com

"Real-deal" Thai, "spiced to your taste", comes via "cheerful", "speedy" staffers at this cash-only Hell's Kitchen duo considered an "excellent pre-theater" choice; the digs are "kinda dumpy" "but who cares" – you're getting "one of the best deals in town."

Paola's *Italian*

23 | 20 | 22 | $61

E 90s | Wales Hotel | 1295 Madison Ave. (92nd St.) | 212-794-1890 | www.paolasrestaurant.com

As a "sophisticated" haunt for "ritzy" Upper Eastsiders, this "attractive" Carnegie Hill Italian wins favor with "*delizioso*" cuisine and "hospitality" via the "gracious" eponymous owner and her "tip-top" staff; wallet-watching wags dub it "Payola's" – but it's "thriving" (and "loud") "for a reason."

Papaya King *Hot Dogs*

20 | 6 | 14 | $9

E 80s | 179 E. 86th St. (3rd Ave.) | 212-369-0648 | www.papayaking.com ●⊅
LaGuardia Airport | US Airways Terminal C, Food Court | LaGuardia Rd. | Queens | No phone 🖴 Ⓜ

"Vital to NYC", this "munch-and-go" Upper East Side "perennial" (with a LaGuardia offshoot) specializes in "awesome", "snappy" hot dogs and "frothy" fruit drinks "done dirt cheap"; you'll "eat standing up" in digs that "aren't fancy, to say the least", but it's a "siren song" for legions of "satisfied" subjects.

Pappardella ● *Italian*

20 | 17 | 19 | $41

W 70s | 316 Columbus Ave. (75th St.) | 212-595-7996 | www.pappardella.com

This "inviting" Upper West Side "neighborhood joint" is a "not-too-expensive" "fixture" for "consistently" "tasty pastas" and other "solid" Italian standards delivered by an "efficient" team; whether you "relax" indoors or "sit outside" and scope the sidewalk scene, count on "no pressure."

Parea Bistro *Greek*

▽ 23 | 20 | 21 | $48

Flatiron | 36 E. 20th St. (bet. B'way & Park Ave. S.) | 212-777-8448

For "traditional Greek favorites" prepared as they "should be" and matched with "attentive but unintrusive" service, Hellenists turn to this "pleasant" if somewhat unheralded Flatiron District haven; it's "fairly priced too", particularly the prix fixe "steals" ($19 at lunch, $22 dinner).

NEW Parish Hall *American*

- | - | - | I

Williamsburg | 109 N. Third St. (bet. Berry St. & Wythe Ave.) | Brooklyn | 718-782-2602 | www.parishhall.net

Hatched by the Egg gang, this Williamsburg newcomer carries on the mission of sourcing from in-state, farm-to-table producers to muster sandwiches at lunch and creatively homespun Americana by night; with its communal tables and light-wood minimalism, the space matches the sensible tabs.

	FOOD	DECOR	SERVICE	COST

The Park ◗ *Mediterranean*　　　　18 | 25 | 17 | $40

Chelsea | 118 10th Ave. (bet. 17th & 18th Sts.) | 212-352-3313 |
www.theparknyc.com

"It's all about" the "magical" atmosphere at this "stylish" multilevel
Chelsea hot spot whose "lovely" glassed-in garden feels like "Central
Park indoors"; the Med menu is "average" and the service iffy, but most
don't mind since you "go for the ambiance" and "High Line proximity."

Ⓩ Park Avenue Spring/Summer/　　25 | 27 | 24 | $77
Autumn/Winter *American*

E 60s | 100 E. 63rd St. (bet. Lexington & Park Aves.) | 212-644-1900 |
www.parkavenyc.com

A "sleek crowd" collects at this East Side "class joint" with a "smart
concept": the "exceptional" New American "menu changes according
to the season", as does the "unforgettable", AvroKO-conceived decor;
add "superior" service, and there's "a compelling reason" to drop "big
bucks" "at least four times a year."

Park Side ◗ *Italian*　　　　25 | 20 | 22 | $49

Corona | 107-01 Corona Ave. (bet. 51st Ave. & 108th St.) | Queens |
718-271-9321 | www.parksiderestaurantny.com

"*Sopranos* jokes aside", when "you want red sauce" it "doesn't get
much better" than this "Corona classic" for "fabulous old-world"
Italiana delivered by tuxedoed waiters; it's an "established" "destination" complete with "a valet", so reserve "way in advance" and expect
a "packed" house.

Parlor Steakhouse *Steak*　　　22 | 21 | 21 | $58

E 90s | 1600 Third Ave. (90th St.) | 212-423-5888 |
www.parlorsteakhouse.com

Carnegie Hill "carnivores" "counter the neighborhood's" dearth of
beef at this "modern" meatery, which tenders "top-notch" steaks and
raw-bar fare amid "enjoyable" ambiance ("lively bar scene"); prices
run "a bit high", but it's "successful" with locals who've "got the money."

NEW Parm ◗ *Italian/Sandwiches*　　24 | 17 | 19 | $29

NoLita | 248 Mulberry St. (bet. Prince & Spring Sts.) | 212-993-7189 |
www.parmnyc.com

They "elevate" chicken, meatball or eggplant parm to "dizzying
heights" at this new NoLita adjunct to Torrisi, turning out "signature
sandwiches" and other "just-right" "Italian soul food"; it's already too
"popular" for the "tiny" '50s diner–inspired space, so expect a "lengthy
wait" to "squeeze in."

Parma *Italian*　　　　22 | 14 | 21 | $58

E 70s | 1404 Third Ave. (bet. 79th & 80th Sts.) | 212-535-3520
This "longtime" UES Northern Italian is a "bastion" of "hearty", "old-
fashioned" cooking delivered by a seasoned staff that's clearly "there
to please"; maybe it's "pricey" and "not much to look at", but "it feels
right" for longtimers who return regularly.

Pascalou *French*　　　　21 | 15 | 19 | $43

E 90s | 1308 Madison Ave. (bet. 92nd & 93rd Sts.) | 212-534-7522
So long as "you don't mind sitting elbow-to-elbow", this UESer is "dependable" for "really good" French fare in the "tiniest" space; given the

| | FOOD | DECOR | SERVICE | COST |

"welcoming" vibe and "cost-conscious" tab ("especially the early-bird"), even "shoehorned" patrons "seem to be enjoying themselves."

Pasha *Turkish*

21 | 19 | 20 | $43

W 70s | 70 W. 71st St. (bet. Columbus Ave. & CPW) | 212-579-8751 | www.pashanewyork.com

It's a bit like being "magically transported" to the "Bosphorus" at this "sedate" UWS "retreat", where "fine" Turkish "staples" are enhanced by "ever-attentive" service and "civilized" surroundings; adherents applaud it as a "fairly priced" "change of pace" "en route to Lincoln Center."

Pasquale's Rigoletto *Italian*

22 | 17 | 21 | $45

Fordham | 2311 Arthur Ave. (Crescent Ave.) | Bronx | 718-365-6644

"For an authentic Bronx experience", this Arthur Avenue "landmark" "never disappoints" with its "generous" helpings of "real Italian" classics seasoned with "a lot of local color"; it's "a post-Yankee favorite", and the "live music on Saturdays" is "definitely a plus."

Pastis ● *French*

22 | 22 | 19 | $51

Meatpacking | 9 Ninth Ave. (Little W. 12th St.) | 212-929-4844 | www.pastisny.com

You feel "cooler just walking in" to Keith McNally's "Parisian" bistro "replica", a "buzzing", "noisy" Meatpacking "perennial" furnishing the "fashion"-forward with "classic" French fare "done well" from "breakfast to late-night"; it's generally a "frenetic" "scene", but if you "relax and enjoy the show" you "won't regret it."

Pastrami Queen *Deli/Kosher*

22 | 6 | 14 | $28

E 70s | 1125 Lexington Ave. (bet. 78th & 79th Sts.) | 212-734-1500 | www.pastramiqueen.com

"Outstanding pastrami" is the claim to fame of this UES deli "staple" that's "the real thing" for "overstuffed sandwiches" and other kosher "basics done right"; seating's "almost an afterthought" in the "cramped and dingy" space, though, so "takeout is best."

Patricia's *Italian*

25 | 21 | 22 | $35

Morris Park | 1082 Morris Park Ave. (bet. Haight & Lurting Aves.) | Bronx | 718-409-9069 | www.patriciasnyc.com

Bronx-based boosters of this Morris Park Italian say it "satisfies" any hankering for "solid" "homestyle cooking" and "excellent" wood-fired pizzas; it's also become "fancier" since a "makeover", though a few "miss the original" and its "bang for the buck."

Patroon ⧉ *American*

23 | 22 | 23 | $73

E 40s | 160 E. 46th St. (bet. Lexington & 3rd Aves.) | 212-883-7373 | www.patroonrestaurant.com

Ken Aretsky's "polished" East Side "business" "oasis" remains a place to "impress clients" with "solid" American fare and "first-class service" in "men's club" digs done up with "classic photos"; "especially nice" are the private rooms and roof bar, "but watch out for those prices."

Patsy's *Italian*

23 | 19 | 23 | $58

W 50s | 236 W. 56th St. (bet. B'way & 8th Ave.) | 212-247-3491 | www.patsys.com

Seemingly "untouched" since its heyday as a "Sinatra favorite", this West Midtown "golden oldie" still satisfies "hefty appetites" via "seasoned waiters" who ferry "old-school" Neapolitan fare doused with "lots of red sauce"; if the "simple" setup seems "dated", for "nostalgia" buffs that's part of the "charm."

Patsy's Pizzeria *Pizza*   21 | 13 | 17 | $27

Chelsea | 318 W. 23rd St. (bet. 8th & 9th Aves.) | 646-486-7400
E 60s | 1279 First Ave. (69th St.) | 212-639-1000
E 60s | 206 E. 60th St. (bet. 2nd & 3rd Aves.) | 212-688-9707
G Village | 67 University Pl. (bet. 10th & 11th Sts.) | 212-533-3500
Harlem | 2287-91 First Ave. (bet. 117th & 118th Sts.) |
212-534-9783 | www.thepatsyspizza.com ⊞
Murray Hill | 509 Third Ave. (bet. 34th & 35th Sts.) |
212-689-7500 ◑

W 70s | 61 W. 74th St. (bet. Columbus Ave. & CPW) | 212-579-3000
Pizzaphiles plug this colorful '30s-era "East Harlem original" and its separately owned offshoots as "family-friendly" faves for "addictive" pies – and "even the salads are awesome"; "raggedy" looks and "iffy" service aside, they appeal to "local tastes" for "economical" eats.

Paul & Jimmy's *Italian*   ▽ 21 | 19 | 22 | $45

Gramercy | 123 E. 18th St. (bet. Irving Pl. & Park Ave. S.) |
212-475-9540 | www.paulandjimmys.com
"It's been there for ages", meaning "they know what they're doing" at this "family-owned" Gramercy Italian supplying "solid", "old-school" staples via a "welcoming" crew; it's "appreciated" hereabouts, not least because the prix fixes are a "deal."

Paulie Gee's Ⓜ *Pizza*   ▽ 26 | 23 | 22 | $27

Greenpoint | 60 Greenpoint Ave. (bet. Franklin & West Sts.) |
Brooklyn | 347-987-3747 | www.pauliegee.com
There's "never a boring pizza" at this Greenpoint "standout", whose "exquisite" Neapolitan pies marry a "perfect" "wood fired" crust with "innovative" locavore-oriented toppings (including "lots of vegan options"); "omnipresent owner" Paulie himself "loves to schmooze" in the "cool, rustic" room while fans brave the "wait" "to be amazed."

Peacefood Café *Kosher/Vegan/Vegetarian*   23 | 17 | 18 | $22

W 80s | 460 Amsterdam Ave. (82nd St.) | 212-362-2266 |
www.peacefoodcafe.com
"Imaginative" (and "kosher") "vegan deliciousness" attracts an "unpretentious" crunchy clientele to this "casual", "Woodstock-like" Upper Westsider; "earnest" but "lackadaisical" service is a weak point, but "guilt-free" grub at "affordable" rates makes it hard not to "feel at peace."

Peaches *Southern*   24 | 21 | 23 | $28

Bed-Stuy | 393 Lewis Ave. (bet. Decatur & MacDonough Sts.) |
Brooklyn | 718-942-4162 | www.peachesbrooklyn.com

Peaches HotHouse Ⓜ *Southern*

Bed-Stuy | 415 Tompkins Ave. (Hancock St.) | Brooklyn |
718-483-9111 | www.peacheshothouse.com
"Peaches, how sweet you are!" gush groupies of this Bed-Stuy pair, where the "buoyant" vibe and "sincere" service are a "win-win" when combined with the "no-nonsense" "Southern comfort" menu; in sum, "your palate will be pleased", and so will your wallet.

Peanut Butter & Co. *Sandwiches*   21 | 15 | 19 | $15

G Village | 240 Sullivan St. (bet. Bleecker & W. 3rd Sts.) |
212-677-3995 | www.ilovepeanutbutter.com
"Kitschy and creative", this Village "niche" "celebrates peanut butter
in all its glory" with sammies spanning the "classics" to "concoctions
you'd never think of"; it's a surefire hit "with the kids", though the
"bare-bones" digs are "tight if you eat in."

Pearl Oyster Bar 🗷 *New England/Seafood*   26 | 16 | 21 | $48

W Village | 18 Cornelia St. (bet. Bleecker & W. 4th Sts.) |
212-691-8211 | www.pearloysterbar.com
There's "no sign of slowing down" at Rebecca Charles' Village version
of a "New England" "seaside shack", a "superior" source for "unreal"
lobster rolls and "exceptionally fresh and unfussy" fish; after all these
years, they still "don't take reservations", so "be ready" to "queue up."

Pearl Room *Seafood*   23 | 21 | 21 | $49

Bay Ridge | 8201 Third Ave. (82nd St.) | Brooklyn | 718-833-6666 |
www.thepearlroom.com
"As fancy as it gets in Bay Ridge", this seafaring "surprise" provides
"excellent preparations" of "fresh" fin fare from an "attentive" crew in
a fetching setting suitable for "romantic" encounters; predictably, the
"attractive" boatload is also "pretty pricey."

Peasant Ⓜ *Italian*   24 | 22 | 20 | $58

NoLita | 194 Elizabeth St. (bet. Prince & Spring Sts.) | 212-965-9511 |
www.peasantnyc.com
From the "warm, inviting space" to the "fabulous" "wood-fired" cuisine
and "professional" service, this "unforgettable" Italian "outshines"
more mainstream NoLita neighbors; it's not cheap, but romeos set on
"romance" really "can't go wrong" – especially in the "cellar" wine bar.

Peels ◑ *American*   21 | 21 | 18 | $35

E Village | 325 Bowery (2nd St.) | 646-602-7015 | www.peelsnyc.com
Staked somewhere "between retro and the new hip", this East Village
American duplex from "the creators of Freemans" caters to the "dis-
cerning nosher" with "well-executed" takes on Southern-style "comfort" classics; the "warm" whitewashed space hosts a "fantastic",
"buttery" brunch – "if you can get in."

Peking Duck House *Chinese*   23 | 15 | 18 | $42

Chinatown | 28 Mott St. (bet. Mosco & Pell Sts.) | 212-227-1810
E 50s | 236 E. 53rd St. (bet. 2nd & 3rd Aves.) | 212-759-8260
www.pekingduckhousenyc.com
Specializing in "Peking duck done right" ("duh"), this "steady" Chinese
twosome's "must-have" "namesake" – complete with the "pageantry of
tableside carving" – easily offsets an otherwise "unremarkable" menu;
maybe the decor's "a bit lame", but the "value couldn't be better."

Pellegrino's *Italian*   25 | 21 | 25 | $46

Little Italy | 138 Mulberry St. (bet. Grand & Hester Sts.) | 212-226-3177
"High-quality" "traditional Italian" cooking and "personal service" from
tuxedoed "pros" foster the "happy ambiance" at this "consistent"
"winner" in the "heart of Little Italy"; "out-of-town guests" will relish
the chance to "sit outside" and take in the Mulberry Street "scene."

	FOOD	DECOR	SERVICE	COST

Penang *Malaysan* 21 | 16 | 18 | $30

W 70s | 127 W. 72nd St. (bet. Amsterdam & Columbus Aves.) |
917-441-4790 | www.penangnewyork.com

Supplying curries, satays and noodle dishes that are "not that easy to
come by" in these parts, this Upper Westsider's "varied" Malaysian
lineup is a "tasty" "change of pace"; it's "nothing fancy", but priced for
"value" – notably the "lunch specials."

Penelope *American* 23 | 19 | 19 | $25

Murray Hill | 159 Lexington Ave. (30th St.) | 212-481-3800 |
www.penelopenyc.com

Murray Hill dwellers "count on" this "adorable" neighborhood "favorite" for "fab", "comfort"-oriented New American plates served in
"country cafe" digs at "reasonable cost"; the "amazing brunch" is in
"high demand", so have "patience" with the inevitable "long waits."

NEW **The Penrose** ● *American* – | – | – | M

E 80s | 1590 Second Ave. (bet. 82nd & 83rd Sts.) | 212-203-2751 |
www.penrosebar.com

A taste of Williamsburg on the UES, this new gastropub from the team
behind The Wren and Wilfie & Nell specializes in old-fashioned cocktails and American bar bites, including a custom-blend LaFrieda
burger; vintage wallpaper, decorative typewriters and antique luggage
give the place a hipster-throwback look.

Pepe Giallo To Go *Italian* 23 | 15 | 18 | $24

Chelsea | 253 10th Ave. (bet. 24th & 25th Sts.) | 212-242-6055
Pepe Rosso Caffe *Italian*

E 40s | Grand Central | Lower level (42nd St. & Vanderbilt Ave.) |
212-867-6054
Pepe Rosso To Go *Italian*

SoHo | 149 Sullivan St. (bet. Houston & Prince Sts.) | 212-677-4555
Pepe Verde To Go *Italian*

W Village | 559 Hudson St. (bet. Perry & W. 11th Sts.) | 212-255-2221
www.peperossotogo.com

For a "budget-conscious" "quick bite", this "friendly" quartet slings
"lotsa pasta" and other "pretty good" Italian "staples" that "go easy on
the wallet"; just know they're "totally unassuming" "joints" where service is "almost DIY."

Z Pepolino *Italian* 27 | 19 | 24 | $62

TriBeCa | 281 W. Broadway (bet. Canal & Lispenard Sts.) |
212-966-9983 | www.pepolino.com

You'll find "bliss in TriBeCa" at this "hidden" Tuscan trattoria, where
"exquisite" Italian dishes are prepared "with love and flair" and delivered by a "personable staff"; "prices are high" given the "unpretentious" setting, but insiders say such "perfection" is worth "a splurge."

Pequena ⌐ *Mexican* ∇ 22 | 20 | 18 | $23

Fort Greene | 86 S. Portland Ave. (Lafayette Ave.) | Brooklyn | 718-643-0000
Prospect Heights | 601 Vanderbilt Ave. (Bergen St.) | Brooklyn |
718-230-5170
www.pequenarestaurant.com

"Authentic zing" makes up for "tiny" dimensions at this "funky" Fort
Greene "micro"-*cucina*, where the "fresh, delicious" Mexican "favor-

ites" come at "decent prices"; those who say the original is "suffocating" will find the Prospect Heights spin-off a relief.

Pera *Mediterranean/Turkish* `21` `21` `19` `$51`

E 40s | 303 Madison Ave. (bet. 41st & 42nd Sts.) | 212-878-6301
NEW **SoHo** | 54 Thompson St. (bet. Broome & Spring Sts.) |
212-878-6305
www.peranyc.com
This "attractive" pair is a "solid" (if "pricey") bet for Turkish-accented Mediterranean fare – including a "lovely range" of meze – served in "modern" surrounds; the Midtown original is a "no-brainer for business", while the stylin' SoHo spin-off sports a "stunning outdoor deck."

Perbacco ● *Italian* `24` `17` `21` `$53`

E Village | 234 E. Fourth St. (bet. Aves. A & B) | 212-253-2038 |
www.perbacconyc.com
"Not your mama's Italian", this "itty-bitty" East Villager specializes in "creatively prepared" versions of the familiar favorites set down by "enthusiastic servers"; maybe the "high prices" don't jibe with the "unassuming" setting, but baccers say foodwise it "outshines" many of its neighbors.

◪ Perilla *American* `27` `21` `25` `$61`

W Village | 9 Jones St. (bet. Bleecker & W. 4th Sts.) | 212-929-6868 |
www.perillanyc.com
"Harold Dieterle proves his *Top Chef* win was no fluke" at this West Village "hideaway", where the "masterful" American menu's merger of "savory" and "satisfying" is a "dream come true"; factor in service and atmosphere that are "warm" and "unpretentious", and most agree it's "fairly priced" for "what you get."

Periyali *Greek* `24` `21` `23` `$59`

Flatiron | 35 W. 20th St. (bet. 5th & 6th Aves.) | 212-463-7890 |
www.periyali.com
"Dependably rewarding" since the '80s, this Flatiron "Greek classic" remains a "refined" refuge for "superb fresh fish" and "gracious service" in "soothing" surrounds where the "low noise level" "enables good conversation"; its "upscale" admirers attest it's still "worth the high price."

NEW Perla ● *Italian* ▽ `22` `20` `23` `$59`

G Village | 24 Minetta Ln. (bet. MacDougal St. & 6th Ave.) |
212-933-1824 | www.perlanyc.com
Gabe Stulman (Joseph Leonard, Fedora) pulls off a "perfect mixture" of "rustic" and "sexy" at this compact new Villager, where an "attentive" team sets down "excellent", hearty Italian fare; with upmarket types filling its banquettes, it can be "a mob scene."

Per Lei ● *Italian* `20` `18` `19` `$52`

E 70s | 1347 Second Ave. (71st St.) | 212-439-9200 |
www.perleinyc.com
"Young" Eurocentric sorts kick up a "fun vibe" at this Upper East Side hangout where the Italian classics are "well prepared", but the "happening" "scene" is even tastier; go for the "sidewalk" seats to "avoid the loud bar", but there's no getting around tabs that run "a bit high."

	FOOD	DECOR	SERVICE	COST

Perry St.   *American*
26 | 25 | 24 | $68

W Village | 176 Perry St. (West St.) | 212-352-1900 |
www.jean-georges.com

It's "worth the trek" to this "elegant" Way West Village outpost,
where Jean-Georges Vongerichten and his culinary scion Cedric "really shine" with "vibrant" New American fare heightened by "discreet
service" and a "tasteful" "modernist" setting by Richard Meier; its
"grown-up" clientele hardly minds the hefty tabs, but the $32 prix fixe
lunch accommodates almost "all budgets."

☑ Per Se   *American/French*
29 | 28 | 29 | $325

W 60s | Time Warner Ctr. | 10 Columbus Circle, 4th fl. (60th St. at B'way) |
212-823-9335 | www.perseny.com

"Elegance at its apex", this "Thomas Keller sensation" in the Time
Warner Center is a jackets-required "epic dining event", where an "in-
tricate" French–New American "symphony" is set against "spectacular"
Central Park views and delivered by a "second-to-none" staff (once again
voted No. 1 in NYC); the prix fixe runs a "heart-stopping" $295, but
"world-class food is worth the cost" – and there's always the "à la carte"
salon to "provide a little peek" at the kitchen's "food-as-art" handiwork.

Persepolis   *Persian*
22 | 16 | 20 | $40

E 70s | 1407 Second Ave. (bet. 73rd & 74th Sts.) | 212-535-1100 |
www.persepolisnyc.com

A "standout" among "the few Persians" in town, this Upper Eastsider
offers its "interesting", "well-spiced" Iranian classics (the "sour-cherry
rice is such a treat") in an "understated" milieu; given the "personal
service" and overall "value", it's "easy to relax and enjoy" being here.

Pescatore   ● *Italian/Seafood*
21 | 18 | 21 | $47

E 50s | 955 Second Ave. (bet. 50th & 51st Sts.) | 212-752-7151 |
www.pescatorerestaurant.com

Eastsiders who "count on" this "reliable" "local Italian" attest that the
"plentiful" portions of fish and pasta are "surprisingly good for the
price"; with its "pleasant" service, "homey feel" and "alfresco" tables
upstairs and down, it's a "sleeper" "date" place.

Petaluma   *Italian*
18 | 17 | 18 | $49

E 70s | 1356 First Ave. (73rd St.) | 212-772-8800 |
www.petalumarestaurant.com

A "longtime" UES "local", this standby supplies brick-oven pizzas and
other Italian "basics" that are "consistently good" if "not particularly
distinctive"; the "open" space is "appealing", though critics contend
it's an "upscale wannabe" that's gotten "a little too pricey."

☑ Peter Luger Steak House   ⊅ *Steak*
27 | 16 | 21 | $83

Williamsburg | 178 Broadway (Driggs Ave.) | Brooklyn |
718-387-7400 | www.peterluger.com

The "undisputed" steakhouse "champeen" for "eons", this Williamsburg
meat lover's "Valhalla" is "duly famous" for "magnificent", "perfectly
aged" porterhouses and "top-flight" sides that devotees "measure
others against"; it's "mad-busy all the time" despite the "notoriously"
"gnarly" waiters and "throwback" German "barroom" setting, not to
mention a "cash or house account"–only policy that requires "raiding
the ATM" before making the "pilgrimage."

Peter's Since 1969 *American*   23 | 16 | 21 | $24

NEW **E 50s** | 667 Lexington Ave. (bet. 55th & 56th Sts.) | 212-308-1969
W 40s | 587 Ninth Ave. (bet. 42nd & 43rd Sts.) | 212-868-0600
Williamsburg | 168 Bedford Ave. (bet. N. 7th & 8th Sts.) | Brooklyn |
718-388-2811
www.peterssince.com

For "comforting" chow "done right", this Williamsburg joint and its
Manhattan siblings dispense "awesome" rotisserie chicken and other
"hearty" American "home cooking" ("don't forget the fixin's"); with
"simple" counter-service setups staffed by a "sweet" crew, they're
"easy, filling" and "well priced."

NEW Pete Zaaz *Pizza*   ▽ 27 | 21 | 22 | $17

Prospect Heights | 766 Classon Ave. (bet. Sterling & St. Johns Pls.) |
Brooklyn | 718-230-9229 | www.petezaaz.com

Prospect Heights denizens "couldn't be luckier" having this arrival
slinging "quirky-yet-delicious" pizzas flaunting "experimental" toppings (e.g. the Cold Fried Chicken, with squash, fontina, collards and
pickled chilies); "friendly folks" man the snippet of space, and there's
now a roomier back patio.

Petite Abeille *Belgian*   20 | 16 | 18 | $32

Flatiron | 44 W. 17th St. (bet. 5th & 6th Aves.) | 212-727-2989
Gramercy | 401 E. 20th St. (1st Ave.) | 212-727-1505
TriBeCa | 134 W. Broadway (bet. Duane & Thomas Sts.) | 212-791-1360
W Village | 466 Hudson St. (Barrow St.) | 212-741-6479
www.petiteabeille.com

"Reliable for moules frites" washed down with beers from an "endless
list", this Belgian bistro chainlet is also a favored "brunch standby"; the
"Tintin-poster" decor is strictly "casual" and service "can be spotty",
but the check "won't empty your pockets."

Petrossian *Continental/French*   24 | 25 | 23 | $75

W 50s | 182 W. 58th St. (7th Ave.) | 212-245-2214 | www.petrossian.com

Come "spoil yourself" at this art deco Carnegie Hall–area "temple" of
"serious luxury", where you get "white-glove service" and a French-
Continental menu starring "wondrous" caviar and "bubbly"; those
lacking "money to burn" can still "go for it" via the "wonderful" cafe/
bakery "next door."

Philip Marie ●Ⓜ *American*   20 | 18 | 20 | $43

W Village | 569 Hudson St. (W. 11th St.) | 212-242-6200 |
www.philipmarie.com

A "standby" for "homestyle cooking" in the "neighborhood", this
"laid-back" West Villager does a "solid" job with its "unpretentious"
New American lineup; admittedly, it's "not quite fine dining", but the
"fair value" has regulars "coming back for more."

Philippe ● *Chinese*   23 | 21 | 21 | $69

E 60s | 33 E. 60th St. (bet. Madison & Park Aves.) | 212-644-8885 |
www.philippechow.com

"Low-lit and high-class", this East Side Chinese channels "Mr. Chow"
with "well-crafted" cuisine in a "cacophonous" setting "for the glamorous"; the $20 prix fixe lunch dodges the "sky-high" tab – but while
you may "run into Lil' Kim", skeptics shrug "better scene than food."

Pho Bang ⊅ *Noodle Shop/Vietnamese* | 23 | 9 | 16 | $15

Little Italy | 157 Mott St. (bet. Broome & Grand Sts.) | 212-966-3797
Elmhurst | 82-90 Broadway (Elmhurst Ave.) | Queens | 718-205-1500
Flushing | 41-07 Kissena Blvd. (Main St.) | Queens | 718-939-5520

Phollowers endorse this Vietnamese trio as a "legit" source for "substantial" "steaming bowls" of the "mmm-mmm" namesake soup; ignore the "tacky" decor and waiters who "communicate in grunts", and just focus on what's clearly a "super deal."

Phoenix Garden ⊅ *Chinese* | 23 | 10 | 15 | $32

Murray Hill | 242 E. 40th St. (bet. 2nd & 3rd Aves.) | 212-983-6666 | www.thephoenixgarden.com

"A real find" in Murray Hill, this "unassuming" BYO is "as good as" C-town for "genuine Cantonese" specialties led by the "excellent salt-and-pepper shrimp"; fans overlook the "attitude", "dreary decor" and "cash-only policy" because you can't beat the "value."

Pho Viet Huong *Noodle Shop/Vietnamese* | ∇ 24 | 11 | 14 | $20

Chinatown | 73 Mulberry St. (bet. Bayard & Canal Sts.) | 212-233-8988 | www.phoviethuongnyc.com

"Superb" pho for "very little dough" leads the "bewilderingly broad" menu of "top-notch" Vietnamese eats at this C-town stalwart; the decor's basic and service "can be iffy", but it's "full of jurors at lunchtime" all the same.

Piadina ●⊅ *Italian* | ∇ 24 | 19 | 20 | $36

G Village | 57 W. 10th St., downstairs (bet. 5th & 6th Aves.) | 212-460-8017 | www.piadinanyc.com

A "quiet" "hideaway" best known to its "local crowd", this "small", cash-only Villager plies "incredible pastas" and other "real-deal" Italiana in "rustic" grotto digs; admirers appreciate that it's "intimate" enough to get amorous, but "not crazy-priced."

Piccola Venezia *Italian* | 25 | 17 | 24 | $56

Astoria | 42-01 28th Ave. (42nd St.) | Queens | 718-721-8470 | www.piccola-venezia.com

"You name it, they prepare it" at this venerable Astoria "charmer", where the "menu's only a suggestion" and the "traditional" Italian dishes are "impeccably" rendered; it's "a little pricey" given the "dated" decor, but "personalized service" ensures everyone feels "like family."

Piccolo Angolo Ⓜ *Italian* | 26 | 16 | 23 | $46

W Village | 621 Hudson St. (Jane St.) | 212-229-9177 | www.piccoloangolo.com

Owner and "character" Renato Migliorini puts "heart and soul" into this "homey" West Village vet, where the "ample portions" of "wonderful" Northern Italian fare and "amiable" service inspire many a "permanent smile"; it's a "tiny" place with "lines outside", so reserve ahead.

ⓩ Picholine Ⓜ *French/Mediterranean* | 27 | 25 | 26 | $103

W 60s | 35 W. 64th St. (bet. B'way & CPW) | 212-724-8585 | www.picholinenyc.com

A "timeless classic" for "old-fashioned pampering", Terry Brennan's "top-drawer" Lincoln Center–area "destination" is a "refined" "marriage" of "*magnifique*" French-Med fare (concluding with an "unbelievable" "artisanal cheese" course) and "exemplary service" in a "lovely", "adult" setting; "costly" it is, but it's "worth cracking open the piggy bank" for what is always a satisfying experience; P.S. it's temporarily closed for renovations.

Pier 9 *Seafood*

20 | 18 | 19 | $45

W 50s | 802 Ninth Ave. (bet. 53rd & 54th Sts.) | 212-262-1299 | www.pier9nyc.com

Supplying "unexpectedly" "solid" shore fare in Hell's Kitchen, this "moderately priced" seafooder is appreciated for its fish-shack classics and "nontraditional" dishes like lobster mac 'n' cheese; the "nautical" setup's staffed by an "accommodating" crew, but a few skeptics shrug "nothing to write home about."

Pies-n-Thighs ⦿ *Soul Food*

25 | 14 | 19 | $21

Williamsburg | 166 S. Fourth St. (Driggs Ave.) | Brooklyn | 347-529-6090 | www.piesnthighs.com

As a "front-runner" for "succulent" fried chicken and sides topped off with "damn-good" pie, this Williamsburg soul fooder is an "artery-clogging" "treat"; maybe the "snug" space is "not so special", but "amiable" service and "even friendlier prices" earn a "thumbs-up."

Pietro's 🗷 *Italian/Steak*

25 | 14 | 23 | $69

E 40s | 232 E. 43rd St. (bet. 2nd & 3rd Aves.) | 212-682-9760

In the Grand Central area since 1932, this "old-school" holdout rests its rep on "excellent steaks" and Italian basics "served in copious amounts" by a "gracious", "been-there-for-years" staff; no, the room's "not glamorous", but its "loyal following" savors the "quiet conversation."

Pig Heaven ⦿ *Chinese*

21 | 15 | 20 | $36

E 80s | 1540 Second Ave. (bet. 80th & 81st Sts.) | 212-744-4333 | www.pigheavennyc.com

"When nothing but pig will do", "sweetheart" hostess Nancy Lee's "aptly named" Upper East Side Chinese vet comes in handy as a "relaxed" "favorite" for affordable "hog-inspired dishes" led by "superior spareribs"; the "cheesy" "pink decor" gets a few grunts, but for devotees, it's "all about taste."

Pinche Taqueria *Mexican*

▽ 22 | 11 | 16 | $15

NoHo | 333 Lafayette St. (Bleecker St.) | 212-343-9977
NoLita | 227 Mott St. (bet. Prince & Spring Sts.) | 212-625-0090
www.pinchetaqueria.us

Pedigreed via a Tijuana original, these "no-frills" NoHo-NoLita taquerias "hit the spot" with "brilliant fish tacos" and other "top-drawer" West Coast–style Mexican eats; the quarters may be "cramped", but for peso-pinchers the prices are "worth an elbow or two."

Ping's Seafood *Chinese/Seafood*

21 | 13 | 15 | $31

Chinatown | 22 Mott St. (bet. Chatham Sq. & Mosco St.) | 212-602-9988
Elmhurst | 83-02 Queens Blvd. (Goldsmith St.) | Queens | 718-396-1238
www.pingsnyc.com

With "first-rate" seafood backed by "varied", "flavorful" dim sum, these Chinatown-Elmhurst Cantonese contenders stay "ping on target"; despite "simple" settings and "not-that-welcoming" service, "they pack 'em in" – "get there early" for "madhouse" Sunday brunch.

Pinocchio *Italian*

24 | 18 | 24 | $49

E 90s | 1748 First Ave. (bet. 90th & 91st Sts.) | 212-828-5810

"Really fine" for a "local place", this "tiny" UES Italian offers a "robust" menu with "special attention" from the "true gentleman" of an owner; the space is "a bit close", but that doesn't deter "devoted" regulars with a nose for a deal.

Pintaile's Pizza *Pizza*

▽ 20 | 7 | 13 | $19

E 80s | 1573 York Ave. (bet. 83rd & 84th Sts.) | 212-396-3479 | www.pintailespizza.com

Proof that pizza can "actually be healthy", this Yorkville "neighbor-hood haunt" produces "well-crafted pies" featuring "unusually thin" "whole-wheat crusts" and "fresh", "inventive toppings"; it's a "real hole-in-the-wall", though, so many go "carryout."

Pio Pio *Peruvian*

23 | 16 | 18 | $28

E 90s | 1746 First Ave. (bet. 90th & 91st Sts.) | 212-426-5800
Murray Hill | 210 E. 34th St. (bet. 2nd & 3rd Aves.) | 212-481-0034
W 40s | 604 10th Ave. (bet. 43rd & 44th Sts.) | 212-459-2929
W 90s | 702 Amsterdam Ave. (94th St.) | 212-665-3000
Mott Haven | 264 Cypress Ave. (bet. 138th & 139th Sts.) | Bronx | 718-401-3300
Jackson Heights | 84-02 Northern Blvd. (bet. 84th & 85th Sts.) | Queens | 718-426-4900
Jackson Heights | 84-21 Northern Blvd. (bet. 84th & 85th Sts.) | Queens | 718-426-1010
Rego Park | 62-30 Woodhaven Blvd. (62nd Rd.) | Queens | 718-458-0606 ⊟
www.piopionyc.com

The "succulent" rotisserie chicken smothered in "killer" green sauce is a "force to be reckoned with" at these "not-fancy" Peruvians, places to "stuff yourself" with Andean "fabulosity" at "super-low" rates; with compadres "coming in droves", "rushed" service and "ear-splitting" decibels are part of the package.

Piper's Kilt ❶ *Burgers/Pub Food*

22 | 16 | 21 | $21

Inwood | 4946 Broadway (207th St.) | 212-569-7071 | www.piperskiltofinwood.com
Kingsbridge | 170 W. 231st St. (Albany Crescent) | 347-602-7880

"Locals gather" for the "best burgers around" at these Bronx-Inwood "mainstays", where the "satisfying" pub fare is best chased with "a mug of beer" or three; their "throwback" Irish bar locales accommo-date "everyone from toddlers to drunken Jets fans."

Pisticci *Italian*

25 | 20 | 22 | $36

W 100s | 125 La Salle St. (B'way) | 212-932-3500 | www.pisticcinyc.com

It "doesn't get much better for local Italian" profess admirers of this "warm, welcoming" Columbia-area "favorite", home to "scrumptious" food at "reasonable prices" and "jazz on Sundays"; the "no-reservations" thing "can be a drag", but "long lines" deter few.

PizzArte *Pizza*

▽ 21 | 20 | 19 | $35

W 50s | 69 W. 55th St. (bet. 5th & 6th Aves.) | 212-247-3936 | www.pizzarteny.com

"True" Neapolitan specialties qualify this bi-level Italian as a "wonder-ful addition to Midtown", turning out "perfectly charred" pizzas from a "wood-burning oven", as well as other "well-priced" Italiana; what's more, the "cool", "modern" space is lined with art, all for sale.

Pizza 33 ❶ *Pizza* | 21 | 10 | 15 | $15 |

Chelsea | 268 W. 23rd St. (bet. 7th & 8th Aves.) | 212-206-0999
Murray Hill | 489 Third Ave. (33rd St.) | 212-545-9191
www.pizza33nyc.com

"After hitting up the local bars", revelers say the "big slices" from these crosstown pizzerias "help soak up the booze" well into the wee hours; they're "not much to look at", but their "weekend" clientele won't remember anyway.

P.J. Clarke's ❶ *Pub Food* | 18 | 17 | 18 | $38 |

E 50s | 915 Third Ave. (55th St.) | 212-317-1616
P.J. Clarke's at Lincoln Square ❶ *Pub Food*
W 60s | 44 W. 63rd St. (Columbus Ave.) | 212-957-9700
P.J. Clarke's on the Hudson *Pub Food*
Financial District | 4 World Financial Ctr. (Vesey St.) | 212-285-1500
www.pjclarkes.com

The "quintessential" East Side "watering hole", this 1884 saloon dishes up "the Cadillac" of "juicy" burgers along with "no-pretenses" pub grub in a "good-natured", "high-energy" vibe; purists scoff at the "pseudo" offshoots, but the Lincoln Center branch suits "for a bite" pre-show, while the FiDi outpost is "nicely located on the marina."

The Place *American/Mediterranean* | 23 | 23 | 22 | $52 |

W Village | 310 W. Fourth St. (bet. Bank & 12th Sts.) | 212-924-2711 | www.theplaceny.com

"Nestled" "below sidewalk level", this "quintessential West Village date spot" is "sure to impress" with its "cozy, quaint", "extremely romantic" fireplace-equipped digs, "decadent" Med–New American cooking and "warm" service; the only quibble is with the "boring name", which the besotted say "doesn't do it justice."

Plaza Food Hall *Eclectic* | 23 | 22 | 19 | $45 |

W 50s | Plaza Hotel | 1 W. 59th St., lower level (5th Ave.) | 212-986-9260 | www.theplazafoodhall.com

A "great way to graze", Todd English's "vibrant" "one-stop shop" below the Plaza provides "lunch counter–style" seating and "outstanding" Eclectic options via "varying food stations" issuing sushi, pizza, grill grub and much more; recently expanded to add more vendors, it remains plenty "popular" despite "so-so" service.

Pó *Italian* | 26 | 18 | 23 | $52 |

W Village | 31 Cornelia St. (bet. Bleecker & W. 4th Sts.) | 212-645-2189 | www.porestaurant.com

Pocket-size but "charming", this Village vet remains an "absolute gem" furnishing "first-quality" Italian fare "without an ounce of pretense"; "repeat customers" confirm "the tight squeeze" is "so worth it" for a rare "culinary delight" that "won't break the bank."

Poke 🗷🞕 *Japanese* | 25 | 15 | 19 | $43 |

E 80s | 343 E. 85th St. (bet. 1st & 2nd Aves.) | 212-249-0569 | www.pokesushinyc.com

"The finest fish" lures UES sushiphiles to this "cash-only" Japanese BYO, a modest standby where the "creative" rolls "compare favorably" with any; "affordable" rates ensure it's "always busy", so critics take a poke at the "no-reservations policy" and "long lines."

NEW Pok Pok Ny *Thai* ▽ 22 | 11 | 17 | $20

Red Hook | 127 Columbia St. (bet. Degraw & Kane Sts.) | Brooklyn | 718-923-9322 | www.pokpokpdx.com

"No frills, but all thrills" is the word on Andy Ricker's Columbia Waterfront outpost "fresh in from Portland", which is far from the nearest subway but lures throngs with its "affordable", "addictive" takes on Thai classics; many of the dishes pack heat, which can be cooled with one of the 'drinking vinegars', and those waiting for a table in the teeny dining room or larger garden can have a drink in an adjacent tented area.

Pomodoro Rosso *Italian* 22 | 17 | 22 | $44

W 70s | 229 Columbus Ave. (bet. 70th & 71st Sts.) | 212-721-3009 | www.pomodororossonyc.com

It's like "mama's in the kitchen" cooking up "hearty" Italian "comfort" classics at this "quaint" UWS "favorite" near Lincoln Center; it's run "with loving care", but "no reservations" means "big waits" – "get there early" if you're going pre-performance.

Pongal *Indian/Kosher/Vegetarian* ▽ 23 | 15 | 18 | $25

Murray Hill | 110 Lexington Ave. (bet. 27th & 28th Sts.) | 212-696-9458 | www.pongalnyc.com

Home to South Indian specialties "not easily found elsewhere", this Curry Hill "dosa nirvana" "surprises" with its "delicious" kosher-vegetarian bounty; the service "can be slow" and there's "no decor" to speak of, so most customers just focus on the "unbeatable" cost.

Pongsri Thai *Thai* 21 | 13 | 18 | $28

Chelsea | 165 W. 23rd St. (bet. 6th & 7th Aves.) | 212-645-8808
Chinatown | 106 Bayard St. (Baxter St.) | 212-349-3132
W 40s | 244 W. 48th St. (bet. B'way & 8th Ave.) | 212-582-3392
www.pongsri.com

Although "unassuming", these "established" Thai standbys pack serious "flavor per dollar" with their "addictive" "basics" reflecting a "knack for the right spice"; since they're "handy", "speedy" and "won't break the bank", regulars readily "ignore the worn decor."

Ponte's ⓈⓂ *Italian* ▽ 25 | 22 | 23 | $72
(fka F.illi Ponte)

TriBeCa | 39 Desbrosses St. (bet. Washington & West Sts.) | 212-226-4621 | www.filliponte.com

Dating to 1967, this way-western TriBeCan is "tried-and-true" for "wonderful" "old-world Italian" and "elegant service" in a "quiet setting" that's *romantico* "for couples"; if the up-to-date prices are a distraction, refocus on the "breathtaking" sunsets "over the Hudson."

Ponticello *Italian* ▽ 25 | 21 | 23 | $53

Astoria | 46-11 Broadway (bet. 46th & 47th Sts.) | Queens | 718-278-4514 | www.ponticelloristorante.com

"Not bad" for a "local" longtimer, this Astoria Northern Italian boasts a "terrific" roster of "classics" served by seasoned waiters who ensure you're "well taken care of"; if it seems "slightly overpriced" for the "old-world" ambiance, habitués still "feel completely at home."

Ponty Bistro *African/French*

22 | 15 | 20 | $45

Gramercy | 218 Third Ave. (bet. 18th & 19th Sts.) | 212-777-1616 | www.pontybistro.com

"Sparking your taste buds", this Gramercy "find" offers "wonderfully original" French-Senegalese cooking "livened up" with African spices and "charming" service; it's also "well priced" (notably the $25 early-bird), but word's "getting out" and the "narrow" room "fills up" fast.

Porchetta *Italian*

25 | 10 | 18 | $18

E Village | 110 E. Seventh St. (bet. Ave. A & 1st Ave.) | 212-777-2151 | www.porchettanyc.com

"The holy grail" for "swine" lovers, chef Sara Jenkins' East Village "one-trick pony" vends only Italian roast pork – whether as "scrumptious" "signature sandwiches" or platters – plus a few sides; given the "tiny", six-seat setup, it's "basically a take-out place."

Porsena *Italian*

22 | 15 | 19 | $50

E Village | 21 E. Seventh St. (bet. 2nd & 3rd Aves.) | 212-228-4923 | www.porsena.com

The "distinctive touch" of chef-owner Sara Jenkins "elevates" the "heavenly pastas" and other "delicious, straightforward" Italian staples at this "friendly" East Villager; it works as a "down-to-earth" "date spot", albeit one that's apt to be "busy"; P.S. a next-door wine bar adjunct is in the works.

Porter House New York *Steak*

26 | 25 | 25 | $77

W 60s | Time Warner Ctr. | 10 Columbus Circle, 4th fl. (60th St. at B'way) | 212-823-9500 | www.porterhousenewyork.com

"Classy" "without a stuffy feel", this "prime" TWC steakhouse from "masterful" chef Michael Lomonaco "gets it right" with a "winning combination" of "phenomenal" cuts, "first-rate" service and "comfortable", "contemporary" digs sporting "fabulous views" of Central Park; it's "not cheap", but hey, "you should treat yourself well."

Portofino *Italian/Seafood*

∇ 23 | 20 | 23 | $45

City Island | 555 City Island Ave. (Cross St.) | Bronx | 718-885-1220 | www.portofinocityisland.com

"A throwback to old-style Italian", this "steady", circa-1975 City Islander is a "staple" for "enjoyable", if familiar, fare centered on "fresh" seafood; longtime loyalists agree "for the meal you get" with an alfresco "view of the water", it's "worth the price."

Post House *Steak*

24 | 21 | 23 | $82

E 60s | Lowell Hotel | 28 E. 63rd St. (bet. Madison & Park Aves.) | 212-935-2888 | www.theposthouse.com

Well "established" among the "well-heeled", this "memorable" East Side meatery's "superb steaks" are "served professionally" in an "old-guard" setting "where women are welcomed"; "you'll pay for it", but it's a "tradition" that brings "a who's who" of "biz" diners "back for more."

Posto *Pizza*

24 | 15 | 18 | $30

Gramercy | 310 Second Ave. (18th St.) | 212-716-1200 | www.postothincrust.com

The "thinnest", "winningest" crust is the hallmark of this Gramercy pizzeria, a "local hot spot" cranking out "splendid" pies at "accessible prices"; it's a "tight space" with "no decor" and "not-so-courteous" service, so the to-go trade stays brisk.

Potbelly Sandwich Shop *Sandwiches* | 20 | 15 | 19 | $12 |

NEW **Chelsea** | 41 W. 14th St. (bet. 5th & 6th Aves.) | 646-289-4209
E 40s | Rockefeller Ctr. | 30 Rockefeller Plaza (bet. 49th & 50th Sts.) |
646-289-4203
Financial District | 101 Maiden Ln. (Pearl St.) | 646-289-4201
NEW **Financial District** | 90 Broad St. (bet. Bridge & Stone Sts.) |
646-289-4211 🖪
NEW **Garment District** | 366 Fifth Ave. (35th St.) | 646-289-4207
NEW **Garment District** | 501 Seventh Ave. (bet. 37th & 38th Sts.) |
646-289-4205
NEW **Murray Hill** | 333 Park Ave. S. (bet. 24th & 25th Sts.) |
646-289-4212 🖪
NEW **TriBeCa** | 280 Broadway (bet. Chambers & Reade Sts.) |
646-289-4206
NEW **Union Sq** | 22 E. 17th St. (bet. B'way & 5th Ave.) | 646-289-4204
NEW **W 50s** | 46 W. 56th St. (bet. 5th & 6th Aves.) | 646-289-4210 🖪
www.potbelly.com
Additional locations throughout the NY area

Recently imported "from the Windy City", these "neat" "grab-and-go" outlets enter the lunchtime "throwdown" with "spot-on" sandwiches served toasted and "priced right" ("the Wreck is the bomb"); they're "a zoo" at midday, but "efficient" counters move the line "pretty fast."

NEW Pounds & Ounces *American* | ▽ 16 | 18 | 17 | $36 |

Chelsea | 160 Eighth Ave. (18th St.) | 646-449-8150 |
www.poundsandouncesnyc.com

This gay-friendly Chelsea arrival offers moderately priced New American fare with luxurious touches and colorful cocktails at the mahogany bar; a DJ spins while those looking to mingle can sit at the communal tables, or outside for prime people-watching.

Pranna ●🖪 *SE Asian* | 20 | 24 | 20 | $42 |

Murray Hill | 79 Madison Ave. (bet. 28th & 29th Sts.) |
212-696-5700 | www.prannarestaurant.com

With its "lovely", multitiered design, this "spacious" Murray Hill Southeast Asian offers a "modern" backdrop for its "tasty" plates; there's also a "lively bar" that takes on a "club vibe" the "later it gets", so never mind if it's "expensive" for what some term "style over substance."

Press 195 *Sandwiches* | 24 | 16 | 19 | $21 |

Bayside | 40-11 Bell Blvd. (bet. 40th & 41st Aves.) | Queens |
718-281-1950 | www.press195.com

The "hardest part is choosing" from the "extensive list" of "creative, satisfying" panini capably pressed at this "affordable" Bayside "casual-eats" standout; "addicting" fries complete the "perfect combination."

Prime Grill *Kosher/Steak* | 24 | 22 | 21 | $68 |

E 40s | 60 E. 49th St. (bet. Madison & Park Aves.) | 212-692-9292 |
www.theprimegrill.com

Prime KO *Kosher/Steak*

W 80s | 217 W. 85th St. (bet. Amsterdam Ave. & B'way) |
212-496-1888 | www.primehospitalityny.com

What every kosher steakhouse "should aspire to be", this "fabulous" Midtown-UWS twosome sets the "gold standard" for "deliciously pre-

pared" beef (plus sushi at KO), well served in "modern" surrounds; the
faithful freely foot "astonishingly high" tabs for "one of the best."

Primehouse

	25	24	24	$65

New York *Steak*

Murray Hill | 381 Park Ave. S. (27th St.) | 212-824-2600 |
www.primehousenyc.com

As a "prime" Murray Hill pick, this "professionally run" cow palace
"doesn't disappoint" given its "first-rate" steaks (not to mention
"awesome" tableside Caesar) from an "outstanding" staff in "roomy",
"sleek" quarters; prices "geared to the expense-account" set come
with the territory.

Prime Meats ● *American/Steak*

24	21	21	$53

Carroll Gardens | 465 Court St. (Luquer St.) | Brooklyn |
718-254-0327 | www.frankspm.com

"The name says it" about this "carnivore"-oriented Carroll Gardens
Frankies Spuntino spin-off, where the "fantastic", "German-inspired"
New American steakhouse fare arrives via an "über-hip" "whis-
kered" staff; the "cool, Prohibition-style" digs get "packed" and they
"don't take reservations", so "arrive early."

Primola ● *Italian*

23	18	20	$63

E 60s | 1226 Second Ave. (bet. 64th & 65th Sts.) | 212-758-1775

"Definitely a neighborhood haunt", this "busy", "clubby" Italian
satisfies its "moneyed Upper East Side" clientele with "dependable" pastas at "steep prices"; count on service "with a smile" if
you're a "regular or a celebrity", but for "first-timers" the "attitude" can be "intimidating."

Print *American*

23	24	23	$64

W 40s | Ink48 Hotel | 653 11th Ave. (bet. 47th & 48th Sts.) |
212-757-2224 | www.printrestaurant.com

Sited just about "as far west as you can go", this "yet-to-be-discovered"
Hell's Kitchen hoteler is "first-rate" for "locavoracious" New American
fare and "smart" service in "stylish" environs via David Rockwell; don't
overlook the "rooftop lounge" with its "skyline view."

Prune *American*

25	17	22	$53

E Village | 54 E. First St. (bet. 1st & 2nd Aves.) | 212-677-6221 |
www.prunerestaurant.com

"Amazing chef" and "writer" Gabrielle Hamilton's East Village "treasure" rests its "enduring cachet" on "inspired, unpretentious" New
American "food for thought" done "with verve" and "graciously served"
in a "tiny", "cheek-by-jowl" space; expect "enormously long lines"
during the weekend "brunch rush."

Public *Eclectic*

23	25	21	$65

NoLita | 210 Elizabeth St. (bet. Prince & Spring Sts.) | 212-343-7011 |
www.public-nyc.com

"Sure to impress" with its "superb", "library"-like AvroKO interior, this
"cool" NoLita Eclectic also "stands up well" with an "Australian/
New Zealand–inspired" menu ("kangaroo appetizer", anyone?);
the "hospitality" brings its "energetic" admirers back, especially
for "outstanding brunch."

	FOOD	DECOR	SERVICE	COST

Pulino's ● *Pizza*   21 | 19 | 19 | $38

NoLita | 282 Bowery (E. Houston St.) | 212-226-1966 |
www.pulinosny.com

Keith McNally's "buzzy" pizzeria is "a boon" to the Bowery for "solid"
pies that "range from classic to inventive" ("breakfast pizza" – "why
not?"); the "efficient service" and "cool" bottles-and-tile interior pull
in an "energetic" crowd, though "your hearing may pay the price."

NEW Pulqueria ● *Mexican*   ▽ 20 | 21 | 16 | $49

Chinatown | 11 Doyers St., downstairs (bet. Bowery & Pell St.) |
212-227-3099 | www.pulquerianyc.com

You'd "never expect it" given the "hidden" Chinatown basement locale, but this "Mexican joint" from the Apothéke folks "authentically"
musters regional eats that venture well "beyond the ordinary"; "interesting cocktails" based on "the namesake spirit", pulque, ease the
pain of paying.

Pure Food & Wine *Vegan/Vegetarian*   25 | 23 | 24 | $52

Gramercy | 54 Irving Pl. (bet. 17th & 18th Sts.) | 212-477-1010 |
www.purefoodandwine.com

Granted, it's "very different", but this Gramercy vegan "revelation" deserves recognition for the "unexpected" "flavor and flair" of its "dazzling" "raw cuisine"; "capable service" and a "lovely" garden enhance the
"pure pleasure", though it's a "quite expensive" way to "feel virtuous."

Pure Thai Cookhouse *Thai*   26 | 17 | 21 | $23

W 50s | 766 Ninth Ave. (bet. 51st & 52nd Sts.) | 212-581-0999 |
www.purethaishophouse.com

Purists plug this Hell's Kitchen "hole-in-the-wall" for the "authenticity"
of its "full-flavored" Thai dishes, many starring "homemade egg noodles" in "perfectly spiced" soups ("watch out for the heat"); the pace
is "fast", with "decent prices" offsetting "elbow-to-elbow" conditions.

NEW Purple Fig *French*   – | – | – | E

W 70s | 250 W. 72nd St. (bet. B'way & West End Ave.) |
212-712-9823 | www.thepurplefignyc.com

Irish celeb chef Conrad Gallagher is behind this upscale UWS modern
French bistro whose opulent interior features plush velvet seating and
a front bar with its own small-plates menu; the inventive, meticulous
fare isn't cheap, but then everything – from the bread and pastries to
the pâtés and terrines – is made in-house, and the $42 pre-theater
prix fixe packs value.

Purple Yam *Asian*   22 | 19 | 21 | $34

Ditmas Park | 1314 Cortelyou Rd. (bet. Argyle & Rugby Rds.) |
Brooklyn | 718-940-8188 | www.purpleyamnyc.com

"A delicate touch" distinguishes the "creative" cookery at this Ditmas
Park Pan-Asian, best known for its "tasty" "takes on traditional Filipino
fare"; customers are tended by "the nicest folks", and the prices are
no less agreeable.

Puttanesca *Italian*   20 | 17 | 18 | $42

W 50s | 859 Ninth Ave. (56th St.) | 212-581-4177 | www.puttanesca.com
"You don't have to spend a fortune" for "decent old-school" Italian and
"efficient service" at this "popular" Hell's Kitchen "standby"; during

the "pre- or post-performance" Lincoln Center crush and brunch with its "bottomless" drinks, expect "noise bouncing off the bricks."

⚡ Pylos ● *Greek*

27 | 23 | 22 | $50

E Village | 128 E. Seventh St. (bet. Ave. A & 1st Ave.) | 212-473-0220 | www.pylosrestaurant.com

"A happy buzz" pervades this East Village haven for Greek "fine dining", which "shines" with "sensational" cuisine including appetizers so "ambitious" they're "all you need"; a ceiling hung "with terra-cotta pots" adds "rustic charm", and "no-attitude" service keeps it "inviting", if "a bit cramped."

Qi *Asian*

22 | 23 | 20 | $28

Union Sq | 31 W. 14th St. (bet. 5th & 6th Aves.) | 212-929-9917

Qi Bangkok Eatery *Thai*

W 40s | 675 Eighth Ave. (43rd St.) | 212-247-8991 www.qirestaurant.com

A Times Square "treasure", this "glam Thai" pairs a "knockout" backdrop with an "amazing", "health-conscious" menu from chef Pichet Ong; the airy Union Square original proffers SE Asian eats that tilt "macrobiotic" – and both locations are rated "way above expectations" given the "excellent price."

Quality Meats *American/Steak*

26 | 24 | 24 | $74

W 50s | 57 W. 58th St. (bet. 5th & 6th Aves.) | 212-371-7777 | www.qualitymeatsnyc.com

For the "urban carnivore" seeking an "other-than-traditional steakhouse" experience, the Stillmans' "smart" Midtowner fills the bill with "quality for sure", from the "top-notch porterhouse" to the "outrageous ice cream" and AvroKO's "vibrant", rustic-meets-"industrial" setting; in sum, "you pay a lot, but you get a lot."

Quantum Leap *Health Food/Vegetarian*

22 | 12 | 19 | $22

G Village | 226 Thompson St. (bet. Bleecker & W. 3rd Sts.) | 212-677-8050 | www.quantumleapwestvillage.com

"One of the original" Greenwich Village health-food havens, this "small", "friendly" '70s survivor still supplies "tasty" vegetarian specialties along with "some fish offerings"; in keeping with the "low-key", "collegey atmosphere", expect "laid-back" service and "affordable" tabs.

Quatorze Bis *French*

21 | 20 | 21 | $62

E 70s | 323 E. 79th St. (bet. 1st & 2nd Aves.) | 212-535-1414

"Steady" and "so French", this "longtime" Upper East Side bistro remains a "local" "favorite" for its "well-done" "Left Bank menu" and "welcoming" atmosphere "redolent" of Paree; though "priced for the neighborhood", it "takes the sting out of aging" for many of its "prosperous clientele."

Quattro Gatti *Italian*

22 | 19 | 21 | $52

E 80s | 205 E. 81st St. (bet. 2nd & 3rd Aves.) | 212-570-1073

Though "not fancy", this "cozy" UES stalwart (since 1985) is favored as a "predictable" fallback for "pretty good" "homestyle Italian" served by "genial" "old-school types"; "sleepy" but "affordable", it's "worth repeat business" for loyalists in the "neighborhood."

	FOOD	DECOR	SERVICE	COST

Queen *Italian*
25 | **17** | **23** | **$47**

Brooklyn Heights | 84 Court St. (bet. Livingston & Schermerhorn Sts.) | Brooklyn | 718-596-5955 | www.queenrestaurant.com

A circa-1958 "Brooklyn Heights institution" "near the courthouses", this "homey" Italian continues its reign as an area "favorite" for "true red-sauce" fare minus "culinary gimmicks"; since it "keeps on giving" with "gracious service" and "reasonable" tabs, most pardon the "dated" decor.

Queen of Sheba ● *Ethiopian*
23 | **17** | **18** | **$28**

W 40s | 650 10th Ave. (bet. 45th & 46th Sts.) | 212-397-0610 | www.shebanyc.com

"Hidden" in Hell's Kitchen, this "neat" Ethiopian is "the real thing" for "flavorful" fare – "numerous" veggie dishes included – noshed using "your hands" and "a heap of injera" bread; even with "small" quarters and "slow" pacing, it's "a repeater" for the cost-conscious.

Queens Kickshaw ● *Coffeehouse/Sandwiches*
∇ **24** | **19** | **22** | **$20**

Astoria | 40-17 Broadway (bet. 41st & Steinway Sts.) | Queens | 718-777-0913 | www.thequeenskickshaw.com

"Specializing in grilled cheese", this saloonish Astoria sandwich "joint" kicks the "gooey" staple "to another level" with its "out-of-this-world" "combinations", served alongside other fromage-focused eats by "friendly" "hipsters"; the "specialty coffees" and craft beers are "a huge plus", as is the "cheap" cost.

Rack & Soul *BBQ/Southern*
22 | **12** | **17** | **$27**

W 100s | 258 W. 109th St. (B'way) | 212-222-4800 | www.rackandsoul.com

Supplying "awesome chicken, meaty ribs" and other "basic BBQ" favorites, this "authentic" Southerner near Columbia racks up points with collegians "craving" an "inexpensive" feed; given the "no-frills" setup and "lackadaisical" service, even fans say it's "better to take out."

Radiance Tea House *Teahouse*
∇ **22** | **21** | **22** | **$33**

W 50s | 158 W. 55th St. (bet. 6th & 7th Aves.) | 212-217-0442 | www.radiancetea.com

Radiating "calm" amid the "Midtown madness", this "delightful" teahouse "retreat" matches an "incredible selection" of "exotic" brews with an affordable lunch menu of "fresh", Chinese-accented "small bites"; the "very Zen" surroundings (which also house a gift shop) "crowd up fast" come noon.

Rai Rai Ken ●🍴 *Japanese/Noodle Shop*
∇ **22** | **11** | **17** | **$16**

E Village | 218 E. 10th St. (bet. 1st & 2nd Aves.) | 212-477-7030

Recently transferred to "bigger digs" down the block, this "Tokyo-style" East Village noodle bar now has a few tables in addition to the counter; it's still cash only and "not the fanciest" joint, but it remains as "quick", "authentic" and "budget"-friendly as ever.

Ramen Setagaya *Japanese/Noodle Shop*
∇ **20** | **12** | **14** | **$19**

E Village | 34 St. Marks Pl. (bet. 2nd & 3rd Aves.) | 212-387-7959

"Reliable" ramen is "served hot and fast" with "no pretension" at this East Village branch of a Japan-based noodle-shop outfit; "inexpensive" rates help make it a "fulfilling" stop, provided you "sit down, slurp" and "ignore the decor."

	FOOD	DECOR	SERVICE	COST

Rao's ⚅⌷ *Italian* | 23 | 17 | 22 | $84 |

Harlem | 455 E. 114th St. (Pleasant Ave.) | 212-722-6709 |
www.raos.com

It practically "takes an act of Congress" to "score" a "coveted table", but if you "get lucky", Frank Pellegrino's East Harlem Italian lives up to the "mystique" with its "terrific" cooking and "central-casting" crowd peppered with real "celebrities"; short of "VIP" connections, "the ordinary person" can visit "the one in Las Vegas" or just "buy the sauce in jars" – when they say 'call ahead', they mean in 2020, when the first rez come available.

Raoul's ◗ *French* | 25 | 21 | 22 | $67 |

SoHo | 180 Prince St. (bet. Sullivan & Thompson Sts.) |
212-966-3518 | www.raouls.com

"The 'it' factor" endures at this "classic", circa-1975 SoHo bistro, which stays "true to itself" and its arty admirers with "surprisingly serious" French fare in a "sexy" "Parisian locale" with a "walk through the kitchen" to the "magical" garden; though it's "noisy and crowded", few rue its "popularity" or high price.

Rare Bar & Grill *Burgers* | 22 | 18 | 18 | $33 |

Chelsea | Fashion 26 Hotel | 152 W. 26th St. (bet. 6th & 7th Aves.) |
212-807-7273

Murray Hill | Shelburne Murray Hill Hotel | 303 Lexington Ave. (37th St.) |
212-481-1999

www.rarebarandgrill.com

Given their "top-notch" "variety" of burgers and fries, these "midscale" patty purveyors are rarely less than "bustling"; if the Murray Hill original's too "packed", the Chelsea follow-up "has a ton of space" – and "hoppin'" roof bars await at both.

Rasputin ◗Ⓜ *Continental/Russian* | ▽ 18 | 22 | 18 | $72 |

Sheepshead Bay | 2670 Coney Island Ave. (Ave. X) | Brooklyn |
718-332-8111 | www.rasputinny.com

"Wannabe czars and czarinas" have "crazy fun" at this Sheepshead Bay Continental cabaret, relishing copious spreads with "traditional Russian" leanings and Vegas-worthy "live entertainment" starring spicy terpsichorniks; while "expensive", there's no disputin' "the show is incredible."

Ravagh *Persian* | 23 | 15 | 19 | $31 |

E 60s | 1237 First Ave. (bet. 66th & 67th Sts.) | 212-861-7900

Murray Hill | 11 E. 30th St. (bet. 5th & Madison Aves.) |
212-696-0300 | www.ravaghmidtown.com

Persian pundits pronounce this "authentic" East Side pair "consistently" "spot-on" for "succulent kebabs" and other "standard" Iranian eats from an "attentive" team; the "generous" portions and "modest pricing" are most "satisfying" if you "don't expect much" decorwise.

𝗡𝗘𝗪 Raymi *Peruvian* | - | - | - | E |

Flatiron | 43 W. 24th St. (bet. 5th & 6th Aves.) | 212-929-1200 |
www.richardsandoval.com

Richard Sandoval does Peruvian at this roomy Flatironer where diners can enjoy their pisco sours and savory dishes in a choice of attractive rooms; prices are predictably expensive given the upscale milieu.

Rayuela *Pan-Latin*

	FOOD	DECOR	SERVICE	COST
	22	24	21	$58

LES | 165 Allen St. (bet. Rivington & Stanton Sts.) | 212-253-8840 | www.rayuelanyc.com

Besides being an eyeful, this "snazzy" Lower Eastsider aims to "wow the palate" with "bold" tapas and Pan-Latin fare in "lovely" duplex digs featuring an "olive tree" "growing through the middle"; "gracious" staffers oversee a milieu that's "sceney" – and accordingly "pricey."

Real Madrid *Spanish*

	FOOD	DECOR	SERVICE	COST
	∇ 22	16	20	$42

Mariners Harbor | 2075 Forest Ave. (Union Ave.) | Staten Island | 718-447-7885 | www.realmadrid-restaurant.com

"You get what you pay for" at this Spanish vet in Staten Island's Mariners Harbor that scores with lobster specials and other "dependable" dishes in "hungry-man–size" helpings; "satisfying meals" at "decent prices" help realists disregard decor that seems to have been kicked around a bit.

Recette ❶ *American*

	FOOD	DECOR	SERVICE	COST
	25	19	21	$73

W Village | 328 W. 12th St. (Greenwich St.) | 212-414-3000 | www.recettenyc.com

The "expertly prepared" if "exceptionally small" servings pack a "superlative" "punch" that'll "make you want to lick the plate" at this West Village New American "gem"; "high prices" and "cramped" quarters don't dampen the "elbow-to-elbow" "foodie scene."

Recipe *American*

	FOOD	DECOR	SERVICE	COST
	25	18	22	$42

W 80s | 452 Amsterdam Ave. (bet. 81st & 82nd Sts.) | 212-501-7755 | www.recipenyc.com

"A rare UWS find", this "postage stamp–size" New American "original" furnishes "phenomenal", "farm-to-fork" cuisine from a "laid-back" staff at prices that run "reasonable"; the "narrow" setup "only accommodates 26", so "make reservations" and be ready to get "cozy."

Red Cat *American/Mediterranean*

	FOOD	DECOR	SERVICE	COST
	23	20	22	$57

Chelsea | 227 10th Ave. (bet. 23rd & 24th Sts.) | 212-242-1122 | www.theredcat.com

"Purrfect" when you're "prowling the Chelsea galleries", this "tried-and-true" "local favorite" "satisfies" "arty types" and other "hepcats" with its "terrific" Med–New American menu and "timely" service; sustaining a "buzzy" but "relaxing" vibe with a "touch of style", it's "pricey" but "definitely a keeper."

Red Egg *Chinese*

	FOOD	DECOR	SERVICE	COST
	21	18	18	$32

Little Italy | 202 Centre St. (Howard St.) | 212-966-1123 | www.redeggnyc.com

"Not nearly as hectic" as the usual dim sum specialists, this "contemporary" Little Italy Chinese dispenses "high-quality" "tidbits" that are "made to order" and served by "competent" sorts with "no carts" in sight; despite the "lounge"-like setting, prices remain egg-ceptably "low."

Redeye Grill ❶ *American/Seafood*

	FOOD	DECOR	SERVICE	COST
	21	20	20	$58

W 50s | 890 Seventh Ave. (56th St.) | 212-541-9000 | www.redeyegrill.com

"Well-prepared seafood" stands out on the "something-for-everyone" New American menu at Shelly Fireman's "energetic" Midtown "mega-room" across from Carnegie Hall; "prompt" and "priced right", it's "handy" for "theatergoers", "tourists" and biz "clients" who keep it "bustling" and "noisy."

RedFarm ● *Chinese* | 26 | 18 | 22 | $54 |

W Village | 529 Hudson St. (bet. Charles & W. 10th Sts.) | 212-792-9700 | www.redfarmnyc.com

A "hot ticket" in the West Village, this "modern Chinese" from impresario Ed Schoenfeld and "inventive" chef Joe Ng "thrills" with the "farmstand" "twist" that renders specialties like its vaunted dim sum "unforgettable"; despite "efficient" service, the "mostly communal seating" in the "trendy"-cum-"homey" space is generally "jammed" and the lines "ridiculous" (they "should take reservations").

The Redhead ● *Southern* | 24 | 16 | 20 | $39 |

E Village | 349 E. 13th St. (bet. 1st & 2nd Aves.) | 212-533-6212 | www.theredheadnyc.com

"Outrageously good" Southern "comfort" classics (e.g. "OMG-delicious" fried chicken) and "perfectly made" cocktails keep this "unassuming" East Village bar/eatery "crowded"; despite the "no-frills", "noisy" setup, it packs serious "value" – " if you can score" a table.

Red Hook Lobster Pound *Seafood* | 26 | 12 | 19 | $26 |

Red Hook | 284 Van Brunt St. (bet. Verona St. & Visitation Pl.) | Brooklyn | 718-858-7650 | www.redhooklobsterpound.com

This Red Hook "storefront" seafooder specializes in "mouthwatering" "fresh" "lobstah rolls" prepared "Maine (cold)" or "Connecticut (warm) style"; the "picnic-area" decor "makes it clear" eating's "the only thing they care about", but it's worth venturing over because it's a "deal."

Red Rooster *American* | 23 | 23 | 23 | $51 |

Harlem | 310 Lenox Ave. (bet. 125th & 126th Sts.) | 212-792-9001 | www.redroosterharlem.com

"Creative gastronomy" comes to Harlem via "masterful chef" Marcus Samuelsson with his "spirited" New American "hot spot" serving a "fab" menu ranging from Swedish meatballs to "Southern homestyle cooking" to a "vivacious" "mix of demographics" filling "delightful" digs overseen by "eager" staffers; "pizzazz" aside, there are a few grumbles that the food is "secondary" and the waits "nothing to crow about."

Regional *Italian* | 20 | 15 | 18 | $35 |

W 90s | 2607 Broadway (bet. 98th & 99th Sts.) | 212-666-1915 | www.regionalnyc.com

"Neighborhood" regulars peg this "friendly" UWS Italian a few "notches above the usual" thanks to a "totally solid" regional lineup featuring pasta-centric choices "from all over" The Boot; it's also highly "affordable", with "special deals" on Monday and Tuesday nights.

Remi *Italian* | 23 | 22 | 22 | $62 |

W 50s | 145 W. 53rd St. (bet. 6th & 7th Aves.) | 212-581-4242 | www.remi-ny.com

"Reliable" "all-around quality" marks this "upscale" Midtown Italian, where "superb" Venetian specialties are "served with panache" for "pre-theater" and "business dining"; the "serene space" is so "pretty to look at" with its "impressive" Grand Canal mural that you may forget the "expense account"-ready prices.

	FOOD	DECOR	SERVICE	COST

Republic *Asian*
20 | **16** | **16** | **$23**

Union Sq | 37 Union Sq. W. (bet. 16th & 17th Sts.) | 212-627-7172 | www.thinknoodles.com

Long a "Union Square standby", this Asian "mess hall" still "does the trick" with "filling" bowls of "noodles galore" and more at "bargain-basement prices"; the "communal-style" setup is "awkward" and "noisy as all get-out", but its "young" votaries eat and exit "in a flash."

Resto ● *Belgian*
21 | **18** | **18** | **$43**

Murray Hill | 111 E. 29th St. (bet. Lexington Ave. & Park Ave. S.) | 212-685-5585 | www.restonyc.com

A "hedonist's delight", this Murray Hill gastropub offers a "refreshing" chance to "pig out" on "really tasty" Belgian eats à la burgers and moules frites, chased with a "tremendous beer selection"; the "low roar" in the room testifies to its "appreciative" following.

NEW Reynard ● *American*
– | **–** | **–** | **E**

Williamsburg | Wythe Hotel | 80 Wythe St. (N. 12th St.) | Brooklyn | 718-460-8004 | www.wythehotel.com

The Williamsburg waterfront grows up with this New American stunner in the new Wythe Hotel, where the team behind Diner and Marlow & Sons turns out upscale, seasonally inspired, impeccably plated plates from an open kitchen; the high-ceilinged, artfully weathered-looking space mixes Manhattan panache with Brooklyn bluster; P.S. have a drink on the rooftop while you're there.

Ricardo Steak House *Steak*
∇ **25** | **21** | **21** | **$41**

Harlem | 2145 Second Ave. (bet. 110th & 111th Sts.) | 212 289-5895 | www.ricardosteakhouse.com

East Harlem has "a real gem" in this "well-done" steakhouse, whose "simply delicious" cuts are served with "flair" to a crowd with "energy" to spare; the art-lined room "gets rather full", but there's a "quiet patio" and the "value" alone is "reason to subway" over.

Rice ⊄ *Eclectic*
22 | **18** | **19** | **$23**

Dumbo | 81 Washington St. (bet. Front & York Sts.) | Brooklyn | 718-222-9880 | www.riceny.com

Turning out "tasty" "combinations" that highlight "different takes on rice", this cash-only Dumbo Eclectic is a "go-to" for "light", relatively "healthy" eats; the interior's "cramped" "enough to let knees touch", but it's "dependable" when you're "trying to save a buck."

Rice 'n' Beans ● *Brazilian*
22 | **12** | **19** | **$26**

W 50s | 744 Ninth Ave. (bet. 50th & 51st Sts.) | 212-265-4444 | www.riceandbeansmidtownwest.com

They "don't have many seats", but this Hell's Kitchen "hole-in-the-wall" furnishes "flavorful" Brazilian "staples" that "easily offset" the "humble" surroundings and "laconic service"; with "more-than-reasonable" tabs, it qualifies as a "casual" "find" for "pre-theater."

Rin Thai Cuisine *Thai*
∇ **24** | **23** | **22** | **$26**

Chelsea | 265 W. 23rd St. (bet. 7th & 8th Aves.) | 212-675-2988 | www.rinthai.com

Besides supplying "really good" Siamese standards, this "cute" "find in the FIT area" boasts "lovely" service and a "Zen-like" vibe that set it

| | FOOD | DECOR | SERVICE | COST |

"apart from the tons of neighborhood Thais"; happily, the "low prices" are more "typical."

Riposo 46 ◐ *Italian*   22 | 19 | 22 | $33
W 40s | 667 Ninth Ave. (bet. 46th & 47th Sts.) | 212-247-8018 | www.riposonyc.com

Riposo 72 ◐ *Italian*
W 70s | 50 W. 72nd St. (bet. Columbus Ave. & CPW) | 212-799-4140
"Welcoming all around", these wine bars offer "above-average", "priced-right" Italian bites ("love their flatbread pizza") that are "well matched" with "fabulous" pours; both the "cute little" Hell's Kitchen original and its "roomier" UWS sequel promote "romantic" meet-ups.

Risotteria *Italian* 23 | 13 | 20 | $26
W Village | 270 Bleecker St. (Morton St.) | 212-924-6664 | www.risotteria.com
A "celiac's delight", this "fairly priced" Village Italian works "gluten-free magic" with its "delish" lineup showcasing "the art of risotto" plus wheatless pizza; the "tiny", "crammed" space is "not much to look at", so just "squeeze in" and "make new friends."

☑ River Café *American* 26 | 28 | 26 | $130
Dumbo | 1 Water St. (bet. Furman & Old Fulton Sts.) | Brooklyn | 718-522-5200 | www.rivercafe.com
The "postcard-ready" Lower Manhattan views "dazzle" at Buzzy O'Keeffe's "only-in-NY" Dumbo "landmark", where the "tantalizing" New American cuisine and "superlative" service "live up to" the "picturesque", "floral"-enhanced setting; the $100 dinner prix fixe will run up a "hefty bill", but the "unforgettable" "special-occasion" atmosphere more than "justifies the cost."

☑ Riverpark *American* 25 | 27 | 25 | $65
Murray Hill | Alexandria Ctr. | 450 E. 29th St. (bet. FDR Dr. & 1st Ave.) | 212-729-9790 | www.riverparknyc.com
It requires a "trek" to a Kips Bay "corporate" lobby, but you're "rewarded" with a "standout" experience at Tom Colicchio's latest "gem", which presents "elegant" New American cuisine and "solicitous" service in "stunning", "modern" surrounds complete with a "remarkable" vegetable garden; "alfresco" tables with "calming water views" and "free parking" are included in the tab.

Riverview ◐ *American* ▽ 23 | 25 | 21 | $57
LIC | 2-01 50th Ave. (enter at Center Blvd. & 49th Ave.) | Queens | 718-392-5000 | www.riverviewny.com
Anchored alongside the East River, this spacious LIC resto-lounge purveys a solid New American menu that skews "pricey" for the location; for a complimentary "romantic" fillip, a walk along the water affords "breathtaking views of the Manhattan skyline."

Rizzo's Pizza *Pizza*   23 | 13 | 18 | $14
E 90s | 1426 Lexington Ave. (93rd St.) | 212-289-0500
Astoria | 30-13 Steinway St. (bet. 30th & 31st Aves.) | Queens | 718-721-9862
www.rizzosfinepizza.com
"Yum, yum", the "distinct and tasty" "square pies" come "thin with a tangy sauce" at this enduring "local pizza joint" in Astoria, now joined

by an anchovy-size Carnegie Hill annex; economical tabs are in line with the strictly functional setups.

Robataya *Japanese* ▽ 25 | 22 | 22 | $53

E Village | 231 E. Ninth St. (bet. 2nd & 3rd Aves.) | 212-979-9674 | www.robataya-ny.com
"It's all about" the "authentic robata" counter at this "transporting" East Village "Japanese experience", where patrons are "entertained" by "the chefs at work" grilling "high-quality" "veggies, meats and fish" served "on long wooden paddles"; while a bit "expensive", it's "something different" and "so much fun."

☑ Robert ❶ *American* 21 | 27 | 22 | $58

W 50s | Museum of Arts and Design | 2 Columbus Circle, 9th fl. (bet. B'way & 8th Ave.) | 212-299-7730 | www.robertnyc.com
High "above the fray", this museum American boasts such "wondrous" views "over Columbus Circle and Central Park" (a window table "is key") that the "pricey" fare is "almost an afterthought"; insiders note the "artsy design" is just as "striking" over "cocktails" in the "comfy lounge."

Roberta's ❶ *Italian/Pizza* 26 | 18 | 19 | $34

Bushwick | 261 Moore St. (Bogart St.) | Brooklyn | 718-417-1118 | www.robertaspizza.com
Redefining "the Brooklyn aesthetic", this "super-popular" Bushwick Italian is known for its "phenomenal" "wood-fired" pies, as well as other "smashing" dishes crafted with "ingredients picked from their own garden"; "throngs of hipsters" descend on its "industrial" digs, but "if you can stomach the wait" it's "worth the extended trip on the L."

Roberto ☒ *Italian* 26 | 20 | 23 | $57

Fordham | 603 Crescent Ave. (Hughes Ave.) | Bronx | 718-733-9503 | www.roberto089.com
"One of the greats", chef Roberto Paciullo's "destination-worthy" Bronx Italian "off Arthur Avenue" "keeps it real" with "abundant" servings of "exceptional" "Salerno"-esque specialties from a "diligent" staff; given the "intimate", "old-style" setting and the no-reservations "headache", "go early" or expect to "wait a while."

Roc ❶ *Italian* 22 | 20 | 21 | $53

TriBeCa | 190 Duane St. (Greenwich St.) | 212-625-3333 | www.rocrestaurant.com
"Year after year", this TriBeCa "standby" remains roc-"solid" for upmarket Italian "classics" courtesy of "delightful owners" who ensure that regulars are "treated like family"; a "peaceful setting" with "outdoor seating" distracts from prices that slant "expensive."

Rock Center Café *American* 20 | 22 | 19 | $49

W 50s | Rockefeller Ctr. | 20 W. 50th St. (bet. 5th & 6th Aves.) | 212-332-7620 | www.patinagroup.com
With its "rink-side" view of "skaters during the winter" and open-air tables "in front of Prometheus" in milder months, this Rock Center American is an "undeniable draw" for "tourists" and your "holiday guests"; "only-average" food just proves "you're paying" for "location, location, location."

NEW Rocket Pig ⑤ *Sandwiches*

- | - | - | I

Chelsea | 463 W. 24th St. (10th Ave.) | 212-645-5660 |
www.rocketpignyc.com

Tucked into an alleyway behind Chelsea's Trestle on Tenth, this inexpensive sandwich slinger keeps things simple, offering one signature (and massive) smoked pork 'wich, plus oysters and charcuterie; there's a small area for dining in, though most choose to grab their pig roll and rocket right out.

Rocking Horse Cafe *Mexican*

22 | 17 | 18 | $37

Chelsea | 182 Eighth Ave. (bet. 19th & 20th Sts.) | 212-463-9511 |
www.rockinghorsecafe.com

"Handy" "in the neighborhood", this "buoyant" Chelsea fixture "rocks on" as a "go-to" for "flavorful Mexican" grub and "sure value", notably the $15 brunch prix fixe; "frequent crowds" fueled by "fab" margaritas create a "lively scene" and mucho "noise."

Rolf's *German*

17 | 21 | 17 | $43

Gramercy | 281 Third Ave. (22nd St.) | 212-477-4750 |
www.rolfsnyc.com

"*Ein* trip" "around the holidays", this Gramercy German "time warp" is a "sight to see" when the "jaw-droppingly" "gaudy" Oktoberfest and Christmas decorations go up ("bring your sunglasses"); then again, "run-of-the-mill" food makes the case for a "drink at the bar."

Roll-n-Roaster ❶ *Sandwiches*

23 | 12 | 17 | $14

Sheepshead Bay | 2901 Emmons Ave. (bet. Nostrand Ave. & 29th St.) |
Brooklyn | 718-769-5831 | www.rollnroaster.com

"Retro fast-food" fans roll into this "busy" Sheepshead Bay "institution" to "chow down on" "bangin'" roast beef sandwiches and "heavenly" cheese fries into the "late" hours; the aging digs are pretty "beat up", but "it isn't Brooklyn without" it.

Roman's *Italian*

▽ 26 | 21 | 23 | $44

Fort Greene | 243 DeKalb Ave. (bet. Clermont & Vanderbilt Aves.) |
Brooklyn | 718-622-5300 | www.romansnyc.com

Its "locally sourced" New American small plates "change every day, but the quality doesn't" at this "hip" Fort Greene sibling to Marlow & Sons, a "memorable" "juxtaposition" of culinary "passion" and "neighborhoody" vibes; no reservations means a "standard" "wait", providing time to size up the bar's "talented mixologists."

Room Service *Thai*

22 | 23 | 20 | $27

Chelsea | 166 Eighth Ave. (bet. 18th & 19th Sts.) | 212-691-0299
W 40s | 690 Ninth Ave. (bet. 47th & 48th Sts.) | 212-582-0999 ❶
www.roomservicerestaurant.com

"Decked out with mirrors and chandeliers", this "eye-popping" Chelsea–West Midtown pair sets a "jazzy" scene for "spot-on" Thai bites and "ultrafast" service at a "fair price"; the "upbeat", "noisy" vibe, "cool cocktails" and "fun-loving" crowd are all part of the "like-a-nightclub" milieu.

② Rosa Mexicano *Mexican*

23 | 22 | 21 | $49

E 50s | 1063 First Ave. (58th St.) | 212-753-7407 ❶
Flatiron | 9 E. 18th St. (bet. B'way & 5th Ave.) | 212-533-3350

(continued)

Rosa Mexicano

W 60s | 61 Columbus Ave. (62nd St.) | 212-977-7700 ◐
www.rosamexicano.com

After "years of success", these "splashy" Mexicans are "still way up
there" for "*delicioso*" dishes preceded by "sensational" "tableside guacamole" and "dynamite" pomegranate margaritas; add "responsive"
service and a "festive" "scene", and the big bucks are "pesos well spent."

Rosanjin ⊠ *Japanese*

▽ 25 | 22 | 25 | $124

TriBeCa | 141 Duane St. (bet. Church St. & W. B'way) |
212-346-0664 | www.rosanjintribeca.com

"Aesthetically" "amazing", this "petite" TriBeCa Japanese is a "top-end
kaiseki" specialist showcasing the "heavenly" tastes and textures of
"exquisitely presented" set menus "deferentially" served by a kimono-
clad staff; the "serene" setting is the "perfect frame" for a "transporting" experience that's (predictably) beyond "expensive."

NEW Rosemary's ◑ *Italian*

▽ 25 | 25 | 24 | $38

W Village | 18 Greenwich Ave. (W. 10th St.) | 212-647-1818 |
www.rosemarysnyc.com

Happening since day one, this West Village Italian "home run" from
the owner of nearby Bobo gets serious locavore cred, sourcing produce from its own "beautiful rooftop garden"; the "light and airy"
space has an au naturel feel, with a staircase to the garden, and a back
bar with Prosecco on tap.

Rose Water *American*

26 | 20 | 25 | $47

Park Slope | 787 Union St. (6th Ave.) | Brooklyn | 718-783-3800 |
www.rosewaterrestaurant.com

Park Slope's "lll'" "locavore heaven", this way-"cozy" New American vet
"remains consistently fabulous" with its "inventive", "seasonally driven"
menu and service "like a finely oiled machine"; it's a "favorite" brunch
pick, where the only thorn is "bumping elbows" in the "tight space."

Rossini's ◑ *Italian*

24 | 19 | 25 | $63

Murray Hill | 108 E. 38th St. (bet. Lexington & Park Aves.) |
212-683-0135 | www.rossinisrestaurant.com

The "good old days" endure at this "upper-end" '70s-vintage Murray
Hill Northern Italian that "will spoil you" with "excellent" cooking and
"seamless" service from "tux"-attired pros; the nightly "piano player"
and live "opera music" on Saturdays should soothe any "sticker shock."

Rothmann's *Steak*

23 | 20 | 22 | $72

E 50s | 3 E. 54th St. (bet. 5th & Madison Aves.) | 212-319-5500 |
www.rothmannssteakhouse.com

Centrally sited "for businesspeople", this Midtown steakhouse lives
"up to expectations", providing "wonderful meat" and "dependable"
service "without fuss and drama"; it's "costly", but the "comfort level"
holds whether you're there to "clinch a deal" or sip "cocktails after work."

Rouge et Blanc *French/Vietnamese*

▽ 25 | 19 | 23 | $62

SoHo | 48 MacDougal St. (bet. Houston & Prince Sts.) |
212-260-5757 | www.rougeetblancnyc.com

"Totally unexpectedly", this SoHo "sleeper" achieves "remarkable
subtlety" with an "innovative" French-Vietnamese lineup that "mar-

ries perfectly" with its "wonderful" wines; a "low-key" space ("think *The Quiet American*") with "never-rushed" service, it's a "hidden gem" – at least until "the masses catch on."

Ⓩ Rouge Tomate Ⓩ *American*　　25 | 26 | 24 | $66

E 60s | 10 E. 60th St. (bet. 5th & Madison Aves.) | 646-237-8977 | www.rougetomatenyc.com

Eastsiders stay "waist-conscious" without "sacrificing on taste" at this "sleek" New American "oasis", where the "healthful" ethos and "sustainable" "culinary delights" are enhanced by "gracious" service and a "pristine" bi-level space; the "ladylike" portions go "for big bucks", but most "love it, love it, love it."

Rub BBQ *BBQ*　　23 | 13 | 18 | $32

Chelsea | 208 W. 23rd St. (bet. 7th & 8th Aves.) | 212-524-4300 | www.rubbbq.net

'Cue hounds "chow down" on "smoky" "slow-cooked meats" at this "no-frills" Chelsea outlet for "damn-fine" Kansas City–style BBQ ("come early for the burnt ends"); it delivers the goods at a "fair price", and "where else can you go for deep-fried Oreos?"

Rubirosa *Italian/Pizza*　　22 | 16 | 19 | $39

NoLita | 235 Mulberry St. (bet. Prince & Spring Sts.) | 212-965-0500 | www.rubirosanyc.com

"Perfecto" "crispy" pizzas and "soulful" pastas offered at "a fair price point" keep this tolerably "trendy" NoLita Italian on "solid footing" with its "funky downtown" following; it's "friendly enough" with a "decent scene" to boot, so expect a "wait" for entree into its "cramped" quarters.

Ruby Foo's *Asian*　　19 | 21 | 19 | $45

W 40s | 1626 Broadway (49th St.) | 212-489-5600 | www.rubyfoos.com

"Lots of tourists" with "kids" in tow "love every cheesy inch" of this "sprawling" Times Square Asian with its "broad menu" and "Grauman's Chinese Theater" decor; while the "Westernized" chow's "surprisingly" "decent", those unmoved by the "gimmicky" "appeal" say "you can do better."

Rucola ◑ *Italian*　　▽ 25 | 23 | 23 | $37

Boerum Hill | 190 Dean St. (Bond St.) | Brooklyn | 718-576-3209 | www.rucolabrooklyn.com

"Wildly popular", this "wonderful addition" to Boerum Hill renders a "decently priced" "rustic Italian" menu with "fresh and light" "farm-to-table" "twists" that appeal to "hipsters and family groups" alike; the lumber-lined space is "tight", so "prepare for close contact" and "a challenge" getting in.

Rue 57 ◑ *French*　　20 | 19 | 19 | $48

W 50s | 60 W. 57th St. (6th Ave.) | 212-307-5656 | www.rue57.com

A "convenient" "pit stop" for "client lunches" and "visitors", this "fast-paced" Midtown brasserie owes its "high traffic" to "dependable, middle-of-the-road" French fare (and sushi) at "reasonable prices"; "iffy" service and "hubbub" aside, it's "not bad" for an "easy" "in and out."

	FOOD	DECOR	SERVICE	COST

Russian Samovar ● *Continental/Russian* | 21 | 19 | 20 | $53 |

W 50s | 256 W. 52nd St. (bet. B'way & 8th Ave.) | 212-757-0168 |
www.russiansamovar.com

"Home away from home" for "Russian-speakers", this "cheerful"
Theater District stalwart serves "well-prepared" Russo-Continental
"staples" amid "live piano"–led "festivity" that "gets louder" as the
night proceeds; for "your money's worth", "throw back" some "infused
vodkas" and ignore the "lackluster" setting.

Russian Tea Room ● *Continental/Russian* | 21 | 25 | 22 | $69 |

W 50s | 150 W. 57th St. (bet. 6th & 7th Aves.) | 212-581-7100 |
www.russiantearoomnyc.com

The "opulent" interior remains as "gawk-worthy" as ever at this "famous" Russo-Continental beside Carnegie Hall, an "over-the-top"
"imperial" venue tailored to caviar-and-blini binges; but with "average
food" for the "sky-high" tabs, those who remember "the original"
deem it a "touristy" "shadow of its former self."

Ruth's Chris Steak House *Steak* | 26 | 22 | 24 | $75 |

W 50s | 148 W. 51st St. (bet. 6th & 7th Aves.) | 212-245-9600 |
www.ruthschris.com

A "slather" of "melted butter" adds "that extra-fab" "sizzle" to the "big
cuts" of "tender" beef at this "first-rate" Theater District link of the
New Orleans steakhouse chain; likewise, the "personalized" service
and "upscale" "woodwork" are as "impressive" as the price is "high."

Rye *American* | ▽ 26 | 22 | 23 | $40 |

Williamsburg | 247 S. First St. (bet. Havemeyer & Roebling Sts.) |
Brooklyn | 718-218-8047 | www.ryerestaurant.com

The "speakeasy-style" setting with a vintage bar "sets the scene perfectly" for "fine cocktails" and "first-rate" grub at this "charming"
Williamsburg American ("meatloaf sandwich" fanciers "won't be
sorry"); it also earns wry praise as a "hipster" hang "without pretension."

Sacred Chow *Vegan/Vegetarian* | ▽ 22 | 14 | 19 | $22 |

G Village | 227 Sullivan St. (bet. Bleecker & 3rd Sts.) | 212-337-0863 |
www.sacredchow.com

For a "lifestyle change", try this "wee" Village health-food niche, where
"ingenious" kosher vegan recipes yield "wholesome" chow with "creative flair"; "earthy" enthusiasts find it "laid-back" and "reasonably
priced", though nonbelievers note it's "very impressed with itself."

Sagaponack *Seafood* | 19 | 19 | 20 | $42 |

Flatiron | 4 W. 22nd St. (bet. 5th & 6th Aves.) | 212-229-2226 |
www.sagaponacknyc.com

When hankering for "the Hamptons", think of this Flatiron seafooder
that serves "simple" but "solid" fin fare (e.g. "lobster in all its forms") in
"peaceful" "beachfront"-esque surrounds; if you're casting for a "reasonable" "respite" with breezy, "accommodating" service, it's "not bad."

Sahara ● *Turkish* | 23 | 15 | 19 | $31 |

Gravesend | 2337 Coney Island Ave. (bet. Aves. T & U) | Brooklyn |
718-376-8594 | www.saharapalace.com

It's "old-school at this point", but this durable Gravesend Turk is "hard
to beat" for "seriously good" grill fare ("kebab is king") at the right

price; the "huge" space is "short on ambiance", but that doesn't hurt its "popularity" with "groups and families."

Saigon Grill ● *Vietnamese* 21 | 11 | 16 | $25

W 90s | 620 Amsterdam Ave. (90th St.) | 212-875-9072

Seemingly "the entire UWS" frequents this "roomy" Vietnamese, a "best bet" for "well-flavored" fare served "in a flash" at "bargain prices" that trump the "functional" decor; still, in the wake of "labor issues", some wonder if it's "losing its touch."

Saju Bistro ● *French* 21 | 20 | 21 | $44

W 40s | Mela Hotel | 120 W. 44th St. (bet. B'way & 6th Ave.) | 212-997-7258 | www.sajubistro.com

A "slice of Paree" in Times Square, this "very French" bistro is "spot-on" for "traditional Provençal dishes" at "fair" prices; it's "especially" "convenient" "pre-theater", with a $28 prix fixe and an "engaging" staff to "get you in and out."

Sakagura *Japanese* 25 | 22 | 22 | $53

E 40s | 211 E. 43rd St., downstairs (bet. 2nd & 3rd Aves.) | 212-953-7253 | www.sakagura.com

"Like Tokyo" but "minus the 14-hour plane ride", this Japanese izakaya tucked "literally underground" in a "nondescript" Midtown building is the "real deal" for "incredible" small plates matched with "exceptional" sakes; its "high quality" comes with a "price tag to match."

Salinas ● *Spanish* 22 | 20 | 20 | $60

Chelsea | 136 Ninth Ave. (bet. 18th & 19th Sts.) | 212-776-1990 | www.salinasnyc.com

"Charmed" Chelsea dwellers hail this "creative" Spaniard for its "terrific tapas" served in an "intimate" space "with a retractable roof" sheltering "a fabulous garden"; it's "pricey", but this is "one to reckon with."

Salt & Fat Ⓜ *Asian* 26 | 17 | 23 | $35

Sunnyside | 41-16 Queens Blvd. (bet. 41st & 42nd Sts.) | Queens | 718-433-3702 | www.saltandfatny.com

The name shows a "sense of humor", but "they take the food seriously" at this Sunnyside "rising star" where "inventive" chef Daniel Yi's small plates present a "delectable" "amalgam" of New American and "Asian flavors" to "share with adventurous friends"; with a "super-helpful" staff and "Queens prices", it's one to "look out for."

Salumeria Rosi Parmacotto *Italian* 25 | 19 | 21 | $47

W 70s | 283 Amsterdam Ave. (bet. 73rd & 74th Sts.) | 212-877-4800 | www.salumeriarosi.com

"The quality shines" at chef Cesare Casella's "*molto Italiano*" UWS enoteca/salumeria, where the cured meats, Tuscan small plates and wines are like "a gift" from "the mother country"; just be ready for a "tight squeeze" and bills that "climb fast"; P.S. a roomier, more upscale Madison Avenue branch is in the works.

Sambuca *Italian* 21 | 19 | 21 | $41

W 70s | 20 W. 72nd St. (bet. Columbus Ave. & CPW) | 212-787-5656 | www.sambucanyc.com

"Italian cooking, family-style" sums up this "trustworthy" UWS fixture, where the "gigantic" platters of "typical" dishes (plus a "gluten-free menu") are "meant for sharing"; "reasonable" tabs compensate for "dated" decor, and it's "a lot easier to get into" than Carmine's.

Sammy's ◐ *Chinese* 21 | 11 | 18 | $27

G Village | 453 Sixth Ave. (11th St.) | 212-924-6688

"Bring your appetite" to this "efficient" Village Chinese that "consistently" "scores" with a "wide menu" of "inexpensive" "comfort" chow, notably noodle soups; seriously "worn-out" digs and service "without a smile" explain why it's a "neighborhood take-out" nexus.

Sammy's Fishbox ◐ *Seafood* 22 | 18 | 20 | $47

City Island | 41 City Island Ave. (Rochelle St.) | Bronx | 718-885-0920 | www.sammysfishbox.com

"You will not leave hungry" should be the motto of this "huge" City Island vet, which has been churning out "generous" servings of seafood since 1966; though not cheap, it's something of a "tourist" magnet, so count on it being "crowded in summer months."

Sammy's Roumanian *Jewish* 20 | 10 | 18 | $60

LES | 157 Chrystie St. (Delancey St.) | 212-673-0330

"Oy! vhat an experience" this LES "heartburn city" is, bringing on "old-fashioned Jewish" staples "covered in schmaltz" and vodka "in ice blocks" amid "grungy basement" trappings where a "keyboardist" spouts "nonstop shtick"; "like a bar mitzvah" that "never ends", the clamorous "cavorting" could cause "cardiac arrest", but it's "a great way to go."

Sammy's Shrimp Box ◐ *Seafood* 24 | 19 | 22 | $38

City Island | 64 City Island Ave. (Horton St.) | Bronx | 718-885-3200 | www.shrimpboxrestaurant.com

Docked "at the end of the strip" near its Fish Box forerunner, this "casual" City Islander dispenses "down-to-earth" "fried seafood" and "lots of it" at a "nice price"; it's a standard "hang in the summer", where you should expect "very crowded" conditions.

Sandro's *Italian* 26 | 16 | 21 | $66

E 80s | 306 E. 81st St. (bet. 1st & 2nd Aves.) | 212-288-7374 | www.sandrosnyc.com

"Never boring", this "cozy" Upper East Side Italian "rises above the ordinary" with "top-notch Roman" cuisine from "mercurial" chef-owner Sandro Fioriti, who "greets diners" in his "pajama bottoms"; "high prices" for the "simple setting" don't deter "lively" locals who "want to save it" for themselves.

Sanford's ◐ *American* 24 | 22 | 22 | $26

Astoria | 30-13 Broadway (bet. 30th & 31st Sts.) | Queens | 718-932-9569 | www.sanfordsnyc.com

Lodged in a "converted diner" flaunting a "contemporary" makeover, this "friendly" Astoria New American makes "higher-caliber" comfort food "available 24/7" at "reasonable" rates; the formula's "deservedly popular", especially at brunch when "the only drawback is the wait."

San Matteo ◐ *Pizza* ∇ 26 | 15 | 20 | $28

E 90s | 1739 Second Ave. (90th St.) | 212-426-6943

(continued)

(continued)

San Matteo Panuozzo ⬤∅ *Italian/Sandwiches*
NEW **E Village** | 121 St. Marks Pl. (Ave. A) | 212-979-8000 |
www.sanmatteopanuozzo.com

This "quaint" UES Italian "wins hearts" with "quality" Neapolitan pizzas and "wonderful" *panuozzi,* panini-esque creations; it's so "cheap" and "charming", most "don't mind" being "squeezed"; P.S. the East Village cubbyhole devotes itself to its namesake.

San Pietro 🖬 *Italian*
25 | 20 | 24 | $89

E 50s | 18 E. 54th St. (bet. 5th & Madison Aves.) | 212-753-9015 | www.sanpietro.net

"Filled with CEO types" at lunch, this "high-end" Italian is acknowledged as a Midtown "class act" that's "as good as it gets" for "sumptuous cuisine" and "customer-centric" service; it's "oriented to expense-account" dining, however, so it helps if "money is no object."

Sant Ambroeus *Italian*
22 | 19 | 20 | $61

E 70s | 1000 Madison Ave. (bet. 77th & 78th Sts.) | 212-570-2211
W Village | 259 W. Fourth St. (Perry St.) | 212-604-9254 |
www.santambroeus.com

"Sophisticated Europeans" are "naturally" drawn to these "Milano-in-NY" cafes on the UES and in the West Village, both "cosseting" sources for "oh-so-delicious" Italian nibbles in a "civilized" milieu; they "deliver" "refinement", but "at a cost" ("what else is new?").

Sapphire Indian *Indian*
21 | 19 | 19 | $40

W 60s | 1845 Broadway (bet. 60th & 61st Sts.) | 212-245-4444 | www.sapphireny.com

"A welcome retreat" off Columbus Circle, this "quiet" Indian's "reliable" kitchen, "courteous service" and "comfortable" quarters leave loyalists "totally satisfied"; though "more expensive" than some, it's "pleasurable" "prior to Lincoln Center", and the $16 buffet lunch is a must-try.

Sarabeth's *American*
21 | 18 | 19 | $37

Chelsea | Chelsea Mkt. | 75 Ninth Ave. (bet. 15th & 16th Sts.) |
212-989-2424 | www.sarabeth.com
E 90s | 1295 Madison Ave. (92nd St.) | 212-410-7335 | www.sarabeth.com
Garment District | Lord & Taylor | 424 Fifth Ave., 5th fl. (bet. 38th & 39th Sts.) | 212-827-5068 | www.sarabeth.com
TriBeCa | 339 Greenwich St. (bet. Harrison & Jay Sts.) |
212-966-0421 | www.sarabeth.com
W 50s | 40 Central Park S. (bet. 5th & 6th Aves.) | 212-826-5959 |
www.sarabethscps.com
W 80s | 423 Amsterdam Ave. (bet. 80th & 81st Sts.) | 212-496-6280 |
www.sarabeth.com

"Forerunners for popularizing brunch", this "inviting" American "mini-empire" still "packs 'em in" to its "cute" locations for "upscale comfort food" and "hard-to-beat" breakfasts; peak-hour "waits" "can be daunting", but "sedate" dinner is also an option.

Saraghina ∅ *Pizza*
∇ 27 | 24 | 23 | $26

Bed-Stuy | 435 Halsey St. (Lewis Ave.) | Brooklyn | 718-574-0010 |
www.saraghinabrooklyn.com

Pizzaphiles "salute" this multiroomed Bed-Stuy "hidden treasure" run by a "superb" staff, where "excellent" wood-fired Neapolitan pies are a "real steal" given the "amazing" quality; the pleasingly "rustic" premises also house a coffee bar – another reason it's counted as a "savior in this neighborhood."

Saravanaa Bhavan *Indian/Vegetarian*
23 | 13 | 16 | $23

Murray Hill | 81 Lexington Ave. (26th St.) | 212-679-0204
W 70s | 413 Amsterdam Ave. (bet. 79th & 80th Sts.) | 212-721-7755
www.saravanabhavan.com

"Packed" at prime times, these UWS–Curry Hill national chain links sling "absolutely delicious" South Indian veggie fare, including "must-try" dosas; "brusque" service and interiors that "need an up-grade" are downsides, but most just focus on the "interesting flavors" and "value" pricing.

Sardi's ●Ⓜ *Continental*
19 | 23 | 21 | $55

W 40s | 234 W. 44th St. (bet. B'way & 8th Ave.) | 212-221-8440 | www.sardis.com

"Tourists" and maybe a "celeb or two" dine amid showbiz "caricatures" on the walls at this "legendary" circa-1921 Theater District ode to "opening nights"; the "high-priced" Continental fare and "old-fashioned" waiters are "just ok", but for "Broadway history", there's "nothing like it."

Sarge's Deli ● *Deli*
21 | 11 | 16 | $26

Murray Hill | 548 Third Ave. (bet. 36th & 37th Sts.) | 212-679-0442 | www.sargesdeli.com

Among the "dwindling legion of old-NY delis", this 24/7 Murray Hill fixture supplies "whopping" pastrami sandwiches and other "quintes-sential" Jewish "fixes" at "decent prices"; "dreary" digs, "rushed service" and the inevitable "food coma" are part of the "classic" experience.

Sasabune ⓏⓂ *Japanese*
29 | 11 | 23 | $113

E 70s | 401 E. 73rd St. (bet. 1st & York Aves.) | 212-249-8583

Once again rated "NYC's best for sushi", Kenji Takahashi's "sublime" UES Japanese is known for an "incredible culinary journey" of an omakase menu, featuring "clearly superior" fish, "chosen and cut by absolute experts" and sure to induce "swoons" (ditto the tab); the quarters are "spartan" and the "knowledgeable" staff can be "brisk", but finatics hardly notice.

ℕ𝔼𝕎 Sauce ●⇆ *Italian*
▽ 26 | 21 | 23 | $31

LES | 78 Rivington St. (Allen St.) | 212-420-7700 | www.saucerestaurant.com

Red gravy and red meat are the focus at this "booming" Lower Eastsider, where the "homestyle" Southern Italian eats come in nonna's-meets-funky hangout quarters; a butcher shop in full view of the dining room makes it a saucier version of siblings Lil' Frankie's and Supper, but with the same "cheap" prices and cash-only policy.

Ⓩ Saul *American*
27 | 21 | 25 | $66

Boerum Hill | 140 Smith St. (bet. Bergen & Dean Sts.) | Brooklyn | 718-935-9844 | www.saulrestaurant.com

"Wonderful from start to finish", chef Saul Bolton's "superb" Boerum Hill "gem" is lauded for "exquisite" New American cuisine brimming with "compelling flavors"; it's "spendy", but to most it's "worth every penny" given the "wonderful" service and "straightforward" but "pleasant" decor – it's "one of Brooklyn's finest."

	FOOD	DECOR	SERVICE	COST

🆕 Saxon & Parole *American*   23 | 24 | 22 | $59

NoHo | 316 Bowery (Bleecker St.) | 212-254-0350 |
www.saxonandparole.com

"Lively and energetic", this "stylish" NoHo "scene" from AvroKO "oozes
cool", drawing deep-pocketed "beautiful people" into its "happening"
"equestrian-themed" digs; happily, it "breaks from the pack of
scenester" haunts with its "sophisticated" meat-centric American fare.

Sazon *Puerto Rican*   ▽ 24 | 22 | 22 | $45

TriBeCa | 105 Reade St. (bet. Church St. & W. B'way) | 212-406-1900 |
www.sazonnyc.com

"High-class Puerto Rican" fare draws "down-home and beautiful"
types to this "upscale" TriBeCa joint, where the popular pernil is "as
good as your *abuela's*"; sangria with "the right amount of flair" and
"upbeat" music boost the "fun" (albeit "noisy") vibe.

Scaletta *Italian*   21 | 19 | 21 | $52

W 70s | 50 W. 77th St. (bet. Columbus Ave. & CPW) | 212-769-9191 |
www.scalettaristorante.com

Inventive it's not, but this "dependable" UWS "favorite" serves "solid"
"old-style" Northern Italian with "simple elegance", drawing locals
back "again and again"; the "spacious seating" and "blissful quiet" make
conversation "a pleasure", and "no one pushes you out the door."

Scalinatella ● *Italian*   25 | 18 | 22 | $88

E 60s | 201 E. 61st St., downstairs (3rd Ave.) | 212-207-8280

"Superb" Capri-style dishes draw a moneyed "'in' crowd" to this one-
of-a-kind UES Italian "hideaway" "situated downstairs" in an "intimate"
grotto; service is as "impressive" as the "incredible" food, but if your
server steers you toward the specials, "be prepared for sticker shock."

🄯 Scalini Fedeli 🅜 *Italian*   27 | 25 | 27 | $92

TriBeCa | 165 Duane St. (bet. Greenwich & Hudson Sts.) |
212-528-0400 | www.scalinifedeli.com

"You can taste the passion in every dish" at Michael Cetrulo's "gorgeous" TriBeCa Northern Italian, a "powerhouse" where "vaulted-
salon" environs, "remarkable wines" and "exemplary service" add up
to an "unforgettable", "romantic" experience; yes, its prix fixe–only
dinner is $65, but when the food arrives, "little else matters."

Scalino *Italian*   ▽ 23 | 14 | 22 | $37

Park Slope | 345 Seventh Ave. (10th St.) | Brooklyn | 718-840-5738

Every neighborhood should have a "wonderful" little "pasta joint" like
this Park Slope Italian turning out "flavorful" "home"-style fare via
"charming" owners who enhance the "friendly" feel; given all that,
most take the "nondescript", somewhat "cramped" digs in stride.

Scarpetta *Italian*   26 | 22 | 23 | $73

Chelsea | 355 W. 14th St. (bet. 8th & 9th Aves.) | 212-691-0555 |
www.scarpettanyc.com

Led by that "extraordinary" spaghetti, the "sophisticated Italian" cuisine
at Scott Conant's 14th Street destination "matches the hype", with the
"pro" service and "beautiful", "skylight"-enhanced space keeping
pace; sure, it's "expensive", but the fact that a rez is still "hard to get"
speaks for itself; P.S. dinner only.

	FOOD	DECOR	SERVICE	COST

Schiller's ● *Eclectic* — 20 | 20 | 19 | $37

LES | 131 Rivington St. (Norfolk St.) | 212-260-4555 |
www.schillersny.com

"Balthazar's younger", "lower-priced" cousin, this "welcoming" LES
Eclectic neo-bistro from Keith McNally is an ever-"packed" source for
"solid, hearty" eats in "buzzing" (i.e. "noisy") environs; whether for
"starting the day" or "ending a long night", it's a perennial "favorite."

Schnipper's Quality Kitchen *American* — 20 | 14 | 17 | $17

NEW **Flatiron** | 23 E. 23rd St. (bet. Madison & Park Aves.) |
212-233-1025 S

W 40s | NY Times Bldg. | 620 Eighth Ave. (41st St.) | 212-921-2400
www.schnippers.com

"All-American" "guilty pleasures" are the thing at these "cafeteria-style"
stops for "juicy" burgers, "awesome shakes" and other "affordable"
diner classics; the look is "chain-joint blah", but the original opposite
Port Authority is an "oasis" in "commuter hell", and the new Flatironer
fills the bill when you can't face the "lines at Shake Shack."

Schnitzel Haus *German* — ∇ 24 | 19 | 22 | $34

Bay Ridge | 7319 Fifth Ave. (74th St.) | Brooklyn | 718-836-5600 |
www.schnitzelhausny.com

"Real", "no-apologies" German "home cooking" and "excellent beers"
on tap make it "impossible to leave hungry" from this Bay Ridge
Bohemian; the "nice price", "laid-back" vibe and live music on weekends further endear it to locals.

Scottadito Osteria Toscana Ⓜ *Italian* — ∇ 23 | 19 | 22 | $37

Park Slope | 788 Union St. (bet. 6th & 7th Aves.) | Brooklyn |
718-636-4800 | www.scottadito.com

It has been "overlooked for too long" insist Park Slope partisans of this
"quiet" "gem" slinging "hearty" Northern Italian fare in "fireplace"-
enhanced "rustic" Tuscan digs; "affordable" tabs, "fantastic service"
and an "unlimited-mimosa brunch" strengthen their argument.

SD26 *Italian* — 25 | 24 | 24 | $74

Murray Hill | 19 E. 26th St. (bet. 5th & Madison Aves.) |
212-265-5959 | www.sd26ny.com

With its "glam" modernist dining room and front bar employing "iPad
wine menus", this San Domenico sequel on Madison Square Park has
gone "downtown"-"chic", but still reflects father-daughter duo Tony
and Marisa May's "commitment" to "glorious" Italian cooking and "incredible" vintages; yes, it's "pricey", but who's complaining when you're
"treated like royalty"?

Sea *Thai* — 23 | 24 | 19 | $29

Meatpacking | 835 Washington St. (Little W. 12th St.) |
212-243-3339
Williamsburg | 114 N. Sixth St. (Berry St.) | Brooklyn |
718-384-8850 ●
www.seathainyc.com

The "awe-inspiring interiors" at these "nightclub"-like Williamsburg-
Meatpacking Thais resemble "dreamy faux temples" replete with "indoor ponds" and "huge Buddhas", plus pulsing "techno"; "party" people report the "served-fast" eats are "delicious", ditto the "bargain" tab.

Sea Grill ⧄ *Seafood* `24` `24` `24` `$74`

W 40s | Rockefeller Ctr. | 19 W. 49th St. (bet. 5th & 6th Aves.) | 212-332-7610 | www.theseagrillnyc.com

The "matchless view" of the skating rink, "golden Prometheus" and the "Christmas tree" at this Rock Center "destination" inspire "even locals" to "act like tourists"; of course, you "pay for the location", but "memorable" seafood, "elegant" service and "exquisite outdoor dining" in summer are sufficient reward.

Sea Shore ◗ *Seafood* ▽ `22` `21` `22` `$42`

City Island | 591 City Island Ave. (Cross St.) | Bronx | 718-885-0300 | www.seashorerestaurant.com

A City Island "place to be" since 1920, this "friendly" seafooder dishes up "tastes-just-caught" finfare amid "old-fashioned" shore-side surrounds; it's "noisy", but the outdoor dining and marina views are compelling attractions for "families" and "weekend" visitors, likewise the relatively moderate prices.

Seäsonal *Austrian* `25` `20` `24` `$70`

W 50s | 132 W. 58th St. (bet. 6th & 7th Aves.) | 212-957-5550 | www.seasonalnyc.com

"Classic Austrian" cuisine gets a "playful twist" and a "seasonal" spin at this "refined" Midtowner overseen by a "well-trained" staff; some wonder "why it's not more beloved" given its "convenient location" near Carnegie Hall and City Center – "expensive" tabs may be a clue.

☒ 2nd Ave Deli ◗ *Deli/Kosher* `23` `14` `18` `$29`

E 70s | 1442 First Ave. (75th St.) | 212-737-1700
Murray Hill | 162 E. 33rd St. (bet. Lexington & 3rd Aves.) | 212-689-9000
www.2ndavedeli.com

A "throwback to kinder, cholesterol-oblivious times", this kosher deli duo supplies epic "food marathons" via "iconic" sandwiches that give "overstuffed a new meaning"; trade-offs include "ambivalent service", "nebbish" decor and "heartburn"-inducing prices, yet these "blasts from the past" remain a "taste of childhood" for many; P.S. the UES outlet is "less claustrophobic" than its more "condensed" Murray Hill cousin.

Seersucker *Southern* `23` `21` `23` `$41`

Carroll Gardens | 329 Smith St. (bet. Carroll & President Sts.) | Brooklyn | 718-422-0444 | www.seersuckerbrooklyn.com

Bringing "the best of the South up north", this Carroll Gardens "escape" turns "wonderful local products" into "soul-pleasing" Southern cooking with a "modern twist"; "sweet" staffers and down-to-earth prices keep the "minimalist"-"chic" space "buzzy."

Sentosa ◗⧄ *Malaysian* ▽ `22` `17` `18` `$18`

Flushing | 39-07 Prince St. (bet. Roosevelt & 39th Aves.) | Queens | 718-886-6331 | www.sentosausa.com

"Spicy" curries and other satisfying Malaysian "home-cooking" classics offered "really cheap" are the draw at this Flushing find; pleasant wood-lined quarters and "warm" service complete the picture; P.S. in summer, "go for the shaved ice desserts."

Serafina ◗ *Italian* `20` `17` `18` `$43`

E 50s | 38 E. 58th St. (bet. Madison & Park Aves.) | 212-832-8888 ☒

(continued)

Serafina

E 60s | 29 E. 61st St. (bct. Madison & Park Aves.) | 212-702-9898
E 70s | 1022 Madison Ave., 2nd fl. (79th St.) | 212-734-2676
NEW Meatpacking | 7 Ninth Ave. (Little W. 12th St.) | 212-898-3800
W 40s | Time Hotel | 224 W. 49th St. (bet. B'way & 8th Ave.) | 212-247-1000
W 50s | Dream Hotel | 210 W. 55th St. (B'way) | 212-315-1700
NEW W 70s | On the Ave Hotel | 2178 Broadway (77th St.) |
212-595-0092
www.serafinarestaurant.com

If "fantastic" pizzas and pastas "like you wish mom had made" are
what you seek, this "rustic" Italian mini-chain "does it right"; depending on the location, it ranges from "private-school" "teeny-bopper"
hangout to "see-and-be-seen" scene, but "quick", "harried" service,
"lively", "loud" atmosphere and moderate prices are constants.

Serendipity 3 ◐ *Dessert*

20 | 21 | 17 | $31

E 60s | 225 E. 60th St. (bet. 2nd & 3rd Aves.) | 212-838-3531 |
www.serendipity3.com

The "ultimate" East Side "dessert spot" and "après-Bloomingdale's
pick-me-up", this circa-1954 "institution" still lures "kids of all ages";
waits are "crazy-long", service "s-l-o-w" and prices "high", but it's
"open late" – and that frozen hot chocolate is "famous for a reason."

Sette Mezzo ⊘ *Italian*

24 | 18 | 22 | $74

E 70s | 969 Lexington Ave. (bet. 70th & 71st Sts.) | 212-472-0400
The "simple, rich" Italian fare is "excellent" but almost beside the
point at this "clubhouse" for the "UES cognoscenti", where "upscale"
"regulars" get "house accounts" and "personable" service, but for everyone else it's "cash only" and "snark, snark, snark"; either way, expect "tight tables" and a "steep" tab.

Settepani *Bakery*

▽ 24 | 21 | 23 | $37

Williamsburg | 602 Lorimer St. (bet. Conselyea St. & Skillman Ave.) |
Brooklyn | 718-349-6524

Ristorante Settepani *Italian*

Harlem | 196 Lenox Ave. (120th St.) | 917-492-4806
www.settepani.com

This "stylish" Harlem cafe and its Billyburg sibling are both known for
"fabulous" desserts, but the former also boasts a "fantastic" menu of
"Italian bites" and a "wonderful wine list"; "friendly" staffers add to
the "inviting", "relaxed" vibe at these neighborhood "gems."

Seva Indian Cuisine *Indian*

▽ 25 | 17 | 21 | $20

Astoria | 30-07 34th St. (30th Ave.) | Queens | 718-626-4440 |
www.sevaindianrestaurant.com

Not your average curry house, this "small-but-cozy" Astoria standout
spotlights "bold and flavorful" Northern Indian cuisine, made "as spicy
as you want"; everyone leaves "happily full", and the "all-you-can-eat
weekend brunch" and prix fixes offer amazing "bang for the buck."

Seven's Turkish Grill *Turkish*

21 | 16 | 21 | $34

W 70s | 158 W. 72nd St. (bet. Amsterdam & Columbus Aves.) |
212-724-4700 | www.seventurkishgrill.com

At this "pleasant" UWS Turk, the "bread is just-baked" and the dishes
are "subtlely spiced", so no surprise it's a "favorite" with locals; ok, the

| | | | FOOD | DECOR | SERVICE | COST |

"cafeteria"-like ambiance feels "anonymous", but the "warm", "attentive" treatment and "fair prices" more than compensate.

Sevilla ◑ *Spanish* `25` `16` `22` `$42`

W Village | 62 Charles St. (W. 4th St.) | 212-929-3189 |
www.sevillarestaurantandbar.com
"They know what they're doing" at this circa-1941 Village "garlic haven" delivering "fabulous paellas" and other low-cost Spanish classics via "efficient" waiters; yes, the decor's "worn", but patrons downing "out-of-this-world sangria" are having too much "fun" to notice.

Sezz Medi' *Mediterranean/Pizza* ▽ `22` `18` `17` `$29`

W 100s | 1260 Amsterdam Ave. (122nd St.) | 212-932-2901 |
www.sezzmedi.com
It's all about the "fresh" pizzas and other Med staples at this "popular", affordable Columbia "hangout"; service can be "inattentive" and the rustic-style digs are nothing fancy, but it's a "plus for the neighborhood."

Sfoglia *Italian* `24` `19` `21` `$65`

E 90s | 1402 Lexington Ave. (92nd St.) | 212-831-1402 |
www.sfogliarestaurant.com
Widely praised for "authentic" Italian cooking, "knowledgeable" servers and "romantic" "farmhouse" digs, this Carnegie Hill standby catty-corner from the 92nd Street Y is "the real deal"; though "pricey", most agree it's "worth the money" – "getting a table" is the real problem.

Shabu-Shabu 70 *Japanese* `23` `13` `23` `$42`

E 70s | 314 E. 70th St. (bet. 1st & 2nd Aves.) | 212-861-5635
"Shabu-shabu cooked at the table" that's "great fun to eat with a crowd" is the main attraction at this UES "Japanese hideout", but you "won't go wrong with sushi" here either; affordable rates and "congenial" service outshine kinda "shabby" digs.

Shabu-Tatsu *Japanese* ▽ `22` `14` `18` `$34`

E Village | 216 E. 10th St. (bet. 1st & 2nd Aves.) | 212-477-2972 |
www.tic-nyc.com
If "cook-your-own" is what you seek, this "authentic", moderately tabbed East Village Japanese lets you simmer "super-tasty" shabu-shabu and sukiyaki in hot pots at your table; service is efficient enough, but diminutive dimensions spell "difficulties in getting a table."

⊠ Shake Shack *Burgers* `22` `13` `16` `$16`

E 80s | 154 E. 86th St. (bet. Lexington & 3rd Aves.) | 646-237-5035
Financial District | 215 Murray St. (bet. North End Ave. & West St.) |
646-545-4600
Flatiron | Madison Square Park | 23rd St. (Madison Ave.) | 212-889-6600
W 40s | InterContinental NY Times Sq. | 691 Eighth Ave. (44th St.) |
646-435-0135 ◑
W 70s | 366 Columbus Ave. (77th St.) | 646-747-8770
NEW Downtown Bklyn | Fulton Street Mall | 409 Fulton St. (Adams St.) |
Brooklyn | 718-307-7590
Flushing | Citi Field | 126th St. & Roosevelt Ave. (behind the scoreboard) |
Queens | No phone
www.shakeshack.com
Unless you go "off peak", you're likely to confront "lines" and "inadequate seating" at Danny Meyer's "ever-growing" empire of neo–fast

fooders best known for "rich, luscious burgers" and "thick" shakes; they're almost always "swarming" with customers who insist that the "buzz" is "well-deserved."

Shalezeh *Persian*

| 23 | 20 | 23 | $45 |

E 80s | 1420 Third Ave. (bet. 80th & 81st Sts.) | 212-288-0012 | www.shalezeh.com

"As close as you get to authentic Persian dining in NYC", this upscale-yet–decently priced Upper Eastsider presents "fragrant, richly flavored" cuisine (notably the rice dishes) in "comfortable" quarters; "gracious" service and those "pomegranate mojitos" boost the "pleasant" experience.

Shanghai Café ⊅ *Chinese*

| 24 | 10 | 11 | $20 |

Little Italy | 100 Mott St. (bet. Canal & Hester Sts.) | 212-966-3988

This "tiny", "cash-only" Little Italy Chinese churns out its signature "succulent soup dumplings" and other Shanghai treats "fast" and "dirt cheap"; the "flavorful" eats help frugal patrons "tune out" the "barking" service and inauspicious "fluorescent-light-and-Formica" setting.

Shanghai Pavilion *Chinese*

| ▽ 22 | 20 | 22 | $34 |

E 70s | 1378 Third Ave. (bet. 78th & 79th Sts.) | 212-585-3388 | www.shanghaipavillionnyc.com

It's hard to say what's most "surprising" about this "elegant" UES Chinese: the "solid" Shanghainese cooking, "welcoming" service or "quiet", "upscale atmosphere"; whatever the case, it's a "welcome combination", especially at the modest price.

Shi *Asian*

| ▽ 25 | 26 | 21 | $37 |

LIC | 47-20 Center Blvd. (Vernon Blvd.) | Queens | 347-242-2450 | www.eatdrinkshi.com

"Fantastic views of the NYC skyline" combine with "stylish, delicious" Pan-Asian cuisine, "amazing cocktails" and a "lovely staff" for a winning overall experience at this "upscale" LIC high-rise dweller; however, the "TVs at the bar" and "disco" on Saturday nights get mixed reviews.

Shiro of Japan *Japanese*

| ▽ 23 | 22 | 24 | $37 |

Glendale | Shops at Atlas Park | 80-40 Cooper Ave. (80th St.) | Queens | 718-326-8704 | www.shiroofjapan.com

A "fun, friendly" crew serves up "well-priced" "hibachi-style" eats plus "delicious" sushi to families and other locals at this "casual" Glendale Japanese; what's more, the "prepared-in-front-of-you" dishes provide a "great show along with your meal."

Shorty's ◐ *Cheesesteaks*

| 23 | 14 | 18 | $19 |

W 40s | 576 Ninth Ave. (bet. 41st & 42nd Sts.) | 212-967-3055
NEW **Murray Hill** | 66 Madison Ave. (bet. 27th & 28th Sts.) | 212-725-3900 | www.shortysnyc.com

Lil' Shorty's *Cheesesteaks*

NEW **Murray Hill** | 133 E. 31st St. (Lexington Ave.) | 212-779-8900 | www.shortysnyc.com

When "homesick for Philly", these "noisy" Midtowners come in handy for "out-of-this-world" cheesesteaks, craft suds and full-time "Philly sports" on the tube (game nights are "earsplitting"); the new Lil' outpost in Murray Hill sticks to takeout and delivery.

	FOOD	DECOR	SERVICE	COST

Shula's Steak House ● *Steak* | 24 | 20 | 23 | $73 |

W 40s | Westin Times Sq. Hotel | 270 W. 43rd St. (bet. B'way & 8th Ave.) | 212-201-2776 | www.westinny.com

Not surprisingly, a "football" theme prevails at this Times Square outlet of legendary coach Don Shula's steakhouse chain; it scores with "tasty" beef and "efficient" service, but while its memorabilia may appeal to "Dolphins fans", for Jets and Giants supporters "nothing's remarkable" enough to come "running back."

Shun Lee Cafe ● *Chinese* | 21 | 18 | 20 | $47 |

W 60s | 43 W. 65th St. (bet. Columbus Ave. & CPW) | 212-769-3888 | www.shunleewest.com

The "dim-scrumptious" Chinese at this "reliable" stalwart is a "tradition" for Lincoln Center–goers who appreciate its "zippy service" and overlook the by-now-"dusty" "checkerboard" digs; it's a "relaxed" alternative to its pricier next-door sibling, but all of those little bites "can add up" to a serious sum.

Shun Lee Palace ● *Chinese* | 24 | 21 | 22 | $59 |

E 50s | 155 E. 55th St. (bet. Lexington & 3rd Aves.) | 212-371-8844 | www.shunleepalace.com

Michael Tong set the standard for "high-end Chinese" with this "handsome", "1970s-era" Midtowner, where "venerable" waiters dispense "delicious" plates in a "white-tablecloth" milieu; the tabs may be "hefty", but you're "well taken care of" and there's no arguing with "quality."

Shun Lee West ● *Chinese* | 23 | 21 | 22 | $58 |

W 60s | 43 W. 65th St. (bet. Columbus Ave. & CPW) | 212-595-8895 | www.shunleewest.com

The "epitome of haute Chinoise", this Lincoln Center standby "takes itself seriously" with "expert servers" dispensing "delectable" dishes; black lacquer–and–"golden dragon" decor amplifies the "elegant" air, which comes justifiably with "prices to match."

Siam Square ▣ *Thai* | ▽ 24 | 19 | 21 | $32 |

Riverdale | 564 Kappock St. (Henry Hudson Pkwy.) | Bronx | 718-432-8200 | www.siamsq.com

Spice-hounds don't mind "trekking to Riverdale" for the "creative specials" and other "well-flavored" Thai dishes at this reasonably priced find; the space isn't much, but it's "quiet", the staff's "welcoming" and locals know they're "lucky to have such quality dining" nearby.

Sidecar ● *American* | 23 | 20 | 23 | $40 |

Park Slope | 560 Fifth Ave. (bet. 15th & 16th Sts.) | Brooklyn | 718-369-0077 | www.sidecarbrooklyn.com

The bartenders "mix a mean drink" at this "warm", "bustling" Park Slope purveyor of "original cocktails" and "amazing" American comfort fare, prepared in an open kitchen visible from the "copper-topped bar"; the ultimate "local haunt", it also gets a "thumbs up" for its late hours.

Sidetracks *American* | 21 | 21 | 21 | $34 |

Sunnyside | 45-08 Queens Blvd. (45th St.) | Queens | 718-786-3570 | www.sidetracksny.com

The "hearty", "standard American" pub grub at this Sunnyside "fixture" is "better than one might expect", as is its "relatively upscale"

| | FOOD | DECOR | SERVICE | COST |

look; it's usually "packed", due in no small part to "twinkle-in-the-eye" staffers and a "clublike" vibe (enhanced by DJs on weekend nights).

Sik Gaek ● *Korean* ▽ 24 | 16 | 21 | $31

Flushing | 161-29 Crocheron Ave. (162nd St.) | Queens | 718-321-7770
Woodside | 49-11 Roosevelt Ave. (50th St.) | Queens |
718-205-4555
www.sikgaekusa.com

"Adventurous" types crowd these low-budget Flushing-Woodside Koreans, where "attentive" servers dole out "authentic" oceanic fare amid "blaring Korean hip-hop"; seafood "still wriggling in the pot" can be "off-putting", but it's "fun" for "big groups" and high on "exotic excitement."

Sinigual *Mexican* 22 | 21 | 21 | $41

E 40s | 640 Third Ave. (41st St.) | 212-286-0250 |
www.sinigualrestaurants.com

Mexican standards and "potent margaritas" get a "modern spin" at this "convivial" contender near Grand Central; the "cavernous" space can get "noisy", especially "after-work" at the bar, but the "tableside guac" alone justifies "the price of admission."

Sip Sak *Turkish* 21 | 14 | 16 | $38

E 40s | 928 Second Ave. (bet. 49th & 50th Sts.) | 212-583-1900 |
www.sip-sak.com

"Solid" Turkish specialties full of flavor come at "fair" rates at this U.N.-area "standby"; the "Montparnasse–meets–the Dardanelles" decor is considered "just ok" , but the food and service shore up an overall "satisfying" experience.

NEW Siro's *American* - | - | - | E

E 40s | 885 Second Ave. (47th St.) | 212-486-6400 |
www.sirosny.com

Saratoga Springs' iconic trackside eatery gallops into Midtown with this swanky New American outpost backed by *Entourage* stars Kevin Connolly and Kevin Dillon and Yankee Mariano Rivera; the pricey menu combines old-school classics (crab cakes) with newfangled flourishes (ratatouille lasagna) in a multiroom space with a well-groomed, equestrian-themed look.

Sistina *Italian* 26 | 20 | 23 | $78

E 80s | 1555 Second Ave. (bet. 80th & 81st Sts.) | 212-861-7660
"Serious diners" gather at this "civilized" Upper East Side "white-tablecloth Italian", where "inspired" cuisine is matched with an "outstanding" wine list; "impeccable" service and attractive decor allow its moneyed "local" regulars to easily accept prices as "mind-blowing" as the extensive "specials."

NEW 606 R&D Ⓜ *American* 24 | 23 | 23 | $36

Prospect Heights | 606 Vanderbilt Ave. (bet. Prospect Pl. & St. Marks Ave.) |
Brooklyn | 718-230-0125 | www.606vanderbiltbklyn.com

Prospect Heights foodies see "great potential" in this new eatery-cum–mini-market serving "farm-to-fork" Americana with "Brooklyn flair" all day long; the small, high-ceilinged space is "sunny" and the service "personable", but it's the mechanical "donut robot" that early visitors find most intriguing.

67 Burger *Burgers*
22 | 17 | 20 | $20

Fort Greene | 67 Lafayette Ave. (Fulton St.) | Brooklyn | 718-797-7150
NEW **Park Slope** | 234 Flatbush Ave. (bet. Bergen St. & 6th Ave) |
Brooklyn | 718-399-6767
www.67burger.com

These "cafeteria"-style Brooklyn burger joints supply "cooked-to-order" beef patties plus "all manner of fixin's" to "hipsters" as well as "BAM" and Barclays Center attendees; no one minds the "sterile" settings what with the "reasonable" tabs and "kid-friendly" vibes.

S'MAC *American*
24 | 11 | 15 | $15

E Village | 345 E. 12th St. (bet. 1st & 2nd Aves.) | 212-358-7912
NEW **E Village** | First Park | 75 E. First St. (1st Ave.) | 212-358-7917
www.smacnyc.com

"Sock-meltingly delicious" mac 'n' cheese "done up fancy" is the thing at these "affordable" East Village "pleasure palaces", which offer "customized", "gluten-free" and "vegan" variants; given "minimal seating", "cheesy" decor and service that's "less than caring", many opt for the "take-and-bake" option.

The Smile ● *Mediterranean*
▽ 22 | 21 | 20 | $28

NoHo | 26 Bond St., downstairs (bet. Bowery & Lafayette St.) | 646-329-5836
NEW **Smile to Go** *Mediterranean/Sandwiches*
SoHo | 22 Howard St. (bet. Crosby & Lafayette Sts.) | 646-863-3893
www.thesmilenyc.com

"Hipsters abound" at this "sweet little" NoHo nook (with a SoHo take-out satellite), which flies a bit under the radar with its "charming", "rustic" basement locale and "basic" Med-American bites; by day, it's the "ideal" coffeehouse to "hole up in", and if the staff can be "spacey", hey – "they always smile."

The Smith ● *American*
21 | 19 | 19 | $40

NEW **E 50s** | 956 Second Ave. (bet. 50th & 51st Sts.) | 212-644-2700
E Village | 55 Third Ave. (bet. 10th & 11th Sts.) | 212-420-9800
www.thesmithnyc.com

"Overflow crowds" mark these East Village–Turtle Bay Americans where "young" "trendy" types down "mean drinks", hone their "competitive shouting" skills and kick up "quite the scene"; they're "brunch favorites" too, with "simple", "reasonably priced" eats that are "surprisingly good" – would that every neighborhood had one of these.

Smith & Wollensky *Steak*
24 | 20 | 23 | $77

E 40s | 797 Third Ave. (49th St.) | 212-753-1530 |
www.smithandwollenskynyc.com

One part "gruff, manly steakhouse", one part "NY institution", this "classic" Midtown beefery delivers "perfectly marbled slabs" and "generous drinks" to a "power-broker" crowd; "old-school" waiters preside over the "noisy, informal" scene, and quickly dispatch the "corporate cards" at meal's end.

Smoke Joint *BBQ*
23 | 15 | 19 | $25

Fort Greene | 87 S. Elliott Pl. (Lafayette Ave.) | Brooklyn |
718-797-1011 | www.thesmokejoint.com

The "sauce is boss" at this cheap, "bare-bones" Fort Greene BBQ standby, "a definite do" for "outstanding", "smoky" ribs and "on-point" wings; it's "rough around the edges", but service is "solid", and the crowds happily "eat while standing" ("'cuz it's so packed").

Smorgasburg ⊠Ⓜ *Eclectic* ▽ 28 | 16 | 19 | $21

Williamsburg | East River Waterfront (bet. 6th & 7th Sts.) | Brooklyn | 718-928-6603 | www.smorgasburg.com

This Williamsburg waterfront food market, an offshoot of the Brooklyn Flea, offers views of the "Manhattan skyline" to go with its "fantastic", "deliciously cheap" eats from "local food purveyors" ("the sheer variety makes the trip essential"); "crazy crowds" comprising everyone from "yupsters" to "hipsters" converge every Saturday – "go early, as things tend to sell out."

Smorgas Chef *Scandinavian* 20 | 17 | 20 | $37

Financial District | 53 Stone St. (William St.) | 212-422-3500 ●
Murray Hill | Scandinavia Hse. | 58 Park Ave. (bet. 37th & 38th Sts.) | 212-847-9745
W Village | 283 W. 12th St. (4th St.) | 212-243-7073
www.smorgas.com

Admirers would "return just for the meatballs", but these "reliable" Scandinavians offer plenty of other "traditional" dishes as well, brought to table by a "lovely" staff; the surroundings are "spare" but "relaxing", and better still the check won't "break the bank."

Snack *Greek* 23 | 16 | 20 | $35

SoHo | 105 Thompson St. (bet. Prince & Spring Sts.) | 212-925-1040

Snack Taverna *Greek*

W Village | 63 Bedford St. (Morton St.) | 212-929-3499
www.snackny.com

It's easy to "gorge" at these "friendly" Greeks dishing up "fresh", "delectable" classics in "large portions"; the slightly roomier West Villager is "a step up" from its "teeny" 12-seat SoHo sibling, but both exude "rustic charm" – and "the price is just right."

sNice *Sandwiches/Vegetarian* 21 | 17 | 18 | $16

SoHo | 150 Sullivan St. (bet. Houston & Prince Sts.) | 212-253-5405
W Village | 45 Eighth Ave. (bet. Horatio & Jane Sts.) | 212-645-0310
Park Slope | 315 Fifth Ave. (bet. 2nd & 3rd Sts.) | Brooklyn | 718-788-2121
www.snicecafe.com

Make fun if you must, but these "chill" sandwich hangouts prove that "delicious", "healthy" and "vegetarian" fare isn't an oxymoron; everyone from "moms-to-be" to "laptop" "hipsters" and "crunchy-granola" vegans finds the "friendly community spirit" soNice.

Soba Nippon *Japanese/Noodle Shop* ▽ 23 | 17 | 21 | $39

W 50s | 19 W. 52nd St. (bet. 5th & 6th Aves.) | 212-489-2525 | www.sobanippon.com

"They grow their own buckwheat" upstate to make the noodles at this "good-value" Midtown Japanese soba standout; "personal" service and a "calm" atmosphere mean it's "perfect for stressed-out afternoons."

Soba Totto *Japanese/Noodle Shop* 25 | 19 | 20 | $47

E 40s | 211 E. 43rd St. (bet. 2nd & 3rd Aves.) | 212-557-8200 | www.sobatotto.com

"Stunning" "housemade soba" and "fresh" yakitori beckon Grand Central commuters to this "dimly lit" Japanese, one of Midtown's

Totto trifecta; the prices are a bit "expensive" for the genre, but it's a pleasure to "sit at the bar and watch the charcoal pros work their magic."

Soba-ya *Japanese/Noodle Shop* | 25 | 19 | 21 | $30 |

E Village | 229 E. Ninth St. (bet. 2nd & 3rd Aves.) | 212-533-6966 | www.sobaya-nyc.com

At this "low-key" East Village "go-to", the "superb" Japanese soba features "refreshing broths" and "delicious noodles"; "no reservations" spells "waits on weekends", but "affordable" price tags and "pleasant" environs mean most don't mind much.

Socarrat Paella Bar *Spanish* | 23 | 18 | 18 | $49 |

Chelsea | 259 W. 19th St. (bet. 7th & 8th Aves.) | 212-462-1000
NEW **E 50s** | 953 Second Ave. (bet. 50th & 51st Sts.) | 212-759-0101
NoLita | 284 Mulberry St. (bet. Houston & Prince Sts.) | 212-219-0101
www.socarratpaellabar.com

The "paella is the star" at these "rustic" Spaniards, but the "seasonal tapas" and "affordable wines" also contribute; the original Chelsea "closet" "has expanded" to include two larger venues, and all three boast "intimate" atmospheres that are "romantic" or "festive", depending on the night.

Social Eatz *Asian/Sandwiches* | 22 | 16 | 17 | $28 |

E 50s | 232 E. 53rd St. (bet. 2nd & 3rd Aves.) | 212-207-3339 | www.socialeatz.com

Top Chef contender Angela Sosa's "inventive" Midtown "burger pub" mixes "American classics" with "Asian twists"; service is "inconsistent" and the "cramped" quarters are one part "*Brady Bunch*", one part "student dining hall", but who cares? – the bill "won't break the bank."

Sofrito ● *Puerto Rican* | 24 | 21 | 20 | $47 |

E 50s | 400 E. 57th St. (bet. 1st Ave. & Sutton Pl.) | 212-754-5999 | www.sofritony.com

"To-die-for" mofongo and pernil get washed down with "fruity vacation drinks" at this "clubby" Sutton Place Puerto Rican, where "loud Latin music" booms, and someone's always "celebrating something"; the "enormous" repasts are "surprisingly affordable", but "bring your earplugs."

Sojourn ● *Eclectic* | ▽ 23 | 19 | 19 | $44 |

E 70s | 244 E. 79th St. (bet. 2nd & 3rd Aves.) | 212-537-7745 | www.sojournrestaurant.com

This "lively" UES Eclectic's "knowledgeable" staffers deliver a "wide range" of "creative" small plates and "unusual beers" to an "attractive clientele"; equally "sexy" is the dark, modern space with a "downtown" vibe, but "order carefully" or the bill may "be a shock."

Solera ⊠ *Spanish* | ▽ 23 | 19 | 22 | $55 |

E 50s | 216 E. 53rd St. (bet. 2nd & 3rd Aves.) | 212-644-1166 | www.solerany.com

No one "feels rushed" at this "civilized" East Midtown Spaniard where "Iberian wines", "terrific" tapas and "plenty of paella" are dispensed by a "friendly" crew; prices are "high", but the "comfortable and spacious" dining room makes sure "conversation is easily possible."

	FOOD	DECOR	SERVICE	COST

Solo *Kosher/Mediterranean* — 26 | 23 | 22 | $69

E 50s | 550 Madison Ave. (bet. 55th & 56th Sts.) | 212-833-7800 |
www.solonyc.com

It's the "crème de la crème" of glatt kitchens say fans of this "quiet"
Midtowner offering an "expansive" menu of "splendid" kosher Med
fare; the "pretty" place and its "unpretentious" staff exude "refinement", but its "captive audience" has to "part with a lot of shekels."

NEW Son Cubano *Cuban/Spanish* — ∇ 23 | 22 | 20 | $45

Chelsea | 544 W. 27th St. (bet. 10th & 11th Aves.) | 212-366-1640 |
www.soncubanonyc.com

Reopened in Way West Chelsea, this eatery/nightclub kept the "old
Havana" supper-club vibe intact, from the glitzy chandeliers to the
checkerboard dance floor; the kitchen turns out midpriced Cuban favorites, best paired with tropical cocktails, and later on the scene
"turns into a Latin dance party."

Song ∌ *Thai* — 24 | 18 | 19 | $22

Park Slope | 295 Fifth Ave. (bet. 1st & 2nd Sts.) | Brooklyn | 718-965-1108

Park Slopers sing the praises of this "family-friendly" Joya sibling, where
"fantastic" Thai dishes are "generously portioned and inexpensive" so
most take the "no-credit-card policy" in stride; if the high "volume of
music and chatter" inside rankles, there's always the "garden in the rear."

NEW Sons of Essex ● *American* — ∇ 21 | 24 | 21 | $45

LES | 133 Essex St. (bet. Rivington & Stanton Sts.) | 212-674-7100 |
www.sonsofessexles.com

The redone Mason Dixon space now sports a "vintage feel" with a
"cool speakeasylike entrance" at this "hip", "pricey" Lower Eastsider;
the "DJ" and "fantastic bar scene" threaten to overshadow the "decadent" New American fare and "the service suffers" at times – but everyone's having too much "fun" to notice.

Sookk *Thai* — 22 | 19 | 21 | $26

W 100s | 2686 Broadway (bet. 102nd & 103rd Sts.) | 212-870-0253 |
www.sookkrestaurant.com

UWS locals leave this "reliable" "neighborhood" Thai "with a full
stomach" thanks to its "innovative" Bangkok-inspired street eats
doled out in "generous portions"; the "calm" digs are "tiny", but those
"sparky flavors" come so "super cheap", "what's not to love?"

Sorella ● M *Italian* — ∇ 24 | 20 | 22 | $59

LES | 95 Allen St. (bet. Broome & Delancey Sts.) | 212-274-9595 |
www.sorellanyc.com

It's "love at first bite" at this LES Italian "charmer" known for "consistently exciting" Piedmontese small plates and regional wines; "helpful" service and a "cool", "inviting", recently expanded space take the
edge off of kinda pricey tabs.

Sosa Borella ● *Argentinean/Italian* — 21 | 16 | 20 | $45

W 50s | 832 Eighth Ave. (50th St.) | 212-262-7774 | www.sosaborella.com

This West 50s vet "just keeps rolling along" with "simple", "tasty"
Argentinean-Italian fare served in "friendly" environs; "value" rates
and a "pleasant" rooftop are other reasons it's an "excellent choice"
pre- or post-theater.

| | | FOOD | DECOR | SERVICE | COST |

Soto ● ⑤ *Japanese*   28 | 20 | 23 | $104

W Village | 357 Sixth Ave. (bet. 4th St. & Washington Pl.) |
212-414-3088 | www.sotonyc.com

It's a "paradise for uni-lovers", but just "don't tell anybody" plead
partisans of chef Sotohiro Kosugi's "tiny", "understated", somewhat
under-the-radar West Village Japanese known for its "urchin artistry";
its "exquisite" sushi "would stand up to any in Tokyo", but comes "with
prices to match."

SottoVoce *Italian*   ▽ 21 | 18 | 21 | $36

Park Slope | 225 Seventh Ave. (4th St.) | Brooklyn | 718-369-9322 |
www.sottovocerestaurant.com

"Reliable pastas" and other Italian basics "done right" keep this "unpretentious" Park Sloper "popular", as do the "can't-beat" $10 prix
fixe lunch and "unlimited-mimosa" brunch; "warm, familial service"
and "pleasant" sidewalk seating ice the cake.

South Brooklyn Pizza *Pizza*   24 | 15 | 18 | $15

E Village | 122 First Ave. (bet. 7th & 8th Sts.) | 212-533-2879 |
www.southbrooklynpizza.com
Carroll Gardens | 451 Court St. (bet. 4th Pl. & Lucquer St.) | Brooklyn |
718-852-6018 Ⓜ 🗫
Park Slope | 447 First St. (bet. 6th & 7th Aves.) | Brooklyn |
718-832-1022 | www.southbrooklynpizza.com ● 🗫
Park Slope | 64 Fourth Ave. (bet. Bergen & Dean Sts.) | Brooklyn |
718-399-7770

With an original location grafted to the Carroll Gardens Irish bar P.J.
Hanley's, this burgeoning mini-chain of "funky" pizzerias dishes up
"incredibly fresh" "NYC-style" thin-crust pies; "you can get slices" –
which many take on the run given the no-frills "hole-in-the-wall" setups.

South Gate *American*   22 | 25 | 19 | $72

W 50s | Jumeirah Essex Hse. | 154 Central Park S. (bet. 6th & 7th Aves.) |
212-484-5120 | www.154southgate.com

Somewhat "under the radar" despite an "unbeatable" Essex House location, this "quiet CPS find" offers Kerry Heffernan's "delightful" New
Americana in "glam" quarters; ok, "you'd expect better service" given
the "stiff price", but most just focus on the "view of Central Park."

Sparks Steak House ⑤ *Steak*   26 | 21 | 24 | $84

E 40s | 210 E. 46th St. (bet. 2nd & 3rd Aves.) | 212-687-4855 |
www.sparkssteakhouse.com

A "carnivore's delight" since 1966, this "classic" Midtown East chop
shop draws "business types" aplenty with its "succulent" steaks and
"fantastic wines" delivered by "pro" waiters; dark, wood-paneled decor and "expense account–only" pricing are just marks of its "old-
school boys' club" authenticity.

Spasso ● *Italian*   24 | 20 | 22 | $53

W Village | 551 Hudson St. (Perry St.) | 212-858-3838 |
www.spassonyc.com

"Fresh, innovative" Italian fare and "excellent" wines come via "friendly"
staffers at this slightly "sceney" West Villager; locals who note it becomes "loud and tight" at prime times "hope it doesn't get more
popular" – prices "on the expensive side" may keep crowds in check.

	FOOD	DECOR	SERVICE	COST

NEW Speedy Romeo ⊠ *Italian/Pizza* ▽ 24 | 24 | 25 | $35

Clinton Hill | 376 Classon Ave. (Greene Ave.) | Brooklyn |
718-230-0061 | www.speedyromeo.com
Housed in a former body shop, this "high-quality" Italian arrival to
Clinton Hill specializes in "excellent" wood-fired pizzas topped with
"housemade mozz" and other "fresh" ingredients, but it also serves up
grill dishes; its casual, brick-lined interior centered on an open kitchen
fills up fast.

Spice *Thai* 21 | 17 | 18 | $27

Chelsea | 199 Eighth Ave. (20th St.) | 212-989-1116
Chelsea | 236 Eighth Ave. (22nd St.) | 212-620-4585
E 70s | 1411 Second Ave. (bet. 73rd & 74th Sts.) | 212-988-5348
E 70s | 1479 First Ave. (77th St.) | 212-744-6374
E Village | 104 Second Ave. (6th St.) | 212-533-8900
E Village | 77 E. 10th St. (4th Ave.) | 212-388-9006
G Village | 39 E. 13th St. (bet. B'way & University Pl.) | 212-982-3758
W 80s | 435 Amsterdam Ave. (81st St.) | 212-362-5861
Park Slope | 61 Seventh Ave. (bet. Berkeley & Lincoln Pls.) | Brooklyn |
718-622-6353
www.spicethainyc.com
"Generous" helpings of "straightforward" Thai fare offered "cheap"
keep this chain "very popular" among the "college" set and others "on
a budget"; "lively"-but-"noisy" environs and distracted service may be
part of the "bargain", but there's always "reliable" delivery.

☑ Spice Market ● *SE Asian* 24 | 26 | 22 | $61

Meatpacking | 403 W. 13th St. (9th Ave.) | 212-675-2322 |
www.jean-georges.com
"Still hitting the mark" after nearly a decade as a "Meatpacking scene",
Jean-Georges Vongerichten's "sumptuous" Southeast Asian plies
"fabulous" street fare and "innovative" cocktails amid "seductive"
"Hollywood-oriental" surrounds; it's "noisy" and tabs are "hefty", but
"tourists" and "NYers" alike call it a "hot place to be" – especially in
the "private cabanas" downstairs.

Spicy & Tasty ⇗ *Chinese* 24 | 12 | 16 | $24

Flushing | 39-07 Prince St. (bet. Roosevelt & 39th Aves.) | Queens |
718-359-1601 | www.spicyandtasty.com
"The name says it all" about this cash-only Flushing Chinese where the
"hot, hot, hot" Sichuan cooking will "open your sinuses" but won't scorch
your wallet; overlook the "nonexistent" decor and any "communication problems" with the staff, because "it's all about the food" here.

Spiga *Italian* 24 | 20 | 22 | $56

W 80s | 200 W. 84th St. (bet. Amsterdam Ave. & B'way) |
212-362-5506 | www.spiganyc.com
Among the "best-kept secrets on the UWS", this "off-the-beaten-
path" trattoria is a "tiny sanctuary" of "rich", "refined" Italian cooking;
ok, the "romantic hideaway" quarters are "tight" and the tabs "a little
pricey", but "gracious" service helps "make up for it."

Spigolo *Italian* 24 | 16 | 21 | $62

E 80s | 1561 Second Ave. (81st St.) | 212-744-1100 | www.spigolonyc.com
Upper Eastsiders squeeze into this "teensy" trattoria for "fantastic" (if
"pricey") Italian classics delivered by "the friendliest" crew, overseen

by "wonderful" owners Scott and Heather Fratangelo; "snagging a reservation" is "tough", but first come, first served outside seats ease the process in summer.

Spina *Italian*   ▽ 25 | 21 | 23 | $46

E Village | 175 Ave. B (11th St.) | 212-253-2250 |
www.spinarestaurant.com
"Fresh pastas like nonna makes" are the "big draw" at this "cute", mid-priced East Village Italian where the noodles are "made right in front of you"; "relaxing" ambiance and "gracious" service help cement its reputation as an "inviting" local "go-to."

Spotted Pig ● *European*   24 | 20 | 19 | $48

W Village | 314 W. 11th St. (Greenwich St.) | 212-620-0393 |
www.thespottedpig.com
Having "started the NYC gastropub" trend, this "raucous" West Villager remains "ridiculously popular" thanks to April Bloomfield's "superlative" Modern European eats; look for a "crazy, noisy" scene with "celeb-spotting" aplenty along with "killer waits", but the "insane burger" alone is "worth it."

S.P.Q.R. *Italian*   21 | 21 | 21 | $48

Little Italy | 133 Mulberry St. (bet. Grand & Hester Sts.) |
212-925-3120 | www.spqrnyc.com
"Well known" in Little Italy "for ages", this '80s vet is still "enjoyable" for "middle-of-the-road Italian" fare from "old-school servers who take good care of you"; the "spacious" wood-paneled setting is "group-friendly", though elitists sniff it's also "touristy."

Spring Natural Kitchen ● *Health Food*   21 | 18 | 18 | $31

NEW **W 80s** | 474 Columbus Ave. (83rd St.) | 646-596-7434 |
www.springnaturalkitchen.com
Spring Street Natural ● *Health Food*
NoLita | 62 Spring St. (Lafayette St.) | 212-966-0290 |
www.springstreetnatural.com
"Not just for the granola crowd", this "wholesome", "affordable" NoLita "standby" and its UWS offshoot sling "very healthy" dishes featuring veggies, fish and fowl, to suit everyone from "vegans to carnivores"; thanks to "large" setups with a "relaxing" "hippie" vibe, "you can sit forever and won't be bothered."

Spunto *Pizza*   ▽ 23 | 15 | 20 | $26

W Village | 65 Carmine St. (7th Ave. S.) | 212-242-1200 |
www.spuntothincrust.com
"Gorgeous thin-crust pizzas" crowned with "departure-from-the-usual" toppings are the calling card of this Village member of the Gruppo/Posto/Vezzo family; the "relaxed" digs are small, so many try for the patio seating – or choose "speedy" delivery.

Square Meal *American*   23 | 16 | 22 | $51

E 90s | 30 E. 92nd St. (bet. 5th & Madison Aves.) | 212-860-9872 |
www.squaremealnyc.com
"A hidden gem – square-cut, of course", this "civilized" Carnegie Hiller is a "favorite" of "older" sorts who appreciate the "wonderful" American staples served by a "friendly" crew; ok, the "spare" space "could use some warmth", but everyone's aglow about its cost-saving BYO policy.

	FOOD	DECOR	SERVICE	COST

☑ Sripraphai ⊄ *Thai*   27 | 14 | 18 | $27

Woodside | 64-13 39th Ave. (bet. 64th & 65th Sts.) | Queens |
718-899-9599 | www.sripraphairestaurant.com
Once again voted NYC's tops-in-genre, you won't find a more "authentic Thai" than this Woodside "mecca", where some of the dishes are "hot and spicy" enough to rate a "fire extinguisher"; just know that "perfunctory" service, "suburban" decor and no rez-induced "long waits" are part of the "incredible bargain."

Stage Deli ⦿ *Deli*   20 | 12 | 16 | $31

W 50s | 834 Seventh Ave. (bet. 53rd & 54th Sts.) | 212-245-7850 |
www.stagedeli.com
"Gargantuan" sandwiches piled "Empire State tall" have made this "stroke-friendly" Jewish "deli on steroids" a Midtown "institution" for more than 75 years; everything comes "served with a side of attitude" from "antique" staffers, and the "tourist"-oriented crowd is "packed in" to learn which is the bagel and which is the lox.

Stage Door Deli   *Deli*   21 | 15 | 18 | $22

Financial District | 26 Vesey St. (bet. B'way and Church St.) |
212-791-5252 | www.stagedoordeli.net
Garment District | 5 Penn Plaza (33rd St.) | 212-868-9655 |
www.stagedoordeli.com ⦿
"Deli food served diner-style" sums up these separately owned "basic Jewish" delis in the Garment and Financial Districts, where the sandwiches are "piled high" with corned beef and pastrami; popular with both "tourists and locals", they offer a taste of "the good old days" in "heart attack city."

Stamatis ⦿ *Greek*   23 | 14 | 18 | $35

Astoria | 29-09 23rd Ave. (bet. 29th & 31st Sts.) | Queens |
718-932-8596
"If you can't get to Greece", this "well-established", "family-oriented" Astoria taverna provides an "authentic" alternative with its "reliable" "traditional" Hellenic cooking; "stark" decor and somewhat "indifferent" service are less transporting, but "reasonable prices" take the edge off.

Standard Grill ⦿ *American*   22 | 22 | 20 | $58

Meatpacking | Standard Hotel | 848 Washington St. (bet. Little W. 12th & 13th Sts.) | 212-645-4100 | www.thestandardgrill.com
Way "above standard", this Meatpacking District "hot spot" under the High Line dispenses "surprisingly good", "pricey" American basics to "beautiful" "Euros" and "A-listers" galore; whether outside, in the "loud" cafe or "happening" main dining room, "long waits", "attitude" and "zoo"-like conditions are part of the "chichi, kiss-kiss" "scene."

St. Andrews ⦿ *Seafood/Steak*   20 | 19 | 20 | $42

W 40s | 140 W. 46th St. (bet. B'way & 6th Ave.) | 212-840-8413 |
www.standrewsnyc.com
A "scotch-drinker's heaven", this atmospheric Theater District pub pours a "tremendous" selection of single malts and draft beers soaked up with "traditional", well-priced surf 'n' turf fare; the staff's "cute kilts" and "accents" boost the mood of being "connected to Scotland."

St. Anselm *American*

▽ 27 | 21 | 24 | $41

Williamsburg | 355 Metropolitan Ave. (Havemeyer St.) | Brooklyn | 718-384-5054

"If you can get a table" at this Williamsburg meatery from the owners of Spuyten Duyvil, you'll find "simple" but "amazing" steaks and other "farm-fresh" American dishes; the "rugged" brick-walled interior is "bare-bones" and the clientele perhaps "a bit too hip", but "affordable" tabs mean all is forgiven.

Stanton Social *Eclectic*

24 | 23 | 20 | $54

LES | 99 Stanton St. (bet. Ludlow & Orchard Sts.) | 212-995-0099 | www.thestantonsocial.com

"Social butterflies" and other "beautiful" types flutter to this "happening" Lower Eastsider for Eclectic small plates and "decadent" cocktails in a "sleek", "sexy" space; "loud" music, lotsa "lively" "groups" and intense pricing are part of the deal, but hey, "who doesn't love a scene?"

Steak Frites *French/Steak*

20 | 18 | 20 | $48

Union Sq | 9 E. 16th St. (bet. 5th Ave. & Union Sq. W.) | 212-675-4700 | www.steakfritesnyc.com

"Like the name says", steak frites is the main attraction at this Union Square French bistro, where the rest of the menu's considered "just ok" and priced a "bit on the high side"; if the "barn"-size room gets "noisy", "sit outside" for some prime people-watching.

NEW Steak 'n Shake ◑ *Burgers*

21 | 15 | 18 | $13

W 50s | 1695 Broadway (bet. 53rd & 54th Sts.) | 212-247-6584 | www.steaknshake.com

Boosters "brave the Times Square crowds" for "juicy burgers" and "unbeatable" shakes at this first NYC link of a Midwestern franchise housed in the Ed Sullivan Theater; given "unbelievably cheap" prices, no surprise "seating's at a premium" in its retro-diner digs – especially when the audience is lined up for the Letterman show.

STK *Steak*

24 | 25 | 22 | $74

Meatpacking | 26 Little W. 12th St. (bet. 9th Ave. & Washington St.) | 646-624-2444 ◑
NEW **W 40s** | 1114 Sixth Ave. (bet. 42nd & 43rd Sts.) | 646-624-2455 🖻
www.stkhouse.com

"The 'S' must stand for 'scene'" at this Meatpacking District "half-nightclub, half-steakhouse" and its Midtown offshoot where the "amazing-looking" crowd is as "breathtaking" as the "sleek" set-ups complete with "rooftop" seating; while the chop-shop fare is "absolutely solid" (and "definitely pricey"), it takes a back seat to the "party atmosphere."

Stonehome Wine Bar ◑ *American*

▽ 22 | 19 | 21 | $40

Fort Greene | 87 Lafayette Ave. (S. Portland Ave.) | Brooklyn | 718-624-9443 | www.stonehomewinebar.com

"Unpretentious" but "romantic", this "cozy" Fort Greene wine bar boasts a 200-strong selection of "fairly priced" vintages paired with an "ever-changing" menu of "really solid" New Americana; equipped with a "pretty back garden", it's "close to BAM" and "perfect" pre- or post-show.

	FOOD	DECOR	SERVICE	COST

Stone Park Café *American* | 24 | 21 | 23 | $50 |

Park Slope | 324 Fifth Ave. (3rd St.) | Brooklyn | 718-369-0082 |
www.stoneparkcafe.com

"Inventive seasonal" New American cooking in a "moderately upscale"
milieu earns "neighborhood favorite" status for this Park Sloper; a
"wonderful" crew, "outdoor tables" and a "fantastic brunch" are further
endearments, and if tabs are "a bit pricey", it's well worth the "splurge."

Strip House *Steak* | 26 | 23 | 23 | $78 |

G Village | 13 E. 12th St. (bet. 5th Ave. & University Pl.) |
212-328-0000 | www.striphouse.com

NEW Strip House Grill *American*

G Village | 11 E. 12th St., downstairs (bet. 5th Ave. & University Pl.) |
212-838-9197 | www.striphousegrill.com

A "carnivore's delight" via Steve Hanson "smack in the middle of the
Village", this meatery vends "top-notch" cuts and "creative" sides in a
"dark, sexy", "bordello"-inspired room complete with "red walls" and
"vintage stripper" photos; the new Grill in an adjacent basement space
rolls out simpler fare, but you can also order from the original's menu.

Sud Vino & Cucina Ⓜ⊅ *Italian* | ▽ 26 | 22 | 24 | $33 |

Bed-Stuy | 1102 Bedford Ave. (Lexington Ave.) | Brooklyn |
718-484-8474 | www.sudnyc.com

"Tasty", affordable offerings and "super-nice" service have Bed-
Stuy locals cheering this "quaint, authentic" Italian wine bar as a
"welcome addition to the neighborhood"; a list of specials beefs up
the pasta-heavy menu, while a backyard patio augments the "small"
brick-walled digs.

Sueños Ⓜ *Mexican* | 23 | 19 | 21 | $48 |

Chelsea | 311 W. 17th St. (bet. 8th & 9th Aves.) | 212-243-1333 |
www.suenosnyc.com

"Superior" Mexican fare with "innovative twists" keeps chef Sue Torres'
"cozy", "off-the-beaten-path" Chelsea favorite busy with those who
tout the "made-to-order guacamole" paired with "excellent" margaritas; tabs may be a touch "expensive", but it's a "friendly place to
explore new flavors."

Sugar Freak *Cajun/Creole* | ▽ 22 | 24 | 22 | $27 |

Astoria | 36-18 30th Ave. (bet. 36th & 37th Sts.) | Queens |
718-726-5850 | www.sugarfreak.com

A change of pace on the busy 30th Avenue strip, this "bit of N'Awlins
in Astoria" traffics in "real-deal" Cajun-Creole favorites, "kickass
cocktails" and "desserts that'll make a sugar freak out of anyone";
"kitschy-cute" decor with a "DIY feel" and "swift", "friendly" service
seal the deal.

Sugiyama ●ⓈⓂ *Japanese* | ▽ 28 | 20 | 26 | $103 |

W 50s | 251 W. 55th St. (bet. B'way & 8th Ave.) | 212-956-0670 |
www.sugiyama-nyc.com

"You'd swear you were in Tokyo" at this "serene", underknown
Midtown Japanese where "skillful" chef Nao Sugiyama's "outstanding" kaiseki meals are ferried by "warm", "wonderful" servers; the "unforgettable experience" is prix fixe–only and "steep", but
the "pre-theater deal" packs "value."

NEW Super Linda *S American* ▽ 19 | 18 | 16 | $50

TriBeCa | 109 W. Broadway (Reade St.) | 212-227-8998 |
www.superlindanyc.com

"Gorgeous people" pack this TriBeCan from Matt Abramcyk (ex Beatrice
Inn) and Serge Becker (Miss Lily's), where "flavorful" South American
fare comes in "hip" surrounds, including a "sexy" basement lounge;
despite predictably "snotty" service, it's "crazy popular."

Supper ●⊄ *Italian* 26 | 21 | 21 | $45

E Village | 156 E. Second St. (bet. Aves. A & B) | 212-477-7600 |
www.supperrestaurant.com

At this no-rez East Villager from the Frank crew, you can look forward
to "delicious", "comfort"-oriented Italiana at more-than-fair prices;
"pleasant" service enhances "rustic" digs that are "always bustling"
despite "tight" tables, "long waits" and a "cash-only" policy.

Surya *Indian* ▽ 21 | 17 | 18 | $37

W Village | 302 Bleecker St. (bet. Grove St. & 7th Ave. S.) |
212-807-7770 | www.suryany.com

"Well-prepared" Indian staples put this West Village vet a "step
ahead" of its competition; a few find the "friendly" service "inconsistent" and the decor "uninspiring", but "reasonable" prices and a "lovely"
back garden compensate.

SushiAnn 🗷 *Japanese* ▽ 26 | 19 | 24 | $69

E 50s | 38 E. 51st St. (bet. Madison & Park Aves.) | 212-755-1780 |
www.sushiann.com

A "business-oriented" crowd converges on this "consistently excellent" Midtown Japanese for "simple", "high-quality" sushi, compe-
tently delivered; the traditionally decorated digs are less notable and
tabs are high – luckily, the "CEOs in training" don't seem to mind.

Sushi Damo *Japanese* 23 | 19 | 22 | $42

W 50s | 330 W. 58th St. (bet. 8th & 9th Aves.) | 212-707-8609 |
www.sushidamo.com

With "consistently fresh" sushi, "friendly", "efficient" service and
"median prices", this "under-the-radar" Japanese Time Warner Center
neighbor "ticks all the boxes"; maybe the kinda "stark" digs "could use
an update", but it's a "reliable" pick for an "easy" meal.

Sushiden *Japanese* 25 | 18 | 23 | $65

E 40s | 19 E. 49th St. (bet. 5th & Madison Aves.) | 212-758-2700
W 40s | 123 W. 49th St. (bet. 6th & 7th Aves.) | 212-398-2800 🗷
www.sushiden.com

"Catering to the Japanese businessman crowd", these "no-frills"
Midtown vets vend "exquisite" sushi and sashimi via an "attentive"
crew; they're "serene" "oases", and as for the "wallet-capturing" tab –
it's sure cheaper than "going to Tokyo."

SushiSamba ● *Brazilian/Japanese* 23 | 21 | 19 | $53

Flatiron | 245 Park Ave. S. (bet. 19th & 20th Sts.) | 212-475-9377
W Village | 87 Seventh Ave. S. (Barrow St.) | 212-691-7885
www.sushisamba.com

Maybe they're "a little dated", but these Flatiron–West Village vets are
still a "scene" thanks to their "creative" Brazilian-Japanese "fusion

fare" and sushi, "loungelike" decor and "festive" vibe abetted by "tropical cocktails"; service skews "erratic" and tabs "pricey", but with a few "fantastic caipirinhas", most don't even notice.

☑ Sushi Seki ●☒ *Japanese* 28 | 14 | 22 | $79

E 60s | 1143 First Ave. (bet. 62nd & 63rd Sts.) | 212-371-0238 | www.sushisekinyc.com

"Master" chef Seki "does spectacular things with fish" at this "top-notch" East Side Japanese – "you can't go wrong" with his "sublime" omakase; "solid" service helps temper stiff tabs and "tight" quarters – and the 2:30 AM closing time can't be beat.

Sushi Sen-nin Ⓜ *Japanese* ▽ 26 | 17 | 21 | $57

Murray Hill | 30 E. 33rd St. (bet. Madison Ave. & Park Ave. S.) | 212-889-2208 | www.sushisennin.com

Though a "neighborhood favorite", this Murray Hill Japanese remains an "under-the-radar" source for "some of the freshest sushi" around at prices "accessible" enough for "semi-regular" dining; "friendly" service is another plus, but don't expect much in the way of decor.

NEW Sushi Shop *Japanese* ▽ 24 | 21 | 19 | $40

E 50s | 536 Madison Ave. (bet. 54th & 55th Sts.) | 212-840-5555 | www.mysushishop.com

Choosing your sushi is "like selecting jewelry out of a catalog" say early adopters of this "creative" midpriced Midtown counter-service Japanese, a Euro chain import; service can be "slow", but the high-design space provides plenty of seats while waiting.

Sushiya *Japanese* ▽ 22 | 16 | 22 | $39

W 50s | 28 W. 56th St. (bet. 5th & 6th Aves.) | 212-247-5760 | www.sushiya56.com

"Solid" sushi at "affordable" rates keeps the lunch hour "busy" at this Midtown Japanese "standby" for "business" types; ok, "it's not hoity-toity", but the "fanfare-free" milieu makes for a "pleasant" everyday repast, and you can't beat the "great location."

☑ Sushi Yasuda ☒ *Japanese* 28 | 22 | 24 | $89

E 40s | 204 E. 43rd St. (bet. 2nd & 3rd Aves.) | 212-972-1001 | www.sushiyasuda.com

Despite losing its eponymous chef, this "stunning" Grand Central–area Japanese is still serving sushi that's among "NYC's best"; equally "flawless" service in "simple" blond-wood digs help justify the "expensive" tabs – though the $23 dinner prix fixe "may be the best deal" in town.

Sushi Zen ☒ *Japanese* 26 | 21 | 23 | $68

W 40s | 108 W. 44th St. (bet. B'way & 6th Ave.) | 212-302-0707 | www.sushizen-ny.com

It's "less touted" than some, but supporters say this Japanese "island of calm" is "one of the Theater District's best" thanks to its "pristine", "beautifully presented" sushi; "excellent" service and "small" but "Zen"-like digs help justify the tab.

Suteishi *Japanese* ▽ 25 | 21 | 23 | $44

Seaport | 24 Peck Slip (Front St.) | 212-766-2344 | www.suteishi.com

A "welcome" find in a "neighborhood filled with Irish pubs", this "charming" Seaport Japanese offers "high-quality sushi" and cooked dishes via an "attentive" crew; in summer its "low-key" space is augmented with "outdoor seating" affording "amazing" "Brooklyn Bridge" views.

Sweet Melissa   *Dessert/Sandwiches*   21 | 18 | 18 | $20

Park Slope | 175 Seventh Ave. (bet. 1st & 2nd Sts.) | Brooklyn | 718-788-2700 | www.sweetmelissapatisserie.com

The "pastries rock" at this "cute" Park Slope bakery/cafe where "decadent desserts", "afternoon tea" and "pleasing" salads and soups win favor; a "casual" vibe and a "nice garden" offset "so-so service" and prices slightly "expensive" for the genre.

Swifty's   *American*   18 | 20 | 20 | $66

E 70s | 1007 Lexington Ave. (bet. 72nd & 73rd Sts.) | 212-535-6000 | www.swiftysnyc.com

The "plastic surgery set" convenes at this "private club"–like UES American where "seating is according to your standing in the Social Register" and the "back room" is "the place to be seen"; its "ok-to-good" staples are priced "big", but it's the perfect stopover for those shuttling between Palm Beach and the Hamptons.

Sylvia's   *Soul Food/Southern*   20 | 16 | 20 | $33

Harlem | 328 Lenox Ave. (bet. 126th & 127th Sts.) | 212-996-0660 | www.sylviasrestaurant.com

Even after half a century, this Harlem soul food "institution" "continues to deliver" with "hearty portions" of "real-deal" Southern cooking dished up by "friendly, patient" servers; beloved founder and namesake Sylvia Woods passed away recently, but her soul lives on here.

Symposium   *Greek*   ∇ 20 | 16 | 21 | $25

W 100s | 544 W. 113th St. (bet. Amsterdam Ave. & B'way) | 212-865-1011 | www.symposiumnyc.com

Serving "students and absentminded Columbia profs" for 40-plus years, this "extremely friendly" Morningside Heights Greek slings "large portions" of "very good" traditional cooking at "rock-bottom prices"; the "kitschy" decor with "paintings on the ceiling" only bolsters its charm.

Szechuan Gourmet   *Chinese*   23 | 13 | 17 | $28

NEW **E 70s** | 1395 Second Ave. (bet. 72nd & 73rd Sts.) | 212-737-1838 | www.szechuangourmetny.info
Garment District | 21 W. 39th St. (bet. 5th & 6th Aves.) | 212-921-0233 | www.szechuangourmetnyc.com
W 50s | 242 W. 56th St. (bet. B'way & 8th Ave.) | 212-265-2226 | www.szechuangourmet56.com
Flushing | 135-15 37th Ave. (bet. Main & Prince Sts.) | Queens | 718-888-9388 | www.szechuangourmetnyc.com

"If you can take the heat", head for these "real Sichuans" whose "fiery" cuisine "beats the wontons off" typical corner Chinese; although the "brusque" service and "dumpy" decor aren't nearly as "sizzling", "low prices" compensate.

Table d'Hôte   *American/French*   ∇ 20 | 14 | 18 | $53

E 90s | 44 E. 92nd St. (bet. Madison & Park Aves.) | 212-348-8125 | www.tabledhote.info

If you're "unable to take that trip to Paris", try this "tiny-but-impressive" Carnegie Hill bistro plying "very good", "expensive" French-American cooking in "neighborly" confines; given the *très* "petite" dimensions, however, you might consider packing a "shoehorn."

Taboon *Mediterranean/Mideastern*   25 | 20 | 22 | $54

W 50s | 773 10th Ave. (52nd St.) | 212-713-0271 |
www.taboonnyc.com

NEW Taboonette *Sandwiches*

G Village | 30 E. 13th St. (bet. 5th Ave. & University Pl.) |
212-510-7881 | www.taboonette.com

It's "out of the way", but this "lively" West Hell's Kitchen outpost is often "jammed" thanks to its "fine" Med–Middle Eastern cuisine, including "fresh, hot" bread from the namesake oven; the new quick-service Village offshoot specializes in flatbread sandwiches with hearty fillings.

Taci's Beyti *Turkish*   26 | 15 | 21 | $31

Midwood | 1955 Coney Island Ave. (bet. Ave. P & Kings Hwy.) |
Brooklyn | 718-627-5750

In a refreshingly "hipster-free corner of Brooklyn", this long-standing BYO Turk is a Midwood "favorite" for "huge portions" of "delicious" classic dishes, including "juicy, flavorful" kebabs; the staff "couldn't be nicer", ditto the prices, and the plain-Jane digs are "more appealing" due to a recent spiff-up.

Tacombi at Fonda Nolita ❶⏎ *Mexican*   ∇ 23 | 18 | 17 | $18

NoLita | 267 Elizabeth St. (bet. Houston & Prince Sts.) |
917 727 0179 | www.tacombi.com

"Taking the concept of a food truck" indoors, this "real-deal" NoLita taqueria plies "delicious" "mini-me-size" tacos from a vintage "VW van" parked inside an "industrial garage"; it's a "fun" and "kitschy" experience, even if the "picniclike" seating "could be nicer."

Taïm ⏎ *Israeli/Vegetarian*   26 | 10 | 17 | $13

NEW NoLita | 45 Spring St. (Mulberry St.) | 212-219-0600
W Village | 222 Waverly Pl. (bet. Perry & W. 11th Sts.) | 212-691-1287
www.taimfalafel.com

Almost "literally a hole-in-the-wall" and "basically a take-out counter" with a few stools, this West Village vegetarian Israeli draws "100-mile-long" lines with its "sublime" falafel rated "best in NYC" – and maybe "the USA"; the much-anticipated new NoLita offshoot offers more elbow room and somewhat later hours.

Takahachi *Japanese*   25 | 17 | 23 | $38

E Village | 85 Ave. A (bet. 5th & 6th Sts.) | 212-505-6524 ●
TriBeCa | 145 Duane St. (bet. Church St. & W. B'way) | 212-571-1830
www.takahachi.net

"Reliable sushi" and "tasty" Japanese "home-cooking" basics offering a favorable "quality-to-price ratio" earn these TriBeCa–East Village twins "favorite-in-the-'hood" status; a "helpful" staff adds warmth to the "nothing-fancy" setups, which "bustle" at prime times.

Takashi *Japanese*   ∇ 27 | 18 | 23 | $64

W Village | 456 Hudson St. (bet. Barrow & Morton Sts.) |
212-414-2929 | www.takashinyc.com

"Fantastic" yakiniku ("cook-your-own" Japanese BBQ) is the draw at this West Villager where "daring", "every-piece-of-the-cow" offerings have "adventurous" carnivores enthusing "welcome to the offal house" –

though timid palates also find plenty to like; "attentive" service and "pleasantly minimalist" decor keep the focus on the "amazing cuts."

NEW Talde ● *Asian*   25 | 21 | 24 | $46

Park Slope | 369 Seventh Ave. (11th St.) | Brooklyn | 347-916-0031 |
www.taldebrooklyn.com

Top Chef contender Dale Talde "reigns" at this "high-energy" new Park Sloper where the "wildly creative", "pork and seafood–heavy" fare is rated a Pan-Asian "triumph"; it's no-rez and the "tavern"-like digs have been "jammed" from day one ("get there early" or "wait") – good thing there's a "patient, helpful" staff to keep everyone "happy."

Tamarind ● *Indian*   26 | 24 | 24 | $58

Flatiron | 41-43 E. 22nd St. (bet. B'way & Park Ave. S.) | 212-674-7400
TriBeCa | 99 Hudson St. (bet. Franklin & Harrison Sts.) | 212-775-9000
www.tamarind22.com

The "heavenly" "nouvelle" Indian cuisine at these "upscale" twins once again earns NYC's tops-in-genre honors, which extends to the "calming", "charming" service; both the "cozy" Flatiron original and the "gleaming", "much larger" TriBeCa follow-up ooze "high style" and not surprisingly "high prices", except for the $24 prix fixe lunch "bargain."

Tang Pavilion *Chinese*   23 | 18 | 23 | $40

W 50s | 65 W. 55th St. (bet. 5th & 6th Aves.) | 212-956-6888 |
www.tangpavilionnyc.com

"Terrific" "traditional Shanghai" cooking has made this "sophisticated" Midtown Chinese a "top choice" near City Center and Carnegie Hall; though aesthetes note its "classy" decor is "getting a little frayed", the service remains "polished" as ever, and "reasonable prices" are the crowning touch.

Z Tanoreen M *Mediterranean/Mideastern*   27 | 20 | 23 | $41

Bay Ridge | 7523 Third Ave. (76th St.) | Brooklyn | 718-748-5600 |

www.tanoreen.com

"Extraordinary" Mediterranean-Mideastern cuisine that's a "feast for the senses" is the forte of this Bay Ridge "favorite", where chef Rawia Bishara herself "makes the rounds to welcome guests"; "decent" prices, "abundant" portions and an all-around "warm, inviting" vibe further justify the "schlep."

Z Tao ● *Asian*   24 | 27 | 21 | $61

E 50s | 42 E. 58th St. (bet. Madison & Park Aves.) | 212-888-2288 |
www.taorestaurant.com

Equal parts "club and restaurant", this "cavernous" Midtowner stands out with its "energizing" vibe and "impressive" decor centered on a "massive Buddha", not to mention its "solid", "pricey" Pan-Asian fare; service is smooth too, if "occasionally snooty", but the "people-watching" is unparalleled – putting the "wow" in Tao.

Tarallucci e Vino *Italian*   21 | 19 | 19 | $38

E Village | 163 First Ave. (bet. 10th & 11th Sts.) | 212-388-1190
Flatiron | 15 E. 18th St. (bet. B'way & 5th Ave.) | 212-228-5400
W 80s | 475 Columbus Ave. (83rd St.) | 212-362-5454
www.tarallucievino.net

When you seek a "drop-in spot for a glass of wine" and a "step-up-from-your-standard-Italian" bite, this "relaxed-but-hip" trio is a "safe" bet; "quality" espresso and pastries (which are the mainstay of the East Village original) make it a morning "favorite" as well.

Taro Sushi *Japanese*   ▽ 24 | 17 | 20 | $38

Prospect Heights | 244 Flatbush Ave. (St. Marks Ave.) | Brooklyn | 718-398-5240 | www.tarosushibrooklyn.com

"Modest" it may be, but this Prospect Heights corner Japanese "never lets you down" when you seek "fresh", "earnest" sushi as well as cooked dishes; "pleasant, comfortable" environs, "polite, prompt" service and "reasonable prices" ensure that you'll get your money's worth.

Tartine ⊟ *French*   23 | 16 | 19 | $34

W Village | 253 W. 11th St. (4th St.) | 212-229-2611

At this "tiny" West Village "cutie", "delectable" French bistro basics and a "could-be-in-Paris" vibe come at prices that are way low for the 'hood – and the BYO policy only sweetens the deal; "long waits" are a given and it's "knees-to-your-nose" "tight" inside, so regulars try for one of the "rickety sidewalk tables."

Taste *American*   ▽ 21 | 17 | 19 | $54

E 80s | 1413 Third Ave. (80th St.) | 212-717-9798 | www.elizabar.com

A "self-service" cafe "without frills" by day, Eli Zabar's UES American makes a chameleonlike evening transition to an "intimate dining room" rolling out seasonal "home cooking for grown-ups"; deep-pocketed locals don't mind paying for the "civilized" experience since Eli makes sure they're getting "top-quality" ingredients.

Tasty Hand-Pulled Noodles ⊟ *Noodle Shop*   22 | 7 | 16 | $12

Chinatown | 1 Doyers St. (Bowery) | 212-791-1817

Soups brimming with "springy, chewy" noodles and "excellent" dumplings are the stars at this Chinatown "hole-in-the-wall"; "quick" service and "cheap" tabs – plus a view of the chefs at work "slamming and pulling" dough – help compensate for seriously "sketchy" decor.

Tatiana ● *Russian*   21 | 17 | 16 | $59

Brighton Bch | 3152 Brighton Sixth St. (Brightwater Ct.) | Brooklyn | 718-891-5151 | www.tatianarestaurant.com

"Close your eyes" and it's "Odessa circa 1985" at this "decadent" Brighton Beach nightclub where the "surprisingly good" Russian food takes a backseat to the "over-the-top" "Vegas-style" floor show; alfresco fans nab a boardwalk table and "take in the scenery."

☑ Taverna Kyclades *Greek/Seafood*   27 | 14 | 20 | $36

Astoria | 33-07 Ditmars Blvd. (bet. 33rd & 35th Sts.) | Queens | 718-545-8666 | www.tavernakyclades.com

"Super-fresh" seafood worthy of the "Greek gods" draws "persistent crowds" to this Astoria Hellenic where "can't-go-wrong" prices have everyone overlooking the "tight, noisy", "rustic" setting; the real rub is the no-rez policy and attendant "horrendous lines" – "go early" or "fight for a place to stand outside."

T-Bar Steak & Lounge *Steak*   22 | 20 | 21 | $59

E 70s | 1278 Third Ave. (bet. 73rd & 74th Sts.) | 212-772-0404 | www.tbarnyc.com

Tony Fortuna's "tony" East 70s steakhouse tenders "delicious", "not-frightfully-overpriced" beef in "pleasant" surrounds via a "gracious" crew; the "UES-housewives-of-NY" crowd at the bar kicks up a "noisy" "scene", so "if you want to hear yourself talk", opt for the back room.

Tea & Sympathy *British*   25 | 20 | 21 | $27
W Village | 108 Greenwich Ave. (bet. 12th & 13th Sts.) |
212-807-8329 | www.teaandsympathynewyork.com
"Anglophiles and expat Brits" make a beeline for this "tiny" West Village teahouse where English "comfort food" comes on "charmingly varied chinaware" in "adorable", "usually packed" digs; "helpful"-but-"cheeky" service is a "hallmark" and a "long wait" de rigueur, but satisfied sippers say it's the "perfect place for afternoon tea."

Z Telepan *American*   27 | 22 | 25 | $71
W 60s | 72 W. 69th St. (bet. Columbus Ave. & CPW) | 212-580-4300 |
www.telepan-ny.com
Chef Bill Telepan's "exquisite" "Greenmarket-centered" cooking is the star at this "understated" UWS New American, but its "wonderful" "pro" service and "calming" environs also add to the "memorable" experience; yes, it's "pricey" – excepting the $22 prix fixe lunch – but it's "perfect" pre–Lincoln Center.

Telly's Taverna ● *Greek/Seafood*   23 | 17 | 20 | $38
Astoria | 28-13 23rd Ave. (bet. 28th & 29th Sts.) | Queens |
718-728-9056 | www.tellystaverna.com
It's "simple perfection" laud lovers of the "freshest" grilled fish at this "old-time" Astoria Greek taverna, where the nothing-fancy digs are "large" and "relaxing" and overseen by a "friendly, never rushed" staff; factor in "fair prices", and no wonder it's a locals' "favorite."

NEW 1066 Eno ● *Asian*   24 | 23 | 23 | $46
E 50s | 1066 First Ave. (bet. 58th & 59th Sts.) | 212-888-8008 |
www.1066eno.com
A playlist of '90s pop songs, koi tanks and a Buddha statue – reminders of the space's previous life as Aja – set the scene at this kinda "expensive" Pan-Asian near the Queensboro Bridge; its "delicious" dressed-up sushi and wok go down well with libations from a full bar.

Tenzan *Japanese*   21 | 17 | 19 | $35
E 50s | 988 Second Ave. (bet. 52nd & 53rd Sts.) | 212-980-5900 |
www.tenzanrestaurants.com ●
E 80s | 1714 Second Ave. (89th St.) | 212-369-3600 |
www.tenzansushi89.com
W 70s | 285 Columbus Ave. (73rd St.) | 212-580-7300 |
www.tenzanrestaurants.com ●
Bensonhurst | 7116 18th Ave. (71st St.) | Brooklyn | 718-621-3238 |
www.tenzanrestaurants.com
These separately owned "neighborhood" Japanese are "reliable" for "fresh" sushi of "consistent quality" and "generous" size, offered at an "unbeatable price"; "fast", "no-nonsense" service and "sparse" but "pleasant"-enough premises are part of the package.

Teodora *Italian*   ▽ 21 | 15 | 21 | $54
E 50s | 141 E. 57th St. (bet. Lexington & 3rd Aves.) | 212-826-7101 |
www.teodorarestaurant.com
It "almost gets lost" in the Midtown "hustle", but this "charming" Northern Italian "hideaway" can be counted on for "very good" pasta-

	FOOD	DECOR	SERVICE	COST

centric Northern Italian cooking; it may be "a bit costly", but "pleasant" service and "comfortable" "no-pretenses" digs make it a "safe" bet for a "quiet evening out."

Teresa's *Diner/Polish* — 21 | 13 | 18 | $23

Brooklyn Heights | 80 Montague St. (Hicks St.) | Brooklyn | 718-797-3996

Sited "steps from the Promenade", this "Brooklyn Heights institution" keeps the neighbors coming with "dependable, hearty" "diner-style Polish grub" dished up in "massive portions"; all appreciate the "incredible prices", though "standoffish" service and basic "coffee-shop" decor are also part of the "bargain."

Terroir ● *Italian* — 21 | 20 | 22 | $42

E Village | 413 E. 12th St. (bet. Ave. A & 1st Ave.) | No phone
NEW **Murray Hill** | 439 Third Ave. (bet. 30th & 31st Sts.) | 212-481-1920
TriBeCa | 24 Harrison St. (bet. Greenwich & Hudson Sts.) | 212-625-9463
www.wineisterroir.com

"If only all bar food could be this good" sigh supporters of these "unstuffy" enotecas, where "tasty" Italian small plates go down well with quaffs from an "enormous" wine list; "well-versed", "down-to-earth" service is another plus, but since all those nibbles "can add up" "don't forget the credit card."

Tertulia ● *Spanish* — 24 | 19 | 20 | $59

W Village | 359 Sixth Ave. (Washington Pl.) | 646-559-9909 | www.tertulianyc.com

"Northern Spain" comes to "Nuevo York" via this Villager from Seamus Mullen (ex Boqueria) where "fabulous" tapas and "Basque cider on tap" are dispensed in "rustic" "stone-walled-tavern" digs; it's a *muy caliente* "scene" with "high prices" and a no-rez policy that "means a long wait", but amigos insist it's "worth it."

Testaccio *Italian* — ▽ 22 | 21 | 20 | $45

LIC | 47-30 Vernon Blvd. (47th Rd.) | Queens | 718-937-2900 | www.testacciony.com

"Well worth the trip to LIC", this brick-walled, multilevel Italian serves "excellent" "cucina Romana" in a "lovely", low lit former warehouse space manned by a "pro" staff; if tabs are "high for the neighborhood", that's the price of "sophistication."

Tevere *Italian/Kosher* — ▽ 26 | 22 | 24 | $61

E 80s | 155 E. 84th St. (bet. Lexington & 3rd Aves.) | 212-744-0210 | www.teverenyc.com

"Truly a find" for the observant, this "high-end" UES kosher Italian "keeps packing 'em in" with "excellent" Roman cooking ferried by an "outstanding" crew; some may gripe that its "pricey" tabs aren't quite orthodox, but there's a reason it's been around for 20-plus years.

Thai Market *Thai* — 24 | 18 | 17 | $25

W 100s | 960 Amsterdam Ave. (bet. 107th & 108th Sts.) | 212-280-4575 | www.thaimarketny.com

Thanks to "authentic" dishes that go way "beyond pad Thai", this "no-frills" UWS Siamese "fills up quick"; the "funky" decor evokes "street carts in Bangkok", as do "very reasonable" prices – no surprise it's a hit with "the college crowd."

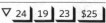
Thai Pavilion *Thai*
▽ 24 | 19 | 23 | $25

Astoria | 23-92 21st St. (bet. 23rd Terr. & 24th Ave.) | Queens | 718-274-2088
Astoria | 37-10 30th Ave. (bet. 37th & 38th Sts.) | Queens | 718-777-5546
www.thaipavilionny.com

"Delicious, reasonably priced" Thai "classics" lure Astorians to these "friendly neighborhood" standbys; there's "no real decor", but "attentive" service boosts their "bang-for-your-buck" factor.

Thalassa *Greek/Seafood*
24 | 25 | 23 | $68

TriBeCa | 179 Franklin St. (bet. Greenwich & Hudson Sts.) |
212-941-7661 | www.thalassanyc.com

"Elegant" Greek seafood is the "star" at this "high-end" TriBeCan; of course, such "fine" fish comes at a price ("you help pay its air fare"), but "first-rate" service and a "beautiful", "expansive", "Santorini"-esque setting soften any sticker shock.

Thalia ◐ *American*
21 | 21 | 21 | $47

W 50s | 828 Eighth Ave. (50th St.) | 212-399-4444 |
www.restaurantthalia.com

"Perfect before or after the theater", this "reliable" Hell's Kitchen vet plies "solid", "well-priced" American fare ferried by "pleasant" staffers who ensure "you'll make your show"; its "lively crowd" can kick up some "noise", but that's all part of the "open, friendly atmosphere."

Thistle Hill Tavern ◐ *American*
21 | 17 | 18 | $38

Park Slope | 441 Seventh Ave. (15th St.) | Brooklyn | 347-599-1262 |
www.thistlehillbrooklyn.com

Already a "neighborhood stalwart", this midpriced Park Slope American rolls out "reliable" gastropub fare in "bustling" corner tavern digs; ok, it can "pack 'em in a little too tight", but the "friendly" staff and kickin' "specialty drinks" keep things "comfortable."

Tía Pol *Spanish*
26 | 17 | 21 | $45

Chelsea | 205 10th Ave. (bet. 22nd & 23rd Sts.) | 212-675-8805 |
www.tiapol.com

"Still amazing" after nearly a decade dispensing "delicious", "authentic" tapas and "well-chosen" Iberian wines, this Chelsea Spaniard keeps devotees squeezing into its "classy" "shoebox" space; most take the "cramped" quarters in stride since it's "crowded for good reason."

Tiella *Italian*
26 | 17 | 24 | $58

E 60s | 1109 First Ave. (bet. 60th & 61st Sts.) | 212-588-0100 |
www.tiellanyc.com

"Marvelous little" namesake pizzas, "housemade pastas" and other "delectable" Neapolitan dishes lure Eastsiders to this "informal", pricey Italian; it's "about the size and shape of a Pullman dining car", but "caring", "efficient" service makes it feel more "charming" than "crowded."

Tiffin Wallah *Indian/Vegetarian/Kosher*
▽ 24 | 15 | 19 | $21

Murray Hill | 127 E. 28th St. (bet. Lexington Ave. & Park Ave S.) |
212-685-7301 | www.tiffindelivery.us

"Love their dosas" and other "deliciously cheap" South Indian fare declare devotees of this "unassuming" Curry Hill veggie-kosher standby; the lunch buffet is such a "deal" that the diminutive digs are "mobbed" at midday, but "fast" service keeps things moving.

	FOOD	DECOR	SERVICE	COST

Tiny's ◑ *American* | 21 | 23 | 19 | $40

TriBeCa | 135 W. Broadway (bet. Duane & Thomas Sts.) |
212-374-1135 | www.tinysnyc.com

"As the name would imply", this "trendy TriBeCan" from nightlife czar
Matt Abramcyk and former NY Ranger Sean Avery is indeed "tiny",
though the "rustic, bohemian" decor tilts more "cute" than "cramped";
the American menu is likewise "small", but showcases an "awesome"
burger served late.

Tipsy Parson *Southern* | 22 | 21 | 19 | $44

Chelsea | 156 Ninth Ave. (bet. 19th & 20th Sts.) | 212-620-4545 |
www.tipsyparson.com

"Too cute for words", this midpriced Chelsea "standout" "by the High
Line" dishes up "decadent" Southern fare "with a twist" backed by
"lovely cocktails"; the " inviting", grandma's-kitchen interior and
"easy-with-a-smile" service keeps the crowed "happy."

☑ Tocqueville ☒ *American/French* | 27 | 26 | 26 | $83

Union Sq | 1 E. 15th St. (bet. 5th Ave. & Union Sq. W.) |
212-647-1515 | www.tocquevillerestaurant.com

A "civilized oasis" off Union Square, this "elegant, understated"
French–New American presents the "genius" cuisine of chef Marco
Moreira via a "flawless" team that has patrons feeling "like royalty";
yes, it's "expensive", but it's "the place" for a very "special occasion",
and the $29 prix fixe lunch is a "steal."

Tolani ◑ *Eclectic* | 21 | 20 | 20 | $47

W 70s | 410 Amsterdam Ave. (bet. 79th & 80th Sts.) | 212-873-6252 |
www.tolaninyc.com

"Global comfort food" served tapas-style is paired with "diverse"
wines at this UWS "secret hideaway"; along with the "consistently
good" Eclectic bites, the "dark, relaxing" vibe and "friendly" service
have earned it "neighborhood favorite" status.

Toledo ☒ *Spanish* | ▽ 23 | 23 | 23 | $58

Murray Hill | 6 E. 36th St. (bet. 5th & Madison Aves.) |
212-696-5036 | www.toledorestaurant.com

With its "waiters in red short coats" and "heavy sauces", this circa-
1975 Murray Hill Spaniard may be "somewhat dated", but locals don't
mind given the "well-executed" classics, "nicely spaced" tables and
"excellent" service; just know the prices are the most up-to-date ele-
ment at this "old-world" bastion.

Toloache *Mexican* | 24 | 18 | 21 | $47

🆕 **E 80s** | 166 E. 82nd St. (bet. Lexington & 3rd Aves.) |
212-861-4505

W 50s | 251 W. 50th St. (bet. B'way & 8th Ave.) | 212-581-1818

Toloache Taqueria ☒ *Mexican*

Financial District | 83 Maiden Ln. (bet. Gold & William Sts.) |
212-809-9800
www.toloachenyc.com

"Modern Mexican with a nod to the traditional" sums up the "upscale"
comida at this "festive" Theater District cantina that's also known for
its "wonderful drinks"; the 82nd Street offshoot is "just what the UES
needed", while the FiDi's Taqueria is a good quick-lunch pick.

| | FOOD | DECOR | SERVICE | COST |

Tommaso *Italian*　　24 | 19 | 23 | $48

Dyker Heights | 1464 86th St. (bet. Bay 8th St. & 15th Ave.) | Brooklyn | 718-236-9883 | www.tommasoinbrooklyn.com
Although its "old-world" "red-sauce" favorites "the way you remember them" "never disappoint", regulars say the real "draw" at this mid-priced Dyker Heights Italian is the "opera floor show" on certain nights; beyond the "festive" vibe and "loving" service, it boasts an "amazing" wine cellar.

Tomoe Sushi *Japanese*　　26 | 11 | 17 | $48

G Village | 172 Thompson St. (bet. Bleecker & Houston Sts.) | 212-777-9346
"Go early" to miss the "lines out the door" at this "tiny" Village Japanese "joint" where the lure is "entertainingly big" slabs of "quality fish" at "value" prices; "tight" digs, "nonexistant" decor and so-so service are trade-offs, but "who cares" – you're "there for the sushi."

Tom's ⊖ *Diner*　　22 | 19 | 24 | $18

Prospect Heights | 782 Washington Ave. (Sterling Pl.) | Brooklyn | 718-636-9738
On weekend mornings the lines wrap "around the block" at this circa-1936 Prospect Heights "institution" beloved as much for its "second-to-none" service and "old-school kitschy vibe" as for its "to-die-for" pancakes and "even better prices"; it's a "favorite" for egg creams and other soda fountain "classics" too, but just don't show up at dinnertime ("breakfast and lunch only").

Tony's Di Napoli ● *Italian*　　23 | 19 | 22 | $41

NEW **E 60s** | 1081 Third Ave. (bet. 63rd & 64th Sts.) | 212-888-6333
W 40s | 147 W. 43rd St. (bet. B'way & 6th Ave.) | 212-221-0100
www.tonysnyc.com
Best enjoyed with a "crowd of red sauce-lovers", this "bustling" Theater District "Carmine's clone" and its new UES sibling dish up "abundant" "family-size platters" of "delish" Italian "basics" at "can't-beat-'em" prices; "unrelenting noise" comes with the territory, but the "friendly" staff "keeps it fun."

Topaz Thai *Thai*　　23 | 14 | 18 | $30

W 50s | 127 W. 56th St. (bet. 6th & 7th Aves.) | 212-957-8020 | www.topazthai.com
"Near Carnegie Hall and City Center", this "simple", "tiny" Thai slings "flavorful" classics priced way "low" for the zip code; "drab" digs with "no elbow room" and variable service are part of the "bargain", but still it's "always packed."

Torishin *Japanese*　　▽ 26 | 19 | 20 | $72

E 60s | 1193 First Ave. (bet. 64th & 65th Sts.) | 212-988-8408 | www.torishinny.com
It's "chicken heaven" at this "super-authentic", "packed" Upper East Side yakitori joint whose "top-notch" skewers showcase poultry in every permutation; "sit at the bar and watch the chefs" for the full "Tokyo" experience – it's expensive, but cheaper than the "plane ride" with almost the same effect.

	FOOD	DECOR	SERVICE	COST

☑ Torrisi Italian
Specialties *Italian*   **27** | **19** | **23** | **$78**

NoLita | 250 Mulberry St. (bet. Prince & Spring Sts.) | 212-965-0955 | www.torrisinyc.com

"Now that it takes reservations", there's "no excuse not to go" to this NoLita "standout" that "lives up to the hype" with its "clever, delightful" takes on the Italian-American classics "mom made", offered in a seven-course, $65 prix fixe–only format; the basic digs are "tiny", but "nimble" staffers keep the feel "friendly"; P.S. it doesn't serve lunch Monday–Thursday, but it's next-door sibling, Parm, does.

Tortilleria Nixtamal ⊅ *Mexican*   ▽ **26** | **13** | **19** | **$16**

Corona | 104-05 47th Ave. (bet. 104th & 108th Sts.) | Queens | 718-699-2434 | www.tortillerianixtamal.com

"It's all about the masa" ground in-house at this Corona Mexican renowned for the freshest tortillas "this side of the Rio Grande", as well as "authentic" tacos and "melt-in-your-mouth" tamales; it's a "hole-in-the-wall", but "friendly" service and budget prices ensure "you can't go wrong."

Tosca Café ◐ *Italian*   **23** | **23** | **23** | **$34**

Throgs Neck | 4038 E. Tremont Ave. (bet. Miles & Sampson Aves.) | Bronx | 718-239-3300 | www.toscanyc.com

"Lines form on weekends" at this "nightclub"-like Throgs Neck "hangout", whose array of "quite good", "straightforward" Italian eats stretches to sushi ("quite a combination"); the "large", "loungey" setup includes a "cool roofdeck" and "happening" bar, and hosts what may be the Bronx's "best brunch."

Totonno's Pizzeria
Napolitano Ⓜ ⊅ *Pizza*   **25** | **11** | **17** | **$22**

Coney Island | 1524 Neptune Ave. (bet. W. 15th & 16th Sts.) | Brooklyn | 718-372-8606

"Fabulous" "coal-oven" thin-crust pies make this circa-1924 "throwback" a "must-stop in Coney Island" and ideal "after a Cyclones' game"; Brooklyn-"colorful" service, paper plates and "oddly decorated" "shoebox" digs only burnish its standing as a one-of-a-kind "New York treasure."

Totto Ramen ⊅ *Japanese/Noodle Shop*   **26** | **12** | **18** | **$18**

W 50s | 366 W. 52nd St. (bet. 8th & 9th Aves.) | 212-582-0052 | www.tottoramen.com

"Insanely delicious" ramen soups sold "cheap" inspire "ridiculous waits" at this teeny, "takes-you-back-to-Tokyo" Hell's Kitchen nook, voted NYC's No. 1 Noodle Shop; skeptics shrug it's over-"hyped", but "there's a reason people stand on line for hours" here – and "it's not" the "bare-bones" decor.

Tournesol *French*   **24** | **16** | **21** | **$41**

LIC | 50-12 Vernon Blvd. (bet. 50th & 51st Aves.) | Queens | 718-472-4355 | www.tournesolnyc.com

Just like finding "Paris in Queens", this "charming" LIC bistro offers "*magnifique*" "real-French" fare at "value" rates; yes, the "cramped space" means "you really have to like your neighbor", but the "warm welcome" from a "most pleasant" staff "more than compensates."

| | FOOD | DECOR | SERVICE | COST |

NEW Toy ❶ *Asian* — | — | — | E

Meatpacking | Gansevoort Hotel | 18 Ninth Ave. (13th St.) | 212-203-5422 | www.hotelgansevoort.com

In the Meatpacking's Gansevoort Hotel, this swanky Asian offers a pricey menu of sushi and small plates, eaten with neon-colored chopsticks and best paired with a whimsical cocktail or two; meant to evoke a 'fantasy playground', its separate areas include an indoor/outdoor oyster bar, patio and bi-level dining room; P.S. after 1 AM, it becomes a full-on club.

Tra Di Noi Ⓜ *Italian* — ▽ 24 | 15 | 24 | $43

Fordham | 622 E. 187th St. (bet. Belmont & Hughes Sts.) | Bronx | 718-295-1784

"Like a meal at grandma's house", this family-run Italian "jewel off Arthur Avenue" offers a "homey, informal atmosphere" warmed by "truly nice and accommodating" service; still, it's the "fresh", "cooked-just-right" classics that make it "worth the trip."

Traif ❶Ⓜ *Eclectic* — 27 | 18 | 21 | $45

Williamsburg | 229 S. Fourth St. (bet. Havemeyer & Roebling Sts.) | Brooklyn | 347-844-9578 | www.traifny.com

With a provocative moniker given its Hasidic Williamsburg proximity, this "pork heaven" proffers "exceptional" Eclectic small plates with a "creative" bent ("bacon donuts, 'nuff said"); "pleasant" service and "cool" digs complete with a verdant back patio help keep the "young foodies" coming.

Trattoria Cinque *Italian* — ▽ 22 | 20 | 20 | $47

TriBeCa | 363 Greenwich St. (bet. Franklin & Harrison Sts.) | 212-965-0555 | www.trattoriacinquenyc.com

"Cavernous" and "good for groups", this TriBeCa "old-world" Italian dishes up "solid" pizzas and pastas in a five-choices-per-course format that skeptics deem "a total gimmick"; still, the "value" price tag and "attentive" service alone make it "worth a return trip – if not *cinque.*"

Trattoria Dell'Arte ❶ *Italian* — 23 | 20 | 21 | $59

W 50s | 900 Seventh Ave. (bet. 56th & 57th Sts.) | 212-245-9800 | www.trattoriadellarte.com

"Always a scene", this "vibrant" Tuscan opposite Carnegie Hall remains "extremely popular" with "power-lunch" types and "theatergoers" for its "exceptional" pizzas, antipasto bar and "whimsical" "body-parts" decor; it's always a "festive" experience – until you see the bill.

Ⓩ Trattoria L'incontro Ⓜ *Italian* — 27 | 21 | 26 | $59

Astoria | 21-76 31st St. (Ditmars Blvd.) | Queens | 718-721-3532 | www.trattorialincontro.com

Once again rated "best Italian in Queens", this "special occasion"-worthy Astorian showcases "genius" chef-owner Rocco Sacramone's "absolutely fantastic" cooking; yes, it's "loud and busy" with debatable decor, but all agree that hearing the "amazing waiters" recite the "mile-long" list of specials alone "is worth the money."

Trattoria Pesce & Pasta *Italian/Seafood* — 21 | 16 | 20 | $36

E 80s | 1562 Third Ave. (bet. 87th & 88th Sts.) | 212-987-4696
W 90s | 625 Columbus Ave. (bet. 90th & 91st Sts.) | 212-579-7970

(continued)

Trattoria Pesce & Pasta

W Village | 262 Bleecker St. (bet. 6th Ave. & 7th Ave. S.) |
212-645-2993 | www.pesce-pasta.com ◗

"Simple, well-done" Italian seafood and pastas "at a price that's fair"
is the "solid, satisfying" formula at these "cozy, old-fashioned" "neighborhood Italians"; they're "not night-out-on-the-town" picks, but they
fill the bill when you "don't want a fuss", e.g. "Sunday supper."

Trattoria Romana   *Italian*   26 | 17 | 24 | $47

Dongan Hills | 1476 Hylan Blvd. (Benton Ave.) | Staten Island |
718-980-3113 | www.trattoriaromana.com

"First-rate" Southern Italian cuisine makes this Dongan Hills "mainstay" a "worthwhile" Staten Island destination; "attentive" service,
"reasonable" prices and a chef-owner who "treats his guests like family" help explain the "throngs" waiting in line.

Trattoria Toscana   *Italian*   ▽ 25 | 17 | 24 | $45

W Village | 64 Carmine St. (bet. Bedford St. & 7th Ave. S.) | 212-675-8736

"Extremely flavorful", "well-priced" Tuscan cooking has made this "informal", "old-world" West Village Italian a "long-standing neighborhood hit"; maybe it's "nothing highly unusual", but they "don't cram
diners cheek-by-jowl", and a "warm, friendly" vibe prevails.

Trattoria Trecolori   *Italian*   22 | 18 | 22 | $44

W 40s | 254 W. 47th St. (bet. B'way & 8th Ave.) | 212-997-4540 |
www.trattoriatrecolori.com

The staffers "make everyone feel at home" at this "warm, inviting" yet
"underrated" Theater District Italian, a "red-sauce" joint that earns
ovations for its "value" pricing and "lively" atmosphere; it "gets packed"
pre- and post-curtain, so rezzies are "a must."

Tre Dici 🅱 *Italian*   ▽ 22 | 20 | 21 | $48

Chelsea | 128 W. 26th St. (bet. 6th & 7th Aves.) | 212-243-8183

Tre Dici Steak 🅱 *Steak*

Chelsea | 128 W. 26th St., 2nd fl. (bet. 6th & 7th Aves.) | 212-243-2085
www.tredicinyc.com

"Eclectic Italian" fare prepared "with flair" is the draw at this "genial"
Chelsea standby with a "modern" look; upstairs is the steakhouse with
a "mysterious entryway" that serves "delicious" beef in "seductive"
red digs that look one part "speakeasy", one part "bordello."

Tre Otto 🅼 *Italian*   ▽ 22 | 18 | 19 | $39

E 90s | 1408 Madison Ave. (bet. 97th & 98th Sts.) | 212-860-8880 |
www.treotto.com

"Solid" Italiana at "fair prices" make this "small", "no-pretenses" Upper
Eastsider a "wonderful" asset in a nabe with "few options" (talk about
"an escape from Mount Sinai!"); when the weather is warm, the "pretty
patio's the place to be."

Trestle on Tenth   *American*   23 | 19 | 22 | $48

Chelsea | 242 10th Ave. (24th St.) | 212-645-5659 |
www.trestleontenth.com

"Rustic" New Americana with Swiss inflections and an "intelligent" wine
list appeal to gallery-goers and High Line hoofers at this "exposed-

brick" Chelsea "oasis"; a "lovely" garden out back and "accommodating" service take the edge off of slightly "pricey" tabs.

Tribeca Grill *American*
23 | 21 | 23 | $60

TriBeCa | 375 Greenwich St. (Franklin St.) | 212-941-3900 |
www.tribecagrill.com

"After all these years", this "still-wonderful" New American from Drew Nieporent and Robert De Niro remains a TriBeCa "top pick", where a "doting staff" delivers "fab" fare and wines from a "standout" list; it's "informal" but with a "continuous buzz" lending an "exciting feel", and while prices are "above average", the $24 prix fixe lunch is a great intro.

Triomphe *French*
24 | 22 | 24 | $69

W 40s | Iroquois Hotel | 49 W. 44th St. (bet. 5th & 6th Aves.) |
212-453-4233 | www.triompheny.com

C'est "*magnifique*" coo admirers of the cuisine at this "high-end" Theater District French "jewel box"; it's "tiny", but the combination of "sublime" food, "quiet atmosphere" and "superb service" makes the experience "well worth" the "extra" euros.

Tulsi *Indian*
24 | 23 | 22 | $57

E 40s | 211 E. 46th St. (bet. 2nd & 3rd Aves.) | 212-888-0820 |
www.tulsinyc.com

Chef Hemant Mathur (ex Dévi) is "fully engaged" at this "tranquil dining treat" near Grand Central dispensing "innovative Indian" with "fusion flair"; "attentive" service and a "beautiful" room with "sheer curtains separating tables" help justify the "pricey" tab.

Turkish Cuisine ● *Turkish*
21 | 15 | 19 | $35

W 40s | 631 Ninth Ave. (bet. 44th & 45th Sts.) | 212-397-9650 |
www.turkishcuisinenyc.com

"Consistent", "tasty" Turkish fare at moderate rates make this "unassuming" Theater District storefront (don't mind the "no-duh name") a worthwhile "pre-curtain choice"; all appreciate the "pleasant" staff, so who cares if the decor "needs freshening up."

Turkish Grill *Turkish*
▽ 24 | 17 | 20 | $30

Sunnyside | 42-03 Queens Blvd. (42nd St.) | Queens | 718-392-3838 |
www.turkishgrillnyc.com

"Excellent", "delicately spiced" kebabs, salads and meze highlight the menu at this "authentic" Sunnyside Turkish "find"; "polite" service and eminently "reasonable" rates compensate for "lackluster" surrounds.

Turkish Kitchen *Turkish*
22 | 18 | 20 | $41

Murray Hill | 386 Third Ave. (bet. 27th & 28th Sts.) | 212-679-6633 |
www.turkishkitchen.com

"Flavorful" Turkish "home cooking" transports patrons' taste buds "to Istanbul" at this reasonably priced Murray Hiller staffed by "friendly" folk; locals declare the "bountiful brunch" one of the "best bargains" "west of Topkapi Palace", and the "recent decor update" is a plus too.

Turkuaz *Turkish*
21 | 20 | 20 | $37

W 100s | 2637 Broadway (100th St.) | 212-665-9541 |
www.turkuazrestaurant.com

"Tasty, filling" and well-priced "Turkish "delights" served by "costumed" waiters amid decor that resembles a "sultan's private tent" draw "armchair travelers" and "belly-dancing" buffs to this "amenable" Upper Westsider; the "plentiful" Sunday buffet is an additional lure.

Tuscany Grill *Italian*   26 | 20 | 24 | $44
Bay Ridge | 8620 Third Ave. (bet. 86th & 87th Sts.) | Brooklyn | 718-921-5633
Beloved in Bay Ridge for "fantastic" contemporary Tuscan food at mid-range prices, this "lovely" "neighborhood" Italian caters to "a mature, upscale crowd"; valet parking and a "welcoming" staff overseeing the "cozy" confines ensure it remains "a winner."

12th St. Bar & Grill ● *American*   22 | 21 | 22 | $39
Park Slope | 1123 Eighth Ave. (12th St.) | Brooklyn | 718-965-9526 | www.12thstreetbarandgrill.com
A locals' "go-to", this South Sloper is an "old reliable" for "well-prepared" yet "affordable" New Americana delivered by an "accommodating" crew; the "pretty" main dining room is fit for a casual "date", while the round-the-corner pub offers the same menu with "sports on the telly."

12 Chairs *American/Mideastern*   23 | 19 | 21 | $33
SoHo | 56 MacDougal St. (bet. Houston & Prince Sts.) | 212-254-8640
The kind of "nice cheapie" that "high-rent" SoHo "could use more of", this "chill" cafe dishes up "value"-priced, "lovingly made" American-Mideastern noshes in "cozy, familial" digs (though it does have "more than 12 chairs"); with so many "basic pleasures", most "can't wait to go back."

⊠ 21 Club ⊠ *American*   24 | 25 | 25 | $74
W 50s | 21 W. 52nd St. (bet. 5th & 6th Aves.) | 212-582-7200 | www.21club.com
Bringing the "glory of yesteryear to the modern day", this "timeless" Midtown "sentimental favorite" parlays *Mad Men*–era dining via a "man's-man" American menu, eclectic "memorabilia hanging from the ceiling" and "efficient, unobtrusive" service from "career waiters"; jackets are required, as is a full wallet – though the $37 prix fixe lunch is a true "bargain"; "extraordinary private rooms" upstairs ice the cake.

26 Seats ⓜ *French*   23 | 18 | 22 | $42
E Village | 168 Ave. B (bet. 10th & 11th Sts.) | 212-677-4787 | www.26seatsbistro.com
A "date night" to remember kicks into gear at this "romantic" Alphabet City "fave", a "cozy" French bistro featuring "delightful" classics, "lovely" service and endearingly "mismatched decor"; yes, it's as "minuscule" as the name implies, but skimpy square footage aside, "great value" abounds.

Two Boots *Pizza*   20 | 13 | 16 | $15
E 40s | Grand Central | 231 Grand Central Station, Lower Level (42nd St. & Vanderbilt Ave.) | 212-557-7992 | www.twoboots.com
E 80s | 1617 Second Ave. (84th St.) | 212-734-0317 | www.twoboots.com ●
E Village | 42 Ave. A (3rd St.) | 212-254-1919 | www.twoboots.com ●
NoHo | 74 Bleecker St. (B'way) | 212-777-1033 | www.twoboots.com ●
W 40s | 625 Ninth Ave. (bet. 44th & 45th Sts.) | 212-956-2668 | www.twoboots.com ●

(continued)

(continued)

Two Boots

W 90s | 2547 Broadway (bet. 95th & 96th Sts.) | 212-280-2668 |
www.twoboots.com ◗

W Village | 201 W. 11th St. (7th Ave. S.) | 212-633-9096 |
www.twoboots.com ◗

Park Slope | 514 Second St. (bet. 7th & 8th Aves.) | Brooklyn |
718-499-3253 | www.twobootsbrooklyn.com

A "Cajun-Italian theme" inspires the "pizzas with pizzazz" at this "trippy" chainlet offering a "cornmeal-crust, spicy-sauce" "alternative" to the "usual" pie; the "quirky" setups are basic and service varies by location, but parents are pleased with the "child-friendly" vibe (particularly at Park Slope's separately owned, full-menu "strollerville").

2 West *American*   23 | 22 | 23 | $53

Financial District | Ritz-Carlton Battery Park | 2 West St. (Battery Pl.) |
917-790-2525 | www.ritzcarlton.com

This Battery Park New American may be "low key" for a Ritz-Carlton resident, but business types value its "peaceful" vibe, not to mention its "delicious" food and "excellent" service; a "beautiful" Hudson River panorama is part of the package, as is an "expensive" tab.

Txikito *Spanish*   24 | 16 | 21 | $51

Chelsea | 240 Ninth Ave. (bet. 24th & 25th Sts.) | 212-242-4730 |
www.txikitonyc.com

"Each dish is a new adventure" at this "friendly", "crowded" Chelsea "Basque gem", where the pintxos pack "big flavor" and the wines send you "back to San Sebastián"; the "vibe is cool", and while prices "vary a lot depending on your order", most agree the "cost-benefit ratio is high."

Umberto's Clam House *Italian/Seafood*   22 | 17 | 19 | $39

Little Italy | 132 Mulberry St. (bet. Grand & Hester Sts.) |
212-431-7545 | www.umbertosclamhouse.com ◗

Fordham | 2356 Arthur Ave. (186th St.) | Bronx | 718-220-2526 |
www.umbertosclamhousebronx.com

Linguine-lovers "dig the clams" and pastas at this "casual" Italian seafooder in new-ish Mulberry Street digs (goodbye, ghost of "Joe Gallo") and its Arthur Avenue sibling; purists knock their "tourist" tendencies, but all appreciate the "fair" pricing.

Uncle Jack's Steakhouse *Steak*   24 | 21 | 23 | $69

Garment District | 440 Ninth Ave. (bet. 34th & 35th Sts.) | 212-244-0005

W 50s | 44 W. 56th St. (bet. 5th & 6th Aves.) | 212-245-1550

Bayside | 39-40 Bell Blvd. (40th Ave.) | Queens | 718-229-1100
www.unclejacks.com

There's "artery-jamming love in every bite" of "juicy steak" at these "traditional" carnivore clubhouses geared toward "fat cats" who purr over the "masculine" digs and "efficient" service; if "not quite in the league of the steakhouse greats", they're "trying real hard."

Uncle Nick's *Greek*   21 | 13 | 18 | $34

Chelsea | 382 Eighth Ave. (29th St.) | 212-609-0500

W 50s | 747 Ninth Ave. (bet. 50th & 51st Sts.) | 212-245-7992
www.unclenicksgreekrestaurant.com

"Ample portions" of "simple" Greek eats at "affordable" rates is the "crowd"-pleasing lure of these "unpretentious", "bustling" Chelsea-

Midtown tavernas known for their dramatic "flaming cheese dish"; "who cares" if there's "so-so" service and "no decor" – "you go for the food."

Union Square Cafe *American* 27 | 23 | 26 | $71

Union Sq | 21 E. 16th St. (bet. 5th Ave. & Union Sq. W.) | 212-243-4020 | www.unionsquarecafe.com

"Danny Meyer's original flagship" in Union Square has locked up "forever-favorite" status, accruing perennial "accolades" for its "expertly prepared" "Greenmarket"-driven New American cuisine, "affable, unpretentious" service and "subdued, stylish" digs; the experience is "worth every penny", and while scoring a rez "isn't always easy", you can always "eat at the bar."

Untitled *American* 21 | 19 | 20 | $38

E 70s | Whitney Museum | 945 Madison Ave., downstairs (75th St.) | 212-570-3670 | www.untitledatthewhitney.com

A "good restaurant in an art museum" is not an oxymoron, and exhibit A is Danny Meyer's "upscale" take on the classic "coffee shop" inside the Whitney; "attractive" and starkly "modern", it vends "comforting" sandwiches, "terrific" java and other light breakfast and lunch fare as well as a more ambitious dinner (Friday–Sunday only).

Ushiwakamaru *Japanese* ▽ 28 | 19 | 24 | $92

G Village | 136 W. Houston St. (bet. MacDougal & Sullivan Sts.) | 212-228-4181

Even if they "can't pronounce the name to their cab driver", "serious" sushiphiles seek out this Village Japanese sleeper for "exquisite", "high-end" fish, especially via the "sublime omakase"; some find the "tiny", no-frills interior "disappointing for the price", but hey, it costs "less than a flight to Tokyo."

Uskudar *Turkish* 22 | 13 | 20 | $39

E 70s | 1405 Second Ave. (bet. 73rd & 74th Sts.) | 212-988-4046 | www.uskudarnyc.com

A "magic carpet ride" for the taste buds, this "tiny", "tempting" Upper East Side Turk may be "cramped" and "narrow", but it does a brisk business thanks to "delicious", "high-quality" cooking and staffers who "go out of their way to please"; "reasonable" prices seal the deal.

Utsav *Indian* 21 | 19 | 20 | $41

W 40s | 1185 Sixth Ave., 2nd fl. (enter on 46th St., bet. 6th & 7th Aves.) | 212-575-2525 | www.utsavny.com

A "find" for ticket-holders, this Theater District Indian delivers "above-average" classics in "civilized" modern digs manned by a "gracious" crew; if prices seem a "little high", the $32 pre-theater prix fixe leaves "bargain"-seekers "happy as a puffed-up papadum."

Uva ● *Italian* 23 | 22 | 20 | $42

E 70s | 1486 Second Ave. (bet. 77th & 78th Sts.) | 212-472-4552 | www.uvanyc.com

"Bevies of beauties" and "metrosexuals" flock to this "trendy" (and "noisy") Upper East Side "date destination" trading in Italian small-plate "yummies" and "wonderful wines"; an "enchanting" back garden, "decent" price tags and "attentive" service have earned it "neighborhood-favorite" status.

Uvarara ⓜ *Italian* ▽ 25 | 23 | 23 | $42

Middle Village | 79-28 Metropolitan Ave. (bet. 79th & 80th Sts.) | Queens | 718-894-0052 | www.uvararany.com

"Quality" midpriced Italian vittles served alongside "lovely wines" in a "cozy" and "hospitable" setting decked out with "murals" make this venue a "welcome addition" to Middle Village; who knew it could "feel like" Italia in Queens?

Valbella ⓩ *Italian* 25 | 24 | 24 | $83

NEW E 50s | 11 E. 53rd St. (bet. 5th & Madison Aves.) | 212-888-8955 | www.valbellamidtown.com
Meatpacking | 421 W. 13th St. (bet. 9th Ave. & Washington St.) | 212-645-7777 | www.valbellanyc.com

With their "excellent" Northern Italian cuisine, "terrific" wines, "lavish" spaces and "solicitous" service, this "classy" Meatpacking "experience" and its East Side offshoot are deemed ideal "celebration" places; just "bring an appetite" and loads of "money" – and don't forget their "perfect private" rooms for "special events."

Valentino's on the Green ⓜ *Italian* ▽ 22 | 24 | 23 | $60

Bayside | 201-10 Cross Island Pkwy. (bet. Clearview Expwy. & Utopia Pkwy.) | Queens | 718-352-2300 | www.valentinosonthegreen.com

Rudolph Valentino's "newly renovated" former residence houses this "pricey" Italian in Bayside that brings upscale dining to an out-of-the-way corner of Queens; a "beautiful" setting with "fantastic" views of Little Bay and the Throgs Neck Bridge and "first-rate" service make the food even tastier.

The Vanderbilt ◑ *American* 22 | 20 | 20 | $41

Prospect Heights | 570 Vanderbilt Ave. (Bergen St.) | Brooklyn | 718-623-0570 | www.thevanderbiltnyc.com

"Soon to be the old standby" on Prospect Heights' burgeoning Vanderbilt strip, Saul Bolton's "stylish" midpriced American trades in "delightful", "strictly in-season" small plates and "delicious cocktails"; locals call it a "go-to" for a "friendly", "no-hassles" experience.

Vanessa's Dumpling House *Chinese* 22 | 8 | 13 | $10

E Village | 220 E. 14th St. (bet. 2nd & 3rd Aves.) | 212-529-1329
LES | 118 Eldridge St. (bet. Broome & Grand Sts.) | 212-625-8008
NEW Williamsburg | 310 Bedford Ave. (bet. S. 1st & 2nd Sts.) | Brooklyn | 718-218-8806 | www.vanessasdumplinghouse.com

Just a few dollars fund a "pig out" at these "always-busy" dumpling dispensers whose "amazing" namesake specialty is fried or steamed "while you wait"; the setups with minimal seating are "utilitarian" and service is "insouciant" at best, but for a "cheap, fast, filling" nosh, you "can't beat it."

Vareli ◑ *Mediterranean* 23 | 21 | 20 | $41

W 100s | 2869 Broadway (bet. 111th & 112th Sts.) | 212-678-8585 | www.varelinyc.com

"Gourmet-ish" Med fare dished up in "wine barrel"–themed digs at this "two-level" standout brings "much-needed" "sophistication" to the "sea of college bars and restaurants" around Columbia; checks are a bit high for the area, so "ask for the bar menu" if "you're on a budget."

	FOOD	DECOR	SERVICE	COST

Vatan *Indian/Vegetarian* — 24 | 24 | 23 | $40

Murray Hill | 409 Third Ave. (29th St.) | 212-689-5666 |
www.vatanny.com

An "incredible variety of flavors" from "delicate" to "spicy" emerges
from the kitchen of this Murray Hill veggie Indian where the "authentic
Gujarati" specialties come in an "all-you-can-eat" Thali format for
$30; "accommodating" service and a transporting "village" setting
complete the "unique experience."

NEW Veatery ◑ *Vietnamese* — ▽ 22 | 18 | 21 | $27

E 80s | 1700 Second Ave. (88th St.) | 212-722-0558 |
www.veatery.com

"Delicious" Vietnamese fare with locally sourced cred makes this
"under-the-radar" UES arrival a "delightful" "find" for classic satays
and noodle dishes; "satisfying" service and "incredible prices" seal the
deal – locals are "so glad to have it" in the neighborhood.

Veniero's ◑ *Dessert* — 24 | 17 | 17 | $18

E Village | 342 E. 11th St. (bet. 1st & 2nd Aves.) | 212-674-7070 |
www.venierospastry.com

"Wildly popular and rightly so", this "old-school" East Village Italian
"pastry palace" has been the reigning "king of cannoli" since 1894;
just "be prepared to stand in line" before savoring one of the gazillion
"mouthwatering" treats, because this "diet breaker" and "tourist"
magnet is generally "overrun."

Z Veritas ⊠ *American* — 25 | 22 | 25 | $95

Flatiron | 43 E. 20th St. (bet. B'way & Park Ave. S.) | 212-353-3700 |
www.veritas-nyc.com

"Masterful" New American cuisine and a "biblical" wine list presided
over by an "exceptional" staff are the hallmarks of this Flatiron
"gem" now in its "second incarnation" under chef Sam Hazen;
"winos nerding it up" appreciate the "contemporary" yet "dark and
romantic" atmosphere – though they're likely to sober up when it's
time to settle the bill.

Veselka *Ukrainian* — 20 | 13 | 17 | $23

E Village | 9 E. First St. (bet. Bowery & 2nd Ave.) | 212-387-7000
E Village | 144 Second Ave. (9th St.) | 212-228-9682 ◑
www.veselka.com

Borscht, pierogi and other "hearty" Ukrainian "staples" draw everyone
from "families" to the "post-party crowd" to these East Villagers appreciated for their "late-night" hours (no wonder the "staff is over-
worked"); there's "no decor" at the 24/7 Second Avenue original, but
the new Bowery outpost has a bit of "modern" polish – happily, prices
are "cheap" at both.

Vesta *Italian* — ▽ 26 | 19 | 24 | $33

Astoria | 21-02 30th Ave. (21st St.) | Queens | 718-545-5550 |
www.vestavino.com

Among the "besta" in its "residential" corner of Astoria, this local
"favorite" serves pizzas and other "perfect, simple" Italian fare with a
"sustainable", "seasonal" bent and "well-chosen wines" at "reasonable prices"; the unpretentious digs are "a little cramped at peak hours",
but the "engaging" staff keeps things simpatico.

			FOOD	DECOR	SERVICE	COST

Vesuvio ● *Italian* — FOOD 21 | DECOR 18 | SERVICE 21 | COST $31
Bay Ridge | 7305 Third Ave. (73rd St.) | Brooklyn | 718-745-0222 |
www.vesuviobayridge.com
It may "not have the name recognition" of other Brooklyn pizza stalwarts, but this "comfortable" "neighborhood" Bay Ridge Italian has been slinging "delicious" pies since 1953, not to mention pastas served "in abundance"; a "friendly" staff, "fair" tabs and "never a long wait" keep regulars regular.

Vezzo *Pizza* — 24 | 15 | 17 | $24
Murray Hill | 178 Lexington Ave. (31st St.) | 212-839-8300 |
www.vezzothincrust.com
"Crispy" "super-thin-crust" pizzas with "toppings to suit any taste" lead to "waits on weekends" at this "funky", "bargain-priced" Murray Hill "joint"; the digs are "tight" and service can be "slooow", but all's forgiven after a bite of that "mushroom-lover's-heaven" Shroomtown pie.

Via Brasil *Brazilian/Steak* — 22 | 15 | 21 | $38
W 40s | 34 W. 46th St. (bet. 5th & 6th Aves.) | 212-997-1158 |
www.viabrasilrestaurant.com
A "mainstay" of 46th Street's "Little Brazil" strip, this circa-1978 stalwart turns out "traditional" meat-centric Brazilian fare chased with "strong drinks"; if the "dark" surroundings are on the "charmless" side, "personable" staffers and "very-reasonable-for-Midtown" tabs more than compensate.

Via Emilia 🗷🍴 *Italian* — ∇ 24 | 17 | 22 | $44
Flatiron | 47 E. 21st St. (bet. B'way & Park Ave. S.) | 212-505-3072 |
www.viaemilianyc.net
"Marvelous", "value"-priced Emilia-Romagnan food and wine (including "excellent Lambruscos") have "attracted a following" at this cash-only Flatiron Italian, cemented by the "friendly" service; the "minimalist" digs may be merely "adequate", but at least the "tables are spaced to give you elbow room."

Via Quadronno *Italian/Sandwiches* — 24 | 18 | 21 | $40
E 70s | 25 E. 73rd St. (bet. 5th & Madison Aves.) | 212-650-9880
Via Quadronno Cafe 🗷 *Italian/Sandwiches*
E 50s | GM Bldg. | 767 Fifth Ave. (59th St.) | 212-421-5300
www.viaquadronno.com
"Rub elbows" with "all the chic Euro moms" while enjoying "to-die-for" Italian panini and espresso at this "seriously clubby" UES rendition of a Milanese bar; the price of admission skews high and the quarters "tight", but that doesn't deter its fab client base; P.S. the GM building spin-off is counter service only.

NEW Vic & Anthony's *Seafood/Steak* — - | - | - | E
Flatiron | 233 Park Ave. S. (19th St.) | 212-220-9200 |
www.vicandanthonys.com
To the Flatiron's former Angelo & Maxie's space comes this first NYC outlet of an upscale steakhouse concept from Texas' Landry's Restaurants; it dishes up pricey surf 'n' turf standards within big, splashy environs whose eye-catching red-ball lighting fixtures and glass wine showcases present a contemporary take on the classic chophouse look.

	FOOD	DECOR	SERVICE	COST

ViceVersa *Italian*
23 | 21 | 23 | $57

W 50s | 325 W. 51st St. (bet. 8th & 9th Aves.) | 212-399-9291 |
www.viceversanyc.com

At this "Theater District favorite", the "solid" Italian cooking garners
as many "bravos" as the "attentive" staffers who'll "get you out in
time" for your curtain; factor in a "sleek" interior augmented with a
"delightful" small patio and it's an all-around "pleasant" repast.

Victor's Cafe ● *Cuban*
22 | 21 | 21 | $53

W 50s | 236 W. 52nd St. (bet. B'way & 8th Ave.) | 212-586-7714 |
www.victorscafe.com

Cuban cooking "as it should be" and "killer mojitos" fuel the "festive"
"old Havana" mood at this "enjoyable" circa-1963 Theater District
"standby"; it's "somewhat pricey", but most don't mind given the "fantastic ambiance" enhanced by waiters "in guayaberas", "slow and
easy ceiling fans" and "first-rate" live Afro-Cuban music.

The View *American*
18 | 24 | 20 | $87

W 40s | Marriott Marquis Hotel | 1535 Broadway, 47th fl. (bet. 45th &
46th Sts.) | 212-704-8880 | www.theviewny.com

"As the name implies", it's all about the "second-to-none" "360-degree
views" of Manhattan at this "revolving" hoteler "high atop Times
Square"; ok, "be prepared to spend" to dine on "so-so" American fare
amid "lots of tourists" – but it proves that the tourists sometimes
know more than the locals, and it's a "must" at least once.

Villa Berulia *Italian*
24 | 21 | 26 | $53

Murray Hill | 107 E. 34th St. (bet. Lexington & Park Aves.) |
212 689-1970 | www.villaberulia.com

One visit and you'll be "greeted as an old family friend" at this "first-
class" Murray Hill vet known for "classic, old-world" Italian fare and
"top-notch" service; upstarts note the room "looks like an ode to 1981",
but to regulars it feels "like coming home."

Villa Mosconi ⊠ *Italian*
24 | 18 | 22 | $48

G Village | 69 MacDougal St. (bet. Bleecker & Houston Sts.) |
212-673-0390 | www.villamosconi.com

"Comforting red-sauce" fanciers endorse this "old-school" Village Italian
"fixture" (since 1976) for its "generous portions" of "smack-your-lips-
good" classics delivered by "delightful waiters"; maybe the "homey"
digs could "use updating", but "decent prices" keep 'em coming back.

Vincent's ● *Italian*
24 | 17 | 20 | $38

Little Italy | 119 Mott St. (Hester St.) | 212-226-8133

A "Little Italy standby" since "before you were born", this circa-1904
Italian is "known far and wide" for its "incredible" "hot" marinara
sauce that "makes the dishes sing"; "quick, pleasant" service, comfy
"old-school" digs and prices "a little more down to earth" than the
neighbors' cement its "standby" status.

Vinegar Hill House *American*
25 | 21 | 20 | $51

Vinegar Hill | 72 Hudson Ave. (bet. Front & Water Sts.) | Brooklyn |
718-522-1018 | www.vinegarhillhouse.com

"Brooklyn to its core", this New American "hipster magnet" in "middle-
of-nowhere" Vinegar Hill is "worth seeking out" for "incredibly crafted"

"market cooking" served in "funky digs"; the only rubs are "cramped" conditions and no rez–induced "long waits."

Virgil's Real Barbecue ● *BBQ* 21 | 16 | 18 | $35

W 40s | 152 W. 44th St. (bet. B'way & 6th Ave.) | 212-921-9494 | www.virgilsbbq.com

"Heaping" portions of "succulent" "down-home" BBQ and "sinful sides" are the "finger-lickin'" lure at this theatrical Times Square "joint" that's "not just for tourists"; it's "very inexpensive" for the neighborhood, although you may have to invest in "extra Lipitor" before showing up.

NEW Viv ● *Thai* ▽ 23 | 26 | 22 | $24

W 40s | 717 Ninth Ave. (49th St.) | 212-581-5999 | www.vivnyc.com

This Hell's Kitchen Thai stands out from the Ninth Avenue pack with its "superb" futuristic design featuring a sleek, "neon-lit" dining room that could've beamed down from a spaceship; the menu doesn't deviate from the usual suspects, however, but the "value" prices and "cute" staffers with a "sense of humor" are refreshing.

Vivolo ⧄ *Italian* 20 | 18 | 20 | $53

E 70s | 140 E. 74th St. (bet. Lexington & Park Aves.) | 212-737-3533

Cucina Vivolo *Italian*

E 70s | 138 E. 74th St. (bet. Lexington & Park Aves.) | 212-717-4700

www.vivolonyc.com

An "old-school" enclave set in a "fireplace"-equipped townhouse, this circa-1977 UES Italian seduces its mature fan base with "simple", "satisfying" repasts, "clubby" looks and "welcoming" service; its next-door cafe is more casual and less expensive.

V-Note *Vegan* 24 | 21 | 22 | $37

E 70s | 1522 First Ave. (bet. 79th & 80th Sts.) | 212-249-5009 | www.v-notenyc.com

When vegans get a craving for "seitan piccata" or "soy-bacon cheeseburgers", they head for this UES herbivore hangout, a Blossom sibling that's also appreciated for its gluten-free menu and "wonderful wines"; its "modern", white banquette–equipped space is decidedly more glam than granola.

Wa Jeal *Chinese* 23 | 14 | 18 | $35

E 80s | 1588 Second Ave. (bet. 82nd & 83rd Sts.) | 212-396-3339 | www.wajealrestaurant.com

For a "10-alarm fire" of the taste buds, diners turn to this "wonderful" UES Chinese whose Sichuan fare's "freshness" and "authentic" fiery flavors "set it apart"; the decor is strictly "drab", but "quick service" and "comfortable prices" make it "worth a visit."

Walker's ● *Pub Food* 19 | 16 | 21 | $32

TriBeCa | 16 N. Moore St. (Varick St.) | 212-941-0142

"As local as it gets in TriBeCa", this "convivial neighborhood pub" is populated by everyone from area "families" to "bankers" and "film people shooting nearby"; "welcoming" vibes and "quality" "bar food" at "value" rates keep the place humming.

Wall & Water *American* ▽ 22 | 23 | 21 | $55

Financial District | Andaz Wall Street Hotel | 75 Wall St. (Water St.) | 212-699-1700 | www.wallandwaterny.com

Another "hushed" "business-meeting" venue in the Financial District, this upscale hoteler features "locavore"-friendly New American cuisine proffered in Rockwell Group–designed digs centered on an "interesting" display kitchen; "expensive" tabs come with the territory.

Wallsé *Austrian* 26 | 22 | 25 | $78

W Village | 344 W. 11th St. (Washington St.) | 212-352-2300 | www.kg-ny.com

"Top-notch" Modern Austrian fare keeps "fans of schnitzel" coming to Kurt Gutenbrunner's "welcoming" "Vienna-in-NYC" Villager that's hung with "artwork by Julian Schnabel"; "absolutely tops" service ensures the "sophisticated" experience is "worth" the steep tab.

Walter Foods ◑ *American* 22 | 22 | 22 | $40

NEW **Fort Greene** | 166 DeKalb Ave. (Cumberland St.) | Brooklyn | 718-488-7800

Williamsburg | 253 Grand St. (Roebling St.) | Brooklyn | 718-387-8783 | www.walterfoods.com

Rated the "Socratic ideal of neighborhood places" by Brooklyn boosters, these Williamsburg–Fort Greene Americans dispense spiffed-up "comfort" offerings via "handsome" staffers; "reasonable" prices and "comfortable" interiors are other pluses, and the Billyburg original boasts outdoor seating in summer.

Watawa *Japanese* ▽ 25 | 23 | 24 | $30

Astoria | 33-10 Ditmars Blvd. (bet. 33rd & 35th Sts.) | Queens | 718-545-9596

"Fresh", "inventive" sushi and "delicious" cooked Japanese dishes are the deal at this "unpretentious" Astorian that also wins praise for its service and "value"; its "modern, chic" space was recently "expanded" and now sports a small pond and Buddha statue.

Ⓩ Water Club Ⓜ *American* 23 | 26 | 24 | $71

Murray Hill | East River & 30th St. (enter on 23rd St.) | 212-683-3333 | www.thewaterclub.com

This "elegant" "floating" eatery on a moored "East River barge" is beloved for its "truly romantic" setting boasting "breathtaking" "water views"; add "courtly" service, "delicious" Traditional American cuisine and a "wonderful" Sunday brunch, and it's well "worth the cab ride" and "expensive" tab; P.S. it's "the best place in NYC to host a party."

Water's Edge Ⓩ *American/Seafood* 22 | 25 | 22 | $65

LIC | East River & 44th Dr. (Vernon Blvd.) | Queens | 718-482-0033 | www.watersedgenyc.com

A "free water taxi" ride kicks off the "romantic" experience at this LIC "special-occasion" favorite where the "magnificent" Manhattan "skyline views" induce swoons; the "decent" American seafood is "expensive for what you get", but not considering the "exceptional ambiance."

Waverly Inn ◑ *American* 22 | 24 | 21 | $67

W Village | 16 Bank St. (Waverly Pl.) | 917-828-1154

Maybe "the celebrity buzz has slowed", but Graydon Carter's "clubby", historic West Village American remains a "lively scene" where "beautiful" types nibble "high-end spins" on "home-cooking" favorites; some say its "elegant", "fireplace"-enhanced confines (complete with Edward Sorel mural) even exude a "neighborly charm" of late – fortunately the neighbors are mostly well-off.

WD-50 *American/Eclectic*   25 | 21 | 25 | $102

LES | 50 Clinton St. (bet. Rivington & Stanton Sts.) | 212-477-2900 | www.wd-50.com

"Blow-your-mind" American-Eclectic "edible experiments" rated "more playful than pretentious" emerge from chef Wylie Dufresne's "science lab" kitchen at this decade-old Lower Eastsider; "superb" service and a "hip, friendly" vibe add up to a "great gustatory experience", albeit "not one for the frugal."

West Bank Cafe ● *American*   20 | 16 | 20 | $45

W 40s | Manhattan Plaza | 407 W. 42nd St. (bet. 9th & 10th Aves.) | 212-695-6909 | www.westbankcafe.com

"Right off Times Square", this "standby" earns applause for "satisfying" American food in "congenial" environs; the menu "may not be the most exciting", but "theatergoers" don't mind much since the prices are "affordable" and they get you "out on time" for your show.

Westville *American*   23 | 14 | 19 | $27

Chelsea | 246 W. 18th St. (bet. 7th & 8th Aves.) | 212-924-2223
W Village | 210 W. 10th St. (bet. Bleecker & W. 4th Sts.) | 212-741-7971

Westville East *American*

E Village | 173 Ave. A (11th St.) | 212-677-2033
www.westvillenyc.com

The "fresh" veggie-centric American "comfort food" suffused with "home-cooked lovin'" and "price-is-right" rates at these "friendly", "no-frills" triplets have regulars raving "don't change a thing"; no wonder there's "likely going to be a wait", but "delivery" is an option too.

NEW Whitehall ● *British*   ▽ 22 | 22 | 24 | $47

W Village | 19 Greenwich Ave. (W. 10th St.) | 212-675-7261 | www.whitehall-nyc.com

The owners of Highlands bring their "brilliant" brown spirits–and–British eats formula to this "cool" West Villager; diners choose between the "buzzy", tile-lined front barroom and rear dining room serving a meat-heavy menu of small plates and mains.

Whole Foods Café *Eclectic*   21 | 13 | 14 | $18

E 50s | 226 E. 57th St., 2nd fl. (bet. 2nd & 3rd Aves.) | 646-497-1222
LES | 95 E. Houston St., 2nd fl. (bet. Bowery & Chrystie St.) | 212-420-1320
TriBeCa | 270 Greenwich St., 2nd fl. (bet. Murray & Warren Sts.) | 212-349-6555
Union Sq | 4 Union Sq. S. (bet. B'way & University Pl.) | 212-673-5388
W 60s | Time Warner Ctr. | 10 Columbus Circle, downstairs (60th St. at B'way) | 212-823-9600
W 90s | 808 Columbus Ave. (bet. 97th & 100th Sts.) | 212-222-6160
www.wholefoods.com

"Crazy-busy at peak times", these in-supermarket cafeterias let you "grab a quick, healthy" meal from a "diverse ethnic" array – "hot, cold, sweet, savory" – as well as the "ne plus ultra of salad bars"; "monstrous" check-out lines "move pretty fast", but given the limited seating, many prefer "takeout."

	FOOD	DECOR	SERVICE	COST

Whym *American*

20 | **18** | **20** | **$38**

W 50s | 889 Ninth Ave. (bet. 57th & 58th Sts.) | 212-315-0088 |
www.whymnyc.com

"The name says it all" about the "whimsical takes" on New American
classics at this "pleasant" eatery "not too far from Lincoln Center"; locals say it "hits the sweet spot" of "decent prices" and "friendly" service, meriting many a "return" visit.

'Wichcraft *Sandwiches*

20 | **12** | **16** | **$17**

Chelsea | 269 11th Ave. (bet. 27th & 28th Sts.) | 212-780-0577 🗷
Chelsea | 601 W. 26th St. (bet. 11th Ave. & Westside Hwy.) |
212-780-0577 🗷
E 40s | 245 Park Ave. (47th St.) | 212-780-0577 🗷
E 40s | 555 Fifth Ave. (46th St.) | 212-780-0577 🗷
Flatiron | 11 E. 20th St. (bet. B'way & 5th Ave.) | 212-780-0577
G Village | 60 E. Eighth St. (Mercer St.) | 212-780-0577
TriBeCa | 397 Greenwich St. (Beach St.) | 212-780-0577
W 40s | 1 Rockefeller Plaza (49th St., bet. 5th & 6th Aves.) | 212-780-0577
W 40s | 11 W. 40th St. (6th Ave.) | 212-780-0577
W 60s | David Rubenstein Atrium at Lincoln Ctr. | 61 W. 62nd St.
(bet. B'way & Columbus Ave.) | 212-780-0577
www.wichcraftnyc.com
Additional locations throughout the NY area

"Wonderfully crafted" sandwiches and "on-the-go" snacks made from
"quality" ingredients justify the "premium price" at this ever-expanding
chain from *Top Chef's* Tom Colicchio; "no-frills" setups and "inconsistent" service don't deter the lunchtime "masses."

Wild Ginger *Asian/Vegetarian*

23 | **19** | **22** | **$27**

Little Italy | 380 Broome St. (Mott St.) | 212-966-1883 |
www.wildgingeronline.com
Cobble Hill | 112 Smith St. (bet. Dean & Pacific Sts.) | Brooklyn |
718-858-3880 | www.wildgingeronline.com
Williamsburg | 212 Bedford Ave. (bet. 5th & 6th Sts.) | Brooklyn |
718-218-8828 | www.wildgingerny.com

It's "vegan paradise" at these separately owned Pan-Asians where the
"creative", "flavorful" dishes star "mock meat" that "even carnivores
will enjoy" for a "healthy change of pace"; "friendly, accommodating"
service and "cheap" prices complete the virtuous picture.

Wildwood Barbeque *BBQ*

20 | **18** | **17** | **$37**

Flatiron | 225 Park Ave. S. (bet. 18th & 19th Sts.) | 212-533-2500 |
www.wildwoodbbq.com

The intoxicating "smell of smoky barbecue" pervades this "cavernous" Flatironer dishing up "tasty" 'cue at "decent prices"; however,
purists citing "impersonal" service, a "chain-restaurant" feel "with
flat-screens everywhere" and "loud" "frat-boy" crowds dismiss it
as "BBQ for beginners."

Wo Hop ●⇗ *Chinese*

23 | **7** | **16** | **$20**

Chinatown | 17 Mott St., downstairs (bet. Chatham Sq. & Mosco St.) |
212-267-2536

This "old-time" Chinatown "classic" (since 1938) satisfies "bargain"-
hunters with "wonderful" Cantonese "standards" at "minuscule" prices
served into the wee hours; it's a "tiny basement" "dump" with "uncom-
municative" service, but those lines out front speak for themselves.

Wolfgang's Steakhouse *Steak*

26 | **22** | **23** | **$79**

E 50s | 200 E. 54th St. (3rd Ave.) | 212-588-9653
Murray Hill | 4 Park Ave. (33rd St.) | 212-889-3369
TriBeCa | 409 Greenwich St. (bet. Beach & Hubert Sts.) |
212-925-0350
W 40s | NY Times Bldg. | 250 W. 41st St. (bet. 7th & 8th Aves.) |
212-921-3720
www.wolfgangssteakhouse.net

For "cooked-to-perfection", "quality" beef that's best "on someone else's expense account", hit these "testosterone"-infused steakhouses manned by "quick" waiters; they're "packed, packed, packed", resulting in a "rushed", "noisy, tight" scene, yet most "will be back soon."

Wollensky's Grill ◖ *Steak*

23 | **18** | **21** | **$62**

E 40s | 201 E. 49th St. (3rd Ave.) | 212-753-0444 |
www.smithandwollenskynyc.com

"Less highfalutin" and somewhat "cheaper" than "big brother" Smith & Wollensky "next door", this "more-intimate" Midtown East offshoot serves "dynamite" steaks and burgers in "high-energy" environs; night owls turn up for "late dining" (it's open till 2 AM every night).

Wondee Siam *Thai*

21 | **12** | **18** | **$23**

W 40s | 641 10th Ave. (bet. 45th & 46th Sts.) | 212-245-4601 |
www.wondeesiam3.com
W 50s | 792 Ninth Ave. (bet. 52nd & 53rd Sts.) | 212-459-9057 |
www.wondeesiam.com
W 50s | 813 Ninth Ave. (bet. 53rd & 54th Sts.) | 917-286-1726 |
www.wondeesiam2.com
W 100s | 969 Amsterdam Ave. (bet. 107th & 108th Sts.) |
212-531-1788 | www.wondeesiamv.com ◖

"Consistently delicious" Thai fare to "bring back memories of Bangkok" at "rock-bottom prices" is the key to the enduring "popularity" of these "hole-in-the-wall" Westsiders; no, they're "not fancy" and "seating is limited", but service is "fast" and "friendly."

NEW Wong ⊠ *Asian*

24 | **16** | **20** | **$56**

W Village | 7 Cornelia St. (bet. Bleecker & W. 4th Sts.) |
212-989-3399 | www.wongnewyork.com

Simpson Wong (Cafe Asean) "has a winner" in this midpriced West Villager whose "inventive", "terrific" small plates combine Pan-Asian flavors with "farm-fresh ingredients"; despite gripes about the "tight squeeze", "fun cocktails" help ease the mood; P.S. "go for the duckavore dinner."

Wu Liang Ye *Chinese*

23 | **12** | **15** | **$35**

W 40s | 36 W. 48th St. (bet. 5th & 6th Aves.) | 212-398-2308

"Just off Rock Center" and "one of the best Chinese restaurants north of C-town" is this source for "real-deal" "fiery", "tingly" Sichuan cooking ("bring tissues to deal with your runny nose"); "bargain prices" outweigh "glum" digs and "rushed" service.

Xi'an Famous Foods ⇶ *Chinese*

24 | **6** | **12** | **$12**

Chinatown | 67 Bayard St. (bet. Bowery & Mott St.) |
212-608-4170
Chinatown | 88 E. Broadway (Forsyth St.) | 212-786-2068
E Village | 81 St. Marks Pl. (1st Ave.) | 212-786-2068

(continued)

Xi'an Famous Foods

Flushing | Golden Shopping Mall | 41-28 Main St., downstairs (41st Rd.) | Queens | 212-786-2068
www.xianfoods.com

"One taste" of the "hand-pulled noodles", "cumin-lamb burgers" and other "insanely cheap" specialties "with real kick" and "you'll understand" the allure of these Western Chinese "bargain base-ments"; just know you "don't come for the service", "paper-plates" milieu or "limited seating."

X.O. ⌐ *Chinese*　　　　▽ 22 | 13 | 17 | $33

Little Italy | 148 Hester St. (bet. Bowery & Elizabeth St.) | 212-965-8645

A "wide variety" of "XOtraordinary" Hong Kong–style dim sum capti-vates comers to this "always-crowded" Chinese standby in Little Italy; service is of the basic-but-"fast" variety and decor nonexistent, but for sheer "value" it's a "find."

Yakitori Totto ● *Japanese*　　25 | 16 | 19 | $46

W 50s | 251 W. 55th St., 2nd fl. (bet. B'way & 8th Ave.) | 212-245-4555 | www.tottonyc.com

"Every skewer is better than the one before" at this "small" Midtown yakitori den where meats, veggies and "chicken parts that you never knew existed" are grilled on sticks; it's a real "excursion to Tokyo" com-plete with "cramped", "noisy" digs and tabs that "add up quickly."

Yama ⊠ *Japanese*　　　　24 | 14 | 18 | $43

E 40s | 308 E. 49th St. (bet. 1st & 2nd Aves.) | 212-355-3370
Gramercy | 122 E. 17th St. (Irving Pl.) | 212-475-0969
W Village | 38-40 Carmine St. (bet. Bedford & Bleecker Sts.) | 212-989-9330

"Whale-size" slices of "fresh" sushi at "bargain" rates turned out at this "solid" Japanese trio outweigh "haphazard" service and "crowded, cramped" conditions in "cubbyhole" spaces; no, they "don't dazzle" decorwise, but those "long lines" speak for themselves ("arrive early to get a seat").

NEW Yefsi Estiatorio *Greek*　▽ 24 | 21 | 22 | $50

E 70s | 1481 York Ave. (bet. 78th & 79th Sts.) | 212-535-0293 | www.yefsiestiatorio.com

"Finally York Avenue has a winner" enthuse Upper Eastsiders of this "excellent" Greek where a "talented" ex-Milos chef sends out "authentic" classics with "wonderful" mezes as a focus; its "warm", "rustic", "like-in-Athens" digs have the "added bonus" of garden seating in summer.

Yerba Buena *Pan-Latin*　　24 | 20 | 22 | $48

E Village | 23 Ave. A (bet. Houston & 2nd Sts.) | 212-529-2919
W Village | 1 Perry St. (Greenwich Ave.) | 212-620-0808
www.ybnyc.com

Chef Julian Medina delivers "delectable", "inventive" Pan-Latin fare while the "mixologists make magic" at these "stylish", "upbeat" cross-town siblings manned by a crisp crew; just be aware that the "noise level rises a few decibels" as the night goes on and space is "tight."

| | FOOD | DECOR | SERVICE | COST |

Yuba *Japanese* ▽ 23 | 18 | 21 | $50

E Village | 105 E. Ninth St. (bet. 3rd & 4th Aves.) | 212-777-8188 |
www.yubanyc.com
"Easily overlooked" in the East Village, this newcomer from "former
Masa chefs" is worth seeking out for "outstanding" sushi and Japanese
cuisine made with "first-rate" luxe ingredients; its "warm" interior and
"pro" staff have early-goers citing favorable "quality-to-price ratio."

Yuca Bar ● *Pan-Latin* 22 | 17 | 19 | $31

E Village | 111 Ave. A (7th St.) | 212-982-9533 | www.yucabarnyc.com
"Lively" and full of "good-looking" things, this well-priced East Villager
mixes "delicious" Pan-Latin fare with "killer" drinks to create a "fun"
scene; it gets "loud" and service can lag, but for "people-watching" by
the open doors and windows it's hard to beat.

Yuka ⊄ *Japanese* 22 | 11 | 17 | $31

E 80s | 1557 Second Ave. (bet. 80th & 81st Sts.) | 212-772-9675
Every neighborhood should have a "reliable" Japanese fallback like this
"busy" Yorkville veteran where the "super-fresh", "all-you-can-stuff-
in" sushi costs just $21 per person; the space and service are just ba-
sic, so most diners imply focus on the "bargain."

NEW **Yunnan Kitchen** *Chinese* ▽ 18 | 19 | 19 | $26

LES | 79 Clinton St. (Rivington St.) | 212-253-2527 |
www.yunnankitchen.com
Offering a "fun take on Modern Chinese", this "welcoming" Lower
Eastsider's wallet-friendly, market-driven fare focuses on the cuisine
of the eponymous province; the "cozy" space is outfitted with vintage
Chinese jewelry and a tiger-skin rug, creating a laid-back vibe that attracts a good-looking crowd.

Yura on Madison *Sandwiches* 20 | 12 | 14 | $24

E 90s | 1292 Madison Ave. (92nd St.) | 212-860-1598 |
www.yuraonmadison.com
A neighborhood "haunt" for nearby "prep school girls" and their
"Madison Avenue moms", this "bustling", "pricey" Carnegie Hill "corner cafe" turns out "consistently delicious" sandwiches, salads and
baked goods; it "needs more seating" and service is just "adequate",
so "takeout" is an attractive option.

Yuva *Indian* ▽ 24 | 19 | 20 | $40

E 50s | 230 E. 58th St. (bet. 2nd & 3rd Aves.) | 212-339-0090 |
www.yuvanyc.com
"Perfectly spiced" cooking, including "excellent tandoori" specialties,
makes this "comfortable", "upscale" Indian "stand out" among its East
58th Street brethren; "modest" prices, "sweet" servers and a "reasonably quiet setting" encourage comers to "linger."

Zabb Elee *Thai* 22 | 13 | 18 | $25

E Village | 75 Second Ave. (bet. 4th & 5th Sts.) | 212-505-9533
Jackson Heights | 71-28 Roosevelt Ave. (72nd St.) | Queens |
718-426-7992 ● ⊄
www.zabbelee.com
"Complex flavors", some "blistering-hot", distinguish these "very affordable" and "delicious" Thais in the East Village and Jackson Heights

supplying "unusual" Northeastern Isan cooking to the "adventurous diner"; "friendly" staffers add warmth to the "sterile" environs.

Zaitzeff *Burgers*
22 | 12 | 16 | $20

Financial District | 72 Nassau St. (John St.) | 212-571-7272
NEW Murray Hill | 711 Second Ave. (bet. 38th & 39th Sts.) | 212-867-3471
www.zaitzeffnyc.com

"Tasty" patties of all persuasions – Kobe beef, sirloin, turkey, vegetable – made with "quality" ingredients and served on "terrific Portuguese rolls" are the draw at these burger-and-beer places; "small", "crowded" settings that really are "not comfortable" suggest getting 'em to go.

Zaytoons *Mideastern*
21 | 14 | 17 | $20

Carroll Gardens | 283 Smith St. (Sackett St.) | Brooklyn | 718-875-1880
Fort Greene | 472 Myrtle Ave. (bet. Hall St. & Washington Ave.) | Brooklyn | 718-623-5522
Prospect Heights | 594 Vanderbilt Ave. (St. Marks Ave.) | Brooklyn | 718-230-3200 ⬮
www.zaytoonsrestaurant.com

For "tasty", "reliable" Middle Eastern fare, stay tooned to this Brooklyn trio staffed by a "pleasant" crew; "tables are close", but the prices are "terrific" – and Carroll Gardens and Fort Greene are BYO, while Prospect Heights boasts an "attractive garden."

Zebú Grill *Brazilian*
∇ 23 | 17 | 21 | $45

E 90s | 305 E. 92nd St. (bet. 1st & 2nd Aves.) | 212-426-7500 | www.zebugrill.com

Upper Eastsiders on a meat binge hit this "relaxed" Brazilian specializing in "fantastic" churrasco dishes; "solicitous" service and "a caipirinha or two" confirm that this somewhat "out-of-the-way" contender is "pleasant for a quiet evening out."

Ze Café *French/Italian*
21 | 24 | 21 | $53

E 50s | 398 E. 52nd St. (bet. FDR Dr. & 1st Ave.) | 212-758-1944 | www.zecafe.com

Step in and you "feel like you're in a flower shop" – and that's no surprise since this French-Italian Sutton Place "jewel box" is run by Zezé, one of NYC's top florists; the "tasty" "light meals" are right for "lunch with the ladies" ("dah-ling!") and service is "charming", so no one "seems to mind" the "steep" pricing.

Zengo *Pan-Latin*
23 | 24 | 20 | $50

E 40s | 622 Third Ave. (40th St.) | 212-808-8110 | www.richardsandoval.com

A "beautiful, airy" tri-level space designed by AvroKO sets the stage for a "special" experience at this Grand Central–area Pan-Latin presenting Richard Sandoval's "imaginative" Asian-accented cuisine; "pricey" tabs and "tiny portions" annoy, but "welcoming" service and the downstairs "tequila library" tip the balance.

Zenkichi ●Ⓜ *Japanese*
26 | 25 | 25 | $61

Williamsburg | 77 N. Sixth St. (Wythe Ave.) | Brooklyn | 718-388-8985 | www.zenkichi.com

Once you find the "secret" location, expect a "fun" experience at this Williamsburg Japanese izakaya where "wonderful", "original" small plates and sake are served in a "date-night nirvana" triplex with "private booths" and "superb" staffers who're summoned "via pushbutton"; just "be prepared to open those wallets."

Zen Palate *Vegetarian*

| | 20 | 16 | 19 | $28 |

Gramercy | 115 E. 18th St. (bet. Irving Pl. & Park Ave. S.) | 212-387-8885 ●
NEW Murray Hill | 516 Third Ave. (bet. 34th & 35th Sts.) | 212-685-6888
W 40s | 663 Ninth Ave. (46th St.) | 212-582-1669
W 100s | 239 W. 105th St. (B'way) | 212-222-2111
www.zenpalate.com

This still-"virtuous" Asian-vegetarian chainlet can be depended on for "creative" dishes starring "mock" meats that "satisfy the palate" and leave you "relieved of bad karma"; naysayers charge that the operation "could use updating", but "price-is-right" tabs get no beefs.

Zero Otto Nove *Italian/Pizza*

| | 24 | 22 | 22 | $42 |

Flatiron | 15 W. 21st St. (bet. 5th & 6th Aves.) | 212-242-0899
Fordham | 2357 Arthur Ave. (186th St.) | Bronx | 718-220-1027 Ⓜ
www.roberto089.com

"Real-deal" housemade pastas and "sublime pizza" ensure there's "something to please everyone" at these "friendly" Southern Italians, whose "reasonable prices" are another reason "loyal fans" "keep comin' back"; with its "piazza"-inspired decor, the Arthur Avenue original "transports" diners to Salerno, while "nothing beats" the new Flatiron offshoot "after an afternoon of shopping."

Zito's
Sandwich Shoppe *Italian/Sandwiches*

| ▽ | 22 | 17 | 20 | $16 |

NEW Park Slope | 195 Fifth Ave. (bet. Sackett & Union Sts.) | Brooklyn | 718-857-1950
Park Slope | 300 Seventh Ave. (bet. 7th & 8th Sts.) | Brooklyn | 718-499-2800
www.zitossandwichshoppe.com

The "old-time Brooklyn" sub shop gets a locavore update via these counter-service Park Slopers vending "tasty, filling" classic Italian heros made with "quality, mostly local ingredients", accompanied by NY beer and wine; the "simple" setups include back patios that add warm-weather appeal.

Zoma *Ethiopian*

| ▽ | 24 | 20 | 21 | $30 |

Harlem | 2084 Frederick Douglass Blvd. (113th St.) | 212-662-0620 | www.zomanyc.com

Mavens say "some of the best Ethiopian in the city" is served in Harlem at this "upscale" contender offering "delicious", "authentic" stews eaten with injera bread; "modern" decor and "friendly" service enhance the experience, as do the affordable checks.

Zum Schneider ●⇪ *German*

| | 22 | 19 | 20 | $30 |

E Village | 107 Ave. C (7th St.) | 212-598-1098 | www.zumschneider.com

It's "all about" the "humongous" Bavarian "steins of beer" and "German brats" at this affordable East Village "slice of Munich", a "boisterous" "haus away from home" where "every day's a party"; prepare to "wait" during "Oktoberfest" and hit the ATM since it's "cash only."

	FOOD	DECOR	SERVICE	COST

Zum Stammtisch *German*

24 | 21 | 22 | $40

Glendale | 69-46 Myrtle Ave. (bet. 69th Pl. & 70th St.) | Queens | 718-386-3014 | www.zumstammtisch.com

Bring your appetite to this Glendale German doling out "hearty" "classics" in "you-won't-leave-hungry" portions; "pleasant frauleins in Alpine costume" toting steins of "terrific", "frosty beer" bolster the kitschy "hofbrauhaus-in-Bavaria" vibe, while affordable prices ensure it won't "bring out the wurst in you."

Zuzu Ramen Ⓜ⇄ *Japanese/Noodle Shop*

∇ 23 | 17 | 21 | $25

Park Slope | 173 Fourth Ave. (Degraw St.) | Brooklyn | 718-398-9898 | www.zuzuramen.com

"First-rate" Japanese noodles to make you forget "the ramen of your college-dorm days" are the "slurp"-worthy stars at this "local favorite" on the Park Slope–Gowanus border; it's an "affordable" and "friendly" standby that just might have you "watching *Tampopo* again."

Latest openings, menus, photos and more on plus.google.com/local